ERRATA

Please note these corrections in your copy of the Third Edition of READINGS IN POPULATION AND COMMUNITY ECOLOGY by William E. Hazen.

1. The credit line for the article by Hett and O'Neill (page 422) was inadvertently omitted. It should read:

   Reproduced with permission from *Arctic Anthropology* 11 (1):31–40. Copyright 1974 by the Regents of the University of Wisconsin System.

2. The correct affiliation of Dr. Hazen, the editor of this volume, is San Diego State *University*.

We extend our apologies for the errors.

W. B. SAUNDERS COMPANY

Readings in Population and Community Ecology

Third Edition

WILLIAM E. HAZEN
Professor of Biology, San Diego State University

W. B. SAUNDERS COMPANY • Philadelphia • London • Toronto

W. B. Saunders Company: West Washington Square
Philadelphia, PA 19105

1 St. Anne's Road
Eastbourne, East Sussex BN21 3UN, England

1 Goldthorne Avenue
Toronto, Ontario M8Z 5T9, Canada

Front cover illustration—Phase diagram of host and
parasite density for a modeled stable structure. From Odum:
Fundamentals of Ecology, Third Edition

Readings in Population and Community Ecology   ISBN 0-7216-4607-7

Last digit is the print number: 9   8   7   6   5   4   3   2

EDITOR'S INTRODUCTION

This is the third set of selections published under this title; the successive changes reflect both my own changing interests and the more objective changes in the field of ecology. Since the purpose of this collection is to introduce students to the literature of ecology as soon as they begin their study of the subject, the principle of selection is a heuristic one. These readings are intended for use by third and fourth year students, in conjunction with lectures, laboratory and field work.

The current focus of interest in ecology that emphasizes population and communities as the proper objects of study in the science can be traced to two books published in the 1920's: Lotka's *Elements of Physical Biology,* and Elton's *Animal Ecology.* Both these volumes stressed the role of populations, with population dynamics or kinematics having central positions. Volterra's classic study should also be mentioned; its influence was more marked after 1931, when a translation of it appeared as an appendix to Chapman's *Animal Ecology.* In the next decade such works as Gause's *The Struggle for Existence* and Bodenheimer's *Problems of Animal Ecology* redirected the attention of investigators to theoretical problems and to their experimental solutions. In plant ecology, the discussions of Tansley, who proposed the term ecosystem for the fundamental ecological unit, had a similar function. It is difficult to point to particular recent authors, but Lindeman should be mentioned as one who directed the activity of working ecologists to the problems of productivity and efficiency.

In the five years since the last edition appeared, the word ecology has become a touchstone for the concerned, a scapegoat for the greedy. I hope to show here that it remains a relevant intellectual discipline.

The collection of papers in this volume attempts to explain some of the avenues that research and speculation have taken. The articles are grouped under four substantive headings, with a short introduction for each part. The sections are: "Single Species Populations," "Relations between Organisms," "Metabolism: Energetics and Productivity," and "Communities of Organisms." I have attempted to place the papers so they can be read sequentially.

By using different criteria, the papers could be grouped differently than they appear here. One of these possible groupings would correspond to the different kinds of activities which the authors undertake. Thus there are theoretical papers, which use the rational processes of logic and mathematics to investigate the possible ways of ordering ecological subject matters, and empirical ones, which investigate the world of art and nature — that is, ecology as studied by experiment or simple observations. I have made no attempt to "cover" ecology. The papers are uneven in difficulty and a few will be too difficult for those undergraduates inadequately prepared in mathematics. For this I offer the defense that it is better for students to be shown the scope of the science in all its difficulty and particularity than to be fed predigested and regurgitated pap.

In ecology, diverse answers can be given to the central question about the relations among the entities studied. A community may be viewed as a statistical assemblage of organisms, each individual essentially living its own life. Or a community may be regarded as the locus of predator-prey, exploiter-exploited relations. Yet another conception is as individuals or groups in such close relation that exchanges of surpluses and needs are facilitated. Here research identifies the routes of matter and energy, the agents and means of exchange. A community may be regarded as an organization, understandable as a set of functions—such as photosynthesis and decomposition—each performed by groups in the community. Here research becomes the search for the particular agency carrying out each function. Finally, the community has been regarded as an organism, and here research may become the working out of the community-organism analogy. The views of the investigator determine the questions asked, the data gathered, and the conclusions reached. In no other science is the intellectual orientation of the investigator more important, nor is the diverse nature of the conclusions reached more apparent.

I wish to acknowledge the help of my colleagues at San Diego State University in preparing this revision. My discussions with John Brooks while I spent a year at the National Science Foundation illuminated many aspects of ecology. I remain indebted to Nelson Hairston, Frederick Smith, and Lawrence Slobodkin, who first introduced me to the nature and scope of ecology.

CONTENTS

Part I

SINGLE SPECIES POPULATIONS

A principal goal of population ecology is to find out how environmental factors and biological characteristics of the population interact to determine the number of organisms of each species found in any particular area. This goal is seldom realized either in terrestrial or aquatic ecology. The data available are not sufficiently detailed, precise, extensive, or accurate, nor have theories been sufficiently comprehensive or applicable. The analysis of the relation of environment to organisms can be attempted in three ways: mathematical studies, experiments, and observations based on field sampling. The most fruitful work employs a combination of these methods to illuminate nature.

In the first, a mathematical model is used in which it is hoped the important biological forces and factors will be expressed not only simply but also with enough accuracy so that manipulation of the model will permit new conclusions to be drawn. In the second, organisms are grown and investigated in the laboratory under simpler and more controlled conditions than in nature, the experimenter manipulating a small number of the possible conditions to ascertain their effects and relative importance. In the last, either simple observations are made and reported, a method that can be regarded as merely anecdotal, or repeated observations of organisms under both similar and different conditions are made, the observer hoping that the information obtained under different and changing conditions will reveal how the populations are controlled. When all attempts at rational analysis fail, a multiple regression can be performed if the observer has no other way to reduce the mass of data.

When mathematics is applied to a natural science, one attempts to form a mathematical model or picture which states the essential values, mimicking nature well enough to furnish new insights. These relations can be further examined by manipulations and may respond by giving information and indicating additional relations which were not originally apparent. The art of establishing a successful model lies in choosing the elements which are truly essential in the relations. Biological relations are usually so complex that most factors, whether environmental or intrinsic, must be ignored. The interpreter should

1

always remain aware of the simplifying assumptions made and should make these explicit to others. These assumptions limit the generality of the conclusions, but in return it is possible to examine a few of the presumably important relations freed from other perturbations. Even the population biology of the simplest organism is complex and variable. The equations derived by Lotka (1925) and Volterra (1928) led to a great deal of research, but it is apparent that the simplifying assumptions have been ignored by many biologists who apply these models to field studies.

The models most often seen in population dynamics — or to employ Lotka's (1925) older and more accurate expression, population kinetics — are based on statements about the biological nature of the populations rather than derived from data about a particular organism. They are, therefore, *a priori* models rather than ones established *a posteriori*. Such a model is the one for exponential growth:

$$\frac{dN}{dt} = rt$$

or for logistic population growth:

$$\frac{dN}{dt} = rN\left(\frac{K-N}{K}\right).$$

Equations of relationships established from regressions are derived directly from data, and are therefore *a posteriori*.

Classified in another way, two sorts of mathematical models may be devised: deterministic and stochastic. In the former, some property is predicted exactly by the model; in the latter, a mean value is predicted, together with a measure of the variability of the prediction. Deterministic models are more common, yet reflect biological reality less adequately. According to Smith's (1974) analysis, the deterministic equation for population growth:

$$dN/dt = rN$$

assumes that in the short interval Δt, each invididual gives rise to a fraction $r\Delta t$. More realistically, the corresponding stochastic model assumes that in the interval Δt, an individual produces an offspring with the probability $r\Delta t$, and no offspring with the probability $(1-r)\Delta t$. Therefore the average population at time t will be:

$$\hat{N}_t = N_0 e^{rt}$$

with the variance:

$$var(N) = N_0 e^{2rt}(1-e^{-rt}).$$

The difference between the two is the added knowledge about variability present in the stochastic model. With infinite populations, no difference exists between the formulation of the stochastic and the deterministic models.

Deterministic models are used in ecology rather than stochastic ones only because they are more convenient — they are an expression of ignorance.

A stochastic model often used in ecology is the Poisson distribution, useful in describing the distribution of organisms in space. Small-scale distribution, or pattern of dispersion, which is a measure of the spatial relationships of individuals in a given area, is a subject of particular interest to those concerned with specific effects of the physical and biological environment on individuals and populations and with problems of sampling error involved in censusing populations (see, for example, Cassie, 1959; Grieg-Smith, 1964; Pielou, 1969). Plants and animals exhibit three basic types of small-scale distribution, the relationships of which can be represented as a continuous spectrum:

Uniform----------Random----------Aggregated.

In practice, statistical methods are used to determine the position of an observed small-scale distribution pattern on this continuum. Evidence from a wide variety of terrestrial and aquatic habitats has shown that both random and uniform (even) spacing of individuals are quite uncommon patterns compared to aggregation. An aggregated distribution pattern is characterized by densities of individuals which are markedly higher than the overall mean density in some parts of the area sampled, and markedly lower in others. This effect is the result of the tendency for individuals to occur in groups which are often called aggregations, clumps, or patches. Thus, the terms clumped, patchy, and contagious also are used in referring to an aggregated small-scale distribution pattern.

Dispersion patterns of organisms may be considered quantitatively by using a device for sampling areas or volumes to obtain replicate density estimates, or by using nearest neighbor distance measurements obtained by a plotless sampling technique. The latter method is of limited value in most aquatic situations where conditions generally dictate the use of volumetric samplers. The observed data are compared statistically with those expected on the basis of a random dispersion pattern. These expected values can be determined from the terms of the Poisson distribution, which has the form:

$$p_n = \frac{\gamma^n e^{-\gamma}}{n\ !}$$

where n is the number of individuals per sampling unit, γ is the mean number of individuals per sampling unit (mean density), e is the base of the natural logarithms, and p_n is the probability or expected frequency of occurrence for n individuals per sampling unit. The expected numbers of sampling units containing 0, 1, 2, 3, . . . ,n individuals are each obtained by multiplying the expected relative frequency (p_n) for each n value by the total number of sampling units; they may then be compared by a chi-square test to determine if the observed pattern, as reflected by a frequency distribution of density data, conforms to a random pattern or departs from it in the direction of uniformity or aggregation.

Another useful property of the Poisson distribution, which allows an alternate method of analysis, is that the variance equals the mean. Thus, using a statistical significance test, one can compare an observed variance-to-mean ratio based on replicate density estimates with the expected Poisson ratio of 1.0 to determine whether the observed data fit or depart from a random dispersion pattern.

Note that no attempt is made to ascertain the position of each individual. Rather the pattern of distribution of the whole population is assessed.

The papers in this section examine a number of aspects of the biology of single species populations, and form an ordered sequence, the order being,

3

I hope, other than a random one. Most of them are self explanatory, and contain enough introductory material so that little exposition is necessary. More attention is given plant populations than in earlier editions; this represents a convergence between plant and animal ecologists, and shows a recasting of old problems such as plant succession as a part of population ecology.

The last paper, the analysis of deterministic population models by Smith, serves as a bridge to the next section, and could equally well belong there. It makes unnecessary a rehearsal of the simple theories of population change.

LITERATURE CITED

Lotka, A. S. 1925. *Elements of Physiological Biology*. Williams, & Wilkins, Baltimore. Reprinted as *Elements of Mathematical Biology*, by Dover Publications, Inc., New York, 1966.

Smith, J. M. 1974. *Models in Ecology*. Cambridge University Press, Cambridge, England.

THE BEHAVIOUR OF *LARREA DIVARICATA* (CREOSOTE BUSH) IN RESPONSE TO RAINFALL IN CALIFORNIA

BY S. R. J. WOODELL, H. A. MOONEY AND A. J. HILL

Botany School, University of Oxford, and
Botany Department, University of California, Los Angeles

INTRODUCTION

One of the most striking aspects of desert vegetation is the apparently regular spacing of shrubs. The species which has been commented on most in this respect is *Larrea divaricata* Cav., the creosote bush (Leopold 1963; Went 1952, 1955; Baker 1966). Its wide-reaching root system is referred to by Cannon (1911), who excavated several systems and showed that in some situations the roots could extend 2 or 3 m in all directions.

Such regular spacing, if it exists (and casual observation certainly suggests that it does) must be the result of some sort of mutually disadvantageous interaction between the individuals. Went suggested that allelopathy was involved in this pattern in a widely quoted statement made in 1955: 'Another Death Valley plant endowed with a remarkable root system is the evergreen creosote bush. It has wide reaching roots which can extract water from a large volume of soil. The creosote bush is spread with amazingly even spacing over the desert; this is especially obvious from an aeroplane. The spacing apparently is due to the fact that the roots of the bush excrete toxic substances which kill any seedlings which start near it. The distance of spacing is correlated with rainfall; the less rainfall the wider the spacing. This probably means that rain leaches the poisons from the soil so that they do not contaminate so wide an area. We commonly find young creosote bushes along roads in the desert, where the road builders have torn up the old bushes.' Rainfall measurements have been carried out at many stations in the California desert for varying numbers of years. We chose our experimental sites as close as possible to rainfall stations, preferably stations where records had been kept for some years (see map, Fig. 1). Eight sites were sampled in the Mojave Desert and four in the Sonoran desert. Each site was selected to be as near to the weather recording station as possible, to be on as level an area as possible, and to have minimum dissection by drainage channels.

METHODS

We used three principles in selecting the methods of sampling of the population: (i) since it was not easy to find a large uniform area, the sample area should be reasonably circumscribed; (ii) we used at least one well-tried and widely accepted method, and another method, based on a different set of measurements, partly as a check on the first; (iii) because of the time involved in sampling such widely dispersed plants we used methods that could use the same sample points, and by which we could gather maximum data.

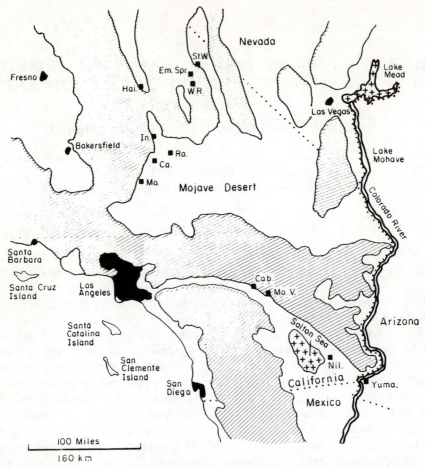

FIG. 1. The location of sample sites. St. W., Stovepipe Wells; Em. Sp., Emigrant Spring; WR, Wildrose; Hai, Haiwee; In., Inyokern; Ra., Randsburg; Ca., Cantil; Mo., Mojave; Cab., Cabazon; Mo. V., Morongo Valley; Nil., Niland.

At each site, a line 100 m long was laid out. Using a table of random numbers, sampling points were chosen by taking a number (from 1 to 100) along the tape, and then by taking another number (from 1 to 100) and pacing out the distance at right angles to our base line. Twenty-five points were taken on each side of the baseline, giving a total of fifty points, in an area 200 × 100 m. This was found to be an adequate area to avoid more than very occasional resampling of the same bushes, even where *Larrea* was very widely spaced.

The two methods used were the variance:mean ratio (Clapham 1936; Blackman 1942 and others), and the point-to-plant distance method of Pielou (1959). The variance:mean ratio method uses a significance test (*t* test) for the difference between the observed and expected variance:mean ratio. The advantages and disadvantages of this method have been discussed by Greig-Smith (1964), but the major possible source of inaccuracy is the effect of the size of quadrat used. Pielou's method was designed to avoid this. She pointed out that in order to test whether or not plants are randomly dispersed, one needs two of the following three observations:

1. An estimate of density.
2. A sample of plant-to-neighbouring-plant distances.
3. A sample of point-to-nearest-plant distances.

She chose (1) and (3) because one obtains a measure of density, which is useful in itself, because the selection of random points is easier than the selection of random plants, and also because an index based on point-to-plant distances will be affected by all scales of non-randomness in the population.

For Pielou's method: r, distance from random point-to-plant nearest to point; D, density of plants/unit area; N, number of sample points; α, statistic (if >1 the plants are aggregated, if <1 the plants are regular). Then

$$\alpha = \pi D \frac{r^2}{N}$$

For $N = 50$, the 95% confidence intervals for α are 0·742–1·296.

Our procedure at each sample point was to measure the distance to the nearest individual of *Larrea*. The central point of the shrub was taken as the position of the individual, to avoid errors that might be introduced by the large size of some plants. Then, with our sample point as centre, a circular quadrat was described, the area being 1000 ft^2 (93 m^2) in all sites except Niland and Stovepipe Wells, where it was 4000 ft^2 (370 m^2). All individuals of *Larrea* within this circle were counted, and the total number of individuals of all other shrub species was recorded. Data on the nature of the substratum were noted at the same time. A brief description of each site is given in Table 1. In addition to

Table 1. *The sites sampled for pattern, density and cover in* Larrea divaricata; *July–August* 1966

Wildrose	In Wildrose Canyon, Death Valley; gravelly substratum, with largest particles 2–3 in. (5–7·5 cm), several inches deep
Emigrant Spring	400 yd (365 m) south of Emigrant Ranger Station, Death Valley; 5° slope to north, dissected by small washes; stony soil with boulders up to 12 in. (30 cm) in diameter
Stovepipe Wells	Very gentle north-facing slope on outwash fan, 400 yd (365 m) south of Stovepipe Wells Hotel, Death Valley; much dissected by small washes; some dead individuals of *Larrea*; rubble between ½ and 6 in. (1·3–15 cm); much of area covered by 'desert pavement'
Randsburg	½ mile (0·8 km) south of Randsburg on gentle (5°) south-east slope; gravelly substratum, several inches deep, with particles up to 1 in. (2·5 cm); some mining disturbance
Haiwee	¼ mile (0·4 km) west of reservoir; 5° slope to east, gravel, with largest particles up to 1 in. (2·5 cm); occasional scattered larger rocks; very shallow soil
Mojave	1½ miles (2·4 km) north of Mojave; level site on deep coarse gravel, few rocks over 1 in. (2·5 cm); heavy grazing; much die-back in *Larrea*
Inyokern	1 mile (1·6 km) south-west of Inyokern; almost level site, coarse gravel with few large particles
Cantil	1 mile (1·6 km) north of Cantil; very gentle east slope; coarse sand; much die-back of *Larrea*
Morongo Valley	½ mile (0·8 km) east of Morongo Valley, south side of road; very sandy soil, much gullied, with hardpan at surface in places; *Larrea* forming huge individuals
Cabazon	1 mile (1·6 km) east of Cabazon; evidence of some grazing; very firm coarse gravel; many seedlings of *Larrea* in the area
Niland	2 miles (3·8 km) north-west of Niland; coarse gravel interspersed with pebbles, with shallow washes; some die-back of *Larrea* and many dead individuals of other species
Yuma	Dunes west of Yuma; level area of soft sand; *Larrea* only shrub species present; very large individuals in large mounds of sand

the twelve *Larrea* sites, an exactly similar procedure was followed in a date grove near Indio, where the palms were almost exactly 30 ft (9 m) apart in rows 30 ft apart. This completely regular arrangement enabled us to check on our methods.

RESULTS

Density

That there is a fairly good correlation of density with the annual rainfall is shown by Fig. 2. Cabazon deviates mostly from the general trend. It is a site with very large and widely spaced individuals of *Larrea*. Many of the shrubs are apparently very old and compact in contrast to the usual straggling growth of the species. This site is in an area of

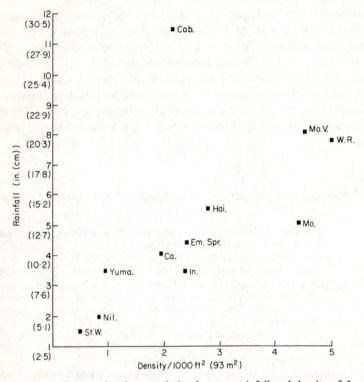

Fig. 2. Scatter diagram showing correlation between rainfall and density of *Larrea*.

almost continuous high wind, funnelled through the gap between the San Jacinto and San Gorgonio Mountains. It is possible that this increases the evapotranspiration level in the area to such an extent that it reduces the effective rainfall to a level below that measured by a rain gauge. If this were so it would bring this site more into line with the others. In general the correlation of density with rainfall is very close.

One striking point concerning the correlation of density with rainfall is that the density of *Larrea* appears to be more or less independent of that of other shrub species (see Table 2). For example, the two sites at Haiwee and Emigrant Spring have densities of other shrubs of 50·7 and 7·1/1000 ft^2 (93 m^2) respectively, yet the density of *Larrea* does not deviate from the general species trend. Some tentative conclusions can be drawn from the data on density of other shrubs; they are: (i) on the coarser, gravelly substrata

8

where there is a moderate amount of rain there is a high density of these shrubs; (ii) on the sandy soils there is a very low density; (iii) at very low rainfall levels there is a very low density.

Table 2. *The density of* Larrea divaricata *and of other shrubs in the sample sites*

Site	Mean annual rainfall			Density/1000 ft² (93 m²) of:	
	(in.)	(cm)		*Larrea*	Other shrubs
Cabazon	11·76	29·9	(32)	2·22	11·7
Morongo Valley	8·52	21·8	(17)	4·54	5·34
Wildrose Canyon	8·14	20·7	(4)	5·0	95·1
Randsburg	5·89	15·0	(24)	1·66	26·0
Haiwee	5·63	14·3	(38)	2·78	50·7
Mojave	5·02	12·8	(59)	4·6	1·28
Emigrant Spring	4·4	11·1	(4)	2·44	7·1
Cantil	3·92	10·0	(6)	1·93	6·92
Inyokern	3·57	9·1	(16)	2·44	69·2
Yuma	3·56	9·1	(40)	1·0	0·0
Niland	1·88	4·8	(19)	0·79	3·49
Stovepipe Wells	1·56	4·0	(10)	0·56	0·44
Date grove				4·52*	

* Density of date palm.
The figures in parentheses after the rainfall figures are the number of years over which rainfall records have been kept.

Table 3. *The pattern of* Larrea divaricata *at twelve sites in California*

Population	Mean annual rainfall		Variance:mean	Pielou's
	(in.)	(cm)		statistic
Wildrose	8·14	20·7	2·955***	1·048
Morongo Valley	8·52	21·8	1·70***	1·162
Randsburg	5·89	15·0	1·512**	0·982
Haiwee	5·63	14·3	1·12	1·015
Cabazon	11·76	29·9	0·837	0·898
Stovepipe Wells	1·56	4·0	0·796	0·973
Niland	1·88	4·8	0·728	0·815
Mojave	5·02	12·8	0·701	0·802
Inyokern	3·57	9·1	0·583*	0·897
Emigrant Spring	4·4	11·1	0·551*	0·798
Cantil	3·92	10·0	0·421**	1·073
Yuma	3·56	9·1	0·408**	0·787
Date grove			0·111***	0·600

Significantly non-random at the following levels: * 5%; ** 1%; *** 0·1%.

Pattern

The data for variance:mean ratio are shown in Table 3, together with those for Pielou's method; the relative merits of the two methods will be discussed later. With one exception (Cantil) they were in agreement as to the type of pattern displayed by *Larrea* in these twelve sites.

These data show that where rainfall is high there is a tendency to aggregation in *Larrea*, very marked in the two populations at Wildrose and Morongo Valley. At moderate rainfall levels there is regularity; the four populations which show a significant departure from randomness in the direction of regularity (by the variance:mean method), all occur when rainfall levels are between 3·5 and 4·5 in. (9–11·5 cm)/annum. Of the remaining populations, Haiwee, with an annual rainfall of 5·63 in. (14·3 cm), departs from randomness in the direction of aggregation; and this might be expected on the basis of rainfall level. The remaining populations do not fit in with the general trend, and require further discussion.

Cabazon, with a rainfall of 11·76 in. (29·9 cm)/annum, is the most striking in its departure from the trend. The reasons cited earlier for its low density may well account for this; it is much more regular than expected. Mojave, with its annual rainfall of 5·02 in. (12·8 cm), and its tendency to regularity, is subject to severe grazing, and we cannot say how much this affects its behaviour. The two populations of areas of very low rainfall (Stovepipe Wells with 1·56 in. (4·0 cm) and Niland with 1·88 in. (4·8 cm)/annum) tend toward regularity. Features that these two populations have in common are extremely low density, which may lead to unreliability of the methods used, and a high degree of dissection of the terrain. These are areas of scarce but often violent rainfall, and they are criss-crossed by well-marked drainage channels, in which no shrubs grow. Presumably the infrequent storms cause such drastic run-off that plants cannot survive in these washes. This must affect the distribution of the shrubs. Taking all these facts into account, there is a surprisingly strong association of aggregation with high and regularity with low rainfall.

DISCUSSION

The density and pattern of *Larrea divaricata* in the Californian desert is generally correlated with rainfall. What are the possible explanations for these relationships? In a habitat in which plants are under high environmental stress, as in the desert, it is perhaps possible to see more clearly the direct effect of major factors than in a complex, less limiting environment. In the desert, there is no doubt that availability of water is one of the most important limiting factors. The variety of drought avoidance, evasion and tolerance mechanisms evolved by desert plants bears witness to this. However, water availability must be considered in the context of the characteristics of the plant as well as the habitat. For example, Walter (1962) states 'the water balance of isolated plants in the desert is not so bad as is generally believed. In effect the density of the vegetational cover is proportional to the precipitation, in such a way that, per unit of transpiring surface, plants receive the same quantity of water as in humid climates.' There is an implication in this statement that because of an increased distance between individuals each individual has an increased volume of soil from which it can obtain the moisture it requires. Thus where moisture is very low the spacing of the plants will be wider than where it is less limiting. Our figures for density of *Larrea*, with the close correlation that they show with rainfall, give some support for Walter's view.

Pattern in desert plants has attracted much attention, but surprisingly very little quantitative work has been carried out on it. Greig-Smith & Chadwick (1965) investigated pattern in *Acacia–Capparis* semi-desert scrub near Khartoum, in the Sudan. They found no evidence of regular pattern resulting from competition between individuals for water. However, they did find some evidence that there was competition between seedlings and between smaller individuals of *Acacia*, and this might result in a more regular spacing in older stands. Anderson (1967) similarly did not find regularity in *Atriplex vesicaria* in Australia, and pointed out that field data were necessary to substantiate the suggestions made in the literature that distributions in arid regions are regular. Pielou (1959) discussing the results she obtained using synthetic populations stated 'A sparse, regular population would be unlikely to occur in nature ... ; regularity in a plant population would be expected to occur only when the available space was almost fully occupied.' These three pieces of information, two the result of field observation, the other of inference, suggest that the situation we have demonstrated for *Larrea*—the occurrence of regular distribution in a very sparse population—is unlikely to be a common one.

Viewed in the light of Walter's and Pielou's statements, however, it is not altogether surprising that a shrub growing under such conditions of low water availability is regularly spaced. If water is scarce, plant cover will be sparse, and the result will be that as far as root spread is concerned, the available space *is* almost fully occupied. In this connection it is worth quoting from Cannon (1911) in his classic account of the root systems of desert plants.

Cannon investigated two plants of *Larrea*, one on a bajada (outwash fan) and the other on a flood plain. The root system of the plant on the flood plain was much deeper, and less spreading than that on the bajada, but the systems occupied about the same volume of soil. As Cannon said, these differences make it imperative that fewer plants occupy a given space on the bajada than on the flood plain. In excavating the plant on the bajada he found that: '60 roots of neighbouring Covillias (Larreas) were encountered at the same level, and frequently in physical contact with the roots of the plant studied, and very many more were met between the levels of these roots and the surface of the ground. Therefore the competition between neighbouring Covilleas on the bajada, for soil water, is presumably keen.' It would be interesting to know what the pattern of *Larrea* was on that site.

It is likely, then, that the regular spacing of *Larrea* in many sites of low rainfall is the result of root competition for available water. What of Went's hypothesis that the regular spacing is the result of toxic exudation from the roots of *Larrea*? Went based this view on the observation (1952) that seedlings in close proximity to established bushes of *Larrea* were seen to die through the season, at first beneath the bushes, and later gradually extending outwards. Very recently some experimental work has been carried out on *Larrea* extracts (Knipe & Herbel 1966) and the relevant portion of their work showed that *Larrea* root extracts do not inhibit germination or growth of *Larrea* seedlings, nor are they detrimental to mature plants. Their observations suggested that there is a high mortality in *Larrea* seedlings from drought, heat and disease, but not toxins.

The effectiveness of the methods used for detecting pattern

Table 3 gives the results for the two methods used in this investigation, the variance: mean ratio, and Pielou's point-to-plant method. For seven of the twelve sample sites, the variance:mean ratio method gives significant deviation from random. Although Pielou's method shows a deviation toward aggregation or regularity in the same direction as the variance:mean method in all cases except one (Cantil), the deviation is not significant. However, the general agreement between the two methods encourages us to believe that our data have some validity.

Pielou comments that her method was most unreliable when her artificial population was sparse, and Hopkins (1954), using a point-to-plant and plant-to-plant method, found the same. Our data suggest that her method is giving the right sort of result, but that our sample size was too small for this sort of population. Of particular interest is the result for the date grove. Here, in a widely spaced, very regular population, her method gives a highly significant non-randomness in the direction of regularity, and it is here in full agreement with the variance:mean ratio.

ACKNOWLEDGMENTS

Our thanks are due to those students who gave valuable help at three of the sites. We are especially grateful to Ernst-Detlef Schülze and Hikmat Al-Ani, who helped in the collection of data at the remaining sites. Useful suggestions have been made by Professor Harlan Lewis.

SUMMARY

At twelve sites in California, the density and pattern of *Larrea divaricata* has been measured. There is a good correlation between density and the amount of rainfall. At high rainfall levels, *Larrea* tends to be clumped, and at low levels it is regularly spaced.

REFERENCES

Anderson, D. J. (1967). Studies on structure in plant communities. V. Pattern in *Atriplex vesicaria* communities in south-eastern Australia. *Aust. J. Bot.* **15**, 451–8.

Baker, H. G. (1966). Volatile growth inhibitors produced by *Eucalyptus globulus*. *Madroño*, **18**, 207–10.

Blackman, G. E. (1942). Statistical and ecological studies in the distribution of species in plant communities. I. *Ann. Bot.* N.S. **6**, 351–70.

Cannon, W. A. (1911). The root habits of desert plants. *Publs Carnegie Instn*, **131**.

Clapham, A. R. (1936). Over-dispersion in grassland communities and the use of statistical methods in plant ecology. *J. Ecol.* **24**, 232-51.

Greig-Smith, P. (1964). *Quantitative Plant Ecology*, 2nd edn. London.

Greig-Smith, P. & Chadwick, M. J. (1965). Data on pattern within plant communities. III. *Acacia–Capparis* semi-desert scrub in the Sudan. *J. Ecol.* **53**, 465–74.

Hopkins, B. (1954). A new method for determining the type of distribution of plant individuals. *Ann. Bot.* N.S. **18**, 213–26.

Knipe, D. & Herbel, C. H. (1966). Germination and growth of some semidesert grassland species treated with aqueous extract from creosote bush. *Ecology*, **47**, 775–81.

Leopold, A. S. (1963). *The Desert*. Amsterdam.

Pielou, E. C. (1959). The use of point-to-plant distances in the study of the pattern of plant populations. *J. Ecol.* **47**, 607–13.

U.S. Weather Bureau (1898–1965). *Climatological Data: Annual Summaries*. Washington D.C.

Walter, H. (1962). Die Wasservergorgung der Wustenpflanzen. *Scientia, Bologna*, **59**, 1–7.

Went, F. W. (1952). The effects of rain and temperature on plant distribution in the desert. *Desert Research: Proceedings International Symposium, Jerusalem*, pp. 220–37.

Went, F. W. (1955). The ecology of desert plants. *Scient. Am.* **192**, 68–75.

(*Received* 28 *March* 1968)

THE CAUSES OF REGULAR PATTERN IN DESERT PERENNIALS

BY T. J. KING* AND S. R. J. WOODELL

Botany School, South Parks Road, Oxford OX1 3RA

INTRODUCTION

Woodell, Mooney & Hill (1969) demonstrated a positive correlation between the density of 'individuals' of *Larrea divaricata* Cav. and rainfall, over twelve sites in the Sonoran and Mojave deserts, California. They also found 'a surprisingly strong association of aggregation with high and regularity with low rainfall', and suggested on the basis of these and other data that the regular spacing of *L. divaricata* in many sites of low rainfall is likely to be the result of root competition for available water. Anderson (1971) rejected this hypothesis. Barbour (1973) re-iterates Anderson's view. Some fallacies are pointed out here in the arguments put forward by Anderson (1971), some new evidence is considered, and some of the possible causes of regular patterns are discussed.

CAN REGULARITY BE DEMONSTRATED?

Regularity has been demonstrated in three species of desert shrubs.

(1) Woodell *et al.* (1969) found significantly regular patterns ($P < 0.05$ by the variance: mean ratio method) in four populations of *Larrea divaricata* in California.

(2) Waisel (1971) found some regular patterns in *Zygophyllum dumosum* Boiss. in Israel. Some of his results are summarized in Table 1. The site where regularity occurred had a somewhat lower rainfall than the site where random patterns were found. East of Mezad Tamar, *Z. dumosum* was aggregated in wadis.

(3) Beals (1968) demonstrated regular patterns of individuals of *Cadaba rotundifolia* Forsk. in the Danikil desert, Ethiopia, by the variance:mean ratio method and by χ^2 tests of goodness to fit to the Poisson model. Anderson (1971) claimed that the results of Beals (1968) suggested a random pattern, not a regular one, because the ratios of observed to expected variance of 0·67 and 0·65 on the Poisson model for 'all shrubs' and 'shrubs > 1 m diameter' fell inside the 95% two-tailed confidence band of 0·64–1·44. However, Beals (1968, and personal communication) chose his site to show quantitatively that the individuals were distributed regularly. Thus the appropriate significance test was one-tailed, and since both these ratios fall outside the 95% one-tailed confidence limit of about 0·68, and even fall outside the shortest unbiased 95% confidence limits for a two-tailed test (Rohlf & Sokal 1969), there is no reason to reject the conclusion reached by Beals. Anderson (1971) did not refer to the goodness to fit test to the expected Poisson distribution (Beals 1968), which showed significant regularity for 'all shrubs' at the 0·1% level.

* Present address: Westminster School Science Laboratories, 20 Great College Street, London SW1 3RU.

Reproduced with permission from *The Journal of Ecology*, 61:761–765. Published by Blackwell Scientific Publications. Oxford and Edinburgh.

It is most likely that significant regularity in desert shrubs at the 5% level would have been demonstrated in many cases at increased sample sizes. Some populations might have had true variance:mean ratios of, say, 0·75, but the 95% confidence limits for a sample of fifty quadrats are 0·64–1·44. Significant regularity in such a population is unlikely to be found.

It is suggested that those using the Poisson model should specify the degree of regularity which they wish to detect. For instance, they might wish to have a high probability of detecting regularity in any population with a true variance:mean ratio of 0·75 or less. By assuming that the population had a true variance:mean ratio of 0·75, and that this ratio is χ^2-distributed, they could calculate the approximate sample size needed to have a given

Table 1. *Some of the variance:mean ratios obtained by Waisel* (1971) *for Zygophyllum dumosum in Israel*

Site sampled	Approximate mean annual rainfall (mm)	Mean no. shrubs/16 m²	Variance: mean ratio	Interpretation
Sede Boquer (A)	91	4·0	0·90 NS	Random
Sede Boquer (C)	91	4·0	2·2 ***	Clumped
Mezad Tamar (D)	80	1·8	0·36***	Regular
Mezad Tamar (E)	80	2·1	0·18***	Regular
Mezad Tamar (F)	80	8·6	0·11***	Regular
E. of Mezad Tamar (G)	60	0·6	5·5 ***	Clumped
E. of Mezad Tamar (H)	60	2·0	2·7 ***	Clumped

Twenty-five quadrats, each 16 m² in area, were examined in each case. NS, $P > 0.05$; ***, $P < 0.001$, when compared with V:M = 1.

probability (say 90%) of obtaining a significant departure from a variance:mean ratio of one. This sample size could then be used in the investigation.

ANDERSON'S OBJECTIONS TO THE INTERPRETATION OF THE EVIDENCE

Woodell *et al.* (1969) based their hypothesis that regularity in *Larrea divaricata* is the consequence of competition for a limiting water resource on (i) the positive correlation between rainfall and shrub density, (ii) the positive correlation between rainfall and variance:mean ratio, and (iii) other evidence, e.g. of shrub root distribution, and against allelopathic influences on pattern (Knipe & Herbel 1966). Anderson (1971) objected to the explanation on the grounds that (i) the assumptions underlying the analysis of the data were invalid, and (ii) calculations on the data suggested that the volume of water available per shrub *increased* with increasing regularity in shrub pattern.

Firstly, the three most important assumptions which Anderson (1971) attributes to Woodell *et al.* (1969) are as follows.

(1) 'that there is a uniform distribution of rainfall (both temporally and spatially) in the sites they examined, and that this is associated with a lack of surface run-off and subsequent infiltration and redistribution of rainfall'. However, the peculiarities of each site were allowed for to some extent in interpreting plant patterns (Woodell *et al.* 1969, p.42).

(2) 'that density of individuals is comparable to Walter's (1962) concept of "density of the vegetational cover," ' i.e. that *L. divaricata* bushes were the same size, and their size distribution was the same, from site to site. Fig. 1 shows the distribution of shrub diameters at each of the twelve sites sampled by Woodell *et al.* (1969). There is considerable variation between sites in shrub size and size-distribution.

(3) 'that the *Larrea* populations they examined contained only even-aged or at least

physiologically comparable individuals'. If age is reflected in size, the data in Fig. 1 show that the *Larrea* populations were not even-aged.

Thus the sites certainly differed in substratum, mean shrub size and shrub size-distribution. Despite these differences, variation in rainfall accounted for much more of the

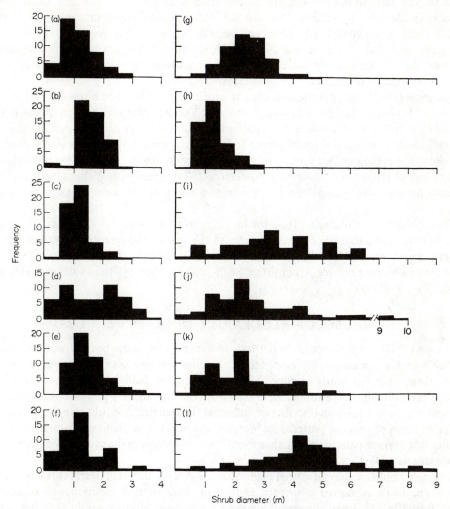

Fig. 1. Histograms illustrating the frequency of shrubs of *Larrea divaricata* in each diameter class at each site sampled by Woodell *et al.* (1969). The height and largest diameter of the shrub nearest each random sampling point were measured. Shrub height was related to diameter over all sites by the regression equation: $H = 0.035 + 0.476D$ in which $H =$ shrub height (m) and $D =$ shrub diameter (m). (a) Inyokern; (b) Emigrant Spring; (c) Stovepipe Wells; (d) Niland; (e) Haiwee; (f) Mojave; (g) Cantil; (h) Wildrose Canyon; (i) Morongo Valley; (j) Cabazon; (k) Randsburg; (l) Yuma.

variation in pattern than any other factor examined. A mere correlation does not imply a causal relationship, but the hypothesis suggested seems the most reasonable.

Secondly, Anderson (1971) calculated the mean rainfall per individual of *L. divaricata* per year ('available water') at each of the four sites at which Woodell *et al.* (1969) had found significantly regular patterns by the variance : mean ratio method. He suggested

15

that the positive correlation between regularity and rainfall per individual was evidence that regularity in *L. divaricata* was not the result of competition for a limiting water resource.

In arranging the four sites in order of regularity, Anderson (1971) was assuming that a variance : mean ratio from a sample of fifty quadrats provides a good indication of the relative regularity of different populations. Yet on the basis of χ^2 tests of the goodness of fit of the raw data to the Poisson model, the order of regularity is different. Moreover, when only the sites at which individuals of *L. divaricata* have significantly ($P < 0.05$) regular patterns are considered, there is no basis for assuming that rainfall (or 'available water per individual') accounts for much of the variation in pattern type which remains between sites. Shrub size, for instance, could now account for much of the variation in pattern through its interaction with 'available water'.

Anderson (1971) arranged the four sites at which *L. divaricata* had a regular pattern in the order: Inyokern, Emigrant Spring, Cantil and Yuma. From Inyokern to Yuma both regularity and the 'available water' per individual increased. Fig. 1 shows that the size of individuals also increased markedly from Inyokern to Yuma. Calculations would doubtless show that as the sampled shrub pattern becomes more regular, there is less rainfall per unit *volume* of foliage of *L. divaricata*. Anderson (1971) agrees with Walter (1962) that in dryland habitats the 'foliage density' is likely to be regulated according to the water supply.

For these reasons, quite apart from the fact that 'available water' per individual cannot be calculated without detailed measurements of the spatial and temporal distribution of rainfall, infiltration and run-off, the hypothesis that regularity might be due to competition for a limited water resource is consistent with, and justified by, the evidence given by Woodell *et al.* (1969).

THE CAUSES OF REGULARITY IN DESERT SHRUBS

Anderson (1971) sought another hypothesis to explain regularity, but did not state one explicitly in his discussion. He emphasized that the younger plants in populations of desert shrubs are frequently clumped. This clumping gradually disappears with time, owing to the elimination of small individuals from the high density phases of the mosaic, and this results in a random distribution amongst the remaining shrubs. He thus regards the production of random patterns as 'normal' in shrubs in dryland environments, and implies that regular patterns are chance events rare in nature, perhaps caused by unusual combinations of factors.

However, regularity has now been demonstrated in three different desert shrub species, and in one of them, *Larrea divaricata*, at four or more sites. The elimination of small plants from the high density phases of a mosaic could easily produce a regular rather than a random pattern in the remaining individuals, especially in homogeneous environments subject to intense stress. Anderson, Jacobs & Malik (1969) demonstrated a progressive reduction in pattern intensity with increasing shrub size in *Atriplex vesicaria* Heward at Oxley, New South Wales (site AV9); as the plants became larger, their pattern was 'trending towards regularity'. Unfortunately no figures were given for rainfall at the sites studied.

In low rainfall climates, like those of the Californian deserts, the lower the mean annual rainfall, the greater its variability. Some of the regular patterns in desert perennials may have originated during long droughts, when intraspecific competition for water became so intense that individuals close to others were selectively eliminated. Subsequently regularity might have been maintained by the inability of young plants, in the face of intense competition, to establish themselves close to older individuals. This hypothesis, touched on by Walter (1962) and Beals (1968), accounts for the fact that regularity of *Larrea divaricata* is more frequent, in general, at sites with the lowest mean annual rainfalls.

Anderson (1971) states that 'if a low rainfall regime is associated with competition between adjacent plants for a limiting water resource, and if these combined factors are the prime determinants of pattern in populations of desert perennials, then it is surprising that so great a diversity of pattern—regular, random and contagious—is detected in the field'. However, if the mechanism discussed by Anderson (1971) is invoked, one would *expect* to find these different patterns in the field (at least in *L. divaricata*) according to the age-structure and droughting history of the shrub population.

ACKNOWLEDGMENTS

We are grateful to Professor D. J. Anderson for his helpful comments on the first draft of this paper.

SUMMARY

The evidence that regular patterns occur in populations of desert shrubs is reviewed. The objections by Anderson (1971) to the hypothesis of Woodell *et al.* (1969) that regularity in *Larrea divaricata* in California is due to competition for a limiting water resource are discussed and refuted.

REFERENCES

Anderson, D. J. (1971). Pattern in desert perennials. *J. Ecol.* **59**, 555–60.
Anderson, D. J., Jacobs, S. W. L. & Malik, A. R. (1969). Studies on structure in plant communities. VI. The significance of pattern evaluation in some Australian dry-land vegetation types. *Aust. J. Bot.* **17**, 315–22.
Barbour, M. G. (1973). Desert dogma re-examined: root/shoot productivity and plant spacing. *Am. Midl. Nat.* **89**, 41–57.
Beals, E. W. (1968). Spatial pattern of shrubs on a desert plain in Ethiopia. *Ecology*, **49**, 744–6.
Knipe, D. & Herbel, C. H. (1966). Germination and growth of some semi-desert grassland species treated with aqueous extract from creosote bush. *Ecology*, **47**, 775–81.
Rohlf, F. J. & Sokal, R. R. (1969). *Statistical Tables*. Freeman, San Francisco.
Waisel, Y. (1971). Patterns of distribution of some xerophytic species in the Negev, Israel. *Israel J. Bot.* **20**, 101–10.
Walter, H. (1962). Die Wasserversorgung der Wüstenpflanzen. *Scientia, Bologna*, **59**, 1–7.
Woodell, S. R. J., Mooney, H. A. & Hill, A. J. (1969). The behaviour of *Larrea divaricata* (creosote bush) in response to rainfall in California. *J. Ecol.* **57**, 37–44.

(*Received 26 February* 1973)

LIFE TABLES FOR NATURAL POPULATIONS OF ANIMALS

By EDWARD S. DEEVEY, Jr.

Osborn Zoological Laboratory, Yale University

(Contribution No. 384 from the Woods Hole Oceanographic Institution)

At sperat adulescens diu se victurum, quod sperare idem senex non potest. Insipienter sperat; quid enim stultius quam incerta pro certis habere, falsa pro veris?

—Cicero, *De Senectute*

INTRODUCTION

"THE certainty of death", remarks Sir Thomas Browne, "is attended with uncertainties, in time, manner, places." The same refrain, audible in classical authors from Horace to Hoffenstein, embodies immutable truth. But the rise of life insurance has taught us to ask the fatal question differently. We now substitute "probability" for "certainty," and have exchanged our fates for parameters of populations. The dictum of Galilei, "to measure what can be measured, to make measurable what can not be measured," has been applied to the product of Lachesis' loom, with interesting results.

There is no evidence that man's maximum life span has been lengthened a particle since antiquity. The celebrated cases of fantastic longevity, from Methuselah to Thomas Parr, do not withstand critical scrutiny. The mean length of life, however, differs widely among the races of men, is notably lower for most primitives than for civilized populations, and has been increasing by leaps and bounds in the United States during the last century. In ancient Rome, according to Macdonell's analysis (1913), the expectation of life at age 10 was an additional 22 years, compared to an additional 55 years for a male resident of the United States in 1929–31 (Dublin and Lotka, 1935).

The Romans, in fact, knew more about such matters than might be supposed from their superstition that "ten times twelve solar years were the term fixed for the life of man, beyond which the gods themselves had no power to prolong it; that

the fates had narrowed the span to thrice thirty years, and that fortune abridged even this period by a variety of chances, against which the protection of the gods was implored" (Hodge, 1857, cited from Niebuhr's *History of Rome*). A table showing the expection of life at birth, at age 20, and at 5-year intervals thereafter, evidently based on real experience and intended for the computation of annuities, was in use in the third century A.D.; it is attributed to Ulpian (Trenerry, 1926). Even the Babylonians seem to have known about insurance contracts, though this does not necessarily imply any actuarial knowledge, and Horace's reference to "Babylonian numbers"—"Tu ne quaesieris (scire nefas) quem mihi, quem tibi finem di dederint, Leuconoe, nec Babylonios temptaris numeros" (*Odes*, I: 11)—may mean more than he intended.

Having gained some idea of the limits circumscribing his own mortality, man has turned to look at the other animals. In 1935 Pearl and Miner, in their discussion of the comparative mortality of lower organisms, attempted to formulate a general theory of mortality. They quickly gave up the attempt upon realizing that the *environmental* determinants of life duration can not, at least as yet, be disentangled from such *biological* determinants as genetic constitution and rate of living. They ended with a plea for "more observational data, carefully and critically collected for different species of animals and plants, that will follow through the life history from birth to death of each individual in a cohort of statistically respectable magnitude." Thus by implication Pearl and Miner appealed to the ecologists, who for the most part have been busy elsewhere. Accounts of the conceptions and methodology of life tables have not yet found their way into textbooks of ecology, and while field naturalists have devoted increasing attention to the dynamics of natural populations

Reproduced with permission from The Quarterly Review of Biology, 22: 283–314, 1947. Published by The Williams and Wilkins Company, Baltimore, Maryland.

most of them have been content to leave the construction of life tables to the statisticians and laboratory ecologists.

This article, which is designed as an introduction to the subject rather than as a formal review, brings together from the ecological literature a mass of information bearing on the survival of animals in nature. This information has not heretofore been considered relevant by biometricians working with human populations, nor has it ever been considered in its context by ecologists. In collecting the material it was immediately obvious that it is still too early to formulate general theories. Serious deficiencies are only too apparent in the data. But the difficulties differ from case to case, and are therefore not insurmountable. Moreover, the bibliography will show that virtually all of this knowledge has been acquired in the twelve years since the appearance of the review by Pearl and Miner. By taking stock now, and by calling attention to gaps in our information, it is hoped that some guidance can be given to ecologists and others in the gathering of new material.

THE MEANING OF THE LIFE TABLE

A life table is a concise summary of certain vital statistics of a population. Beginning with a cohort, real or imaginary, whose members start life together, the life table states for every interval of age the number of deaths, the survivors remaining, the rate of mortality, and the expectation of further life. These columns are symbolized by d_x, l_x, q_x and e_x, respectively, where x stands for age. Additional columns which may be tabled include the age structure (L_x) or the number of persons living who are between ages x and $x + 1$.

Because all the life table functions can be calculated from each other, it makes little difference where one begins in summarizing the method of construction. It is convenient to begin with deaths at given ages (d_x), since these usually make up the "raw data." A curve obtained by plotting number of deaths against age is obviously a histogram showing the frequency distribution of deaths. It is customary to reduce the data to a relative basis by expressing the observed number of deaths at any age as a fraction of the total number of deaths. Such fractions stated as percentages and carried out to three figures include a decimal place; in this review and elsewhere where small samples are involved, it is the practice to drop the decimal

point and put deaths, etc., on a "per thousand" basis. Starting, then, with a cohort of 1000 individuals born together, survivorship (l_x) is obtained by successive subtraction of deaths in the age interval from survivors at the beginning of the age interval. Mortality rate (q_x) is the fraction of those living at the beginning of the age interval who die during the interval, $q_x = d_x/l_x$, and is usually expressed here on a per thousand basis, $1000\ q_x = 1000\ d_x/l_x$.

The calculation of expectation of life is more complicated. For individuals at age 0 (at the beginning of their life span), it is the same as the mean length of life of the cohort. For older individuals, it is the mean life span remaining to those attaining a given age. It could therefore be calculated for any age x by measuring the area under the survivorship curve beyond x and dividing by the number of survivors attaining age x,

$$e_x = \frac{\int_x^{\omega} l_x \cdot dx}{l_x}$$

However, a life table, among other things, is a device for obtaining such integrals arithmetically, being divided into age intervals so small that changes between age x and $x + 1$ can be regarded as linear functions of x. It is therefore assumed that the *age structure*, L_x, or the number of persons alive who are between ages x and $x + 1$, which is exactly given by

$$L_x = \int_x^{x+1} l_x \cdot dx$$

is in practice given by

$$L_x = \frac{l_x + l_x + 1}{2} \qquad *$$

Successive values of L_x obtained in this way are then summed from the bottom of the column up to each age x. This gives T_x, the total number of (persons × age units), or person-years if age is expressed in years still to be lived by persons of age x. Dividing by l_x, the number of persons, gives the expectation of life in age units,

$$e_x = \frac{T_x}{l_x}$$

Farner (1945) calculates e_x directly for each year of a bird's age by obtaining the mean after lifetime

---

*Author's note: Corrected equation is $\qquad L_x = \dfrac{l_x + l_{x+1}}{2}$

of birds alive on their first November 1, doing the same for birds alive on their second November 1, and so on. This procedure is cumbersome, and is more accurate than the method given here only if the deaths in any year are so unequally distributed through the year that a serious error results from ignoring the fact (Lack, 1943b).

Nice (1937) gives, as Table XXVIII, the "theory as to age composition of a population of breeding birds; theoretical numbers of each age according to annual survival rate." As this table has been frequently used by students of bird populations, it is as well to understand its construction. Actually, it consists of a group of life table d_z columns, constructed on the assumption of mortality rates

the number of deaths. For the ratio of the living at any age to the total number living must equal the ratio of the dead at any age to the total number of deaths,

$$\frac{l_z}{\Sigma l_z} = \frac{d_z}{\Sigma d_z}.$$

But $\Sigma d_z = 100$, by convention; therefore

$$100\,\frac{l_z}{\Sigma l_z} = d_z.$$

By the same reasoning it can be shown that

$$100\,\frac{L_z}{\Sigma L_z} = d_z.$$

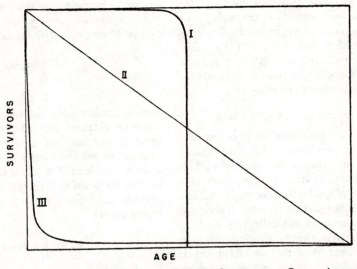

Fig. 1. Schematic Representation of Theoretical Types of Survivorship Curve, Adapted from Pearl and Miner (1935)

The survival axis can be graduated either arithmetically or logarithmically, but the logarithmic scale is more instructive, in that a straight line implies equal *rates* of mortality with respect to age.

which are *constant with respect to age*, but change from column to column between 75 and 25 per cent per year. It may seem surprising that a table of deaths should show the age composition of the living, but this is merely a consequence of starting with a round number of births, 100 in this case. Nice takes a cohort of 100 individuals and obtains their survivorship by successive applications of the assumed mortality rate until the number of survivors is reduced to 1. She then expresses the number living at any age as a percentage of the total number living at all ages, and thus the age composition of the living becomes identical with

Nice's table is convenient for ornithologists, since the assumption of constant age-specific mortality rates proves to be approximately true for adult birds. When mortality rates change with age, as they normally do, the table is inapplicable, though of course the age composition computed as percentage will always bear the same relationship to the d_z column. Nice states that her table applies to species breeding at one year of age, but this is not a necessary condition, as Farner (1945) has pointed out: it merely implies that the birth rate cannot be deduced from the life table age composition unless all members of the population breed every year.

The fact that the various life table columns are interconvertible makes it unnecessary to discuss all of them in dealing with a given species. Usually it is sufficient to focus attention on the survivorship curve, since this is most readily comprehensible. Pearl and Miner (1935; see also Pearl, 1940) have made it clear that there are three possible sorts of distribution of survivorship with respect to age, as shown diagrammatically in Fig. 1. Type I, the *negatively skew rectangular*, is shown by members of a cohort which, having been born at the same time, die more or less simultaneously after a life span which is presumably characteristic of the species. Type II is *diagonal* (when the logarithm of the number of survivors is plotted against age), implying a constant mortality rate for all age groups, or no one age as a favored time of dying. Type III, the *positively skew rectangular*, shows extremely heavy mortality beginning early in life, but the few individuals which survive to advanced ages have a relatively high expectation of further life.

Most survivorship curves hitherto published, including those for man, *Drosophila, Hydra, Agriolimax*, the mouse (Pearl and Miner, 1935), the vole (Leslie and Ranson, 1940), the black widow spider (Deevey and Deevey, 1945), *Tribolium* (Pearl Park, and Miner, 1941), and other laboratory animals, are variants of the diagonal type, or rather are intermediate between Type I and Type II. Type III has never been obtained with a laboratory population, though marine species with pelagic eggs and larvae, such as the oysters, would doubtless fall here if complete data were available. Type I has been observed in the case of adult *Drosophila* which were given no food, but this sort of survivorship is probably to be thought of as a laboratory curiosity.

KINDS OF LIFE TABLES

Life tables for human populations, which differ in certain important respects from animal populations in nature, are calculated by roundabout methods, most of which have little relevance to ecology. Some understanding of them is nonetheless essential. Census data show the number of persons born in a given year living in various political areas. Published vital statistics give the number of deaths in the same areas each year and the ages of those dying. By combining the two sets of figures it is possible to arrive at estimates of the rate of mortality (q_x) suffered by persons of a given age *at the time of the census*. Using a smooth curve fitted with exquisite precision to the q_x data,

a life table can be constructed on the assumptions: (1) that a standard cohort (100,000 persons) is born alive uniformly throughout the year of the census; (2) that its members will be exposed throughout life to these particular mortality rates; and (3) that there is no immigration or emigration.

A life table so derived exposes to view a purely theoretical population, one which might have existed at the time of the census, but which ceased to exist even before the census was complete. For human populations are notably subject to immigration and emigration; the best known ones are growing, and their age structure is therefore changing; and what is even more important, the mortality rates observed at the time of the census are certain to change with the passage of time. An example will make clear how ordinary life table procedure crystallizes an imaginary population from a series of "time-specific" death rates.

This example is a paraphrase of Merrell's lucid exposition delivered at the symposium on "Life Tables and Their Application" held at Boston on December 27, 1946.

In 1940 the individuals, born in 1890 and now living in a certain state, were exposed to a risk of death at their current age (50 years) which works out at 12.58 per thousand. By 1950 the survivors of these same individuals, now aged 60 years, will be exposed to a different risk of death, say 27.03 per thousand. Eventually the last survivor will be dead, having been subject, in his last year of life, to a mortality rate of 1000 per thousand, and at that time it will be theoretically possible to construct a survivorship curve for the original group of individuals born in the state in 1890 and suffering age-specific mortality rates which changed systematically throughout their lives. But this will be impossible to do in practice, since (1) the birth records for 1890 are incomplete, and (2) many of those whose births were recorded will have left the state and died elsewhere. Moreover, (3) they will have been replaced by a number (probably a larger number) of persons born elsewhere in 1890, subjected to different mortality risks for varying fractions of their lives, who appear in the death records merely as "born in 1890."

In 1940, however, we also know the mortality rate for individuals born in 1900, and now 40 years of age. By 1950, when these persons are 50 years old, their age-specific mortality rate at age 50 will be obtainable. It will not be 12.58 per thousand, but probably a slightly lower figure. In fact, the mortality rates for all ages will have changed slightly, some more, some less, by 1950, partly because of immigration and emigration and partly because of improvements in public health technique. The same applies, mutatis mutandis, to 1960, when the 1900 year-class are 60 years old. In actuarial practice *this does not matter*. By drawing a vertical line, as it were, through all the age-classes present in 1940, and taking their age-specific mortality rates as the basis of a life table, the actuary seizes the only way out of a troublesome situation. He erects a hypothetical population and tables its survivorship, its mortality rates, its age structure, and the expectation of life of its members, and his figures serve for ordinary purposes. In any case they are the best available until the next census, when they have to be completely revised.

A very different life table would result if, instead of arbitrarily halting the flow of events at some particular time, as 1940, we followed all the individuals born in a certain state in a particular year, and recorded their deaths as they occurred. This would be a "horizontal" life table. Human biologists are less interested in this type, for from their standpoint, life being long and patience short, it is more worth while to be able to predict the future than to describe the past. The life table for persons born in 1840 is not of pressing concern to medical scientists (or to insurance salesmen) in 1940, conditions having meanwhile changed profoundly. The two sorts of life table approach identity as the age structure of the population approaches stability in a uniform environment, but these considerations have no real meaning to the actuary, who deals with expanding populations in which births exceed deaths and which are constantly improving their own environmental conditions. The ecologist, on the other hand, is bound to be interested in both kinds of life table. If there is no change in the environment from year to year, and if the natural population is at equilibrium, with recruitment of each age class always kept exactly balanced by deaths, a horizontal life table for the year-class born in 1940 or any other year will be identical with a vertical life table drawn up for all year-classes present in 1940 or any other year. But normally there will be good years and bad years, both the birth rate and the age-specific death rates will oscillate more or less reciprocally, and the

resulting differences in the two sorts of life tables will be large.

Since the data necessary for a vertical life table include both a census of the age distribution of the living members of the population and a record of the deaths by ages, the horizontal life table is easier to construct. The experimental ecologist, in particular, can go at the problem directly, by allowing a large cohort to be born at the same time, keeping its members under observation throughout their lives, and recording deaths as they occur. Thus survivorship (l_x) and deaths (d_x) make up the raw data of his experiment. Mortality rates are then easily obtained as the ratio of the dying to the living at any age, and other life table functions follow just as readily. The environment having been maintained constant artificially, there should be no difference between such a life table and one built up vertically from a census made when the age structure becomes stable.

ECOLOGICAL LIFE TABLES

The field ecologist deals with populations which are by no means so elementary as those inside *Drosophila* bottles. Even the total size of the population of a species cannot be easily ascertained for an area large enough to be representative, and calculations of the birth rate and death rate are uncertain at best, largely owing to immigration and emigration. It is seldom indeed that the ecologist knows anything of the age structure of a natural population. In a few cases, growth rings on the scales or otoliths (fish) or horns (ungulates) make it possible to determine the age of an animal. Moore (1935) has shown that annual growth rings occur in the genital plates of sea-urchin tests, as they do in the shells of some molluscs. Moore checked the validity of the age determination by reference to the size-frequency distribution in his catches, and the separation of modal size classes in a population often affords a clue to age, particularly for younger age groups. The age of adult females can be determined in the case of certain mammals (whales, Wheeler, 1934, Laurie, 1937; seals, Bertram, 1940) by counting the corpora lutea in the ovaries. But for most animals it is possible to find out the ages of individuals only by marking them in some way.

Even when the age of a member of a natural population is known, it is not a simple matter to obtain accurate vital statistics. The source of greatest confusion lies in the impracticability of keeping the individuals under continuous observation. Migratory birds, for example, are easy to band as nestlings, but nearly impossible to find between fledging and the time they leave for winter quarters. Often they can not be found at all unless they return to the same area to breed, when they can be trapped in nest boxes. Their mortality between fledging and breeding can be calculated, but the calculation is rendered uncertain by the tendency of young birds not to return to their birthplaces as breeding adults.

As sources of data for the construction of life tables, the ecological information falls into three groups: (1) cases where the age at death (d_x) is directly observed for a large and reasonably random sample of the population; (2) cases where the survival (l_x) of a large cohort (born more or less simultaneously) is followed at fairly close intervals throughout its existence; (3) cases where the age structure is obtained from a sample, assumed to be a random sample of the population, and d_x is inferred from the shrinkage between successive age classes. It should be noticed that only the second sort of information is statistically respectable, since in so far as the breeding can safely be assumed to be simultaneous, it is comparable to that obtained from a *Drosophila* bottle. The first and third types can be used only if one is prepared to assume that the population is stable in time, so that the actual age distribution and the life table age distribution are identical. This assumption would certainly not be true of a human population; it may be approximately true for many natural populations of animals. When it is definitely not true, e.g., when certain age classes are stronger or weaker than they should be, to take the ages at death or the actual age structure as observed at any "instant" of time will give erroneous estimates of the age-specific mortality rates. In these cases it would be better to construct a series of horizontal life tables, one for each year class. A vertical life table could be constructed from the average age composition observed over many years, if the ages at death were also known. But the ecological information does not yet give both the census by ages and the deaths by ages for any one population.

In making comparisons between species that have widely different life spans, Pearl's device is very useful. This consists in shifting the origin of the age axis from zero to the mean length of life and regraduating the age scale so that age is expressed as percentage deviation from the mean.

In this way l_x values (and other life table functions, should they be desired) can be shown on the same graph in equal detail for rotifers, which live for a matter of days, and for birds, which live for many years. In connection with this method it has been customary to work with a fitted curve, the life table functions being calculated for equal percentage deviations, as −80%, −60%, −40%, etc. This procedure, applied to the natural populations considered in this review, would entail an enormous amount of arithmetical labor which does not seem to be justified by the end in view. Curve fitting minimizes observational error and generalizes the sweep of the observations, but in this case the generalization goes too far, in that it seems to confer a universality on the resulting life table which is not supported by the facts. The published life tables for *Drosophila*, the flour beetle, and other lower organisms apply only to the particular experimental conditions under which they were obtained. Under other conditions, e.g., with different population densities, the longevity will be different and different life tables will result. Accordingly, all life tables presented below have been treated simply, and age intervals, though expressed as percentage deviation from the mean longevity, have been entered in the tables only for values corresponding to the original observations. The only exception is the life table for *Balanus balanoides* (see footnote, Table 6).

Age at Death Directly Observed

In the course of his careful investigation of the wolves of Mt. McKinley, Murie (1944) picked up the skulls of 608 Dall mountain sheep (*Ovis d. dalli*) which had died at some time previous to his visit, and an additional 221 skulls of sheep deceased during the four years he spent in the Park. The age of these sheep at death was determinable from the annual rings on the horns. "Time, which antiquates antiquities, and hath an art to make dust of all things, hath yet spared these minor monuments" (Sir Thomas Browne, *Urn Burial*). Most of the deaths presumably occurred directly as a result of predation by wolves. Many skulls showed evidence of a necrotic bone disease, but it is not possible to say whether death was due solely to the disease or whether the disease merely ensured death by predation.

The mean longevity of the later sample is significantly greater (7.83 years) than that of the earlier (7.09 years), but the interpretation of this fact is not clear. The form of the distribution of deaths is sensibly the same in the two samples. As the survival of the members of this population is astonishingly great, it seems best to be conservative, and attention has been focussed on the larger, earlier sample. Except for the "lamb" and "yearling" classes, which are doubtless under-represented in the data owing to the perishability of their skulls, there is no reason to suppose that either group is anything but a fair sample of the total population, i.e., the probability of finding a

predation and that only the very young, which have not learned by experience, and the very old, which are too feeble to escape, suffer heavy losses. This survivorship curve is decidedly not of the positively skew rectangular type.

The second case to be discussed is that of an aquatic invertebrate, the sessile rotifer *Floscularia conifera*. This species has been studied by Edmondson (1945) under conditions which are fully as natural as those enjoyed by Murie's mountain sheep. *Floscularia* lives attached to water plants,

TABLE 1

Life table for the Dall Mountain Sheep (Ovis d. dalli) based on the known age at death of 608 sheep dying before 1937 (both sexes combined)*. Mean length of life 7.09 years
Data from Murie (1944)

x	x'	d_x	l_x	$1000\ q_x$	e_x
AGE (years)	AGE AS % DEVIATION FROM MEAN LENGTH OF LIFE	NUMBER DYING IN AGE INTERVAL OUT OF 1000 BORN	NUMBER SURVIVING AT BEGINNING OF AGE INTERVAL OUT OF 1000 BORN	MORTALITY RATE PER THOUSAND ALIVE AT BEGINNING OF AGE INTERVAL	EXPECTATION OF LIFE, OR MEAN LIFE-TIME REMAINING TO THOSE ATTAINING AGE INTERVAL (years)
0–0.5	−100	54	1000	54.0	7.06
0.5–1	−93.0	145	946	153.0	—
1–2	−85.9	12	801	15.0	7.7
2–3	−71.8	13	789	16.5	6.8
3–4	−57.7	12	776	15.5	5.9
4–5	−43.5	30	764	39.3	5.0
5–6	−29.5	46	734	62.6	4.2
6–7	−15.4	48	688	69.9	3.4
7–8	−1.1	69	640	108.0	2.6
8–9	+13.0	132	571	231.0	1.9
9–10	+27.0	187	439	426.0	1.3
10–11	+41.0	156	252	619.0	0.9
11–12	+55.0	90	96	937.0	0.6
12–13	+69.0	3	6	500.0	1.2
13–14	+84.0	3	3	1000	0.7

* A small number of skulls without horns, but judged by their osteology to belong to sheep nine years old or older, have been apportioned *pro rata* among the older age classes.

skull is not likely to be affected by the age of its owner. A life table for the 608 sheep has accordingly been prepared (Table 1). The survivorship curve, plotted logarithmically in Fig. 2, is remarkably "human" in showing two periods of relatively heavy mortality, very early and very late, with high and nearly constant survival ratios at intermediate ages.

The adult sheep have two principal methods of defense against wolves, their chief enemies: flight to higher elevations, where wolves can not pursue; and group action or herding. It is clear that these recourses confer a relative immunity to death by

especially *Utricularia*, surrounded by a tube constructed by itself out of pellets of detritus. The tube is added to at the top continuously throughout life, and Edmondson was able to identify all the members of a population living in a pond by dusting the *Utricularia* plant with a suspension of powdered carmine. On subsequent visits the *Floscularia* present at the time of dusting were conspicuously marked by bands of carmine-stained pellets in the walls of their tubes, each band being surmounted by new construction of varying widths. Thus in one operation the stage was set for an analysis of growth, age, birth-plus-immigration, and death in a natural population. Among other spectacular results, Edmondson found that the expectation of life of solitary individuals was only half as great as that of members of colonies of two or more, and he presented separate life tables for each component of the population, calculated from the age at death. To facilitate comparison with other species, however, solitary and colonial individuals have been lumped together (for Edmondson's "Experiment 1") in the life table of Table 2.

The survivorship curve (Fig. 2), like that of the Dall sheep, shows unexpectedly good survival. As Edmondson has pointed out, it is not so good as that of other rotifers reared in the laboratory under

(*Larus argentatus*) has recently been prepared by Paynter (*in press*). These gulls, banded as chicks at the Bowdoin Scientific Station, Kent Island, Bay of Fundy, have been recovered dead from all over North America. No special effort was made to recover banded gulls at their birthplace, and the colony is a large one (ca. 30,000 birds). The fact remains, however, that the first-year birds are perhaps more likely to be picked up than older birds near the place of banding, and perhaps less likely to be picked up elsewhere, so that some doubt can be cast on the reliability of the first-year recoveries as truly representative of the deaths in the first year. This troublesome point is probably

TABLE 2

Life table for the sessile rotifer Floscularia conifera based on the known age at death of 50 rotifers, both solitary and colonial. Mean length of life 4.74 days From Edmondson (1945), Experiment 1

x	x'	d_x	l_x	$1000\,q_x$	e_x
AGE (*days*)	AGE AS % DEVIATION FROM MEAN LENGTH OF LIFE	NUMBER DYING IN AGE INTERVAL OUT OF 1000 ATTACHING	NUMBER SURVIVING AT BEGINNING OF AGE INTERVAL OUT OF 1000 ATTACHING	MORTALITY RATE PER THOUSAND ALIVE AT BEGINNING OF AGE INTERVAL	EXPECTATION OF LIFE, OR MEAN LIFE TIME REMAINING TO THOSE ATTAINING AGE INTERVAL (*days*)
0–1	−100	20	1000	20	4.76
1–2	−78.9	200	980	204	3.78
2–3	−57.8	60	780	77	3.70
3–4	−36.7	0	720	0	2.98
4–5	−15.6	300	720	416	1.97
5–6	+5.4	140	420	333	2.02
6–7	+26.7	60	280	214	1.79
7–8	+47.7	140	220	636	1.14
8–9	+68.8	40	80	500	1.25
9–10	+90.0	20	40	500	1.00
10–11	+111.0	20	20	1000	0.50

standard conditions (*Proales decipiens, P. sordida, Lecane inermis*), but it is only a little less good, and life tables for these rotifers are notorious (Pearl and Miner, 1935) for their close approach to a Type I distribution.

The case of *Floscularia* is almost above reproach as an example of a life table obtained under natural conditions. It is, of course, open to the objection that only the age at death is known, and the age structure of the living animals must be assumed to be constant. Apart from this deficiency, it should also be realized that the origin of the life table is not at birth. The pelagic larval life of the rotifer, like the larval life of barnacles and insects, is omitted from consideration in such a table.

A life table for a population of herring gulls

less serious than with the songbirds to be discussed below; moreover, it is overshadowed by another difficulty, the fact that the study is not complete, and many of the banded birds are still alive. Paynter minimized this error by a compensatory adjustment; since banding began ten years ago and is still being carried out, first-year recoveries were divided by 10, second-year recoveries by 9, etc. Birds dying at ages greater than 10 years have naturally not yet been recorded, though a few are to be expected.

That these older birds will probably not change the life table appreciably is shown by Marshall's independent study (1947) of the longevity of the herring gull. Marshall used all available records of American herring gulls banded as young during

25

the last 25 years and subsequently recovered dead. Thus his data probably include most of the returns from the Kent Island population. Returns before September 1 of the first year of life were excluded, so that the life table refers to adult birds only. It differs from Paynter's chiefly in that it includes birds older than 10 years, one bird having lived as long as 17 years. Despite two factors which might be supposed to enhance the apparent longevity (exclusion of juvenile mortality; inclusion of older birds) the expectation of life is markedly lower than that of the Kent Island colony, 1.5 years on the first

tality before 1936, and Marshall's recoveries may have been predominantly from the earlier years, before banding started at Kent Island. The simplest explanation is that (3) an appreciable number of bands are lost by older birds, so that the mean age at death is actually higher than appears from the returns of banded birds.

These questions will doubtless be discussed by Paynter on the basis of direct observation of juvenile mortality, planned for the coming summer (1947) at Kent Island. Meanwhile, taking his life table at face value, the figures have been entered in

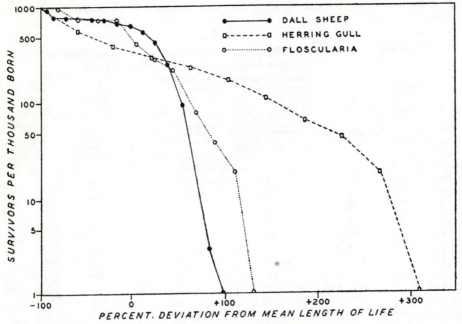

FIG. 2. SURVIVORSHIP (l_x) CURVES FOR THE DALL MOUNTAIN SHEEP, THE SESSILE ROTIFER FLOSCULARIA CONIFERA, AND THE HERRING GULL, AGE BEING EXPRESSED AS PERCENTAGE DEVIATION FROM THE MEAN LENGTH OF LIFE

September 1 of life as against 2.44 years at banding age.

Probably neither set of data for the herring gull is wholly reliable. Paynter's calculations suggest that the Kent Island population is just replacing its losses, assuming a rather high reproductive potential and a rather low rate of mortality between hatching and fledging, while a similar calculation applied to Marshall's figures implies that the population as a whole must be declining. Several reasons may be suggested for the discrepancy between the two life tables: (1) the mortality of the Kent Island gulls may actually be lower than average; (2) there may have been greater total mor-

Table 3, and the survivorship curve is plotted in Fig. 2 for comparison with the Dall sheep and the rotifer. In contrast to those cases, the curve for the gulls is of the diagonal type, the mortality rate being approximately constant throughout life. This feature seems to be characteristic of birds, as will appear below. The causes of death of these birds have been discussed in detail by Paynter, who finds that there is no significant difference in mean length of life between gulls dying through human interference (shooting, trapping, etc.) and those dying through "natural" or unknown causes.

In his delightful book, *The Life of the Robin* (1943a) and in two admirable papers, Lack (1943b,

26

c) has investigated the age at death of certain British birds, as obtained by recoveries of individuals banded as nestlings. Because banded nestlings are likely to be picked up near the banding stations or not at all, it is impossible to estimate the whole of the mortality in the first year of life with any accuracy, and Lack begins his life tables on August 1. The proportion of birds banded which are later recovered is small, ranging from 1.0 per cent for the robin to 18.4 per cent for the cormorant; but after August 1 of the first year it is considered that the ages at death of birds recovered are not likely to differ from the ages at death among the total population. The samples are small and of course become progressively smaller with increasing age,

they suffer more or less severe depredations from shooting.

The striking feature of these survivorship curves is their diagonal form. The mortality in the first year varies from 380 per thousand for the lapwing to 723 per thousand for the robin, but for a given species the mortality remains approximately constant throughout life, or at least for as long as the data are reliable.

When the ages of these birds are transformed into percentage deviations from the mean, as in Fig. 4, it becomes obvious that the mortality per unit of life span is constant for all the birds studied. This does not tell us anything new, for any series of diagonal lines will become the same when replotted

TABLE 3

Life table for the Herring Gull (Larus argentatus) based on returns of 1252 birds banded as chicks at Kent Island, Bay of Fundy, 1936–1945. Mean length of life 2.44 years

From Paynter (in press)

x	x'	d_x	l_x	$1000\ q_x$	e_x
AGE (years)	AGE AS % DEVIATION FROM MEAN LENGTH OF LIFE	NUMBER DYING IN AGE INTERVAL OUT OF 1000 BORN	NUMBER SURVIVING AT BEGINNING OF AGE INTERVAL OUT OF 1000 BORN	MORTALITY RATE PER THOUSAND ALIVE AT BEGINNING OF AGE INTERVAL	EXPECTATION OF LIFE, OR MEAN LIFE TIME REMAINING TO THOSE ATTAINING AGE INTERVALS (years)
0–1	−100	419	1000	419	2.44
1–2	−59	181	581	312	2.84
2–3	−18	95	400	238	2.90
3–4	+23	65	305	213	2.65
4–5	+64	69	240	288	2.22
5–6	+105	60	171	351	1.92
6–7	+146	45	111	405	1.68
7–8	+187	21	66	318	1.48
8–9	+228	26	45	578	0.93
9–10	+269	19	19	1000	0.53

so that Lack does not regard the mortality rates and expectation of life as reliable beyond the fourth or fifth year.

Several of Lack's life tables are reproduced in Table 4, and the survivorship curves are shown in Fig. 3. Three of the species are familiar British songbirds belonging to the Turdidae, the robin (*Erithacus rubecula melophilus*), the blackbird (*Turdus m. merula*), and the song thrush (*T. e. ericetorum*). The others are the starling (*Sturnus v. vulgaris*) and the lapwing (*Vanellus vanellus*), taxonomically though not ecologically a "shorebird" (Charadriidae). Lack's remaining species, the woodcock, black-headed gull, lesser blackbacked gull, and cormorant, have been omitted, as

in this way, but it is helpful none the less. A line fitted by eye to the survivorship points plotted in this figure has a slope corresponding to a mortality of about 320 per thousand per 100 per cent deviation. If the divergence of the points for older ages is ignored as being due to inadequate data, and this line projected, it cuts the age axis at about +560 per cent, implying that if the mortality of birds is really constant throughout life, the oldest bird in a group of 1000 adults should survive about 6.6 times as long as the average bird.

The American robin (*Turdus m. migratorius*), a larger bird than its distant English relative, has been studied by Farner (1945), using U. S. Fish and Wildlife Service data on 855 birds banded as young

TABLE 4

Life tables for several British birds, based on returns from all Britain of birds banded as nestlings and known to be alive on August 1 of their first year. Age reckoned from August 1

From Lack (1943a, b, c)

SPECIES; SIZE OF SAMPLE; MEAN LENGTH OF LIFE AFTER FIRST AUGUST 1	x AGE (years)	x' AGE AS % DEVIATION FROM MEAN LENGTH OF LIFE	d_x NUMBER DYING IN AGE INTERVAL OUT OF 1000 ALIVE ON AUGUST 1	l_x NUMBER SURVIVING AT BEGINNING OF AGE INTERVAL OUT OF 1000 ALIVE ON AUGUST 1	$1000\,q_x$ MORTALITY RATE PER THOUSAND ALIVE AT BEGINNING OF AGE INTERVAL	e_x EXPECTATION OF LIFE, OR MEAN LIFE-TIME REMAINING TO THOSE ATTAINING AGE INTERVAL (years)
Blackbird (352) 1.58 years	0–1	−100	545	1000	545	1.57
	1–2	−37	170	455	374	1.85
	2–3	+27	142	285	498	1.66
	3–4	+90	57	143	398	1.82
	4–5	+153	34	86	396	1.80
	5–6	+216	20	52	385	1.65
	6–7	+280	17	32	531	1.38
	7–8	+343	9	15	600	1.33
	8–9	+405	0	6	0	1.50
	9–10	+470	6	6	1000	0.50
Song Thrush (374) 1.44 years	0–1	−100	556	1000	556	1.44
	1–2	−31	185	444	417	1.61
	2–3	+39	136	259	525	1.40
	3–4	+108	72	123	585	1.39
	4–5	+178	21	51	411	1.65
	5–6	+245	13	30	433	1.43
	6–7	+316	11	17	647	1.12
	7–8	+385	3	6	500	1.17
	8–9	+455	3	3	1000	0.67
Robin (130) 1.01 years	0–1	−100	723	1000	723	1.03
	1–2	−2	131	277	472	1.41
	2–3	+97	108	146	740	1.23
	3–4	+196	23	38	605	2.29
	4–5	+294	8	15	533	4.0
	5–6	+392	0	15	0	3.0
	6–7	+491	0	15	0	2.0
	7–8	+590	0	15	0	1.0
	8–9	+689	8	7	1000	0.5
Starling (203) 1.49 years	0–1	−100	487	1000	487	1.49
	1–2	−33	261	513	509	1.43
	2–3	+34	113	252	448	1.40
	3–4	+102	89	139	640	1.12
	4–5	+168	25	50	500	1.22
	5–6	+236	20	25	800	0.92
	6–7	+302	0	5	0	1.60
	7–8	+370	5	5	1000	0.60
Lapwing (460) 2.36 years	0–1	−100	380	1000	380	2.37
	1–2	−58	213	620	344	2.51
	2–3	−15	128	407	314	2.56
	3–4	+27	78	279	280	2.50
	4–5	+70	67	201	334	2.28
	5–6	+112	56	134	418	2.17
	6–7	+154	24	78	308	2.37
	7–8	+196	20	54	370	2.20
	8–9	+239	7	34	206	2.20
	9–10	+282	9	27	333	1.63
	10–11	+324	7	18	389	1.17
	11–12	+366	11	11	1000	0.55

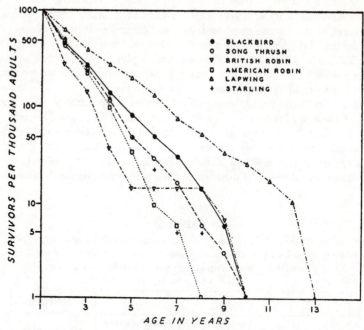

FIG. 3. SURVIVORSHIP (l_x) CURVES FOR THE BRITISH ROBIN, SONG THRUSH, BLACKBIRD, STARLING, LAPWING AND AMERICAN ROBIN, AGE BEING EXPRESSED IN YEARS

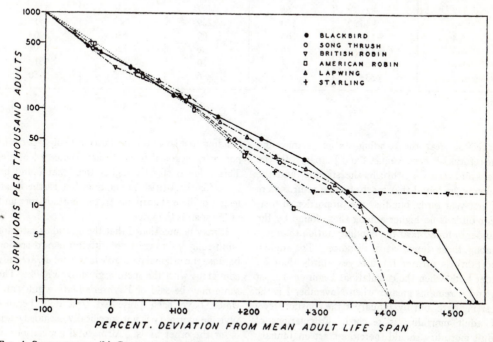

FIG. 4. SURVIVORSHIP (l_x) CURVES FOR THE SAME SPECIES AS IN FIG. 3, AGE BEING EXPRESSED AS PERCENTAGE DEVIATION FROM THE MEAN LENGTH OF LIFE

within the breeding range of the type subspecies between 1920 and 1940, and subsequently recovered dead. Farner's method of treatment of the data is analogous to Lack's, except that November 1 is taken as the starting point for the life table. The figures for the American robin have been entered in Table 5, and Figs. 3 and 4 indicate that this species suffers a mortality which is not only uniform with respect to age but is approximately the same as that of the British birds with respect to units of the mean life span.

Lack (1946) has recently discussed anew the question whether the disproportionately high mortality found among birds in their first year of life is real, or is due to the greater likelihood of their being

portionate" mortality in the first year, starting from August 1, is really very little greater than in later years; it is scarcely visible on a logarithmic plot of survivorship (Figs. 3 and 4). The significant differences between juvenile and adult mortality, which would give a marked initial dip on such a plot, have been left out of account altogether, and August 1 is not too early, but too late a starting point.

Additional information on the lapwing is given by Kraak, Rinkel, and Hoogerheide (1940), who studied the age at death of 1333 continental birds banded as juveniles. The life table is not published, but the survivorship curve is reproduced, and is shown to be closely fitted by a line corres-

TABLE 5

Life table for the American Robin (Turdus m. migratorius), based on returns of 568 birds banded as nestlings and known to be alive on November 1 of their first year. Age reckoned from November 1. Mean length of life after November 1—1.37 years
From Farner (1945)

x	x'	d_x	l_x	$1000\,q_x$	e_x
AGE (years)	AGE AS % DEVIATION FROM MEAN LENGTH OF LIFE	NUMBER DYING IN AGE INTERVAL OUT OF 1000 ALIVE ON NOVEMBER 1	NUMBER SURVIVING AT BEGINNING OF AGE INTERVAL OUT OF 1000 ALIVE ON NOVEMBER 1	MORTALITY RATE PER THOUSAND ALIVE AT BEGINNING OF AGE INTERVAL	EXPECTATION OF LIFE, OR MEAN LIFE TIME REMAINING TO THOSE ATTAINING AGE INTERVAL (years)
0–1	−100	503	1000	503	1.38
1–2	−27	268	497	539	1.26
2–3	+46	130	229	567	1.16
3–4	+119	63	99	636	1.03
4–5	+192	26	36	722	0.94
5–6	+265	4	10	400	1.10
6–7	+338	5	6	1000	0.50

picked up near the banding station. Analysing the returns between August 1 and January 1 for the blackbird, the song-thrush, the starling, and the lapwing, he found that most of these returns were of first-year birds, but that the proportion of first-year birds is no higher among those found by the bander or found near the banding station than it is among those found at a distance. The annual mortality is greater for first-year birds than for older birds when the calculations begin on August 1, and it remains greater when November 1 is the starting date, but by January 1 the constant level of adult mortality is reached. Calculations of adult mortality should therefore start on January 1, but from a comparative point of view this adjustment is of minor importance. The "dispro-

ponding to a constant mortality rate of 40 per cent per year, reckoned from the first January 1 of life. This value is slightly higher than that found by Lack for the British population, but as the mean length of life is slightly lower, the mortality per unit of life span is the same.

It may be mentioned that the mortality rates for adult song sparrows, dealt with in the next section because the original data give l_x and not d_x, are fully consistent with the picture given by Fig. 4. The same may be said of Paynter's herring gull data, which have been presented separately because juvenile mortality is not specifically excluded, as it is for the other birds. All natural populations of birds so far investigated in any detail appear, therefore, to be alike in suffering a constant annual risk of death from early adult life to the end of the life span, this mortality being constant for birds at about 320 per thousand per hundred centiles of life span. Little is known of the seasonal distribution of these deaths, and it will be very interesting to discover whether non-migratory tropical birds suffer death in similar fashion.

Survivorship Directly Observed

The cases now to be discussed differ from the preceding in the character of the original observations.

observations, so that births can be assumed to be simultaneous, as in a *Drosophila* bottle, a horizontal life table can be directly constructed from the survivorship data. Unfortunately, most of the species which have been studied in this way have short spans of natural life, and when census data are obtained only once a year the number of points on the survivorship curve is too small to be satisfactory.

The best example of such observed survivorship comes from Hatton's work (1938) with the barna-

TABLE 6

Life table for a typical population of Balanus balanoides, based on the observed survival of adult barnacles settling on a cleaned rock surface in the spring of 1930. The population is that at Cité, (St. Malo, France), a moderately sheltered location, at Level III, at half-tide level. The initial settling density (2200 per 100 cm²) is taken as the maximum density attained on May 15. Mean length of life 12.1 months

Data from Hatton (1938)

x	x'	d_x	l_x	$1000\,q_x$	e_x
*AGE (months)	*AGE AS % DEVIATION FROM MEAN LENGTH OF LIFE	NUMBER DYING IN AGE INTERVAL OF 1000 ATTACHING	NUMBER SURVIVING TO BEGINNING OF AGE INTERVAL OUT OF 1000 ATTACHING	MORTALITY RATE PER THOUSAND ALIVE AT BEGINNING OF AGE INTERVAL	EXPECTATION OF FURTHER LIFE (months)
0–2	−100	90	1000	90	12.1
2–4	−83.5	100	910	110	11.3
4–6	−67.0	50	810	62	10.5
6–8	−50.4	60	760	79	9.1
8–10	−33.9	80	700	114	7.8
10–12	−17.4	160	620	258	6.7
12–14	−0.9	80	460	174	6.7
14–16	+16.0	100	380	263	5.9
16–18	+32.2	50	280	179	5.7
18–20	+49.0	40	230	174	4.7
20–22	+65.4	100	190	526	2.4
22–24	+82.0	60	90	667	1.9
24–26	+98.8	20	30	667	1.8
26–28	+115.0	8	10	800	1.4
28–30	+132.0	2	2	1000	1.0

* Survivorship data given graphically by Hatton were smoothed by eye, and values at every other month were then read from the curve. The original observations were made at irregular intervals during three years.

Instead of a fairly large sample of individuals about which little or nothing can be told except their age at death, we have a group of individuals known to have been born at a particular time and to have been present or absent at some later time. Their presence gives their survivorship, their absence implies death in the interval since they were last observed. This is the best sort of information to have, since it does not require the assumption that the age composition of the population is stable in time. Provided only that the season of birth is a small fraction of the age interval between successive

cle, *Balanus balanoides*. This work will be examined in great detail in a later section, and it is here necessary to say only that the case is very nearly ideal. The barnacle settles on rocks during a short time (two to six weeks) in early spring. Test areas were scraped clean one winter, and after new populations had settled, the survival of their members was followed at intervals of one to four months for three years. Barnacles which disappeared from the areas between observations were certainly dead, for emigration does not complicate the problem. Immigration, however, does present difficulties, though since it is confined to the attachment seasons of subsequent years it should be possible to control it in subsequent work. There is one further disadvantage in that the life tables necessarily start at metamorphosis, leaving out of account mortality during pelagic larval stages. A life table for a typical population of barnacles is presented in Table 6.

The remaining examples suffer from more serious defects, and the data do not justify extended treatment. Green and Evans (1940) in their important study of the snowshoe rabbit (*Lepus americanus*) in Minnesota, followed the survival of marked individuals of several year classes, the total population present on the area and the number in each age-class being obtained by the mark-and-recapture method—also known as the "Lincoln index" (Jackson, 1939). Marking was done during most of the winter, and the annual census was made in February. It is perhaps unnecessary, and certainly uncharitable, to point out two sources of error in this excellent and ingenious work. In the first place, when marked individuals are released into a population and later recaptured, the calculation of the total population from the fraction

$$\frac{\text{size of sample when recapturing}}{\text{number recaptured}} \times \text{number marked}$$

depends on two assumptions, neither of which is likely to be true in this case: that there is no mortality between marking and recapturing; and that the marked individuals disperse at random through the whole population. Secondly, the flow of vital events in this population was so rapid, very few rabbits more than three years old ever having been found, that observations made annually can give only a very rough idea of the life table.

The latter objection applies with equal force to the study of a pheasant population made by Leopold et al. (1943) in Wisconsin. The former objection, though doubtless it could be urged, has less validity here, since the population, as ascertained by trapping, was checked by census drives. Nice's thoroughgoing work (1937) on the song sparrow (*Melospiza melodia*) included a consideration of the survival of banded birds from year to year. The number of individuals which could be kept under continuous observation was necesarily* small, and to find a sample large enough to use as the basis of a life table, it is necessary to take the 144 males banded in the breeding season between 1928 and 1935. Unfortunately, some of these

males were of unknown age when first banded. Even if one assumes, (and the assumption is not far from the truth) that all new males appearing are first-year birds born elsewhere, the survival ratios from year to year will be too low if any adult males were still alive but failed to return to the area. Evidently such emigration is of minor importance with adult male song sparrows. With adult females, however, it is so serious that Nice did not think it worth while to publish the data on their return. Clearly, work on the survival of migratory birds is full of uncertainties, though the same may be said of resident species such as the wren-tit (Erickson, 1938) and the robin (Lack, 1943a).

All of these cases, snowshoe rabbit, pheasant, and song sparrow have one defect in common. This is the necessity of calculating the survival between birth and the first year of adult life from other data than those given by banding. For the snowshoe rabbit, the initial strength of the year-class is calculated from the estimated breeding population present and its known fertility. Leopold et al., lacking observations of their own on the pheasant mortality between birth and the first census period, used the estimates given by Errington for pheasants in another state. Nice calculates the survival of fledged young song sparrows to their first breeding season, by assuming a stable population and combining the estimated mean length of life of adults with their average nesting success. These procedures, while perfectly defensible as approaches to the problem, are inadequate substitutes for direct observation.

The three sets of data, with all their uncertainties, have been used as bases for synthetic life tables, and the survivorship curves are presented in Fig. 5. The snowshoe rabbit curve is that for the 1933 year class, the only one for which data are available on rabbits as old as four years. The juvenile mortality for 1933 is calculated by Green and Evans as 77 per cent between birth and the following February; for most other years it was higher, and for a few it was lower. Adult mortality, amounting to 70 per cent per year, was essentially constant throughout the study. The data for the pheasant are the average survival values for adults (30 per cent per year), combined with Errington's estimate of 84 per cent mortality between hatching and maturity. The song sparrow curve is calculated in two ways, the first including only the estimated mortality between fledging and the first breeding season (80 per cent) and the

---

* Corrected spelling is: necessarily

second also including the loss (40 per cent) between the laying of the eggs and fledging. The adult part of the life span is taken from the survival of the 144 males banded in 1928–1935.

The three curves show a pronounced diagonality from the adult stage onward. Initially, however, since the juvenile mortality in all cases is greater than the adult mortality, the curves show a dip which is most emphatic for the song sparrow reckoned from the egg, but which is invariably present. Here, then, we have for the first time sur-

between successive age classes, has not been directly observed. This kind of information lends itself just as well as either of the others to the computation of life tables. As in the group where only the age at death is known, of course, it is necessary to assume the age composition to be unchanged with time. When this assumption is unreasonable, as it often is for fish populations, with their outrageous fluctuation in strength of year-classes, average age compositions obtained from several years' work can often be used. As it happens,

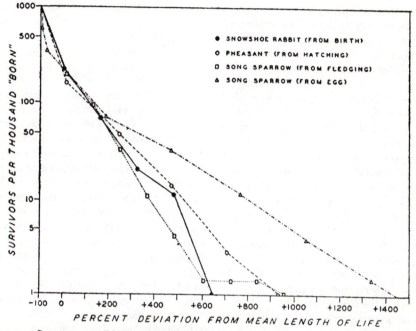

Fig. 5. Synthetic Survivorship (l_x) Curves for the Snowshoe Rabbit, the Pheasant, and the Song Sparrow, the Latter Calculated from Two Different Biological Ages
Data for different parts of the life spans are derived in different ways, as explained in the text.

vivorship curves which approach the positively skew rectangular type expected in theory from animals in nature. It is surprising that the approach is not closer, but it may well be true that the theoretical curve, in its most extreme form, is not to be looked for among terrestrial vertebrates.

Age Structure Directly Observed

Ecological information of a third sort is available for a number of natural populations, principally of fishes and birds. In these cases the investigator has been able to determine how many individuals of each age are living in the population, and the age at death, though calculable from the shrinkage

however, all the life tables which fall in this third group are incomplete for one reason or another, and the data do not bear close comparison with such examples of natural life tables as those of the Dall sheep and the barnacle.

Kortlandt (1942) has recently given a very elaborate analysis of the Netherlands population of cormorants (*Phalacrocorax carbo sinensis*). Birds banded as nestlings were later observed in their breeding and playing colonies, the numbers on the bands being read with the aid of a telescope. The age distribution of the banded birds being known in 1940 and 1941, it should be possible to infer the age distribution of the total population and from this to compute the annual mortality suffered by each year-class. A number of complicating conditions are present in this case, however, making direct calculation unreliable and necessitating a more circuitous approach: (1) the size of the Dutch cormorant population is not constant, but has been increasing by about 10 per cent per year, as estimated by counts of nests at the breeding colonies; (2) differences between the observed sex ratio among sexually mature birds and the sex ratio predicted on the basis of estimated mortality by sex and age class show clearly that there is some *band mortality*; that is, some birds either lose bands or die because of the band, making estimates of natural mortality too high by a factor of about 2; (3) it is not possible to infer the complete age structure from observations made at breeding colonies, since the one- and two-year-old birds occupy "colonies" elsewhere, returning to their birthplaces to breed no sooner than their third year.

In view of these difficulties, and others which need not be discussed here, Kortlandt's results must be regarded as schematic and preliminary only, and scarcely warrant the construction of a life table. His computations suggest that cormorants suffer mortality somewhat as follows: 17 per cent between fledging and the first May 1; 8 per cent in the first year; 6 per cent in the second year; and about 4 per cent per year in the third to twelfth years. These are astonishingly low figures for a natural population, but it must be remembered that the population is increasing rapidly. It is interesting to find that the slight differential death rate between the sexes from the third year onward appears to favor the female rather than the male sex. It is not known whether this is true of birds generally, in contrast to most other animals (Geiser, 1923, 1924). MacArthur and Baillie (1932) have maintained that there is no evidence that differential mortality is correlated with the sex-determining chromosome mechanism, and that among moths and birds the male longevity is generally lower in conformity with the "rate of living" theory.

Huge numbers of returns of the common tern (*Sterna hirundo*) have been obtained at the Austin Ornithological Research Station on Cape Cod (Austin, 1942), where terns have been banded for over twenty years. Unfortunately the data are inadequately published, and in any case can yield only an incomplete life table, since terns, like other sea birds, scatter widely after birth and do not return to their birthplace until breeding age. Inspection of Austin's table, in which all returns are given by ages for the four years 1938–1941, suggests that the annual mortality is not constant from the fourth year onward, but varies from 178 to 636 per thousand even between the fourth and eighth years, when the numbers are large. It is not clear, however, whether or not the tern population has remained statistically constant during the period of study, i.e., whether the table really reflects the true natural mortality of an average or of any one year-class.

The literature of fisheries biology is full of attempts to estimate the mortality of fishes, to distinguish natural mortality from rate of exploitation, and to determine the rate of exploitation which, given certain mortality rates and certain relationships between age and size, will steadily yield an optimum catch. These complex questions are fully discussed in the important works of Russell (1942), Thompson and Bell (1934), and Ricker (1940, 1944), and by various authors in the *Rapports et Procès-Verbaux of the International Council for the Study of the Sea*, Volume 110, 1939. Little of this information can be directly used for our purpose. The explanation is as simple as it is regrettable: although the age of a caught fish can be ascertained with more or less complete confidence, fishes of all ages can not be caught with equal facility. Inevitably the methods so skilfully developed for catching fish of desirable sizes will fail to catch fish of undesirable sizes. It is true that on various occasions the whole fish population of a lake has been removed by poisoning or drainage. The estimates given by Eschmeyer (1939) for the abundance of large-mouth black bass (*Huro salmoides*) in Howe Lake, Michigan, at the time of its poisoning in 1937, may be cited as an example:

Age	Number
0	18,374
0 (cannibals)	229
I	25
II	10
III	105
IV	7
V and older	9
Total	18,759

The implication of enormously greater mortality in the first year of life is plain from these figures, but such data can not be taken as they stand, partly because of very variable annual recruitment, and partly because young of the year were removed from the lake at various times for hatchery purposes.

Lacking satisfactory observations of the complete age structure of the population, and faced with the obstacle of variable yearly recruitment in its most massive form, it is not surprising that fisheries workers have not attempted the construction of life tables, and have so far been content with the estimation of natural mortality among fishes of certain sizes only. This mortality is generally assumed to be constant with respect to age, and it may well be so for middle-aged fishes exposed to fishing; but a life table constructed from the available observations would certainly be lacking both head and tail.

As an example of the kind of information yielded by fisheries statistics, and of the methods used in their analysis, we may first take the data given by Ricker (1945) for the bluegill sunfish (*Lepomis macrochirus*) in Muskellunge Lake, Indiana. This is an especially instructive case, for it shows that despite great technical advantages not enjoyed by students of marine fisheries (a small, isolated, self-contained population; size and character of catch known with certainty by the investigator; age structure of the population checked by tagging methods), the difficulties remaining are still embarrassing.

Ricker first determined the rate of exploitation and the total mortality between one year and the next by what he called (rather inappropriately) the "direct" method, involving marked fish. In 1942, of 140 fish 145 mm. and larger (mostly 3 years old and older) marked prior to the opening of the season, 25 were recaptured by fishermen during the season, giving a rate of exploitation of 18 per cent. Estimated autumn fishing raises this figure to 19 per cent. Of 230 blue-gills 125 mm. and larger, marked prior to the 1942 season, 14 were recaptured in 1943. The rate of exploitation of fish in the same size group (then 155 mm. and larger) in 1943 was 15.1 per cent. It is necessary to calculate the number of 1942-marked fish present at the beginning of the 1943 season; this number is given by dividing the number recaptured in 1943 by the rate of exploitation in 1943, or $\frac{14}{0.151} = 93$. These 93 fish were the survivors of 230 marked fish present before the 1942 season, so the rate of mortality from one season to the next was $\frac{230 - 93}{230} = 60$ per cent. Subtracting the 19 per cent rate of exploitation leaves 41 per cent as the natural mortality.

Ricker's "indirect" method is the life-table method in a crude form. A collection of scales from 529 blue-gills caught by fishermen in 1942 gave the following as the age structure of the sample:

Age	I	II	III	IV	V	VI	VII	VIII
Number	1	293	151	54	20	7	2	1

The age I fish was presumably caught by accident, and those of age II were not equally vulnerable to fishing during the first part of the season. From age III onward the age structure may be used to yield an estimate of the age-specific mortality rates (assuming uniform recruitment and mortality rates from year to year). These mortality rates in early ages, where the data are more reliable, are nearly constant at about 65 per cent. A weighted geometric mean by Jackson's method gives

$$\frac{1 + 2 + 7 + 20 + 54}{2 + 7 + 20 + 54 + 151} = 36\% \text{ survival}$$

$$= 64\% \text{ mortality.}$$

This is close to the 60 per cent mortality calculated by the "direct" method. However, both methods contain unproved and rather unlikely assumptions, and the agreement merely shows the order of magnitude of the total annual mortality. Moreover, the natural mortality as calculated so far is too low, as some of the fish caught by anglers would have died anyway. By making the additional assumption that the natural mortality is synchronized with the fishing mortality, Ricker calculates the former to be of the order of 50 per cent per year for blue-gills age III and older in four Indiana lakes. This is an important result, and one which will doubtless surprise many fisheries supervisors. It is not sufficient as the basis for a life table, however, since it does not include the mortality from birth to the third year of life, and since the method of weighting underrates the age-specific mortality at advanced ages. Ricker, in fact, thinks it not unlikely that the older fish are subject to a still higher mortality, but his data give no clear answer to the question.

It is a generally accepted conclusion that *adult* fishes, from the time they enter a fishery to the age at which they cease to be caught in significant numbers, suffer a more or less constant mortality with respect to age. Thus for these intermediate ages the survivorship curves, whether constructed vertically for a series of year-classes in any one fishing season, or horizontally for particular year-classes followed through several seasons, tend to fall on straight lines when plotted logarithmically. Such straight lines, with slopes changing according to the rate of exploitation, are implicit in Raitt's treatment of the statistics on the haddock (1939) and are conspicuous in Jensen's review (1939) of data on the cod, haddock, plaice, and herring in the North Sea. Whether the natural mortality, as distinguished from the fishing mortality, also is constant at all adult ages is an open question, but most fisheries workers would probably be prepared to assume that this is the case, in the absence of evidence to the contrary.

Direct observations of *juvenile* mortality in fishes are not easy to make, but a mass of indirect evidence points to the conclusion that it must be very much greater than adult mortality in many species. Some idea of this mortality can be had from Sette's work (1943) on the mackerel. Eggs and larvae of this pelagic species were caught on several systematically conducted cruises over the continental shelf between Martha's Vineyard and the Chesapeake Capes. Several broods spawned at short intervals during the season of 1932 were recognizable at later times and at geographically remote stations as separate modes in the frequency distributions of size and age. Assuming that the technique of plankton sampling gives a reliable estimate of the abundance of eggs and larvae of particular stages in the sea, their reduction in numbers gives a measure of their mortality. Sette's calculations show that the mortality is very great, and is substantially the same per unit time at all egg and larval stages. There is a noticeable rise in mortality rate, from about 10 to 14 per cent per day up to about 30 to 45 per cent per day, at the transition from larval to post-larval stages, when the fins are developing rapidly, but it falls again to the original level. The total mortality from the beginning of development to the 50 mm. stage, when the baby fish school like the adults and seek out their nursery grounds, is 99.9996 per cent. This fantastically high figure refers to a time interval of about *70 days*, and may be compared with values of 50 to 90 per cent *per year* estimated as the total mortality suffered by several species of commercial fishes as adults. Clearly, Pearl was correct in supposing that the survivorship curve for pelagic fishes may be of the J-shaped or positively skew rectangular form.

Though it can not be doubted that survivorship curves for fishes in nature will in general have an initial dip, it would be incorrect to conclude that this dip is invariably as pronounced as in the case of the mackerel. Barnaby (1944), for example, has considered the mortality of the Karluk River population of red salmon (*Oncorhynchus nerka*). Marking experiments suggest a total mortality in the ocean of about 79 per cent, while a calculation based on the reproductive potential yields a figure for the mortality in fresh water, between birth and seaward migration, of 99.55 per cent. The problem is complicated by the fact that the salmon may spend their lives in fresh water and in the ocean in various combinations of years, as 3 + 2 years, 3 + 3 years, 4 + 2 years, etc., so that these mortality rates refer to varying intervals of age. Thus there is no proof that the *annual* mortality rate is other than constant, and while no such deduction should be made from the data, it is evident that the age-specific mortality in fresh water can not be *very much* greater than in the ocean.

The data just presented have been grouped together because they give some conception of the form of the life table for certain species of fish, and the fact has been ignored that some of the information is not based on the age structure of the population, but on other kinds of evidence. This section may logically be concluded with a brief reference to the data for the fin whale, in which, as recent investigations have shown, the age of the female can be determined from the number of old corpora lutea in the ovary. By this method Wheeler (1934) arrived at the following as the age structure, observed over five seasons, 1926–1931, of the catch of female fin whales in the Antarctic:

Age	Number caught
3–4 years	130
5–6 years	95
7–8 years	72
9–10 years	53
11–12 years	37
13–14 years	28
15–16 years	10
17–18 years	4
19–20 years	1
21–22 years	1

The data imply (subject to the usual qualifications) a biennial mortality of about 26 per cent, increasing beyond the 15th year to much higher values. The author considers that the increased rate of loss with age is not real, but is due to failure of the older whales to return from their winter quarters in the north. This belief may or may not be well founded, but one suspects it to be predicated on the idea that mortality, at least when it is primarily due to exploitation, is constant among animals with respect to age. Edser (to whom the statistical analysis is credited) assumed, for the purpose of a rough calculation of the necessary rate of replacement, that the mortality between birth and breeding age is also 26 per cent. The improbability of this assumption may be surmised by reference to the life table for the Dall sheep (Table 1). Edser's calculation has the great merit of yielding a minimal estimate of the alarming exploitation being conducted by the whaling industry in the Antarctic. More realistic assumptions would darken the picture even more. In any case the data can not yet be cast into a life table.

Miscellaneous Survivorship Data

By means of the mark-and-recapture method, Jackson (1936, 1939) has given an analysis of the population of a tsetse fly (*Glossina morsitans*) in Tanganyika. Jackson was chiefly interested in determining the size of the population and its fluctuations from season to season. The death of flies in the one-week intervals between marking and recapturing struck at the foundation of the method, which assumes no such mortality. But by taking a geometric average of the survival of marked flies in successive weeks, and extrapolating backward one week, the number theoretically recapturable on the date of marking was calculable. From this figure, the first term in a geometric survival series, the population could be directly calculated for each week during the year over which the study was conducted. But the flies were of unknown ages when first marked, being recognizable simply as adult males (plus a few females) having had their first meal. Evidently the operation was designed to smooth out of existence those systematic changes in age-specific mortality in which we are interested here. A few males were marked *before* their first meal, and the returns of these should permit the construction of a life table beginning at early adult life, but the data are not published separately, and in any case are probably inadequate statistically.

Two other points of interest are raised by this resourceful study. The first deals with the sex ratio in the wild population. Data on the return of marked females are not numerous, but so far as they go they suggest a considerably lower mortality

than among males, the calculated survival ratio being 0.716 for females and ranging from 0.307 to 0.622 (depending on the season) for males. Expressed as mortality rates, these values are equal to 284, and between 693 and 378 per thousand flies per week, respectively. As a result, the normal sex ratio among the wild flies must vary from 1.5 to 2.0 in favor of females. Yet the sex ratio at emergence from the pupa is unity. There is no evidence that emigration, though always a complicating factor, is performed differentially by the two sexes, and it is not improbable that here also, as in man and in so many other animals studied in the laboratory, the female is significantly more long-lived than the male. The oldest fly captured lived $13\frac{1}{2}$ weeks after marking, and was a female.

The second point is that Jackson used two methods for the calculation of *a*, the initial term in a survivorship series. "Instead of considering the survival curve of flies marked in any one week and recaptured in subsequent weeks . . . we can equally well consider the recaptures of flies marked in previous weeks and recaptured in any one week. Subject to sampling errors, both methods should give the same value of *a*." The difference between the latter "negative" method and the former "positive" method is essentially the difference between a vertical and a horizontal life table. The two methods, while equally applicable to a series of mortality rates assumed to be constant and equal to the geometric mean, as in this case, will give different results for animals of known ages if the age-specific mortality rates change with time. Inasmuch as the smoothed mortality rates for flies of all ages in the population appear to change regularly with the season, being greater in the dry season, real life tables constructed for similar populations would have to be distinguished with care.

An elaborate program of trapping and marking has been carried out with a population of long-tailed field mice (*Apodemus sylvaticus*) by Hacker and Pearson (1946). This sort of work is full of pitfalls, arising mainly from the fact that the traps are attractive to the mice and tend to drain them from distances which are frequently too great to be safely negotiated a second time. As the mice were of unknown ages when first marked, the results need not be summarized in any detail here, but some of the conclusions are of interest in giving an indication of the form of the field mouse life table in nature.

The "standard" survival ratio for mature mice,

as determined from repeated recaptures between December 1938 and April 1939, was 0.879, i.e., the mortality was 121 per thousand per month. But returns of these same mice in December and in March of the following year were much lower than expected from this ratio, implying that the mortality rate increases with age. Data for other years also show that the survival of the winter population is lower in the summer. Moreover, a study of returns of small, middle-sized, and large mice over three winter periods shows that the rates of loss are higher at both ends of the size distribution. Such scanty information can not be cast into a life table, but it is noticeable that a survivorship curve with two inflections fits well with that of the vole (*Microtus agrestis*), as established in the laboratory by Leslie and Ranson (1940).

Survival of Barnacles

Some of the advantages of the life table notation will now be illustrated by an analysis of the survivorship of the barnacle *Balanus balanoides*, as studied at St. Malo by Hatton (1938). The technical advantages presented by intertidal barnacles as objects of population research have been discussed in an earlier section, and a typical example of a barnacle life table has been given in Table 6. The relevant information about the biology of the species, as elucidated by Runnström (1925), Moore (1934), and Hatton, may be briefly summarized:

Balanus balanoides is a typical intertidal species, occurring primarily within the mean range of neap tides, where it often makes dense incrustations on all solid objects. It breeds in the fall, the nauplii being held in the mantle cavity for some time before liberation, while attachment and metamorphosis of the cyprid larvae takes place in the early spring, the exact time doubtless depending on the temperature. The attachment season lasts about six weeks. The intensity of attachment varies with the exposure to surf and the tidal level, being greatest at most exposed localities and at lower levels. The growth rate after attachment is greatest at lower tidal levels in the first year of life, but in subsequent years the growth at higher levels surpasses that at lower levels. Mortality, however, is also greater at lower levels, as shown by survival of barnacles of known ages from year to year, and thus the few barnacles at high levels (up to the mean level of high-water neap tides) are larger after a year's growth and live longer than those lower down. The maximum longevity appears to be about 5 years, but is much less at lower levels.

It is not clear which of these facts are simple responses to the physical ecology of the intertidal zone, and which are biotic effects. It is easy to suppose that the growth rate might be best at lower levels, where the barnacles are more continuously submerged and therefore take food more frequently. It is not so easy to explain the decline of growth rate with age at these levels (or the increase of growth rate with age at higher levels), unless it is in some way related to the population density; yet the growth differences are said to be observable in the absence of crowding. The low attachment densities at high levels presumably reflect the time necessary for a cyprid to attach, for the time available on any one tide decreases with the height. But after attachment the higher levels are exposed for longer periods to desiccation, direct sunlight, and rainwater, and the enhanced survival under these conditions is difficult to understand except as a function of the low population density.

The relation between population density and longevity is well known for certain laboratory animals. In general the length of life is curtailed by overcrowding (Pearl, 1946; Davis, 1945). In certain well-studied cases, however, the mean length of life has been found to increase at densities above the minimum, to decrease at very high densities, and to be greatest at some intermediate density (Pearl, Miner, and Parker, 1927). Pratt's proof of an optimum density for longevity of *Daphnia magna* (1943) is particularly convincing, since the densities were actually maintained constant throughout the life of the animals, and were not permitted to decrease with the gradual extinction of the initial cohort.

It is of considerable importance, therefore, to examine Hatton's data, which fortunately are published in full, for evidence of the relationship between longevity and population density in *Balanus balanoides*. Hatton studied nine different populations, allowed to settle on cleaned areas in 1930, and followed for three years. Three different levels were chosen at each of three localities as follows:

Localities	*Levels*
Décollé Ouest, exposed	II—mean high-water neap tide
Décollé Est, sheltered	III—half-tide
Cité, moderately sheltered	IV—mean low-water neap tide

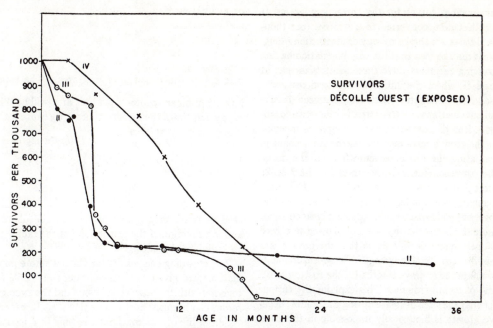

FIG. 6. SURVIVORSHIP (l_x) CURVES FOR THREE OF THE NINE POPULATIONS OF BALANUS BALANOIDES STUDIED AT
ST. MALO BY HATTON (1938)

The locality, Décollé Ouest, is exposed to surf. The initial density of attachment, taken as the maximum density attained on May 15, 1930, was as follows: II (at mean high-water neap tide level), 790 per 100 cm²; III (at half-tide level), 2330 per 100 cm²; IV (at mean low-water neap tide level), 1500 per 100 cm².

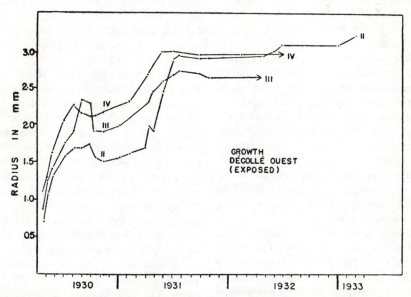

FIG. 7. GROWTH CURVES FOR BARNACLES CORRESPONDING TO THE THREE POPULATIONS OF FIG. 6, BUT OBTAINED
FROM UNCROWDED SPECIMENS

The measurements began on April 1, 1930, and the points plotted are the average lengths (at the base, in the rostro-carinal axis), divided by 2. Each point represents an average of about 50 measurements.

Survivorship curves for the three populations at Décollé Ouest, converted to a relative (per thousand) basis, are shown by way of illustration in Fig. 6. It may be seen that the only population having surviving members after three years was that at Level II, where the initial population density was also least. The same relationship between density and survival was observed at the other two localities. But the matter is not so simple as it looks, for the growth rates must be taken into account in evaluating the degree of crowding on the areas. The corresponding growth curves for the Décollé Ouest populations are shown in Fig. 7. The measurements were made, not on the original populations, but on barnacles from adjacent cleaned areas, where the initial density was not allowed to exceed 100 per square decimeter, so that the growth was uninfluenced by crowding. The measurements given are the average lengths (in the rostro-carinal axis) of 50 individuals. This explains the curious fact that the sizes decrease during the winter: negative growth is biologically impossible in this case, and evidently there was a relatively great loss of older barnacles each winter. For purposes of calculation the radius of a barnacle has been taken to equal half the length, and the reasonable growth figures (ignoring negative increments) have been fitted to equations of the form

$$r = at^b$$

where r is the radius and t is the time in months.

Hatton's survivorship curves give the population per unit area at any time. The area at the base of an average uncrowded member of the population at any time can be calculated from the growth curve on the assumption, which is sufficiently accurate for the purpose, that the barnacles grow as expanding circles. The degree of crowding attained at any time can be evaluated as follows: (Grateful acknowledgment is due to Dr. John Ferry, of the University of Wisconsin, for the elegant following formulation.)

If barnacles of radius r settle at random within distance D of each other, and grow as expanding circles, so that at any time the radii r are equal, any barnacle which settles within distance $2r$ will be in contact with or overlap another. The number of binary contacts per barnacle will be given by:

$$\int_0^{2r} \frac{N}{A} \cdot 2\pi D \cdot dD$$

or, evaluating:

$$4\pi r^2 \frac{N}{A}.$$

where $\frac{N}{A}$ is the density per unit area. The total number of binary contacts per unit area will be this expression times the density times $\frac{1}{2}$ (because each contact is counted twice):

$$C = 2\pi r^2 \left(\frac{N}{A}\right)^2$$

This value C, the *crowding coefficient*, can be evaluated in terms of contacts per square centimeter, and is a function of the density and of the radius of an individual barnacle.

The crowding coefficients for Hatton's nine populations are given for selected times in Table 7, together with the observed density and the average radius of a barnacle at the same times. The expectation of life of a barnacle at the time in question is calculated by ordinary life table methods. Plotting C against e_x gives the graph shown in Fig. 8.

Evidently the population density, when considered in this way, has a definite effect on the survival of *Balanus balanoides*. The effect is not linear, but becomes less marked at higher degrees of crowding. Evidently, too, the relationship between survivorship and crowding is less definite at advanced ages, for the points for 18 months diverge from the curve.

It seems fairly certain that this discrepancy is due to the fact that the treatment has ignored the new settlements of barnacles which were added to the populations in subsequent years. The new arrivals can be treated by an extension of Dr. Ferry's mathematical approach, but it becomes necessary to decide whether there is any superincrustation, i.e., whether the area exposed to settlement, A, is (1) the same as the original area, (2) equal to the unoccupied area, or (3) has some intermediate value. No decision can be reached on this point from Hatton's account, which moreover gives only the second-year settlements, without subsequent data on the survival of the 1931 year-class or any information on the 1932 year-class. The data, however, are suggestive in that all the populations which diverge widely at 18 months from the curve of Fig. 8 received high second-year settlements, while the "good" points are from populations which received relatively little

recruitment in 1931. Since in general the populations with highest initial densities will receive the most considerable reinforcement in subsequent

such as the one drawn in Fig. 8, is an illusion. But only further work will permit a deeper analysis of this exceptionally interesting case.

TABLE 7

Population density, calculated radius, crowding coefficients, and expectation of life at selected times for nine populations of Balanus balanoides at St. Malo

Original data from Hatton (1938)

POPULATION (Locality and Level)	t TIME (months)*	N/A DENSITY PER CM²	r RADIUS (mm.)	C CROWDING COEFFICIENT: contacts per cm² = $2\pi r^2(N/A)^2$	e_x EXPECTATION OF FURTHER LIFE (months)†	POPULATION (Locality and Level)	t TIME (months)*	N/A DENSITY PER CM²	r RADIUS (mm.)	C CROWDING COEFFICIENT: contacts per cm² = $2\pi r^2(N/A)^2$	e_x EXPECTATION OF FURTHER LIFE (months)†
Décollé Est II	0	4.0	1.08	1.17	23.1	Décollé Ouest IV	0	15.0	1.74	42.55	12.6
	6	2.4	1.65	0.98	29.6		6	12.6	2.20	48.41	8.2
	12	2.1	1.92	1.02	27.2		12	7.3	2.40	19.35	5.6
	18	1.9	2.11	1.01	23.7		18	3.0	2.54	3.65	3.7
	24	1.5	2.27	0.73	23.1		24	0.6	2.64	0.16	2.9
	30	1.5	2.39	0.81	17.7		30	0.08	2.73	0.03	2.0
Décollé Est III	0	11.9	1.12	11.24	13.8	Cité II	0	10.0	1.24	9.61	14.3
	6	8.3	1.59	10.87	12.8		6	3.4	1.67	2.03	28.6
	12	5.4	1.80	5.92	12.6		12	2.9	1.89	1.88	27.2
	18	4.2	1.94	4.09	9.1		18	2.8	2.00	1.97	22.5
	24	2.0	2.06	1.07	9.9		24	2.5	2.10	1.73	19.0
	30	1.0	2.16	0.29	12.2		30	2.2	2.19	1.45	15.2
Décollé Est IV	0	15.0	1.41	27.91	9.5	Cité III‡	0	22.0	1.32	53.22	12.1
	6	8.4	1.80	14.35	7.5		6	16.7	1.66	48.05	9.1
	12	4.8	1.97	5.61	4.9		12	10.1	1.80	20.70	6.7
	18	1.8	2.08	0.88	1.2		18	5.1	1.89	5.85	4.7
							24	0.7	1.96	0.11	1.8
Décollé Ouest II	0	7.9	1.34	7.07	11.0						
	6	1.9	1.82	0.75	31.2	Cité IV	0	23.8	1.44	74.10	11.2
	12	1.7	2.03	0.75	28.5		6	12.9	1.71	30.68	12.2
	18	1.5	2.18	0.67	24.5		12	11.0	1.82	25.29	7.9
	24	1.4	2.29	0.65	20.3		18	6.1	1.90	8.41	5.4
	30	1.3	2.38	0.61	15.8		24	2.6	1.95	1.62	2.5
Décollé Ouest III	0	23.3	1.50	76.28	7.0						
	6	6.3	1.94	9.34	8.7						
	12	4.9	2.12	6.81	4.7						
	18	1.2	2.25	0.46	1.0						

* These are the times corresponding to the density figures (read from the survivorship curves), beginning at 0 = 15 May. The growth curves begin on 1 April, and the time values for radius as stated are actually 1.5, 7.5, 13.5, 19.5, 25.5, and 31.5 months.

† Computed on the assumption that those populations still having surviving members after 3 years would have terminated at 5 years.

‡ Life table for this population given in Table 6.

years, it is easy to imagine that over the years the effect of unit change of crowding on survival, $\dfrac{de_x}{dC}$, will be greatest for these populations. This argument carries the implication that a single curve,

Returning to the original question, whether there is a density above the minimum which is optimal for the longevity of *Balanus balanoides* in nature, Fig. 8 indicates that there is not. The expectation of life is greatest when the crowding coefficient is least, and the curve does not rise before it falls. This negative evidence is probably not conclusive, and a larger body of data, preferably obtained under conditions which are less variable as regards factors other than crowding, might give a different answer. But there is no particular reason to expect that a species such as this one would benefit greatly from mutual support. It is possible to point to another barnacle in which the case may be otherwise. This is *Chthamalus stellatus*, which flourishes best at an intertidal level above that of

this phenomenon was never observed with *Chthamalus*.

Hatton's work included survival studies of *Chthamalus* as well as of *B. balanoides*, but as the longevity of the former is greater (see also Moore and Kitching, 1939), few of the populations had run their courses when the experiments were terminated at the end of three years. As a result, the expectation of life cannot be calculated with any confidence. Annual mortality rates for six populations (three at Level I, above the *B. balanoids*

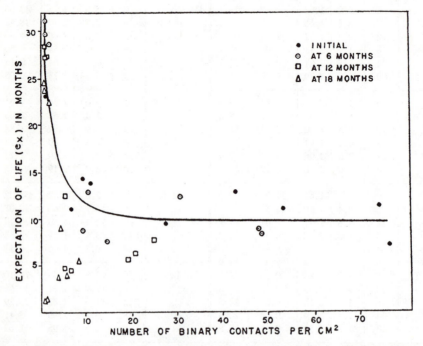

FIG. 8. RELATION BETWEEN EXPECTATION OF LIFE (e_x) OF BALANUS BALANOIDES AT SELECTED TIMES AND THE CROWDING COEFFICIENT (CONTACTS PER SQUARE CENTIMETER) AT THE SAME TIME
Data in Table 7, calculated from data of Hatton.

B. balanoides. Here it is exposed to sun and drought for long periods, and Monterosso (1930) has found that it is remarkably hardy, specimens having survived for three years on a laboratory table with only one or two days' immersion in sea water each month. Hatton suggests that the chances of survival of a young *Chthamalus* are improved if it settles in the shade of a larger individual; at any rate, the larvae tend to attach in the shade in greater numbers, when ridges of cement are built upon the rocks. Moreover, while attached and growing *B. balanoides* were frequently found to dislodge each other from the substratum,

zone; and three at Level II, where densities of *B. balanoides* were low) are arranged in Table 8 for direct comparison with the density. The table shows that the populations having very low densities suffered higher mortality rates on the average than those below the dashed line in the table, which had higher densities. The difference is more pronounced when the first year's mortality is omitted, but in neither case is the difference significant statistically. The predicted relation between density and survivorship of *Chthamalus* is therefore not proven, and the question remains open.

Mention has been made in an earlier section of a

defect inherent in the life tables calculated from experiments like Hatton's, in that the observations much greater, reaching 95 per cent (survival ratio 0.05) at the greatest densities observed.

TABLE 8

Annual mortality of Chthamalus stellatus at St. Malo in relation to population density
Data from Hatton (1938), Tables XXXVI–XXXVIII

POPULATION (LOCALITY AND LEVEL)	FIRST YEAR		SECOND YEAR		THIRD YEAR	
	Initial density per 100 cm²	Mortality %	Density per 100 cm²	Mortality %	Density per 100 cm²	Mortality %
Décollé Ouest I.	21	4.8	20	10.0	18	16.6
Décollé Est II.	39	10.3	35	20.0	28	28.6
Cité I.	44	9.1	40	17.5	33	9.1
Décollé Est I.	48	31.2	33	9.1	30	36.7
Cité II.	184	11.4	163	13.5	141	8.5
Décollé Ouest II.	270	17.4	223	11.2	198	14.1

start with metamorphosis, and the pelagic larval life is neglected. Some idea of the mortality during the earliest attachment stage, the interval between attachment of the cyprid and its transformation to an adult barnacle, can be gained from the unpublished studies of Weiss at Miami Beach, Florida.

Permission to present these results in advance of publication has been courteously granted by Mr. C. M. Weiss of the Woods Hole Oceanographic Institution.

Weiss observed the daily attachment of cyprid larvae (mainly *Balanus improvisus*) to glass slides exposed each twenty-four hours for more than three years. At the same time, records were kept of the attachment of adult barnacles to glass panels exposed each month at the same locality. The time required for a cyprid to grow into an adult barnacle large enough to be counted varies from one to two weeks according to the season. By summing the daily cyprid attachments over a two- to three-week period, therefore, and comparing the figures with the number of adult barnacles found on the panels at the end of the month, a measure of the survival between cyprid and adult stages was obtained. The results are shown in Fig. 9, the ratio of surviving barnacles to cyprids being plotted against the intensity of cyprid attachment. The curve shows clearly that a cyprid's chances of successful growth to maturity vary inversely with the density of attachment: when few cyprids attach most or all of them survive to become barnacles, but when cyprid densities are high the mortality is

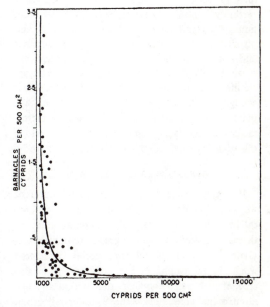

FIG. 9. RELATION BETWEEN SURVIVAL OF BARNACLES TO MATURITY AND THE INTENSITY OF CYPRID ATTACHMENT AT MIAMI BEACH, FLORIDA

Cyprid attachment was observed on glass slides exposed for twenty-four hours; the barnacles were counted on glass panels exposed for twenty-eight days. Daily cyprid attachment figures have been summed over two or three weeks, according to the season, for comparison with the number of surviving barnacles. From unpublished results of C. M. Weiss, Woods Hole Oceanographic Institution.

Inspection of the scale of barnacle:cyprid ratios in Fig. 9 brings out an apparent paradox in that ratios above 1.0 were frequently observed, i.e., in some months more barnacles survived than can be accounted for from the cyprids attaching. Weiss takes this to mean that the longer exposure of the one-month panels made them more suitable for the attachment of barnacles than the twenty-four-hour slides. Such a result of exposure can reasonably be attributed to the facilitating effect of a "slime film" (of diatoms and bacteria) on the attachment of larvae of fouling organisms, an effect of which there is independent evidence. This complication, interesting as it is, makes it impossible to use the data further for an analysis of the mortality of barnacles in early stages. For if in any month more cyprids attached to the panels during certain days than the daily figures show, the barnacle:cyprid ratio will give too low an estimate of the mortality; but such an error is not likely to be systematic, and would have to be evaluated separately.

Although it is abundantly clear that much of the mortality suffered by natural stands of barnacles is directly related to population density, much of it certainly is not. Predators, such as whelks and limpets, account for many deaths at all ages, and physical factors, including desiccation in summer and abrasion by boulders in winter, are also important. We are not yet able to dissect the barnacle life tables to expose the causes of death. It is enough for the purposes of this review to have pointed out: (1) the attraction of barnacle incrustations as objects for population research; and (2) the advantages of life table methods in their study.

COMPARISONS AND CONCLUSIONS

It is now apparent that, owing to the different ways in which data have been collected, all ecological life tables are not strictly comparable among themselves, and a summary graph containing survivorship curves for all the species considered would be misleading in the extreme. It is also true, though not so obvious, that within any one group of life tables, such as the "d_x observed" group or the "l_x observed" group, comparisons are also apt to lead us astray. For the various life tables so far constructed *take their origin at different biological ages*. Is it fair to compare a bird life table, beginning at early adult life, with the Dall sheep life table, which begins at birth, or with the life table of a sessile invertebrate, beginning at attachment or metamorphosis? Evidently not; birth itself is not an age of universal biological equivalence outside the placental mammals, and for a broader view of comparative mortality the only safe point of reference would be the fertilized ovum.

This reservation should perhaps not be applied too literally. Human and insect survivorship curves have been compared in the past, and the comparison is instructive, despite the very different origins and statistical foundations of the life tables. It is possible to compare the survivorship of an insect such as *Drosophila*, beginning at sexual maturity, with that of a laboratory population of black widow spiders (Deevey and Deevey, 1945) which enter their life table at the antepenultimate instar when the sexes become distinguishable. The comparison, which of course is purely qualitative, suggests that organisms are born at different points on their survivorship curves, so to speak, and that heavy juvenile mortality may be carried over into later life as a neotenic character. This is the statistical aspect of that ancient proverb which Cicero quotes disparagingly, "grow old early if you would be old long."

The cognate suggestion has been made that altricial and praecocial birds should be examined in the light of this hypothesis. Unfortunately, such a comparison cannot yet be made. We now have life tables of a sort for several altricial species, (song sparrow, Turdidae, etc.) and for at least one markedly praecocial bird (the pheasant), but the data are lacking for those early ages at which the comparison might have some meaning.

If bird life tables cannot even be compared with one another except from adult ages onward, we can hardly make very enlightening comparisons between birds and other animals. The ecological information is deficient, to a variable degree it is true, but still deficient, for the early ages; and this is the segment of the life curve on which future investigators must concentrate their efforts. The most that can be said at present is that the more nearly complete natural life tables (Dall sheep, barnacle, rotifer) give no ground for supposing that ecological life tables are invariably diagonal, as is so often assumed *faute de mieux* in fisheries work. Increases and decreases in mortality rate must be expected at any age, as the laboratory populations also show.

Related to the paucity of data near the beginning of life is the remarkable absence, among the examples adduced, of life curves approaching Pearl's "Type III" distribution. Only the synthetic survivorship curve for the song sparrow calculated from the egg stage (Fig. 5) shows the pronounced dip in early life associated with this form. But Sette's data for the mackerel show that pelagic fishes actually fall here; the barnacle and the rotifer might also fall here if their life tables were complete, and ecologists will await with interest the construction of a life table for the oyster.

It is pertinent to inquire whether the ecological life tables throw any light on the relation between the different theoretical types of survivorship curve (Fig. 1). It is a well known property of human longevity that while the mean age at death shows extreme variation among different populations, ancient and modern, and has shown a marked increase in Europe and the United States in recent decades, the maximum life span is fixed (Dublin and Lotka, 1935; Pearl, 1946). In other words, the human survivorship curve is like a rubber band, fixed at points corresponding to birth and about the 115th year, and while medical science has succeeded in stretching the band more and more toward the upper side of Fig. 1, the termini have remained fixed as they were in Roman times.

If the maximum life span is fixed for all species by physiological considerations, as it probably is, the mean life span is not. Lack (1943b) points out that a young blackbird in nature can expect to live for but 8 per cent of its potential life span, compared to some 60 per cent for a juvenile human. Evidently there is much room for improvement in the expectation of life of species in the wild, to judge from the known longevity of some of them in captivity. As has been shown, birds as a group seem to have remarkably diagonal survivorship curves, the mortality being constant for a given bird with respect to age, and for all birds so far studied with respect to units of mean life span. This means that experience of life is of no use to a bird in avoiding death, although Farner (1945) raises the question whether the apparent diagonality may not be a result of insufficient data.

The case is quite otherwise with the Dall sheep, with its low mortality during middle life. This species seems to have evolved a mechanism for stretching its mean life span toward the maximum. Whether this has come about because of intimate demographic contact with a single important predator or for some other reason is a "puzzling question." Such an enhancement of survival during the years of maximum reproductive efficiency has important implications for the whole population problem, including the question of the nature of internally generated cycles; but on this matter little

more can be said than that the mathematical methods are available for a study of the relation between the fertility schedule and the death rate structure when the data come to hand (Leslie, 1945).

Bodenheimer (1938) has maintained that not only is the maximum life span fixed for a species, but that the potential mean longevity is the same as the maximum. On this view a species has a "physiological life table" of the negatively skew rectangular type, and a more diagonal or positively skew "ecological life table" which is the result of premature mortality. All such mortality is thus regarded as environmentally produced. This position is probably not tenable as a basis for a general theory of mortality, since there appears to be no reason why "endogenous senescence" (in Pearl's phrase) should be strictly confined to the end of the life span. Even in genetically homogeneous populations the members are not identical, and endogenous senescence must have a probability distribution which is not necessarily regular, though it may well be more so than that of "exogenous senescence." In any case, since we can not observe physiological survivorship except in an environment of some sort, Bodenheimer's conception would appear to be non-operational.

The question at issue resolves itself into the relation between the mean and the maximum life span. In theory there is a simple answer: the ratio of the maximum to the mean approaches 1.0 as a limit for Type I, approaches infinity for Type III, and its actual value for Type II depends on the level at which we permit the abscissa of Figure 1 to intersect the ordinate. If we decide to terminate the diagram when a cohort of 1000 individuals has been reduced to 1, a diagonal survivorship line will intersect the age axis at some point above 1.0, but if we start with 100,000 individuals the same line projected will give a higher maximum age for the last survivor. Reference to Figs. 2, 4, and 5 will make the matter plain, when it is realized that an age value of +100 per cent deviation from the mean corresponds to a maximum: mean ratio of 2.0, one of +500 per cent corresponds to a ratio of 6.0, etc. In all cases we have started with 1000 individuals, simply because the samples were of less than 1000 to begin with, and only three places at most can be significant. Had we larger samples available the maximum life span, as shown on the abscissas of Figs. 2, 4, and 5, would have been higher for a given mortality rate.

It should now be clear that we cannot yet formulate the relationship exactly. One stumbling block is that with a cohort of 1000 individuals the 1 per thousand level has lost all semblance of reliability: taking Fig. 4 as an illustration, we might well find that the last hundred birds in a cohort of 100,000 really have gained some benefit from their accumulated experience of life, and die at decreasing rates. This would mean that the true survivorship curve is concave. It is equally possible that these hypothetical survivors of a larger cohort would be found to be decrepit, and to die at greatly accelerated rates, giving a convexity to the tail of the survivorship curve.

The other obstacle to an exact formulation is that the mean length of life is calculated from different starting points in the cases before us, so that an observed relation between maximum and mean has no quantitative significance as a basis of comparison between species. Empirically, it will eventually be possible to divide animals into three groups, somewhat as follows: those in which the maximum length of life is between two and six times the mean may be called "thrifty" (the Dall sheep, rotifer, and barnacle might fall here, along with most of the populations studied in the laboratory); those in which the ratio lies between 6.0 and 15.0 (as perhaps in song birds) might be called "indifferent"; those which on the average realize less than one-fifteenth of their maximum life span might be called "prodigal." These limits would have to be arbitrarily defined by the age (in units of mean life span) attained by the oldest individual in a cohort of 1000. But such limits can not yet be specified, and the values assigned are pure guesses, based on data which we know to be inadequate, and intended simply for illustration.

So far we have confined our attention almost exclusively to the *form* of the life table, and have said very little about the *causes* of death other than to imply that they are suitable subjects for ecological investigation. Authors who have discussed the matter in some detail for particular cases have not reached very satisfactory general conclusions. Thus Ricker (1945) decides that "senile death is an everyday occurrence among bluegills and crappies," and Lack (1943a) says, "Who killed cock robin is, for the most part, still a mystery." Errington (1945, 1946) has argued energetically against the generally accepted view that predation is responsible for the maintenance of population size among vertebrates, believing that intraspecific competition demands more attention than it has received. Predation, in Errington's opinion, falls principally on the very young, the very old, and the diseased, i.e., on the insecure members of the population, who might otherwise have died in any event. Clearly, the task of constructing better life tables for natural populations, though an important prerequisite to the study of mortality, is not a substitute for such a study. Even so interesting a series of life tables as is available for *Balanus balanoides* proves to be unsatisfactory when it is realized that they all start at the same season, and the survivors are exposed to winter conditions at the same ages. What would happen to the survivorship curves if such animals were caused to be born out of season can only be found out by painstaking work. And until such questions, and many others, are answered, we will not be ready to establish a general theory of mortality.

"Sed omnes una manet nox
et calcanda semel via leti."

SUMMARY

Materials for the study of the age distribution of mortality are available from several natural populations of animals. Attempts are made, in most instances for the first time, to condense this information into life tables, showing for each age interval the number of deaths, the number of survivors, the mortality rate, and the expectation of further life of members of an initial cohort of 1000 individuals. These life table functions, especially when age is expressed in terms of units of the mean life span rather than in years, months, or days, should afford the best basis for comparing populations of the same and of different species in respect to their order of dying. Unfortunately, the ecological information is of unequal value in the various cases, and only limited and tentative comparisons can be made.

According to the methods used in collecting the information, the species studied fall into three groups: (a) those in which the *age at death* (d_x) is known, with fair accuracy, at least beyond certain ages (Dall mountain sheep, the sessile rotifer *Floscularia conifera*, and several species of birds); (b) those in which the *number of survivors* (l_x) out of a definite initial number has been directly observed at frequent intervals (barnacles, song sparrow, pheasant, snowshoe rabbit); (c) those in which the *age structure* (L_x) of the population is observed at a specified time, and the age at death is inferred from the shrinkage between age classes (cormorant, many fish, fin whale). Information of type (*b*) is comparable to that obtainable from a laboratory experiment, provided only that the season of birth is sharply defined, and can be used without qualification for the construction of a life table. Information of types (*a*) and (*c*) can be so used only upon the assumption that the age structure of the population does not change with time.

Both in nature and in the laboratory, animals differ characteristically in their order of dying. When the mortality rate at all ages is constant, the survivorship (l_x) curve is diagonal on semi-logarithmic graph paper. Such a curve is found for many birds from adult stages onward; the mortality of adult birds is about 320 per thousand per hundred centiles of mean life span. If the constant age-specific mortality rate observed for the first few years of adult life is really maintained throughout life, the oldest bird in a cohort of 1000 lives 6.6 times as long as the average bird. Not all animals resemble birds in this respect, however, although many (e.g., fish) are assumed to do so. The Dall sheep, the rotifer, and possibly the barnacle are more like civilized man in that they seem to have evolved a mechanism for stretching the mean life span toward the maximum, so that the survivorship curve is convex. In these cases the maximum life span (among a sample of 1000) is only two or three times the mean. On the other hand there are undoubtedly species in which juvenile mortality is very heavy, but the few survivors to advanced ages die at reduced rates. This J-shaped or concave survivorship line, with the maximum longevity perhaps 15 or more times the mean, is presumed to characterize the oyster and other species, but it has not yet been formally recognized either in the laboratory or in nature. The closest approach to it, so far, is found when the survival of song sparrows is reckoned from the egg stage; but the mackerel will almost certainly provide an even better example.

Detailed comparisons between species cannot yet be made, partly because of the diverse statistical foundations of the life tables and partly because the data begin at different biological ages (birth, hatching, metamorphosis, sexual maturity, etc.) in the different cases. In all cases it is the youngest ages about which we know least, and ecologists should therefore concentrate their efforts on this segment of the life span of animals in nature.

The best examples of ecological life tables come from Hatton's work with the barnacle *Balanus balanoides*, which is a very favorable object for population research. By way of emphasizing the advantages of life table notation, Hatton's data are manipulated so as to show the relationship between longevity and population density. A theory of two-dimensional crowding by radially growing circular objects is first derived from geometric considerations, and it is then possible to relate the expectation of life (e_x) of a barnacle to a factor, called the *crowding coefficient*, which incorporates both the population density and the rate of growth. The number of barnacle populations available for study is limited, and Hatton's experiments were designed for a different purpose, but so far as the data go there is no evidence of an optimum density for survival of *B. balanoides*. Reasons are given for supposing that *Chthamalus stellatus* may prove to have such an optimum density.

ACKNOWLEDGMENTS

This article had its inception as part of a symposium, entitled "Life Tables and Their Application," held at Boston on December 27, 1943, under the joint auspices of the Ecological Society of America and the American Statistical Association. The present version has been completely reworked in the light of other contributions to the symposium. Remarks made at the meeting by Margaret Merrell, C. P. Winsor, and W. E. Ricker have been particularly helpful. Much has been learned also from later conversations with David Lack, G. E. Hutchinson, and Daniel Merriman. The author retains sole responsibility, however, for errors which may still remain.

LIST OF LITERATURE

Austin, O. L. 1942. The life span of the common tern (*Sterna hirundo*). Bird-Banding, 13: 159–176.

Barnaby, J. T. 1944. Fluctuations in abundance of red salmon, *Oncorhynchus nerka* (Walbaum) of the Karluk River, Alaska. *U. S. Fish & Wildlife Service, Fishery Bull.*, 50 (39): 235–295.

Bertram, G. C. L. 1940. The biology of the Weddell and Crabeater Seals, with a study of the comparative behaviour of the Pinnipedia. *Brit. Mus.*

(*Nat. Hist.*): *British Graham Land Expedition 1934–37, Sci. Rep.*, 1 (1): 139 pp., pls. 1–10.

BODENHEIMER, F. S. 1938. *Problems of animal ecology.* vi + 183 pp. Oxford Univ. Press, London.

DAVIS, M. B. 1945. The effect of population density on longevity in *Trogoderma versicolor* Creutz. (= *T. inclusa* Lec.). *Ecology*, 26: 353–362.

DEEVEY, G. B., and E. S. DEEVEY. 1945. A life table for the black widow. *Trans. Conn. Acad. Arts Sci.*, 36: 115–134.

DUBLIN, L. I., and A. J. LOTKA. 1935. *Length of life. A study of the life table.* xxii + 400 pp. Ronald Press, New York.

EDMONDSON, W. T. 1945. Ecological studies of sessile Rotatoria, Part II. Dynamics of populations and social structures. *Ecol. Mon.*, 15: 141–172.

ERICKSON, M. M. 1938. Territory, annual cycle, and numbers in a population of wren-tits (*Chamaea fasciata*). *Univ. Calif. Pub. Zool.*, 42 (5): 247–334, pls. 9–14.

ERRINGTON, P. L. 1945. Some contributions of a fifteen-year local study of the northern bobwhite to a knowledge of population phenomena. *Ecol. Mon.*, 15: 1–34.

——. 1946. Predation and vertebrate populations. *Quart. Rev. Biol.*, 21: 144–177, 221–245.

ESCHMEYER, R. W. 1939. Analysis of the complete fish population from Howe Lake, Crawford County, Michigan. *Papers Mich. Acad. Sci. Arts Lett.*, 24 (II): 117–137.

FARNER, D. S. 1945. Age groups and longevity in the American robin. *Wilson Bull.*, 57: 56–74.

GEISER, S. W. 1923. Evidences of a differential death rate of the sexes among animals. *Amer. Midl. Nat.*, 8: 155–163.

——. 1924. The differential death-rate of the sexes among animals, with a suggested explanation. *Wash. Univ. Stud.*, 12: 73–96.

GREEN, R. G., and C. A. EVANS. 1940. Studies on a population cycle of snowshoe hares on the Lake Alexander area. I. Gross annual censuses, 1932–1939. *J. Wildl. Man.*, 4: 220–238. II. Mortality according to age groups and seasons. Ibid., 4: 267–278. III. Effect of reproduction and mortality of young hares on the cycle. Ibid., 4: 347–358.

HACKER, H. P., and H. S. PEARSON. 1946. The growth, survival, wandering, and variation of the long-tailed field mouse, *Apodemus sylvaticus*. II. Survival (By H. P. Hacker). *Biometrika*, 33: 333–361.

HATTON, H. 1938. Essais de bionomie explicative sur quelques espèces intercotidales d'algues et d'animaux. *Ann. Inst. Océanogr.*, 17: 241–348.

HODGE, W. B. 1857. On the rates of interest for the use of money in ancient and modern times. (Part I). *Assurance Mag. & J. Inst. Act.*, 6: 301–333.

JACKSON, C. H. N. 1936. Some new methods in the study of *Glossina morsitans*. *Proc. Zool. Soc. Lond.*, 1936: 811–896, pls. 1–12.

——. 1939. The analysis of an animal population. *J. Anim. Ecol.*, 8: 238–246.

JENSEN, A. J. C. 1939. On the laws of decrease in fish stocks. *Cons. Per. Intern. Explor. Mer, Rapp. Proc.-Verb.*, 110 (8): 85–96.

KORTLANDT, A. 1942. Levensloop, samenstelling en structuur der Nederlandse aalscholver bevolking. *Ardea*, 31: 175–280.

KRAAK, W. K., G. L. RINKEL, and J. HOOGERHEIDE. 1940. Oecologische bewerking van de Europese ringgegevens van de Kievit (*Vanellus vanellus* (L.)). *Ardea*, 29: 151–175.

LACK, D. 1943a. *The life of the robin.* 200 pp. H. F. & G. Witherby, London.

——. 1943b. The age of the blackbird. *Brit. Birds*, 36: 166–175.

——. 1943c. The age of some more British birds. *Brit. Birds*, 36: 193–197, 214–221.

——. 1946. Do juvenile birds survive less well than adults? *Brit. Birds*, 39: 258–264.

LAURIE, A. H. 1937. The age of female blue whales and the effect of whaling on the stock. *Discov. Rep.*, 15: 223–284.

LEOPOLD, A., T. M. SPERRY, W. S. FEENEY, and J. S. CATENHUSEN. 1943. Population turnover on a Wisconsin pheasant refuge. *J. Wildl. Man.*, 7: 383–394.

LESLIE, P. H. 1945. On the use of matrices in certain population mathematics. *Biometrika*, 33: 183–212.

——, and R. M. RANSON. 1940. The mortality, fertility, and rate of natural increase of the vole (*Microtus agrestis*) as observed in the laboratory. *J. Anim. Ecol.*, 9: 27–52.

MACARTHUR, J. W., and W. H. T. BAILLIE. 1932. Sex differences in mortality in *Abraxas*-type species. *Quart. Rev. Biol.*, 7: 313–325.

MACDONELL, W. R. 1913. On the expectation of life in ancient Rome, and in the provinces of Hispania and Lusitania, and Africa. *Biometrika*, 9: 366–380.

MARSHALL, H. 1947. Longevity of the American herring gull. *Auk*, 64: 188–198.

MONTEROSSO, B. 1930. Studi cirripedologici, VI. Sul comportamento di "Chthamalus stellatus" in diverse condizioni sperimentali. *Atti. R. Accad. Naz. Lincei Rend., Ser. 6, Cl. Sci. Fis. Mat. Nat.*, 11 (5): 501–505.

MOORE, H. B. 1934. The biology of *Balanus balanoides*. I. Growth rate and its relation to size, season, and tidal level. *J. Mar. Biol. Ass.*, n. s., 19: 851–868.

MOORE, H. B. 1935. A comparison of the biology of *Echinus esculentus* in different habitats. Part II. *J. Mar. Biol. Ass.*, n. s., 20: 109–128.

——, and J. A. KITCHING. 1939. The biology of *Chthamalus stellatus* (Poli). *J. Mar. Biol. Ass.*, n. s., 23: 521–541.

MURIE, A. 1944. *The wolves of Mount McKinley*. (Fauna of the National Parks of the U. S., Fauna Series No. 5, xx + 238 pp.) U. S. Dept. Int., Nat. Park Service, Washington.

NICE, M. M. 1937. Studies on the life history of the song sparrow. Vol. I. A population study of the song sparrow. *Trans. Linn. Soc. N. Y.*, 4: vi + 247 pp.

PAYNTER, R. A. (*in press*). The fate of Kent Island herring gulls. *Bird-Banding*, (in press).

PEARL, R. 1940. *Introduction to medical biometry and statistics*. 3rd ed. xv + 537 pp. W. B. Saunders, Philadelphia and London.

——. 1946. *Man the animal*. 128 pp. Principia Press, Bloomington.

——, and J. R. MINER. 1935. Experimental studies on the duration of life. XIV. The comparative mortality of certain lower organisms. *Quart. Rev. Biol.*, 10: 60–79.

——, ——, and S. L. PARKER. 1927. Experimental studies on the duration of life. XI. Density of population and life duration in *Drosophila*. *Amer. Nat.*, 61: 289–318.

——, T. PARK, and J. R. MINER. 1941. Experimental studies on the duration of life. XVI. Life tables for the flour beetle *Tribolium confusum* Duval. *Amer. Nat.*, 75: 5–19.

PRATT, D. M. 1943. Analysis of population development in *Daphnia* at different temperatures. *Biol. Bull.*, 85: 116–140.

RAITT, D. S. 1939. The rate of mortality of the haddock of the North Sea stock. *Cons. Perm. Intern. Explor. Mer, Rapp. Proc.-Verb.*, 110 (6): 65–79.

RICKER, W. E. 1940. Relation of "catch per unit effort" to abundance and rate of exploitation. *J. Fish. Res. Bd. Canada*, 5: 43–70.

——. 1944. Further notes on fishing mortality and effort. *Copeia*, 1944: 23–44.

——. 1945. Natural mortality among Indiana bluegill sunfish. *Ecology* 26: 111–121.

RUNNSTRÖM, S. 1925. Zur Biologie und Entwicklung von *Balanus balanoides* (Linné). *Bergens Mus. Aarbok* 1924-25, *Naturvid. Raekke*, (5). 46 pp.

RUSSELL, E. S. 1942. *The overfishing problem*. viii + 130 pp. Cambridge Univ. Press, Cambridge.

SETTE, O. E. 1943. Biology of the Atlantic mackerel (*Scomber scombrus*) of North America. Part I: Early life history, including the growth, drift, and mortality of the egg and larval populations. *U. S. Fish Wildl. Serv. Fish. Bull.*, 50 (38): 147–237.

THOMPSON, W. F., and F. H. BELL. 1934. Biological statistics of the Pacific halibut fishery. (2) Effect of changes in intensity upon total yield and yield per unit of gear. *Rep. Intern. Fish. Comm.*, 8: 49 pp.

TRENERRY, C. F. 1926. *The origin and early history of insurance, including the contract of bottomry*. xiv + 330 pp. P. S. King & Son, London.

WHEELER, J. F. G. 1934. On the stock of whales at South Georgia. *Discov. Rep.*, 9: 351–372.

THE INTRINSIC RATE OF NATURAL INCREASE
OF AN INSECT POPULATION

By L. C. BIRCH*, *Zoology Department, University of Sydney*

CONTENTS

1. INTRODUCTION

The intrinsic rate of increase is a basic parameter which an ecologist may wish to establish for an insect population. We define it as the rate of increase per head under specified physical conditions, in an unlimited environment where the effects of increasing density do not need to be considered. The growth of such a population is by definition exponential. Many authors, including Malthus and Darwin, have been concerned with this and related concepts, but there has been no general agreement in recent times on definitions. Chapman (1931) referred to it as 'biotic potential', and although he does state in one place that biotic potential should in some way combine fecundity rate, sex ratio and survival rate, he never precisely defined this expression. Stanley (1946) discussed a somewhat similar concept which he called the 'environmental index'. This gives a measure of the relative suitability of different environments, but it does not give the actual rate of increase of the insect under these different conditions. An index for the possible rate of increase under different physical conditions would at the same time provide a measure of the relative suitability of different environments. Birch (1945 c) attempted to provide this in an index combining the total number of eggs laid, the survival rate of immature stages, the rate of development and the sex ratio. This was done when the author was unaware of the relevance of cognate studies in human demography. A sounder approach to insect populations based on demographic procedures is now

suggested in this paper. The development of this branch of population mathematics is principally due to A. J. Lotka. From the point of view of the biologist, convenient summaries of his fundamental contributions to this subject will be found in Lotka (1925, Chapter 9; 1939 and 1945). A numerical example of the application of Lotka's methods in the case of a human population will be found in Dublin & Lotka (1925). The parameter which Lotka has developed for human populations, and which he has variously called the 'true' or 'inherent' or 'intrinsic' rate of natural increase, has obvious application to populations of animals besides the human species. The first determination of the intrinsic rate of increase of an animal other than man was made by Leslie & Ranson (1940). They calculated the 'true rate of natural increase' of the vole, *Microtus agrestis*, from age-specific rates of fecundity and mortality determined under laboratory conditions. With the use of matrices Leslie has extended these methods and, as an example, calculated the true rate of natural increase of the brown rat, *Rattus norvegicus* (Leslie, 1945). The author is much indebted to Mr Leslie for having drawn his attention to the possible application of actuarial procedures to insect populations. He has been completely dependent upon him for the methods of calculation used in this paper.

Before proceeding to discuss the reasons for the particular terminology adopted in this paper, it is necessary first to consider the true nature of the parameter with which we are concerned.

* This investigation was carried out at the Bureau of Animal Population, Oxford University, during the tenure of an overseas senior research scholarship from the Australian Science & Industry Endowment Fund.

2. BIOLOGICAL SIGNIFICANCE OF THE INTRINSIC RATE OF NATURAL INCREASE

The intrinsic rate of increase is best defined as the constant 'r' in the differential equation for population increase in an unlimited environment,

$$dN/dt = rN,$$

or in the integrated form $N_t = N_0 e^{rt}$,

where N_0 = number of animals at time zero,

N_t = number of animals at time t,

r = infinitesimal rate of increase.

The exponent r is the difference between the birth-rate (b) and the death-rate (d) in the population ($r = b - d$). In some circumstances it may be more useful to know the finite rate of increase, i.e. the number of times the population multiplies in a unit of time. Thus, in a population which is increasing exponentially, if there are N_t individuals at time t then in one unit of time later the ratio

$$\frac{N_{t+1}}{N_t} = e^r$$
$$= \text{antilog}_e r = \lambda.$$

Hence the finite rate of increase (λ) is the natural antilogarithm of the intrinsic (infinitesimal) rate of increase.

Any statement about the rate of increase of a population is incomplete without reference to the age distribution of that population, unless every female in it happens to be producing offspring at the same rate at all ages, and at the same time is exposed to a chance of dying which is the same at all ages. In such an inconceivable population the age of the individuals obviously has no significance. In practice, a population has a certain age schedule both of fecundity and of mortality. Now a population with *constant* age schedules of fecundity and mortality, which is multiplying in an unlimited environment, will gradually assume a fixed age distribution known as the stable age distribution' (Lotka, 1925, p. 110). When this age distribution is established the population will increase at a rate $dN/dt = rN$. Thus the parameter r refers to a population with a stable age distribution. The consideration of rates of increase in terms of the stable age distribution was one of the most important advances in vital statistics. In any other sort of population the rate of increase varies with time until a stable age distribution is assumed. There is, for example, no simple answer to the question: what is the rate of increase of x newly emerged adult insects in an unlimited environment? The rate will vary with time as immature stages are produced until the population has a stable age distribution. The rate of increase in the first generation might be given, but that is a figure of limited value. On the other hand, the maximum rate that it can ever maintain over an indefinite period of time is given by the rate of increase in a population of stable age distribution. That rate is therefore the true intrinsic capacity of the organism to increase. Thompson (1931) rejected the use of the exponential formula in the study of insect populations in preference for a method of dealing with the rate of increase as a 'discontinuous phenomenon'. His paper should be consulted for the reasons why he considers a single index unsatisfactory in relation to the particular problems with which he was concerned.

If the 'biotic potential' of Chapman is to be given quantitative expression in a single index, the parameter r would seem to be the best measure to adopt, since it gives the intrinsic capacity of the animal to increase in an unlimited environment.[*] But neither 'biotic potential' nor 'true rate of natural increase' can be regarded as satisfactory descriptive titles. The word 'potential' has physical connotations which are not particularly appropriate when applied to organisms. There is a sense in which it might be better used with reference to the environment rather than the organism. Contrary to what it seems to imply, the 'true rate of natural increase' does not describe the actual rate of increase of a population at a particular point in time, unless the age distribution of that population happens to be stable. But it does define the intrinsic capacity of that population, with its given regime of fecundity and mortality, to increase. This point is clearly made by Dublin & Lotka (1925). More recently, Lotka (1945) has dropped the use of 'true rate of natural increase' for the more precise 'intrinsic rate of natural increase'. It would seem desirable that students of populations should adopt the same terminology, irrespective of the animals concerned, and as 'intrinsic rate of natural increase' is more truly descriptive of the parameter r than other alternatives, its use is adopted in this paper.

The intrinsic rate of increase of a population may be calculated from the age-specific fecundity[†] and survival rates observed under defined environmental conditions. For poikilothermic animals these rates vary with physical factors of the environment such as temperature and humidity. Furthermore, within any

---

[*] For a discussion of the relative merits of this and other parameters in human demography reference should be made to Lotka (1945).

[†] Fecundity rate is used to denote the rate at which eggs are laid by a female. Some eggs laid are infertile and so do not hatch. The percentage 'infertility' is included in the mortality rate of the egg stage. It is usual amongst entomologists to denote the percentage of fertile eggs as the 'fertility rate'. Demographers, on the other hand, use 'fertility rate' to denote the rate of live births. Since 'fertility rate' has this other usage in entomology the term 'fecundity rate' is used throughout this paper as synonymous with the 'fertility rate' of the demographers.

given combination of physical factors, the fecundity and survival rates will vary with the density of the animals. Hence it is possible to calculate an array of values of r at different densities. But particular significance attaches to the value of r when the fecundity and survival rates are maximal, i.e. when density is optimal, for this gives the maximum possible rate of increase *within* the defined physical conditions. *Between* the whole array of physical conditions in which the animal can survive there is a zone where fecundity and survival rates are greatest and where, therefore, the intrinsic rate of increase will be greatest too. The zone within which the intrinsic rate of increase is a maximum may be referred to as the optimum zone. This is an arbitrary use of the word optimum and it does not imply that it is always to the advantage of the animal to increase at the maximum possible rate. The maximum intrinsic rate of increase under given physical conditions has importance from two points of view. It has a theoretical value, since it is the parameter which necessarily enters many equations in population mathematics (cf. Lotka, 1925; Volterra, 1931; Gause, 1934; Crombie, 1945). It also has practical significance. The range of temperature and moisture within which the insect can multiply is defined most precisely by that range within which the parameter exceeds zero. This will define the maximum possible range. In nature the range of physical conditions within which the species may be found to multiply may be less, since it is possible that effects of density and interspecific competition may reduce this range, and also the range of the optimum zone. These considerations are, however, beyond the scope of this paper; some discussion of them will be found in a review paper by Crombie (1947).

There are some important differences in the orientation with which the demographer and the student of insect populations face their problems. In human populations the parameter r varies in different civilizations and at different times in one civilization, depending upon customs, sanitation and other factors which alter mortality and fecundity rates. The maximum possible value of r does not enter into most demographic studies. In a population which is growing logistically the initial rate of increase is theoretically the maximum intrinsic rate of increase, and this latter value can be determined indirectly by calculating the appropriate logistic curve. Lotka (1927) has done this for a human population and so arrived at an estimate of a physiological maximum for man. This has theoretical interest only. In insect populations, on the other hand, the maximum value for the intrinsic rate of increase does assume considerable theoretical and practical significance, as has already been pointed out. The entomologist can readily determine the maximum values and this is his

obvious starting-point. But the determination of r at different stages in the population history of an insect, whether in an experimental population or in the field, offers many practical difficulties which have not yet been surmounted for any single species. The values which the entomologist has difficulty in determining are those which are most readily obtained for human populations. The crude birth-rates and crude death-rates of the population at specific stages in its history are precisely those indices with which the demographer works. His census data provides him with the actual age distribution which is something not known empirically for a single insect species. He can have a knowledge of age distribution even at intercensal periods, and under civilized conditions he can also determine the age-specific rates of fecundity and mortality which were in operation during any particular year. In insect populations this is at present impossible; one can only keep a number of individuals under specified conditions and determine their age-specific rates of fecundity and survival, and from these data r can be calculated.

The fact that populations in nature may not realize the maximum value of their intrinsic rate of natural increase, does not negate the utility of this parameter either from a theoretical or a practical point of view. Having determined this parameter, the next logical step is to find out the extent to which this rate of increase is realized in nature. It is conceivable that some species, such as those which infest stored wheat or flour, may increase exponentially when liberated in vast quantities of these foodstuffs. This would imply that the insects could move out of the area in which they were multiplying with sufficient speed to escape density effects and that they had no gregarious tendencies. An exponential rate of increase may also occur in temperate climates in some plant-feeding species which only multiply in a short period of the year in the spring. In seasons with abundant plant growth the insect population may be far from approaching any limitation in the resources of the environment before the onset of summer retards the rate of increase. The population counts of *Thrips imaginis* in some favourable seasons in South Australia suggest such a picture (Davidson & Andrewartha, 1948).

3. CALCULATION OF THE INTRINSIC RATE OF NATURAL INCREASE

(a) Experimental data required

The calculation of r is based on the female population; the primary data required being as follows:

(1) The female life table giving the probability at birth of being alive at age x. This is usually designated l_x ($l_0 = 1$).

(2) The age-specific fecundity table giving the

mean number of female offspring produced in a unit of time by a female aged x. This is designated m_x.

In the calculation of the stable age distribution the age-specific survival rates (l_x) of both the immature stages and the reproductive stages are required. For the calculation of r the life table of the adult and only the total survival of the immature stages (irrespective of age) are needed. In practice, the age-specific fecundity rates m_x will be established for some convenient interval of age, such as a week. If N eggs are laid per female alive between the ages x to $x+1$ in the unit of time chosen, then m_x simply equals $\frac{1}{2}N$ when sex ratio is unity. It is assumed that this value occurs at the mid-point of the age group.

A numerical example is worked out for the rice weevil *Calandra* (*Sitophilus*) *oryzae* (L.) living under optimum conditions (29° C. in wheat of 14% moisture content). Data for the rates of development and survival of the immature stages, and the age-specific fecundity rates were obtained from Birch (1945 *a*, *b*). The life table of adult females has not been determined experimentally, only the mean length of adult life being known. However, an estimate was obtained for purposes of these calculations by adapting the known life table of *Tribolium confusum* Duval (Pearl, Park & Miner, 1941) to *Calandra oryzae*, making the necessary reduction in the time scale. Since the mean length of life of *Tribolium confusum* in this life table was 198 days and the mean length of life of *Calandra oryzae* at 29° was 84 days, one 'Calandra day' has been taken as equivalent to 2·35 'Tribolium days'. To this extent the example worked out is artificial, but, for reasons which will become evident later in the paper, it is unlikely that the error so introduced in the estimate of r is of much significance.

Before proceeding to outline direct methods of estimating r two other parameters must first be mentioned: the net reproduction rate and the mean length of a generation.

(b) The net reproduction rate

This is the rate of multiplication in one generation (Lotka, 1945) and is best expressed as the ratio of total female births in two successive generations. This we shall call R_0 and so follow the symbolism of the demographers. R_0 is determined from age-specific fecundity and survival rates and is defined as

$$R_0 = \int_0^\infty l_x m_x dx,$$

where l_x and m_x are as already defined.

The method of calculating R_0 is set out in Table 1. The values of l_x are taken at the mid-point of each age group and age is given from the time the egg is laid. Since the survival rate of the immature stages was 0·90 the life table of adults reckoned from 'birth',

i.e. oviposition, was the product: l_x for adults $\times$ 0·90. Development from the egg to emergence of the adult from the grain lasts 28 days and 4·5 weeks is the mid-point of the first week of egg laying. The product $l_x m_x$ is obtained for each age group and the sum of these products $\Sigma l_x m_x$ is the value R_0. In this particular example $R_0 = 113$·6. Thus a population of *Calandra oryzae* at 29° will multiply 113·6 times *in each generation.*

Table 1. *Showing the life table (for oviposition span) age-specific fecundity rates and the method of calculating the net reproduction rate* (R_0) *for* Calandra oryzae *at* 29° *in wheat of* 14% *moisture content. Sex ratio is equal*

Pivotal age in weeks (x)	(l_x)	(m_x)	($l_x m_x$)
4·5	0·87	20·0	17·400
5·5	0·83	23·0	19·090
6·5	0·81	15·0	12·150
7·5	0·80	12·5	10·000
8·5	0·79	12·5	9·875
9·5	0·77	14·0	10·780
10·5	0·74	12·5	9·250
11·5	0·66	14·5	9·570
12·5	0·59	11·0	6·490
13·5	0·52	9·5	4·940
14·5	0·45	2·5	1·125
15·5	0·36	2·5	0·900
16·5	0·29	2·5	0·800
17·5	0·25	4·0	1·000
18·5	0·19	1·0	0·190

$$R_0 = 113·560$$

The comparison of two or more populations by means of their net reproduction rates may be quite misleading unless the mean lengths of the generations are the same. Two or more populations may have the same net reproduction rate but their intrinsic rates of increase may be quite different because of different lengths of their generations. Consider, for example, the effect of moving the $l_x m_x$ column in Table 1 up or down by a unit of age, R_0 remains the same but it is obvious that the generation times are now very different. For these reasons the parameter R_0 has limited value and it must always be considered in relation to the length of the generation (T).

(c) The mean length of a generation

The relation between numbers and time in a population growing exponentially is given by

$$N_T = N_0 e^{rT}.$$

When T = the mean length of a generation, then from the definition of net reproduction rate $N_T/N_0 = R_0$, hence

$$R_0 = e^{rT},$$

and

$$T = \frac{\log_e R_0}{r}.$$

It follows that an accurate estimate of the mean length of a generation cannot be obtained until the value of r is known. For many purposes, however, an approximate estimate of T which can be calculated independently of r may be of use. Thus, although oviposition by the female is extended over a period of time, it may be considered as concentrated for each generation at one point of time, successive generations being spaced T units apart (Dublin & Lotka, 1925). For approximate purposes therefore it may be defined as

$$T = \frac{\Sigma x l_x m_x}{\Sigma l_x m_x}.$$

We may thus consider the figures for the product $l_x m_x$ given in the last column of Table 1 as a frequency distribution of which the individual items are each concentrated at the mid-point of each age group. The mean of this distribution is the approximate value of T. In this particular example

$$T = \frac{943 \cdot 09}{113 \cdot 56} = 8 \cdot 3 \text{ weeks.}$$

If this were an accurate estimate of T we could proceed to calculate the value of r since, from the above equation relating R_0, r and T, we have

$$r = \frac{\log_e R_0}{T}$$

$$= \frac{\log_e 113 \cdot 56}{8 \cdot 30} = 0 \cdot 57 \text{ per head per week.}$$

It will become evident in what follows that this is an underestimate of r owing to the approximate estimate of T. The procedure does, however, serve to illustrate the nature of the parameter, and in some cases where r is small it may be a sufficiently accurate means of calculation (cf. for example, Dublin & Lotka, 1925). We shall proceed in the next section to an accurate method for the calculation of r.

(d) The calculation of 'r'

A population with constant age schedules of fecundity and mortality will gradually approach a fixed form of age distribution known as the stable age distribution (p. 16). Once this is established the population increases at a rate $dN/dt = rN$ and the value of r may be calculated from the equation

$$\int_0^\infty e^{-rx} l_x m_x dx = 1.$$

For the derivation of this formula reference must be made to Lotka (1925) and the bibliography therein. The usual methods of calculation may be found in Dublin & Lotka (1925, Appendix) or Lotka (1939, p. 68 et seq.). For high values of r, these methods may not be particularly satisfactory (Leslie & Ranson, 1940; Leslie, 1945, Appendix), and the computations, moreover, become very tedious. Some approxima-

tions to the rigorous procedures are justified in so far as the determination of the primary data which enter the above formula is of course subject to considerable error, arising from the normal variation in the organisms and conditions to which they are subjected in the experiments. It was considered that an estimate of r, calculated to the second decimal place, was sufficient in these circumstances. The following approximate method was therefore adopted. It has the merit of being both simple and fast.

As an approximation we may write

$$\Sigma e^{-rx} l_x m_x = 1.$$

Here x is taken to be the mid-point of each age group and the summation is carried out over all age groups for which $m_x > 0$. A number of trial values are now substituted in this equation, in each case calculating a series of values e^{-rx} and multiplying them by the appropriate $l_x m_x$ values for each age group. By graphing these trial values of r against the corresponding summation values of the left-hand side of the above expression, we may find the value of r which will make

$$\Sigma e^{-rx} l_x m_x \rightarrow 1.$$

The whole procedure is greatly simplified by the use of 4-figure tables for powers of e (e.g. Milne-Thomson & Comrie 1944, Table 9). Since these tables only give the values of $e^{\pm x}$ at intervals of 0·01 in the argument x up to $e^{\pm 6}$, it may be convenient to multiply both sides of the equation by a factor e^k in order to work with powers of e which lie in the more detailed parts of the table. Thus, in the present example, k was taken as 7:

$$e^7 \Sigma e^{-rx} l_x m_x = e^7$$

$$\Sigma e^{7-rx} l_x m_x = 1097.$$

A value of r was now sought which would make the left-hand side of this expression equal to 1097. The actual process of carrying out this simple computation is exemplified in Table 2. The summation of the expression is not carried beyond the age group centred at 13·5 because of the negligible contribution of the older age groups. It has already been mentioned that r is an infinitesimal rate of increase not to be confused with a finite rate of increase λ which equals antilog$_e r$. In this particular example $r = 0·76$ and λ therefore has a value 2·14. In other words the population will multiply 2·14 times per week.

By reference to Table 2 it is clear that the relative weights with which the different age groups contribute to the value of r are given by the values $l_x m_x e^{7-rx}$ at each age group. It is of particular interest to observe the relation between values at successive age intervals (Table 3). The value of r is 56% accounted for by the first week of adult life. The first 2 weeks combined contribute 85% towards the final value and the first 3 weeks combined total 94%. The 13·5th week, on the other hand, contributes 0·02%. It should not be inferred that adults 13·5 weeks old are of no importance since their eggs will eventually give rise to adults in the productive age categories. The biological significance of Table 3 is that the intrinsic rate of increase is determined to a much greater extent by the rate of oviposition in the first couple of weeks of adult life than by the total number of eggs laid in the life span of the adult, even although only 27 % of the total number of eggs are laid in the first 2 weeks. With

Table 2. *Showing the method of calculating* r *for Calandra oryzae at* 29° *by trial and error substitutions in the expression* $\Sigma e^{7-rx}l_x m_x = 1097$

Pivotal age group (x)	$l_x m_x$	$7-rx$	e^{7-rx}	$7-rx$	e^{7-rx}
		r = 0·76		*r = 0·77*	
4·5	17·400	3·58	35·87	3·53	34·12
5·5	19·090	2·82	16·78	2·76	15·80
6·5	12·150	2·06	7·846	1·99	7·316
7·5	10·000	1·30	3·669	1·22	3·387
8·5	9·875	0·54	1·716	0·45	1·5683
9·5	10·780	−0·22	0·8025	−0·32	0·7261
10·5	9·250	−0·98	0·3753	−1·09	0·3362
11·5	9·570	−1·74	0·1755	−1·86	0·1557
12·5	6·490	−2·50	0·0821	−2·62	0·0728
13·5	4·940	−3·26	0·0384	−3·39	0·0337
$\sum_{4\cdot5}^{13\cdot5} e^{7-rx}l_x m_x =$			1108		1047

r lies between 0·76 and 0·77 and by graphical interpretation = 0·762.

Table 3. *The contribution of each age group to the value of* r *when* r = 0·76

Pivotal age group (x)	$l_x m_x e^{7-rx}$	Percentage contribution of each age group
4·5	624·1	56·33
5·5	320·3	28·91
6·5	95·3	8·60
7·5	36·7	3·31
8·5	17·0	1·53
9·5	8·7	0·78
10·5	3·5	0·32
11·5	1·7	0·15
12·5	0·5	0·05
13·5	0·2	0·02
	1108·0	100·00

each successive week, eggs laid make a lessened contribution to the value of r. In this particular case this can be expressed by stating that for each egg laid in the first week of adult life it would require 2·1 times as many in the second week to make the same contribution to the value of r, $(2·1)^2$ in the third week and $(2·1)^{n-1}$ in the nth week. The ratio 2·1 : 1 is the ratio between successive weighting values e^{7-rx} (per egg) in Table 2. The importance of the first few weeks is further intensified by the fact that egg laying is at a maximum then. From these considerations it

follows that in determining oviposition rates experimentally, the rates in early adult life should be found with the greatest accuracy. Of corresponding importance is the accurate determination of the pivotal age for the first age category in which eggs are laid. In the example being cited an error of half a week causes an error of 8 % in the estimate of r.

The calculations were repeated ignoring the adult life table. The value of r was then 0·77. Since the imposition of an adult life table only makes a difference of 1 % in the value of r it is evident that the life table is of little importance in this example. This is due to the fact already noted that the major contribution to the value of r is made by adults in early life, and during early adult life survival rate is at a maximum. The life table may assume quite a different importance in a species with a different type of age schedule of fecundity or when the value of r is lower.

4. THE STABLE AGE DISTRIBUTION

With a knowledge of the intrinsic rate of increase and the life table it is possible to calculate the stable age distribution and the stable female birth-rate of the population. Thus if c_x is the proportion of the stable population aged between x and x + dx, and b is the instantaneous birth-rate

$$c_x = be^{-rx}l_x,$$

and

$$1/b = \int_0^\infty e^{-rx}l_x dx.$$

For the usual methods of computation reference should be made again to Dublin & Lotka (1925). Mr Leslie has, however, pointed out to me another method of calculation which saves much of the numerical integration involved in the more usual methods. At the same time it is sufficiently accurate for our present purpose. If at time t we consider a stable population consisting of N_t individuals, and if during the interval of time t to t + 1 there are B_t female births, we may define a birth-rate

$$\beta = B_t/N_t.$$

Then if we define for the given life table (l_x) the series of values L_x by the relationship $L_x = \int_x^{x+1} l_x dx$ (the stationary or 'life table' age distribution of the actuary),[*] the proportion (p_x) of individuals aged between x and x + 1 in the stable population is given by

$$p_x = \beta L_x e^{-r(x+1)},$$

$$1/\beta = \sum_{x=0}^{m} L_x e^{-r(x+1)},$$

where x = m to m + 1 is the last age group considered in the complete life table age distribution. It will be noticed that the life table (l_x values) for the complete

* For a discussion of L_x see Dublin & Lotka (1936).

age span of the species are required for the computation of p_x and β. But where r is high it will be found that for the older age groups the terms $L_x e^{-r(x+1)}$ are so small and contribute so little to the value of β that they can be neglected.

The calculations involved are quite simple and are illustrated in the following example for *Calandra oryzae* at 29° (Table 4). Actually, in the present example, instead of calculating the values of L_x, the values of l_x were taken at the mid-points of each age group. This was considered sufficiently accurate in the present instance. It should also be pointed out that whereas only the total mortality of immature stages was required in the calculation of r, the age specific mortality of the immature stages is needed

Table 4. *Calculation of the stable age distribution of* Calandra oryzae *at 29° when* $r = 0.76$

Age group (x)	L_x	$e^{-r(x+1)}$	$L_x e^{-r(x+1)}$	Percentage distribution $100\beta L_x e^{-r(x+1)}$	
0—	0·95	0·4677	0·4443150	54·740	95·5 %
1—	0·90	0·2187	0·1968300	24·249	total
2—	0·90	0·10228	0·0920520	11·341	immature
3—	0·90	0·04783	0·0430470	5·304	stages
4—	0·87	0·02237	0·0194619	2·398	
5—	0·83	0·01046	0·0086818	1·070	
6—	0·81	0·00489	0·0039609	0·488	
7—	0·80	0·002243	0·0017944	0·221	
8—	0·79	0·001070	0·0008453	0·104	4·5 %
9—	0·77	0·000500	0·0003850	0·047	total
10—	0·74	0·000239	0·0001769	0·022	adults
11—	0·66	0·000110	0·0000726	0·009	
12—	0·59	0·000051	0·0000301	0·004	
13—	0·52	0·000024	0·0000125	0·002	
14—	0·45	0·000011	0·0000050	0·001	

$$1/\beta = 0.8116704 \qquad 100.000$$

for the calculation of the stable age distribution. In this example the total mortality of the immature stages was 10 %—and 98 % of this mortality occurred in the first week of larval life (Birch, 1945 *d*). Hence the approximate value of L_x for the mid-point of the first week will be 0·95 and thereafter 0·90 for successive weeks of the larval and pupal period (column 2, Table 4). The stable age distribution is shown in the fifth column of Table 4. This column simply expresses the fourth column of figures as percentages. It is of particular interest to note the high proportion of immature stages (95·5 %) in this theoretical population. This is associated with the high value of the intrinsic rate of natural increase. It emphasizes a point of practical importance in estimating the abundance of insects such as *C. oryzae* and other pests of stored products. The number of adults found in a sample of wheat may be quite a misleading representation of the true size of the whole insect population. Methods of sampling are required which will take account of the immature stages hidden inside the grains, such, for example, as the 'carbon dioxide index' developed by Howe & Oxley (1944). The nature of this stable age distribution has a bearing on another practical problem. It provides further evidence to that developed from a practical approach (Birch, 1946) as to how it is possible for *C. oryzae* to cause heating in vast bulks of wheat, when only a small density of adult insects is observed. It is not an unreasonable supposition that the initial rate of increase of insects in bulks of wheat may approach the maximum intrinsic rate of increase and therefore that the age distribution may approach the stable form. Nothing, however, is known about the actual age distribution in nature at this stage of an infestation.

5. THE INSTANTANEOUS BIRTH-RATE AND DEATH-RATE

We have already defined a birth-rate β by the expression

$$1/\beta = \sum_{x=0}^{m} L_x e^{-r(x+1)}.$$

This is not, however, the same as the instantaneous birth-rate (*b*) where $r = b - d$. In personal communications Mr Leslie has provided me with the following relationship between these two birth-rates.

$$b = \frac{r\beta}{e^r - 1}.$$

Thus, in the example for *C. oryzae*, we have $1/\beta = 0.81167$ (Table 4), $r = 0.76$ and thus $b = 0.82$ and the difference between r and b is the instantaneous death-rate $(d) = 0.06$.

The instantaneous birth-rate and death-rate are widely used by students of human populations. The insect ecologist is more likely to find greater use for the finite rate of increase λ (natural antilog$_e$).

6. THE EFFECT OF TEMPERATURE ON 'r'

As an illustration of the way in which the value of r varies with temperature and the corresponding changes in rate of development, survival and fecundity, an estimate of r for *C. oryzae* has been made for two temperatures (23° and 33·5° C.) on either side of the optimum (29°). The span of adult life at 23° is about the same as at the optimum 29° and so the same life table has been applied. Even although the egg laying is more evenly distributed throughout adult life the life table makes little difference to the value of r. Furthermore, the first 2 weeks of adult life carry a weight of 59 % of the total weight of all age groups in the determination of the value of r. For every egg laid in the first week of adult life it would require 1·5 times as many eggs in the second week to make the same contribution to the value of r, and 2·3 times as many eggs in the third week to have the same effect. The relative weight of each week decreases less with successive weeks at 23° than at 29°. This is associated with the lower oviposition rates and the longer duration of the immature stages at 23°.

At 33·5° egg laying ceases after the fourth week of adult life, the mortality of adults during these 4 weeks is not high and so the estimate of r obtained without a life table may not be very different from the true value.

Table 5. *Showing the values of l_x, m_x and the estimate of r for* Calandra oryzae *at 23° and 33·5°*

23°			33·5°		
Pivotal age in weeks (x)	l_x	m_x	Pivotal age in weeks (x)	l_x	m_x
0·5 · · · · 6·5 } Immature stages 0·90		—	0·5 · · · 8·5 } Immature stages 0·25		—
7·5	0·87	9·0	9·5	0·25	6·0
8·5	0·83	11·0	10·5	0·25	3·5
9·5	0·81	11·5	11·5	0·25	3·0
10·5	0·80	12·0	12·5	0·25	1·0
11·5	0·79	11·5			
12·5	0·77	13·0	$r=$0·12 per head per week		
13·5	0·74	11·5			
14·5	0·66	11·0			
15·5	0·60	10·0			
16·5	0·52	11·0			
17·5	0·45	12·5			
18·5	0·36	10·5			
19·5	0·29	11·5			
20·5	0·25	4·0			
21·5	0·19	2·0			

With adult life table $r=$0·43 per head per week.
Without adult life table $r=$0·44   ,,   ,,

7. DISCUSSION

In order for a species to survive in a particular environment it may need to have evolved a certain minimum value for its intrinsic rate of natural increase. If its rate of increase is less than this it may succumb in the struggle for existence. It does not necessarily follow that the higher the intrinsic rate of increase the more successful will the species be. Evolution may operate to select species with an intrinsic rate of increase which is both large enough to enable them to compete successfully with other species and small enough to prevent a rate of multiplication which would exhaust the food supply in the environment. Whatever is the minimum necessary value of 'r' it could be attained along more than one route,

since r has a number of component variables; the length of development of the immature stages, the survival rate of the immature stages, the adult life table and the age-specific fecundity schedule. These components enter into the value of r with various weights, and it is suggested in the discussion which follows that a knowledge of their relative contributions may provide a clue to the significance of the life patterns characteristic of different species. There is clearly a pattern in the seasonal environment too, which must be considered at the same time. A hot dry period, for example, may necessitate a prolonged egg stage. In an environment which has relatively uniform physical conditions all the year round, these complicating factors are at a minimum, e.g. a tropical forest or the micro-environment of a stack of wheat.

(1) Consider first the length of the immature stages (non-reproductive period) in relation to the span of egg laying and the age schedule of fecundity. The earlier an egg is laid in the life of the insect the greater is the contribution of that particular egg to the value of r. In illustration we may consider the age schedule of fecundity for *C. oryzae* at 29°. Since over 95 % of the value of r is determined by the eggs laid in the first 4 weeks of adult life (Table 3) we can, for purposes of illustration, ignore the remaining period.

At 29° the immature stages of *C. oryzae* last 4 weeks and the maximum rate of egg laying is 46 eggs per week (Table 1). Now the same value of r (0·76) is given in a number of imaginary life cycles by reducing the length of the immature stages along with a reduction in the rate of egg laying and alternatively by increasing both the length of the immature stages and the number of eggs laid (ordinary figures, Table 6). In Table 6 the age schedule of fecundity is kept proportionate in each case. In the extreme examples if the immature stages could develop in a week, an oviposition maximum of 5 eggs per week would give the same rate of increase as the imaginary insect which took 6 weeks to develop and had an oviposition maximum of 204 eggs per week. The imaginary life cycles have been calculated from the ratio (2·1:1) for successive weighting values (e^{7-rx}) in Table 2.

The question might now be asked, what determines the particular combination which the species happens to possess? In the specific example in question, if the larva took 6 weeks to develop the adult would need to lay 200 eggs per week. But it now becomes necessary to consider the behaviour pattern, for *C. oryzae* bores a hole in the grain of wheat for every egg which is laid. The whole process of boring and egg laying occupies about 1 hr. per egg. So that with this particular mode of behaviour 24 eggs per day would be an absolute maximum. There must of course also be some physiological limit to egg production. For a larger insect the physiological limit might be less restrictive provided that the size of the egg does not increase proportionately with the size of the insect. In considering this possibility, ecological considerations are important, for *C. oryzae* is adapted to complete its development within a grain of wheat and a size limit is set by the length of the grain. There is, in fact, a strain which is found in maize kernels in Australia and this is considerably larger than the so-called 'small strain' (Birch, 1944). Furthermore, the larger insect would probably require a longer time to complete development (which is actually the relationship observed between the small and large strains) and this would operate to reduce the value of *r*. In considering the possibilities in the opposite direction, there is obviously a limit below which the length of development could not be reduced any further. A species of smaller size could doubtless develop in a shorter time and on this merit might be a more successful mutation. But the question then arises whether a smaller species could command muscles and mandibles of sufficient strength to chew whole

The relative advantage of this type of fecundity schedule is less, the smaller the value of *r*. At 23° the value of *r* for *C. oryzae* is 0.43 and the eggs laid in the first week of adult life are worth $(1.5)^{n-1}$ eggs in the *n*th week (compare this with the value of $(2.1)^{n-1}$ when $r = 0.76$). The actual oviposition time curve at 23° has no distinct peak as at 29° (Tables 1 and 5).

There is a wide variation in the nature of the age schedule of fecundity amongst different species of insects with perhaps the tsetse fly and the lucerne flea illustrating contrasting extremes. Whereas tsetse flies (*Glossina*) deposit single larvae spaced at intervals of time, the 'lucerne flea' (*Smynthurus viridis*) deposits its eggs in one or two batches of as many as 120 at a time (Maclagan, 1932). The particular advantage of this mode of oviposition must be tremendous, and is probably responsible in part for the great abundance of this collembolan and possibly other members of the same order, which, as a whole, are among the most

Table 6. *Showing the actual relation between the length of the immature stages and the age schedule of fecundity for* Calandra oryzae *at 29° (black figures) and some theoretical possibilities which would give the same intrinsic rate of increase (r = 0.76). The length of the immature stages is shown in the left of the table; figures in the body of the table are number of eggs per week*

Pivotal age in weeks

	0·5	1·5	2·5	3·5	4·5	5·5	6·5	7·5	8·5	9·5	Total
1 week	4	5	3	3	—	—	—	—	—	—	15
2 weeks		9	10	7	6	—	—	—	—	—	32
3 weeks			19	22	14	12	—	—	—	—	67
4 weeks				40	46	30	25	—	—	—	141
5 weeks					84	97	63	53	—	—	297
6 weeks						117	204	132	111		564

grain. Grain-feeding species of beetles which are smaller than *C. oryzae* are in fact scavengers rather than feeders on sound grain. Thus it would seem that a balance is struck somewhere between the minimum time necessary for development and the maximum possible rate of egg laying, and this is conditioned by the behaviour pattern of the insect and the particular ecology of its environment.

For a maximum value of *r* the optimum age schedule of fecundity is one which has an early maximum. In an imaginary schedule for *C. oryzae* a concentration of 71 eggs in the first week of egg laying would give the same value of *r* (0.76) as 141 eggs distributed over 4 weeks.

Age schedule of fecundity of Calandra oryzae
at 29°

Weeks	1	2	3	4	Total
Actual	40	46	30	25	141
Imaginary	71	0	0	0	71

abundant insects in nature. This is of course speculative and much more information is required before any generalizations can be made. Another interesting category are the social insects, since only one female of the population (in termites and the hive-bee) or a few (in social wasps) are reproductives. A theoretical consideration of the relative merits of one queen and many queens might throw more light on the evolution of these systems, especially as they relate to differences in behaviour.

The relation between the length of the pre-reproductive stages and the nature of the age-fecundity schedule is in part dependent upon the nature of the seasonal changes in the environment. Life histories may be timed so that the reproductive and feeding stages coincide with the least hostile season of the year. Diapause, aestivation and hibernation are some of the adaptations which ensure this. They have particular significance too in determining the age distribution of the initial population in the reproductive season. Consideration of this is left to a later section of the discussion.

(2) For the calculation of the maximum intrinsic rate of increase the life table of the species from deposition of the egg (or larva) to the end of egg-laying life in the adult must be known. The starting-point of this life table is thus the stage which corresponds to the point of 'birth'. Deevey (1947) has noted that the point of universal biological equivalence for animals is doubtless fertilization of the ovum. But, from the point of view of the number of animals in the population and for purposes of calculating r, a knowledge of pre-birth mortality is not required. For the calculation of r the life table beyond the end of reproductive life has no significance, but a knowledge of age-specific post-reproductive survival until the point of death is needed, on the other hand, for the calculation of the stable age distribution and the instantaneous birth-rate. This is evident from a consideration of the method of calculation shown in Table 4. The post-reproductive life assumes negligible significance in this particular example, but its importance in such calculations increases as r approaches a value of zero.

The relative importance of the survival pattern (i.e. the shape of the l_x curve) in determining the value of r is itself a function of r. When r is small its value may be dependent to a significant extent on the oviposition in late adult life, when it is large it is mostly determined by the oviposition rates of adults in early adult life. When the intrinsic rate of increase is high and the life table of the adult follows the typical diagonal pattern (e.g. Pearl *et al.* 1941) with no high mortality in early adult life, consideration of the adult life table is of little importance in calculating r. This is because survival rate is high in the ages which contribute most to the value of r. In species which have a low intrinsic rate of increase the life table may assume more significance in determining the value of that rate of increase. More data are required before the importance of this point can be established. The pattern of survival which gives a maximum value of r has its maxima in the pre-reproductive and early reproductive stages. A knowledge of total survival of the immature stages is of course essential in all cases. More attention might well be given by entomologists to securing life table data than has been given in the past. Without it no true picture of the intrinsic rate of increase can be obtained.

(3) There remains to be considered the age distribution of the population in relation to its capacity to increase in numbers. In a population in an unlimited environment the stable age distribution is the only one which gives an unvarying value of r. For this reason the stable age distribution is the only sound basis on which to make comparisons between different values for rates of increase (whether between different species or one species under different physical conditions). The actual age distribution of a population in nature may be quite different and its consideration is of importance in determining the initial advantage one form of distribution has over another. In an unlimited environment these initial differences in age composition are eventually ironed out. A population which initiates from a number of adults at the peak age of egg laying clearly has a higher initial rate of increase than one which starts from the same number in all different stages of development.

These considerations may be of most importance in temperate climates where there is a definite seasonal occurrence of active stages. The stage in which the insect overwinters or oversummers will determine the age distribution of the population which initiates the seasonal increase in the spring or in the autumn (whichever the case may be). The pea weevil, *Bruchus pisorum*, in California hibernates as an adult. With the first warm days in the spring the adults leave their overwintering quarters under bark and fly into the pea fields (Brindley, Chamberlin & Hinman, 1946). Following a meal of pollen they commence oviposition on the pea crops. This mode of initiating the spring population would be far more effective than one which started with the same number of insects in the egg stage. The overwintering adults begin their reproductive life at a much later age than the adults in the next generation. It would be of interest to know whether the age schedule of fecundity (taking the commencement of egg laying as zero age) is the same for both generations. This is a point which does not appear to have been investigated for insects which hibernate as adults. It is clearly of much importance in determining the intrinsic rate of increase of successive generations.

Overwintering as pupae must theoretically rank as the second most effective age distribution for initiating spring increase. Many species which overwinter as pupae would have a higher mortality if they overwintered as adults. The corn-ear worm, *Heliothis armigera*, for example, can hardly be conceived as overwintering as an adult moth in the North American corn belt. In the northern part of this belt even the pupae which are protected in the soil are unable to survive the winter. Recolonization evidently takes place each year from the warmer south (Haseman, 1931).

Overwintering in the egg stage (in hibernation or in diapause) is common in insects. Here again it is difficult to imagine the other stages of these orders as successfully hibernating. The grasshopper, *Austroicetes cruciata* (Andrewartha, 1944), and the majority of aphids are examples of this. A minority of aphid species are, however, able to overwinter as apterae by finding protection in leaf axils and similar niches (Theobald, 1926), some others are enabled to survive as adults by virtue of their symbiosis with ants (Cutright, 1925). The relatively vulnerable aphids find protection in the nests of ants. The ants not only carry them to their nests, but feed them during the winter months and with the return of spring plant them out on trees again!

Overwintering as nymphs or larvae is a rarer phenomenon except with species which can feed and grow at low temperatures and so are not hibernators. The active stages of the lucerne flea, *Smynthurus viridis*, for example, can be found in the winter in Australia (Davidson, 1934). The seasonal cycle of the reproducing population commences with the first rains in autumn; this population being initiated with oversummering eggs. The eggs are the only stage which are resistant to the dryness and high temperatures of the summer months. Species of insects with hardy adult stages like the weevil, *Otiorrhynchus cribricollis* (Andrewartha, 1933), aestivate as adults. An interesting case of a butterfly, *Melitaea phaeton*, aestivating as a quarter-grown larva at the base of its food plant is described by Hovanitz (1941).

The preceding examples illustrate how the age distributions of initiating populations vary in seasonal species. This depends on the nature of the overwintering or oversummering stage. The particular stage may have been selected in nature not only by virtue of its resistance to unfavourable physical conditions but also in relation to its merits in initiating rapid establishment of a population in the spring and autumn. The calculation of the initial and subsequent rates of increase of populations with these different types of age distribution is considerably more complicated than the calculation of intrinsic rates of increase for populations with stable age distributions. This problem is not dealt with in this paper and the reader is referred to Leslie (1945, p. 207 *et seq.*) for an outline of the principles involved in such calculations.

The length of the developmental stages, the age schedule of fecundity, the life table of the species and the age distribution of initiating populations present a pattern which has adaptive significance for the species. The analytic study of the intrinsic rate of increase of a species (as exemplified by *Calandra oryzae*) may throw light on the evolutionary significance of the life pattern of different species. Such a study must necessarily be related to the behaviour pattern of the insect and the type of environment it lives in. Nor can the importance of effects of density and competition be overlooked. These are, of course, studies in themselves beyond the scope of this paper.

8. SUMMARY

The parameter known as the intrinsic rate of natural increase, which was developed for demographic analyses by A. J. Lotka, is introduced as a useful concept for the study of insect populations. It is suggested that for the sake of uniformity of terminology in population biology and for precision of definition, that the term 'intrinsic rate of natural increase' might be considered more appropriate than an alternative term 'biotic-potential' which is more frequently used in relation to insect populations. The intrinsic rate of natural increase is defined as the exponent 'r' in the exponential equation for population increase in an unlimited environment. The rate of increase of such a population is given by $dN/dt = rN$. The parameter r refers to the rate of increase of a population with a certain fixed age distribution known as the stable age distribution. Both the intrinsic rate of natural increase and the stable age distribution may be calculated from the age-specific survival rates (life table) and age-specific fecundity rates. The methods of calculation are exemplified with data for the rice weevil, *Calandra oryzae* (L.), and some adapted from the flour beetle, *Tribolium confusum* Duval. It is shown in this example that the intrinsic rate of natural increase is determined to a much greater extent by the rate of oviposition in the first 2 weeks of adult life than by the total number of eggs laid in the entire life time. The oviposition rates in the first 2 weeks account for 85% of the value of r whereas only 27% of the total number of eggs are laid in that time. With each successive week in the life of the adult, eggs laid make a lessened contribution to the value of r. The methods of calculation of r provide a means of determining the extent to which the various components—the life table, the fecundity table and the length of the pre-reproductive stages—enter into the value of r. It is suggested that analyses of this sort may provide a clue to the life patterns characteristic of different species.

The importance of the age distribution of populations which initiate seasonal increase in the autumn and spring is discussed. These age distributions depend on the nature of the overwintering or oversummering stage. It is suggested that this particular stage, whether it be adult, larva, pupa or egg, has been selected by virtue not only of its resistance to the unfavourable season, but also in relation to its merits in initiating rapid establishment of a population in the succeeding season.

It is shown how the value of r for *Calandra oryzae* varies with temperature. Four other parameters are also defined: the net reproduction rate, the mean length of a generation, the infinitesimal birth-rate and the infinitesimal death-rate. The methods of calculation of these parameters are also exemplified with data for *C. oryzae*.

9. ACKNOWLEDGEMENTS

Grateful acknowledgement is made to the Director of the Bureau of Animal Population, Oxford University, Mr C. S. Elton, for the facilities of the Bureau which were placed at the author's disposal during his term there as a visiting worker. Mr Elton provided much encouragement during the investigation. It is a pleasure to acknowledge too the inspiration and help of Mr P. H. Leslie of the Bureau of Animal Popula-

tion. His direction was indispensable in all mathematical and actuarial aspects of the paper and his critical examination of the manuscript was much to its advantage.

REFERENCES

Andrewartha, H. G. (1933). 'The bionomics of *Otiorrhynchus cribricollis* Gyll.' Bull. Ent. Res. 24: 373–84.

Andrewartha, H. G. (1944). 'The distribution of plagues of *Austroicetes cruciata* Sauss. (Acrididae) in relation to climate, vegetation and soil.' Trans. Roy. Soc. S. Aust. 68: 315–26.

Birch, L. C. (1944). 'Two strains of *Calandra oryzae* L. (Coleoptera).' Aust. J. Exp. Biol. Med. Sci. 22: 271–5.

Birch, L. C. (1945a). 'The influence of temperature on the development of the different stages of *Calandra oryzae* L. and *Rhizopertha dominica* Fab. (Coleoptera).' Aust. J. Exp. Biol. Med. Sci. 23: 29–35.

Birch, L. C. (1945b). 'The influence of temperature, humidity and density on the oviposition of the small strain of *Calandra oryzae* L. and *Rhizopertha dominica* Fab.' Aust. J. Exp. Biol. Med. Sci. 23: 197–203.

Birch, L. C. (1945c). 'The biotic potential of the small strain of *Calandra oryzae* and *Rhizopertha dominica*.' J. Anim. Ecol. 2: 125–7.

Birch, L. C. (1945d). 'The mortality of the immature stages of *Calandra oryzae* L. (small strain) and *Rhizopertha dominica* Fab. in wheat of different moisture contents.' Aust. J. Exp. Biol. Med. Sci. 23: 141–5.

Birch, L. C. (1946). 'The heating of wheat stored in bulk in Australia.' J. Aust. Inst. Agric. Sci. 12: 27–31.

Brindley, T. A., Chamberlin, J. C. & Hinman, F. G. (1946). 'The pea weevil and methods for its control.' U.S. Dept. Agric. Farmers' Bull. 1971: 1–24.

Chapman, R. N. (1931). 'Animal ecology with especial reference to insects.' New York.

Crombie, A. C. (1945). 'On competition between different species of graminivorous insects.' Proc. Roy. Soc. B, 132: 362–95.

Crombie, A. C. (1947). 'Interspecific competition.' J. Anim. Ecol. 16: 44–73.

Cutright, C. R. (1925). 'Subterranean aphids of Ohio.' Ohio Agric. Exp. Sta. Bull. 387: 175–238.

Davidson, J. (1934). 'The "lucerne flea" *Smynthurus viridis* L. (Collembola) in Australia.' Bull. Coun. Sci. Industr. Res. Aust. 79: 1–66.

Davidson, J. & Andrewartha, H. G. (1948). 'Annual trends in a natural population of *Thrips imaginis* Bagnall (Thysanoptera).' (In the Press.)

Deevey, E. S. (1947). 'Life tables for natural populations of animals.' Biometrics, 3: 59–60.

Dublin, L. I. & Lotka, A. J. (1925). 'On the true rate of natural increase as exemplified by the population of the United States, 1920.' J. Amer. Statist. Ass. 20: 305–39.

Dublin, L. I. & Lotka, A. J. (1936). 'Length of life.' New York.

Gause, G. F. (1934). 'The struggle for existence.' Baltimore.

Haseman, L. (1931). 'Outbreak of corn earworm in Missouri.' J. Econ. Ent. 24: 649–50.

Hovanitz, W. (1941). 'The selective value of aestivation and hibernation in a Californian butterfly.' Bull. Brooklyn Ent. Soc. 36: 133–6.

Howe, R. W. & Oxley, T. A. (1944). 'The use of carbon dioxide production as a measure of infestation of grain by insects.' Bull. Ent. Res. 35: 11–22.

Leslie, P. H. (1945). 'On the use of matrices in certain population mathematics.' Biometrika, 33: 183–212.

Leslie, P. H. & Ranson, R. M. (1940). 'The mortality, fertility and rate of natural increase of the vole (*Microtus agrestis*) as observed in the laboratory.' J. Anim. Ecol. 9: 27–52.

Lotka, A. J. (1925). 'Elements of physical biology.' Baltimore.

Lotka, A. J. (1927). 'The size of American families in the eighteenth century and the significance of the empirical constants in the Pearl-Reed law of population growth.' J. Amer. Statist. Ass. 22: 154–70.

Lotka, A. J. (1939). 'Théorie analytique des associations biologiques. Deuxième Partie. Analyse démographique avec application particulière à l'espèce humaine.' Actualités Sci. Industr. 780: 1–149.

Lotka, A. J. (1945). 'Population analysis as a chapter in the mathematical theory of evolution.' In LeGros Clark, W. E. & Medawar, P. B., 'Essays on Growth and Form', 355–85. Oxford.

Maclagan, D. S. (1932). 'An ecological study of the "lucerne flea" (*Smynthurus viridis*, Linn.)–I.' Bull. Ent. Res. 23: 101–90.

Pearl, R., Park, T. & Miner, J. R. (1941). 'Experimental studies on the duration of life. XVI. Life tables for the flour beetle *Tribolium confusum* Duval.' Amer. Nat. 75: 5–19.

Stanley, J. (1946). 'The environmental index, a new parameter as applied to *Tribolium*.' Ecology, 27: 303–14.

Theobald, F. V. (1926). 'The plant lice or the Aphididae of Great Britain.' Vol. 1. Ashford.

Thompson, W. R. (1931). 'On the reproduction of organisms with overlapping generations.' Bull. Ent. Res. 22: 147–72.

Thomson, L. M. Milne- & Comrie, L. J. (1944). 'Standard four-figure mathematical tables.' London.

Volterra, V. (1931). 'Leçons sur la théorie mathématique de la lutte pour la vie.' Paris.

SUGAR MAPLE (*ACER SACCHARUM* MARSH.) SEEDLING MORTALITY

BY JOAN M. HETT AND ORIE L. LOUCKS*

Ecological Sciences Division, Oak Ridge National Laboratory, Oak Ridge, Tennessee 37830, U.S.A.

INTRODUCTION

Analysis of population age models has been useful in many studies in entomology, animal ecology and fisheries (Birch 1948; Ricker 1958; Watt 1961; Snyder 1962; Kabot & Thompson 1963; Keith 1963; Morris 1963; Larkin, Raleigh & Wilimovksy 1964). The negative exponential or power function relationships often found are not unique to animal studies, however, since previous workers have recognized a negative exponential depletion in size classes of trees for forest stands (de Liocourt 1898; Goodman 1930; Hough 1936; Knuchel 1953; Bliss & Reinker 1964; Leak 1964; Goff 1966). Although Clements (1916) recognized the usefulness of age relationships, such principles have been used little in the study of plant populations or communities (Hawksworth 1965).

One of the sampling techniques used in animal population studies is the time specific life table, where one sample of the total population present is used to describe the age structure of that population, and the mortality rates are calculated from the life table. Investigations utilizing the time specific life table approach to describe the probability of a plant individual surviving to the next year require species having age distributions which remain stable over long periods. Sugar maple (*Acer saccharum* Marsh.) seemed appropriate because, both ecologically and commercially, it is one of the more important members of the deciduous forests of North America (Godman 1957; Curtis & McIntosh 1951). Sugar maple is a dominant member of the sugar maple–basswood community considered the stable endpoint of a compositional sequence. As such, sugar maple is believed to have a continuous reproductive input into the youngest age class and a resulting stable age structure.

Plants, more than most animals, tend to saturate the surrounding environment with progeny (Salisbury 1942). Although sugar maple seed crops may be highly variable from one year to the next, there is almost always ample seed to fill the available growing sites with seedlings. Thus, establishment and related factors are considered more important in producing the one year age class than factors affecting germination (Fisher 1935).

There have been few studies on the germination and establishment of sugar maple, but some information is available. In southern Wisconsin, Curtis (1959) found a direct correlation between seed viability and the amount of seed produced. In low seed years, there was very low germination. Nonetheless, in the decade in which Curtis collected data, the lowest yield was 10^5 seeds/ha, certainly enough seed to establish that age class in the communities studied. Most of the literature on seed germination and seedling establishment indicates that moisture availability and temperature of the seed bed are

* Present address: University of Wisconsin, Department of Botany, Madison, Wisconsin, U.S.A.

dominant factors in initial establishment (Hough 1937). Darlington (1930) suggests that sugar maple shows highest percentage germination on maple leaf mould, and lowest on areas covered with hemlock needles. Tubbs (1965) found that April temperatures in upper Michigan are extremely important in germination of sugar maple. Temperatures near freezing resulted in a doubling of the number germinating compared to temperatures above 5° C. The roots of sugar maple seedlings are relatively short for the first growing season, thus requiring a season with relatively high moisture in the humus layer. Adequate light is a further factor to be considered in survival analysis, even in a species as shade tolerant as sugar maple. Curtis (1959) and others have reported patches of older sugar maple seedlings under canopy gaps.

This paper reports on investigations of the age structure of sugar maple seedlings in three major climatic regions within Wisconsin. It was undertaken, as Salisbury (1942) has suggested, in order to assess the factors influencing survival and to understand the ways in which a species perpetuates itself in a community.

STUDY AREAS AND METHODS

Bray (1956) defined a stable plant community as one having individuals of the dominant species present in all size classes. To use the time specific approach, it is imperative that stability be approached as closely as possible within the sample areas. Since climatic differences were chosen as one of the variables to be investigated, the study sites also had to have a minimal variation in edaphic factors. Thus, stands were selected if, and only if, there was sugar maple present in all strata, assuring mature stands which had established continuous understorey inputs for a considerable period of time. Also, stands having coniferous species in the upper strata were not included. To minimize the differential effects of edaphic factors on germination and establishment, all stands selected were on silt loams, reducing as much as possible the variation in available water.

Three southern stands were selected in Green County near the southern border of Wisconsin. The stands were located on soils which had formed in the loess cap. Two stands were sampled in Menominee County in the central portion of the state. These stands are approximately 257 km north and slightly east of the Green County stands. Both were on soils formed in aeolian silts over glacial till. In Bayfield County, the most northerly county in the state, three stands on light silt loams were sampled. These stands are approximately 225 km north-west of Menominee County.

The major climatic differences between these three areas are the length of the growing season, the amount and type of precipitation and the temperature. The length of the annual growing season decreases from 156 days in Green County to 138 days in Menominee County to 128 days inland and 116 days along the Lake Superior shore in Bayfield County. Although there is not a great difference in amount of precipitation, southern regions most frequently receive their rainfall in the form of thunder showers. The intervals between storms are commonly 2–3 weeks in duration accompanied by high temperatures. The precipitation ranges from a mean annual 85·5 cm in the south to 68·3 cm along the shores of Lake Superior. The same decrease can be found in the mean July temperatures. Green County has a mean July temperature of 23° C, Menominee County 20° C and inland Bayfield County is characterized by 19·6° C with the lakeshore having a mean July temperature of 19·2° C (United States Department of Agriculture 1941).

Sampling was carried out in June and July 1965, first in Green County, then at 1 week intervals in Menominee and Bayfield Counties. Within each of the selected stands, a smaller area of approximately $\frac{1}{2}$ ac (0·2 ha) was marked for intensive study. The smaller area was then stratified into ten equal-area blocks and two random circular quadrats were located within each of the blocks. For each quadrat, numbers and ages of the sugar maple seedlings present were recorded. Since germinating seedlings greatly outnumbered the older seedlings, quadrat size varied with age class and density of the population. In a dense population of germinating seedlings, 1 m² was sufficient to obtain an adequate sample. The older seedlings required larger quadrats, 4–8 m², which were superimposed over the smaller ones.

Ageing the younger sugar maple seedlings in the field is relatively easy. Young, healthy and undamaged individuals can be aged by counting the annual bud scars. Those which could not be aged directly in the field were returned to the laboratory for ageing under a microscope by counting annual rings.

Within each quadrat, all stems under 92 cm in height and <0·7 cm in diameter at the root crown were cut or aged directly. The upper size limit of the seedlings was selected because: (1) at heights and diameters greater than this limit, it is exceedingly difficult to tell whether the seedlings are of seed or sprout origin; (2) a sample of stems with diameters of 0·9 cm at the root crown were aged in different woods in the same area and found to be older than 15 years. It was assumed that only a small percentage of stems, if any, would be missed in the zero to 15 year age classes of interest to this study.

The initial sampling in the early summer included ages and numbers of seedlings present. Early in the autumn, each stand was revisited and another count made of that year's germinants, using twenty randomly placed quadrats within the same stratified site. Sampling of the overstorey also was made on an area larger than the marked site in order to include all the trees which could be influencing the understorey in the study site. Within this larger site, all stems >10 cm dbh were recorded by basal area and species. Stems between 2·5 and 10 cm dbh were sampled with ten 100 m² circular quadrats.

Warm spring temperatures were the first variable considered because of the experiments by Tubbs (1965) on the effect of high temperatures on germination of sugar maple. To investigate the effects of extremely warm April temperatures, the temperatures of those years for which seedling numbers showed the greatest deviation from the negative exponential age model for southern Wisconsin were examined in relation to minimum daily temperatures above 7·1 °C and 10° C. Because the southern Wisconsin sugar maple populations have undoubtedly adapted to higher temperatures, temperatures much higher than those used by Tubbs were examined.

The United States Weather Bureau (Palmer 1965) has developed drought stress indices for several geographic areas in Wisconsin. Monthly indices incorporate precipitation, temperature, humidity, run-off and soil moisture into a single cumulative drought index. Regional indices are available for the counties where observations were made. Each of these monthly indices was examined to determine differences in moisture availability during the growing season of each year represented by seedling age classes.

Rainfall is sporadic in southern Wisconsin, and may vary widely in amount and duration over short distances. For this reason, a third environmental consideration, rainfall distribution, was assessed through a closer examination of daily rainfall records from the closest weather station (Brodhead) to the stands in Green County. This detailed precipitation study also allowed a comparison of local moisture conditions with the more generalized drought indices for the region.

Since the three study areas chosen are on a regional environmental gradient, temperature, drought and rainfall are environmental variables which could have an influence on local survival. In addition, however, stand structure, as it relates to amount of light and rainfall interception imposed on the understorey should be investigated as an environmental influence on the seedling layer. Stand structural profiles were plotted for each stand to allow an examination of species and numbers in each stratum.

RESULTS AND DISCUSSION

Two major methods for analysing survival within a population are available. Life table analyses using age distributions have been used in animal studies (Deevey 1947; Hickey 1952; L. B. Keith, personal communication 1964). Forest analyses have used size distributions (Hough 1936; Meyer 1952; Bliss & Reinker 1964). Although survival is not calculated *per se* in forestry, de Liocourt's Law (1898) states that the number of stems in an old-growth forest geometrically decreases with increasing diameter classes, with the percentage survival approximately constant between adjacent diameter classes.

Direct application of life table analyses to sugar maple populations appears unjustified as the methods make assumptions which cannot be met in dealing with a tree population of extremely long life span and unequal recruitment. However, the life table can be considered a method of tabulating individuals in consecutive age classes. Thus, the life table becomes valuable as a budget accounting of the population, and can be a valuable initial tool for further analyses.

Survival

(a) *Summer*

By use of the results of the germinating seedlings in the early summer and those counted in the autumn, it is possible to look at summer survival in the three areas. Per cent survival was calculated as

$$\% \text{ Summer survival} = \frac{\text{Number/unit area in autumn}}{\text{Number/unit area in spring}} \times 100$$

Survival in Bayfield County is more than double that found in the other two counties (Table 1). Also, Bayfield County averaged 904 800 germinants/ha surviving until September: Menominee County averaged 84 000 and Green County 132 720/ha. A *t*-test between

Table 1. *Survival of sugar maple seedlings during the summer of* 1965

Green County Stands		Menominee County		Bayfield County	
Abraham's	25·1%	Neopit	36·2%	Nourse's	41·0%
Brodhead	16·1%	Dutchman's		Two Lakes	77·6%
Peedee	42·2%	Lookout	10·6%	Drummond	76·0%
Mean	27·8%*		23·4%		64·9%

* Significantly different at the 0·05 level.

the averages from Green and Bayfield County showed a significant difference ($P<0·05$), indicating that conditions in the most northern portion of the state seem more favourable for initial survival.

(b) *Annual*

Deevey (1947) describes three kinds of survival curves found in animal populations. Two of these may be applicable to plant populations which have life spans greater than one season. The first is the diagonal or negative exponential depletion, of the form

$$y = y_0 e^{-bx} \tag{1}$$

which when transformed by taking the natural logarithm becomes a straight line

$$\log_e y = \log_e y_0 - bx$$

where b is the mortality constant and the slope of the line, y is the number of individuals at any time, t, y_0 is the initial population number and x is the age in years. Harper (1967) found that this model had a good fit to the populations of perennial herbs which he investigated.

The second model, Type III by Deevey's definition, can be described by several models; the simplest one is

$$y = y_0 \, x^{-b} \qquad (2)$$

a power function which can be transformed to a straight line by taking the natural logarithm of the equation to give

$$\log_e y = \log_e y_0 - b \log_e x$$

This model, with slope b being the mortality rate, implies that mortality is not constant; rather it decreases as the individuals in the population age.

Although a scatter about the linear relationship for a natural population is likely, significant deviations from the model can be examined for possible effects of climate or size of seed crops during that year.

Linear regression analyses using transformations appropriate for first the negative exponential and the power function models were calculated for the data in each county. The distribution of numbers in each age class and the fitted curves are shown in Figs. 1 and 2. The zero age class in each county represents the number of sugar maple remaining in the autumn of the study year 1965. The use of this value rather than the spring value takes into account the summer mortality, a value comparable with the rest of the data. Points deviating from the regression line by more than two standard deviations are indicated and each was compared to those environmental parameters thought to have a possible influence on sugar maple survival. None of the environmental parameters investigated seemed to explain these departures. With one exception, the deviations are in either the youngest or the oldest age class. In the case of the youngest age class, the seedlings have not yet been subjected to winter mortality. In the oldest age class, the sample is probably inadequate. No explanation can be supported for the deviation of the 5-year class at Bayfield.

A comparison of the adequacies of the two models can be seen in Table 2. In nearly all cases, the power function model shows higher correlation coefficients than the negative exponential model, although a z-test indicated that there were no significant differences between any of the coefficients. The probabilities of the correlation coefficient from the power function model showed that all were significant at the 0·05 level. For these reasons, the remainder of this paper will include only those analyses done using the power function.

Environmental stresses

(a) *Minimum April temperatures*

Green County, the most southerly county, is most likely to have extended periods of above normal April temperatures. The only data point which represented nearly a week of daily minimum April temperatures greater than 7° C and showed a negative (but not significantly different) deviation from the regression line was for 1952. All the other points showing negative deviations represented normal April temperatures during the spring in which the corresponding seeds germinated. Years which did have periods of more than 7 days with high temperatures included 1954, 1955 and 1957. Yet each of these years was within two standard deviations from the regression line. Therefore, from the data available, minimum temperatures greater than 7° C during the month of April do not seem to affect the number of stems established in southern sugar maple populations. Since high April temperatures did not affect seedling establishment in the most southern county, data from more northern counties were not analysed.

66

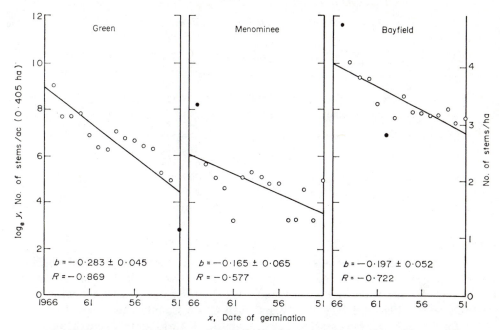

FIG. 1. Linear regression analyses of survival using the negative exponential model $y = xe^{-bt}$ on the data from the three counties. The mortality rate and the standard error of estimate are given for each set of data. Filled points are those which are more than two standard deviations from the regression line.

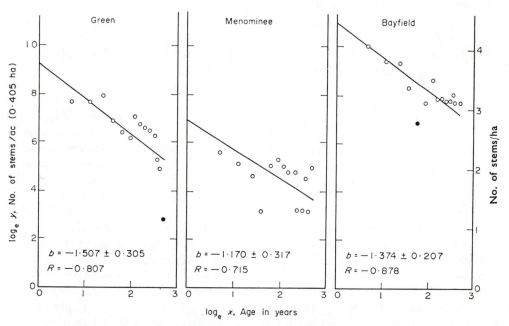

FIG. 2. Linear regression analyses of survival using the power function model $y = x^{-bt}$ on the data from the three counties. The mortality rate and the standard error of estimate are given for each set of data. Filled points are those which are more than two standard deviations from the regression line.

Table 2. *A comparison of the correlation coefficients from the negative exponential model and the power function model*

	Negative exponential model	Power function model	z-Test
Green County	−0·869***	−0·807***	n.s.
Abraham's	−0·740*	−0·765*	n.s.
Brodhead	−0·736***	−0·747***	n.s.
Peedee	−0·654*	−0·697***	n.s.
Menominee County	−0·577*	−0·715*	n.s.
Neopit	−0·437n.s.	−0·608**	n.s.
Dutchman's Lookout	−0·641*	−0·796***	n.s.
Bayfield County	−0·722*	−0·878***	n.s.
Nourse's	−0·779***	−0·906***	n.s.
Two Lakes	−0·639**	−0·826***	n.s.
Drummond	−0·379n.s.	−0·552*	n.s.

Significance of *r*: *0·05; **0·01; ***0·001.

(b) *Drought indices*

The south-central region of Wisconsin is the only area of the three examined which is subjected to droughts lasting a complete growing season. Drought indices, as calculated by the United States Weather Bureau (Palmer 1965), of less than −2·00 are considered relatively severe. 1958 and 1964 were years when Green County had indices less than −2·00 for the entire growing season. The drought in 1964 was more severe than any of the drought years during the 1930s. The seedling numbers surviving to 1965 show a negative deviation from the regression line but are within two standard deviations. Abraham's Woods appeared most affected by the drought, for in 1965 there were no 1-year-old seedlings. The 1958 drought did not appear to have any effect on the seedling population germinating during that season.

Menominee County, in the central part of the state, had only 1 month (June 1958) with a severe drought stress, and there was not a significant reduction in stems surviving from that year. None of the recorded drought stress records for Bayfield County indicated that moisture in this county was a limiting factor.

(c) *Precipitation*

A comparison of precipitation and drought stress is important in southern Wisconsin because of the periodicity of rainfall and the occurrence of local thunder showers. Fig. 3, a graph of two representative years, 1956 and 1958, indicates an extended period of dry warm weather in early June 1956 (recorded at the Brodhead weather station in Green County). The drought indices for this region are nearly normal for this period, suggesting that drought indices alone, because of the large area encompassed in the calculations, are not the best indicators of local climatic conditions. The distribution of precipitation in 1956 also shows large inputs of moisture over short periods of time.

The 1958 precipitation record is of interest because this is the year one might have expected a reduction in germination or establishment of sugar maple due to the very dry growing season indicated by the drought indices. However, the dry growing season was accompanied by below normal temperatures. Thus, the severe drought stress may have been compensated by a more uniform distribution of rainfall and low temperatures which gave a regular moisture input to the humus layers along with low evaporation.

(d) *Stand structure*

Although sugar maple is considered the most shade tolerant of tree species in Wisconsin, there is some indication that even sugar maple does not grow well under a dense sugar maple canopy (Curtis 1959). The influence of a dense, sugar maple stratum of intermediate

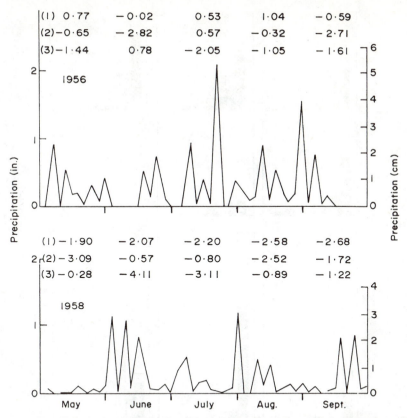

FIG. 3. The precipitation pattern and (1) monthly drought stresses, (2) deviation from the mean monthly precipitation, and (3) deviation from mean monthly temperatures are shown for 2 years which could have had an influence on sugar maple seedlings.

height on the seedling layer as well as stability, maturity and past history of a stand can be estimated by examining the structural profile to determine different size class densities and species composition. Fig. 4 shows the structural profile of each stand studied using 10·16 cm dbh size classes. The number of sugar maple present in each class, for all stands, shows an inverse J-shaped distribution of stems characteristic of forests at equilibrium (Leak 1965). The major differences in the profiles are numbers of stems in the various strata, the age of the stands (as age and size are probably correlated in the larger size classes) and the past history of the stand.

In Green County, Peedee Woods appears to be the oldest stand but has lower than expected numbers of sugar maple and other species in one of the small tree classes. As this is a farmer's woodlot, there is a strong possibility that the reduction of stems may have been influenced by grazing. The increased light and throughfall precipitation due to the lower density of stems in the middle strata may also account for the greater number of saplings and older seedlings. Abraham's Woods is the youngest of the three stands. Sugar maple is well represented in the smaller classes, with elm (*Ulmus* spp.) and red oak (*Quercus rubra* L.) more prominent in the larger classes. The stand profile representing the most stable structural dynamics is Brodhead Woods. Also a farmer's woodlot, Brodhead may have had some light grazing in the past leading to the increase of elm in the middle size classes. Ecologically, one might expect a lower mortality rate at Brodhead. The more stable size distribution (Fig. 4) of sugar maple probably indicates that no past disturbance has upset the stand equilibrium. Fig. 5 allows a comparison of mortality

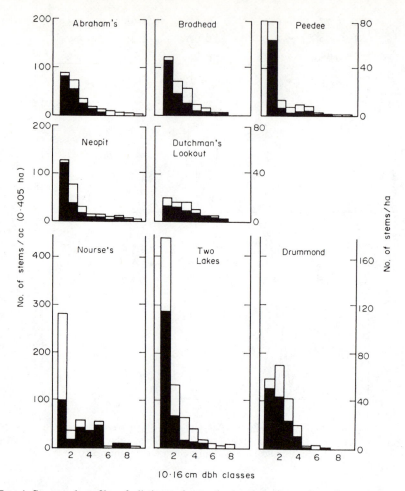

FIG. 4. Structural profiles of all the study stands showing the number of stems of sugar maple (closed columns) and of all other species (open columns) present in each size class.

rates for these three stands. A z-test showed that there was no significant difference ($P<0.05$) between the slopes of the regression lines. The two stands in Menominee County also have similar mortality rates (Fig. 5) and these rates are not significantly different from those in Green County. Again, the more structurally stable stand, Neopit (Fig. 4), has a lower mortality rate.

Bayfield County stands have much higher densities in each size class than those in the other two counties. In this county, Drummond has a significantly ($P<0.05$) lower mortality rate than either of the other stands; however, there is no significant difference when comparing the mortality rates of these three stands to those in other counties. The structural profile of the Drummond stand shows a small number of stems in the smallest size class. This sparse understorey may account for the decreased mortality rate but this stand is also the one having a nearly J-shaped size distribution. Also, the gap in sugar maple stem distribution in the second largest size class is occupied by red oak suggesting the stand may be of fire origin (Eggler 1938).

Two Lakes and Nourse's Woods have high, but not significantly different, mortality rates; yet, these stands have very dissimilar histories. Two Lakes is a relatively young

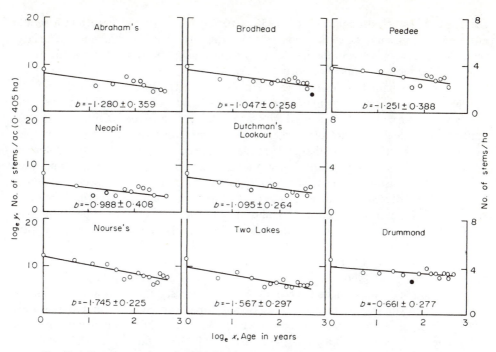

FIG. 5. A linear regression of survival in each stand using the power function model. The slope or mortality rate of each population is given ±1 S.E.

stand and has a high percentage of red oaks in the middle size classes indicating some past disturbance. Nourse's Woods is regularly used as a 'sugar bush' with light selective cutting for non-sugar producing species. Therefore, not only is Nourse's Woods one of the older stands, it has a much heavier weighting of sugar maple in the overstorey than might be expected naturally. The differences in mortality between Two Lakes and Drummond may be a result of the high numbers of sugar maple in the smallest size class at Two Lakes which act as an intermediate canopy decreasing light and throughfall precipitation (Anderson, Loucks & Swain 1969). In Nourse's Woods, the wave of sugar maple in the middle classes also may contribute to increased mortality, but there is no indication that this stand has suffered a severe disturbance within the life of the oldest trees.

CONCLUSIONS

Curtis & McIntosh (1951) suggest that sugar maple qualifies as a suitable species for the study of seedling survival and factors involved in sustained input of tree seedlings into the forest community because it is the most shade tolerant tree species in Wisconsin. It is reasonable to assume that large deviations from exponential or geometric relationships can be examined for the effects of external factors acting upon the seedling input. The fact that the sugar maple data do not permit direct use of the 'classical' types of life table analyses does not preclude the use of regression analyses of age depletions as a methodology in plant population biology. None of the environmental stresses examined appeared to have any influence on sugar maple seedlings. The number of seedlings remaining which germinated in 1954, 1955 and 1957 did not show any correlation with the above normal April temperatures of those years. There was also no evidence that the drought in southern Wisconsin in 1958 had a detrimental effect on the survival of the germinating seedlings. A 2-week drought in June 1956, a period which should have had a serious effect on seedling survival, evoked no noticeable response in seedling numbers. The large numbers in each age class in Bayfield County stands may, however, be a response to the more regular moisture supply in northern Wisconsin.

The survival characteristics of sugar maple in southern Wisconsin (a prairie–forest border region) are probably influenced by the restriction of sugar maple to deep silt loams which have characteristically high water retention capacities (Curtis 1959). Also contributing to high moisture availability in these sugar maple stands is their topographic position. Harper (1963) found that all the sugar maple communities in southern Wisconsin are situated on northern slopes where they are subjected to a minimum evaporation stress. The long history of sugar maple on these sites suggests that the species is adapted for successful establishment under moderate fluctuations in climate, and probably only severe climatic extremes influence survival of the younger stems. An example of this may be the complete elimination of germinating seedlings in Abraham's Woods during the unusual drought of 1964.

Documentation of the forest structure allows an examination of stresses imposed by the overstorey (Goff 1966) including the penetration of light and precipitation. Sugar maple, although the most shade tolerant of Wisconsin trees, does not establish well in the dense shade of younger sugar maple trees. Canopy openings, common in mature stands, have patches of younger sugar maple saplings, but the small seedling layer is often independent of openings (Bray 1956; Curtis 1959). If the stand is young or has had a recent disturbance which permits the development of a dense canopy of younger trees, light as well as rainfall interception may be important in the survival of the lower strata (Anderson *et al.* 1969).

Of the eight stands sampled, two have a prominent sapling size class. These include Peedee Woods in Green County and the Two Lakes stand in Bayfield County. The overstocking in this size class did not appear to influence seedling survival in Peedee Woods. Abraham's Woods in Green County, Dutchman's Lookout in Menominee County and the Drummond stand in Bayfield County have low densities in the smaller size classes. Seedling survival both in the older age classes and in the establishing germinants is sporadic in these stands. The intermittent establishment may indicate that the recent history of the stand is important in determining seedling survival. The expected exponential depletion of stems against diameter can be seen best in Brodhead Woods in Green County and Neopit in Menominee County. These stands are approaching a stable structure that appears to favour a higher survival of maple seedlings.

There is a suggestion that survival is related to overstorey stresses which reduce light and throughfall precipitation, but the wide range in stand structure needed to draw this conclusion firmly has not been studied. Drummond, a relatively stable woods, had statistically higher seedling survival, while in the same region other stands undergoing change had lower survival. The data further suggest that factors susceptible to modification by canopy density (as interpreted from stand structure) assume more importance as the seedlings become older. Moisture stress, particularly in southern Wisconsin, appears limiting to the germinating seedlings.

The power function model for describing age depletions in sugar maple populations seems to be the better model for most of the data. The assumption that mortality remains constant throughout the life history of a population, as suggested by the negative exponential model, is not sound biologically for long-lived species. As an individual ages, the probability of it surviving should increase until senescence. Each year the plant gains more height, reducing the light competition on the forest floor, and it develops deeper root systems with less reliance on the surface input of moisture.

In summer, during years experiencing moderate climatic deviations, initial establishment of sugar maple seedlings is not affected by external environmental influences.

Deviations in the survival of sugar maple in Green County could not be accounted for by spring temperatures or drought stresses. Examination of stand structural profiles indicated that the stresses imposed by the canopy trees may be instrumental in determining whether or not a seedling survives in the community in the years after initial establishment. Age distribution of seedlings is therefore concluded to be an effective way for studying establishment and survival rates of sugar maple and, in the final analysis, community process itself.

ACKNOWLEDGMENTS

The authors gratefully acknowledge the support of the U.S. National Science Foundation through research grant GB-4940 to Dr Loucks and Davis Fellowship, University of Wisconsin, to Joan Hett which made the study possible. We also are grateful for the assistance of the University of Wisconsin Statistical Advising Service and Dr Donald G. Watts of the Statistics Department.

SUMMARY

The several views on variability in seedling establishment of sugar maple and on its mortality rates over the first decade are reviewed and compared with the negative exponential and power function models for describing the age distribution of seedlings. The age distribution for sugar maple seedlings was obtained for three different locations in Wisconsin, one northern, one southern, and one central. Analysis shows that the power function adequately describes the seedling depletion and that the effects of drought, warm spring temperatures and other environmental influences are not detectable in the surviving numbers of seedlings. The organization of the forest canopy above the seedling layer, particularly in relation to the presence of multiple strata in old growth forests, appears to have some influence on seedling survival.

REFERENCES

Anderson, R. C., Loucks, O. L. & Swain, A. M. (1969). Herbaceous response to canopy cover, light intensity, and throughfall precipitation in coniferous forests. *Ecology*, **50**, 255–63.

Birch, L. L. (1948). The intrinsic rate of natural increase of an insect population. *J. Anim. Ecol.* **17**, 15–26.

Bliss, C. I. & Reinker, K. A. (1964). A lognormal approach to diameter distributions in even-aged stands. *Forest Sci.* **10**, 350–60.

Bray, J. (1956). Gap phase replacement in maple–basswood forests. *Ecology*, **37**, 598–600.

Clements, F. E. (1916). *Plant Succession.* Carnegie Institution, Washington, D.C.

Curtis, J. T. (1959). *The Vegetation of Wisconsin.* University of Wisconsin Press, Madison, Wisconsin.

Curtis, J. T. & McIntosh, R. P. (1951). An upland forest continuum in the prairie forest border region of Wisconsin. *Ecology*, **32**, 476–96.

Darlington, H. T. (1930). Vegetation of the Porcupine Mountains, northern Michigan. *Pap. Mich. Acad. Sci.* **13**, 9–84.

Deevey, E. S. (1947). Life tables for natural populations of animals. *Q. Rev. Biol.* **22**, 283–314.

Eggler, W. A. (1938). The maple–basswood forest type in Washburn County, Wisconsin. *Ecology*, **19**, 243–63.

Fisher, G. M. (1935). Comparative germination of tree species on various kinds of surface-soil material in the western white pine type. *Ecology*, **16**, 606–11.

Godman, R. M. (1957). Silvical characteristics of Sugar Maple. *Forest Exp. Stn Lake States*, No. **50**.

Goff, F. G. (1966). *Dynamic relations in Wisconsin upland forests.* Ph. D. thesis, University of Wisconsin, Madison, Wisconsin.

Goodman, R. B. (1930). Conditions essential to selective cutting in northern Wisconsin hardwoods and hemlocks. *J. For.* **28**, 1070–5.

Harper, J. L. (1967). A Darwinian approach to plant ecology. *J. Ecol.* **55**, 247–70.

Harper, K. T. (1963). *Structure and dynamics of the maple–basswood forests of southern Wisconsin.* Ph. D. thesis, University of Wisconsin, Madison, Wisconsin.

Hawksworth, F. G. (1965). Life tables for two species of dwarf mistletoe. I. Seed dispersal, interception and movement. *Forest Sci.* **11**, 142–51.

Hickey, J. J. (1952). Survival studies of banded birds. *Spec. Scient. Rep. U.S. Fish Widl. Serv.* No. **15**.

Hough, A. F. (1936). A climax forest community on east Tionesta Creek in northwest Pennsylvania. *Ecology*, **17**, 9–28.

Hough, A. F. (1937). Study of natural tree reproduction in the birch–maple–hemlock type. *J. For.* **35,** 376–8.

Kabot, C. & Thompson, D. R. (1963). Wisconsin Quail, 1834–1962. Population dynamics and habitat management. *Tech. Bull. Wis. Conserv. Dep.* **30,** 1–135.

Keith, L. B. (1963). *Wildlife's Ten-year Cycle.* University of Wisconsin Press, Madison, Wisconsin.

Knuchel, H. (1953). *Planning and Control in the Managed Forest.* Oliver and Boyd, Edinburgh.

Larkin, P. A., Raleigh, R. F. & Wilimovsky, N. J. (1964). Some alternative premises for constructing theoretical reproduction curves. *J. Fish. Res. Bd Can.* **21,** 477–84.

Leak, W. B. (1964). An expression of diameter distribution for unbalanced, uneven-aged stands and forests. *Forest Sci.* **10,** 39–50.

Leak, W. B. (1965). The J-shaped probability distribution. *Forest Sci.* **11,** 405–9.

de Liocourt, F. (1898). De l'aménagement des Sapinières. *Bull. Soc. for. Franche-Comté*, 396–406.

Meyer, W. H. (1952). Structure, growth and drain in balanced uneven-aged forests. *J. For.* **50,** 85–92.

Morris, R. F. (Ed.) (1963). The dynamics of epidemic Spruce Budworm populations. *Mem. ent. Soc. Can.* **31,** 1–332.

Palmer, W. C. (1965). Meteorological drought. *Res. Pap. U.S. Weath. Bur.* **45.**

Ricker, W. E. (1958). *Handbook of Computations for Biological Statistics of Fish Populations.* Fisheries Research Board of Canada. *Bull.* **119,** 1–300.

Salisbury, E. J. (1942). *The Reproductive Capacity of Plants.* G. Bell, London.

Snyder, R. L. (1962). Reproductive performance of a population of woodchucks after a change in sex ratio. *Ecology*, **43,** 507–15.

Tubbs, C. H. (1965). Influence of temperature and early spring conditions on sugar maple and yellow birch germination in upper Michigan. *Res. Notes Forest Exp. Stn Lake States*, LS-72.

United States Department of Agriculture (1941). *Climate and Man; Year Book of Agriculture.*

Watt, K. E. F. (1961). The conceptual formulation and mathematical solution of practical problems in population input–output dynamics. *Exploitations of Natural Animal Populations* (Ed. by E. D. Le Cren & M. W. Holdgate), pp. 191–203. Blackwell Scientific Publications, Oxford.

AN EXPERIMENTAL APPROACH TO THE DYNAMICS OF A NATURAL POPULATION OF *DAPHNIA GALEATA MENDOTAE*

Donald James Hall

Department of Entomology and Limnology, Cornell University, Ithaca, New York

INTRODUCTION

In general, populations have been studied either in the laboratory under experimental conditions with environmental variables controlled, or in their natural habitat where variables are uncontrolled. In laboratory investigations the analyses are often powerful and yield knowledge of the fundamentals of population growth but are limited to specific conditions seldom found in nature. In field studies, analyses are limited to correlations of population phenomena with environmental variables and frequently involve large errors in estimates of the inferred rates.

The apparent paradox of many field and laboratory population studies can be reconciled in part by manipulating laboratory populations in such a manner that information appropriate to an analysis of the natural population is obtained. To manipulate experimental populations properly, some a priori knowledge of influential variables in the natural population is necessary.

This study is directed to combining an experimental approach with a field description. The purpose of such an analysis is to predict natural population growth of *Daphnia,* and, consequently, to focus attention on the factors which control it.

Because of the difficulties encountered in determining population rate processes and the role of underlying environmental variables, predictive models of population growth have been limited to controlled laboratory populations or unusual natural situations with relatively constant environmental conditions. Predictive schemes applied to natural populations are more likely to succeed the more information they utilize; but such models become hopelessly complicated, requiring vast amounts of empirical information. It is not yet clear whether simple models, requiring relatively little information, can adequately predict population growth in natural situations. However, comparison of a model with the observed population growth focuses attention upon the kinds and amounts of information absolutely essential for prediction. Inappropriate models may prove valuable by emphasizing the effect of disregarding important variables.

Few investigations of this sort have been attempted on plankton populations. Elster (1954) in studying the population dynamics of the copepod, *Eudiaptomus gracilis,* utilized the ratio of eggs-to-females to obtain a reproductive index for the population. By determining the developmental rate of eggs at different temperatures he was able to estimate the increase of the population. Edmondson (1960) applied the experimental-field approach to several rotifer populations, placing great emphasis on the eggs-to-female ratio as a useful tool for determining the birth rates of populations. A model based on birth alone was then used to predict population growth and size.

Although not concerned with zooplankton populations, 2 other studies are pertinent because the approaches are similar. Reynoldson (1961) made a quantitative population study of the triclad, *Dugesia lugubris.* Laboratory experiments allowed Reynoldson to assess the effects of temperature and food on the reproduction of *Dugesia,* and to conclude that population growth was often food-limited. Subsequent field experiments strengthened his conclusion. Morris (1959) in a study of 2 spruce-defoliating insects constructed a predictive model based on a single key factor. The incidence of parasitism in a larval stage of a given generation of defoliators could be used to predict the density of the next generation. This approach proved quite successful, in both a predictive and analytic sense.

Daphnia was selected for the present study because much is known of its biology and population attributes (Banta, Wood, Brown, and Ingle 1939; Slobodkin 1954; Edmondson 1955; Frank, Boll, and Kelly 1957). *Daphnia* reproduces parthenogenetically and at frequent intervals, is easily maintained under laboratory conditions, and is usually an important constituent of the zooplankton in lakes and ponds.

The decision on what variables to include was influenced by several sources. Previous investigations of *Daphnia* as well as pilot studies of *Daphnia galeata mendotae* indicate that food and temperature strongly influence population growth rate. Other variables, such as alkalinity, dissolved gases, and light, either tend to remain relatively constant in the zone of the lakes inhabited by *Daphnia* or seem to be of little importance. Predation undoubtedly affects growth rate in many *Daphnia* populations. This variable is intentionally ignored in this study because the necessary labor of estimating predation rates was prohibitive. The difference between observed and predicted population growth, if carefully evaluated, can indicate the extent of predation upon the *Daphnia* population.

Laboratory experiments were performed to determine rate functions of *Daphnia* under controlled conditions and to obtain relevant descriptive population data so that rates could be inferred from similar data on natural populations.

The experiments deal with the effects of food and temperature upon reproduction, development, individual growth, and survival. The choice of experimental temperature conditions was determined by the range of environmental temperatures throughout the year in the natural habitat. Food levels were selected high enough to permit nearly maximal growth, and low enough (it was hoped) to include the range of food levels existing in the lake. The population of *Daphnia galeata mendotae* in Base Line Lake, Michigan, was selected for study because of its dominant position in the zooplankton, and because of the relatively simple morphometric features of the lake.

MATERIALS AND METHODS

Laboratory Experiments

Daphnia were raised individually from the newborn state in "old-fashion" glasses containing 150 cm³ medium (surface area: 30 cm²; depth: 7 cm) at 25 ± 0.5, 20 ± 1, and $11 \pm 1°C$.

Three different food levels or concentrations were used at each temperature. Animal responses

TABLE I. Instantaneous rates of population increase (r) of *Daphnia galeata mendotae* with associated standard errors at 3 temperatures and 3 food levels

Temperature (°C)	Food level (Klett units)	r
25	16	0.51±0.006
	1	0.46±0.013
	1/4	0.36±0.015
20	16	0.33±0.016
	1	0.30±0.002
	1/4	0.23±0.002
11	16	0.12±0.006
	1	0.10±0.093
	1/4	0.07±0.005

were so uniform that samples of only a few individually raised *Daphnia* yield a very small sampling error to the population rate of increase data (Table I). With 2 exceptions at 11°C, the sample size for each experimental condition was 10. In addition to these 9 experimental conditions 21 *Daphnia* were grown at $5 \pm 1°C$.

Before the experiments *Daphnia* were maintained for several generations at the experimental conditions to account for effects of acclimatization and conditioning to food level.

Food consisted of mixed green algae (*Chlorella, Ankistrodesmus,* and other small species) grown at room temperature in large aquaria exposed to natural as well as fluorescent light. No attempt was made to provide pure or uni-algal sources of food. Consequently, some bacteria and detritus were also included, but at all times the algae represented the major food source. The aquaria contained fish and snails. Food rations were passed through a #25 silk bolting cloth in order to remove undesirable large material. At each feeding the optical density of a sample of the algal culture was measured with a Klett-Summerson photometer equipped with a #42 blue filter. The sample was then centrifuged for 15 min at 3,500 rpm in a clinical centrifuge, after which the optical density of the supernatant liquid was measured. The difference in readings was considered the optical density of centrifugable (and, hence, probably filterable) material. Tap water, conditioned for about one week in large aerated aquaria containing various plants and invertebrates, was passed through an HA Millipore filter and used to dilute the stock algae to 3 concentrations representing 16, 1, and 1/4 Klett units. Sixteen Klett units equal approximately one million algal cells per cm³. The relationship of optical density of cells to cell count over this range of Klett units appears to be linear. This procedure of quantifying the food resulted in uniform responses as reflected by the uniform brood size of daphnids reared at any given food level in the laboratory during the course of 2 years. This food suspension was then brought to the experimental temperature. The medium was changed daily for the 20 and 25° conditions, bidaily for the 11°, and every 4 days for the 5° conditions.

Daphnia were examined at every change of medium. Molting rate was determined by the frequency of appearance of cast skins. The maximum carapace length of the cast skin was the criterion used to measure size. The duration of egg development and duration of adult instar are nearly identical. *Daphnia* carry eggs in their brood chamber which are released as fully developed young during the molting process, at which time a new batch of eggs enters the brood chamber. Reproduction was measured as the number of newborn present at each change of medium. Calculations of the instantaneous rates of increase (r) were made by combining age-specific survival (l_x) and age-specific birth rates (m_x) following the technique of Evans and Smith (1952). Once data for the rate of increase were complete, experiments were terminated even though not all daphnids were dead.

Field Data

Morphometric information was obtained from the contour map of Base Line Lake published by the Institute for Fisheries Research, Michigan Department of Conservation. Temperature conditions were measured with a Whitney resistance thermometer. Water samples were taken periodically and analyzed for oxygen content according to the PKA modification of the Winkler method. A pigmy Gurley current meter was used to estimate current velocities of the river at the outlet of the lake. Current profiles were then constructed from which flow rates were calculated. Two such estimates were made, one during spring high water and another in midsummer. Stomach analyses were made of fish collected in April 1961 from Base Line Lake.

A #6 mesh, 12-in. diameter plankton net equipped with a Clarke-Bumpus flow meter served as the quantitative sampler. It possessed no closing device, however. Calibration of this instrument indicated that one revolution represents 33.4 liters of water through a range of towing speeds from one to 4 knots. A #6 mesh net retains the smallest *Daphnia galeata mendotae* but allows most of the phytoplankton and much of the zooplankton to pass through, thus facilitating the counting procedure. Collections were made from a rowboat moving at a speed of from one to 2

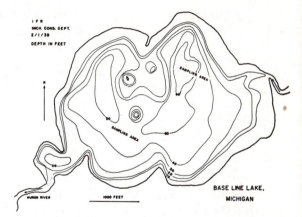

Fig. 1. Contour map of Base Line Lake, Michigan.

knots. With few exceptions, samples were not taken on windy days. The sampling procedure consisted of making long oblique tows through each of 3 strata: upper, middle, and deep. This ensured a stratified but extensive sampling of the population. The meter of water immediately overlying the lake bottom was not sampled. The vertical depth of the tows was calculated, using an angle measurer attached to the tow line. Occasionally in homothermous periods a complete oblique tow (from top to bottom of the lake) was made, while during the winter months vertical hauls were taken under the ice.

The 1960 samples were taken in duplicate at one station. The 1961 samples were taken in duplicate but from opposite sides of the lake (Fig. 1). Samples were also taken at the inlet and outlet of the lake. Each sample represented the contents of 2,000 liters or more of water, excepting those taken in the winter. Thirty-five collections were made during the period from July 1960 to July 1961. *Daphnia* samples were immediately preserved in 95% alcohol. Formalin or less concentrated alcohol caused carapaces to balloon with the consequence that appreciable numbers of eggs fell out of the brood chambers, and it became difficult to assess carapace length.

Samples were too large (about one liter) for complete analysis. After thoroughly mixing the sample, 2 ml subsamples were taken and counted in their entirety until at least 100 *Daphnia* had been counted. Subsamples were placed in a narrow rectangular counting chamber and examined under a dissecting microscope equipped with an ocular micrometer. The maximum carapace length and brood size of each specimen of *Daphnia galeata mendotae* were recorded. Other daphnids were noted if found.

The following equation was used to obtain the density estimate of *Daphnia* in each stratum:

$$\frac{\# \, Daphnia}{100 \text{ liters}} = \frac{\text{average } \# \, Daphnia \text{ in subsample} \times \# \text{ subsamples in concentrate}}{\# \text{ revolutions of flow meter} \times 33.4 \text{ liters}} \times 100$$

The density for the total water column was obtained by taking an average of the upper, middle, and lower strata density estimates, weighted according to the thickness of the strata.

Identification and classification of *Daphnia* follow the monograph of Brooks (1957).

RESULTS

Laboratory Studies

Survivorship and fecundity tables were constructed from the age-specific survival (l_x) and reproductive rates (m_x) under 9 experimental conditions. These tables are then combined into an $l_x m_x$ column which is used to solve the following equation for r, the instantaneous rate of population increase:

$$\Sigma \, l_x m_x e^{-rx} = 1.00$$

Birch (1948) gives an excellent discussion of the calculation of r. Since survival through the juvenile and early adult stages is nearly perfect, mortality has little effect on the estimates of r. Consequently, only fecundity tables are presented in Appendix A; l_x values are 1.00 throughout. This treatment permits quantitative evaluation of the effects of food and temperature on the population rate of increase. Population rates of increase (r per day) for each food level are plotted in Figure 2 as a function of temperature. For the chosen conditions, temperature shows a much greater effect upon r than does food level. Obviously, low enough food levels would also have a profound effect upon r. It is clear by inspection of the range of r values (r = 0.07 to r = 0.51) that any reference to the rate of increase of a

TABLE II. Temperature effects upon duration of instar, egg development, and the ratio of duration of juvenile period to duration of adult instar for *Daphnia galeata mendotae*

Temperature	Duration of instar or duration of egg development	Duration of juvenile period / Duration of adult instar
°C	Days	
25	2.0	3.0 (6/2)
20	2.6	2.9 (7.5/2.6)
15	4.5	
13	6.0	
11	8.0	3.0 (24/8)
9	10.8	
8	12.3	
7	14.2	
5	18.0	
4	20.2	
2	?	

population should be accompanied by a statement of the environmental conditions under which the value was determined.

Temperature

Temperature affects the frequency of molting and hence the frequency with which young are produced (Table II). Reproduction occurs every 2.0 days at 25°C; every 2.6 days at 20°C; and every 8.0 days at 11°C. A single adult at 5°C gave birth to young 18 days after producing the eggs.

For each temperature condition the food level had no observable effect upon the frequency of molting and reproduction. Under conditions of near-starvation, however, Banta, Wood, Brown, and Ingle (1939) have demonstrated that the frequency of molting and reproduction is somewhat reduced.

The duration of egg development is identical to the duration of the adult instars at the food levels used. The ratios of the juvenile periods (time from birth to reproductive maturity of instar V) to the duration of adult instars seem temperature-independent (Table II).

Growth is discontinuous in *Daphnia*, for size increases only during and immediately following ecdysis. The amount of growth at each ecdysis does not seem to be dependent upon temperature.

The median lifespan of *Daphnia* is 30 days at 25°C; 60-80 days at 20°C; and about 150 days at 11°C. *Daphnia* grown at 5°C showed no mortality over a 2-month period. These survival estimates suggest that the physiological mortality rate is quite low, probably less than 3% per day

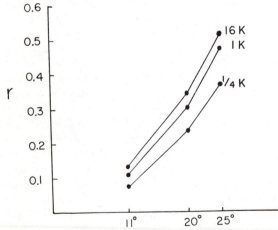

FIG. 2. Instantaneous rates of population increase (r) in relation to temperature (°C) and Klett units of food (K).

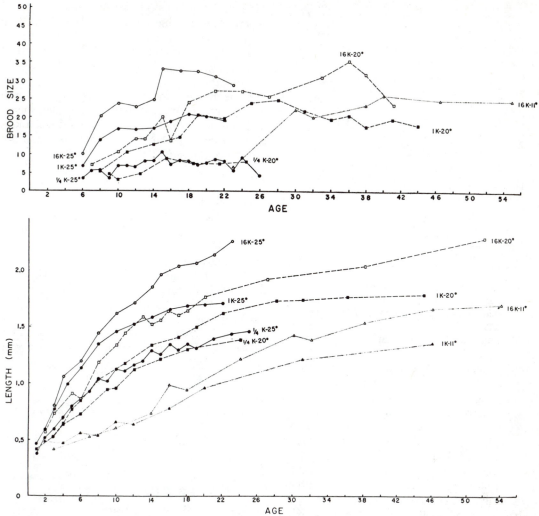

FIG. 3. Upper figure: mean brood size in relation to age (days) under different temperature (°C) and food conditions (Klett units). Lower figure: mean length in relation to age (days) under different temperature (°C) and food conditions (Klett units).

throughout the year. The survival curves were incomplete, but indicate the near-rectangular shape reported for *Daphnia* by Frank, Boll, and Kelly (1957) and Banta, Wood, Brown, and Ingle (1939).

Food

Food level affects reproduction through the number of young per brood (Fig. 3). This effect may appear to be slightly temperature-dependent. When a difference in average brood size does occur for a given food level, the larger size is always associated with a higher temperature. Two features of these experiments might have some bearing on the results. First, at higher temperatures food levels might have been effectively higher than at lower temperatures because the algae seemed to

remain suspended better in the warmer water. Second, had the experiments been carried out for the same number of instars, the curves representing brood size at lower temperatures might have reached the same heights as the curves representing brood size at higher temperatures.

Food level also affects the amount of growth per instar (Fig. 3). Adult stages are affected more by different food levels than are juvenile stages. This effect may appear slightly temperature-dependent, but the 2 reservations mentioned in connection with reproduction apply here also.

Since food level strongly affects both brood size and body size, the relation of brood size to body size (Fig. 4) in daphnids is a poor criterion for inferring food level. *Daphnia* from the different food levels show similar trends, although low food

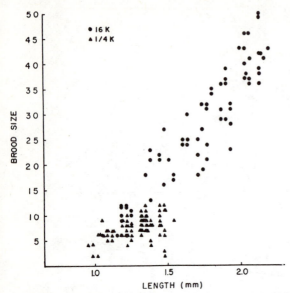

FIG. 4. Brood size in relation to length under high (16 Klett units) and low (¼ Klett unit) food levels at 25°C.

animals remain at the lower end of the distribution.

Although numerous age and size categories are usually present in any natural population, the maximum length and brood size attained by *Daphnia* is apparently determined by the abundance of food. Therefore, an estimate of natural food conditions might be obtained by matching maximum length and brood size from field data to experimentally determined length and brood maxima obtained under specified food levels. Applying this criterion to the collection from Base Line Lake indicates a natural food level of about ¼ Klett unit for much of the year. This technique may prove useful in analyses of other zooplankton populations.

Different food levels did not affect the median

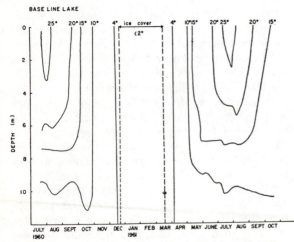

FIG. 5. Base Line Lake isotherms (°C) in 1960-1961.

life span. Banta, Wood, Brown, and Ingle (1939) report that extremely low food levels (near-starvation) increase median longevity.

The separability of the effects of food and temperature greatly facilitates the application of these data to the field collections. Temperature alone may be utilized to predict frequency of molting and reproduction, duration of egg development, and physiological life span. Food level may be inferred from the largest carapace sizes and brood sizes encountered.

Field Studies

Limnological measurements

Base Line Lake in southeastern Michigan (T. 1S.—R. 5E.—Sec. 5, 6; T. 1N.—R. 5E.—Sec. 31, 32) is the last downstream member of a chain of lakes connected by the Huron River. The lake is oval in outline and generally steep-sided, forming a relatively uniform basin ¾ mile long by ½ mile wide (Fig. 1). About 70% of the surface area of the lake overlies water of greater than 8 m depth.

TABLE III. Estimates of volume outflow, lake volume, and flushing rates of Base Line Lake, 1961

VOLUME OUTFLOW	
Spring	1.07 x 10⁶ m³ / day
Midsummer	1.63 x 10⁵ m³ / day
LAKE VOLUME	
Spring	8.73 x 10⁶ m³
Midsummer	8.10 x 10⁶ m³ (total lake)
	5.67 x 10⁶ m³ (epilimnion only)
FLUSHING RATES	
Spring	12.3% / day
Midsummer	3.0% / day (epilimnion only)

Shoal areas are covered with fine marl and are generally devoid of aquatic vegetation. Base Line Lake is a hard-water lake (average surface total alkalinity 155 ppm). Temperature conditions are shown in Figure 5. Stratification occurs from May into October and again from December into March. Oxygen depletion occurred in the hypolimnion in both summers but not during the winter. By June 25, 1961, oxygen concentration was reduced to 1.0 ppm in the hypolimnion; on July 12, 1961, less than 0.10 ppm remained. The effect of summer depletion on *Daphnia* is to reduce the habitable zone of the lake to the epilimnion and thermocline. Prevailing winds are westerly. Circulation patterns within the lake seem to be primarily wind-determined, although the effect of the river flowing through the lake may be considerable during periods of high water.

Table III indicates the volume outflow from the

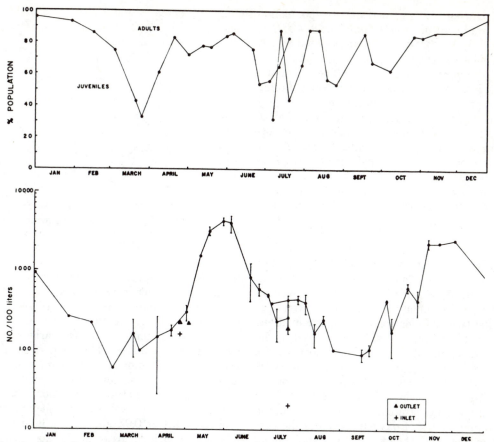

Fig. 6. Upper figure: per cent juveniles and adults in the population. Lower figure: population size (# *Daphnia galeata mendotae* / 100 liters) in 1960-1961. Vertical bars represent standard deviations.

lake at spring high-water level and at summer low-water level. The volume outflow per day is compared with the lake volume yielding a turnover or flushing rate. During May the flushing rate was 12% of the total lake per day. By midsummer the rate had decreased to 3% of the epilimnion per day or 2% of the total lake per day. It is assumed that the outflow rate equals the inflow rate, which is true if the lake level does not fluctuate violently. An annual fluctuation in lake volume of ±3.7%, based on extremes in lake level, lends support to this argument.

Population Attributes

Population size

Population size of *Daphnia galeata mendotae* throughout the course of a year is indicated in Figure 6. The values given are densities (numbers/100 liters) rather than estimates of total population size. Since the densities were determined as an average for all depths, the only assumption involved in converting densities to total numbers is that the densities apply to all parts of the lake. Samples were taken in duplicate, which

should be considered the minimum allowable for population studies. However, samples were very large when compared to most sampling procedures utilizing plankton traps or Clarke-Bumpus samplers. The average coefficient of variability of the population for the pairs of samples is 17.3%, which is relatively low as far as field studies go. Subsamples represented a very small fraction of the total sample (1/200 or less). If any subsample has an equal (but very small) probability of including a given daphnid from the concentrate, then the distribution of the daphnids in the concentrate may be considered a Poisson distribution in which the variance is equal to the mean. Comparing the variance to the mean from samples taken in spring, summer, and fall yields a chi-square value with a probability of 0.10-0.250. The conclusion is that the method of mixing the concentrate ensured randomness, and that the subsampling error was random. The average coefficient of variability associated with subsampling is 18.5%.

Two population maxima occurred; one in late spring, the 2d in late fall. The maximum densities were 4331/100 liters and 2556/100 liters, respectively. During the summer months population density gradually decreased from about 400/100 liters in July to 100/100 liters in September. A large number of *Daphnia galeata mendotae* were present throughout the winter. The minimum density of 60/100 liters occurred in early March just as reproduction was commencing.

Exceedingly few individuals were observed to carry ephippia. All ephippia obtained from bottom samples proved to be *Daphnia pulex*. A few males were observed in fall and spring. *Daphnia galeata mendotae* apparently overwinters largely in the free-swimming stage in Base Line Lake. No reproduction occurred between January 1 and March 4. The water temperature was less than 2°C during the period. Although reproduction occurred in the laboratory at 5°C, it is possible that at 2°C reproduction is prevented. Such a low temperature may also alter the mortality rate.

The vertical distribution of the population seemed dependent upon the temperature stratification of the lake. Under homothermous conditions nearly equal densities of *Daphnia* occurred in the upper, middle, and deep strata. As soon as the lake began to stratify, however, the majority of the daphnids were found in the upper and middle strata. Densities during summer were 10 times greater in the upper stratum than they were in the deep stratum. Lack of oxygen precludes the permanent existence of *Daphnia* in the hypolimnion, and thus few, if any, *Daphnia* would be expected from the deep stratum. Their occurrence in samples from this stratum may be a sampling artifact, since the sampler lacked a closing device. This would bias the density estimates, but the bias would be quite small because the time spent in ascending through the upper and middle strata is very short compared with the time spent in the deep stratum. Another explanation may be that the deep samples frequently included the lower limits of the thermocline where daphnids could live.

Diurnal vertical migration of *Daphnia galeata mendotae* is probably confined to the epilimnion and the thermocline. Attempts to demonstrate vertical migration showed no pattern whatsoever. If vertical migration does occur, it probably does not markedly change the daily temperature environment of the population as a whole. McNaught and Hasler (1961) believe that this species migrates vertically through one m or less of water in Lake Mendota, Wisconsin.

Reproduction

The average brood size (ratio of eggs to mature *Daphnia*) served as a population reproductive index. The criterion of reproductive maturity is

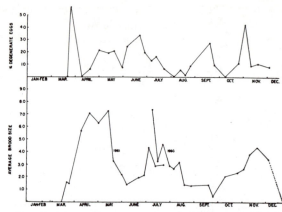

Fig. 7. Upper figure: per cent degenerate eggs in the population. Lower figure: average brood size (average number of eggs per adult).

somewhat arbitrary, since no morphological distinction can be made between mature and immature *Daphnia* unless the adults are reproductive. Carapace length at the onset of reproduction (instar V) was determined under various food and temperature conditions. The range of such lengths was from 0.97 mm to 1.25 mm. All shorter lengths occurred at low food levels. Since it appears that the natural population also experienced a low food level, the size at maturity was arbitrarily set at 0.97 mm. At a high food level this would include many of the last juvenile instars, but would nevertheless yield a very high average brood size.

Average brood sizes are plotted in Figure 7. Three distinct peaks occur. The spring and fall brood size maxima immediately precede the two population density maxima. The summer increase in brood size is not accompanied by an increase in daphnids. The average brood size ranged from 2.0 to 4.0 eggs throughout most of the reproductive season. The largest average brood size was 7.5 eggs.

The per cent reproductive adult females was usually high, especially during peak egg production, but dropped to 50% or less after the spring and summer reproductive peaks and immediately after the onset of reproduction in March. If degenerate broods were also included the per cent would be higher.

Degenerate eggs were frequently observed in the brood chambers of *Daphnia* taken from Base Line Lake. These eggs were a dark gray-brown color and often appeared to be disintegrating. Normal eggs appeared blue-green or yellow-green in color and were of a firm, less fragile texture. Degenerate eggs were excluded from the calculation of average brood size. The percentage degenerate eggs in relation to the total eggs present is shown in Figure 7. There is no suggestion of any relationship with normal brood size. The frequency of entire broods appearing degenerate was greater than the frequency of only a fraction of the brood appearing degenerate, whereas under laboratory conditions the few degenerate eggs observed occurred singly.

The stage of development of the eggs in the brood chamber was also noted. Three stages were defined: the egg stage (no segmentation), first embryo stage (segmentation, but no eyespot), and 2d embryo stage (possession of an eyespot). This classification is similar to Edmondson's (1955). Although the 3 stages are not of identical duration, the relative frequency of their occurrence may still be used to evaluate the question of reproductive periodicity. All 3 stages were present in roughly equal numbers in all samples, indicating that no diurnal periodicity in reproduction occurs under natural conditions. This observation permits reproduction to be treated as a continuous function of the population.

Size structure

Knowledge of the age and size structure of metazoan populations is necessary to analyze properly population growth (Slobodkin 1954). *Daphnia* exhibit no age-specific characters, making it difficult to describe the age structure of the population. A method of estimating the age structure of a population would be to determine, under laboratory conditions, the length of *Daphnia* grown under a variety of experimental conditions, and then to apply the appropriate length-age relationship to the observed field size distribution. The validity of such an estimate depends upon how well the laboratory-determined length-age relationship can be applied.

In this study an attempt was made to estimate the instar structure of the population (later, using temperature data from the laboratory, ages of immature instars will be estimated). The ranges of lengths of instars grown in the laboratory were used to construct a series of size categories, which, when applied in the field samples, probably represent distinct instars at least for the immature period. Once maturity is reached the individual growth rate (increases in length per molt) decreases and becomes more strongly dependent upon food level. Thus, it becomes increasingly difficult to assign an individual to a specific instar. The size structure is therefore based upon 4 immature instars and 3 mature "categories." Figure 6 represents the frequency distribution of adults and juveniles throughout one year. The increase in the proportion of adults from January through March was caused by the absence of reproduction

coupled with the slow maturation of the existing immature daphnids. However, as reproduction commenced in late March the population size structure shifted rapidly until by mid-April less than 20% of the *Daphnia* were mature. For 2 months the proportion of mature daphnids remained at this level with only minor fluctuations. This period coincides with the spring period of rapid population growth. By mid-June the proportion of adults began to increase, reaching 46% of the population before again decreasing to the 20% level. A series of 3 rather violent fluctuations in all size categories occurred during the summer and early fall. Each increase in percentage of adults was followed by a decrease to the 10 to 20% level. In October a 4th such decrease occurred, but this time the proportion of adults reached the 15% level and remained there for more than a month. This last period of stable age structure coincides with the fall period of rapid population growth.

Population size structure in relation to depth showed little variation among the upper, middle, and lower strata. The juveniles were slightly more frequent in the upper and middle strata in the summer. Because most of the population was located in the epilimnion (upper and middle strata), the small differences of size frequency categories in relation to depth are considered unimportant. The population size structure was similar at all depths in spring and fall. The size structure of samples taken at the outlet at spring high water was very similar to the size structure of the population in the lake. The size structure of outlet samples taken in midsummer was composed entirely of juveniles and did not correspond to the size structure of the lake population.

Population losses

Observations on the abundance and feeding habits of several predators indicate that *Leptodora* (a cladoceran), *Chaoborus* (phantom midge

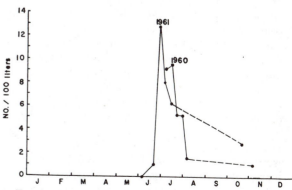

Fig. 8. Population size of *Leptodora* (# / 100 liters) in 1960-1961.

larva), and fish prey upon *Daphnia*. Population density was estimated for *Leptodora* only. *Leptodora* appears in June and reaches peak numbers in July (Fig. 8). Andrews (1949) reports a similar seasonal abundance of *Leptodora* in Lake Erie, but with a 2d minor peak of males in October. *Chaoborus* appear in the upper waters only at night, spending the day in or just above the bottom of the lake. Stomach analyses of adult cisco (*Leucichthys artedi*) and crappies (*Pomoxis nigromaculatus*) taken from Base Line Lake indicate that these fish feed extensively on large *Daphnia pulex* in early spring, but not upon the smaller adults of *Daphnia galeata mendotae*.

Another population loss is caused by the Huron River. This loss may be considered the net effect of passive immigration and emigration of *Daphnia*. Once carried out of the lake, *Daphnia* are lost to the system and soon die (Chandler 1939). The net loss of the population was determined by subtracting the density of *Daphnia* in the river immediately below the lake from the density in the river immediately above the lake. During late April and early May the high flushing rate of the lakes was accompanied by considerable but nearly identical immigration and emigration (Fig. 6). The net loss was low (perhaps as high as 3% of the population per day). During midsummer the low flushing rate of the lake was accompanied by lower immigration and emigration rates. The net loss was one per cent of population per day. These estimates indicate that the river flowing through Base Line Lake exerts a relatively constant and small source of mortality.

Other zooplankton populations

Four other species of *Daphnia* were found in Base Line Lake: *Daphnia pulex, D. retrocurva, D. ambigua,* and *D. longiremis*. Only the first 2 species ever reached appreciable numbers. *D. pulex* reaches a peak abundance in spring after which numbers become sparse. At no time was *D. pulex* more abundant than *D. galeata mendotae*. During summer *D. pulex* is found only in the colder regions of the lake, i.e., the thermocline, where it is the dominant daphnid. The fact that this species does not appear in the warmer epilimnion, and often possesses considerable haemoglobin which is an adaptation to enable it to withstand low oxygen concentration (Fox 1948), would indicate that this species occupies a restricted habitat during much of the year. *D. retrocurva* appeared in the plankton only after the lake had warmed to 20°C. Population size of this species increased during July and early August, and, by late August, this species became the most abundant cladoceran. On September 24, 1960, *D. retrocurva* occurred at a density of 730/100 liters in the epilimnion compared to a density of about 175/100 liters of *D. galeata mendotae*. By late October *D. galeata mendotae* again dominated other cladocera. Indeed, during spring and fall maxima, this species was far more abundant than any species of copepod. *Cyclops* is the predominant copepod. *Diaptomus* is present also. *Bosmina* appears as an important member of the zooplankton during the colder months.

PREDICTIONS

A first-order prediction of *Daphnia* population growth may now be attempted utilizing much of the information obtained from the field and laboratory observations. Such a prediction will indicate if important variables have been overlooked in the population analysis, and may prove a valuable means of gaining insight into this biological system.

Two related kinds of predictions are made: predicted rates of increase and predicted population size or density.

Population growth rate

The rate of increase of the population may be estimated if the birth, death, emigration and immigration rates are known. Although no animal reproduces continuously, many do reproduce frequently enough so that the instantaneous growth equation,

$$(1) \qquad N_t = N_o e^{rt}$$

is a close approximation to natural population growth. N_o and N_t denote initial population size and size t time units later; e is the base of natural logarithms; t represents time units; and r denotes the instantaneous rate of increase and is determined by the 4 rates mentioned above.

If the effects of death, emigration, and immigration are ignored, the growth equation becomes,

$$N_t = N_o e^{bt}$$

in which b is the instantaneous rate. Although the symbols r, b, and d (instantaneous death rate) have been defined under stable age conditions (see Lotka 1925), they may be applied to populations without a stable age distribution as well. The only distinction is that under stable age conditions r, b, and d remain constant; whereas under a continually changing age distribution the instantaneous rates will change accordingly. The instantaneous birth rate, b, may be estimated if the finite birth rate, B is known:

$$b = \ln (1 + B)$$

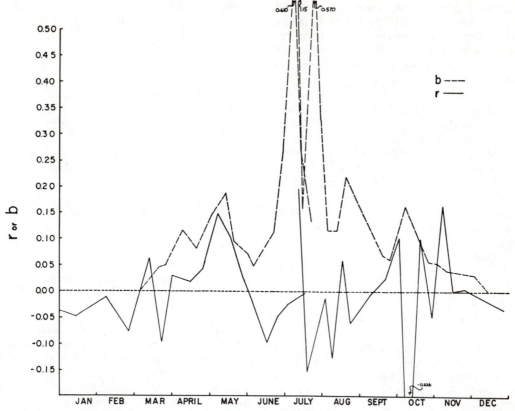

FIG. 9. Observed (r) and estimated (b) instantaneous rates of population increase of *Daphnia galeata mendotae* in Base Line Lake.

The finite birth rate is defined as the number of newborn occurring during an interval of time divided by the number of animals already existing:

(2)

$$B = \frac{\text{number of newborn (during interval } t \text{ to } t+1)}{\text{population size at } t}$$

The problem then is to predict the number of newborn during any interval of time. Four kinds of information are used for this prediction: the population size (N_o); the number of adults (N_A); the average brood size of adults ($\bar{E}$); and the rate of development of the eggs expressed as the fraction of development accomplished per day ($1/D$). The finite birth rate or number of newborn per individual per day is given by the equation:

$$(3) \qquad B = \frac{N_A \cdot \bar{E} \cdot 1/D}{N_o}$$

The values of N_A, $\bar{E}$, and N_o are estimated from a sample of the natural population. In order to determine $1/D$, the temperature at which the eggs develop must be known. Table II indicates values of D for various temperatures. The lengths of

TABLE IV. Average temperatures (°C) during different periods of the year in the upper, middle, and lower strata of Base Line Lake

Periods	Strata		
	Upper	Middle	Deep
1960			
July-Aug.	25	20	15
Sept.	20	20	15
Oct.	13	13	11
Nov.	7	7	7
1961			
Jan.-March	2	2	2
1/2 March	4	4	4
April	6	6	6
1/2 May	11	11	8
1/2 May	15	15	9
June	20	15	9
July	25	15	11

time required for development (D) at 25, 20, 11, and 5°C were determined under constant laboratory conditions. The remainder of the values were obtained by curvilinear interpolation, but not by logarithmic interpolation, since Q_{10} changed considerably throughout this temperature range. Table IV indicates the estimated average temperatures for the 3 strata of Base Line Lake for various months of the year. These average temperatures were determined from the annual temperature profile of Base Line Lake (Fig. 5). During periods of rapid temperature changes in Base Line Lake the averages were based on shorter periods. When the 3 strata differed in average temperatures, 3 separate values of b were calculated from which a weighted average of the 3 was determined. The calculated values of b for the 28 dates are plotted in Figure 9.

Successive pairs of points from Figure 6 yield values of N_o and N_t, from which an average r for each time period can be calculated.

From equation (1):

$$(4) \qquad r = \frac{1_nN_t - 1_nN_o}{t}$$

The 32 points of r in Figure 9 were calculated in this manner.

The properties of b include a lower limit of zero (whenever reproduction ceases). Rapid shifts in the age structure of the population as well as sampling errors produce large changes in the value of b. The lower limit of r is—∞. Values of b should always exceed values of r, since $r = b - d$. Population rate of increase based on b alone is, except for 2 periods of time, always higher than the observed rate of increase.

Despite fluctuations in b and r definite trends in the 2 sets of points are apparent. During spring and fall months r and b values are both positive and nearly equal. Maximum values of b are attained in the summer months, whereas r is negative during this period indicating a population decrease. During the winter b is zero, and r is negative.

Obviously, the curve of r is related to the population numbers from which it was derived. The maximal densities of spring and fall are preceded by maximal r values whereas the minimal summer and winter densities are preceded by minimal r values. The seasonal curve for b is very different. Values of b reach a single large peak during the summer months rather than 2 peaks in spring and fall.

Comparison of birth rates and rates of population change show that in spring and fall, predation, natural death, and net loss to the Huron River are not important variables affecting population growth. Average total population losses of 3.9 and 5.6% per day for April-May and October-November respectively were determined by subtracting r from b during these periods. During

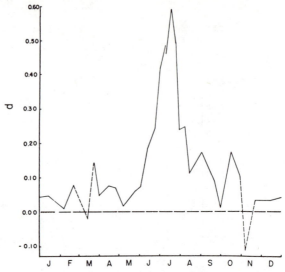

FIG. 10. Estimated instantaneous death rate (d) of *Daphnia galeata mendotae* in Base Line Lake obtained by subtracting r from b in Fig. 9.

the winter a 4.4% loss per day occurs, which probably reflects natural death and loss to the river alone. From mid-June through mid-September the very large difference between r and b indicates that the total population loss is very high (Fig. 10). An average total loss of 28.5% per day was determined by subtracting r from b during July and early August.

Since the net loss to the population due to the river system is 3% per day or less in the spring and 1% in the summer (0.03 and 0.01 daphnids lost per daphnid per day respectively), the effect of animals entering and leaving the population in this manner is small and reasonably constant. Physiological mortality as discussed above is probably low also. Predation then would seem to be the cause of the negative population growth rate throughout most of the summer.

A 2d method of estimating the loss rate is to construct survivorship curves for the population from the size distributions for various periods of the year. A survivorship curve yields the rate of survival (or conversely the death rate) if plotted as a semilogarithmic graph. Knowledge of the age structure and growth rate of the population is necessary to construct a survivorship curve from field data. Laboratory data on the length-age relationship under different food and temperature conditions were here employed to estimate the age and instar of *Daphnia* taken from the natural population. If population size remains unchanged for a length of time greater than one generation period, then the survival curve will become identical or nearly identical to the stable age distribution curve. To obtain a survival curve when the

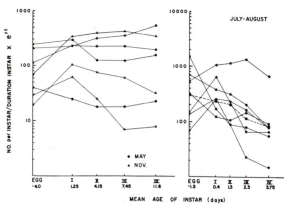

FIG. 11. Estimated survivorship curves relating numbers (# per instar / duration of instar X e^rt) to age (days) for May, November, and July-August. Average survivorship in July-August is represented by the dotted line.

population is changing size, the number of animals in each age category of the age distribution must be multiplied by a correction factor which is based upon the population rate of change and the age of the animal. This method should work providing the rate of population change is known and remains relatively constant over a length of time greater than the generation period.

Figure 11 represents survival curves estimated by the above technique for May, July-August, and November. These periods were chosen because population rate of change was relatively constant (Fig. 6). On the abscissa are plotted the mean ages of the eggs and estimated instars I-IV. The numbers of daphnids within each of these categories was determined by (1) dividing the number of individuals existing as eggs, instar I, etc., by the duration of the category (to adjust for different instar durations), and (2) multiplying this by the finite rate of population change over the time period between birth (t = o) and mean age of category. In the case of eggs, negative time units were employed since the eggs had not entered the population yet. This procedure adjusts the numbers in each category so that they represent the estimated survival in time of a population of the size that exists at t = o. The slope of the line indicates the survival rate since a logarithmic scale was used to plot numbers. A horizontal line indicates perfect survival. It is interesting to note that during May survival appears to be complete; in other words, the death rate is negligible. The survivorship curves for November indicate much the same thing, although not so clearly. In both cases sampling error may produce an apparent increase in numbers with age, which is unrealistic, but the average horizontal trend is obvious. During July and August the curves are no longer

horizontal. Their negative slopes reflect a high death rate. The average summer survivorship curve indicates a death rate of 0.259 daphnids per daphnid per day. Since net immigration-emigration effects indicate a loss of 0.01 daphnids per daphnid per day and the physiological death rate amounts to no more than 3% per day, the conclusion is again reached that predation is the most important factor controlling population size in the summer.

The average summer survivorship curve indicates a reasonably constant loss rate for all age categories. This suggests that predation viewed for the entire period is not age-specific.

Population size

Population size was predicted for 4 intervals; May 1-May 19, June 5-June 28, July 8-August 4, and September 24-November 10. The rate of increase, r, was estimated for one generation period by estimating the number of *Daphnia* that would be produced during the period that it took for a newborn *Daphnia* present at t = o to mature. Thus mature daphnids present at the beginning of each interval were assumed to produce young throughout the entire interval at a rate dependent upon the average brood size and developmental rate 1/D. Daphnids in the last immature instar at the onset of the period were treated in the same manner except the number of "reproductive days" in the period for these animals was shortened by the time it took to reach the mature instar. All subsequent immature instars were treated in the same manner with the number of reproductive days decreased by how many days short of maturity they were. The estimated duration of immature instars at various temperatures was determined from the laboratory experiments. The total number of *Daphnia* born during this generation period was added to the initial number to obtain a predicted population size for the end of the generation period. The instantaneous rate of increase was then determined by solving equation (4), in which t equals the number of days from birth to maturity at the given temperature. The 4 values of r were then utilized to solve for predicted population size at the end of each of the 4 intervals of prediction.

If but one generation occurred during the interval (owing to a low temperature or the shortness of the interval) then the estimated population size would be a good estimate of the expected population size based upon birth rate alone. However, if several generations occurred during the interval, then the r associated with the initial population size structure would be insensitive to changes in size structure occurring during the in-

TABLE V. Observed population size compared to estimated population size of *Daphnia galeata mendotae* at the end of 4 intervals

Time interval	Population size (#/100 liters)	
	Observed	Estimated
May 1-May 19	3,225	2,661
June 5-June 28	607	114,723
July 8-August 4	413	8,745,000
Sept. 24-Nov. 10	2,337	3,663

terval. It is impossible to assume that the initial size structure would not change during some of these intervals (Fig. 6); therefore, this method must be criticized for this shortcoming. However, population size estimated in this manner (Table V) indicates much the same thing as the estimate of population growth did when compared to the observed population growth.

The estimated population size of 2,661 *Daphnia*/100 liters is similar to the observed population size of 3,225 *Daphnia*/100 liters present at the end of the interval May 1-May 19. The estimated population size of 3,663 *Daphnia*/100 liters is also similar to the observed population size of 2,337 *Daphnia*/100 liters present at the end of the interval from September 24-November 10. However, the 144,723 *Daphnia*/100 liters estimated from June 5-June 28 is far greater than the observed population of 607 *Daphnia*/100 liters. An even greater discrepancy exists at the end of the period of July 8-August 4 when the estimated population is 8,745,000 *Daphnia*/100 liters compared to observed 413 *Daphnia*/100 liters.

DISCUSSION

The population growth model based on birth rate alone is an adequate expression of population growth of *Daphnia galeata mendotae* in Base Line Lake during spring and fall, but is inadequate during the summer. Predation seems to be a key variable affecting the population throughout the summer.

Population losses during the summer, estimated by determining the average difference between the expected and observed population growth (b-r) for this period, amount to 28.5% of the population per day. This estimate is remarkably similar to the loss rate of 25.9% of the population per day obtained from the estimated survivorship curves for the same period.

Although both estimates make use of the parameter r, the effect of r in correcting the numbers in each age category in the construction of the survivorship curves is small. The 2 estimates of population loss may be considered virtually independent, since they utilize mainly different information in different ways. Confidence in the reality of such a high population loss rate is increased by the agreement of the estimates.

An average predation rate of just over 25% of the population per day when the population is decreasing very slowly implies that the population turnover time is about every 4 days during July and early August. The turnover rate applies to biomass as well as numbers since the slope of the average summer survival curve is nearly constant (Fig. 11). This appears to be an exceptionally high turnover rate for a microcrustacean population. Stross *et al.* (1961) estimated the turnover time of *Daphnia longispina* in a lime-treated lake to be 2.1 weeks, whereas the estimated turnover time of a *Daphnia pulex* population in the untreated control lake was 4.6 weeks. The slightly lower average temperature of these lakes in comparison to Base Line Lake would, in itself, increase the population turnover time.

Under laboratory conditions *Daphnia galeata mendotae* exhibits a maximal rate of increase of 0.51 at 25°C. If we assume that predation rates would be proportional to the age frequency classes (i.e., predation does not change the age distribution), the theoretical minimum turnover time for *Daphnia* would be slightly less than 1.5 days. This is the length of time necessary to double population size calculated from the exponential growth equation (1).

Temperatures frequently reach 25°C in the surface waters of lakes but not for long periods of time. Food levels in natural habitats rarely, if ever, reach the levels associated with a maximal rate of increase. Even at the lowest laboratory food level, which is approximately the same as that of the lake, the maximum rate of increase is 0.36. Thus, a higher predation rate than that estimated (0.25) is possible, although the daphnids might risk extinction.

The turnover rate of once every 4 days observed in *Daphnia galeata mendotae* indicates that practically all the biomass produced by this population is passed on rapidly to the next trophic level. Since this species is a major component of the zooplankton, it must play a major role in the food chain of the lake during the summer. The role of *Daphnia galeata mendotae* as food would be much less important in spring and fall, since predation appears to be negligible at these times.

The bimodal curve representing population size of *Daphnia galeata mendotae* throughout a period of one year (Fig. 6) is typical of many zooplankton populations. This pattern of population growth is generally interpreted as a reflection of a food-limited system, in which phytoplankton become abundant as the result of increased nutrients following spring and fall mixing of the lake. The zooplankton respond to this increased food level by an increase in numbers until the food supply is essentially exhausted. A decline in numbers results from the shortage of food. In summer the phytoplankton (mainly blue-green and filamentous green algae) may be abundant but are considered unavailable as food for the zooplankton, resulting in low zooplankton densities. In winter phytoplankton growth is limited so that food is again a limiting factor in the growth of zooplankton populations.

The bimodal population curve of *Daphnia galeata mendotae* in this study is not simply the result of a food-limited system. This conclusion stems from considerations of reproductive potential and age-size structure of the *Daphnia* population.

The carrying capacity of the environment in terms of food is not reached during the summer because considerable energy is still available for the production of eggs. A very low average brood size is expected in an equilibrium population (which has reached the carrying capacity of the environment in terms of food supply), for at equilibrium only one egg, on the average, will be produced by each daphnid, and yet the life expectancy of daphnids includes several adult instars. Slobodkin (1954) has observed that equilibrium laboratory populations of *Daphnia* exhibit very little egg production. The average brood size in his equilibrium populations was less than 0.5 eggs/adult.

On one date only (September 24, 1960) did the average brood size fall below 1.0 egg/adult in Base Line Lake. During July and early August the average brood size ranged between 2 and 5 eggs per adult, which is much too large a brood size to be associated with a completely food-limited population.

The population growth rate in spring and fall is initially slowed by a decrease in reproduction indicating lower food levels, but only low enough to reduce the rate of increase and not to cause the rapid decline in population size that was observed in late May and early June.

Thus population size in summer is probably regulated more by predation pressure than by the scarcity of food. The predators are removing the center portion out of what otherwise would be a unimodal population curve. Without predation *Daphnia* would become food limited, but at a considerably higher population density.

Other zooplankton populations may show the same bimodal population curve as a result of similar heavy predation pressures in the summer

months. Nelson and Edmondson (1955) report that following the fertilization of Bare Lake, Alaska, the phytoplankton increased rapidly in density. This was followed by increased reproduction of the zooplankton (especially rotifers), but the size of the zooplankton population increased very little. The interpretation is that most of the increased growth of zooplankton populations was immediately consumed by the next trophic level (Nelson 1958).

In a study of *Daphnia retrocurva* in Bantam Lake, Connecticut, Brooks (1946) reports a population maximum of 3,650 *Daphnia*/100 liters in late spring. The density rapidly decreased thereafter, reaching 340 *Daphnia*/100 liters by July 9, and remained at this level for more than one month. The average brood size (mean number of eggs/adult) increased from less than 1.0 in mid-June to 2.5 on July 21. The mean water temperature during this period was 20°C. The similarity of his observations to those of the present study is striking. Again, the interpretation is that the rapid population growth in the spring is initially slowed by a food shortage, but the population size is drastically reduced by predation during the summer. Brooks did not estimate predation rates, however.

Stross *et al.* (1961) report a rapid increase in population size of *Daphnia longispina* in July. Average brood size exceeded 1.0 egg/adult during most of the period of population increase. However, before the population maximum was reached the brood size dropped to about 0.2 eggs/adult and remained at this size for 2 weeks while the population density decreased by a factor of 10. In this case food scarcity may have played a larger role in the control of population size than in the other studies discussed, although predation would still have to play a major role to account for the observed rate of decrease of population size.

A population with constant age-specific survival and reproductive rates will eventually reach a stable age distribution (Lotka 1931). Slobodkin (1954) found that a stable age-size population structure is not achieved in laboratory populations of *Daphnia* because of time lags inherent in the populations. In natural populations a stable age distribution is unlikely because the age-specific survival and reproductive rates change in association with changing environmental conditions.

The high, relatively constant proportions of juveniles in the spring and fall are certainly reflective of a population growing under relatively stable conditions. However, these periods are followed by a rapid shift toward an adult-dominated population indicative of lowered reproduction and /or selection predation upon the juveniles. These interpretations are borne out by observation of the brood size and estimates of population loss (Figs. 7 and 9).

The role of fungal diseases and other parasites conceivably could contribute greatly to the high summer loss rate. However, extensive examinations of field collections during the summer indicated no visibly parasitized *Daphnia*.

Applying developmental rates obtained from but a few clones of *Daphnia* to the entire natural population assumes that no significant genetic variability of developmental rate exists. The validity of this assumption has not been examined.

The frequent occurrence of degenerate eggs in the natural population (Fig. 7) was unexpected from the results of the laboratory studies. Brooks (1946) reports a similar finding in a natural population of *Daphnia retocurva*. He suggests that egg degeneration is caused by inadequate nutrition. He also postulates that brood size is indicative of nutritional level. However, a comparison of brood size and frequency of degenerate eggs in both his and the present investigations indicates that these 2 criteria of nutritional level are inconsistent. Laboratory studies show that brood size is a reflection of the amount of food or energy available. Degenerate eggs may reflect a specific nutritional deficiency, a change in food level, temporary anoxia, or other conditions.

Causal analyses of natural population growth have frequently been attempted using the correlation approach. Although correlations are valuable in indicating the degree of relationship between variables, their biological significance is often difficult to evaluate. Hazelwood and Parker (1961) examined the effect of various environmental factors upon population size of *Daphnia* and *Diaptomus* (Copepoda). Their approach was based entirely upon correlations of several factors with population size. Accurate population estimates are essential if correlations are to be meaningful. Their analyses are based upon single samples at one depth at one station, and, may thus confound distributional variation with population density. Considerable distributional variation was, in fact, borne out by a single series of samples taken August 13, 1959, from different parts of the lake. Little, if any, experimental evidence was obtained about the effects of variables upon population parameters which would have permitted a stronger analysis of the system.

To perform adequate analyses of natural populations, experimental approaches must be utilized. In the present study the effects of different food and temperature conditions upon various attributes of *Daphnia* were found to be important. The range of laboratory temperatures tested was probably adequate to discern the effects on *Daphnia* of the ambient temperature conditions throughout the year. The laboratory food levels extended to much higher levels than those occurring in Base Line Lake. Testing the effects of food levels lower than ¼ Klett unit would have improved the present study.

Reduction of the complexity of natural population systems to a minimal number of variables is needed before any generalities can be made about the operation of such systems. The birth rate model is a beginning in this direction. Its value does not lie so much in the actual prediction of population growth (in the sense of forecasting), for the model requires empirical information about the population during the interval of prediction. Instead, the model is valuable in testing the effects upon population growth of omitting all but a few variables.

Where the model fails to predict growth rates adequately, attention is then focused upon those variables which seem most influential. An experimental analysis of these suspect variables in both the laboratory and the field will provide further insight into the dynamics of the system. Because reproduction appears to be so labile in most zooplankton populations, the birth rate model may prove of widespread use.

Summary

The dynamics of the population of *Daphnia galeata mendotae* in Base Line Lake, Michigan, were analyzed by combining field and laboratory studies. Life-table and fecundity-table experiments were performed at 25, 20, and 11°C. Three food levels were tested at each temperature. Daily or bidaily observations enabled determination of the frequency of molting, duration of egg development, number of newborn per day, individual growth rate, and median life span.

Calculated population rates of increase, r, ranged from 0.07 to 0.51. Temperature influences r more strongly than food level does under the conditions examined. The effects of food and temperature are separable, thereby facilitating the application of experimental data to the field collection. Frequency of molting and reproduction, duration of egg development, and physiological life span are influenced principally by temperature. Growth per instar, maximum carapace length, and brood size are influenced principally by food.

The population in Base Line Lake was sampled for one year. All samples were examined permitting the estimation of population density, size structure, and average brood size. Population density shows a bimodal annual curve with maximal number in late spring and fall. Average brood size shows a trimodal annual curve. Two peaks in brood size precede and apparently cause the density maxima, whereas the 3d peak occurs in midsummer and is not followed by an increased population size. Average brood size ranged between 2 and 4 eggs per brood during most of the reproductive season. Population loss rates caused by the Huron River are relatively constant and small (3% and 1% population loss/day in spring and summer).

Population rates of increase based on birth rate alone, b, are estimated and compared with observed rates of increase, r. In spring, fall, and winter the small differences between b and r (3.9, 5.6, and 4.4% per day respectively) are accounted for by physiological mortality and river loss. Average summer population loss rate of 28% per day seems primarily due to predation. Summer survival curves estimated from field data indicate an average loss rate of 25% per day.

The summer population turnover rate of both numbers and biomass is estimated to be once every 4 days. *Daphnia galeata mendotae* plays an important role in the food chain of the lake during the summer. Population size does not appear to be solely determined by food. Predation pressure prevents the population from being large in the summer.

The birth rate model focuses attention upon the effect of ignoring important variables and should prove valuable in analyzing other zooplankton populations.

ACKNOWLEDGMENTS

The author wishes to acknowledge the advice and encouragement of Dr. Frederick E. Smith, Department of Zoology, University of Michigan. Also, appreciation goes to the Horace H. Rackham, School of Graduate Studies, University of Michigan, which awarded the author a scholarship and fellowships during this study.

LITERATURE CITED

Andrews, T. F. 1949. The life history, distribution, growth and abundance of *Leptodora kindtii* (Focke) in western Lake Erie. Abstracts of Doctoral Dissertations, 57. Ohio State University Press.

Banta, A. M., T. R. Wood, L. A. Brown, and L. Ingle. 1939. Studies on the physiology, genetics, and evolution of some Cladocera. Carnegie Inst. Wash., Dept. Genetics, Paper no. 39. 285 pp.

Birch, L. C. 1948. The intrinsic rate of natural increase of an insect population. Jour. Anim. Ecol. 17: 15-26.

Brooks, J. L. 1946. Cyclomorphosis in *Daphnia*. I. An analysis of *D. retrocurva* and *D. galeata*. Ecol. Monog. 16: 409-447.

——. 1957. The systematics of North American *Daphnia*. Mem. Conn. Acad. Arts & Sci. 13. 180 pp.

Chandler, D. C. 1939. Plankton entering the Huron River from Portage and Base Line lakes, Michigan. Trans. Am. Micro. Soc. 58: 24-41.

Edmondson, W. T. 1955. The seasonal life history of *Daphnia* in an arctic lake. Ecology 36: 439-455.

——. 1960. Reproductive rates of rotifers in natural populations. Mem. Inst. Ital. Idrobiol. 12: 21-77.

Elster, H. J. 1954. Über die Populationsdynamik von *Eudiaptomus gracilis* Sara und *Heterocope borealis* Fischer im Bodensee-Obersee. Arch. für Hydrobiol., Suppl. 20: 546-614.

Evans, F. C., and F. E. Smith. 1952. The intrinsic rate of natural increase for the human louse, *Pediculus humanus* L. Amer. Nat. 86: 299-310.

Fox, H. M. 1948. *Daphnia* hemoglobin. Roy. Soc. London Proc. Ser. B., 135: 195-212.

Frank, P. W. 1960. Prediction of population growth form in *Daphnia pulex* cultures. Amer. Nat. 94: 357-372.

——, C. D. Boll, and R. W. Kelly. 1957. Vital statistics of laboratory cultures of *Daphnia pulex* De Geer as related to density. Physiol. Zool. 30: 287-305.

Hazelwood, D. H., and R. A. Parker. 1961. Population dynamics of some freshwater zooplankton. Ecology 42: 266-273.

Lotka, A. J. 1925. Elements of physical biology. Baltimore: Williams and Wilkins. 460 pp.

——. 1931. The structure of a growing population. Human Biol. 3: 459-493.

McNaught, D. C., and A. D. Hasler. 1961. Surface schooling and feeding behavior in the white bass, *Roccus chrysops* (Rafinesque), in Lake Mendota. Limnol. and Oceanogr. 6: 53-60.

Morris, R. F. 1959. Single-factor analysis in population dynamics. Ecology 40: 580-588.

Nelson, P. R. 1958. Relationship between rate of photosynthesis and growth of juvenile red salmon. Science 128: 205-206.

Nelson, P. R., and W. T. Edmondson. 1955. Limnological effects of fertilizing Bare Lake, Alaska. U.S. Fish and Wildlife Service Fishery Bull. no. 102, 56: 415-436.

Reynoldson, T. B. 1961. A quantitative study of the population biology of *Dugesia lugubris* (O. Schmidt) (Turbellaria, Tricladida). Oikos 12: 111-125.

Slobodkin, L. B. 1954. Population dynamics in *Daphnia obtusa* Kurz. Ecol. Monog. 24: 69-88.

Stross, R. G., J. C. Neess, and A. D. Hasler. 1961. Turnover time and production of the planktonic crustacea in limed and reference portion of a bog lake. Ecology 42: 237-244.

APPENDIX A

Age-specific reproduction of *Daphnia galeata mendotae* under 9 different conditions of food and temperature expressed as total number of offspring per day. The values of N remain unchanged with respect to age in these tables.

Age (days)	Food levels (Klett units)		
	1/4 (N=12)	1 (N=10)	16 (N=10)
TEMPERATURE: 25°C			
6.0	31	75	100
7.0	33	0	0
8.0	27	138	202
9.0	18	0	0
10.0	46	168	237
11.0	48	0	0
12.0	33	166	227
13.0	41	0	0
14.0	58	153	248
15.0	42	0	229
16.0	57	170	36
17.0	33	0	260
18.0	40	185	0
19.0	28	0	258
20.0	38	161	0
21.0	0	0	248
22.0		152	

Age (days)	(N=8)	(N=9)	(N=10)
TEMPERATURE: 20°C			
7.5	0	0	28
8.5	0	36	6
9.5	8	0	8
10.5	13	12	86
11.5	3	56	42
12.5	22	12	98
13.5	14	7	24
14.5	1	66	80
15.5	45	14	64
16.5	25	8	25
17.5	0	82	171
18.5	45	15	43
19.5	13	117	33
20.5	0	18	193
21.5	21	36	18
22.5	8	98	48
23.5	5	31	141
24.5	14	18	21
25.5	8	92	46
26.5	21	39	129
27.5	0		
28.5	0		
29.5	9		
30.5			

Age (days)	(N=2)	(N=5)	(N=9)
TEMPERATURE: 11°C			
22	0	5	13
24	0	7	44
26	0	7	4
28	0	7	0
30	8	11	88
32	0	25	80
34	0	0	0
36	0	20	0
38	10	11	140
40	0	21	52
42	0	0	16
44	0	21	0
46	11	12	156
48	0	20	41
50			0
52			0
54			182

APPENDIX B

Daphnia galeata mendotae, Base Line Lake, 1960-1961

Date	(1)[a] Stratum	(2) N_0	(3) N_A	(4) $\bar{E}$	(5) 1/D	(6) b	(7) r observed
8 July 1960	U	667	395	7.3	0.50	1.15	
	M	341	290	7.8	0.39	1.27	
	D	107	88	6.8	0.22	0.81	
(8) Weighted average		N_0^a:401		$\bar{E}$:7.4		b:1.15	0.20
14 July 1960	U	1492	146	3.0	0.50	0.14	
	M	2255	333	3.5	0.39	0.18	
	D	194	14	2.8	0.22	0.04	
	(8)	N_0:1313		$\bar{E}$:3.3		b:0.16	0.15
21 July 1960	U	497	95	4.6	0.50	0.37	
	M	750	571	4.7	0.39	0.87	
	D	94	76	4.0	0.22	0.54	
	(8)	N_0:447		$\bar{E}$:4.6		b:0.66	0.00
29 July 1960	U	778	52	0.5	0.50	0.02	
	M	722	459	3.9	0.39	0.67	
	D	77	31	3.1	0.22	0.25	
	(8)	N_0:450		$\bar{E}$:2.9		b:0.33	0.01
4 Aug. 1960	U	458	0	0	0.50	0.00	
	M	693	142	2.6	0.39	0.19	
	D	89	19	3.3	0.22	0.15	
	(8)	N_0:413		$\bar{E}$:2.7		b:0.12	0.13
11 Aug. 1960	U	245	5	2.0	0.50	0.02	
	M	217	35	3.8	0.39	0.21	
	D	39	16	2.3	0.22	0.19	
	(8)	N_0:167		$\bar{E}$:3.2		b:0.12	0.06
18 Aug. 1960	U	265	118	1.8	0.50	0.34	
	M	400	154	1.1	0.39	0.15	
	D	85	57	1.3	0.22	0.18	
	(8)	N_0:250		$\bar{E}$:1.4		b:0.22	0.06
26 Aug. 1960	(8)	N_0:103					0.01
18 Sept. 1960		128	17	1.4	0.39	0.07	
	(8)	N_0:91					0.03
24 Sept. 1960		143	45	0.5	0.39	0.06	
	(8)	N_0:106					0.10
8 Oct. 1960	U	827	283	2.3	0.22	0.16	
	M	322	162	2.2	0.22	0.22	
	D	155	49	1.3	0.17	0.07	
	(8)	N_0:434		$\bar{E}$:2.1		b:0.16	0.23
25 Oct. 1960		647	97	2.4	0.17	0.06	
	(8)	N_0:647					0.05
2 Nov. 1960		438	70	2.7	0.13	0.05	
	(8)	N_0:438					0.16
10 Nov. 1960		2337	304	3.4	0.09	0.04	
	(8)	N_0:2337					0.00
19 Nov. 1960	(8)	N_0:2348					0.01

Date	(1)[a] Stratum	(2) N_0	(3) N_A	(4) $\overline{E}$	(5) 1/D	(6) b	(7) r observed
3 Dec. 1960		2256	332	3.5	0.07	0.03	
	(8)	N_0:2256					0.03
1 Jan. 1961							
	(8)	N_0:941					0.05
28 Jan. 1961							
	(8)	N_0:264					0.01
15 Feb. 1961							
	(8)	N_0:222					0.08
4 Mar. 1961							
	(8)	N_0: 60					0.06
20 Mar. 1961		162	92	1.6	0.05	0.05	
	(8)	N_0:162					0.10
25 Mar. 1961		99	66	1.5	0.05	0.05	
	(8)	N_0: 99					0.03
8 Apr. 1961		152	58	5.7	0.05	0.11	
	(8)	N_0:148					0.02
19 Apr. 1961		180	31	7.1	0.07	0.08	
	(8)	N_0:180					0.04
1 May 1961		307	84	6.2	0.09	0.15	
	(8)	N_0:307					0.15
12 May 1961		1576	342	7.6	0.13	0.19	
	(8)	N_0:1576					0.10
19 May 1961		3225	744	3.4	0.13	0.10	
	(8)	N_0:3225					0.03

Date	(1)[a] Stratum	(2) N_0	(3) N_A	(4) F	(5) 1/D	(6) b	(7) r observed
30 May 1961	U&M	11597	1939	2.2	0.22	0.08	
	D	1728	242	2.0	0.09	0.03	
	(8)	N_0:4331				b:0.07	0.01
5 June 1961	U	9177	1379	0.9	0.39	0.05	
	M	2478	426	1.4	0.22	0.06	
	D	667	80	1.5	0.09	0.02	
	(8)	N_0:4124				b:0.05	0.10
21 June 1961	U	1664	306	2.0	0.39	0.13	
	M	776	213	1.8	0.22	0.10	
	D	198	44	1.5	0.09	0.03	
	(8)	N_0:854				b:0.11	0.05
28 June 1961	U	1204	511	2.3	0.39	0.32	
	M	524	237	2.4	0.22	0.22	
	D	170	77	2.7	0.09	0.11	
	(8)	N_0:607				b:0.27	0.03
5 July 1961	U	1275	562	4.8	0.50	0.72	
	M	229	106	3.4	0.22	0.30	
	D	150	46	3.9	0.13	0.14	
	(8)	N_0:510				b:0.61	
12 July 1961	U	709	166	2.1	0.50	.022	
	M	184	141	3.8	0.22	0.50	
	(8)	N_0:238				b:0.28	0.04
21 July 1961	U	831	81	2.5	0.50	0.12	
	M	114	45	2.5	0.22	0.20	
	D	129	59	3.8	0.13	0.20	
	(8)	N_0:268				b:0.13	

[a] (1) Upper, middle, and lower strata of lake; (2) total population size (total/100 liters); (3) total adults (adults/100 liters); (4) average brood size; (5) developmental rate of eggs which is the reciprocal of duration of egg development from Table II; (6) instantaneous birth rate $b = \ln(1+B)$; (7) observed instantaneous rate of population increase from equation (1); (8) weighted average of N_0, $\overline{E}$, and b for the entire water column.

Population Cycles in Small Rodents

Demographic and genetic events are closely coupled in fluctuating populations of field mice.

Charles J. Krebs, Michael S. Gaines, Barry L. Keller, Judith H. Myers, Robert H. Tamarin

Outbreaks of small rodents were recorded in the Old Testament, in Aristotle's writings, and in the pages of European history. Charles Elton (1) summarized the colorful history of rodent plagues, and described the general sequence of outbreaks, from rapid multiplication to the destruction of crops and pastures, and the decline of the plague into scarcity. This cycle of abundance and scarcity is a continuing rhythm in many small rodents, although not all high populations reach plague proportions. The population cycles of small rodents have always been a classic · problem in population ecology, and speculation on the possible causes of rodent outbreaks has long outstripped the available scientific data. Both for practical reasons and because of our innate curiosity we would like to understand the mechanisms behind the rise and fall of these rodent populations.

Population cycles present an ideal situation in which to study population regulation. One question that has occupied biologists since the time of Malthus and Darwin has been this: What stops population increase? Cyclic populations, which follow a four-step pattern of increase–peak–decline–low, are thus useful in presenting a sequence of contrasting phases and then repeating the phases again and again. In small rodents the period of this cycle

Dr. Krebs is at the University of British Columbia, Vancouver 8; Dr. Gaines is at the University of Kansas; Dr. Keller is at Idaho State University; Dr. Myers is at the University of British Columbia; and Dr. Tamarin is at Boston University.

(2) is usually 3 to 4 years, although 2-year and 5-year cycles sometimes occur.

Since Charles Elton first kindled interest in population cycles in 1924 (3), a great amount of effort has been expended in trying to describe and to explain these fluctuations. Two general facts have emerged from this work. First, many species of microtine rodents (lemmings and voles) in many different genera fluctuate in numbers. These species have not all been studied for long time-periods, but it is striking that in no instance has a population been studied in detail and found to be stable in numbers from year to year. Second, these cycles are found in a variety of ecological communities: lemmings on the tundras of North America and Eurasia, red-backed voles in the boreal forests of North America and Scandinavia, meadow voles in New York, field voles in coastal California, New Mexico, Indiana, Britain, Germany, and France. The list grows long and includes rodents from north temperate to arctic areas. No cyclic fluctuations have been described for tropical rodents or for South American species, but almost no population studies have been done on these species.

The phenomenon of population cycles is widespread but there is disagreement about whether we should seek a single explanation for the variety of situations in which it occurs. We adopt here the simplest hypothesis, that a single mechanism underlies all rodent cycles, from lemming cycles in Alaska to field vole cycles in southern Indiana. The only empirical justification we can give for this approach is that demographic events are similar in a variety of species living in different climates and in different plant communities; but the expectation of a single explanation for rodent cycles is only an article of faith.

There are two opposing schools of thought about what stops population increase in small rodents. One school looks to extrinsic agents such as food supply, predators, or disease to stop populations from increasing. The other looks to intrinsic effects, the effects of one individual upon another. We have abandoned a search for extrinsic agents of control for reasons discussed elsewhere (4, 5). This is not to say that extrinsic factors such as weather and food are not influencing microtine populations to varying degrees, but we believe that more important than the variable effects of extrinsic factors are the intrinsic factors which act in a common way in cycling rodents. We have turned our attention toward intrinsic effects, particularly those of behavior and genetics hypothesized by Chitty (6). Two essential elements of Chitty's hypothesis are (i) that the genetic composition of the population changes markedly during a cycle in numbers; and (ii) that spacing behavior (or hostility) is the variable which drives the demographic machinery through a cycle.

The suggestion that genetical mechanisms might be involved in the short-term changes in rodent populations has opened a new area of investigation. Population ecologists have traditionally been concerned with quantity rather than quality, and have only recently begun to realize the importance of individual variation (7). The genetical basis of the control of population size was discussed as early as 1931 by Ford (8) but most geneticists have assumed that population control is an ecological problem and not a genetic one. Lerner (9) attempted to bridge the gap between genetics and ecology by showing how the solution of ecological problems might be helped by genetical insights. Although population genetics and population ecology have developed as separate disciplines, we have tried to utilize both these disciplines in our attempts to determine the causes of population cycles in rodents.

From 1965 to 1970 we studied the relationships among population dynamics, aggressive behavior, and genetic composition of field vole populations in southern Indiana. The two species of

Microtus (*M. pennsylvanicus* and *M. ochrogaster*) that we studied fluctuate strongly in numbers with peak densities recurring at intervals of 2 or 3 years (*10*). The purposes of our investigations were to (i) describe the mechanics of the fluctuations in population size, (ii) monitor genetic changes with polymorphic marker loci, and (iii) measure changes in male aggressive behavior during a population fluctuation. We here synthesize our findings on the demography and genetic composition of *Microtus* populations, and summarize the results of our behavioral studies that have been reported elsewhere (*11*).

Demographic Changes

In *M. pennsylvanicus* changes in population size can be grouped into three phases, each of which lasts several months or more: an increase phase in which the rate of population increase (r) is greater than 0.03 per week (maximum observed, 0.13 per week); a peak phase in which the rate of increase is zero (between −0.02 and +0.03 per week) and density is high and essentially constant; and a decline phase in which r is negative (−0.03 per week or less; maximum observed, −0.12 per week). Figure 1 illustrates these phases for one population of *M. pennsylvanicus*.

Detailed information on changes in population size is available for several species of voles (*4, 5, 10, 12*). The increase phase is typically the most con-

stant phase of the cycle, and once begun may continue through the winter, as shown in Fig. 1. The peak phase often begins with a spring decline in numbers, and a summer or fall increase restores the population to its former level. The

Table 1. Components of population fluctuations in *M. pennsylvanicus* in southern Indiana, 1965 to 1970. The data are expressed as mean values for more than 2000 individuals from four populations. The survival of early juvenile animals is determined from the number of unmarked young per lactating female; survival of subadults and adults is measured as a probability of survival per 14 days.

Phase	Birth rate (% lactating females)	Early juveniles	Subadult and adult	
			Males	Females
Increase	45	1.31	0.78	0.86
Peak	29	0.96	0.79	0.85
Decline	27	0.88	0.71	0.72

decline phase is most variable. It may begin in the fall of the peak year or be delayed until the next spring. The decline may be very rapid, so that most of the population disappears over 1 to 2 months, but often the decline is gradual and prolonged over a year or more. A phase of low numbers may or may not follow the decline, and little is known of this period, which may last a year or longer.

Changes in birth and death rates are the immediate cause of the population fluctuations in *M. pennsylvanicus* in Indiana. Table 1 shows that the birth rate,

measured by the percentage of adult females captured that are visibly lactating, is reduced both in the peak phase and in the decline phase. The principal reason for this is that the breeding season is shortened in the peak and decline phases. Changes in weight at sexual maturity also contribute to a reduced birth rate in peak populations (*13*).

The death rate of small juvenile animals seems to increase dramatically in the peak and declining populations of *M. pennsylvanicus*. By contrast, the death rate of subadult and adult animals is not increased in peak populations but is increased in declining populations (*14*). Thus, in a peak population, if an animal is able to survive through the early juvenile stage, it has a high survival rate as an adult. Declining populations suffer from a low birth rate and a high mortality rate of both juveniles and adults (*14*).

What is the nature of the mortality factor acting during the population decline? The older animals seem to bear the brunt of the increased mortality during the population decline. Also, periods of high mortality during the decline are not always synchronous in males and females (see Fig. 2). Therefore, the mortality factors that are affecting the age groups and sexes during the population decline can be very selective, which argues against the overwhelming influence of extrinsic agents such as predation and disease.

These changes in birth and death rates are not unique to *M. pennsylvanicus*. Birth rates are higher in the phase of increase for all vole and lemming populations that have been studied (*5, 12, 13, 15*). The most common method of increasing the reproductive rate is by extending the breeding season, which may continue through the winter in both lemmings and voles. Extended breeding seasons are also accompanied by lowered ages at sexual maturity in some species. These trends are reversed in peak and declining populations, and the breeding season may be particularly short in some peak populations. Litter sizes seem to be essentially the same during the increase phase and the decline phase.

Death rate measurements are available for relatively few small rodent populations (*4, 5, 10, 16*). Juvenile losses are often high in peak populations and especially high in declining populations. Adult death rates are not unusually high in dense populations, but may be very high during the decline phase. The demographic changes which cause these rodent populations to fluctuate are thus a syndrome of reproduc-

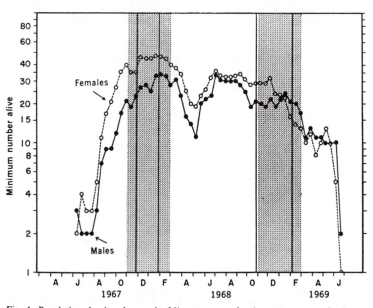

Fig. 1. Population density changes in *Microtus pennsylvanicus* on one grassland area in southern Indiana. Winter months are shaded. Vertical lines separate "summer" breeding period from "winter" period. An increase phase occurred from June to October 1967, and a decline phase from November 1968 to June 1969. [By permission of the Society for the Study of Evolution]

95

Fig. 2. Detailed breakdown of a population decline in *M. pennsylvanicus* during the spring of 1969. The critical observation is the difference in timing of male losses (highest in early March) and female losses (highest in mid-April). This timing is reflected in the gene frequency changes shown on the lowest graph (*r* is the instantaneous rate of population increase).

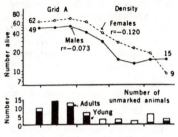

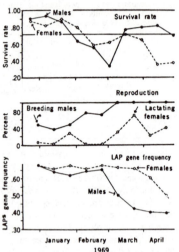

tive shifts and mortality changes. Reproduction and early juvenile survival seem to deteriorate first, and only later is adult survival impaired. This syndrome of changes is common to situations as diverse as lemmings in northern Canada, voles in England, and field voles in Indiana.

Growth rates of individual animals are also affected by the population fluctuations. Both males and females in increasing populations grow more rapidly than individuals in peak populations, who in turn grow more rapidly than individuals in declining populations. Figure 3 illustrates this change in growth for *M. pennsylvanicus* from southern Indiana. The higher growth rates of individuals in increasing populations, coupled with higher survival rates, produce animals of larger than average body size in increasing and peak populations (10). These large animals are characteristic of all peak populations of small rodents.

Fencing Experiments

The first hint we obtained about how the demographic changes are brought about in field populations came from an experiment designed to answer the question: Does fencing a population of *Microtus* effect its dynamics? We constructed three mouse-proof enclosures in the field, each measuring 2 acres (0.8 hectare), and used these to study populations constrained by the fence, which allowed no immigration or emigration of *Microtus*. Figure 4 shows population changes on two adjacent fields, one of which was fenced in July 1965. Both populations increased in size but diverged sharply in the early peak phase. The fenced population (grid B) continued to increase in the summer of 1966 to 310 animals on the 2-acre plot, a density about three times as high as that on control grid A. The overpopulation of the fenced *M. pennsylvanicus* on grid B resulted in habitat destruction and overgrazing, and led to a sharp decline with symptoms of starvation. The result was

the same with enclosed populations of *M. ochrogaster* (10), and during the course of our studies four introductions of *M. ochrogaster* to the fenced areas resulted in abnormally high densities. Thus we conclude that fencing a *Microtus* population destroys the regulatory machinery which normally prevents overgrazing and starvation.

Dispersal (immigration and emigration) is the obvious process which is

prevented by a fence, and we suggested that dispersal is necessary for normal population regulation in *Microtus*. We could see no indication that predation pressure was changed by the small fence around the large areas we studied. Foxes, cats, weasels, and snakes were known to have entered the fenced areas, and hawks and owls were not deterred.

Dispersal Experiments

If dispersal is important for population regulation, how might it operate? We could envisage two possible ways. First, dispersal might be related to population density, so that more animals would emigrate from an area in the peak phase and especially in the decline phase. These emigrants we would presume to be at a great disadvantage from environmental hazards such as other voles, predators, and bad weather. Second, the number of dispersers might not be as important as the quality of the dispersers. If only animals of a certain genetic type are able to tolerate high densities, dispersal may be one mechanism for sorting out these individuals.

We measured dispersal by maintaining two areas free of *Microtus* by trapping and removing all animals caught for 2 days every second week. Voles were free to colonize the areas for 12 days between each episode of trapping. We defined dispersers as those animals colonizing these vacant habitats (17). We thus determined the loss rate of individuals from control populations and the number of colonizers entering the trapped areas, and could calculate the

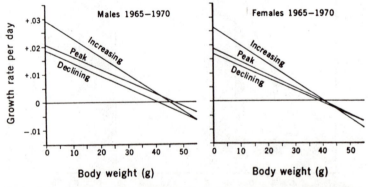

Fig. 3. Instantaneous relative growth rates for *M. pennsylvanicus* in southern Indiana. Regression lines for increase, peak, and decline phases are based on 691, 1898, and 333 observations for males and 776, 1696, and 322 observations for females (all pregnant animals excluded). Slope and elevation of the three regression lines are significantly different (*P* < .01) in both sexes.

fraction, in control populations, of losses attributable to dispersal.

Dispersal was most common in the increase phase of a population fluctuation and least common in the decline phase (Fig. 5). Most of the loss rate in increasing populations seems to be due to emigration (Table 2). Conversely, little of the heavy loss in declining populations is due to animals dispersing into adjacent areas, and hence most losses must be deaths in situ.

Thus dispersal losses from *Microtus* populations were not heaviest during the peak and decline, which supports the view that the role of dispersal is related to the quality of dispersing animals. We present evidence of genetic differences in dispersing *Microtus* in the next section.

Genetic Changes

Polymorphic serum proteins have been used as genetic markers to study the possible role of natural selection in population fluctuations of *Microtus*. We have used the genes *Tf* (transferrin) and *LAP* (leucine aminopeptidase) as markers (18, 19). The electrophoretically distinguishable forms of the products of these genes are inherited as if controlled by alleles of single autosomal loci.

We have found evidence of large changes in gene frequency at these two loci in association with population changes. Some of these changes are

Table 2. Percentage of losses known to be due to dispersal for control populations of *M. pennsylvanicus* in southern Indiana. Total numbers lost are shown in parentheses.

Population phase	Males (%)	Females (%)
Increase	56(32)	69(16)
Peak	33(157)	25(127)
Decline	15(53)	12(42)

repetitive and have been observed in several populations (18, 19). Figure 2 shows the details of one decline in *M. pennsylvanicus* in the late winter and early spring of 1969. The survival rate of males during this decline dropped to a minimum in early March; female survival dropped 6 weeks later. These periods of poor survival coincided with the onset of sexual maturity in many of the adult males and the approximate dates of weaning first litters in adult females. The frequency of the *LAP^s* allele (distinguished by slow electrophoretic mobility) dropped about 25 percent in the males beginning at the time of high losses, and 4 to 6 weeks later declined an equal amount in the females. This type of observation supports strongly the hypothesis that demographic events in *Microtus* are genetically selective and that losses are not distributed equally over all genotypes. Because we may be studying linkage effects and because we do not know how selection is acting, we cannot describe the mechanisms which would explain the associations shown in Fig. 2. We

cannot therefore assign cause and effect to the observations.

We have also used the *Tf* and *LAP* variation to investigate possible qualitative differences between dispersing *Microtus* and resident animals. Since dispersal is particularly important in the increase phase (Fig. 5, Table 2), we looked for qualitative differences at this time. Figure 6 shows the genotypic frequencies at the locus of the *Tf* gene for control populations and dispersing animals during an increase phase. Heterozygous females (*Tf^C/Tf^E*, where *C* and *E* are alleles of the *Tf* gene) are much more common in dispersing *Microtus* than in resident populations and 89 percent of the loss of heterozygous females from the control populations during the population increase was due to dispersal. Certain genotypes thus show a tendency to disperse, a possibility suggested by several authors (20) but not previously demonstrated in natural populations.

The polymorphic genes that we have used for markers in *M. pennsylvanicus* and *M. ochrogaster* are subject to intensive selection pressure, but we have not been able to determine how these polymorphisms are maintained. For example, let us consider the *Tf* polymorphism in *M. ochrogaster*. Two alleles are found in Indiana populations. The common allele *Tf^E* has a frequency of 97 percent in female and 93 percent in male *M. ochrogaster*. This polymorphism does not seem to be maintained by heterosis. We have not found any component of fitness (survival, reproduction, or growth) in which heterozygote voles (*Tf^E/Tf^F*) are superior to homozygote voles (*Tf^E/Tf^E*), except in declining and low populations when the male heterozygotes survive better than the homozygotes. Increasing populations are always associated with strong selection for the *Tf^E* allele (18, 19). Homozygote *Tf^F/Tf^F* females had higher prenatal mortality in field experiments (21). We do not know if this *Tf* polymorphism is maintained by density-related changes in fitness or by frequency-dependent variations in fitness (22).

An alternative explanation for the associations we have described between population density changes and gene frequency changes has been provided by Charlesworth and Giesel (23). Population fluctuations result in continual shifts in age structure. Genotypes with differing ages at sexual maturity and differing survival rates will thus change in frequency as a result of population fluctuations, and genetic changes could

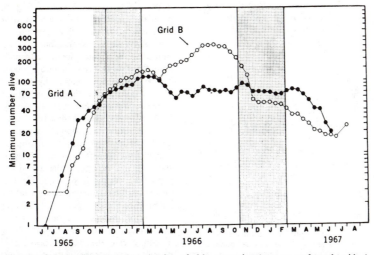

Fig. 4. Changes in population density of *M. pennsylvanicus* on unfenced grid A (control) and fenced grid B. Both are 2-acre (0.8-hectare) grassland fields. Grid B is surrounded by a mouse-proof fence extending 2 feet (0.6 meter) into the soil and projecting 2 feet above the ground. Signs of severe overgrazing were common on grid B by August 1966. [By permission of the Ecological Society of America]

97

Fig. 5. Rate of population change in *M. pennsylvanicus* control population from southern Indiana in relation to dispersal rate from that population, 1968 to 1970. Rate of population change is the instantaneous rate of change per week, averaged over "summer" and "winter" periods shown in Fig. 1. Dispersal rate is the mean number of voles dispersing from the control population to the trapped grid per 2 weeks, averaged over the same time periods. Populations increasing rapidly show the highest dispersal rates.

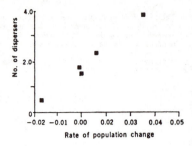

thus be the side effect of population cycles caused by any mechanism. We do not know whether the genetic changes we have described are causally related to population changes or merely side effects, but we question whether they are adequately explained by the Charlesworth and Giesel model. The size of the changes in gene frequency we observed (for example, Fig. 2) is several times larger than the size of the changes obtained in the Charlesworth and Giesel model (1 to 9 percent). Also, Charlesworth and Giesel obtained relatively little effect on gene frequencies by changing death rates in their model; we have found that changes in death rates of different genotypes are a major component of shifts in gene frequency (*11, 19*). We suggest that field perturbation experiments may help to resolve these alternative explanations (*24*).

Behavioral Changes

If behavioral interactions among individual voles are the primary mechanism behind population cycles, the behavioral characteristics of individuals would change over the cycle. We have tested this hypothesis only for male *M. pennsylvanicus* and *M. ochrogaster* in our Indiana populations. Males were tested by paired round-robin encounters in a neutral arena in the laboratory. Males of both species showed significant changes in aggressive behavior during the population cycle, so that individuals in peak populations were most aggressive (*11*). Male *M. pennsylvanicus* which dispersed during periods of peak population density tended to be even more aggressive than the residents on control areas (*17*).

Laboratory measurements of behavior can be criticized because we have no way of knowing how such measures might apply to the field situation. There is no doubt that aggression does go on in field populations of voles and lemmings because skin wounds are found,

particularly in males (*5, 25*). Field experiments could be designed to test the effects of aggression on mortality and growth rates, but none has been done yet on lemmings or voles. In the deer mouse (*Peromyscus maniculatus*) field experiments have demonstrated that aggressive adult mice can prevent the recruitment of juveniles into the population (*26*).

Conclusions

We conclude that population fluctuations in *Microtus* in southern Indiana are produced by a syndrome of changes in birth and death rates similar to that found in other species of voles and lemmings. The mechanisms which cause the changes in birth and death rates are demolished by fencing the population so that no dispersal can occur. Dispersal thus seems critical for population regulation in *Microtus*. Because most dispersal occurs during the increase phase of the population cycle and there is little dispersal during the decline phase, dispersal is not directly related to population density. Hence the quality of dispersing animals must be important, and

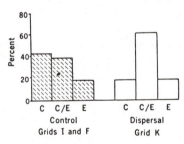

Fig. 6. The increase phase of *M. pennsylvanicus*, fall 1969. Transferrin genotype frequencies of dispersing females on trapped grid K (*N = 39*) compared with those of resident females on control grids immediately adjacent in the same grassland (*N = 224*). Dispersing voles in the increase phase are not a random sample from the control population. C, CIE, and E represent the three transferrin genotypes.

we have found one case of increased dispersal tendency by one genotype.

The failure of population regulation of *Microtus* in enclosed areas requires an explanation by any hypothesis attempting to explain population cycles in small rodents. It might be suggested that the fence changed the predation pressure on the enclosed populations. However, the fence was only 2 feet (0.6 meter) high and did not stop the entrance of foxes, weasels, shrews, or avian predators. A striking feature was that the habitat in the enclosures quickly recovered from complete devastation by the start of the spring growing season. Obviously the habitat and food quality were sufficient to support *Microtus* populations of abnormally high densities, and recovery of the habitat was sufficiently quick that the introduction of new animals to these enclosed areas resulted in another population explosion. Finally, hypotheses of population regulation by social stress must account for the finding that *Microtus* can exist at densities several times greater than normal without "stress" taking an obvious toll.

We hypothesize that the prevention of dispersal changes the quality of the populations in the enclosures in comparison to those outside the fence. Voles forced to remain in an overcrowded fenced population do not suffer high mortality rates and continue to reproduce at abnormally high densities until starvation overtakes them. The initial behavioral interactions associated with crowding do not seem sufficient to cause voles to die in situ.

What happens to animals during the population decline? Our studies have not answered this question. The animals did not appear to disperse, but it is possible that the method we used to measure dispersal (movement into a vacant habitat) missed a large segment of dispersing voles which did not remain in the vacant area but kept on moving. Perhaps the dispersal during the increase phase of the population cycle is a colonization type of dispersal, and the animals taking part in it are likely to stay in a new habitat, while during the population decline dispersal is a pathological response to high density, and the animals are not attracted to settling even in a vacant habitat. The alternative to this suggestion is that animals are dying in situ during the decline because of physiological or genetically determined behavioral stress.

Thus the fencing of a population prevents the change in rates of survival and reproduction, from high rates in the increase phase to low rates in the decline phase, and the fenced populations resemble "mouse plagues." A possible explanation is that the differential dispersal of animals during the phase of increase causes the quality of the voles remaining at peak densities in wild populations to be different from the quality of voles at much higher densities in enclosures. Increased sensitivity to density in *Microtus* could cause the decline of wild populations at densities lower than those reached by fenced populations in which selection through dispersal has been prevented. Fencing might also alter the social interactions among *Microtus* in other ways that are not understood.

The analysis of colonizing species by MacArthur and Wilson (27) can be applied to our studies of dispersal in populations of *Microtus*. Groups of organisms with good dispersal and colonizing ability are called *r* strategists because they have high reproductive potential and are able to exploit a new environment rapidly. Dispersing voles seem to be *r* strategists. Young females in breeding condition were over-represented in dispersing female *Microtus* (17). The Tf^C/Tf^E females, which were more common among dispersers during the phase of population increase (Fig. 6), also have a slight reproductive advantage over the other *Tf* genotypes (19). Thus in *Microtus* populations the animals with the highest reproductive potential, the *r* strategists, are dispersing. The segment of the population which

remains behind after the selection-via-dispersal are those individuals which are less influenced by increasing population densities. These are the individuals which maximize use of the habitat, the *K* strategists in MacArthur and Wilson's terminology, or voles selected for spacing behavior. Thus we can describe the population cycles in *Microtus* in the same theoretical framework as colonizing species on islands.

Our work on *Microtus* is consistent with the hypothesis of genetic and behavioral effects proposed by Chitty (6) (Fig. 7) in that it shows both behavioral differences in males during the phases of population fluctuation and periods of strong genetic selection. The greatest gaps in our knowledge are in the area of genetic-behavioral interactions which are most difficult to measure. We have no information on the heritability of aggressive behavior in voles. The pathways by which behavioral events are translated into physiological changes which affect reproduction and growth have been carefully analyzed by Christian and his associates (28) for rodents in laboratory situations, but the application of these findings to the complex field events described above remains to be done.

Several experiments are suggested by our work. First, other populations of other rodent species should increase to abnormal densities if enclosed in a large fenced area (29). We need to find situations in which this prediction is not fulfilled. Island populations may be an important source of material for such

an experiment (30). Second, if one-way exit doors were provided from a fenced area, normal population regulation through dispersal should occur. This experiment would provide another method by which dispersers could be identified. Third, if dispersal were prevented after a population reached peak densities, a normal decline phase should occur. This prediction is based on the assumption that dispersal during the increase phase is sufficient to ensure the decline phase 1 or 2 years later. All these experiments are concerned with the dispersal factor, and our work on *Microtus* can be summarized by the admonition: study dispersal.

References and Notes

1. C. Elton, *Voles, Mice and Lemmings: Problems in Population Dynamics* (Clarendon Press, Oxford, 1942).
2. The term "cycle" is used here as a convenient shorthand for the more technically correct term "periodic fluctuation." We do not mean to imply a physicist's meaning of the word "cycle" because both the amplitude and the period of population fluctuations in small rodents are variable.
3. C. S. Elton, *Brit. J. Exp. Biol.* **2**, 119 (1924).
4. D. Chitty, *Phil. Trans. Roy. Soc. London Ser. B* **236**, 505 (1952); *Can. J. Zool.* **38**, 99 (1960).
5. C. J. Krebs, *Arctic Inst. N. Amer. Tech. Pap. No. 15* (1964).
6. D. Chitty, *Proc. Ecol. Soc. Aust.* **2**, 51 (1967).
7. L. C. Birch, *Amer. Natur.* **94**, 5 (1960); W. G. Wellington, *Can. J. Zool.* **35**, 293 (1957); *Can. Entomol.* **96**, 436 (1964).
8. E. B. Ford, *Mendelism and Evolution* (Methuen, London, 1931).
9. I. M. Lerner, *Proc. Int. Congr. Genet. 11th* **2**, 489 (1965).
10. C. J. Krebs, B. L. Keller, R. H. Tamarin, *Ecology* **50**, 587 (1969).
11. C. J. Krebs, *ibid.* **51**, 34 (1970); *Proceedings of the NATO Advanced Study Institute, Oosterbeek, 1970,* P. J. den Boer and G. R. Gradwell, Eds. (Center for Agricultural Publishing and Documentation, Wageningen, Netherlands, 1971), pp. 243–256.
12. D. Chitty and H. Chitty, in *Symposium Theriologicum, Brno, 1960,* J. Kratochvíl and J. Pelikán, Eds. (Czechoslovak Academy of Sciences, Prague, 1962), pp. 67–76; F. B. Golley, *Amer. Midland Natur.* **66**, 152 (1961); O. Kalela, *Ann. Acad. Sci. Fenn. Ser. A 4,* 34 (1957); C. J. Krebs, *Ecol. Monogr.* **36**, 239 (1966); E. P. Martin, *Univ. Kans. Publ. Mus. Natur. Hist.* **8**, 361 (1956); J. Zejda, *Zool. Listy* **13**, 15 (1964); G. O. Batzli and F. Pitelka, *J. Mammalogy* **52**, 141 (1971).
13. B. L. Keller and C. J. Krebs, *Ecol. Monogr.* **40**, 263 (1970).
14. We describe here our findings on *M. pennsylvanicus*. We have similar results for *M. ochrogaster* in Indiana, but we do not present these data here because they provide essentially the same conclusions.
15. G. S. Greenwald, *Univ. Calif. Publ. Zool.* **54**, 421 (1957); W. J. Hamilton, Jr., *Cornell Univ. Agric. Exp. Stat. Mem.* **237** (1941); T. V. Koshkina, *Bull. Moscow Soc. Nat. Biol. Sect.* **71**, 14 (1966); G. O. Batzli and F. A. Pitelka, *J. Mammal.* **52**, 141 (1971).
16. D. Chitty and E. Phipps, *J. Anim. Ecol.* **35**, 313 (1966); G. O. Batzli, thesis, Univ. of California, Berkeley (1969).
17. J. H. Myers and C. J. Krebs, *Ecol. Monogr.* **41**, 53 (1971).
18. R. H. Tamarin and C. J. Krebs, *Evolution* **23**, 183 (1969).
19. M. S. Gaines and C. J. Krebs, *ibid.* **25**, 702 (1971).
20. W. E. Howard, *Amer. Midland Natur.* **63**, 152 (1960); W. Z. Lidicker, *Amer. Natur.* **96**, 29 (1962).
21. M. S. Gaines, J. H. Myers, C. J. Krebs, *Evolution* **25**, 443 (1971).

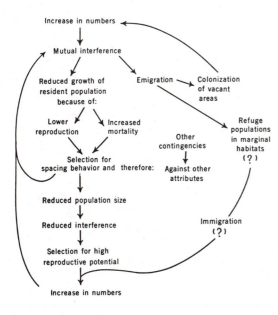

Fig. 7. Modified version of Chitty's hypothesis to explain population fluctuations in small rodents. Density-related changes in natural selection are central to this hypothesis. Our data indicate that selection through dispersal is more important than originally proposed by Chitty.

22. Density-related changes in fitness might be mediated by dispersal. The very rare Tf^p/Tf^p homozygote in *M. ochrogaster* occurred more frequently among dispersing males than in resident populations (*17*).
23. B. Charlesworth and J. T. Giesel, *Amer. Natur.* **106**, 388 (1972).
24. R. P. Canham and D. G. Cameron (personal communication) have obtained evidence for selection against certain *Tf* genotypes in declining populations of *Clethrionomys* and *Peromyscus* which have discrete annual generations in northern Canada. The Charlesworth and Giesel model (*23*) can apply only to species with overlapping generations.
25. J. J. Christian, *J. Mammal.* **52**, 556 (1971).
26. R. M. F. S. Sadleir, *J. Anim. Ecol.* **34**, 331 (1965); M. C. Healey, *Ecology* **48**, 337 (1967).
27. R. H. MacArthur and E. O. Wilson, *The Theory of Island Biogeography* (Princeton Univ. Press, Princeton, N.J., 1967).
28. J. J. Christian, *Biol. Reprod.* **4**, 248 (1971); J. J. Christian, J. A. Lloyd, D. E. Davis, *Recent Progr. Hormone Res.* **21**, 501 (1965); J. J. Christian, *Proc. Nat. Acad. Sci. U.S.A.* **47**, 428 (1961).
29. J. R. Clarke, *Proc. Roy. Soc. London Ser. B* **144**, 68 (1955); P. Crowcroft and F. P. Rowe, *Proc. Zool. Soc. London* **129**, 359 (1957); J. B. Gentry, *Res. Population Ecol.* **10**, 21 (1968); W. Z. Lidicker, *ibid.* **7**, 57 (1965); K. Petrusewicz, *Ekol. Pol. Ser. A* **5**, 281 (1957); R. L. Steecker and J. T. Emlen, *Ecology* **34**, 375 (1953).
30. The population of *M. californicus* on Brooks Island in San Francisco Bay may be acting in the same way as a fenced population, maintaining densities higher than mainland populations (W. Z. Lidicker, personal communication).
31. This research was conducted when all of us were at Indiana University. We thank the National Science Foundation and the Public Health Service for financial support of the research.

The Population Biology of Dandelions

These common weeds provide experimental evidence for a new model to explain the distribution of plants

Otto T. Solbrig

The common garden dandelion (*Taraxacum officinale* L. *sensu latu*) is one of the best known and perhaps also one of the most disliked plants. Its propensity to grow in lawns and its great tenacity make the plant particularly odious to the suburbanite who likes to manicure his lawn on weekends.

Dr. Otto T. Solbrig has been interested in the patterns of variability of plants since his undergraduate days when he initiated studies on the population biology of the wild relatives of the cultivated verbenas. A native of Argentina, he did his undergraduate work there and received his Ph.D. from the University of California at Berkeley. From 1960 to 1966 he was an associate curator at the Gray Herbarium of Harvard University; from 1966 to 1969 he was associate professor and then professor of botany at the University of Michigan in Ann Arbor. Since 1969, he has been professor of biology at Harvard University. He is the author of three books, Evolution and Systematics, Plant Biosystematics, *and* Biosystematic Literature *(the last in collaboration with T. W. J. Gadella), and more than 70 articles. In 1963 he was awarded the Cooley Prize by the American Society of Plant Taxonomists. The author gratefully acknowledges the help of Dr. Beryl Vuilleumier in the conduct of the Cambridge experiments discussed in this paper. Address: Gray Herbarium, Harvard University, 22 Divinity Avenue, Cambridge, MA 02138.*

The dandelion is not an object of dislike everywhere; it was probably brought to this country by the early settlers, not inadvertently as in the case of other weeds, but on purpose as a garden plant. There are indications that seeds of dandelions were carried by the *Mayflower* pilgrims. Even today its leaves are used as salad greens and are greatly appreciated by a diminishing number of enthusiasts. Since the dandelion is a relative of the lettuce (genus *Lactuca*), this is not surprising. Another use of the plant is in the preparation of "dandelion wine," in whose manufacture the flowers are used to impart a bright yellow color to the finished product. Finally, it should be mentioned that dandelions were used in the past as medicinal plants.

Other characteristics of this plant make it an interesting experimental organism for the population biologist. Primary among them are its short life cycle, its relatively small size, its asexual reproduction, and its tremendous plasticity—but above all, its ubiquitousness and its capacity to adapt to so many different ecological situations, many of them man-

Reproduced with permission from *American Scientist*, 59:686–694, 1971.

Figure 1. Dandelion plant grown without competition or disturbance.

made. The combination of these characteristics makes the dandelion almost ideal material to test adaptation and competition of plant species under different environmental conditions.

Structure and ontogeny

Dandelions are rosette-leaved plants with one central tap root. The seed germinates forming a primary root and two specialized first leaves called cotyledons. The first true leaf grows close to the insertion of the cotyledons, due to the fact that the internode (what the layman would call the shoot) separating the insertion of the leaf from the cotyledons is extremely short (less than 1 mm). All following leaves are formed in the same way, on extremely short internodes. If the insertion of the leaves on this short shoot is noted, it will be seen that they form a spiral, and thus do not exactly overlap (only every sixth leaf will overlap). Although the shoot does not grow in length, it increases in width, particularly at its base where it can be up to 3 cm wide. The result is that a flat cone is produced on which the leaves are spirally arranged with the largest on the outside (Fig. 1).

This arrangement leads under undisturbed conditions to the formation of a flattened upside-down bowl, known by the botanist as a globose rosette. Note that I said under undisturbed conditions. In the more normal disturbed conditions of lawns and abandoned fields, where the plants are subjected to trampling, the leaves flatten to the ground and form the more familiar flat rosette (Fig. 2). The arrangement of the leaves on the stem is not affected by the flattening of the leaves.

The development of the root is equally simple. Soon after germination the primary root becomes dominant and as more leaves are added it increases in size, keeping pace with the shoot. Eventually a large (30 cm or more in length, up to 3 cm in width) root is formed that serves as a storage organ similar to a carrot. It is not palatable, however, due to the existence of lactiferous tubes (the so-called "milk"). The white, viscous liquid that fills these tubes contains a suspension of various substances, including rubber. The rubber content of the latex is high enough in a close relative of the common dandelion, *Taraxacum koksaghiz*, a native of central Asia, to permit its use, with mixed success, as a source of commercial rubber, particularly by the Russians, and also by this country during World War II.

If the root gets injured or broken near its upper portion, an undifferentiated tissue called a callus tissue is formed to plug the wound. Following this step, one or more buds are formed on the tissue from which new leaves or an entire new plant then grows. For example, when a dandelion plant is plucked by tugging at its leaves, the usual result is that the upper third of the root breaks off. The part that remains in the ground grows a callus tissue to close the wound, and eventually two to five new plants arise from this callus tissue! Grazing animals and natural accidents that destroy the aerial portions of the plant accomplish the same effect. If one observes lawns and fields where dandelions grow, one can often observe them growing in rings. In such cases, it is probable that at one time there was a single plant in the center of the ring; on the loss of its aerial rosette, the remaining root produced a series of new plants.

Reproductive biology

In the spring and fall, mature dandelion plants form the colorful, attractive flowers well known to everybody. The process, however, is more involved than a casual glance at the lawn reveals. The dandelion is a short-day plant; that is, it does not bloom whenever there are more than twelve hours of light (or less than twelve hours of night). This applies to the majority of the plants of a population. A few occasional plants can be seen blooming in the long summer days of July.

The first sign that a plant is about to start blooming is the formation of a bud in the middle of the rosette. Yet the process leading to blooming has started much earlier, after the plant has formed its first six leaves. At that point the plant starts storing its excess energy in the tap root, which commences to enlarge. Once enough storage materials have accumulated in the root, the plant is ready to bloom whenever the right light conditions are present.

The actual process of blooming is

Figure 2. Dandelion plant grown in a lawn under disturbed conditions. Note the difference with Figure 1.

very rapid. The development of the bud, which takes place in the center of the rosette, takes approximately a week. After that, a special leafless shoot called the scape starts forming between the base of the bud and the tip of the shoot. As the scape enlarges the bud is thrust upwards and it opens and blooms. The entire process of scape formation usually takes only about 48 hours. The flower remains open one day on the average, and then it closes again. In most dandelions, following blooming, the scape and the flower flatten to the ground. After a couple of days, the scape straightens itself again, and the involucral leaves surrounding the closed flower

open revealing a round white ball of seeds, each with a "parachute" of hairs—the so-called pappus, which is a modification of the calyx and aids in the dispersion of the seeds.

Apomixis. Most flowering plants reproduce by the usual sexual process. Pollen grains are transported to the stigma of the flower by insects or wind (or other agents such as water in a few cases). The pollen grain then produces a simple tube which grows down the style and into the opening of the ovule. It then discharges two sperm cells; one fertilizes the egg cell to give rise to the zygote, the first cell of the new embryo. The other

Figure 3. View of the site of Population 1 at the Mathei Botanical Gardens in Ann Arbor, Michigan.

sperm cell fuses with two (in 70 percent of the cases, one to six in the other 30 percent of the cases) cells called "polar cells." The ensuing tissue, which is triploid, is the endosperm. It is a storage tissue which is eventually digested by the growing embryo.

In dandelions and some other plants, the embryo develops without the aid of fertilization. The early stages of ovule formation are normal and so is the first half of the meiotic cell division, the division that produces the egg cell by dividing the number of chromosomes in the cell in half. However, the process is interrupted soon after its inception, and a "restitution nucleus" is formed. This nucleus has the normal 24 chromosomes of a dandelion plant, and it continues to develop into an embryo and a seed without recourse to fertilization. Because the dandelion is a triploid (three sets of chromosomes) of hybrid origin, most pollen grains are abortive and sterile, and are not in a condition to form a pollen tube.

The effect of asexual reproduction is to produce offspring that are genetically identical (barring mutations) to the parent plant. The ability of a population to produce new types of plants that are better adapted to the ever-changing physical and biological environment is consequently impaired. On the other hand, it also reduces the production of types that are less well adapted than the parents to the present environment. This has led many plant evolutionists to consider apomictic plants as evolutionary dead ends, because they are very well adapted to present conditions but lack the flexibility to evolve new biotypes speedily as the environment deteriorates.

Population structure

So far we have considered the life cycle of individual dandelion plants. However, to appreciate the significance of organisms and of the biological characteristics they exhibit, organisms have to be considered in the context of the environment in which they grow. Furthermore, we seldom, if ever, encounter an individual living by itself; instead we find associations of a few pairs to hundreds or even thousands of individuals, which we call populations. Among sexual organisms, a population is a group of interbreeding or potentially interbreeding individuals at any one place. Among asexual organisms, a population is defined by analogy as those individuals that occupy more or less continuously an area of space.

A population of plants occupies an area of varying dimensions. The same space is usually also occupied by other plants. In any area the density of the plants will vary with the species involved and with the physical conditions of the place. So, for example, the total density of plants in the wet forests of the northeastern United States will be many plants per square foot. The density of all plants in an area is an indication of the total amount of resources available, that is, of the carrying capacity of the environment. The most important resources for plants are water, temperature, light and its distribution throughout the year, and minerals in the soil. On the other hand, individual species may be abundant or rare in an area regardless of what the carrying capacity of the environment is. For example, the creosote bush, *Larrea divaricata*, is the most abundant plant in the very dry areas of the Sonoran and Chihuahuan desert, on occasion being the only shrubby species found, although there may be only a few plants per acre absolute density. In the northeastern United States, the common beech, *Fagus sylvestris*, probably has more individuals per acre, and certainly a greater biomass than the creosote bush, but it is proportionally less abundant than the creosote bush because it grows in an area where there are many other species. The relative abundance, or degree of dominance, of a species is determined not by the carrying capacity of the environment but by the ability of the species to compete with others for the available resources, as well as its capacity to defend itself successfully from herbivorous animals and from parasites.

Any organism, be it a plant or an animal, is constantly faced with the struggle for survival and the need to leave offspring. The struggle for survival entails coping successfully with the many and varied rigors of the environment: cold, heat, drought, floods, and all the other density-independent causes of mortality. The struggle for survival also entails the successful harvest of the necessary resources from the environment in competition with other species, as well as the successful avoidance of predators and parasites.

To cope with all these factors, organisms have developed over time a great array of morphological structures and physiological mechanisms in order to adapt themselves better to the struggle for existence. In mammals, layers of fat and hibernation are means of coping with the cold; thick carapaces of turtles protect them against predators; bitter or poisonous substances in many plants

Figure 4. View of the site of Population 2 at the Mathei Botanical Gardens in Ann Arbor, Michigan.

are unpalatable to herbivores, and so on. All these structures and processes allow the organism to stay alive in order to mate and reproduce. However, to produce these structures, energy has to be consumed, and the amount of energy that an organism can harvest from the environment is always limited. Consequently, if the struggle for survival consumes a great proportion of the available energy, the organism is forced to reduce or postpone the production of offspring, another energy consuming activity.

The most successful individuals in a population leave the largest number of offspring that live to reproductive age. Since there is a period after birth when an organism cannot reproduce, a first condition for success is the ability to survive until reproductive age. And since coping with the vagaries of the environment consumes energy, reproductive age will often be postponed in order to grow to a larger size, which allows production of more or of larger offspring. Another strategy is to invest the minimum of energy in energy-consuming adaptive characteristics in order to produce early a greater number of offspring. Mortality will be high, but enough offspring will survive to reproductive age to maintain the species.

Both of these strategies can be observed in nature. Large mammals, such as man or elephants, are a good example of the first; a lot of energy is devoted to the production of a phenotype that is capable of successfully competing for the environmental resources. The price paid is a long developmental time and a very small offspring rate of not more than a couple dozen live births per generation. Such strategy has been called a *K* strategy by MacArthur and Wilson. The opposite strategy is that of many fish; they lay millions of eggs that are essentially defenseless. Most of the young die shortly after birth, but some survive to reproductive age. This strategy is called an *r* strategy because it maximizes reproductive growth. Obviously both of these strategies can lead to success in an evolutionary sense. The question is, When will one strategy be selected and when will the other?

Dandelions are basically *r* strategists; they invest a high proportion of their energy in seed production, as compared to an oak which will take many years before it produces any seed at all. Dandelions grow mostly in disturbed places, such as vacant lots, fallow fields, roadsides, etc. Such disturbed places favor *r* plants with short life cycles and a high seed set. But dandelions are also found in more stable areas, such as meadows, lawns, mountain-slopes, and over great expanses of the Arctic area. The presence of dandelions over such a diversity of habitats presents another problem on account of their asexual nature.

Genetic variability

Most, if not all, species of plants grow in more than one kind of environment. This statement needs qualification because it depends on how environments are defined. If we use a narrow definition in terms of the value taken by the main controlling factors—evapotranspiration, temperature, minerals in the soil—the statement holds. If an even narrower definition is used, then each individual plant in the population faces a different environment because exposure, topography, texture, insolation, drainage, etc. are always slightly different from site to site and from time to time.

Plants cope with these fluctuations in two main ways. Small fluctuations in time and space are dealt with by the capacity of plants to change their phenotype in response to the environment. Such mechanism is called "plasticity." For example, many plants lose their leaves in winter when the temperature goes below freezing and grow a new crop in the spring; many grasses roll their leaves inward when water is temporarily

Figure 5. Close-up view of the vegetation at the site of Population 3. Note the undisturbed nature of the vegetation, particularly in contrast with Population 1.

absent, to decrease evaporation. The plasticity of species varies and is correlated with the degree of variability of the environment where the species grows.

The other way by which plants adjust to the environment is genetically; this response involves the whole population. Every organism possesses several thousand genes arranged on the chromosome in a given order, each position being called a locus. Since every higher plant has a pair of identical sets of chromosomes, at each locus there are two possible combinations of genes occupying any one locus (called allelic genes, or alleles): either the two are identical, a situation called homozygosity, or they are not, a condition called heterozygosity. But only one of them will be realized in any given individual. If, however, the population is considered, and if just one locus and two alleles are taken into account, then three kinds of plants can exist: homozygous for each of the two alleles, and heterozygous. If this scheme is enlarged to include the thousands of loci in the population, and if note is taken that for some loci there may be tens of alleles in the population (although at many there is only one), it will be evident that the number of different combinations that can be formed is almost infinite.

Since each new plant is formed by the union of two gametes, usually from different plants, each gamete containing one set of chromosomes with a unique arrangement of alleles, the exact composition of genotypes in each generation varies. As seeds are broadcast over the population and germinate, in each spot seedlings with slightly different genotypes appear. Those genotypes producing phenotypes best adapted to the particular environment of a site survive, and the others die. This sexual mechanism, called recombination, produces a constant flow of new phenotypes. If conditions in the population are similar from year to year and from site to site, by a constant elimination of variant genotypes (and their genes) the population will become genetically uniform. If, on the other hand, the environmental conditions in the population are variable in space and time, selection will tend to maintain a greater store of alleles. We refer collectively to the different kinds of genotypes in the population as the genetic variability of the population.

We have mentioned that dandelions, being asexual, produce seed without fertilization. Consequently, barring mutation, all the offspring will be genetically identical to the mother plant. Since the process of recombination just explained does not take place in dandelions, then it would appear that they have to rely solely on plasticity to cope with the environment. Furthermore, at any one site over a period of time, by chance and by direct selection, certain genotypes will become eliminated, so that in addition the population will continuously become more uniform unless new genotypes (in the form of seed) are introduced by animals and wind. It consequently would be of interest to know exactly how many genotypes are found in a population.

To answer this question I set up two sets of experiments.

The Ann Arbor experiments

In the first set of experiments, seeds were assembled with the help of correspondents from various parts of the world: Osaka, Mexico City, Buenos Aires, Munich, and Leicester, England. These were grown in the greenhouse and compared with the local Ann Arbor, Michigan, plants. What we wanted to know was whether the genotypes of these plants were identical or not. We did not expect them to be, but we wanted to establish the fact experimentally. Since we were interested in the genotypes, we looked at the enzymes these plants produced. Each gene is characterized by the production of a unique enzyme, and by analyzing enzymes with the help of gel electrophoresis, it is possible to establish the similarity or lack of similarity of the genes at a given locus. The results, as expected, were negative: no two dandelions from different sites were identical, but all the plants from a given site were. However, my correspondents had sent only a handful of seeds, which I suspected came from just one plant. In order to establish exactly the variability (if any) at a given site, a more elaborate experiment was performed.

Three 10 × 10 m quadrats were established on the grounds of the Mathei Botanical Gardens of the University of Michigan. The quadrats were separated by less than 500 m from each other, but each occupied as different a habitat as was found on that meadow. The first sample came from an area (Fig. 3) that was highly disturbed; people walked over it and there was even a path through the area. The soil was comparatively dry and highly compacted. The second sample came from the same general habitat as far as soil and general moisture were concerned, but it was to one side, under an oak tree, where people rarely went. The soil was

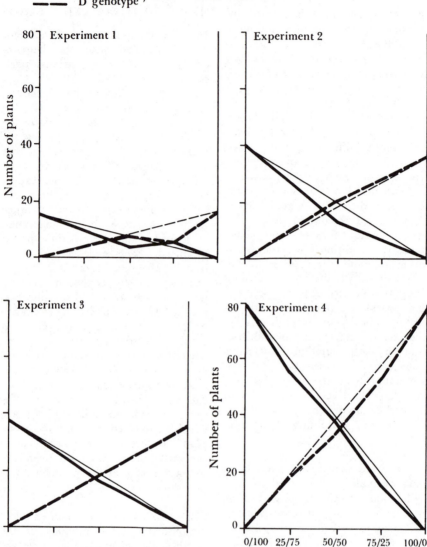

Figure 6. Replacement diagrams showing the average number of surviving plants after one year of competition, as shown in the ordinate. 80 plants were grown to a flat in five different mixtures, as indicated in the abscissa. It can be seen that the values for the D genotype are consistently above expectation, while those for the A genotype are below expectation. For conditions of experiments, see Table 2 and text.

consequently less compacted and the vegetation more dense (Fig. 4).

The third and final sample came from a site close to a creek that periodically overflows its banks. The soil was more humid and, contrary to the other two sites, the area was not mowed weekly. Instead, once a year the grass and weeds were cropped a foot above the ground with a hay mower (Fig. 5). From each population one hundred plants were selected (one from each 1 × 1 m square), transplanted to a uniform garden and, once they had become established, typed as to

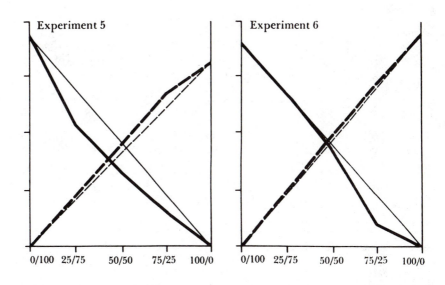

Table 1. Percentage of each of four biotypes in three Ann Arbor populations

Population and habitat	No.	Biotypes			
		A	B	C	D
1. Dry, full sun, highly disturbed	94	73%	13%	14%	...
2. Dry, shade, medium disturbed	96	53%	32%	14%	1%
3. Wet, semishade, undisturbed	94	17%	8%	11%	64%

Table 2. Physical arrangement of competition experiments

Exp. No.	Soil	Light	Water	Initial Mixtures					Repl.
				100A 0D	75A 25D	50A 50D	25A 75D	0A 100D	
1	Loam	Low intensity	50 cc/day	x	x	x	—	x	2
2	Loam	Daylight	100 cc/day	x	x	x	—	x	1
3	Loam	Daylight	unlimited	x	—	x	—	x	2
4	Sand	Daylight	100 cc/day	x	x	x	x	x	2
5	Lime	Daylight	100 cc/day	x	x	x	x	x	2
6	Peat	Daylight	100 cc/day	x	x	x	x	x	2

Table 3. Number of surviving plants after one year (actual number of plants **and** percentage)

Initial Composition		Exp. 1		Exp. 2		Exp. 3		Exp. 4		Exp. 5		Exp. 6	
No.	%	No.	%	No.	%	No.	%	No.	%	No.	%	No.	%
80*A*	100	16	20	40	50	38	48	80	100	74.5	93	72.5	91
60*A*	75	0	0	—	—	—	—	55.5	93	43	72	55	92
20*D*	25	16	80	—	—	—	—	19	95	19	95	20	100
40*A*	50	4	10	13	33	17	43	37.5	94	26	65	35	88
40*D*	50	8	20	20	50	19	48	33.5	84	35.5	89	39	98
20*A*	25	6	30	—	—	—	—	16	80	9	45	8	40
60*D*	75	6	10	—	—	—	—	54	90	54.5	91	57.5	96
80*D*	100	17	22	35.5	44	35.5	44	78	98	65.5	82	77.5	97

Table 4. Estimated biomass after one year (in relative percentage)*

Initial Composition	Exp. 1	Exp. 2	Exp. 3	Exp. 4	Exp. 5	Exp. 6
80A (100%)	47.5	79.5	100	46.5	57.0	79.5
60A (75%)	33.3	—	—	23.3	34.0	42.7
20D (25%)	148.0	—	—	108.0	108.0	146.0
40A (50%)	10.0	16.0	100	31.0	42.0	36.0
40D (50%)	40.0	137.0	127	69.0	73.0	152.0
20A (25%)	—	—	—	8.0	10.0	6.0
60D (75%)	—	—	—	48.6	88.0	142.0
80D (100%)	58.5	55.0	85	53	67	80

* Taking the biomass of the all *A* flat of Exp. 3 as 100% and calculating the relative biomass of each biotype in each flat.

——— A genotype ⎫ Expected values under a model of no competition
- - - D genotype ⎭

▬▬▬ A genotype ⎫ Actual values obtained
▬ ▬ ▬ D genotype ⎭

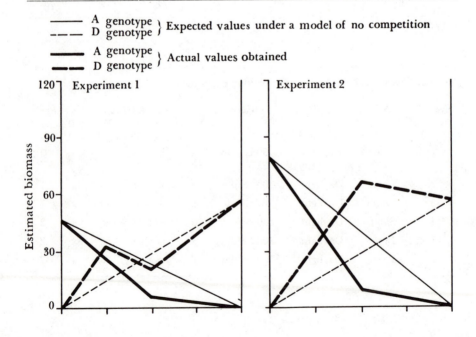

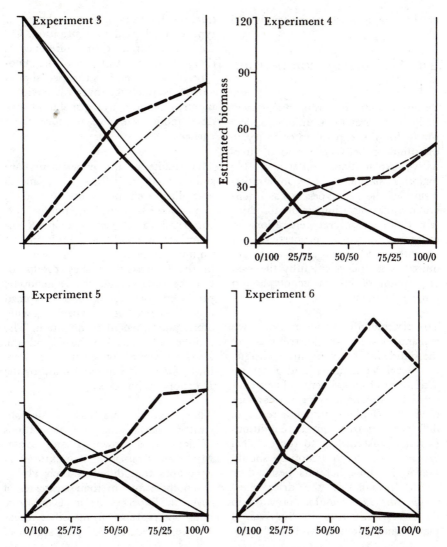

Figure 7. Replacement diagrams showing the average estimated biomass of surviving plants after one year of competition. 80 plants were grown to a flat in five different mixtures, as indicated in the abscissa. The ordinate shows biomass in arbitrary units.

It can be seen that the values for the *D* genotype are consistently above expectation, while those for the *A* genotype are below expectation. For conditions of experiments, see Table 2 and text.

genotype, using once more their pattern of enzymes. The results are outlined in Table 1.

Two points emerge from the experiment. First, there was more than one genotype in the population; as a matter of fact, four were identified in an area of only 100 m². Second, the three populations studied differed in the relative proportion of their genotypes, most notably genotypes *A* and *D*. In populations 1 and 2, the *A* genotype was the most abundant, while in the third population the *D* genotype was most abundant. This immediately leads to the question, why? The two alternative explanations are (1) the classical one that would explain the preference of the *A* and *D* genotypes in terms of microenvironmental requirements, and (2) an alternative explanation that would explain the difference in terms of the *r* and *K* strategies explained above.

The Cambridge competition experiments

Because dandelions reproduce asexually, they present a unique opportunity for the experimenter to try to discriminate between the two alternative explanations. Indeed, in the majority of plants, recombination reshuffles the genotypes in each generation, making it impossible to maintain them for several generations in order to test their properties. Not so with dandelions: all that is required is to collect carefully the seed of a plant of known genotype and propagate them.

To discriminate between the two explanations for the distribution of the dandelion biotypes, my colleague Dr. Beryl Vuilleumier and I set up a number of experiments. They consisted in growing varying proportions of *A* and *D* plants under a series of different environmental conditions (Table 2). According to the classical explanation, the *A* genotype should prevail in those habitats best suited for it (presumably the drier ones) while the *D* should prevail in those best suited to it. Survival of plants and biomass and seed pro-

duction should be higher in the genotype best adapted to a situation. On the other hand, if the difference is due to different strategies of the genotypes, then the *K* strategist should win in competition over all environments, but the *r* strategist should produce more seed, and produce them earlier.

The results of the experiments are summarized in Tables 3, 4, and 5 and illustrated in Figures 6 and 7. We can see that the *D* genotype outcompeted the *A* genotype in *all* environmental conditions, both in the number of plants that survived and in the biomass that they produced. On the other hand, the *A* genotype produced more seed, and produced them earlier, both when growing alone and when in competition. The number of seeds per head and the average weight of each seed were lower for the *A* genotype than for the *D* genotype, however.

These experiments clearly demonstrated that at least the populations of dandelions grown in Ann Arbor, Michigan, consisted of mixtures of genotypes that differ in their ability to compete and in their strategies of survival. Experiments in Cambridge and observations from other areas I have visited, as well as a search of

Table 5. Seed production in dandelions

Pop. 1	% Plants	Heads/plant	% Heads/population
Biotype A	73	3.6	84
Biotype B	13	2.3	9
Biotype C	14	1.5	7
Biotype D	. . .	. . .	. . .
Pop. 2			
Biotype A	53	2.6	59
Biotype B	32	2.1	29
Biotype C	14	1.9	12
Biotype D	1	. . .	. . .
Pop. 3			
Biotype A	17	3.8	40
Biotype B	8	2.3	11
Biotype C	11	0.6	4
Biotype D	64	1.2	45

the literature, indicate that populations of dandelions throughout the world are formed by mixtures of genotypes. Whether in every case they separate solely on the basis of degree of r and K strategy is unlikely, but presumably it always is a factor.

Environmental disturbance and selection

We now must ask, What is the environmental factor that is selecting for and against each of these two reproductive strategies? That factor is, in my opinion, environmental disturbance. By disturbance we mean that plants in a given place are periodically eaten, injured, uprooted, killed, or kept in any other way from growing. Under such circumstances, the ability to compete successfully is not of much use to an organism, since the opportunity to survive long enough to take advantage of the higher competitive ability is absent. However, under such circumstances, the ability to produce a great deal of seed early is of real advantage. This ensures a store of seed to replace the ones that are being eliminated by the environmental disturbance.

Dandelions as a group are adapted to taking advantage of environmental disturbance. That is why they are such successful weeds. Whenever man disturbs the environment through cultivation, land clearing, road building, etc. the dandelion seeds are there to germinate and take advantage of the situation. The present studies have shown that the species is not only adapted to the general situation, but very finely tuned to it, so that it can survive through some of its many genotypes in situations with differing amounts of disturbance. No wonder it is so hard to get rid of unwanted dandelions!

The studies with dandelions show that species of plants are responding not only to the physical factors of the environments (minerals, water, light) but also to biological factors such as interactions with other species. This is of course known and expected. That plants use different reproductive strategies in the allocation of energy between reproduction and competition was suspected but had not been demonstrated empirically. Since dandelions are adapted to disturbed conditions, it would be interesting to see whether the results of this study apply only to plants of disturbed sites (e.g. weeds) or to all plants.

EXPERIMENTAL METHODS IN POPULATION DYNAMICS: A CRITIQUE

FREDERICK E. SMITH

Department of Zoology, University of Michigan, Ann Arbor, Michigan

INTRODUCTION

Until very recently, deterministic theory has been the source of mathematical models for population dynamics. Simple equations have been proposed as suitable representations of sigmoid growth, competition, predation, etc., and these have been fitted to various data. The studies of Gause (1934) epitomize this field.

Stochastic theory provides a kind of model that expresses, not only the general sequence of events, but also the inherent variability of the system. While the deterministic function may represent the "pure" curve of maximum likelihood, the stochastic function permits an evaluation of the actual, observed curve, regardless of its irregularities. Since this ability to handle chance variations and their sequential effects during dynamic processes is relatively new, one must conclude that its future effect upon the approach to population dynamics will be one of progressive increase.

As the theoretical approach is shifting its base, it would be well to look closely to the experimental methods that are in use. The intent of such a critique is two-fold: to determine what has actually been accomplished by such methods, as opposed to what is supposed to have been accomplished, and to launch the newer theoretical approach upon a somewhat better methodology.

Only a few aspects of the experimental techniques are discussed, serving to emphasize phenomena that may well be extended to other aspects. Those discussed fall into the following sections: the mechanisms of culture, the responses of the population, certain properties of deterministic theories, and the application of theories to data. It is the methods that are criticized; such criticisms as occur on the usefulness of particular theories are more or less incidental.

While this paper represents the views of one individual, its existence is very much a result of discussions with E. S. Deevey, G. A. Riley, L. B. Slobodkin, D. W. Calhoun, and especially with G. E. Hutchinson, all at Yale University. Later developments reflect the influence of many others in several places.

THE EXPERIMENTAL ENVIRONMENT

Experiments in population dynamics are accomplished in cultures, and associated with these cultures are specific environments. One advantage of an experiment over field studies is the possibility of simplifying the environment through appropriate manipulation of the culture.

The culture can be treated in many ways, producing various qualitative effects in the environment and hence upon the population. If the experiment is designed as a test of some theory, the manipulations should be such as to simulate the conditions implied by the theory. Thus, if one were to test the

---

predation theory of Lotka (1925) and Volterra (1928), the environment would have to be such that the growth of the prey were in no way inhibited by prey density.

Surprisingly little attention has been paid to the possibility that a given theory, under investigation, defines certain properties for the experiment. In an attempt to emphasize such relationships, a very crude system of classification is given for several culture techniques that may be used in the laboratory. To these will be related the corresponding environments, and the latter will be associated with particular theories.

From the standpoint of ease of interpretation, the simplest culture technique is the *unlimited* culture. Either the population is continually so rarefied or the culture is so rapidly enriched that the organisms never suffer any inhibitive effects upon each other, at least not during the course of study.

Among culture techniques that have limited capacities for growth, the *unrenewed* culture is most frequently used, especially in bacteriology and protozoology. The culture is inoculated, and the subsequent history of the population is recorded. Nothing is added or subtracted by the experimenter.

A variant of this technique is the *periodically renewed* culture. At regular intervals, either the entire population is transferred to a new culture (as is done with flour beetles) or the culture is given booster shots of concentrated medium (as has been done with protozoa).

A still further refinement is the *continuously renewed* culture. The intervals between renewals are so small as to be ineffective, and the system can be treated as though fresh medium is being flushed through at a constant rate all of the time.

While these are but a few techniques, they are simple, and adequate for the present purpose.

Associated with each culture, and determined by the particular factors that are limiting, is a corresponding environment. In the unlimited culture, of course, since nothing is limiting, the environment is of the same type, an unlimited environment.

If the limiting factor is an expendable component of the medium, such as sugar or amino acid, the environment will follow the pattern of the culture.

If the limiting factor is non-expendable, such as space, the environment will in all cases follow the continuously renewed pattern, since the factor is resupplied automatically by the death of individuals. If spatial organization is involved, however, the rhythmic disturbance of the periodically renewed environment may produce a significant effect.

If the limiting factor is a freely diffusable substance like oxygen or carbon dioxide, again the system will in all cases regulate toward the continuously renewed pattern.

If the limiting factor is a noxious metabolite, the environment will follow the pattern of the culture, except that adding booster shots accomplishes little, and this type of culture will be modified toward the unrenewed type.

While these are but a few possibilities, they are enough to indicate some patterns that may occur. Combinations of limiting factors will complicate these patterns, so that, for example, it is not unlikely for an unrenewed culture to be temporarily regulated toward a continuously renewed environment by the supply of oxygen, only to revert to type later as the food is exhausted.

If we now examine some of the published theories, the implied environmental types (extrinsic to the interspecies relation when two populations are involved) are as follows:

1. Unlimited environment: exponential growth (Malthus 1798), predation (Lotka 1925; Volterra 1928), and the host-parasite relation

(Nicholson and Bailey 1935; Thompson 1939).

2. Unrenewed environment: sigmoid growth (Klem 1933).
3. Periodically renewed environment: none.
4. Continuously renewed environment: sigmoid growth (Verhulst 1838; Pearl and Reed 1920; Gompertz and Wilson, both in Wilson 1934) and indirect competition (Volterra 1928; Gause 1934).

In experiments on exponential growth, the culture has usually been so manipulated as to provide the proper environment. This is not known to be so for any of the experiments on predation; in those of Gause (1934, 1935) and of Gause, Smaragdova, and Witt (1936) the prey definitely reached densities that inhibited their own rate of growth. The same is true for most of the experiments on the host-parasite relation. Only one, an experiment by DeBach and Smith (1947), specifically eliminated self-inhibition in the growth of the prey population.

Klem's theory of sigmoid growth was developed for his experiments on yeast. The event appears to be unique, since no one else has applied a theory of growth in an unrenewed environment to data from an unrenewed environment.

While no theories have been developed to include the rhythmic effects of periodic renewal, many experiments have been recorded in which such effects probably existed. This would apply especially to studies of flour insects.

No ecological experiment has been conducted in a continuously renewed culture, although such techniques can be adapted from the work of Novick and Szilard (1950) or of Myers and Clark (1944). No experimental environment has ever been proved to be continuously renewed. While the chances are very good that in some experiments the unrenewed or periodically renewed culture technique that was used was modified by the limiting factors toward a continuously renewed type, this cannot be said with assurance for any particular case.

In summary, from the point of view that an experiment should simulate the conditions of the theory to which it is compared, very few of the published comparisons are known to be suitable. It is known for only one experiment on sigmoid growth (in which the theory did not fit the data well), one experiment on the host-parasite relation (in which the fit of theory to data is fair), and for many experiments on exponential growth. All of the remaining comparisons are open to question.

The Experimental Population

While theories developed in population dynamics are admittedly oversimplified, a general awareness of this in experimental terms seems to be deficient. For, again, if the data are to be used as a "test" of a theory, they should be derived from an appropriate ecological system.

An almost universal simplification in theories is that the unit of the population, the organism, always bears the same relation to the environment. While this is never true, if the distribution of (qualitative) variations among the units is always similar, the approximation is satisfactory.

But stability or constancy of such properties as size-distribution, age-distribution, sex-ratio, etc. is surprisingly rare. Even in the most simple case of population dynamics, exponential growth, marked changes in the population during a recorded phase of such growth are frequent. Demonstrations of such changes are relatively infrequent, since more than one measure of the population has to be taken if a change is to be discerned.

Hershey (1938) demonstrated that, during the period that the cell count was increasing along a good exponential curve, the rate of nitrogen uptake in the population was increasing along a different curve, having a rate function at least 30% smaller. Obviously some character of the population was changing with time; the organism did not stay the same.

The most striking demonstration of this phenomenon was found by Richards (1932) in yeast. During the thirty hours of exponential increase in cell count, the percentage of budding cells increased steadily from 10 to 25, the percentage of moribund cells fell exponentially from 7 to 1, and the surface-volume ratio increased from about 2.9 to 3.4. Richards remarked that the sigmoid growth of yeast was too complicated for comparison to "formulae with arbitrary constants which over simplify the various influences that determine the extent of natural unlimited growth of the cells"; this remark applies equally well to the exponential phase of growth.

Finally, it is a commonplace in bacteriology that cell-count curves and colorimetric curves do not agree.

The conclusion from these demonstrations is that, although the culture is mechanically of the proper type, insufficient time is allowed for the population to adjust to exponential growth. Before the population is able to "settle down," it becomes crowded and passes into plateau. This may be avoided (Hershey 1939) by subculturing from very young cultures. Effectively the period of exponential growth is prolonged, and a steady state of population characteristics is able to develop. In an adjusted culture, all estimates of the growth rate (number, total volume, nitrogen uptake, etc.) must be the same. Most of the published observations of exponential growth are probably inaccurate estimates of the "true" rate of increase.

The concept of unchanging population characteristics in sigmoid growth or in other ecological relations is absurd. This has been recognised, and such "simple" organisms as yeast, protozoa, and bacteria have been used with the assumption that, here, at least, qualitative changes are minimal. It would now appear that such an assumption is unwarranted. The reactions of yeast to environmental stress, as recorded by Richards (1932), are fully as complicated from a mathematical point of view as those of any higher organism.

It is unfortunate that just those species which culture easily (yeast, flour insects, fruit flies, etc.) come from naturally unstable environments. Their complex adaptabilities, which facilitate culture, are precisely what complicate the population experiment. A simpler system would be one using species (not necessarily simple) from stable, uniform environments—species that usually are difficult to culture. Another possible solution is to present the traditional laboratory species with totally new limiting factors, and gamble that the population response will be relatively simple.

It is possible that in some experiments physiological adaptation to stress has combined with an unsuitable environmental type to produce a deceptive result. This is especially likely in comparisons of sigmoid growth with the Verhulst-Pearl theory. In many yeasts and bacteria, as growth proceeds in the unrenewed culture, the population shifts progressively to an inactive state. In an unrenewed environment one would expect the upper part of the sigmoid curve to be small, since it is curtailed by a falling capacity in the culture. After the peak of growth the population, if it could not adapt, would fall, perhaps along a negative exponential. But in these cases, the sum of inactive and active cells enlarges the upper portion of the growth curve and postpones the fall almost indefinitely.

While the result may be described closely by the mathematical form of the Verhulst-Pearl logistic, such a description is not useful. Either the combination of two errors has produced a fortuitous result, or their interaction is regulated by a process as yet unsuspected. In either case the theory does not describe the underlying biology.

Other complications that may be introduced by the organisms cannot be treated lightly. These include environmental conditioning, changes in the age structure of the population, and mutation with a complete replacement of the population (as occurs frequently in the chemostat of Novick and Szilard 1950). Whatever the specific complications, they must be reconciled in any comparison of theory and experiment.

PROPERTIES OF DETERMINISTIC THEORIES

Any equation in population dynamics has specific properties, properties which are obvious to the mathematician, but which seem to have escaped any degree of experimental application. Many of these properties are useful, in that some of them may show immediately that the theory has limitations, while others may provide tools for study. These properties will be discussed by examples.

The theory of Verhulst (1838) and Pearl and Reed (1920) has the following form:

$$\frac{dN}{dt} = rN\left(1 - \frac{N}{K}\right)$$

where N = population size,

t = time,
r = intrinsic (net, maximum, exponential) rate of increase,
K = saturation level or plateau,

expressing the rate of change of the population (dN) with respect to change in time (dt). The equation can also be written as the average rate of change for the individual (dN/N) with respect to the change in time:

$$\frac{dN}{Ndt} = r\left(1 - \frac{N}{K}\right).$$

In this latter form, the average growth rate is seen to be a linear function of the degree of saturation (N/K). Thus, when this ratio is nearly zero, the growth rate is maximal (r), when it is one-half, the growth rate is one-half, and when the system is just saturated, the growth rate is zero.

In unrenewed environments, and in competitive and predative relationships, the possibility of a population level exceeding the current saturation level must be considered. In the Verhulst-Pearl theory, the linear relation continues; when the system is twice saturated, the growth rate is minus r, when it is ten times saturated, the rate is minus $9r$. Thus, the rate of decrease is not a limited function. Lotka (1925) indicated that this property may not be suitable for some situations.

The Verhulst-Pearl theory stands up under this kind of analysis better than most. In the Gompertz theory (Wilson 1934), the equation can be stated:

$$\frac{dN}{dt} = rN \log_e\left(\frac{K}{N}\right)$$

or:

$$\frac{dN}{Ndt} = r \log_e\left(\frac{K}{N}\right).$$

This equation has the same limitation as the Verhulst-Pearl theory, setting no limit to the rate of decrease. It has the more serious fault, however, of setting no limit to the rate of increase. When the ratio, N/K, is small, the rate of growth approaches infinity. It is only between about one-third saturation (where $\log_e K/N$ is 1.0) and full saturation (where $\log_e K/N$ is 0.0) that the constants of the equation can be interpreted biologically.

As a final example, the predation equations of Lotka (1925) and Volterra (1928) are:

$$\frac{dN_1}{dt} = r_1 N_1 - k_1 N_1 N_2$$

$$\frac{dN_2}{dt} = k_2 N_1 N_2 - d_2 N_2$$

where N_1 = prey population,
$\quad\quad N_2$ = predator population,
$\quad\quad r_1$ = intrinsic rate of increase for the prey,
$\quad\quad d_2$ = exponential death rate of the predators,
$\quad\quad k_1, k_2$ = predation constants.

If the predation constants are taken as simple, as they were in the development of an intrinsic cyclic relation, some of the properties are as follows:

$$\frac{dN_1}{N_1 dt} = r_1 - k_1 N_2,$$

$$\frac{dN_2}{N_2 dt} = k_2 N_1 - d_2.$$

1. Neither species enters in its own average growth function; hence, neither ever inhibits its own growth; the environment extrinsic to the relation is unlimited.
2. Prey density has no effect upon the likelihood of a prey being eaten; there is no safety in numbers.
3. Predator density has no effect upon the likelihood of a predator catching a prey; there is no competition for food.
4. The predators have an unlimited rate of increase.

While (1) can be arranged mechanically, and (2) may be true if the predators are certain filter-feeders, (3) and especially (4) are biologically unknown. These simple interpretations of the predation constants must be considered useless. To do so at once invalidates the predation "laws" of Volterra and the regular intrinsic cyclic relation developed by both Lotka and Volterra.

A more complex interpretation of the predation constants is that:

$$k_1 = a + bN_1 + cN_2 + \ldots$$

$$k_2 = a' + b'N_1 + c'N_2 + \ldots$$

defining each as a power series (Lotka 1925). If we consider only the second

function, k_2, it is evident that a power series is most inept for its purpose.

For the growth function of the predators to be satisfactory, the average rate of growth ($dN_2/N_2 dt$) must rise to some asymptote (r_2) as the prey are made more numerous. To describe such a curve by a power series that will handle all values of prey up to infinity, an infinite number of terms and constants are needed. Even to handle the numbers of prey that are likely to develop in an experiment requires several terms of the series. Furthermore, the function fails markedly should the prey density exceed that expected and allowed for. The use of exponential functions, as suggested by Gause (1934), offers a much higher efficiency in terms of the number of constants that would be required to describe this relation.

So far in this section only the deficiencies of theories have been emphasized. The second use of such an analysis of equations is to develop experimental tools. These will be discussed at the end of the following section.

THE APPLICATION OF THEORIES TO DATA

Actually, little can be said in favor of the fitting of deterministic theoretical curves to empirical data. The technique, as a means of "testing" theories, is indefensible on at least three independent counts:

(1) Judgment has to be subjective. Deviations from the best-fit curve always occur, and statistical methods for evaluating these deviations are lacking.

(2) The prior probability of the method is high. This aspect of probability is too often ignored; regardless of the calculated probability of a particular fit, if it is likely to be good before the fit is made, the test itself is inefficient. The method is uncritical; while it may exclude extreme misfits, it fails to discriminate among a host of similar but basically different situations.

Kavanagh and Richards (1934), among others, demonstrated that a variety of theoretical curves could be fitted to the same data on sigmoid growth, and with equal felicity. An even more powerful criticism of this weak method is the fact that the theory of Verhulst and Pearl, for example, has been accepted as a satisfactory fit to a remarkably heterogeneous set of ecological situations. The heterogeneity emphasizes, not the generality of the theory, as is usually assumed, but the weak method of application. The problems discussed in the preceeding sections have not caused difficulty in the past because the established method of fitting theories is not powerful enough to discriminate them.

This weakness is related to the number of constants fitted in the process of comparing a curve to data. With more than two such constants, the prior probability of a "nice" fit (a subjective term to match the subjective basis of judgment) is already high, and with more than four constants to be fitted to one population curve it is hardly necessary to make the comparison.

(3) The method centers attention on the whole rather than on the parts. A direct result has been a general satisfaction with the wholes, without the realization that at least some of the parts in the comparison are not of the right kind. If the overall fit is "nice," a prejudice is established against a rejection of the comparison through some particular fault.

The best fit of a theory to data has been said to be that of the Verhulst-Pearl theory to the growth curve of a yeast culture (Allee *et al.* 1949). The data were gathered by Carlson (1913), and the fit was made by Pearl (1930). In spite of this belief, the culture was unrenewed, the limiting factors were probably at first the food supply (sugar) and the waste accumulation, shifting later to the lower usefulness of the wastes as foods and the re-use of material from burst cells; the culture ended by converting to resting cells!

These three arguments are an unfortunate combination. A high prior probability leaves one at a loss in subjective judgement; the usual standards are not adequately strict. The lack of objective evaluation in whole comparisons, which has been accepted as a necessary evil, has forestalled any degree of partial analysis, in which objective methods are indeed possible. The lack of partial analyses has in turn promoted the habit of fitting all constants, whether some can be calculated independently or not, thus pushing the prior probability to its maximum.

For the comparison of whole theories to the history of a culture, the developing field of stochastic processes offers the only reasonable approach.

But whole comparisons may not be the best way to test theories. The danger still remains that the whole need not be the sum of the right parts. Rigorous testing of the separate aspects of the theories would not only simplify the mathematics, but would eliminate, at least to some degree, this last criticism.

In the Verhulst-Pearl theory, two basic concepts are combined. One is that the exponential rate of growth has a maximum (r), and the other is that the degree of saturation (N/K) is a linear depressant of the rate of growth (dN/Ndt).

The first concept is well supported and established. To measure it in a particular case, however, may be difficult. If there is to be any assurance of its accuracy it should be obtained from at least two kinds of measures in the growing population. Such estimates can be made "deterministic," in the sense that the average of many observations of a constant will approach its deterministic value. Furthermore, the empirical range of error would, with a suitable distribution, provide a means of probability evaluation. The two measures can be tested for the absence of trend and for agreement with each other.

The second concept has never been analysed. Rate curves derived from growth curves are not adequate, since they contain the same stochastic processes as the original data. But the problem can be handled in a different way. In the equation:

$$\frac{dN}{Ndt} = r\left(1 - \frac{N}{K}\right) = r - \frac{r}{K}(N)$$

a graph of the rate of change (dN/Ndt) plotted against the population size (N) shows a straight line, with a y-intercept of r, and x-intercept of K, and a slope of $-r/K$.

Points for this graph could be obtained from a modified chemostat. Keeping the composition of the inflow constant, its rate (the washing-out rate, V/W) can be set at various levels between r and zero. At r, the system will be unstable, but for any rate of flow less than this the population will increase until its growth rate is density-depressed to the rate of flow ($dN/Ndt = V/W$). At each level of this flow, after the system comes to a steady state, a series of observations can be made on the population size (N). The data can then be put through the standard statistical test (again, if a suitable distribution is found) to determine whether the regression of population size (N) upon the rate of growth (dN/Ndt) is linear. This would be a first test of the basic principle of the theory.

Needless to say, this method will apply to other theories of sigmoid growth. In the Gompertz curve, the linear plot becomes:

$$\frac{dN}{Ndt} = r \log_e K - r \log_e N.$$

The procedure can be turned about, to use the methods of partial analysis as a means of finding simple functions for theories. If, for example, none of the functions in established theories worked,

a search with the aid of these partial systems may produce suitable relationships. Any experimental technique which will produce a steady state should yield information that can be used in deterministic theory.

The Lotka-Volterra predation theory indicates that:

1. A plot of dN_1/N_1dt against N_2 is a straight line, with a y-intercept of r_1 and a slope of $-1/k_1$.
2. A plot of dN_2/N_2dt against N_1 is a straight line, with a y-intercept of $-d_2$ and a slope of $1/k_2$.
3. dN_1/N_1dt, for one value of N_2, is constant for all values of N_1.
4. dN_2/N_2dt, for one value of N_1, is constant for all values of N_2.

Even these partial analyses, however, are not foolproof. Straight lines are easier to obtain than most people believe. If the data conform to a straight line "except at one end," or if they conform to two straight lines with a "break" in the middle, a linear relation is probably absent. Furthermore, small deviations toward one end of a curve may reflect large discrepancies in the dynamic processes of growth. For the faith that is put into population theories, the experimental examination will have to be rigorous.

DISCUSSION

The preceding sections point to one conclusion: very little in this field of population dynamics is beyond the hypothetical stage. With the possible exception of the concept of exponential growth, it is a misuse of terms to refer to any of the interpretations as "theories." Almost all of the evidence used in support of various interpretations is, at best, inconclusive.

Yet, the field has provided a considerable fund of interesting material, enough to have profound effects upon allied areas. Perhaps, more than anything else, this influence urges an intense and cautious re-examination of our concepts.

The degree of acceptance of such concepts as, for examples, the Verhulst-Pearl logistic and the Lotka-Volterra equations, is astonishing.

Concepts do not appear easily. Although logic teaches that an infinite number of curves can be fitted to data on sigmoid growth, very few such equations have been set down, and of these only two, the Verhulst-Pearl and the Klem equations, have been expressed adequately in ecological terms. We have only one well-known theory of predation, one of competition, and two or three for parasitism. Sparse as it may be, this collection is the accumulated work of many people for many years.

Hence, even though the present stock of concepts is but a collection of hypotheses, it is a valuable collection. It contains what must be considered progress of the most difficult kind. For the future, also, the continued development of hypothetical relationships will be useful; the armchair is still a necessary piece of equipment.

The experimental side of population dynamics is in a different situation. In spite of the many curves recorded, the many fits made, the work will have to be largely discounted as evidence in support of any particular theories. A repetition of all of it, with more appropriate and more carefully detailed designs, will have to be initiated.

Regardless of the use to be made of stochastic processes, deterministic theory will continue to play a major role. It is a way of thinking; inevitably one considers, not the sequential range of values, but the most likely course of events. Most important, thinking in deterministic terms is a way of producing concepts.

SUMMARY

The methods for experimental verification of deterministic theories in population dynamics are criticized from several points of view.

The mechanism of control in the culture should conform to the conditions implied in the theory. This is often not the case; the most notable instance of disagreement concerns the Verhulst-Pearl logistic, which has never been supported by an experiment known to be made in an appropriate environment. Several kinds of culture control are classified.

The reactions of the population should be limited to those provided in the theory. Most equations are admittedly simplified, but such an admission should be coupled with a much more successful restriction to simplified responses by the organisms. Many laboratory species are highly complex in their reactions to environmental control; physiological adaptation is especially common. A simple response is probably unrelated to evolutionary complexity. Two possible means of finding ideally simple reactions are indicated.

Theoretical equations are manipulated to show various of their properties. The method is useful as a means of "*a priori*" evaluation of equations, especially of their limitations. It is also useful as a means of discovering more simple but vital aspects of theories for specific analysis.

The common method of fitting deterministic curves to data is criticized from three points of view, any one of which raises a serious objection. One solution to the problem in the use of stochastic theory is mentioned, but methods are also discussed for the application of sound experimental techniques to deterministic theory.

The general conclusion is that we have a useful and valuable stockpile of concepts, but that up to the present little of the experimental work is at all conclusive. Most of the ideas in this field should be regarded as hypotheses, not theories.

REFERENCES

Allee, W. C., A. E. Emerson, O. Park, T. Park, and K. P. Schmidt. 1949. Principles of animal ecology. Phila. and London: Saunders.

De Bach, P., and H. S. Smith. 1947. Effects of parasite population density on the rate of change of host and parasite populations. Ecology, 28: 290–298.

Carlson, T. 1913. Über Geschwindigkeit und Grösse der Hefevermehrung in Würze. Biochem. Ztschr., 57: 313–334.

Gause, G. F. 1934. The struggle for existence. Baltimore: Williams & Wilkins.

——. 1935. Vérifications expérimentales de la théorie mathématique de la lutte pour la vie. Actual. Sci. Industr., 277: 1–61.

Gause, G. F., N. P. Smaragdova, and A. A. Witt. 1936. Further studies of interaction between predators and prey. J. Anim. Ecol., 5: 1–18.

Hershey, A. D. 1938. Factors limiting bacterial growth. II. Growth without lag in Bacterium coli cultures. Proc. Soc. Exp. Biol. Med., 38: 127–128.

——. 1939. Factors limiting bacterial growth. IV. The age of the parent culture and the rate of growth of transplants in Escherichia coli. J. Bact., 37: 285–299.

Kavanagh, A. J., and O. W. Richards. 1934. The autocatalytic growth curve. Amer. Nat., 68: 54–59.

Klem, Alf. 1933. On the growth of populations of yeast. Norske Vetensk.-Akad., Oslo, Hvalrådets Skrifter, 7: 55–91.

Lotka, A. J. 1925. Elements of physical biology. Baltimore: Williams & Wilkins.

Malthus, T. R. 1798. An essay on the principle of population. London.

Myers, J., and L. B. Clark. 1944. Culture conditions and the development of the photosynthetic mechanism. II. An apparatus for the continuous culture of Chlorella. J. Gen. Physiol., 28: 103–112.

Novick, A., and L. Szilard. 1950. Experiments with the chemostat on spontaneous mutations of bacteria. Proc. Nat. Acad. Sci., 36: 708–719.

Nicholson, A. J., and V. A. Bailey. 1935. The balance of animal populations. Part I. Proc. Zool. Soc. London, 1935, Part III: 551–598.

Pearl, Raymond. 1930. The biology of population growth. New York: Knopf.

Pearl, Raymond, and L. J. Reed. 1920. On the rate of growth of the population of the United States since 1790 and its mathematical representation. Proc. Nat. Acad. Sci., 6: 275.

Richards, O. W. 1932. The second cycle and subsequent growth of a population of yeast. Archiv Protistenkunde, 78: 263–301.

Thompson, W. R. 1939. Biological control and the theories of the interaction of populations. Parasitology, 31: 299–388.

Verhulst, P. F. 1838. Notice sur la loi que la population suit dans son accroissement. Corr. Math. et Phys., 10: 113.

Volterra, Vito. 1928. Variations and fluctuations of the number of individuals in animal species living together. J. du Conseil intern. pour l'explor. de la mer III vol. I, reprinted in: Animal Ecology, by R. N. Chapman, McGraw-Hill, New York, 1931.

Wilson, E. B. 1934. Mathematics of growth. Cold Spring Harbor Symp. on Quant. Biol., 2: 199–202.

Part II

RELATIONS
BETWEEN
ORGANISMS—
COMPETITION
AND PREDATION

It is a truism that organisms do not exist alone in nature; a web of inter-connections forms the matrix of their existence. The most direct evidence for this is that population sizes are different in the presence and absence of other species.

Of the possible ways in which populations of organisms can interact, those which seem to be of the greatest theoretical and practical interest are competition and predation. In competition, some resource of the environment is not sufficient to allow the individual organisms or the populations in it to flourish as they would if they were living alone. In predation, one set of organisms provides food—that is, energy and substances—for other organisms. Parasitism, which grades imperceptibly into predation, has often been treated as a special case of predation.

That competition has received so much attention is not surprising in view of the importance accorded it by Darwin, who refers to "the infinitely various ways beings have to obtain food by struggling with other beings, to escape danger at various times of life, to have their eggs or seeds disseminated etc., etc." In this list, competition appears first, and means interaction between populations inhabiting a common environment, such as for food or nest sites.

In studies of population growth, competition between two coexisting species, and predation, Gause (1934) combined mathematical modeling and experimentation. The equations for competition are derived from the logistic equation, as are those for predation. Gause's formulation for the growth of the two species occurring alone is:

$$\frac{dN_1}{dt} = r_1 N_1 \left(\frac{K_1 - N_1}{K_1} \right) \qquad \frac{dN_2}{dt} = r_2 N_2 \left(\frac{K_2 - N_2}{K_2} \right)$$

127

with
N_1 = population size of 1st species
N_2 = population size of 2nd species
r_1, r_2 = intrinsic rate of natural increase of the two species
K_1, K_2 = the carrying capacities of the environment for the two species independently
t = time

This model assumes that r_1, r_2, K_1, and K_2 are constants, that all organisms are equivalent, and the responses of the population to change occur instantaneously. The lack of reality in these assumptions shows how unlikely it is that the model can be applied to nature in detail.

The right-hand side consists of two parts: rN, the potential rate of growth of the population in the environment considered, and $\dfrac{K-N}{K}$, the extent to which this potential is realized.

When the two species are grown together, their growth may be affected not only by their own species but likewise by interaction with the other. When competitive interaction occurs, the extent to which the potential is realized is further reduced, and the formulation becomes:

$$\frac{dN_1}{dt} = r_1 N_1 \left(\frac{K_1 - N_1 - \alpha N_2}{K_1} \right) \qquad \frac{dN_2}{dt} = r_2 N_2 \left(\frac{K_2 - N_2 - \beta N_1}{K_2} \right)$$

Here the coefficients α and β convert the population numbers of the competitive species into numbers equivalent to the species itself, taking into account such factors as body size.

This model was tested, though not rigorously, by Gause performing experiments with two species of *Paramoecium* living together in a culture, utilizing the same food. *Paramoecium caudatum* grew more rapidly than *P. aurelius* in the early stages of a mixed culture but was finally eliminated. The precise mechanism of competition was not determined. A more complete analysis of competitive relation between pairs of species is given by Slobodkin (1963).

In the readings provided here, a second kind of interaction, predation, is discussed thoroughly enough so that the essential relation and ideas can be grasped with but little introduction. Smith's paper treats the mathematical relation, and the remainder treat experimental or natural studies of predation.

To study predation quantitatively, one must measure its extent and its effects. This is difficult — so difficult that there has been little agreement among ecologists about the relevance of predation to the control of the population size of prey species. One can find statements by students of predation that predators consume only the unfits; in this view predation functions in natural selection, benefiting the prey populations. Other statements claim that nearly every possible prey organism is consumed, whether healthy or sick, young or old, halt, lame or blind. Here the emphasis shifts to the effect of predation on population size. Differences among known predator-prey systems are not sufficient to account for such diverse opinions. The examples chosen here emphasize the importance of predators as a control of the prey. For a contrary view, the work of Errington (1963) might be read.

LITERATURE CITED

Errington, P. L. 1963. *Muskrat Populations*. Ames: Iowa State University Press. 665 pp.
Gause, G. F. 1934. *The Struggle for Existence*. New York: Hafner. 163 pp.
Slobodkin, L. B. 1963. *Growth and Regulation of Animal Populations*. New York: Holt, Rinehart & Winston. 184 pp.

THE INFLUENCE OF INTERSPECIFIC COMPETITION AND OTHER FACTORS ON THE DISTRIBUTION OF THE BARNACLE *CHTHAMALUS STELLATUS*

Joseph H. Connell

Department of Biology, University of California, Santa Barbara, Goleta, California

Introduction

Most of the evidence for the occurrence of interspecific competition in animals has been gained from laboratory populations. Because of the small amount of direct evidence for its occurrence in nature, competition has sometimes been assigned a minor role in determining the composition of animal communities.

Indirect evidence exists, however, which suggests that competition may sometimes be responsible for the distribution of animals in nature. The range of distribution of a species may be decreased in the presence of another species with similar requirements (Beauchamp and Ullyott 1932, Endean, Kenny and Stephenson 1956). Uniform distribution is space is usually attributed to intraspecies competition (Holme 1950, Clark and Evans 1954). When animals with similar requirements, such as 2 or more closely related species, are found coexisting in the same area, careful analysis usually indicates that they are not actually competing with each other (Lack 1954, MacArthur 1958).

In the course of an investigation of the animals of an intertidal rocky shore I noticed that the adults of 2 species of barnacles occupied 2 separate horizontal zones with a small area of overlap, whereas the young of the species from the upper zone were found in much of the lower zone. The upper species, *Chthamalus stellatus* (Poli) thus settled but did not survive in the lower zone. It seemed probable that this species was eliminated by the lower one, *Balanus balanoides* (L), in a struggle for a common requisite which was in short supply. In the rocky intertidal region, space for attachment and growth is often extremely limited. This paper is an account of some observations and experiments designed to test the hypothesis that the absence in the lower zone of adults of *Chthamalus* was due to interspecific competition with *Balanus* for space. Other factors which may have influenced the distribution were also studied. The study was made at Millport, Isle of Cumbrae, Scotland.

I would like to thank Prof. C. M. Yonge and the staff of the Marine Station, Millport, for their help, discussions and encouragement during the course of this work. Thanks are due to the following for their critical reading of the manuscript: C. S. Elton, P. W. Frank, G. Hardin, N. G. Hairston, E. Orias, T. Park and his students, and my wife.

Distribution of the species of barnacles

The upper species, *Chthamalus stellatus,* has its center of distribution in the Mediterranean; it reaches its northern limit in the Shetland Islands, north of Scotland. At Millport, adults of this species occur between the levels of mean high water of neap and spring tides (M.H.W.N. and M.H.W.S.: see Figure 5 and Table I). In southwest England and Ireland, adult *Chtham-*

TABLE I. Description of experimental areas*

Area no.	Height in ft from M.T.L.	% of time sub-merged	Population Density: no./cm² in June, 1954			Remarks
			Chthamalus, autumn 1953 settlement		All barnacles, undisturbed portion	
			Undisturbed portion	Portion without *Balanus*		
MHWS	+4.9	4	—	—	—	—
1	+4.2	9	2.2	—	19.2	Vertical, partly protected
2	+3.5	16	5.2	4.2	—	Vertical, wave beaten
MHWN	+3.1	21	—	—	--	—
3a	+2.2	30	0.6	0.6	30.9	Horizontal, wave beaten
3b	"	"	0.5	0.7	29.2	" " "
4	+1.4	38	1.9	0.6	—	30° to vertical, partly protected
5	+1.4	"	2.4	1.2	—	" " " " "
6	+1.0	42	1.1	1.9	38.2	Horizontal, top of a boulder, partly protected
7a	+0.7	44	1.3	2.0	49.3	Vertical, protected
7b	"	"	2.3	2.0	51.7	" "
11a	0.0	50	1.0	0.6	32.0	Vertical, protected
11b	"	"	0.2	0.3	—	" "
12a	0.0	100	1.2	1.2	18.8	Horizontal, immersed in tide pool
12b	"	100	0.8	0.9	—	" " " " "
13a	−1.0	58	4.9	4.1	29.5	Vertical, wave beaten
13b	"	"	3.1	2.4	—	" " "
14a	−2.5	71	0.7	1.1	—	45° angle, wave beaten
14b	"	"	1.0	1.0	—	" " " "
MLWN	−3.0	77	—	—	--	—
MLWS	−5.1	96	—	—	- .	—
15	+1.0	42	32.0	—	--	*Chthamalus* of autumn, 1954 settlement; densities of Oct., 1954.
7b	+0.7	44	5.5	3.7	--	

* The letter "a" following an area number indicates that this area was enclosed by a cage; "b" refers to a closely adjacent area which was not enclosed. All areas faced either east or south except 7a and 7b, which faced north.

Chthamalus were in each portion. One portion was chosen (by flipping a coin), and those *Balanus* which were touching or immediately surrounding each *Chthamalus* were carefully removed with a needle; the other portion was left untouched. In this way it was possible to measure the effect on the survival of *Chthamalus* both of intraspecific competition alone and of competition with *Balanus*. It was not possible to have the numbers or population densities of *Chthamalus* exactly equal on the 2 portions of each area. This was due to the fact that, since *Chthamalus* often occurred in groups, the *Balanus* had to be removed from around all the members of a group to ensure that no crowding by *Balanus* occurred. The densities of *Chthamalus* were very low, however, so that the slight differences in density between the 2 portions of each area can probably be disregarded; intraspecific crowding was very seldom observed. Censuses of the *Chthamalus* were made at intervals of 4-6 weeks during the next year; notes were made at each census of factors such as crowding, undercutting or smothering which had taken place since the last examination. When necessary, *Balanus* which had grown until they threatened to touch the *Chthamalus* were removed in later examinations.

To study the effects of different degrees of immersion, the areas were located throughout the tidal range, either *in situ* or on transplanted stones, as shown in Table I. Area 1 had been under observation for 1½ years previously. The effects of different degrees of wave shock could not be studied adequately in such a small area

TABLE I. Description of experimental areas*

Area no.	Height in ft from M.T.L.	% of time sub-merged	Chthamalus, autumn 1953 settlement		All barnacles, undisturbed portion	Remarks
			Undisturbed portion	Portion without Balanus		
MHWS..............	+4.9	4	—	—	—	—
1..................	+4.2	9	2.2	—	19.2	Vertical, partly protected
2..................	+3.5	16	5.2	4.2	—	Vertical, wave beaten
MHWN..............	+3.1	21	—	—	--	—
3a.................	+2.2	30	0.6	0.6	30.9	Horizontal, wave beaten
3b.................	"	"	0.5	0.7	29.2	"　　"　　"
4..................	+1.4	38	1.9	0.6	—	30° to vertical, partly protected
5..................	+1.4	"	2.4	1.2	—	"　"　"　"　"　"
6..................	+1.0	42	1.1	1.9	38.2	Horizontal, top of a boulder, partly protected
7a.................	+0.7	44	1.3	2.0	49.3	Vertical, protected
7b.................	"	"	2.3	2.0	51.7	"　　"
11a................	0.0	50	1.0	0.6	32.0	Vertical, protected
11b................	"	"	0.2	0.3	—	"　　"
12a................	0.0	100	1.2	1.2	18.8	Horizontal, immersed in tide pool
12b................	"	100	0.8	0.9	—	"　　"　　"　　"
13a................	−1.0	58	4.9	4.1	29.5	Vertical, wave beaten
13b................	"	"	3.1	2.4	—	"　　"　　"
14a................	−2.5	71	0.7	1.1	—	45° angle, wave beaten
14b................	"	"	1.0	1.0	—	"　"　"　"
MLWN..............	−3.0	77	—	—	--	—
MLWS..............	−5.1	96	—	—	--	—
15.................	+1.0	42	32.0	—	--	{Chthamalus of autumn, 1954 settlement; densities of Oct., 1954.
7b.................	+0.7	44	5.5	3.7	--	

* The letter "a" following an area number indicates that this area was enclosed by a cage; "b" refers to a closely adjacent area which was not enclosed. All areas faced either east or south except 7a and 7b, which faced north.

Chthamalus were in each portion. One portion was chosen (by flipping a coin), and those *Balanus* which were touching or immediately surrounding each *Chthamalus* were carefully removed with a needle; the other portion was left untouched. In this way it was possible to measure the effect on the survival of *Chthamalus* both of intraspecific competition alone and of competition with *Balanus*. It was not possible to have the numbers or population densities of *Chthamalus* exactly equal on the 2 portions of each area. This was due to the fact that, since *Chthamalus* often occurred in groups, the *Balanus* had to be removed from around all the members of a group to ensure that no crowding by *Balanus* occurred. The densities of *Chthamalus* were very low, however, so that the slight differences in density between the 2 portions of each area can probably be disregarded; intraspecific crowding was very seldom observed. Censuses of the *Chthamalus* were made at intervals of 4-6 weeks during the next year; notes were made at each census of factors such as crowding, undercutting or smothering which had taken place since the last examination. When necessary, *Balanus* which had grown until they threatened to touch the *Chthamalus* were removed in later examinations.

To study the effects of different degrees of immersion, the areas were located throughout the tidal range, either *in situ* or on transplanted stones, as shown in Table I. Area 1 had been under observation for 1½ years previously. The effects of different degrees of wave shock could not be studied adequately in such a small area

Fig. 1. Area 7b. In the first photograph the large barnacles are *Balanus*, the small ones scattered in the bare patch, *Chthamalus*. The white line on the second photograph divides the undisturbed portion (right) from the portion from which *Balanus* were removed (left). A limpet, *Patella vulgata*, occurs on the left, and predatory snails, *Thais lapillus*, are visible.

of shore but such differences as existed are listed in Table I.

The effects of the predatory snail, *Thais lapillus*, (synonymous with *Nucella* or *Purpura*, Clench 1947), were studied as follows: Cages of stainless steel wire netting, 8 meshes per inch, were attached over some of the areas. This mesh has an open area of 60% and previous work (Connell 1961) had shown that it did not inhibit growth or survival of the barnacles. The cages were about 4 × 6 inches, the roof was about an inch above the barnacles and the sides were fitted to the irregularities of the rock. They were held in place in the same manner as the transplanted stones. The transplanted stones were attached in pairs, one of each pair being enclosed in a cage (Table I).

These cages were effective in excluding all but the smallest *Thais*. Occasionally small *Thais*, ½ to 1 cm in length, entered the cages through gaps at the line of juncture of netting and rock surface. In the concurrent study of *Balanus* (Con-

nell 1961), small *Thais* were estimated to have occurred inside the cages about 3% of the time.

All the areas and stones were established before the settlement of *Balanus* began in late April, 1954. Thus the *Chthamalus* which had settled naturally on the shore were then of the 1953 year class and all about 7 months old. Some *Chthamalus* which settled in the autumn of 1954 were followed until the study was ended in June, 1955. In addition some adults which, judging from their large size and the great erosion of their shells, must have settled in 1952 or earlier, were present on the transplanted stones. Thus records were made of at least 3 year-classes of *Chthamalus*.

Results

The effects of physical factors

In Figures 2 and 3, the dashed line indicates the survival of *Chthamalus* growing without contact with *Balanus*. The suffix "a" indicates that the area was protected from *Thais* by a cage.

In the absence of *Balanus* and *Thais,* and protected by the cages from damage by water-borne objects, the survival of *Chthamalus* was good at all levels. For those which had settled normally on the shore (Fig. 2), the poorest survival was on the lowest area, 7a. On the transplanted stones (Fig. 3, area 12), constant immersion in a tide pool resulted in the poorest survival. The reasons for the trend toward slightly greater mortality as the degree of immersion increased are unknown. The amount of attached algae on the stones in the tide pool was much greater than on the other areas. This may have reduced the flow of water and food or have interfered directly with feeding movements. Another possible indirect effect of increased immersion is the increase in predation by the snail, *Thais lapillus,* at lower levels.

Chthamalus is tolerant of a much greater degree of immersion than it normally encounters. This is shown by the survival for a year on area 12 in a tide pool, together with the findings of Fischer (1928) and Barnes (1956a), who found that *Chthamalus* withstood submersion for 12 and 22 months, respectively. Its absence below M.T.L. can probably be ascribed either to a lack of initial settlement or to poor survival of newly settled larvae. Lewis and Powell (1960) have suggested that the survival of *Chthamalus* may be

favored by increased light or warmth during emersion in its early life on the shore. These conditions would tend to occur higher on the shore in Scotland than in southern England.

The effects of wave action on the survival of *Chthamalus* are difficult to assess. Like the degree of immersion, the effects of wave action may act indirectly. The areas 7 and 12, where relatively poor survival was found, were also the areas of least wave action. Although *Chthamalus* is usually abundant on wave beaten areas and absent from sheltered bays in Scotland, Lewis and Powell (1960) have shown that in certain sheltered bays it may be very abundant. Hatton (1938) found that in northern France, settlement and growth rates were greater in wave-beaten areas at M.T.L., but, at M.H.W.N., greater in sheltered areas.

At the upper shore margins of distribution *Chthamalus* evidently can exist higher than *Balanus* mainly as a result of its greater tolerance to heat and/or desiccation. The evidence for this was gained during the spring of 1955. Records from a tide and wave guage operating at this time about one-half mile north of the study area showed that a period of neap tides had coincided with an unusual period of warm calm weather in April so that for several days no water, not even waves, reached the level of Area 1. In the period

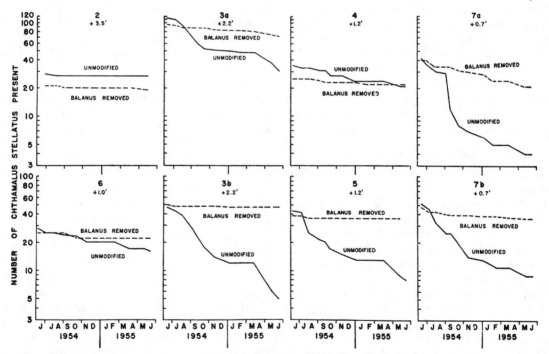

Fig. 2. Survivorship curves of *Chthamalus stellatus* which had settled naturally on the shore in the autumn of 1953. Areas designated "a" were protected from predation by cages. In each area the survival of *Chthamalus* growing without contact with *Balanus* is compared to that in the undisturbed area. For each area the vertical distance in feet from M.T.L. is shown.

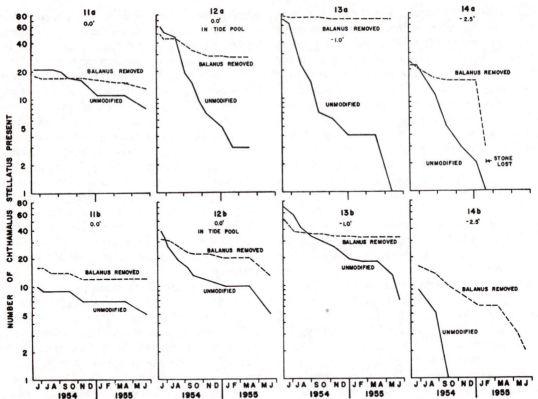

Fig. 3. Survivorship curves of *Chthamalus stellatus* on stones transplanted from high levels. These had settled in the autumn of 1953; the arrangement is the same as that of Figure 2.

between the censuses of February and May, *Balanus* aged one year suffered a mortality of 92%, those 2 years and older, 51%. Over the same period the mortality of *Chthamalus* aged 7 months was 62%, those 1½ years and older, 2%. Records of the survival of *Balanus* at several levels below this showed that only those *Balanus* in the top quarter of the intertidal region suffered high mortality during this time (Connell 1961).

Competition for space

At each census notes were made for individual barnacles of any crowding which had occurred since the last census. Thus when one barnacle started to grow up over another this fact was noted and at the next census 4-6 weeks later the progress of this process was noted. In this way a detailed description was built up of these gradually occurring events.

Intraspecific competition leading to mortality in *Chthamalus* was a rare event. For areas 2 to 7, on the portions from which *Balanus* had been removed, 167 deaths were recorded in a year. Of these, only 6 could be ascribed to crowding between individuals of *Chthamalus*. On the undisturbed portions no such crowding was

observed. This accords with Hatton's (1938) observation that he never saw crowding between individuals of *Chthamalus* as contrasted to its frequent occurrence between individuals of *Balanus*.

Interspecific competition between *Balanus* and *Chthamalus* was, on the other hand, a most important cause of death of *Chthamalus*. This is shown both by the direct observations of the process of crowding at each census and by the differences between the survival curves of *Chthamalus* with and without *Balanus*. From the periodic observations it was noted that after the first month on the undisturbed portions of areas 3 to 7 about 10% of the *Chthamalus* were being covered as *Balanus* grew over them; about 3% were being undercut and lifted by growing *Balanus*; a few had died without crowding. By the end of the 2nd month about 20% of the *Chthamalus* were either wholly or partly covered by *Balanus*; about 4% had been undercut; others were surrounded by tall *Balanus*. These processes continued at a lower rate in the autumn and almost ceased during the later winter. In the spring *Balanus* resumed growth and more crowding was observed.

134

In Table II, these observations are summarized for the undistributed portions of all the areas. Above M.T.L., the *Balanus* tended to overgrow the *Chthamalus,* whereas at the lower levels, undercutting was more common. This same trend was evident within each group of areas, undercutting being more prevalent on area 7 than on area 3, for example. The faster growth of *Balanus* at lower levels (Hatton 1938, Barnes and Powell 1953) may have resulted in more undercutting. When *Chthamalus* was completely covered by *Balanus* it was recorded as dead; even though death may not have occurred immediately, the buried barnacle was obviously not a functioning member of the population.

TABLE II. The causes of mortality of *Chthamalus stellatus* of the 1953 year group on the undisturbed portions of each area

Area no.	Height in ft from M.T.L.	No. at start	No. of deaths in the next year	Percentage of Deaths Resulting From:			
				Smothering by *Balanus*	Undercutting by *Balanus*	Other crowding by *Balanus*	Unknown causes
2.........	+3.5	28	1	0	0	0	100
3a........	+2.2	111	81	61	6	10	23
3b........	"	47	42	57	5	2	36
4.........	+1.4	34	14	21	14	0	65
5.........	+1.4	43	35	11	11	3	75
6.........	+1.0	27	11	9	0	0	91
7a........	+0.7	42	38	21	16	53	10
7b........	"	51	42	24	10	10	56
11a........	0.0	21	13	54	8	0	38
11b........	"	10	5	40	0	0	60
12a........	0.0	60	57	19	33	7	41
12b........	"	39	34	9	18	3	70
13a........	−1.0	71	70	19	24	3	54
13b........	"	69	62	18	8	3	71
14a........	−2.5	22	21	24	42	10	24
14b........	"	9	9	0	0	0	100
Total, 2- 7..	—	383	264	37	9	16	38
Total, 11-14..	—	301	271	19	21	4	56

In Table II under the term "other crowding" have been placed all instances where *Chthamalus* were crushed laterally between 2 or more *Balanus,* or where *Chthamalus* disappeared in an interval during which a dense population of *Balanus* grew rapidly. For example, in area 7a the *Balanus,* which were at the high population density of 48 per cm², had no room to expand except upward and the barnacles very quickly grew into the form of tall cylinders or cones with the diameter of the opercular opening greater than that of the base. It was obvious that extreme crowding occurred under these circumstances, but the exact cause of the mortality of the *Chthamalus* caught in this crush was difficult to ascertain.

In comparing the survival curves of Figs. 2 and 3 within each area it is evident that *Chthamalus* kept free of *Balanus* survived better than those in the adjacent undisturbed areas on all but areas 2 and 14a. Area 2 was in the zone where adults of *Balanus* and *Chthamalus* were normally mixed; at this high level *Balanus* evidently has no influence on the survival of *Chthamalus.* On Stone 14a, the survival of *Chthamalus* without *Balanus* was much better until January when a starfish, *Asterias rubens* L., entered the cage and ate the barnacles.

Much variation occurred on the other 14 areas. When the *Chthamalus* growing without contact with *Balanus* are compared with those on the adjacent undisturbed portion of the area, the survival was very much better on 10 areas and moderately better on 4. In all areas, some *Chthamalus* in the undisturbed portions escaped severe crowding. Sometimes no *Balanus* happened to settle close to a *Chthamalus,* or sometimes those which did died soon after settlement. In some instances, *Chthamalus* which were being undercut by *Balanus* attached themselves to the *Balanus* and so survived. Some *Chthamalus* were partly covered by *Balanus* but still survived. It seems probable that in the 4 areas, nos. 4, 6, 11a, and 11b, where *Chthamalus* survived well in the presence of *Balanus,* a higher proportion of the *Chthamalus* escaped death in one of these ways.

The fate of very young *Chthamalus* which settled in the autumn of 1954 was followed in detail in 2 instances, on stone 15 and area 7b. The *Chthamalus* on stone 15 had settled in an irregular space surrounded by large *Balanus.* Most of the mortality occurred around the edges of the space as the *Balanus* undercut and lifted the small *Chthamalus* nearby. The following is a tabulation of all the deaths of young *Chthamalus* between Sept. 30, 1954 and Feb. 14, 1955, on Stone 15, with the associated situations:

Lifted by *Balanus*	: 29
Crushed by *Balanus*	: 4
Smothered by *Balanus* and *Chthamalus*	: 2
Crushed between *Balanus and Chthamalus*	: 1
Lifted by *Chthamalus*	: 1
Crushed between two other *Chthamalus*	: 1
Unknown	: 3

This list shows that crowding of newly settled *Chthamalus* by older *Balanus* in the autumn mainly takes the form of undercutting, rather than of smothering as was the case in the spring. The reason for this difference is probably that the *Chthamalus* are more firmly attached in the spring so that the fast growing young *Balanus* grow up over them when they make contact. In the autumn the reverse is the case, the *Balanus* being firmly attached, the *Chthamalus* weakly so.

Although the settlement of *Chthamalus* on Stone 15 in the autumn of 1954 was very dense, 32/cm², so that most of them were touching another, only 2 of the 41 deaths were caused by intraspecific crowding among the *Chthamalus*. This is in accord with the findings from the 1953 settlement of *Chthamalus*.

The mortality rates for the young *Chthamalus* on area 7b showed seasonal variations. Between October 10, 1954 and May 15, 1955 the relative mortality rate per day × 100 was 0.14 on the undisturbed area and 0.13 where *Balanus* had been removed. Over the next month, the rate increased to 1.49 on the undisturbed area and 0.22 where *Balanus* was absent. Thus the increase in mortality of young *Chthamalus* in late spring was also associated with the presence of *Balanus*.

Some of the stones transplanted from high to low levels in the spring of 1954 bore adult *Chthamalus*. On 3 stones, records were kept of the survival of these adults, which had settled in the autumn of 1952 or in previous years and were at least 20 months old at the start of the experiment. Their mortality is shown in Table III; it was always much greater when *Balanus* was not removed. On 2 of the 3 stones this mortality rate was almost as high as that of the younger group. These results suggest that any *Chthamalus* that managed to survive the competition for space with *Balanus* during the first year would probably be eliminated in the 2nd year.

Censuses of *Balanus* were not made on the experimental areas. However, on many other areas in the same stretch of shore the survival of *Balanus* was being studied during the same period (Connell 1961). In Table IV some mortality rates measured in that study are listed; the *Balanus* were members of the 1954 settlement at population densities and shore levels similar to those of the present study. The mortality rates of *Balanus* were about the same as those of *Chthamalus* in similar situations except at the highest level, area 1, where *Balanus* suffered much greater mortality than *Chthamalus*. Much of this mortality was caused by intraspecific crowding at all levels below area 1.

TABLE III. Comparison of the mortality rates of young and older *Chthamalus stellatus* on transplanted stones

Stone No.	Shore level	Treatment	Number of *Chthamalus* present in June, 1954		% mortality over one year (or for 6 months for 14a) of *Chthamalus*	
			1953 year group	1952 or older year groups	1953 year group	1952 or older year groups
13b	1.0 ft below MTL	*Balanus* removed	51	3	35	0
		Undisturbed	69	16	90	31
12a	MTL, in a tide pool, caged	*Balanus* removed	50	41	44	37
		Undisturbed	60	31	95	71
14a	2.5 ft below MTL, caged	*Balanus* removed	25	45	40	36
		Undisturbed	22	8	86	75

TABLE IV. Comparison of annual mortality rates of *Chthamalus stellatus* and *Balanus balanoides*[*]

Area no.	Height in ft from M.T.L.	Population density: no./cm² June, 1954	% mortality in the next year
Chthamalus stellatus, autumn 1953 settlement			
1	+4.2	21	17
3a	+2.2	31	72
3b	"	29	89
6	+1.0	38	41
7a	+0.7	49	90
7b	"	52	82
11a	0.0	32	62
13a	−1.0	29	99
12a	(tide pool)	19	95
Balanus balanoides, spring 1954 settlement			
1 (top)	+4.2	21	99
1:Middle Cage 1	+2.1	85	92
1:Middle Cage 2	"	25	77
1:Low Cage 1	+1.5	26	88
Stone 1	−0.9	26	86
Stone 2	"	68	94

* Population density includes both species. The mortality rates of *Chthamalus* refer to those on the undisturbed portions of each area. The data and area designations for *Balanus* were taken from Connell (1961); the present area 1 is the same as that designated 1 (top) in that paper.

In the observations made at each census it appeared that *Balanus* was growing faster than *Chthamalus*. Measurements of growth rates of the 2 species were made from photographs of the areas taken in June and November, 1954. Barnacles growing free of contact with each other were measured; the results are given in Table V. The growth rate of *Balanus* was greater than that of *Chthamalus* in the experimental areas; this agrees with the findings of Hatton (1938) on the shore in France and of Barnes (1956a) for continual submergence on a raft at Millport.

TABLE V. Growth rates of *Chthamalus stellatus* and *Balanus balanoides*. Measurements were made of uncrowded individuals on photographs of areas 3a, 3b and 7b. Those of *Chthamalus* were made on the same individuals on both dates; of *Balanus*, representative samples were chosen

	CHTHAMALUS		BALANUS	
	No. measured	Average size, mm.	No. measured	Average size, mm.
June 11, 1954	25	2.49	39	1.87
November 3, 1954..............	25	4.24	27	4.83
Average size in the interval.......	3.36		3.35	
Absolute growth rate per day x 100	1.21		2.04	

After a year of crowding the average population densities of *Balanus* and *Chthamalus* remained in the same relative proportion as they had been at the start, since the mortality rates were about the same. However, because of its faster growth, *Balanus* occupied a relatively greater area and, presumably, possessed a greater biomass relative to that of *Chthamalus* after a year.

The faster growth of *Balanus* probably accounts for the manner in which *Chthamalus* were crowded by *Balanus*. It also accounts for the sinuosity of the survival curves of *Chthamalus* growing in contact with *Balanus*. The mortality rate of these *Chthamalus*, as indicated by the slope of the curves in Figs. 2 and 3, was greatest in summer, decreased in winter and increased again in spring. The survival curves of *Chthamalus* growing without contact with *Balanus* do not show these seasonal variations which, therefore, cannot be the result of the direct action of physical factors such as temperature, wave action or rain.

Seasonal variations in growth rate of *Balanus* correspond to these changes in mortality rate of *Chthamalus*. In Figure 4 the growth of *Balanus* throughout the year as studied on an intertidal panel at Millport by Barnes and Powell (1953), is compared to the survival of *Chthamalus* at about the same intertidal level in the present study. The increased mortality of *Chthamalus* was found to occur in the same seasons as the in-

creases in the growth rate of *Balanus*. The correlation was tested using the Spearman rank correlation coefficient. The absolute increase in diameter of *Balanus* in each month, read from the curve of growth, was compared to the percentage mortality of *Chthamalus* in the same month. For the 13 months in which data for *Chthamalus* was available, the correlation was highly significant, P = .01.

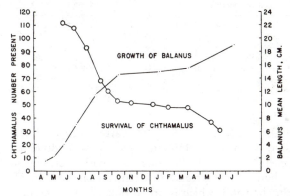

FIG. 4. A comparison of the seasonal changes in the growth of *Balanus balanoides* and in the survival of *Chthamalus stellatus* being crowded by *Balanus*. The growth of *Balanus* was that of panel 3, Barnes and Powell (1953), just above M.T.L. on Keppel Pier, Millport, during 1951-52. The *Chthamalus* were on area 3a of the present study, one-half mile south of Keppell Pier, during 1954-55.

From all these observations it appears that the poor survival of *Chthamalus* below M.H.W.N. is a result mainly of crowding by dense populations of faster growing *Balanus*.

At the end of the experiment in June, 1955, the surviving *Chthamalus* were collected from 5 of the areas. As shown in Table VI, the average size was greater in the *Chthamalus* which had grown free of contact with *Balanus*; in every case the difference was significant (P < .01, Mann-Whitney U. test, Siegel 1956). The survivors on the undisturbed areas were often misshapen, in some cases as a result of being lifted on to the side of an undercutting *Balanus*. Thus the smaller size of these barnacles may have been due to disturbances in the normal pattern of growth while they were being crowded.

These *Chthamalus* were examined for the presence of developing larvae in their mantle cavities. As shown in Table VI, in every area the proportion of the uncrowded *Chthamalus* with larvae was equal to or more often slightly greater than on the crowded areas. The reason for this may be related to the smaller size of the crowded *Chthamalus*. It is not due to separation, since *Chthamalus* can self-fertilize (Barnes and Crisp

137

Area	Treatment	Level, feet above M.T.L.	Number of Chthamalus	Average	Range	% of individuals which had larvae in mantle cavity
3a	Undisturbed	2.2	18	3.5	2.7-4.6	61
"	Balanus removed	"	50	4.1	3.0-5.5	65
4	Undisturbed	1.4	16	2.3	1.8 3.2	81
"	Balanus removed	"	37	3.7	2.5-5 1	100
5	Undisturbed	1.4	7	3.3	2.8-3.7	70
"	Balanus removed	"	13	4.0	3.5-4.5	100
6	Undisturbed	1.0	13	2.8	2.1-3.9	100
"	Balanus removed	"	14	4.1	3.0-5.2	100
7a & b	Undisturbed	0.7	10	3.5	2.7-4.5	70
"	Balanus removed	"	23	4.3	3.0-6.3	81

TABLE VI. The effect of crowding on the size and presence of larvae in *Chthamalus stellatus,* collected in June, 1955

Area	Height in ft from M.T.L.	a: Protected from predation by a cage			b: Unprotected, open to predation		
		With Balanus	Without Balanus	Difference	With Balanus	Without Balanus	Difference
Area 3	+2.2	73 (112)	25 (96)	48	89 (47)	6 (50)	83
Area 7	+0.7	90 (42)	47 (40)	43	82 (51)	23 (47)	59
Area 11	0	62 (21)	28 (18)	34	50 (10)	25 (16)	25
Area 12	0†	100 (60)	53 (50)	47	87 (39)	59 (32)	28
Area 13	−1.0	98 (72)	9 (77)	89	90 (69)	35 (51)	55

TABLE VII. The effect of predation by *Thais lapillus* on the annual mortality rate of *Chthamalus stellatus* in the experimental areas*

% mortality of *Chthamalus* over a year (The initial numbers are given in parentheses)

*The records for 12a extend over only 10 months; for purposes of comparison the mortality rate for 12a has been multiplied by 1.2.
†Tide pool.

1956). Moore (1935) and Barnes (1953) have shown that the number of larvae in an individual of *Balanus balanoides* increases with increase in volume of the parent. Comparison of the cube of the diameter, which is proportional to the volume, of *Chthamalus* with and without *Balanus* shows that the volume may be decreased to ¼ normal size when crowding occurs. Assuming that the relation between larval numbers and volume in *Chthamalus* is similar to that of *Balanus,* a decrease in both frequency of occurrence and abundance of larvae in *Chthamalus* results from competition with *Balanus.* Thus the process described in this paper satisfies both aspects of interspecific competition as defined by Elton and Miller (1954): "in which one species affects the population of another by a process of interference, i.e., by reducing the reproductive efficiency or increasing the mortality of its competitor."

The effect of predation by Thais

Cages which excluded *Thais* had been attached on 6 areas (indicated by the letter "a" following the number of the area). Area 14 was not included in the following analysis since many starfish were observed feeding on the barnacles at this level; one entered the cage in January, 1955, and ate most of the barnacles.

Thais were common in this locality, feeding on barnacles and mussels, and reaching average population densities of 200/m² below M.T.L. (Connell 1961). The mortality rates for *Chthamalus* in cages and on adjacent areas outside cages (indicated by the letter "b" after the number) are shown on Table VII.

If the mortality rates of *Chthamalus* growing without contact with *Balanus* are compared in and out of the cages, it can be seen that at the upper levels mortality is greater inside the cages,

at lower levels greater outside. Densities of *Thais* tend to be greater at and below M.T.L. so that this trend in the mortality rates of *Chthamalus* may be ascribed to an increase in predation by *Thais* at lower levels.

Mortality of *Chthamalus* in the absence of *Balanus* was appreciably greater outside than inside the cage only on area 13. In the other 4 areas it seems evident that few *Chthamalus* were being eaten by *Thais.* In a concurrent study of the behavior of *Thais* in feeding on *Balanus balanoides,* it was found that *Thais* selected the larger individuals as prey (Connell 1961). Since *Balanus* after a few month's growth was usually larger than *Chthamalus,* it might be expected that *Thais* would feed on *Balanus* in preference to *Chthamalus.* In a later study (unpublished) made at Santa Barbara, California, *Thais emarginata* Deshayes were enclosed in cages on the shore with mixed populations of *Balanus glandula* Darwin and *Chthamalus fissus* Darwin. These species were each of the same size range as the corresponding species at Millport. It was found that *Thais emarginata* fed on *Balanus glandula* in preference to *Chthamalus fissus.*

As has been indicated, much of the mortality of *Chthamalus* growing naturally intermingled with *Balanus* was a result of direct crowding by *Balanus.* It therefore seemed reasonable to take the difference between the mortality rates of *Chthamalus* with and without *Balanus* as an index of the degree of competition between the species. This difference was calculated for each area and is included in Table VII. If these differences are compared between each pair of adjacent areas in and out of a cage, it appears that the difference, and therefore the degree of competition, was greater outside the cages at the upper shore levels and less outside the cages at the lower levels.

Thus as predation increased at lower levels, the degree of competition decreased. This result would have been expected if *Thais* had fed upon *Balanus* in preference to *Chthamalus*. The general effect of predation by *Thais* seems to have been to lessen the interspecific competition below M.T.L.

DISCUSSION

"Although animal communities appear qualitatively to be constructed as if competition were regulating their structure, even in the best studied cases there are nearly always difficulties and unexplored possibilities" (Hutchinson 1957).

In the present study direct observations at intervals showed that competition was occurring under natural conditions. In addition, the evidence is strong that the observed competition with *Balanus* was the principal factor determining the local distribution of *Chthamalus*. *Chthamalus* thrived at lower levels when it was not growing in contact with *Balanus*.

However, there remain unexplored possibilities. The elimination of *Chthamalus* requires a dense population of *Balanus*, yet the settlement of *Balanus* varied from year to year. At Millport, the settlement density of *Balanus balanoides* was measured for 9 years between 1944 and 1958 (Barnes 1956b, Connell 1961). Settlement was light in 2 years, 1946 and 1958. In the 3 seasons of *Balanus* settlement studied in detail, 1953-55, there was a vast oversupply of larvae ready for settlement. It thus seems probable that most of the *Chthamalus* which survived in a year of poor settlement of *Balanus* would be killed in competition with a normal settlement the following year. A succession of years with poor settlements of *Balanus* is a possible, but improbable occurrence at Millport, judging from the past record. A very light settlement is probably the result of a chance combination of unfavorable weather circumstances during the planktonic period (Barnes 1956b). Also, after a light settlement, survival on the shore is improved, owing principally to the reduction in intraspecific crowding (Connell 1961); this would tend to favor a normal settlement the following year, since barnacles are stimulated to settle by the presence of members of their own species already attached on the surface (Knight-Jones 1953).

The fate of those *Chthamalus* which had survived a year on the undisturbed areas is not known since the experiment ended at that time. It is probable, however, that most of them would have been eliminated within 6 months; the mortality rate had increased in the spring (Figs. 2

and 3), and these survivors were often misshapen and smaller than those which had not been crowded (Table VI). Adults on the transplanted stones had suffered high mortality in the previous year (Table III).

Another difficulty was that *Chthamalus* was rarely found to have settled below mid tide level at Millport. The reasons for this are unknown; it survived well if transplanted below this level, in the absence of *Balanus*. In other areas of the British Isles (in southwest England and Ireland, for example) it occurs below mid tide level.

The possibility that *Chthamalus* might affect *Balanus* deleteriously remains to be considered. It is unlikely that *Chthamalus* could cause much mortality of *Balanus* by direct crowding; its growth is much slower, and crowding between individuals of *Chthamalus* seldom resulted in death. A dense population of *Chthamalus* might deprive larvae of *Balanus* of space for settlement. Also, *Chthamalus* might feed on the planktonic larvae of *Balanus*; however, this would occur in March and April when both the sea water temperature and rate of cirral activity (presumably correlated with feeding activity), would be near their minima (Southward 1955).

The indication from the caging experiments that predation decreased interspecific competition suggests that the action of such additional factors tends to reduce the intensity of such interactions in natural conditions. An additional suggestion in this regard may be made concerning parasitism. Crisp (1960) found that the growth rate of *Balanus balanoides* was decreased if individuals were infected with the isopod parasite *Hemioniscus balani* (Spence Bate). In Britain this parasite has not been reported from *Chthamalus stellatus*. Thus if this parasite were present, both the growth rate of *Balanus*, and its ability to eliminate *Chthamalus* would be decreased, with a corresponding lessening of the degree of competition between the species.

The causes of zonation

The evidence presented in this paper indicates that the lower limit of the intertidal zone of *Chthamalus stellatus* at Millport was determined by interspecific competition for space with *Balanus balanoides*. *Balanus*, by virtue of its greater population density and faster growth, eliminated most of the *Chthamalus* by directing crowding.

At the upper limits of the zones of these species no interaction was observed. *Chthamalus* evidently can exist higher on the shore than *Balanus* mainly as a result of its greater tolerance to heat and/or desiccation.

The upper limits of most intertidal animals are probably determined by physical factors such as these. Since growth rates usually decrease with increasing height on the shore, it would be less likely that a sessile species occupying a higher zone could, by competition for space, prevent a lower one from extending upwards. Likewise, there has been, as far as the author is aware, no study made which shows that predation by land species determines the upper limit of an intertidal animal. In one of the most thorough of such studies, Drinnan (1957) indicated that intense predation by birds accounted for an annual mortality of 22% of cockles (*Cardium edule* L.) in sand flats where their total mortality was 74% per year.

In regard to the lower limits of an animal's zone, it is evident that physical factors may act directly to determine this boundary. For example, some active amphipods from the upper levels of sandy beaches die if kept submerged. However, evidence is accumulating that the lower limits of distribution of intertidal animals are determined mainly by biotic factors.

Connell (1961) found that the shorter length of life of *Balanus balanoides* at low shore levels could be accounted for by selective predation by *Thais lapillus* and increased intraspecific competition for space. The results of the experiments in the present study confirm the suggestions of other authors that lower limits may be due to interspecific competition for space. Knox (1954) suggested that competition determined the distribution of 2 species of barnacles in New Zealand. Endean, Kenny and Stephenson (1956) gave indirect evidence that competition with a colonial polychaete worm, (*Galeolaria*) may have determined the lower limit of a barnacle (*Tetraclita*) in Queensland, Australia. In turn the lower limit of *Galeolaria* appeared to be determined by competition with a tunicate, *Pyura,* or with dense algal mats.

With regard to the 2 species of barnacles in the present paper, some interesting observations have been made concerning changes in their abundance in Britain. Moore (1936) found that in southwest England in 1934, *Chthamalus stellatus* was most dense at M.H.W.N., decreasing in numbers toward M.T.L. while *Balanus balanoides* increased in numbers below M.H.W.N. At the same localities in 1951, Southward and Crisp (1954) found that *Balanus* had almost disappeared and that *Chthamalus* had increased both above and below M.H.W.N. *Chthamalus* had not reached the former densities of *Balanus* except

at one locality, Brixham. After 1951, *Balanus* began to return in numbers, although by 1954 it had not reached the densities of 1934; *Chthamalus* had declined, but again not to its former densities (Southward and Crisp 1956).

Since *Chthamalus* increased in abundance at the lower levels vacated by *Balanus,* it may previously have been excluded by competition with *Balanus*. The growth rate of *Balanus* is greater than *Chthamalus* both north and south (Hatton 1938) of this location, so that *Balanus* would be likely to win in competition with *Chthamalus*. However, changes in other environmental factors such as temperature may have influenced the abundance of these species in a reciprocal manner. In its return to southwest England after 1951, the maximum density of settlement of *Balanus* was 12 per cm^2; competition of the degree observed at Millport would not be expected to occur at this density. At a higher population density, *Balanus* in southern England would probably eliminate *Chthamalus* at low shore levels in the same manner as it did at Millport.

In Loch Sween, on the Argyll Peninsula, Scotland, Lewis and Powell (1960) have described an unusual pattern of zonation of *Chthamalus stellatus*. On the outer coast of the Argyll Peninsula *Chthamalus* has a distribution similar to that at Millport. In the more sheltered waters of Loch Sween, however, *Chthamalus* occurs from above M.H.W.S. to about M.T.L., judging the distribution by its relationship to other organisms. *Balanus balanoides* is scarce above M.T.L. in Loch Sween, so that there appears to be no possibility of competition with *Chthamalus,* such as that occurring at Millport, between the levels of M.T.L. and M.H.W.N.

In Figure 5 an attempt has been made to summarize the distribution of adults and newly settled larvae in relation to the main factors which appear to determine this distribution. For *Balanus* the estimates were based on the findings of a previous study (Connell 1961); intraspecific competition was severe at the lower levels during the first year, after which predation increased in importance. With *Chthamalus,* it appears that avoidance of settlement or early mortality of those larvae which settled at levels below M.T.L., and elimination by competition with *Balanus* of those which settled between M.T.L. and M.H.W.N., were the principal causes for the absence of adults below M.H.W.N. at Millport. This distribution appears to be typical for much of western Scotland.

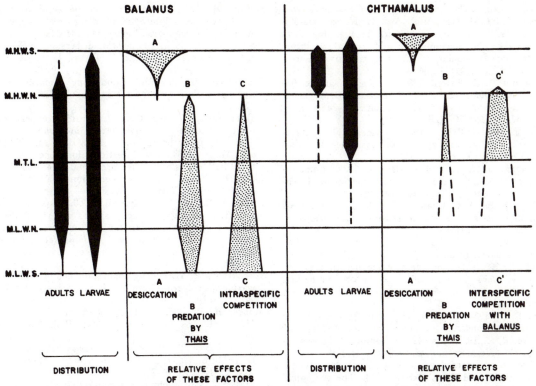

BALANUS   CHTHAMALUS

ADULTS LARVAE   A DESICCATION   C INTRASPECIFIC COMPETITION   ADULTS LARVAE   A DESICCATION   C' INTERSPECIFIC COMPETITION WITH BALANUS
                 B PREDATION BY THAIS   B PREDATION BY THAIS

DISTRIBUTION   RELATIVE EFFECTS OF THESE FACTORS   DISTRIBUTION   RELATIVE EFFECTS OF THESE FACTORS

FIG. 5. The intertidal distribution of adults and newly settled larvae of *Balanus balanoides* and *Chthamalus stellatus* at Millport, with a diagrammatic representation of the relative effects of the principal limiting factors.

SUMMARY

Adults of *Chthamalus stellatus* occur in the marine intertidal in a zone above that of another barnacle, *Balanus balanoides*. Young *Chthamalus* settle in the *Balanus* zone but evidently seldom survive, since few adults are found there.

The survival of *Chthamalus* which had settled at various levels in the *Balanus* zone was followed for a year by successive censuses of mapped individuals. Some *Chthamalus* were kept free of contact with *Balanus*. These survived very well at all intertidal levels, indicating that increased time of submergence was not the factor responsible for elimination of *Chthamalus* at low shore levels. Comparison of the survival of unprotected populations with others, protected by enclosure in cages from predation by the snail, *Thais lapillus*, showed that *Thais* was not greatly affecting the survival of *Chthamalus*.

Comparison of the survival of undisturbed populations of *Chthamalus* with those kept free of contact with *Balanus* indicated that *Balanus* could cause great mortality of *Chthamalus*. *Balanus* settled in greater population densities and grew faster than *Chthamalus*. Direct observations at each census showed that *Balanus* smothered, undercut, or crushed the *Chthamalus;* the greatest mortality of *Chthamalus* occurred during the seasons of most rapid growth of *Balanus*. Even older *Chthamalus* transplanted to low levels were killed by *Balanus* in this way. Predation by *Thais* tended to decrease the severity of this interspecific competition.

Survivors of *Chthamalus* after a year of crowding by *Balanus* were smaller than uncrowded ones. Since smaller barnacles produce fewer offspring, competition tended to reduce reproductive efficiency in addition to increasing mortality.

Mortality as a result of intraspecies competition for space between individuals of *Chthamalus* was only rarely observed.

The evidence of this and other studies indicates that the lower limit of distribution of intertidal organisms is mainly determined by the action of biotic factors such as competition for space or predation. The upper limit is probably more often set by physical factors.

References

Barnes, H. 1953. Size variations in the cyprids of some common barnacles. J. Mar. Biol. Ass. U. K. **32**: 297-304.

141

———. 1956a. The growth rate of *Chthamalus stellatus* (Poli). J. Mar. Biol. Ass. U. K. **35**: 355-361.

———. 1956b. *Balanus balanoides* (L.) in the Firth of Clyde: The development and annual variation of the larval population, and the causative factors. J. Anim. Ecol. **25**: 72-84.

——— and H. T. Powell. 1953. The growth of *Balanus balanoides* (L.) and *B. crenatus* Brug. under varying conditions of submersion. J. Mar. Biol. Ass. U. K. **32**: 107-128.

——— and D. J. Crisp. 1956. Evidence of self-fertilization in certain species of barnacles. J. Mar. Biol. Ass. U. K. **35**: 631-639.

Beauchamp, R. S. A. and P. Ullyott. 1932. Competitive relationships between certain species of freshwater Triclads. J. Ecol. **20**: 200-208.

Clark, P. J. and F. C. Evans. 1954. Distance to nearest neighbor as a measure of spatial relationships in populations. Ecology **35**: 445-453.

Clench, W. J. 1947. The genera *Purpura* and *Thais* in the western Atlantic. Johnsonia **2**, No. 23: 61-92.

Connell, J. H. 1961. The effects of competition, predation by *Thais lapillus,* and other factors on natural populations of the barnacle, *Balanus balanoides.* Ecol. Mon. **31**: 61-104.

Crisp, D. J. 1960. Factors influencing growth-rate in *Balanus balanoides.* J. Anim. Ecol. **29**: 95-116.

Drinnan, R. E. 1957. The winter feeding of the oyster-catcher (*Haematopus ostralegus*) on the edible cockle (*Cardium edule*). J. Anim. Ecol. **26**: 441-469.

Elton, Charles and R. S. Miller. 1954. The ecological survey of animal communities: with a practical scheme of classifying habitats by structural characters. J. Ecol. **42**: 460-496.

Endean, R., R. Kenny and W. Stephenson. 1956. The ecology and distribution of intertidal organisms on the rocky shores of the Queensland mainland. Aust. J. mar. freshw. Res. **7**: 88-146.

Fischer, E. 1928. Sur la distribution geographique de quelques organismes de rocher, le long des cotes de la Manche. Trav. Lab. Mus. Hist. Nat. St.-Servan **2**: 1-16.

Hatton, H. 1938. Essais de bionomie explicative sur quelques especes intercotidales d'algues et d'animaux. Ann. Inst. Oceanogr. Monaco **17**: 241-348.

Holme, N. A. 1950. Population-dispersion in *Tellina tenuis* Da Costa. J. Mar. Biol. Ass. U. K. **29**: 267-280.

Hutchinson, G. E. 1957. Concluding remarks. Cold Spring Harbor Symposium on Quant. Biol. **22**: 415-427.

Knight-Jones, E. W. 1953. Laboratory experiments on gregariousness during setting in *Balanus balanoides* and other barnacles. J. Exp. Biol. **30**: 584-598.

Knox, G. A. 1954. The intertidal flora and fauna of the Chatham Islands. Nature Lond: **174**: 871-873.

Lack, D. 1954. The natural regulation of animal numbers. Oxford, Clarendon Press.

Lewis, J. R. and H. T. Powell. 1960. Aspects of the intertidal ecology of rocky shores in Argyll, Scotland. I. General description of the area. II. The distribution of *Chthamalus stellatus* and *Balanus balanoides* in Kintyre. Trans. Roy. Soc. Edin. **64**: 45-100.

MacArthur, R. H. 1958. Population ecology of some warblers of northeastern coniferous forests. Ecology **39**: 599-619.

Moore, H. B. 1935. The biology of *Balnus balanoides*. III. The soft parts. J. Mar. Biol. Ass. U. K. **20**: 263-277.

———. 1936. The biology of *Balanus balanoides*. V. Distribution in the Plymouth area. J. Mar. Biol. Ass. U. K. **20**: 701-716.

Siegel, S. 1956. Nonparametric statistics. New York, McGraw Hill.

Southward, A. J. 1955. On the behavior of barnacles. I. The relation of cirral and other activities to temperature. J. Mar. Biol. Ass. U. K. **34**: 403-422.

——— and D. J. Crisp. 1954. Recent changes in the distribution of the intertidal barnacles *Chthamalus stellatus* Poli and *Balanus balanoides* L. in the British Isles. J. Anim. Ecol. **23**: 163-177.

———. 1956. Fluctuations in the distribution and abundance of intertidal barnacles. J. Mar. Biol. Ass. U. K. **35**: 211-229.

COMPETITION FOR NUTRIENTS AND LIGHT BETWEEN THE ANNUAL GRASSLAND SPECIES *BROMUS MOLLIS* AND *ERODIUM BOTRYS*

Robert L. McCown[1] and William A. Williams

Department of Agronomy, University of California, Davis, Calif.

(Accepted for publication April 3, 1968)

Abstract. Experiments showed that when competition between the common grass resident, *Bromus mollis,* and an associated forb, *Erodium botrys,* was primarily for sulfur and crowding was not intense, *Erodium* growth was much greater than in pure stands, and *Bromus* growth was markedly less. With competition under a low sulfur regime, *Erodium* acquired a disproportionate share of the available sulfur because of its more rapid root extension. At high sulfur levels, *Bromus* became increasingly competitive as its population density was increased, and wide ratios of *Bromus* to *Erodium* virtually eliminated *Erodium.* Leaf area and illumination profiles revealed that *Bromus* became the superior competitor for light because of its greater stature and more erect leaf habit when exposed to favorable nutrition and population density, and that *Erodium* supremacy at low sulfur levels and sparse population densities was closely associated with reduced leaf-area production by *Bromus.*

Introduction

Bromus mollis and *Erodium botrys* are among the most abundant species in the annual grasslands of the Great Central Valley and the low hot valleys of the inner Coast Ranges of California (Burcham 1957). Both are alien species that were introduced in the 19th century. They, along with other annuals of Mediterranean origin, have largely supplanted the perennial grasses of the pristine California prairies and now constitute a major grazing resource. Recent studies have shown that forage production of the annual grasslands is increased markedly by fertilizers containing nitrogen or combinations of nitrogen with sulfur and phosphorus (McKell, Jones, and Perrier 1962, Jones 1963b, Walker and Williams 1963). The unfertilized range usually contains *Erodium* species (Geraniaceae) as the major forb component, but the vegetation becomes dominated by grasses, often *Bromus* species, when the major nutrient deficiencies are eliminated.

Martin (1958) reported that *Bromus mollis* is a particularly responsive species to sulfur fertilization when nitrogen is in good supply. Walker and Williams (1963) found that nitrogenous fertilizers increased the growth of *Bromus mollis* and *Erodium botrys* without altering their proportions in the standing crop. When sulfur was applied too, however, dominance shifted to *B. mollis.* Two alternate hypotheses were suggested for the response to sulfur: a higher sulfur requirement

for *B. mollis;* or the elimination of all nutrient deficiencies permitted *B. mollis* to overtop and shade the *E. botrys.*

Experiments were conducted to study the mechanisms by which *Bromus* species and other tall grasses dominate annual grassland vegetation when fertilized, while Erodiums dominate under more typical infertile conditions. Specifically, the effect of sulfur fertility on competition for light and nutrients between *Bromus mollis* and *Erodium botrys* was investigated.

Materials and Methods

Seeds of *Bromus mollis* L. (soft chess) were collected from a typical annual range site on the San Joaquin Experimental Range, Coarsegold, California. Seeds of *Erodium botrys* (Cav.) Bertol. (broad-leaf filaree) were obtained from ant colonies of the species *Veromesser andrei* Mayr. (black harvester ant) on annual range 10 miles west of Dunnigan, California, in the foothills west of the Sacramento Valley.

Plants were grown in a sandy loam soil of the Hebron series. This soil has a pH of 6.1 and a cation exchange capacity of 10.5 meq/100 g soil. It contains 3.6 ppm LiCl (M/10) extractable sulfate sulfur.[2] Nitrogen was added as NH_4NO_3, phosphorus as KH_2PO_4, and sulfur as K_2SO_4. Equivalent amounts of potassium were applied as KCl to the nil and low rate of sulfur treatments.

---

[1] Present address: CSIRO Pastoral Research Laboratory, Townsville, Qld., Australia.

[2] Data supplied by W. E. Martin, Soils Specialist, University of California Agricultural Extension Service.

All salts were applied in solution prior to planting. The plants were watered with distilled water.

Experiment 1 was done in a controlled environment cabinet maintained at 21°C during the 10-hr light period and at 10°C during the dark period. Average illumination at the soil surface was 2,300 ft-c, as measured with a Weston illuminometer, Model 756. Light was supplied by fluorescent tubes supplemented with incandescent bulbs. Plants were grown in clay pots 20 cm in diameter and 10 cm deep lined with a polyethylene sleeve. Pots were placed on saucers and free drainage was permitted. Each pot contained 1,700 g Hebron soil mixed with 1,500 g washed river sand. Fertilizer treatments were sulfur at 0, 15, and 50 ppm soil, and nitrogen at 25 and 125 ppm soil, in factorial combinations. Each species was grown in pure stands and also in a 1:1 mixture with each fertilizer treatment, in three replications. Seeds were sown on the soil surface and covered 5 mm deep with washed sand. After emergence, a wire ring, 10.8 cm in diameter, was placed in the center of each pot, delimiting the future harvest area. Stands were thinned to 31 plants/dm² so that all pots contained the same total number of plants. Plants were harvested 30 days after emergence, and dry weights, Kjeldahl nitrogen, total sulfur, and sulfate-sulfur were determined on the plant material.

Experiment 2 was done in the open during April and May 1965, a period of high radiation (mean 606 cal/cm² per day) and moderate temperatures (mean maximum 26°C), except for the 7 days just after emergence (263 cal/cm² per day and 16°C). Containers used were steel cans 10.5 cm in diameter by 35 cm tall lined with a polyethylene sleeve. Free drainage was permitted. Each container was filled with 3,225 g of a Hebron sandy loam soil and fertilized at the rate of 100 ppm nitrogen and 38 ppm phosphorus. There were two levels of sulfur: none added and 30 ppm. In experiment 2a three plants of *Erodium* were grown surrounded by 3, 12, 48, or 192 *Bromus* plants. Experiment 2b consisted of pure cultures of *Erodium* at 3, 12, and 48 plants per pot and pure cultures of *Bromus* at 3, 12, 48, and 192 plants per pot. Plants were protected from birds by cages made from 1-inch poultry net.

Artificial borders were constructed from galvanized window screen covered by black nylon to simulate the effects of border plants in light interception. The borders were raised as the plants grew so that the upper edge of the screen was at the maximum height of the vegetative canopy. The screen alone transmitted 73% of lateral light. The cloth and screen transmitted 3% of lateral light. The height of the borders was adjusted to provide the outermost plants with a light environment similar to that of the central plants.

Just prior to harvesting, light measurements were made in full sunlight above the canopy and at the soil surface of all pots. In addition, in mixtures of species, the amount of light transmitted to the top of the canopy of *Erodium* was measured. All measurements were made between 10 AM and 2 PM, when the incident radiation was roughly perpendicular to the soil surface. For the measurements, an unfiltered selenium cell, 12.5 mm by 22 mm, attached to a Weston microammeter, Model 1951, was used and calibrated with a Weston illumination meter, Model 756.

At harvest the plants were clipped at the soil surface, placed in polyethylene bags, and stored at slightly above 0°C for subsequent laboratory measurements. The leaf area of the *Bromus* above the *Erodium*, the remaining *Bromus* leaf area, and the leaf area of the *Erodium* were determined with an airflow planimeter (Jenkins 1959). Dry weights were determined for shoots of each species at 14, 28, and 42 days after emergence. Shoot tissue was ground and wet-ashed for the determination of total sulfur.

The low planting densities were irrigated whenever the surface soil appeared dry. Stands of high densities were irrigated once or twice daily, depending on the weather, but appreciable drainage was avoided. During the third harvest interval, high-density high-sulfur treatments received Hoagland's solution, minus micronutrients, at alternate irrigations, and low-density treatments received the same solution less frequently in an attempt to prevent any limitation on growth as a result of nutrient shortages.

In both experiments dry weights were determined after samples had been in a forced-draft oven at 65°C for at least 48 hr. Sulfur determinations were made according to the technique of Johnson and Nishita (1952). Since this method estimates sulfate-sulfur, the analyses for this fraction were made on ground plant material. For determinations of total sulfur, the plant material was wet-ashed to oxidize all reduced sulfur to sulfate before analysis.

Relative growth rate was calculated in the usual manner from $(\log_e W_2 - \log_e W_1)/(t_2 - t_1)$, in which W is the shoot dry weight at time t (Williams 1963). The increase in shoot dry weight is regarded as a process of continuous compound interest, with each growth increment being added to the "capital" for further growth, and is expressed as milligrams increased weight per gram total weight per day.

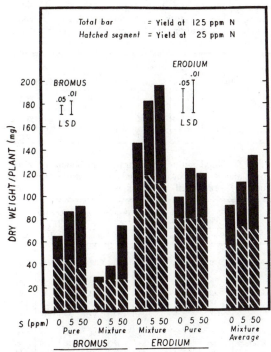

Total bar = Yield at 125 ppm N
Hatched segment = Yield at 25 ppm N

FIG. 1. The effect of sulfur and nitrogen fertilization on *Bromus* and *Erodium* shoot dry weight of individual plants in pure stands and in 1:1 mixtures (experiment 1).

RESULTS

Competition for nutrients in mixtures of equal numbers of Bromus and Erodium (experiment 1)

Competitive abilities of the species were assessed by comparing growth in mixtures of equal numbers of each species with their growth in pure stands. At the high nitrogen level, maximum dry weight was almost achieved with 5 ppm sulfur (S_5) for both species in pure cultures (Fig. 1). In the mixture, S_5 produced a highly significant increase in *Erodium* yield and a small but significant increase in *Bromus* yield. Sulfur at 50 ppm (S_{50}) resulted in no significant increase in *Erodium* over the S_5 treatment, whereas the yield of *Bromus* in the S_{50} treatment was nearly double that at the S_5 treatment, a difference significant at the .01 probability level.

The interpretation of these growth responses is aided by chemical analysis of plant tissue. Jones (1963a) found the critical concentration of sulfate-sulfur for the shoots of these species to be in the range of 200 to 400 ppm dry basis. i.e., growth is a function of sulfate-sulfur concentration at tissue levels less than 200 ppm dry basis, while growth becomes limited by other factors at concentrations above 400 ppm.

TABLE 1. Sulfate-sulfur concentration in shoots of *Bromus* and *Erodium* in pure stands and in 1:1 mixtures (experiment 1)

Nutrient additions		Sulfate-sulfur (ppm)			
		Bromus		Erodium	
N(ppm)	S(ppm)	Pure	Mixture	Mixture	Pure
25	0	170	40	100	130
25	5	1,520	1,040	1,120	1,370
25	50	2,000	1,540	1,580	1,860
125	0	40	40	50	50
125	5	320	130	400	380
125	50	1,320	1,400	1,700	1,200

At the high nitrogen level plus S_0 the concentration of sulfate-sulfur in both species was 40–50 ppm both in pure stands and in the mixture, indicating severe sulfur deficiency (Table 1). In the S_5 treatment the *Bromus* component of the mixture, which had a moderate dry weight increase, had a sulfate-sulfur concentration of 130 ppm. The *Erodium* component contained 400 ppm. The S_{50} treatment, which produced a marked increase in *Bromus* dry weight, had a sulfate-sulfur concentration of 1,400 ppm. Figure 1 and Table 1 indicate that, at the high nitrogen level with sulfur in short supply, *Erodium* was able to increase in dry weight at the expense of *Bromus*. With *Bromus,* maximum growth response to sulfur occurred only when sulfur was added in amounts in excess of the requirements of the associated *Erodium*.

At the low nitrogen level there were no significant dry-weight increases in pure stands as a result of additions of sulfur (Fig. 1). In the mixture the addition of 5 ppm sulfur produced an increase of 25% in *Erodium* weight. However, weight of the *Bromus* component of the mixture did not increase. Although it might seem that competition for nitrogen occurred here, this interpretation was not supported by tissue analysis.

The response to nitrogen was strikingly different for the two species grown in mixture (Fig. 1). Increases in *Erodium* yield due to the applied nitrogen did not differ significantly among sulfur levels, and all yields were significantly higher than at low nitrogen. On the other hand, *Bromus* responses to nitrogen increased significantly with increasing sulfur levels. At S_0 the nitrogen response was not significant. Although the response to nitrogen at S_5 was significant at the .05 level, the increase was greatest at the highest sulfur level (S_{50}). This is further evidence that *Erodium* was able to exploit the limited sulfur pool to the detriment of the associated *Bromus*.

145

Effect of Bromus *population density and sulfur fertility on growth of* Erodium (experiment 2a)

Under natural conditions *Bromus* plants greatly outnumber *Erodium* plants generally (Biswell and Graham 1956, Sumner and Love 1961). In this experiment the effect of density of *Bromus* plants on the growth of associated *Erodium* at high and low sulfur levels was measured with particular attention to the structure of the leaf canopy and competition for light. Ideally, there would have been one *Erodium* plant per pot in order to eliminate *Erodium* intraspecific effects. It was judged, however, that random variation among single *Erodium* plants might have been excessive. Thus, three plants were used as a compromise between minimizing intraspecific competition and minimizing error variation. The densities of 3 *Erodium* and 3, 12, 48, and 192 *Bromus* plants per pot are equivalent to 3.8 *Erodium* and 3.8, 15.5, 62, and 248 *Bromus* plants per dm^2, respectively.

Shoot yields of *Erodium* in mixtures, relative to the control (3 *Erodium*, 0 *Bromus*), were suppressed by increasing population density and duration of growth (Fig. 2). At both sulfur levels, shoot yields of *Erodium* were a function of the number of associated *Bromus* plants. At successive harvest dates, progressively lower densities of *Bromus* suppressed *Erodium* yields relative to the *Erodium* control. The effects of *Bromus* density and duration of growth period were much greater, however, at the high sulfur level than at the low sulfur level. The mixtures with high sulfur tended toward grass dominance, culminated

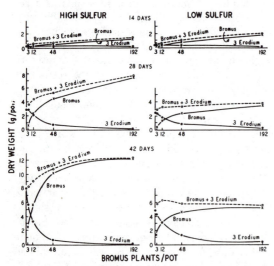

Fig. 2. Effect of number of *Bromus* plants in mixtures with three *Erodium* plants on the shoot dry weight of each species component and their sum at two sulfur levels (experiment 2a).

TABLE 2. Percentage dry weight of *Erodium* in mixtures of three *Erodium* plus various numbers of *Bromus* plants per pot after 14, 28, and 42 days (experiment 2a)

Number of Bromus plants	High sulfur			Low sulfur		
	14 days	28 days	42 days	14 days	28 days	42 days
3	87	82	70	84	84	77
12	53	47	37	53	58	50
48	25	15	6.3	26	29	23
192	4.6	2.5	0.1	7.7	7.2	7.3

TABLE 3. Total sulfur concentration in shoots of *Erodium* and *Bromus* in pure stands and mixtures (experiment 2)—expressed in percentage

	Plants per pot		High sulfur			Low sulfur		
	Bromus	Erodium	14 days	28 days	42 days	14 days	28 days	42 days
Pure Erodium	0	3	0.37	0.30	0.26	0.21	0.15	0.07
Erodium in mixture	3	3	.32	.30	.25	.20	.14	.04
	12	3	.36	.33	.34	.20	.12	.07
	48	3	.38	.32	.40	.18	.12	.07
	192	3	.33	.45	.32	.12	.10	.13
Bromus in mixture	3	3	.25	.34	.21	.20	.16	.06
	12	3	.34	.32	.24	.18	.10	.06
	48	3	.29	.32	.26	.28	.11	.07
	192	3	.32	.33	.26	.19	.09	.06
Pure Bromus	3	0	.31	.28	.23	.28	.24	.07
	12	0	.27	.33	.21	.30	.10	.07
	48	0	.31	.32	.27	.25	.09	.06
	192	0	.31	.27	.24	.18	.11	.06
						LSD 5% = .05*		

*LSD for the low sulfur mixtures and the three plants per pot pure stands for both species.

at the highest *Bromus* density by high *Erodium* mortality by 42 days. In contrast to this progressive decline in the *Erodium* component in all mixtures at high sulfur, there was evidence of the establishment of a rather stable *Erodium* content in the low-sulfur mixtures (Table 2).

At the high sulfur level, the total sulfur concentration in the plants was never less than 0.2% for either species (Table 3), the approximate critical concentration of total sulfur for these species (McCown 1966). Hence, it is very unlikely that growth of *Erodium* was limited by sulfur deficiency. Rather, the taller growing grass assumed a competitive role in controlling *Erodium* growth by shading. With the high sulfur level, *Bromus* developed a substantial leaf canopy above the *Erodium* foliage (Fig. 3). At the higher population densities the leaf-area index values (leaf area, one side only, subtended per unit ground area) of *Bromus* foliage above the *Erodium* foliage were several to many times those for the *Erodium*.

Description of the light environment of *Erodium*

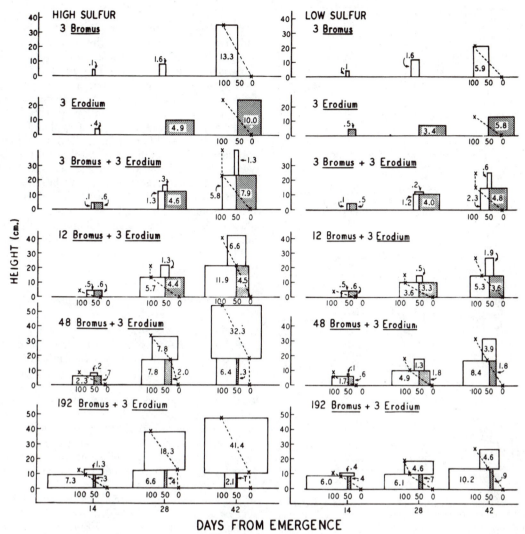

FIG. 3. Foliage canopy structure of pure stands and mixtures of *Bromus* and *Erodium* (hatched). The areas of the rectangles are proportional to the indicated leaf-area index values. In mixtures, *Bromus* leaves were measured in two strata, above and below the average height of the associated *Erodium*. Dotted lines represent illumination as percentage of full daylight (experiment 2).

was difficult because insertion of the photo cell into the canopy of very erect grass laminae produced an opening, resulting in erroneously high readings. Nevertheless, the illumination diagrams in Fig. 3 are useful for qualitative interpretation of the *Erodium* growth responses. The ability of *Bromus* to intercept light and, hence, cast deep shade on the associated *Erodium* is evident. Thus, increases in superior *Bromus* leaf area with increases in *Bromus* density and age appear to account for the corresponding suppression of *Erodium* yields.

At the low sulfur level, sulfur deficiencies were acute in both species in the mixture, but there was no evidence of either species gaining a dispropor-

tionate share of available sulfur (Table 3). The degree of shading of the *Erodium* by the associated grass was markedly less at low sulfur than at the high level (Fig. 3). This was reflected in the relative growth rates (Fig. 4). In contrast to the results at high sulfur, relative growth rates of *Erodium* generally exceeded those of *Bromus* at low S during the 14–28-day interval, and were exceeded by *Bromus* by only a moderate degree at low S during the 28–42-day interval.

Yield-density relationships of pure cultures of Bromus and Erodium (experiment 2b)

Pure culture yield-density relationships were determined as one means of predicting the influ-

147

$$I = I_o e^{-kL}$$

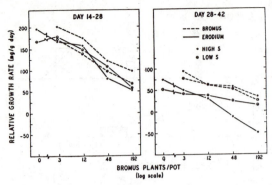

FIG. 4. Relative growth rates of the components of mixtures of three *Erodium* plants + various numbers of *Bromus* plants at two sulfur levels (experiment 2a).

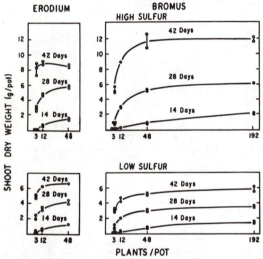

FIG. 5. The relationship of total shoot dry weight to population density in pure stands of *Bromus* and *Erodium* at two sulfur levels (experiment 2b).

where I and I_o refer to the illumination beneath and above the foliage, k is the extinction coefficient, and L is the leaf area index (Loomis, Williams, and Duncan 1967). The lower extinction coefficient for *Bromus* is a consequence of its upright habit of leaf display and is associated with more uniform vertical distribution of light in the foliage and improved efficiency of light utilization in dense foliage. The optimum leaf area index (producing the maximum growth rate) was between 20 and 25 for *Bromus,* and between 5 and 10 for *Erodium.* Hence, under light-limiting conditions, *Bromus* was more productive than *Erodium,* because of an upright leaf arrangement that allowed deeper penetration of light into the leaf canopy, allowing a much higher leaf-area index and greater net photosynthesis.

DISCUSSION

Competition between Bromus mollis *and* Erodium botrys

In the present study, when dry weight yields produced by *Erodium* and *Bromus* in mixtures were compared with the production by equivalent numbers of plants in pure stands, *Erodium* was always favored and *Bromus* was depressed at least slightly by the mixture (Fig. 1). Such comparisons between mixtures and pure stands cannot be made directly in the case of the addition mixtures of experiment 2a. Even so, "actual yields" in mixtures can be compared with "expected yields" in pure stands of comparable density by interpolation from pure stand yield-density curves (Fig. 6) according to the method suggested by Black (1960). Actual yields exceeded expected yields for *Erodium,* while the opposite was true for *Bromus* (Table 4).

In 75% of the studies that Donald (1963) reviewed concerning associated growth of species in pairs, the production per plant of one of the species was increased and that of the other decreased relative to plants in pure stands of equal density. In his words, "One of the species is the aggressor, able to exploit more than its 'share' of the factors of the environment, while the other is suppressed because it is able to secure only a lesser part of the light, water, or nutrients." On the basis of the above comparisons we might state that *Erodium* was the "aggressor" and that the growth of *Bromus* was lessened by its association with *Erodium.* This tentative conclusion, in view of the demonstrated superiority of *Bromus* in competing for light in mixtures, raises the question of whether comparison of performance in mixtures with that in pure cultures is an appro-

ence of density on the competition of species in mixtures. At all harvest dates, *Erodium* was more productive than *Bromus* at the lower densities (Fig. 5). At low sulfur, *Erodium* was more productive than *Bromus* at all comparable densities, and moreover, 48 *Erodium* plants were more productive than 192 *Bormus* plants at the later harvest dates. At high sulfur, however, *Bromus* yield exceeded maximum *Erodium* yield by 33%.

This marked difference in production under light-limiting conditions appears to be related to differences in relations between leaf-canopy structure and light interception. The average extinction coefficients were 0.4 for *Bromus* and 0.9 for *Erodium.* These values were calculated from light-interception data and the amount of leaf area penetrated (Fig. 3) using the Bougeur-Lambert function:

TABLE 4. Comparisons of shoot dry weight of *Bromus* and *Erodium* components of mixtures (actual) with estimated yield[a] of an equivalent number of plants per pot in pure stands (expected) in experiment 2

Plants per pot	High sulfur			Low sulfur		
	Expected[a] (g/pot)	Actual (g/pot)	Diff. (%)	Expected[a] (g/pot)	Actual (g/pot)	Diff. (%)
3 *Bromus*	3.45	2.52	−27	1.86	1.26	−32
3 *Erodium*	4.20	5.83	+39	2.85	4.23	+48
12 *Bromus*	7.20	5.76	−20	3.72	3.12	−16
3 *Erodium*	1.74	3.24	+86	.42	3.06	+143
48 *Bromus*	11.00	10.00	− 9	4.80	4.66	− 3
3 *Erodium*	.51	.69	+35	.39	1.35	+246

[a]Interpolated by means of plant weight: density curves in Fig. 6.

priate measure of the interspecific competitive relationships in this case where *Bromus* and *Erodium* differ markedly in their responses to crowding in pure cultures.

Figure 7 shows the relationships between the logarithm of the weight of individual plants and the logarithm of population density in the mixtures. The slope of the log/log regression is proportional to the intensity of competition (Harper 1961). Although *Erodium* plants were always larger than *Bromus* plants at the low sulfur level, the slopes of their log weight-log density curves were similar over the range of population densities studied. This indicates that increase in *Bromus* density resulted in increases in competition which had the same relative effect on both species. However, at high sulfur, increasing the number of

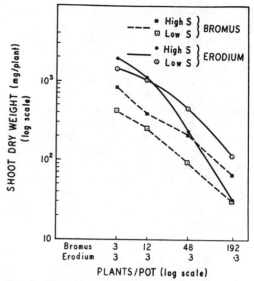

FIG. 7. The effect of sulfur level on the shoot dry weight per plant in *Bromus* and *Erodium* mixtures 42 days after emergence (experiment 2a).

Bromus plants in the mixture reduced weight per plant of *Erodium* more than increasing the number of *Erodium* plants (from comparison of Fig. 6 and 7). Evidently, *Bromus* was able to exploit the light environment in pure stands much more successfully than could *Erodium*. Hence, the relative advantage to *Erodium* in the mixture was due not to any "aggressive" characteristics but rather to the fact that *Erodium* was merely a poorer competitor in pure culture than in equivalent population densities in mixtures.

Another fruitful approach to the competitive relationships of mixtures of *Bromus* and *Erodium* can be made through use of the growth rates of each species component in relation to various environmental factors. In experiment 2a, although there were three *Erodium* plants, the effects of competition among *Erodium* plants in most instances was small in relation to competition with the associated *Bromus*. When competition was for light only (with high sulfur), relative growth rates for *Bromus* exceeded those for *Erodium* at all densities during both harvest intervals, with the difference increasing with increases in *Bromus* density and age (Fig. 4). When sulfur supply was limiting to growth, relative growth rates for *Erodium* exceeded those for *Bromus* at low densities during the first harvest interval. With increased *Bromus* density, age, or both, relative growth rates for *Bromus* exceeded those for *Erodium*. Although *Erodium* was the aggressor when competition for light was minimal, presumably because of its initially greater leaf area (McCown

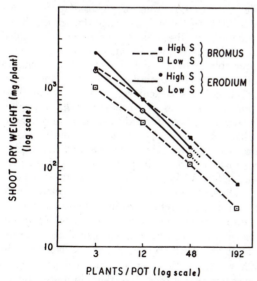

FIG. 6. The effect of sulfur level on shoot dry weight per plant at several population densities in pure stands of *Bromus* and *Erodium* 42 days after emergence (experiment 2b).

1966), *Bromus* always became the aggressor when competition for light became appreciable.

A major purpose of these studies was to determine whether *Erodium* is a more successful competitor for sulfur than *Bromus*. In experiment 1 *Erodium* was depriving *Bromus* of sulfur when the supply was limited (Fig. 1). In an ancillary experiment, rates of root elongation of isolated plants were measured in sand-filled glass tubes inclined at 60° from horizontal. One week from the onset of germination *Erodium* had penetrated 18 cm, while *Bromus* had reached a depth of only 6 cm (Fig. 8). It is reasonable to conclude that *Erodium* exploited limited sulfur supplies to the detriment of *Bromus* simply because *Erodium* roots "got there first."

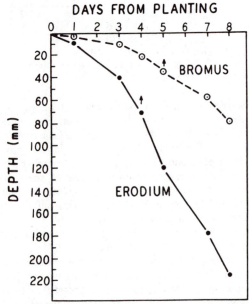

FIG. 8. Penetration of roots of *Bromus* and *Erodium* into moist sand. Arrows indicate seedling emergence.

When the soil supply of one or more nutrients is inadequate, leaf canopy above the *Erodium* is restricted. Under such conditions the handicap of *Erodium*'s low stature is minimized. On the other hand, an early rapid growth rate and a deep rooting habit provide *Erodium* an advantage when nutrients are scarce. It has been shown in lysimeter studies that sulfate is leached readily from coarse-textured soils (McKell and Williams 1960). Annual plants with shallow rooting habits may experience sulfur deficiency early in the season, but recover later as sulfate is released by the decay of organic matter. Deep-rooted perennial plants on the same soils may never experience any deficiency, having access to sulfate accumulated in the clay subsoil (Jordan and Bardsley 1958). In the present studies, the pots provided an environment in which the normally deeper rooted *Erodium* had access only to the same sulfur reservoir as did the *Bromus*, and *Erodium* excelled in competing for sulfur because of its more rapid early growth. This same situation presumably occurs in many areas of annual vegetation where only a few inches of soil overlie bedrock (Storie 1951), or in early season when rainfall may have wetted only a shallow portion of the profile.

Comparisons of benefits of mixtures and pure stands

Unlike sown crops, *Bromus mollis* and *Erodium botrys* rarely exist in pure stands except on relatively small areas (as part of the mosaic pattern of the vegetation). However, the relative proportions of grass and *Erodium* in a sward may vary tremendously.

Any association of species that results in greater utilization of the environmental resources, and consequently in greater yield than a pure stand of any component, is a beneficial mixture. However, such mixtures occur only infrequently (Donald 1963). In the studies reported here there was no instance in which a mixture produced significantly more dry matter than a pure culture at the same density.

The total density of the mixtures and of each pure stand must be equal in order to make comparisons as above. In experiment 2b, yields of pure stands of densities equal to the mixtures can be extrapolated from the yield:density curves (Fig. 6). Comparisons of yields of pure stands and mixtures (Table 5) revealed that although the production by the mixture occasionally equaled that of the better pure stand, it never exceeded it appreciably. These results indicate that maximum production under optimum nutrient (and moisture) conditions is achieved with pure stands of *Bromus*. Mixtures of *Bromus* and *Erodium* under such conditions tended to become pure stands of *Bromus* (Table 2). At low sulfur, the maximum aboveground yield of *Erodium* was higher than that of *Bromus* in pure stands and, in general, slightly higher than in the mixtures (Table 5). Thus, from the standpoint of dry matter production under adverse fertility conditions, a large *Erodium* component would seem to be beneficial.

Even when a mixture is not beneficial in terms of total dry matter yield, it may be beneficial in other ways. If the average mutual depression of species in mixtures is less than in pure stands, the mixture might be considered beneficial. A means of assessing this was proposed by G. A. McIntyre and discussed by Donald (1963). This

TABLE 5. Shoot dry weight (grams/pot) of pure stands and of mixtures of *Bromus and Erodium* (experiment 2)

Plants/pot	High sulfur			Low sulfur		
	Pure *Bromus*[a]	Mixture[b]	Pure *Erodium*[a]	Pure *Bromus*[a]	*Mixture*[b]	Pure *Erodium*[a]
6....................................	6.9	8.4	8.3	3.7	5.5	5.7
15....................................	9.0	9.0	8.6	4.7	6.3	6.3
51....................................	11.5	10.8	8.7	5.4	6.0	6.7
195....................................	12.2	12.3	—	5.9	5.5	—

[a] Yields in pure stands were obtained by interpolation from yield: density curves in Fig. 6.
[b] Actual yields of mixtures of three *Erodium* plants with 3, 12, 48, and 192 *Bromus* plants.

technique can be illustrated using the data from the "3 *Bromus* + 3 *Erodium*" mixture at low sulfur in experiment 2b. The dry weight of a single *Erodium* plant was 1.41 g (Fig. 7). It can be interpolated from Fig. 6 that a plant this size would have developed in a pure stand of 3.7 plants per pot. Considering that there were three *Erodium* plants in the mixture, the three *Bromus* plants in the mixture had an effect equivalent to 0.70 *Erodium* plants. Similarly, the mean yield of *Bromus* plants in the mixture was 0.42 g, a weight which would have been obtained in a pure stand of 10 plants per pot. Thus, three *Erodium* plants had an effect equivalent to seven *Bromus* plants. In symbolic terms:

Competitive effect on 3 E plants: $3B = 0.70E$; $(E/B)_1 = 4.3$

Competitive effect on 3 B plants: $3E = 7.0B$; $(E/B)_2 = 2.3$

The ratio E/B expresses the competitive effect of one plant of *Erodium* in terms of *Bromus* equivalents. The $(E/B)_1$ indicates that 4.3 *Bromus* plants had an effect on an *Erodium* plant equivalent to that of another *Erodium* plant. The $(E/B)_2$ indicates that one *Erodium* plant had an effect on a *Bromus* plant equivalent to that of 2.3 *Bromus* plants. In other words, in this mixture *Bromus* had a small effect on *Erodium,* and *Erodium* had a large effect on *Bromus,* as demonstrated by the difference between the equivalence factors (E/B). An index of the overall benefit of the mixture can be calculated as the ratio of the equivalence factors 1 and 2. Thus the "competition index" $[(E/B)_2/(E/B)_1]$ in this case is 0.54. The competition index can be calculated independent of the equivalence factors as

$$\frac{\text{Pure culture equivalents}}{\text{Actual number of plants}} =$$
$$\frac{7.0 \times 0.70}{3 \times 3} = \frac{4.9}{9} = 0.54$$

The equivalence factors and competition indices of the mixtures of experiment 2a are presented in

TABLE 6. The equivalence factors (E/B) and competition indices (CI) for mixtures of *Bromus* (B) and *Erodium* (E) (experiment 2)

Mixture	High sulfur		Low sulfur	
	E/B	CI	E/B	CI
3 *Bromus*........ 3 *Erodium*........	1) 2.3 2) 2.3	1.0	1) 4.3 2) 2.3	0.54
12 *Bromus*........ 3 *Erodium*........	1) 2.5 2) 2.8	1.1	1) 4.6 2) 2.2	.48
48 *Bromus*........ 3 *Erodium*........	1) 1.4 2) 2.7	1.9	1) 4.4 2) 2.0	.45

Table 6. A competition index of less than 1.0 indicates that the interplant competition is less than would be predicted by the yields in pure stands when comparisons are made on the basis of the products of the numbers. A value of 1.0 or larger indicates a mixture of no benefit or one of detrimental effect. Hence, mixtures of *Bromus* and *Erodium* at a high sulfur level were not beneficial, but at low sulfur were beneficial.

The method devised by Black (1960) for assessing the effects of interspecific competition in a mixture by comparison with pure-stand yields is useful in understanding the meaning of McIntyre's competition index (Table 4). In general, *Erodium* was favored by being in a mixture (positive differences), while *Bromus* was depressed (negative differences). The effect of *Erodium* on *Bromus* was about the same at high as at low sulfur. However, the enhancement of *Erodium* growth in the mixture was markedly greater at low sulfur than at high sulfur. At low sulfur the increase in *Erodium* was much greater than the decrease in the grass. This net favorable interaction is reflected in competition index values of less than 1.0. Since no direct correspondence is apparent between the schemes of Black and McIntyre, it is not surprising that, although the effects of competition were qualitatively similar, the ratio of *Erodium* increase to *Bromus* decrease at high sulfur was so much less than at low sulfur that the competition indices exceeded 1.0.

An inference of practical import can be drawn from these results. The maintenance of *Erodium* as a component of annual grassland vegetation is desirable particularly on soils where fertilization to enhance grass production is uneconomical. Moreover, a large part of the grazeable forage is contributed by *Erodium* in years when the growth of grasses is curtailed by drought (Heady 1961). Thus, a mixture of these species is beneficial in that it provides a buffering effect against moisture or nutritional inadequacies of the environment.

Literature Cited

Biswell, H. H., and C. A. Graham. 1956. Plant counts and seed production on California annual-type ranges. J. Range Manage. 9: 116–118.

Black, J. N. 1960. An assessment of the role of planting density in competition between red clover (*Trifolium pratense* L.) and lucerne (*Medicago sativa* L.) in the early vegetative stage. Oikos 11: 26–42.

Burcham, L. T. 1957. California range land. Calif. Dep. Nat. Res., Sacramento, Calif. 261 p.

Donald, C. M. 1963. Competition among crop and pasture plants. Adv. Agron. 15: 1–118.

Harper, J. L. 1961. Approaches to the study of plant competition, p. 1–39. *In* F. L. Milthorpe [ed.] Mechanisms of biological competition. Symp. Soc. Exp. Biol. XV. Academic Press, New York.

Heady, H. F. 1961. Continuous vs. specialized grazing systems; a review and application to the California annual type. J. Range Manage. 14: 182–193.

Jenkins, H. V. 1959. An airflow planimeter for measuring the area of detached leaves. Plant Physiol. 34: 532–536.

Johnson, C. M., and H. Nishita. 1952. Microestimation of sulfur. Anal. Chem. 24: 726–742.

Jones, M. B. 1963a. Effect of sulfur applied and date of harvest on yield, sulfate concentration, and total sulfur uptake of five annual grassland species. Agron. J. 55: 251–254.

——. 1963b. Yield, percent nitrogen, and total nitrogen uptake of various California annual grassland species fertilized with increasing rates of nitrogen. Agron. J. 55: 254–257.

Jordan. H. V., and C. E. Bardsley. 1958. Response of crops to sulfur on southeastern soils. Soil Sci. Soc. Amer. Proc. 22: 254–256.

Loomis, R. S., W. A. Williams, and W. G. Duncan. 1967. Community architecture and the productivity of terrestrial plant communities, p. 291–308. *In* A. San Pietro, F. A. Greer, and T. J. Army [ed.] Harvesting the sun: photosynthesis in plant life. Academic Press, New York.

Martin, W. E. 1958. Sulfur deficiency widespread in California soils. Calif. Agr. 12(11): 10–12.

McCown, R. L. 1966. Competition for light and nutrients by *Bromus mollis* and *Erodium botrys*. Ph.D. Thesis. University of California, Davis, Calif.

McKell, C. M., M. B. Jones, and E. R. Perrier. 1962. Root production and accumulation of root material on fertilized annual range. Agron. J. 54: 459–462.

McKell, C. M., and W. A. Williams. 1960. A lysimeter study of sulfur fertilization of an annual-range soil. J. Range Manage. 13: 113–117.

Storie, R. E. 1951. Grassland soils, p. 9–11. *In* A. W. Sampson, A. Chase, and D. W. Hendrick. California grasslands and range forage grasses. Calif. Agr. Exp. Sta. Bull. 724.

Sumner, D. C., and R. M. Love. 1961. Seedling competition from resident range cover. Calif. Agr. 15(2): 6.

Walker, C. F., and W. A. Williams. 1963. Responses of annual-type range vegetation to sulfur fertilization. J. Range Manage. 16: 64–69.

Williams, W. A. 1963. Competition for light between annual species of *Trifolium* during the vegetative phase. Ecology 44: 475–485.

EXPERIMENTAL STUDIES ON PREDATION: DISPERSION FACTORS AND PREDATOR-PREY OSCILLATIONS[1,2]

C. B. HUFFAKER[3]

INTRODUCTION

THIS PAPER is the second covering a series of experiments designed to shed light upon the fundamental nature of predator-prey interaction, in particular, and the interrelations of this coaction with other important parameters of population changes, in general. In the first of this series (Huffaker and Kennett, 1956),[4] a study was made of the predatory mites, *Typhlodromus cucumeris* Oudemans[5] and *Typhlodromus reticulatus* Oudemans, and their prey species, *Tarsonemus pallidus* Banks, the cyclamen mite which attacks strawberries. In that paper the authors discussed in a broad way the need for detailed studies of this kind and the implications of such results for theories of population dynamics, particularly the role of predation—which role has been minimized by a number of researchers (e.g., Uvarov, 1931; Errington, 1937, 1946; Leopold, 1954).

A significant result of the experiments of Huffaker and Kennett (1956) was the demonstration of two types of fluctuations in density. Where predators were excluded there was a regularized pattern of fluctuations of **decreasing** amplitude, a result of reciprocal density-dependent interaction of the phytophagous mite and its host plant. The other, sharply contrasting type of regularized fluctuation occurred as a primary result of predation on the phytophagous mite by the predatory form. The interacting reciprocal dependence of the prey and predator populations resulted in greatly reduced densities and amplitude of fluctuations, comparing this with the status when predators were absent.

In the present effort a considerable body of quantitative data is presented. Also, the outlines of an experimental method and design sufficiently flexible for use in studying some of the principles of population dynamics are delineated. The specific results are discussed with respect to the much-debated question of whether the predator-prey relation is inherently self-annihilative, and the bearing on this of the type of dispersion and hazards of searching. Certain trends are exhibited; if these are further verified by later experiments they may be theoretically significant, but such possibilities will be covered only after the accumulation of additional data from this continuing series of studies.

The immediate objective in the present effort has been the establishment of an ecosystem in which a predatory and a prey species could continue

---

[1] Received for publication August 16, 1957.

[2] These results were obtained during a period of sabbatical leave in 1955. The generous assistance of C. E. Kennett and F. E. Skinner in the preparation of the illustrations is gratefully acknowledged.

[3] Entomologist in Biological Control in the Experiment Station, Berkeley.

[4] See "References" on page 383.

[5] H. Womersley and C. E. Kennett now consider that this predator is really *Typhlodromus bellinus* Womersley.

Reproduced with permission from Hilgardia, 27: 343-383, 1958. Published by the California Agricultural Experiment Station, University of California, Berkeley, California.

living together so that the phenomena associated with their interactions could be studied in detail. Once conditions are established giving a measure of assurance against overexploitation, various other features could be introduced to study their relations to the periods and amplitudes of such oscillations in density as are demonstrated. This could include such factors as differences in temperature, humidity, or physical terrain, for example. Also, the effects could be studied of using two or more predatory species competing for the one prey species, or the simultaneous employment of two species of prey acceptable to the one predator. Many variations along these lines could be expected to furnish valuable information, and the present data represent only a beginning.

Some of the many questions that could ultimately be answered include:

1. Are such oscillations inherently of **increasing** amplitude?

2. Even if so, are there commonly present forces which act to cancel this tendency, and if so, what are these forces?

3. Is the predator-prey relation adequately described by the Gause theory of overexploitation and auto-annihilation except under conditions involving immigration from other ecosystems?

4. Does the presence of other significant species in addition to the two primary or original coactors introduce a stabilizing or disturbing effect?

5. What may be the effect of changes in the physical conditions upon the degree of stability or permanence of the predator-prey relation?

6. Can evidence be obtained supporting or refuting the concept that the prey, as well as the predators, benefits from the relation?

7. What is the order of influence on stability of population density of such parameters as shelter (from physical adversity of environment), food, disease, and natural enemies of other kinds?

There are no published accounts wherein the predator-prey relation has been followed under controlled conditions beyond a single wave or "oscillation" in density. Authorities differ as to whether this relation is inherently disoperative, leading inevitably to annihilation of either the predatory species alone or both the predator and its prey in the given universe or microcosm employed. In this controversy there is confusion as to what constitutes a **suitable** experimental microcosm. Published examples of such studies have been contradictory or inconclusive.

In the classic experiments of Gause (1934) and Gause *et al.* (1936), the predator and prey species survived together only under quite arbitrary conditions—either when a portion of the prey population was protected by a "privileged sanctuary" or when reintroductions were made at intervals. Gause concluded that such systems are self-annihilative, that predators characteristically overexploit their prey, and that in nature immigrants must repopulate the local environments where this has occurred. He argued against the theory that repeated waves or oscillations conforming to mathematical formulae have an inherent meaning in the absence of immigrations.

Nicholson (1933, 1954) advocates the contrary view, and he and Winsor (1934) criticized Gause's experiments on the grounds that the universes or microcosms he employed were too small to even approximate a **qualitative**, to say nothing of a **quantitative**, conformity to theory.

DeBach and Smith (1941) conducted a stimulating experiment with a special type of predator (an entomophagous "parasite") in which they tested the biological parameter of searching capacity against Nicholson's formula. The results conformed to theory very neatly. Ecologists consider the results as based upon too arbitrary assignments or omission of other biological parameters—such as length of a generation, fecundity, undercrowding phenomena at very low densities, et cetera. However, their work remains a strikingly successful pioneer endeavor in this field, and their method of isolating the variables other than **searching** was productive.

In the present study an effort was made to learn if an adequately large and complex laboratory environment could be set up in which the predator-prey relation would not be self-exterminating, and in which all the biological parameters are left to the free play of the interacting forces inherent in the experiment, once established. Consequently, the procedure was to introduce the prey species and the predator species only at the initiation of an experiment and to follow population trends afterward without any further introductions or manipulations. No assignments of biological parameters were made. Furthermore, no areas restrictive to the predators were furnished. Food "conditioning" is the only complicating variable and this disturbance was minimized by the methods used. However, as experiments were terminated because of the annihilative force of predation in the initial, limited universes employed, the conditions set up for subsequent experiments were made progressively more complex in nature and the areas larger.

EXPERIMENTAL DESIGN AND PROCEDURE

General Aspects

The six-spotted mite, *Eotetranychus sexmaculatus* (Riley), was selected as the prey species and the predatory mite *Typhlodromus occidentalis* Nesbitt as the predator. These species were selected because successful methods of rearing them in the insectary were already known, and because earlier observations had revealed this *Typhlodromus* as a voracious enemy of the six-spotted mite. It was known to develop in great numbers on oranges infested with the prey species, to destroy essentially the entire infestation, and then to die *en masse*. At this author's suggestion, Waters (1955) had studied the detailed biology of both species and had followed population trends on individual oranges as a problem in predator-prey dynamics.[6] This work was valuable in the conduct of the present research.

Uniformity in certain characteristics was maintained throughout the course of these experiments. Temperature was maintained constant at 83°F. Relative humidity varied some but was not allowed to fall below 55 per cent. There were no means of dehumidifying the room, but automatic humidity controls assured against the damaging action of low humidity. The room was kept dark.

Uniformity in total areas of the universes was achieved by utilizing various combinations of oranges and rubber balls equivalent to them in size (see figs. 1, 2, 3, and 4, for examples). This made it possible to change either or both the total primary food substrate (orange surface) and the degree of dispersion of that substrate without altering the total area of surfaces in the universes or the general distribution of units of surface in the systems. The object was to make it possible to vary the surface of orange utilized and its distribution in order to complicate the search for food by both the prey and predator. Thus, a simple environment where all the food was concentrated to a maximum degree (fig. 3) could be compared with one in which the food was dispersed according to arbitrary degrees (fig. 4) throughout the system

---

[6] The design of Waters' experiments, however, was not such as to answer some of the questions posed by this study. His universes were restricted and simple, with no possibility for return to oranges by individuals leaving them by "dropping off." His results were similar to those of Gause, but he drew several conclusions which are more generally applicable than some of Gause' generalizations.

Fig. 1. Orange wrapped with paper and edges sealed, ready for use with sample areas delineated. (Photograph by F. E. Skinner.)

(the oranges being arranged or randomly dispersed among the rubber balls). Also, the quantity of food as well as the nature of the dispersion were varied by covering the oranges with paper to whatever degree desired, the paper being wrapped tightly, twisted and tied, and with circular holes then cut to expose the required areas of orange surface. The edges of the holes and the twisted ends were then sealed with paraffin to exclude the mites from gaining entrance to the covered surfaces. An example of an orange ready for use is shown in figure 1.

Fig. 4. Four oranges, each with half-surfaces exposed (see fig. 2), randomized among the 40 positions, remainder of positions occupied by waxed, linted rubber balls—a 2-orange feeding area on a 4-orange dispersion, widely dispersed. (Photograph by F. E. Skinner.)

Considerable difficulty was encountered in arriving at a proper means of limiting the feeding area on a given orange. The first method tried was to dip the naked oranges in hot paraffin, leaving the desired areas clean. Considerable time was lost during the operation of the first two series of experiments because the oranges which were almost completely coated with paraffin or,

156

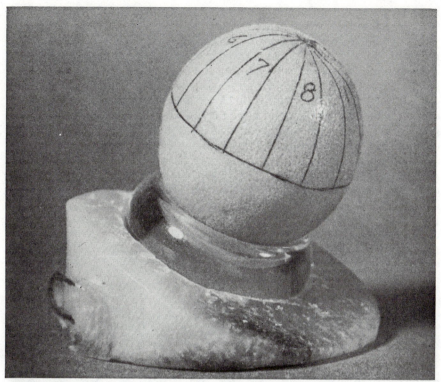

Fig. 2. Orange with lower half covered with paraffin and exposed upper half with sample areas delineated. Fuzzy surface is due to lint used. Paraffin base serves to bring all areas into focus under the microscope (see text). (Photograph by F. E. Skinner.)

later, even those covered with polyethylene bags, rotted before results could be obtained. It was only subsequent to this difficulty that a good grade of typing paper was tried. The paper proved to be an excellent material but somewhat difficult to form to an adequately smooth, mite-excluding covering. This fault was corrected by very slightly dampening the paper before wrapping and by using paraffin as a sealing material.

A primary difficulty foreseen in this study was that of replenishing the food material as it is used or becomes conditioned. Under the conditions employed, oranges last from 60 to 90 days as suitable food for the prey species if not fed upon to the extent of conditioning. However, a heavy infestation can deplete an orange of suitable nourishment and thus condition

Fig. 3. Four oranges, each with half-surfaces exposed (see fig. 2), grouped and joined with a wire loop, remainder of positions occupied by waxed, linted rubber balls, a 2-orange feeding area on a 4-orange dispersion, grouped. (Photograph by F. E. Skinner.)

it within three to five days. It is relatively impracticable to remove the food factor as a limiting feature. Also, localized food depletion by the prey species just as much as food depletion by the predator species is inherent to the natural scene. Yet, it was hoped that depletion of food could be evaluated and reduced to a minor position in limiting the populations. It was desirable to build into the design a schedule of removal of old oranges, whether or not conditioned, and their replacement by fresh ones. This would make possible a continuing system which would not automatically end if and when the original oranges became too old or conditioned. Also, by the use of careful notes on conditioning and by comparing universes where predators were introduced with universes which had none, conclusions could be drawn as to the relative importance of any interference occasioned by the conditioning of the oranges. The schedule consisted of removing ¼ of the oranges (the oldest or obviously most unsuitable ones) at intervals of 11 days. This gave a complete change of oranges every 44 days—a period amply in advance of general unsuitableness because of age alone. One restriction was imposed. No **significant last** of a population in a subsection was removed—any such orange otherwise. "due" being held another 11 days.

Fig. 5. 120 oranges, each with 1/20 orange-area exposed (method of fig. 1), occupying all positions in a 3-tray universe with partial-barriers of vaseline and wooden posts supplied—a 6-orange feeding area on a 120-orange dispersion with a complex maze of impediments (see text). Trays are broadly joined by use of paper bridges. (Photograph by F. E. Skinner.)

An estimate was made from general observations and the results of Waters (1955) that an orange area equivalent to that of two oranges, each 2½ inches in diameter, would be adequate, as a beginning, to study the predator-prey relation. With this premise, the smallest working basis for this design would utilize four oranges with each orange half-covered. This is because it was not desired to change more than ¼ of the food surfaces at a given time; that is, one of the four oranges used. This made it impossible to go to the ultimate in simplicity of searching and greatest concentration of the orange surfaces by utilizing only two whole, uncovered oranges.

Each universe in the earlier experiments conformed to this pattern, but certain other changes were made later. Each universe consisted of a flat metal tray, 40 inches long and 16 inches wide, with a side wall 1 inch in height and with 40 Syracuse watch glasses on each of which rested either an orange or a rubber ball (see figs. 3, 4, and 5). The positions were arbitrarily arranged in rows to conform to the dimensions of the trays—10 oranges and/or balls along the long dimension and four along the short dimension. This gave a center to center distance of 4 inches. The upper rim of the bordering wall of each tray was kept coated with white petroleum jelly to prevent movement of mites into or out of the trays. The predators and prey were therefore free to move onto or leave oranges or rubber balls but were not permitted to leave or enter the universes.

Lint-covered oranges as used by Finney (1953) to culture the six-spotted mite were used in all the experiments. The lint gives an ideal physical environment for propagation of the species employed. It produces an orange surface similar to the covering of fine hairs and setae on the surfaces of many plant leaves. However, it also adds to the complexity of the searching problem for the predator and increases the maximal potentials in populations of both species. In addition, it was noted that populations on well-linted oranges were less subject to the adverse effects of low humidity.

Initially, experiments were arranged in duplicate; check units having the prey species alone were carried along with those having both the prey and predator species. However, as the experiments developed, certain universes automatically terminated, and new ones not synchronized chronologically or exactly comparable in other respects were substituted. With each new universe employed, some change designed to give a better chance for perpetuation of the predator and prey in the system was incorporated. These changes were based on deductive thought and trial and error processes. During this study, the author had the good fortune to have Dr. A. J. Nicholson of Australia, one of the world's leading theoreticians on population dynamics, examine the experiments, and he confirmed the view that these changes must largely be decided upon by trial and error processes. Concerning some points it was not known whether a given change would detract or add to the chances of perpetuation of the predator-prey relations—such is the reciprocal interdependence of some actions.

The exposed area of an orange was in the form of a circle which was stamped on the orange by use of a shell vial of the proper size and an inking pad. The space between the outer edge of this line was then covered with hot paraffin and joined with the edge of the paper surrounding the hole. Several layers of hot paraffin were laid down as a seal by use of a small camel's hair brush. The oranges were then placed in a refrigerator for about 1 hour to chill the surfaces. Upon removal to the laboratory, only two or three oranges at a time, condensation on the surfaces was sufficient for dampening the point of an indelible pencil as lines were drawn on the surfaces of the exposed circular areas. Diameter lines were drawn in this way, dividing the area into 16 or more sampling sections with each section numbered. This greatly facilitated the counting of the populations. The counting had to be done under a stereoscopic microscope.

When the populations reached very low levels, total populations were counted, but normally the populations were counted on only $\frac{1}{4}$ or $\frac{1}{8}$ of the total surfaces. The sample areas were taken in each case so as to be distributed evenly around the face of the "clock," but the first section to be counted was always taken at random.

Considering the universes employing oranges with all or one half their surfaces exposed, much difficulty was initially encountered in manipulating the oranges under the microscope so that the populations in the sample areas could be viewed fully, and without disturbance of the populations. However, the device shown in figure 2 solved this problem. It consists of a paraffin block cut so that one side at its highest point is $1\frac{1}{2}$ inches and is tapered to the other side which is only $\frac{1}{8}$ inch high. An orange placed on the Syracuse watch glass, which sits loosely in a depression in the block, can then be turned by rotating the watch glass so that any desired sample area can be brought into focus without touching or awkwardly manipulating the orange.

Sampling Procedure

Sampling of partial areas and populations in the present study was necessary in order to reduce the time required in counting large populations. Hence, the populations in most cases were sampled. Statistical analyses of test examples furnished estimates of the loss in confidence occasioned by such sampling.

It was found that a population estimate based upon a subsample of a given size on an orange is more reproducible if composed of two or more non-contiguous areas evenly distributed among the position (see fig. 1). This method was used in all sampling.

TABLE 1

ANALYSIS OF VARIANCE FOR DATA OF APRIL 26 IN FIGURE 8.

Orange no.	1	2	3	4	5	6	7	8	9	10	11	12	13	14	15	16	17	18	19	20
Subsample																				
1................	20	2	1	1	2	2	8	1	20	15	17	0	16	7	6	2	1	0	2	0
2................	17	2	5	1	2	4	6	5	30	8	9	4	5	2	7	8	0	0	0	4
3................	21	2	9	3	0	3	0	0	32	4	8	7	1	0	8	1	0	0	0	1
4................	23	1	1	5	0	2	4	3	24	2	15	5	2	4	7	1	0	0	1	1
Sums...........	81	7	16	10	4	11	18	9	106	29	49	16	24	13	28	12	1	0	3	6

Source V.	d.f.	S.S.	M.S.	
Total	79	4,160		Standard error general mean, $S\bar{x}_g = 0.81$, or 14.6% of $\bar{x}_g$.
Between oranges	19	3,679	194*	Standard error between oranges, $S\bar{x}_o = 6.9$, or 31.2% of $\bar{x}_o$.
Within oranges	60	481	8	

Using this method of assignment of the positions of the subsamples on an orange, examples of data were analyzed to establish whether the within-orange variance which is associated with subsampling is significantly greater than the variance between the oranges. The data of Table 1 for April 26 illustrate the nature of the variance, and show that the within-orange variance, which is associated with the subsamples, is very small, and that if greater accuracy were required, it could best be achieved by counting populations on more oranges rather than by altering the technique of subsampling on a given orange.

It was therefore decided that the samples include every orange, but the subsamples on each orange would be varied with the approximate densities of the populations encountered, the usual proportion being ½ or ¼ the total exposed area on each orange.

Early in the study in deciding upon the technique of sampling, the **entire** population of the prey species was counted on a representative group of 44 orange units, with each unit exposing ¹⁄₂₀ of an orange area. This population was thus finite and known. The data used were for July 5 from the experiment illustrated in figure 18. The mean, x, for the 44 items was 6.95 mites per exposed area, with a standard error of ± 1.09, which is 15.7 per cent of the mean. This standard error reflects the variance inherent to the particular type of conglomerate distribution exhibited by such populations.

In order to determine if the subsamples could be used to estimate the total populations, half-area counts were first used. Series of six half-area random lots of the component items were drawn from the aforementioned total population on the 44 representative oranges. The means, standard errors, and the coefficient of variation were then compared with the values based upon the total known population. These statistical parameters were little changed: the standard errors being ± 0.52, ± 0.68, ± 0.65, ± 0.63, ± 0.56, and ± 0.64, respectively, as compared with a half-value of ± 0.55 for the total population; the coefficient of variation varying from 16.2 per cent to 19.3 per cent compared with 15.7 per cent (the coefficient of variation of the whole population); and the means, as estimates of the mean of the total population, averaging only 4.7 per cent higher or lower than the corresponding half-value for the total population—the range being from 3.3 to 7.8.

A test was also made to determine if a further reduction in the counting (to $\frac{1}{4}$ the total area) would give adequate estimates of the population when large universes or high populations were encountered. Both the predator and prey populations on August 1 (see fig. 18) were analyzed for this purpose.

It should be noted that some basic change had occurred between July 5 and August 1 contributing to greater skewness of distribution. This is revealed by an increase in the coefficient of variation from 15.7 per cent for the whole population count of July 5 (analysis just discussed) to 22.3 per cent for the large sample count on August 1. The six subsamples of reduced size taken on August 1 closely approximated the large sample in coefficient of variation, these being 23.3 per cent, 23.9 per cent, 23.3 per cent, 22.8 per cent, 23.3 per cent, and 23.5 per cent, respectively.

There are two probable reasons for this change in the nature of the variation. In the former instance, the predators had not yet been introduced while they were significantly active on August 1. The predator-prey relation characteristically contributes to skewness, colonial, or conglomerate distribution. Also, the prey were introduced into the universe in equal numbers on all oranges at the initiation of the experiment, and some time is necessary for the typical conglomerate distribution to become manifested, even disregarding predation. Therefore, the larger, although uniform coefficient of variation of the samples on August 1 are not the result of inadequate sampling technique but express the nature of the distribution of the population.

Comparing the prey populations of the $\frac{1}{4}$-area samples with the composite "total" or $\frac{1}{2}$-area sample on August 1, the standard errors were little changed: these being $\pm$ 2.43, $\pm$ 2.63, $\pm$ 2.70, $\pm$ 2.67, $\pm$ 2.60, and $\pm$ 2.48, respectively, for the six $\frac{1}{4}$-area samplings, as compared with a half-value of $\pm$ 2.39 for the $\frac{1}{2}$-area sample; the coefficient of variation, previously listed, varied only from 22.8 per cent to 23.9 per cent, compared with 22.3 per cent for the sample of double size; and the means, as estimates of the mean of the population present on twice the area, averaging only 4.7 per cent higher or lower than the corresponding half-value for the larger sample—the range being from 1.6 to 9.2.

Predator populations were more variable than were the prey populations. The standard error for total counts of the large ($\frac{1}{2}$ area) sample was $\pm$ 0.254, with a half-value of $\pm$ 0.127, while the values for the counts made on six $\frac{1}{4}$-area samples were $\pm$ 0.117, $\pm$ 0.150, $\pm$ 0.155, $\pm$ 0.167, $\pm$ 0.153, and $\pm$ 0.151. The coefficient of variation also varied more than the corresponding values for the prey population, these being 24.6 per cent, 34.6 per cent, 32.6 per cent, 29.0 per cent, 32.8 per cent, and 27.2 per cent, compared with 26.7 per cent for the sample of double size. The same was true for the means, these values, as estimates of the mean of the population on the larger area, averaging 5.7 per cent higher or lower, but having a range from 0.0 to 12.1.

When such ranges of error relating to the various observed points in the illustrations are considered, comparing positions of high and low densities, it is obvious that there is adequate accuracy in the estimates to establish the validity of the major trends or patterns of population change exhibited with respect to the predators and their prey in the various experiments. Yet, obviously, some of the minor, inconsistent changes following no general trend in time may be the result of inadequacy of sampling, and hence have a random character independent of predation.

RESULTS

A group of eight universes was started on February 4 and February 10. These were duplicates of an earlier group—which, as previously stated, had to be discarded because the oranges were rotting—except that the covering used on the oranges was part polyethelene material and part paraffin, rather than paraffin alone. This group also had to be discarded except for certain universes which utilized four oranges each, and these were half-covered with paraffin. Oranges only half-covered with paraffin proved satisfactory, and those units were retained.

A basic idea in this study has been the comparison of results when the plant food (oranges) is readily accessible (massed in one location in the universes) with other examples having the food widely dispersed, with the problems of dispersal and searching thus made more difficult for both the predators and the prey. The control universes which reveal the approximate levels of density of the prey species in the **absence** of predation, thus limited by the availability of food, were followed under several conditions of dispersion of the food material. These are considered representative of densities permitted by the respective levels of availability of food; and the degree to which the prey fail to reach these densities under the pressure of predation in the other universes is a measure of the effect of that predation.

The specific designs of experiments which differ from the general methods and procedures discussed previously will be covered, along with the results obtained, under each type of universe employed.

I. Densities of Prey and Fluctuations
in the Absence of Predation

The following three universes were used as a measure of the population dynamics of the prey species in the absence of predators.

A. Predators Absent, Simplest Universe, Four Large Areas of Food, Grouped at Adjacent, Joined Positions. In this universe a 2-orange feeding area on a 4-orange dispersion was employed, and the unit was started February 10 and ended July 1 (see figs. 3 and 6). The initial colony was established by placing 20 female six-spotted mites, *E. sexmaculatus* (the prey species), on one of the four oranges. Movement to the other oranges was delayed until the period between March 4 and March 8 at which time the orange originally colonized was beginning to become conditioned and migrants had started moving. Thus, on a feeding area as large as a half orange, overpopulation may be delayed for about three weeks. This is significant with respect to attempts to establish self-sustained existence of both the predator and its prey in a universe. If the prey do not move readily or at least are not moving from some arenas rather readily most of the time, the predators only have to locate a colony arena and stay with it until it is overexploited, resulting in its own extinction and possibly that of its prey as well. On a given orange, this predator commonly overexploits such a colony in much less than the three week period required for conditioning pressure under these conditions (see figs. 9, 10, and 11). This question will be discussed further in relation to the data of Subsections F, G, H, and I of Section II, and it led to the arrangements used in those universes.

Regarding densities, the approximate mean population reached in this universe (fig. 6) was 9,400 *E. sexmaculatus* (all stages), or 4,700 per orange-area. Two major peaks above that level, once population growth had progressed that far, and two subsequent, resultant depressions below it occurred. These indicate a trend of a somewhat "oscillatory" nature due to occurrence of waves of maximal or excessive utilization of the food, followed by in-

162

adequate food to support the high levels. This trend may be only a carry-over result of the arbitrary unnaturally high abundance of entirely "unconditioned" or unutilized food at the initiation of the experiment, in interaction with the pattern of orange replacement. This example was not continued long enough to learn if the degree of such fluctuations would continue undiminished in amplitude or whether an inherent oscillation associated with factors of dispersal and population density under related conditions is a real feature of well-established, long-term system—i.e., ones which have reached internal balance, or relative calm.

These results do establish that a relatively high mean population is characteristic of this experimental arrangement, contrasted to that which results when predators are present. Perhaps a sizeable part of the large fluctuations may be the result of variations in the nutritional qualities of the oranges supplied during the course of the experiment. It is known that oranges do vary in nutritional value for this mite. Beginning with March 30, at which time the population had first attained maximal utilization of the food, the oranges afterward removed in the replacement scheme were in-

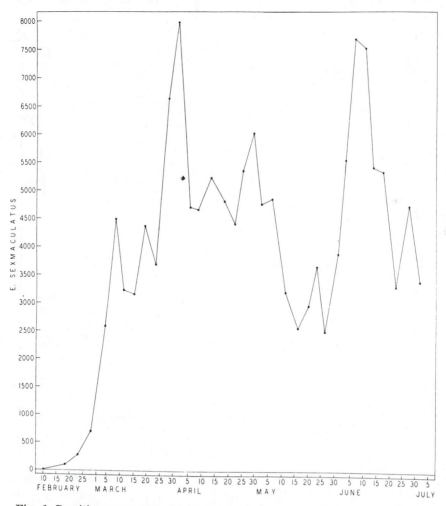

Fig. 6. Densities per orange-area of *Eotetranychus sexmaculatus* in the absence of predators in the simplest universe used, with four large areas of food (orange surface) grouped at adjacent, joined positions—a 2-orange feeding area on a 4-orange dispersion (see fig. 3 and text, Subsection A, Section I of "Results").

163

variably fully utilized or conditioned. This full utilization is probably the most important reason why the mean level of this population was higher than that in the next two universes discussed. In fact, it was characteristic that the populations on these oranges reached conditioning levels well in advance of the dates for removal of the respective oranges, and such conditioning pressure, sometimes from two oranges at once, accomplished very prompt natural colonization of each new orange added, and thus little loss of time in utilization of the food was occasioned. Also, even after such prompt conditioning, the oranges continued to support for some time a much reduced but sizeable population of mites, and these factors support the position that in this universe the more complete utilization accounted for the higher mean level of density, comparing this universe with those of Subsections B, figure 7, and C, figure 8, of this section.

B. Predators Absent, Four Large Areas of Food Widely Dispersed. In this universe, as in the last, a 2-orange feeding area on a 4-orange dispersion was employed (in this case, not grouped), and the unit was started on April 5 and ended July 18 (see figs. 4 and 7).

The mean level of density of *E. sexmaculatus* subsequent to the initial period prior to May 20 was 7,000, or 3,500 per orange-area. It is seen, there-

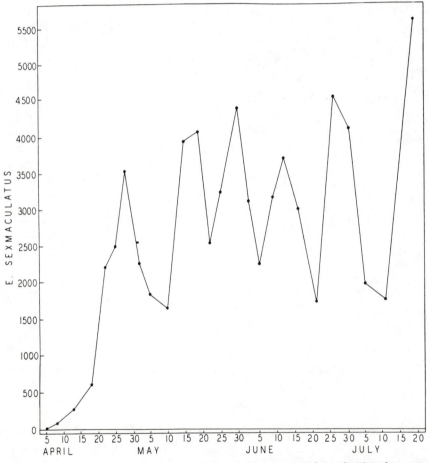

Fig. 7. Densities per orange-area of *Eotetranychus sexmaculatus* in the absence of predators, with four large areas of food (orange surface) widely dispersed among 36 foodless positions—a 2-orange feeding area on a 4-orange dispersion (see fig. 4 and text, Subsection B, Section I of "Results").

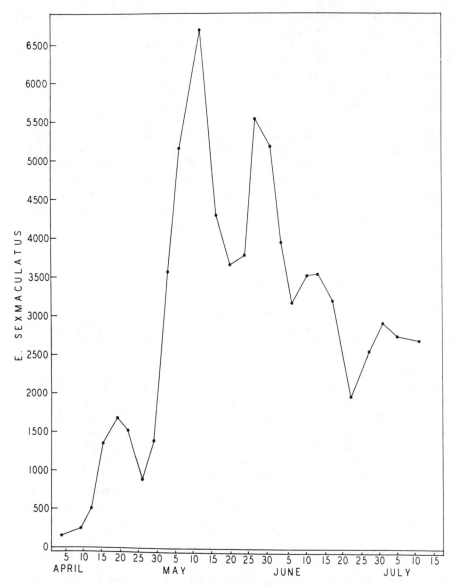

Fig. 8. Densities per orange-area of *Eotetranychus sexmaculatus* in the absence of predators with 20 small areas of food alternating with 20 foodless positions occupied by rubber balls—a 2-orange feeding area on a 20-orange dispersion (no photograph of this exact arrangement, but see text, Subsection C, Section I of "Results").

fore, that although the same quantity of food was supplied, the utilization was somewhat lower due to the difficulty the mites had in quickly locating the new orange units and the resulting loss in population in doing so, with reduced utilization during the time the oranges were in the universe.

There was also a different pattern of fluctuation in numbers, the changes being somewhat more regular in occurrence, and less marked maxima exhibited, than was so when the four oranges were placed adjacent and joined at one arena in the universe. The interaction between the difficulty of dispersal and the supply of food appears to have had a slightly stabilizing effect, compared with the condition when the supply of food alone was the primary feature and problems of dispersal minimal in effects. Unquestionably, the known variation in the quality of the oranges used is a source of error—but doubtfully sufficient to nullify this indication.

Tracing this population, 20 female mites were placed on a single orange and the population growth occurred almost entirely on the single originally stocked orange until just prior to April 28 at which time conditioning of that orange had forced migrants to search for food. By May 2 they had located the other three oranges, but not in sufficient numbers to forestall the decline in the general population resulting from conditioning of the orange originally stocked. The second ascent followed an expected course and was also short-circuited by conditioning on one of the first naturally colonized oranges on which the population first got well under way, at a time before the numbers which had located the other two oranges had increased enough to offset the decline. Subsequent events were similar; the distances between positions with food, and the difficulty the mites had in locating them were such that usually only one orange was highly productive at a time and occasionally an orange came due for removal prior to full utilization. However, none was removed which harbored a major portion of the total population. This would account for the mean density being somewhat lower than that which was experienced in the universe of Subsection A, figure 6, of this section, in which relatively full utilization was experienced.

Unusually high levels of density were the result of a partial chance occurrence of simultaneous productivity on two or more of the four oranges, but the resultant steep ascents such as those occurring during the last half of June and again between July 12 and July 18 are certain to be followed swiftly by corresponding declines in density.

C. Predators Absent, 20 Small Areas of Food Alternating with 20 Positions with No Food. In this universe, also, a 2-orange feeding area was employed, but this was segmented into 20 parts of $\frac{1}{10}$ orange-area each, with one part on each of 20 oranges. The 20 oranges were placed in alternate positions with 20 rubber balls. The universe was started on March 31 and ended on July 11, but the first count was made on April 4 (see fig. 8).

It should be noted that although the food material was segmented into 20 parts and dispersed over 20 oranges (equalizing to a much greater degree the variation in orange quality) and 20 positions in the universe, each orange was only one position distant from another and the positions having no food (the rubber balls) were much fewer in number. Consequently, although the food was widely dispersed it was readily accessible and sources of migrants were close at hand to any new orange added. In this respect the unit more nearly resembled those universes in which all the food was massed at one arena in the universe and on adjacent oranges.

The mean level of density of mites subsequent to the initiation period prior to May 20 was 6,600, or 3,300 per orange-area. This is slightly lower than the results of the previously discussed universe. It is likely that the differences in the actual levels of the means in these last two instances do not have real meaning, but the patterns of change in density are probably meaningful of an inherent relation to the types of dispersion employed. Yet, if the initial extreme high in density, occurring during the middle of May, is **included,** the mean level would be approximately 3,800 per orange-area—still somewhat below the mean level of the universe in which the oranges were grouped and joined (fig. 6), but slightly higher than that exhibited in the universe just discussed.

Tracing the history of this population, it was initiated by placing 10 female *E. sexmaculatus* on each of two of the 20 oranges. The first count on April 4 showed a mean population of 152 per orange-area, and these were still located only on the two colonized, or stocked, oranges. Not until April 19, at which time the population on these two oranges was first noted as causing conditioning and under competitive pressure, had migrants generally moved to other oranges; only one other orange had a few mites prior to that time. That date also marked the decline of the population, and this decline was due to the conditioning on the two oranges stocked originally, before the other 18 oranges had been located and population growth on them gotten under way. In this universe nearly all the oranges were found at this same initial period of migrants and the subsequent very steep population increase was the result of simultaneous utilization of the unused oranges in the entire universe. The second depression in the middle of May was due to rather general conditioning of many of those oranges, and the next increase was made possible by the replacement of utilized oranges by new ones according to the predetermined schedule.

There was in this case a strong indication that the period of initiation and establishment of a balance between density and the schedule of supplying food is prolonged much beyond a period of 45 days. The large amplitude of fluctuations in the early stages of the experiment, considered in relation to the successive **steady decrease** in this amplitude, and in view of the much reduced probable source of error associated with variations in orange quality, makes it likely that a position around 5,500, or 2,750 mites per orange-area, is nearer to a true equilibrium, and that the wide fluctuations and high densities which persisted during the early course of the experiment were adjustments prior to establishment of a semblance of such balance.

In contrast to this, the data illustrated in figure 7 probably represent a meaningful difference in patterns of population change. In that case the large fluctuations did **not** diminish with time. In the universe illustrated in figure 7, a position with food is found with great difficulty, but each such position has a supply five-fold in quantity. In the present example, figure 8, there are five times as many positions with food, but each has only $\frac{1}{5}$ the quantity. The positions with food are more readily located but each is depleted more rapidly. Additional replicates would need to be run and continued over a longer period of time in order to answer the questions raised.

II. Population Changes under Predator and
Prey Interactions

A. Predators Present, Simplest Universe, Four Large Areas of Food, Grouped at Adjacent Joined Positions. In this universe a 2-orange feeding area on a 4-orange dispersion was employed. The unit was started February 4 by stocking with 20 female six-spotted mites. It ended April 5 (fig. 9). The arrangement was the same as the control universe of Subjection A of Section I (see also figs. 3 and 6) except that in this universe the predatory species was present. Two female predators were introduced 11 days after the introduction of the six-spotted mites. Both predators were placed on a single orange. This scheme was followed with all the universes except as otherwise stated.

The stocked orange spoiled between February 7 and February 11, and, consequently, the prey then declined in numbers and only increased after moving to the adjacent oranges. The prey then increased to a level of 500, or 250 per orange-area, at which time it was preyed upon so severely that it was reduced to a nil density within 10 days and all the predators subsequently starved. The consequent characteristic, very gradual increase in the numbers of the prey was then prolonged for about 15 days before there was attained a state of vigorous population growth (see "Discussion").

B. Predators Present, Eight Large Areas of Food, Grouped at Adjacent Joined Positions. In this universe a 4-orange feeding area on an 8-orange dispersion was employed, and the unit was started February 10 and ended

March 28 (fig. 10). The eight oranges were grouped in one end of the tray and joined with wire loops. In this case, because of the larger quantity of food supplied, 40 female six-spotted mites, or prey, were colonized initially, 20 on each of two of the eight oranges. Two female predators were added 11 days later.

The notes taken during the early days of this universe reveal that the female six-spotted mites used for colonizing were old and not from the usual stock colony of vigorous young females. These females died quickly without producing the usual quota of eggs after colonizing. Hence, the population could not increase at the usual rate until the first daughters became fecund. By the time that occurred and the normal population increase would otherwise have ensued, the predators had become sufficiently abundant that the increase never occurred at all, even though migrants had moved to and populated at least six of the eight oranges. Hence, the population reached a maximal level of only 451 mites, or 113 per orange-area.

In this universe the predators overexploited the prey by March 14 to the extent that not only did they annihilate themselves but they also annihilated the prey species, even though the latter had dispersed successfully throughout the universe.

C. Predators Present, Six Whole Oranges as Food, Grouped at Adjacent Joined Positions. In this universe a 6-orange feeding area on a 6-orange dispersion was employed. The unit was started with 20 female six-spotted mites on April 26 and ended July 11 (fig. 11). The prey were introduced on two oranges, the two female predators on only one of them.

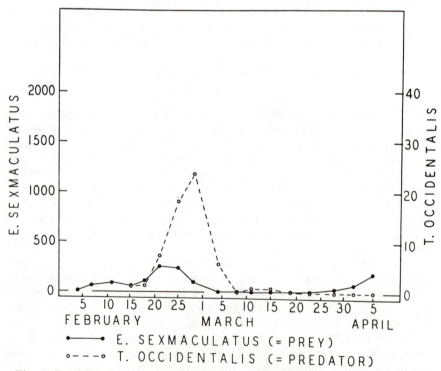

Fig. 9. Densities per orange-area of the prey, *Eotetranychus sexmaculatus*, and the predator, *Typhlodromus occidentalis*, with 4 large areas of food for the prey (orange surface) grouped at adjacent, joined positions—a 2-orange feeding area on a 4-orange dispersion (see fig. 3 and text, Subsection A, Section II of "Results").

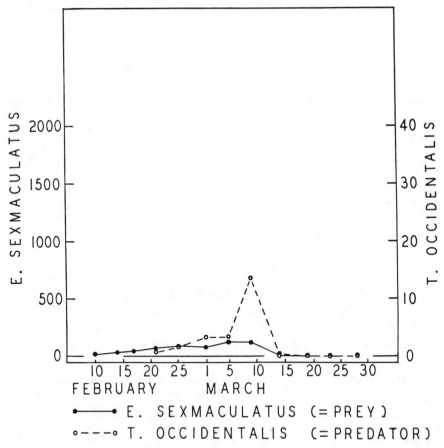

Fig. 10. Densities per orange-area of the prey, *Eotetranychus sexmaculatus*, and the predator, *Typhlodromus occidentalis*, with 8 large areas of food for the prey (orange surface) grouped at adjacent, joined positions—a 4-orange feeding area on an 8-orange dispersion (no photograph of this exact arrangement, but it was similar to that of figure 3 except that 8 oranges were used; see also text, Subsection B, Section II of "Results").

The prey temporarily thus escaped severe predator action on one of the oranges and a few migrants moved onto some of the other oranges, but this was not until about May 15, and before these were able to effect an appreciable general population growth, the predators reached all the infested oranges. The peak population reached was 3,900 mites, or 650 per orange-area. After May 18 to 20, the prey suffered the characteristic crash effect. Contrary to what happened in most similar universes, there was limited temporary survival of the prey **and** the predator species. The prey increased very slightly from June 5 to June 13, and this was followed by a corresponding increase in the predators, after which time the predators quickly annihilated their prey and thus themselves.

D. Predators Present, Four Large Areas of Food Widely Dispersed. In this universe a 2-orange feeding area on a 4-orange dispersion was used (see figs. 4 and 12). The oranges were placed at randomized positions among rubber balls as shown in figure 4. Twenty female six-spotted mites were colonized on one orange on February 4, and two female predators were put on the same orange on February 11. The universe was ended May 17.

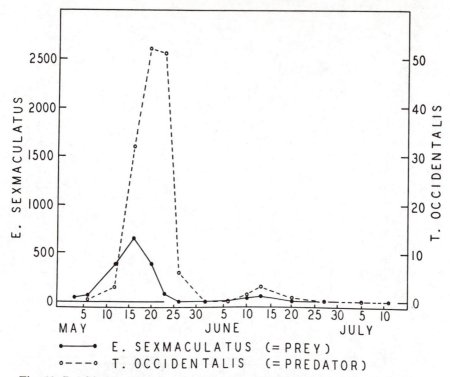

Fig. 11. Densities per orange-area of the prey, *Eotetranychus sexmaculatus*, and the predator, *Typhlodromus occidentalis*, with 6 large areas of food for the prey (orange surface) grouped at adjacent joined positions—a 6-orange feeding area on a 6-orange dispersion (no photograph of this exact arrangement, but it was similar to that of figure 3 except that 6 whole oranges were used; see text, Subsection C, Section II of "Results").

The wide dispersal of the food among the 40 positions presented an obstacle to movement of both the prey and the predators. In fact, neither species reached the unstocked oranges until March 28 when both did and, thus, densities on the other oranges were never substantial. The colonized orange was apparently phenomenal in nutritional quality for on it the prey reproduced at a very high rate, so much so that the predators did not quickly overtake it even though the latter were present on that orange from the eleventh day. The population of predators did not increase rapidly at first, although at the low density at that time it is probable that the numbers missed in the counting may have been enough to explain a part or most of this retarded increase in the midst of an abundance of prey.

At any rate, the prey population reached the high level of 8,113, or 4,056 per orange-area. This level could not be maintained on the single orange longer than a few days even in the absence of predation; thus, both conditioning of that orange and intense predation jointly accounted for the very abrupt crash which followed. Nearly all the predators then starved but a very few survived and prevented any resurgence of the prey until after April 8 at which time the last predator died and the prey began a very gradual increase in numbers (see "Discussion").

E. Predators Present, Eight Large Areas of Food Widely Dispersed. In this universe a 4-orange feeding area on an 8-orange dispersion was utilized, the remainder of the 40 positions being occupied by rubber balls. The unit was started February 10 and ended May 11 (fig. 13). Twenty female six-

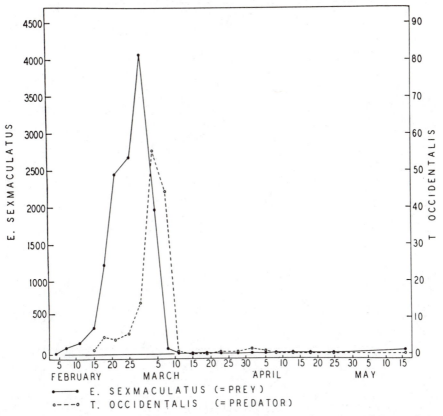

Fig. 12. Densities per orange-area of the prey, *Eotetranychus sexmaculatus,* and the predator, *Typhlodromus occidentalis,* with 4 large areas of food for the prey (orange surface) widely dispersed among 36 foodless positions—a 2-orange feeding area on a 4-orange dispersion (see fig. 4 and text, Subsection D, Section II of "Results").

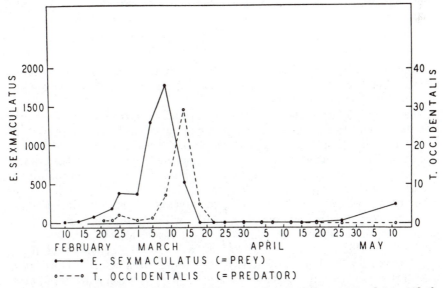

Fig. 13. Densities per orange-area of the prey, *Eotetranychus sexmaculatus,* and the predator, *Typhlodromus occidentalis,* with 8 large areas of food for the prey (orange surface) widely dispersed among 32 foodless positions—a 4-orange feeding area on an 8-orange dispersion (no photograph of this arrangement, but it was similar to that of figure 4 except that 8 oranges were used; see also text, Subsection E, Section II of "Results").

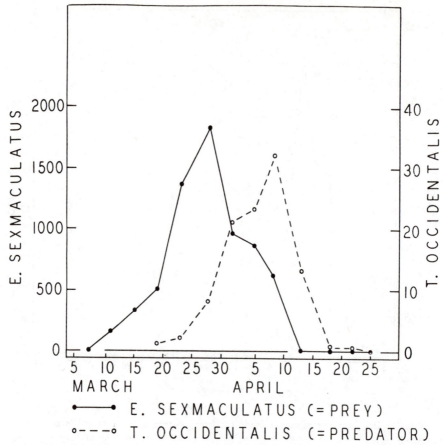

Fig. 14. Densities per orange-area of the prey, *Eotetranychus sexmaculatus*, and the predator, *Typhlodromus occidentalis*, with 20 small areas of food for the prey (orange surface) alternating with 20 foodless positions—a 2-orange feeding area on a 20-orange dispersion (no photograph of this exact arrangement, but see text, Subsection F, Section II of "Results").

spotted mites were colonized on each of two of the eight oranges, whereas the two female predators were introduced 11 days later on one of the oranges colonized with the prey species.

There was a logical delay of about 14 days between the ascent in the prey population and the ascent in the predator population. Thus, the prey could increase unabated on the oranges which did not receive predators until such time as the latter moved onto them. The dispersed condition of the oranges made more likely such a lag in general predator action. In the examples of the universes otherwise comparable except that the food was grouped in one area and joined (figs. 9, 10, and 11), the ascents in predator densities followed the respective ascents in prey densities within intervals of two or three days. Also, in those universes the prey never reached such high levels.

The lag period in this universe was sufficient for the general prey population to reach a level of 7,046, or 1,761 per orange-area before the predators moved through the universe and reduced the prey to a very low level, after which all the predators starved. The very gradual subsequent increase in the numbers of the prey up to May 25 is obvious in figure 13. After that date the undercrowding effects from the intense predator action had been overcome and a *substantial* increase followed.

F. Predators Present, 20 Small Areas of Food Alternating with 20 Food-less Positions. Two universes of this arrangement were used. In each, a 2-orange feeding area on a 20-orange dispersion was used and both were started on March 7. One was ended on April 25, the other on April 26 (figs. 14 and 15). In each universe, 10 female six-spotted mites were introduced onto each of two of the oranges, and in each, two female predators were introduced onto one of the two oranges 11 days later.

In these universes the feeding area employed on a given orange was reduced to a 1/10-orange area. Large areas support the prey species for long periods of time. Dispersal pressure, or overpopulation—which is now known to cause practically all movement from orange to orange—is delayed. It was felt that by decreasing the feeding surface at each orange position—thus having more positions—the prey would be kept on the move from more individual sources so that following a localized crash from predation, there would occur sooner a subsequent population pressure which would cause more rapid dispersal and resultant repopulation on a broader spatial basis in the universe. This seemed to offer a better possibility for achieving perpetuation of the predators and prey than would wider dispersal of the smaller number of larger areas of food.

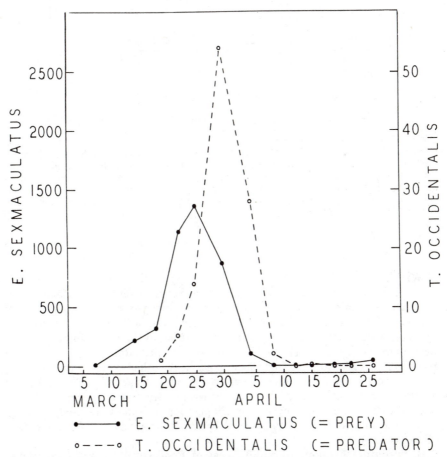

Fig. 15. Densities per orange-area of the prey, *Eotetranychus sexmaculatus*, and the predator, *Typhlodromus occidentalis*, with 20 small areas of food for the prey (orange surface) alternating with 20 foodless positions—a 2-orange feeding area on a 20-orange dispersion (no photograph of this exact arrangement, but see text, Subsection F, Section II of "Results").

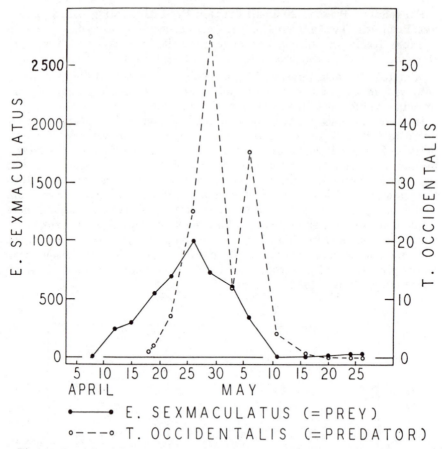

Fig. 16. Densities per orange-area of the prey, *Eotetranychus sexmaculatus*, and the predator, *Typhlodromus occidentalis*, with 40 small areas of food for the prey (orange surface) occupying all 40 positions—a 2-orange feeding area on a 40-orange dispersion, but with units of food thus adjacent (no photograph of this exact arrangement, but it was similar to ⅓ of the universe shown in figure 5 except that the wooden posts were not used and the maze of vaseline partial-barriers was much less complex; see also text, Subsection G, Section II of "Results").

With one of the examples, the period of lag in the increase in predators was just as long, and, with the other, it was three to four days shorter than it was for the units just previously discussed. However, the prey populations did not reach levels quite so high. The higher level, however, occurred in the universe where there was the longer period of lag in the predator response to prey increase (see fig. 14). In this universe the predators exterminated the prey by April 18 and then died themselves. In the other example (see fig. 15), the prey was almost, but not entirely, exterminated by April 8. The predators quickly starved after that date and subsequently the prey gradually increased in numbers. Thus, even when 20 positions of food were used, the prey was exterminated in one instance although it survived in the other (see "Discussion").

G. Predators Present, 40 Small Areas of Food Occupying All Positions. In this universe a 2-orange area was again utilized, but the feeding area on each orange was further reduced to ¹⁄₂₀-orange area; thus, all 40 positions were occupied by oranges (a 40-orange dispersion)—i.e., no rubber balls were used. The unit was started April 8 and ended May 26 (fig. 16). Ten female six-spotted mites were colonized on each of two of the oranges and 10 days later two female predators were colonized on one of them.

The tray used was also divided into three areas, mostly, but not entirely, separated by vaseline barriers as an impediment but not an exclusion to movement. The barrier pattern was not as complicated as that used in the later experiments such as those shown in figure 19. It was felt that the presence of the barriers would introduce greater difficulty for the predators in contacting all general positions of prey at a time, and the smaller areas of food would insure quicker movement of the prey and repopulation of depopulated areas by migrants from areas missed at the time of greatest predator abundance and pressure.

Subsequent to the expected initial increase, there was a sharp decline in the predators between April 29 and May 3 to a level below that which could be supported by the prey population in the total universe at the time. There was then a second sharp increase in the predators as they moved into one of the areas where they had not previously made contact with the prey. The second decline in predators and prey was general throughout the universe and the predators then starved since the prey reached a level which would not support a single predator. The prey population then began a gradual increase in numbers.

In this universe it became obvious that the history of events could not be properly illustrated by use of a simple line graph plotting densities, and this became increasingly true when still greater complexity was introduced. The counts made on the individual oranges revealed, unquestionably, that the sharp drop in predator abundance between April 29 and May 3, and the immediately subsequent sharp increase in numbers, were reliable reflections of the changes in the total populations in the universe. Only a pictorial record of the densities of the predators and the prey in the specific geographic areas in which the predators were active, and in which they were not active, could be expected accurately to portray the situation. Otherwise, the data reveal a sharp decline in predators, followed by a rapid increase, and then followed again by a rapid decline—all taking place synchronously with a rather steady general decline in density of the prey, if the data for the whole universe are plotted as a single unit as in figure 16.

Such events are contrary to the known fact of specific dependence of this predator upon this prey in these universes and, as well, contrary to the fact of the predator's rapid response to changes in the numbers of its prey by corresponding changes in its own numbers if it contacts its prey. Such a pictorial record was constructed for the data of the most important of these experiments (see fig. 18), but the time required to do this for each universe would be excessive. In any event, this does not appear to be necessary when simple universes are used (see "Discussion").

H. Predators Present, 120 Small Areas of Food Occupying All 120 Positions, a 6-Orange Area. In this universe the area of orange exposed at a position was the same as that used in the universe just discussed and the food occupied all positions (no rubber balls were used), but the need for an increase in the total potentials and complexity had become obvious. Hence, in this unit, the food potential and the total areas required to be covered in searching were trebled, i.e., a 6-orange area was used on a 120-orange dispersion. The universe consisted of three of the trays (previously used singly) joined together (see fig. 5). An arrangement of vaseline partial-barriers was again used (see fig. 19). The universe was started with 10 female six-spotted mites, placed on each of two oranges in one of the trays on May 5. Two female predators were added on one of these oranges on May 16. The universe was ended June 27 (fig. 17).

In this universe the predator action was again delayed. However, move-

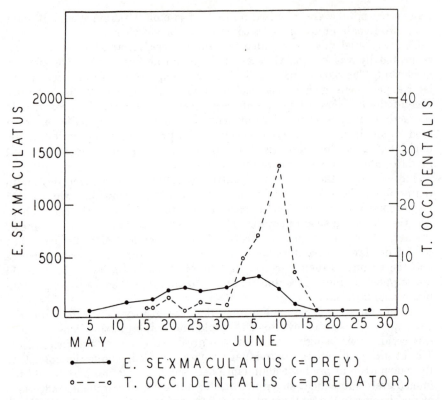

Fig. 17. Densities per orange-area of the prey, *Eotetranychus sexmaculatus*, and the predator, *Typhlodromus occidentalis*, with 120 small areas of food for the prey (orange surface) occupying all 120 positions in a 3-tray universe—a 6-orange feeding area on a 120-orange dispersion, with a simple maze of vaseline partial-barriers utilized (no wooden posts), but with the stocking done in a very restricted manner (see fig. 5 and text, Subsection H, Section II of "Results").

ment of the prey from the one tray in which the initial colonies of both species were introduced never occurred, and it thus became obvious that with the use of such universes a wider arbitrary spread of the initial stock should be employed. Otherwise, the data of this universe added nothing new.

I. Predator-Prey Oscillations, 120 Small Areas of Food Occupying all 120 Positions, a 6-orange Area. This universe was basically like that of the last discussed but greater complexity and a different scheme of introducing the initial colonizing stock were employed. The universe was a three-tray arrangement, and a 6-orange feeding area on a 120-orange dispersion was again used. The partial barriers of vaseline were also used (see fig. 19). Contrary to previous procedure, 120 female six-spotted mites were introduced on June 30 (the graph of fig. 18 shows the first count date, July 5). That is, one mite was placed on each of the 120 oranges. In this universe also, the predators were added only five days later so as to permit them to become effective prior to general conditioning of the stocked oranges by the prey. Also contrary to the previous procedure, 27 female predators were introduced, and these were distributed, one on each of 27 oranges, these being representative of all major sections of the universe. This scheme assured that the populations would not become annihilated prior to dispersal to all parts of the universe—such as happened in the unit previously discussed. This experiment was ended March 27, although because of engraving difficulties, the data were plotted only to February 28 (see fig. 18).

Prey: 0-5 nil density (white); 6-25 low density (light stipple); 26-75 medium density (horizontal lines); 76 or over, high density (solid black). Predator: 1-8 (one white circle).

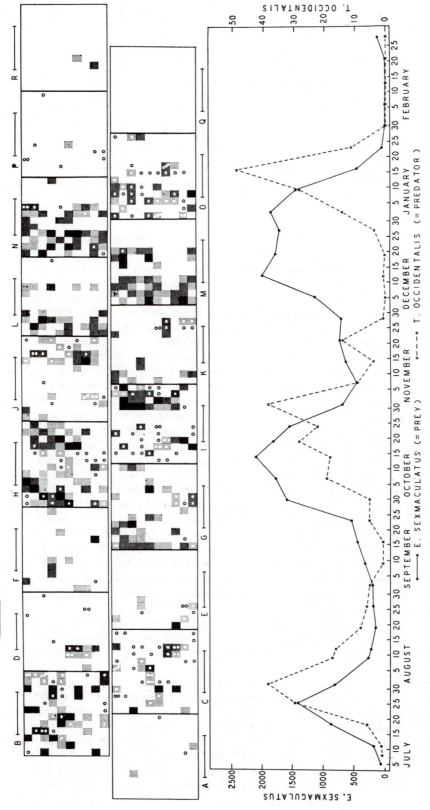

Fig. 18. Three oscillations in density of a predator-prey relation in which the predatory mite, *Typhlodromus occidentalis*, preyed upon the orange feeding six-spotted mite, *Eotetranychus sexmaculatus*.

The graphic record below shows the sequence of densities per orange-area, while the pictorial record, charts A to R, above, shows both *densities* and *positions* within the universe. The horizontal line by each letter "A," "B," et cetera, shows the period on the time scale represented by each chart. A photograph of the arrangement of this universe is shown in figure 5 and a sketch of the complex maze of vaseline partial-barriers in figure 19——a 6-orange feeding area on a 120-orange dispersion (see text, Subsection I, Section II of "Results").

177

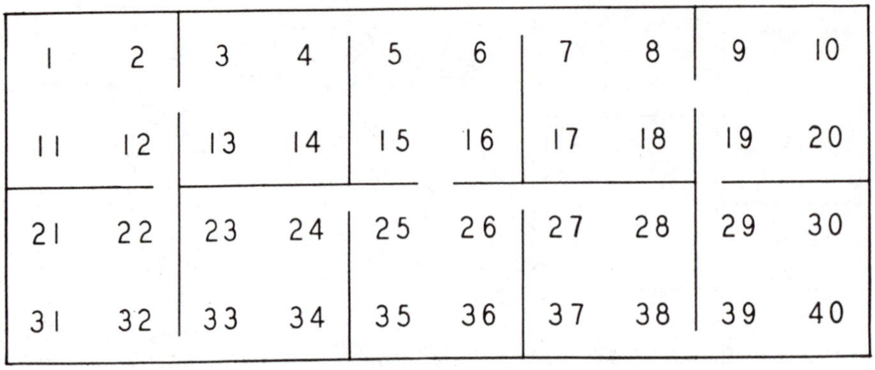

1	2	3	4	5	6	7	8	9	10
11	12	13	14	15	16	17	18	19	20
21	22	23	24	25	26	27	28	29	30
31	32	33	34	35	36	37	38	39	40

Fig. 19. Diagram of a tray used in the complex 3-tray universes (see figs. 17 and 18) with the positions of vaseline barriers shown by black lines.

In addition, small wooden posts were placed in upright positions in each of the major sections of the universe. This was to give the prey species a maximal opportunity to disperse over the vaseline barriers, thus utilizing its adaptive ability to drop by silken strands and be carried by air currents to new locations. An electric fan was used to create a mild air movement in the room. Although the predators have superior dispersal ability within a **limited** environment where movement by wind is not involved, they do not utilize this method of movement. On the other hand, by virtue of such adaptations the prey species has very superior abilities to disperse over greater distances to entirely new areas and environments. Therefore, a restricted environment or universe of the kind used in these experiments utilizes the superior dispersal power of the predator within local areas without giving chance for expression of the equally important superior dispersal power of the prey across greater distances and obstacles. The wooden posts were introduced in an effort to partially correct this condition in these experiments. They did not prove entirely satisfactory, and a more elaborate arrangement to accomplish this purpose should be employed.

Although they were joined into a single universe, the three trays may be looked upon as adjacent microenvironments, and so may the smaller subdivisions within the trays. By this scheme the changes in various areas or the geographic waves in distribution (see charts A to R of fig. 18), as well as the general density changes in the whole universe were followed. It should be noted that the horizontal dimensions of these charts were reduced (relative to the vertical dimensions) because of difficulties in reproduction on a single page. The horizontal dimension of each universe was 50 inches, the dimension shown vertically was 40 inches.

It is obvious in the charts of figure 18 that the divisions between trays, although not covered with a barrier, were an impediment to movement of somewhat greater effect than that caused by the vaseline barriers used **within** each tray.

The charts, A to R of figure 18 represent a compromise with the ideal of showing the exact locations in the universe and the densities of the entire population **on each** date of sampling. In order to have the charts on the same page and running synchronously with the linear graphs of density on the same time scale, the data for each pair of sampling dates were combined. The horizontal lines by each letter "A," "B," "C," et cetera indicate the corresponding time period of the two dates of counting. Note that the chart for the first period, "A," is below, the second, above, the third, below, the fourth, above, et cetera. The classes of density used for the predators and for the prey were limited in number.

In some instances a few prey were present but not enough to be shown. In some instances of predators being shown in areas where no prey are shown, that is a true condition; in others, it may mean only that although the prey were present, there were too few to justify shading. In either instance, such rarity of the prey means that the predators there would be doomed shortly to starvation, and the charts reveal this fact. Note also that the predators are shown in such "white" areas by white circles (ringed), whereas within the shaded areas indicating prey densities, they are shown by white circles also, but no bordering rings are used.

Considering the trays individually, or any sections of the trays individually, the predators either moved away or died in every case just as was true in Gause's experiments with protozoa and with cheese mites, or has been so in all the universes previously discussed herein. However, by utilizing the large and more complex environment so as to make less likely the predators' contact with the prey at all positions at once, or essentially so, it was possible to produce three waves or oscillations in density of predators and prey. That these waves represent a direct and reciprocal predator-prey dependence is obvious.

The maximal density of prey during the first oscillation was 8,550, or 1,425 per orange-area. The predator population responded quickly to the increase in abundance of the prey since the two species occupied the same arenas by virtue of the manual distribution in stocking of the oranges initially (see "Discussion").

The second peak density of prey occurred about October 15 and was somewhat higher than the first at 12,624, or 2,104 per orange-area. The higher level was an automatic effect of the greater lag in response by the predator population during the initial period of this oscillation—i.e., from September 10 to September 30 or somewhat beyond. This lag resulted from the predator's lack of contact with the main masses of the prey which were present in two of the three trays (left third and right third—see charts F and G, fig. 18), although they were in substantial contact with the prey of the center tray (lower center area of chart G) and slightly so with the much larger population in the left tray, or section. Thus the prey were able to sustain a marked increase in density in two of the three trays, as is shown by the progress seen from chart F to chart H and as seen in the graph for this period. More general contact with the prey was eventually achieved but the pattern of achievement reveals the reason for the rather erratic changes in density of the prey * during the process (from October 7 to October 31). On October 7 the predators had reached a moderate density in the universe of 19 per orange-area, but most of these were located in the lower section of the middle tray (chart G), the aftereffect of which is shown in chart H in the elimination of most of the prey in that area and the numbers of predators still present in that area but without food. This chart also shows that their general movement had been partly onto oranges where their prey was abundant and partly onto ones where they found little or no food. As shown in this chart, also, the predators had made substantial contact with the main mass of prey in the left tray but still had not done so in the right tray in which the prey were now rapidly increasing in numbers. It was not until later (chart I) that the right tray also was reached and general population decline of both predators and prey ensued. Thus, localized discontinuity in contact accounts for the zig-zag pattern of increase in the density of the predators during the period involved. A smoothed curve of densities of the predators would correspond to the usual pattern of a predator-prey relation.

*The word "prey" should read "predator."

During the third major increase in the population of the prey, the maximal density reached was 11,956, or 1,993 per orange-area. In this instance, the prey had escaped substantial predation for a long period. Using chart K of figure 18 to represent the end of the second oscillatory wave, it is seen that the predators survived only in the lower right area of the universe where only a minor portion of the prey was present. With the near annihilation of this localized center of population by the predators, the latter then starved as is shown in the subsequent chart L, although one female predator had wandered off into an area where there was no food but from which position it later moved to the left and located the edge of the main mass of prey (chart M). During this time (charts K to M), the prey increased greatly in the absence of predators in the large area it inhabited. Considering the universes having predators, conditioning of the oranges for the first time became a dominant depressive feature for the prey population.

Shortage of food was the principal reason why the population leveled off at a high density of approximately 1,800 mites per orange-area between December 12 and January 2. Except for the fact that the main masses of the population encountered a shortage of food at that time because of the predators' loss of contact with it (charts L, M, and N of fig. 18), the numbers almost certainly would have increased to a position approximating at least 2,500 per orange-area. It is probable that such an increase would have contributed to a compensating, slightly earlier rise in the predator population and, consequently, a slightly earlier decline in the prey population. The resultant crash recorded just subsequent to January 2 was largely an effect of predation, although, as stated, the level from which it was initiated would have been higher (and the resultant aftereffect correspondingly more drastic) except for the ameliorating effect of the shortage of food for the prey just prior to that time. During this time and just subsequently, the approximate proportion of conditioned oranges among those which had reached the age for replacement was 38 per cent (see also "Discussion").

Also, during the peak period of the second oscillation there was a substantial but not principal contribution toward leveling off of the prey population at the approximate position of 1,700 mites per orange-area. In this instance, the proportion of conditioned oranges among those removed from the universe was 25 per cent, but the period of this influence was of shorter duration, and the predators earlier achieved more significant contact with the main masses of the prey, thus preventing a greater degree of food conditioning by the prey. In this instance, it is doubtful whether the prey would have increased to a significantly higher level even if the food had not become limiting to this degree. Thus, 75 per cent of the oranges remained unused to a damaging degree for the 56 days they were present in the universe, and predator action was the principal reason for this.

During the initial oscillatory wave, shortage of food did not enter as a contributive factor. Only six of the 120 oranges removed from the universe were conditioned, i.e., 5 per cent, 95 per cent remaining unconditioned for the 56 days (in this experiment only) each was present in the universe.

The data of this universe with relation to certain points will be covered further under the section on "Discussion."

DISCUSSION

The Experimental Data

Discussed in this section are certain topics pertaining to the data of the various universes (figs. 1 to 18), collectively, and, as well, the significance of these results as exemplifying the role of dispersion in the predator-prey relation.

Since the universe illustrated in figure 18 approaches in result one of the main objectives of this study, those data will be compared with the results in various of the other universes. The arbitrary imposition of wide distribution of both interacting species throughout all sections of the universe in the initial stocking of this universe had several effects which bear a relation to the subsequent events in this universe and to those occurring in other universes otherwise similar: 1) Both species found favorable quantities of food readily at hand for population growth, for during the initial period neither the predator nor the prey faced impediments. 2) The increase in density of the predator in response to increase in density of its prey was immediate. 3) There was very little conditioning of the oranges by the prey during this early phase, for the predators increased their action swiftly and precluded this. 4) The changes in general density of both species during this phase represent rather smooth curvilinear regressions, for the changes in density were relatively simultaneous throughout the universe, with few localized departures from the general pattern (the data thus support the contention that the actual error of sampling is small—see subsection on "Sampling Procedures"). Some of these interrelated points require clarification.

Since in this first oscillation it was not necessary that the predators overcome substantial impediments (with consequent lag effects and losses in numbers) in locating sources of prey, this oscillation is perhaps typical of one where dispersion of food and habitat and the hazards associated with finding them are minimal. In general, the simple universes previously used where the food was massed in one area gave similar results.

On the other hand, the lag effect of predator action exhibited in most of the complex universes discussed earlier, where the colonizing stock of predators was introduced at only a single or very restricted number of positions, is typical of the **second** and **third** oscillatory waves in density as shown for this universe (see fig. 18). Furthermore, the gradual, progressive change in the nature of the distributions (from one oscillation to another) in this universe was such that introductions of the predators into more than a limited number of arenas or introductions of the prey into all sections or arenas of universes would appear to create a condition of distribution not at all natural to such interactions of predators and prey. In this still-too-restricted universe, the predators survived the two critical, post-crash periods only at a single arena and in extremely small numbers, perhaps only a single female in each instance, certainly so in the second. During the third critical, post-crash phase, all the predators perished. Thus, the time required for the interacting populations to adjust to patterns of spatial and quantitative distribution more characteristic of a predator-prey relation which has come closer to **internal** balance may be the principal reason why the lag effect was accumulative from oscillation to oscillation.

Regarding the results of the universes illustrated in figures 14 and 15, the significant fact is that the exact course which may be taken locally at such very low levels of density is a product of chance events, the course of which could be best expressed as a probability of occurrence under various stipulated conditions. In the one instance, the prey were annihilated by the predators, whereas in the other identical universe the predators starved before all the prey were dead, and the prey population then gradually recovered.

Thus, generally, as to whether the participants survive the critical phase and thus make possible the second oscillation is locally a matter of chance, but as the universe considered is increased in complexity and total potentials, the probability that the participants **will** survive is increased.

In this connection it is obvious that the prey must survive the exploitation by the predator as a prerequisite to any possibility of the predator's survival. Thus, the first object is to devise an ecosystem in which there is a near certainty that the prey will survive. In the first universes employed, this condition was not even approached, but the larger, more complex universe employed (see fig. 18) comes closer to this requirement (but, considering the position of the predator, is still far from adequate).

Obviously, for given conditions, the probability that three or four successive oscillations will occur is progressively more remote and is the **product** of the separate probabilities of survival of both participants through **each** component critical phase. This would be true even disregarding the view of Nicholson (1933, 1954) that the amplitude of such oscillations will increase with time. If his view is correct and its tenets **not** modified by damping features, the probability of such a relation continuing for a successively longer number of oscillations would be correspondingly even more reduced. Yet, this cannot be interpreted as contrary to the principle that as density of the prey decreases, the pressure of predator action on it will also decrease.

In this connection, Huffaker and Kennett (1956), as previously stated, demonstrated that biotic interaction between a phytophagous form and its plant host, (with examples which feed in a way as to cause **reaction** by the plant in a manner as to alter the food potential produced subsequently) may be such that the oscillations in the absence of predation may be of **decreasing** amplitude, due to progressive weakening of the plants. Franz (in press) also showed that such interaction may predetermine in a rather subtle way the potentials of subsequent populations of plant feeding forms and, correspondingly, the natural enemies which attack them. Such mechanisms tend to reduce the amplitude of predator-prey oscillations as interactions occur between predator actions and nutritional limitations in time and place.

Shortage of food was also discussed in Subsection I of Section II in relation to damping of the amplitude in a predator-prey universe. It should be noted also that in the universe illustrated in figure 12, there was substantial shortage of food for the prey in local arenas, such was the interaction of problems of dispersal (in this universe where the oranges were widely dispersed) and predator action (see also Subsection D of Section II). While ¼ of the orange supply was fully utilized at its replacement, the predators prevented the utilization of the other ¾ of the food.

Thus, it is obvious that even though action of a predator may be **locally** insignificant at a given time and compensatory in nature (only a substitute for food conditioning which would surely limit the density **there** anyway), the predation may be **far more significant** throughout the larger sphere which would be reached by migrants from the nutritionally overpopulated area. That is, such migrants could proceed to overpopulate the new areas as well but for the predators which preclude the possibility in an example such as this.

This type of control by predation, associated or not with shortage of food for the prey in local arenas, is generally illustrated by the data of this study. The degree of lag in appearance or introduction of the predators into the ecosystem or local arenas is the critical feature of how much of the plant food may be depleted prior to effective curtailment of the plant feeding form. Significantly, in the presence of an effective predator, overpopulation by the plant feeding form in one arena is to a marked degree an assurance against such overpopulation in other arenas. Thus, the common contention by biological control specialists that the farmer should be willing to accept some crop injury is theoretically sound and has been practically demonstrated many times.

In the universes of Subsections A, B, and C of Section II (illustrations of figures 9, 10, and 11), the food of the prey was readily accessible, joined and grouped (a minimum of dispersion). In those universes the predators readily found their prey, responded more quickly to changes in density of the prey and were able quickly to destroy them. This condition appears to offer greater likelihood that **both** the predators and the prey will be annihilated, although in one of the three examples the prey escaped that end.

The occurrence of an almost imperceptible second wave or increase in the universe in which six whole oranges were used (see fig. 11) does not justify the conclusion that simple increase in the area or quantity of food used necessarily greatly increases the chances of creating a self-perpetuating predator-prey system. It is logical to assume that increased complexity is a more important element of the prerequisites than increased area or quantity of food for the prey. Such complexity creates greater relative refuge or protection against the prey's being overexploited, and also reduces its effective reproduction, but it is significant that refuges **restrictive** to the predators such as envisaged by Gause (1934) and Gause, *et al.* (1936) are not implied as essential.

Comparatively, increase of a prey population recovering from the effects of extreme predation is much less rapid than that which results when an original colony is started with an equally low number of colonizing individuals. This has been a characteristic feature in these experiments. Examples of this may be seen in figures 9, 12, 15, 16, and 18 by comparing the steepness of the curves, at the initiation of the universes, with the obviously very gradual increases which resulted from the small numbers which escaped the predators at the end of the crashes in the populations and subsequent to starvation of all the predators.

The reason seems to lie with certain undercrowding phenomena and with the fact that very few females escape the predators, and these are often unmated. Unless copulation occurs later they produce only male offspring. If the female survives long enough and remains in the area, promoting likelihood of contact, she may then copulate with one of her own sons or perhaps another male, and female progeny would result. Two or more generations may be required for the population to attain a favorable proportion of fertilized females and, thus, vigorous population growth, even when predators are no longer present.

Another partial explanation is the observed fact that the females which survive are more commonly found on partially or heavily conditioned oranges. On these oranges the presence of a much greater quantity of webbing, cast skins, and bodies of dead mites affords a relative sheltering effect and thus reduces the probability of the predators' destroying the last survivors. These heavily conditioned oranges are very poor sources of food for population increase; hence, a slow recovery results from the survivors.

CONCLUSIONS

The aforestated considerations suggest that the most satisfactory universe employed (see fig. 18) is still far too restricted, and that, for a perpetuating system, sufficient potentialities must be incorporated to assure several or many such arenas of "last survivors" of predators. This system would leave little probability that all such "last survivors" will simultaneously starve and none find new arenas inhabited by the prey. Thus, there is envisaged in such a system many intergrading, larger, nearly self-sustaining subuniverses or ecosystems, each one as adequate or more adequate than the one illustrated in figure 18.

A major difficulty in demonstrating the existence of reciprocal predator-prey oscillations in nature is associated with the patchy or wavelike occurrence of the predation in time and place, particularly true with examples which are wingless such as the mites and which may have limited extensive dispersal power over distances or from tree to tree, for example. In such studies an inherent oscillatory relation would be confused if the sample area taken to reveal the dynamics of a population unit is too large and, obviously, if it is too small.

Nearly any field entomologist who has studied the action of natural enemies of insect pests has noted that the pattern of action is often patchy in occurrence, proceeding in irregular waves from one or more centers. It is obvious that in one local arena the predator-prey relation may be in one phase of an oscillation while in an adjacent arena it may be in a diametrically opposed phase. Therefore, any combining of two such populations into one would not give a reliable picture of the inherent oscillatory nature of the relation.

Thus, in selecting an environmental area it must be large enough to permit the continued existence of both the predator and its prey, yet not so large that the populations in its several sections may proceed asynchronously, due to too limited interchange of the biotic participants.

It is thus more philosophical than factual to discuss whether or not the predator-prey relation is "inherently" disoperative or self-exterminative in arbitrarily restricted environments. To use an extreme example, the end result would be certain if a small universe or enclosure were employed in which only one pair of mountain lions was confined with only one pair of mule deer. Although in the case of this predatory mite and its prey, an orange is a far more nearly adequate base for a suitable ecosystem, yet, on a single orange the predator has invariably overexploited its prey and become exterminated as a local population. With many examples, the prey has been exterminated also, but with others the prey has been able to recover after the starvation of all the predators. Obviously, if the area is sufficiently small and arbitrarily simple, the biological parameters which have been present during the long evolutionary origins of the relations involving the participants are absent, and capture is so simple that the coaction is disoperative. It is necessary that a system be adequate to assure a high probability that some prey will be missed and that somewhere reasonably accessible, but not too readily so, there are local populations of prey which are thriving and sending emigrants to repopulate the depopulated areas. Also, this predator cannot survive on very low populations (although it requires many fewer prey than does the beetle, *Stethorus* spp., which feeds on the same prey— see also Kuenen, 1945), but must contact a fair density of prey at least at small micro-arenas in order to reproduce and survive.

That self-sustaining predator-prey coactions cannot be maintained without "migration" is self-evident. In this type of study the distinction between migration and any movement at all becomes rather ephemeral. The author disagrees that these migrations must be from beyond the limits of a reasonably adequate system. They may be a result of normal movements within the system—if the system is adequate to give expression to the inherent balance in the biological relations of the predator, its prey, and their coinhabited environment. In an unpublished study, the author and C. E. Kennett have demonstrated that a single strawberry plant is an adequate universe during its life span to sustain a predator-prey coaction. No smaller universe utilizing strawberries is conceivable since a single leaf or flower is not a self-perpetuating living unit.

The speed of local-arena extermination by a predator does not define the period of an oscillation. In fact, it appears to bear little relation to that period. Local extermination of the prey on an orange exposing only $\frac{1}{20}$ orange area has often occurred within three days of the entry of a female predator in that area. Even if the density of the prey population is high, with several hundreds on such an area, they are often exterminated within a period of five or six days. If the environment considered is increased to a single half-orange unit, the time required for self-extermination has been, on the average, longer. In most of the more complicated environments, and involving at least a 2-orange area, the time required to produce the drastic decline in population sufficiently general to jeopardize the predator's existence or cause its extermination has been greatly extended—20 to 40 days for a complicated arrangement involving a single-tray universe and a 2-orange feeding area widely dispersed. The same interval was increased to 30 to 60 days for the most complicated system employing a 6-orange feeding area dispersed over 120 oranges and including a maze-effect of vaseline partial-barriers.

It seems, therefore, that the complexity of the dispersal and searching relationships, combined with the period of time required for the prey species to recover in local arenas from the effects of severe predation and accomplish general repopulation, is more important in determining the period of oscillation than is the intensity of predation once contact is made with local arenas of prey. The rapid recovery of the prey is essential to maintain the predator unless there are arenas of high population which are missed.

It is thought that the existence of barriers increases the chances that the prey species will survive at a level conducive to its rapid recovery. However, it is recognized that the barriers may act as a double-edge sword and defeat the purpose of their use. They do increase the incompleteness of contact and cause marked delay in predator increase. This delay also subsequently causes a greater predator population, which then tends to offset the purpose of the barriers during the crash period. Only further experimentation would really prove whether the barrier feature of this experiment has been a deterrent or an aid to continuance of the coaction. Theoretically, the greater violence of oscillation caused by the barriers would be disoperative in nature, but, on the other hand, they do create the partial asynchrony in geographic position and promote earlier population recovery of the prey species. These features are essential to survival of the predator. They may be more than enough to offset the disoperative pressure created by the higher populations achieved at the crests of population densities. Perhaps, also, the partial ameliorating effect from conditioning of the food in local arenas tends to cancel the greater amplitude otherwise occasioned by the use of the barriers.

The complexity of the environment being searched by both predators and prey lends to the relations a marked inconstancy of hazards from micro-area to micro-area. The idea of a constant area of discovery for the predator or of a constancy in dispersal effectiveness for the prey is difficult to visualize in this environment or in nature. There is not only inconstancy, but nothing resembling a progressive gradation in the hazards. The area of discovery, or that area effectively covered and in which all prey are destroyed by a predator of this species, would vary with its hunger, the density of the prey population independently of hunger of the predator (due to the greater webbing, the added cast skins, debris, et cetera present), the complexity of the general environment with respect to the variability of physical barriers or restrictions of all kinds, and the degree of synchrony in responses, preferences, and tolerances between predator and the prey to such conditions as gravity, light, temperature, moisture, the physical surfaces, air movements, et cetera. The idea of a constant area of discovery has theoretical meaning, particularly where simple, uniform areas are involved to which both predators and prey are rigidly restricted and no chance afforded them to express the broad or narrow ranges of asynchrony in behavior and ecology.

The author feels that the balance or stability observed in nature is characteristic of the total environments in which the evolution of a relation occurred, and forms related to one another in a manner notable for the lack of stability in the community would tend to be replaced by others whose relations are more stable and, thus, the assets of the environment more efficiently utilized. The same effect would be achieved if they were forced by better adjusted competitors to occupy progressively less significant niches within which adequate stability does prevail. It cannot be overstressed that what happens with one predator-prey relation, in one ecosystem, or under a given environmental complex, as to seasons or period of years, for instance, does not necessarily apply to others.

While these data indicate that, other things being equal, simplified monocultures of crops are likely to have greater problems with insect pests than are diversified plantings, it is, nevertheless, known that a single species of introduced natural enemy has in many cases throughout the world permanently solved the most severe problems relating to such pests of monocultures. In this connection, it is interesting to note that Taylor (1955) expressed the opinion that because of the variety and mosaic of small plantings in Britain, the complex of forces for solid natural control are more favorable than in regions where extensive acreages of monocultures are the rule—the reasons for which he considered are yet unknown.

SUMMARY

An experimental study of the role of dispersion in the predator-prey relation was made, using the predatory mite, *Typhlodromus occidentalis,* and the phytophagous mite, *Eotetranychus sexmaculatus,* as the prey. Earlier experimental work by G. F. Gause and associates had led to some acceptance among ecologists of the view that the predator-prey relation is inherently self-annihilative and that continuation of this relation or coaction is dependent upon either: 1) immigrations into the depopulated areas from without, or 2) the existence of definite refuges restrictive to the predators.

In this study, a wide variety of different arrangements in dispersion of plant food (and microhabitat) was tested experimentally. In all the simple universes employed the conclusions of Gause with respect to the predator, but not to the prey, seemed to apply. The unacceptability of that view was demonstrated by the use of a larger, much more complex universe utilizing wide dispersion and incorporating also partial barriers, thus increasing still further the relative dispersion while still not incorporating restrictive refuges. By this method, predator-prey coaction was maintained for three successive oscillations. It is thus quite probable that a controlled, experimental ecosystem can be established in which the predator-prey coaction would not be inherently self-annihilative. It is believed also that various damping mechanisms would come into play which would serve to ameliorate the theoretically sound concept that oscillations arising from this coaction are inherently of increasing severity in amplitude.

The whole controversy becomes rather more philosophical than factual, considering that the earlier view incorporated the purely relative concept of immigration of new stock from without, and any distinction between immigration or emigration and any movement at all on the part of the participants can hardly be upheld. The suggestion seems more appropriate that artificial universes are inadequate if they do not give possibility of expression of the major parameters intrinsic to the specific predator-prey coaction in the natural habitat, and that conclusions drawn from such data as to principles have limited value. The success we have in sustaining such a coaction under experimental conditions is probably a measure of the degree to which we have duplicated the inherent essentials.

In this study, arbitrary selection of different degrees of dispersion and segmentation of the units of food for the prey was accomplished without altering the total surfaces to be searched, and, when desired, without altering the total amounts of food used. This was done by covering oranges to various degrees, leaving known exposed portions, and dispersing them as desired among waxed rubber balls of the same size. The technique offers possibilities of elaborate and varied studies along these lines. For example, further modifications could make it possible to study the predator-prey relation with greater assurance against overexploitation, and, thus, various other features, such as the introduction of a competing predatory species or a competing prey species, could be introduced in order to study their relations to the periods and amplitudes of the oscillations. By elaboration along these lines it should be possible to establish empirically whether employment of quite diversified agricultures may offer prospects of relief from insect pests—in comparison with extensive cultivations of single crops.

REFERENCES

DeBach, P., and H. S. Smith
  1941. Are population oscillations inherent in the host-parasite relations? Ecology 22: 363–69.
Errington, P.
  1937. What is the meaning of predation? Smithsn. Inst. Ann. Rpt. 1936:243–52.
  1946. Predation and vertebrate populations. Quart. Rev. Biol. 21:144–77.
Finney, G. L.
  1953. A technique for mass-culture of the six-spotted mite. Jour. Econ. Ent. 46:712–13.
Franz, J.
  In Press. The effectiveness of predators and food as factors limiting gradations of *Adelges* (*Dreyfusia*) *piceae* (Ratz.) in Europe. Tenth Inter. Cong. Ent., 1956.
Gause, G. F.
  1934. The struggle for existence. (163 pp.) Williams & Wilkins, Baltimore. Md.
Gause, G. F., N. P. Smaragdova, and A. A. Witt
  1936. Further studies of interaction between predators and prey. Jour. Anim. Ecol. 5:1–18.
Huffaker, C. B., and C. E. Kennett
  1956. Experimental studies on predation: Predation and cyclamen-mite populations on strawberries in California. Hilgardia 26(4):191–222.
Kuenen, D. J.
  1945. On the ecological significance of *Metatetranychus ulmi* C. L. Koch (Acari, Tetranychidae). Tijdschr. v. Ent. 88:303–12.
Leopold, A. S.
  1954. The predator in wildlife management. Sierra Club Bul. 39:34–38.
Nicholson, A. J.
  1933. The balance of animal populations. Jour. Anim. Ecol. 2, Supp.:132–78.
  1954. An outline of the dynamics of animal populations. Austral. Jour. Zool. 2:9–65.
Taylor, T. H. C.
  1955. Biological control of insect pests. Ann. Appl. Biol. 42:190–96.
Uvarov, B. P.
  1931. Insects and climate. Ent. Soc. London, Trans. 78:1–247.
Waters, N. D.
  1955. Biological and ecological studies of *Typhlodromus* mites as predators of the six-spotted mite. (Unpublished Ph.D. dissertation, University of California, Berkeley.)
Winsor, C. P.
  1934. Mathematical analysis of growth of mixed populations. Cold Spring Harbor Symposia on Quant. Biol. 2:181–89.

The Components of Predation as Revealed by a Study of Small-Mammal Predation of the European Pine Sawfly[1]

By C. S. HOLLING

Forest Insect Laboratory, Sault Ste. Marie, Ont.

INTRODUCTION

The fluctuation of an animal's numbers between restricted limits is determined by a balance between that animal's capacity to increase and the environmental checks to this increase. Many authors have indulged in the whimsy of calculating the progressive increase of a population when no checks were operating. Thus Huxley calculated that the progeny of a single *Aphis* in the course of 10 generations, supposing all survived, would "contain more ponderable substance than five hundred millions of stout men; that is, more than the whole population of China", (in Thompson, 1929). Checks, however, do occur and it has been the subject of much controversy to determine how these checks operate. Certain general principles—the density-dependence concept of Smith (1955), the competition theory of Nicholson (1933)—have been proposed both verbally and mathematically, but because they have been based in part upon untested and restrictive assumptions they have been severely criticized (e.g. Andrewartha and Birch 1954). These problems could be considerably clarified if we knew the mode of operation of each process that affects numbers, if we knew its basic and subsidiary components. Predation, one such process, forms the subject of the present paper.

Many of the published studies of predation concentrate on discrete parts rather than the whole process. Thus some entomologists are particularly interested in the effect of selection of different kinds of prey by predators upon the evolution of colour patterns and mimicry; wildlife biologists are similarly interested in selection but emphasize the role predators play in improving the condition of the prey populations by removing weakened animals. While such specific problems should find a place in any scheme of predation, the main aim of the present study is to elucidate the components of predation in such a way that more meaning can be applied to considerations of population dynamics. This requires a broad study of the whole process and in particular its function in affecting the numbers of animals.

Such broad studies have generally been concerned with end results measured by the changes in the numbers of predator and prey. These studies are particularly useful when predators are experimentally excluded from the environment of their prey, in the manner adopted by DeBach and his colleagues in their investigations of the pests of orchard trees in California. This work, summarized recently (DeBach, 1958) in response to criticism by Milne (1957), clearly shows that in certain cases the sudden removal of predators results in a rapid increase of prey numbers from persistently low densities to the limits of the food supply. Inasmuch as these studies have shown that other factors have little regulatory function, the predators appear to be the principal ones responsible for regulation. Until the components of predation are revealed by an analysis of the processes leading to these end results, however, we will never know whether the conclusions from such

[1]Contribution from the Dept. of Zoology, University of British Columbia and No. 547, Forest Biology Division, Research Branch, Department of Agriculture, Ottawa, Canada. Delivered in part at the Tenth International Congress of Entomology, Montreal, 1956.

studies apply to situations other than the specific predator–prey relationship investigated.

Errington's investigations of vertebrate predator–prey situations (1934, 1943, 1945 and 1956) suggest, in part, how some types of predation operate. He has postulated that each habitat can support only a given number of animals and that predation becomes important only when the numbers of prey exceed this "carrying capacity". Hence predators merely remove surplus animals, ones that would succumb even in the absence of natural enemies. Errington exempts certain predator-prey relations from this scheme, however, and quotes the predation of wolves on deer as an example where predation probably is not related to the carrying capacity of the habitat. However logical these postulates are, they are only indirectly supported by the facts, and they do not explain the processes responsible.

In order to clarify these problems a comprehensive theory of predation is required that on the one hand is not so restrictive that it can only apply in certain cases and on the other not so broad that it becomes meaningless. Such a comprehensive answer requires a comprehensive approach, not necessarily in terms of the number of situations examined but certainly in terms of the variables involved, for it is the different reactions of predators to these variables that produce the many diverse predator-prey relations. Such a comprehensive approach is faced with a number of practical difficulties. It is apparent from the published studies of predation of vertebrate prey by vertebrate predators that not only is it difficult to obtain estimates of the density of predator, prey, and destroyed prey, but also that the presence of many interacting variables confuses interpretation.

The present study of predation of the European pine sawfly, *Neodiprion sertifer* (Geoff.) by small mammals was particularly suited for a general comprehensive analysis of predation. The practical difficulties concerning population measurement and interpretation of results were relatively unimportant, principally because of the unique properties of the environment and of the prey. The field work was conducted in the sand-plain area of southwestern Ontario where Scots and jack pine have been planted in blocks of up to 200 acres. The flat topography and the practice of planting trees of the same age and species at standard six-foot spacings has produced a remarkably uniform environment. In addition, since the work was concentrated in plantations 15 to 20 years of age, the closure of the crowns reduced ground vegetation to a trace, leaving only an even layer of pine needles covering the soil. The extreme simplicity and uniformity of this environment greatly facilitated the population sampling and eliminated complications resulting from changes in the quantity and kind of alternate foods of the predators.

The investigations were further simplified by the characteristics of the prey. Like most insects, the European pine sawfly offers a number of distinct life-history stages that might be susceptible to predation. The eggs, laid in pine needles the previous fall, hatch in early spring and the larvae emerge and feed upon the foliage. During the first two weeks of June the larvae drop from the trees and spin cocoons within the duff on the forest floor. These cocooned sawflies remain in the ground until the latter part of September, when most emerge as adults. A certain proportion, however, overwinter in cocoons, to emerge the following autumn. Observations in the field and laboratory showed that only one of these life-history stages, the cocoon, was attacked by the small-mammal predators, and that the remaining stages were inaccessible and/or unpalatable and hence completely escaped attack. These data will form part of a later paper dealing specifically with the impact of small mammal predation upon the European pine sawfly.

Cocooned sawflies, as prey, have some very useful attributes for an investigation of this kind. Their concentration in the two-dimensional environment of the duff-soil interface and their lack of movement and reaction to predators con-

189

siderably simplify sampling and interpretation. Moreover, the small mammals' habit of making a characteristically marked opening in the cocoon to permit removal of the insect leaves a relatively permanent record in the ground of the number of cocooned sawflies destroyed. Thus, the density of the destroyed prey can be measured at the same time as the density of the prey.

Attention was concentrated upon the three most numerous predators—the masked shrew, *Sorex cinereus cinereus* Kerr, the short-tail shrew, *Blarina brevicauda talpoides* Gapper, and deer mouse, *Peromyscus maniculatus bairdii* Hoy and Kennicott. It soon became apparent that these species were the only significant predators of the sawfly, for the remaining nine species trapped or observed in the plantations were either extremely rare or were completely herbivorous.

Here, then, was a simple predator-prey situation where three species of small mammals were preying on a simple prey—sawfly cocoons. The complicating variables present in most other situations were either constant or absent because of the simple characteristics of the environment and of the prey. The absence or constancy of these complicating variables facilitated analysis but at the expense of a complete and generally applicable scheme of predation. Fortunately, however, the small-mammal predators and the cocoons could easily be manipulated in laboratory experiments so that the effect of those variables absent in the field situation could be assessed. At the same time the laboratory experiments supported the field results. This blend of field and laboratory data provides a comprehensive scheme of predation which will be shown to modify present theories of population dynamics and to considerably clarify the role predators play in population regulation.

I wish to acknowledge the considerable assistance rendered by a number of people, through discussion and criticism of the manuscript: Dr. I. McT. Cowan, Dr. K. Graham and Dr. P. A. Larkin at the University of British Columbia and Dr. R. M. Belyea, Mr. A. W. Ghent and Dr. P. J. Pointing, at the Forest Biology Laboratory, Sault Ste. Marie, Ontario.

FIELD TECHNIQUES

A study of the interaction of predator and prey should be based upon accurate population measurements, and in order to avoid superficial interpretations, populations should be expressed as numbers per unit area. Three populations must be measured—those of the predators, prey, and destroyed prey. Thus the aim of the field methods was to measure accurately each of the three populations in terms of their numbers per acre.

Small-Mammal Populations

Since a complete description and evaluation of the methods used to estimate the density of the small-mammal predators forms the basis of another paper in preparation, a summary of the techniques will suffice for the present study.

Estimates of the number of small mammals per acre were obtained using standard live-trapping techniques adapted from Burt (1940) and Blair (1941). The data obtained by marking, releasing and subsequently recapturing animals were analysed using either the Lincoln index (Lincoln, 1930) or Hayne's method for estimating populations in removal trapping procedures (Hayne, 1949). The resulting estimates of the number of animals exposed to traps were converted to per acre figures by calculating, on the basis of measurements of the home range of the animals (Stickel, 1954), the actual area sampled by traps.

The accuracy of these estimates was evaluated by examining the assumptions underlying the proper use of the Lincoln index and Hayne's technique and by comparing the efficiency of different traps and trap arrangements. This analysis

190

showed that an accurate estimate of the numbers of *Sorex* and *Blarina* could be obtained using Hayne's method of treating the data obtained from trapping with bucket traps. These estimates, however, were accurate only when the populations had not been disturbed by previous trapping. For *Peromyscus*, Lincoln-index estimates obtained from the results of trapping with Sherman traps provided an ideal way of estimating numbers that was both accurate and unaffected by previous trapping.

N. sertifer Populations

Since small-mammal predation of *N. sertifer* was restricted to the cocoon stage, prey populations could be measured adequately by estimating the number of cocoons containing living insects present immediately after larval drop in June. This estimate was obtained using a method outlined and tested by Prebble (1943) for cocoon populations of the European spruce sawfly, *Gilpinia hercyniae* (Htg.), an insect with habits similar to those of *N. sertifer*. Accurate estimates were obtained when cocoons were collected from sub-samples of litter and duff distributed within the restricted universe beneath the crowns of host trees. This method was specially designed to provide an index of population rather than an estimate of numbers per acre. But it is obvious from this work that any cocoon-sampling technique designed to yield a *direct* estimate of the number of cocoons per acre would require an unpractically large number of sample units. It proved feasible in the present study, however, to convert such estimates from a square-foot to an acre basis, by stratifying the forest floor into three strata, one comprising circles with two-foot radii around tree trunks, one comprising intermediate rings with inner radii two feet and outer radii three feet, and one comprising the remaining area (three to five feet from the tree trunks).

At least 75 trees were selected and marked throughout each plantation, and one or usually two numbered wooden stakes were placed directly beneath the crown of each tree, on opposite sides of the trunk. Stakes were never placed under overlapping tree crowns. The four sides of each stake were lettered from A to D and the stake was placed so that the numbered sides bore no relation to the position of the trunk. Samples were taken each year, by collecting cocoons from the area delimited by one-square-foot frames placed at one corner of each stake. In the first year's sample the frames were placed at the AB corner, in the second year's at the BC corner, etc. Different-sized screens were used to separate the cocoons from the litter and duff.

Cocoons were collected in early September before adult sawflies emerged and those from each quadrat were placed in separate containers for later analysis. These cocoons were analysed by first segregating them into "new" and "old" categories. Cocoons of the former category were a bright golden colour and were assumed to have been spun in the year of sampling, while those of the latter were dull brown in colour and supposedly had been spun before the sampling year. These assumptions proved partly incorrect, however, for some of the cocoons retained their new colour for over one year. Hence the "new" category contained enough cocoons that had been spun before the sampling year to prevent its use, without correction, as an estimate of the number of cocoons spun in the year of sampling. A correction was devised, however, which reduced the error to negligible proportions.

This method provided the best available estimate of the number of healthy cocoons per acre present in any one year. The population figures obtained ranged from 39,000 (Plot 1, 1954) to 1,080,000 (Plot 2, 1952) cocoons per acre.

Predation

Small-mammal predation has a direct and indirect effect on *N. sertifer* populations. The direct effect of predation is studied in detail in this paper. The indirect effect, resulting from the mutual interaction of various control factors (parasites, disease, and predators) has been discussed in previous papers (Holling, 1955, 1958b).

The direct effect of predation was measured in a variety of ways. General information was obtained from studies of the consumption of insects by caged animals and from the analysis of stomach contents obtained from animals trapped in sawfly-infested plantations. More particular information was obtained from the analysis of cocoons collected in the regular quadrat samples and from laboratory experiments which studied the effect of cocoon density upon predation.

The actual numbers of *N. sertifer* cocoons destroyed were estimated from cocoons collected in the regular quadrat samples described previously. As shown in an earlier paper (Holling, 1955), cocoons opened by small mammals were easily recognized and moreover could be classified as to species of predator. These estimates of the number of new and old cocoons per square foot opened by each species of predator were corrected, as before, to provide an estimate of the number opened from the time larvae dropped to the time when cocoon samples were taken in early September.

It has proved difficult to obtain a predation and cocoon-population estimate of the desired precision and accuracy. The corrections and calculations that had to be applied to the raw sampling data cast some doubt upon the results and conclusions based upon them. It subsequently developed, however, that a considerable margin of error could be tolerated without changing the results and the conclusions that could be derived from them. In any case, all conclusions based upon cocoon-population estimates were supported and substantiated by results from controlled laboratory experiments.

LABORATORY TECHNIQUES

Several experiments were conducted with caged animals in order to support and expand results obtained in the field. The most important of these measured the number of cocoons consumed by *Peromyscus* at different cocoon densities. These experiments were conducted at room temperature (ca. 20°C) in a screen-topped cage, 10' x 4' x 6". At the beginning of an experiment, cocoons were first buried in sand where the lines of a removable grid intersected, the grid was then removed, the sand was pressed flat, and a metal-edged levelling jig was finally scraped across the sand so that an even 12 mm. covered the cocoons. A single deer mouse was then placed in the cage together with nesting material, water, and an alternate food—dog biscuits. In each experiment the amount of this alternate food was kept approximately the same (i.e. 13 to 17 gms. dry weight). After the animal had been left undisturbed for 24 hours, the removable grid was replaced, and the number of holes dug over cocoons, the number of cocoons opened and the dry weight of dog biscuits eaten were recorded. Consumption by every animal was measured at either four or five different densities ranging from 2.25 to 36.00 cocoons per sq. ft. The specific densities were provided at random until all were used, the consumption at each density being measured for three to six consecutive days. Ideally the size of the cage should remain constant at all densities but since this would have required over 1,400 cocoons at the highest density, practical considerations necessitated a compromise whereby the cage was shortened at the higher densities. In these experiments the total number of cocoons provided ranged from 88 at the lowest density to 504 at the highest. At all densities, however, these numbers represented a surplus and no more than 40 per cent were ever consumed in a single experiment. Hence consumption was not limited by shortage of cocoons, even though the size of the cage changed.

The sources and characteristics of the cocoons and *Peromyscus* used in these experiments require some comment. Supplies of the prey were obtained by collecting cocoons in sawfly-infested plantations or by collecting late-instar larvae and allowing them to spin cocoons in boxes provided with foliage and litter. Sound cocoons from either source were then segregated into those containing healthy, parasitized, and diseased prepupae using a method of X-ray analysis (Holling, 1958a). The small male cocoons were separated from the larger female cocoons by size, since this criterion had previously proved adequate (Holling, 1958b). To simplify the experiments, only male and female cocoons containing healthy, living prepupae were used and in each experiment equal numbers of cocoons of each sex were provided, alternately, in the grid pattern already described.

Three mature non-breeding male deer mice were used in the experiments. Each animal had been born and raised in small rearing cages 12 x 8 x 6 in. and had been isolated from cocoons since birth. They therefore required a period to become familiar with the experimental cage and with cocoons. This experience was acquired during a preliminary three-week period. For the first two weeks the animal was placed in the experimental cage together with nesting material, water, dog biscuits and sand, and each day was disturbed just as it would be if an experiment were in progress. For the final week cocoons were buried in the sand at the first density chosen so that the animal could learn to find and consume the cocoon contents. It has been shown (Holling, 1955, 1958b) that a seven-day period is more than ample to permit complete learning.

THE COMPONENTS OF PREDATION

A large number of variables could conceivably affect the mortality of a given species of prey as a result of predation by a given species of predator. These can conveniently be classified, as was done by Leopold (1933), into five groups:

(1) density of the prey population.
(2) density of the predator population.
(3) characteristics of the prey, e.g., reactions to predators, stimulus detected by predator, and other characteristics.
(4) density and quality of alternate foods available for the predator.
(5) characteristics of the predator, e.g., food preferences, efficiency of attack, and other characteristics.

Each of these variables may exert a considerable influence and the effect of any one may depend upon changes in another. For example, Errington (1946) has shown that the characteristics of many vertebrate prey species change when their density exceeds the number that the available cover can support. This change causes a sudden increase in predation. When such complex interactions are involved, it is difficult to understand clearly the principles involved in predation; to do so we must find a simplified situation where some of the variables are constant or are not operating. The problem studied here presents such a situation. First, the characteristics of cocoons do not change as the other factors vary and there are no reactions by the cocooned sawflies to the predators. We therefore can ignore, temporarily, the effect of the third factor, prey characteristics. Secondly, since the work was conducted in plantations noted for their uniformity as to species, age, and distribution of trees, there was a constant and small variety of possible alternate foods. In such a simple and somewhat sterile environment, the fourth factor, the density and quality of alternate foods, can therefore be initially ignored, as can the fifth factor, characteristics of the predator, which is really only another way of expressing factors three and four. There are thus only two basic variables affecting predation in this instance, i.e., prey density and predator density. Furthermore, these are the only essential ones, for the remainder, while possibly important in affecting the amount of predation, are not essential to describe its fundamental characteristics.

The Basic Components

It is from the two essential variables that the basic components of predation will be derived. The first of these variables, prey density, might affect a number of processes and consumption of prey by individual predators might well be one of them.

The data which demonstrate the effect of changes of prey density upon consumption of cocooned sawflies by *Peromyscus* were obtained from the yearly cocoon quadrat samples in Plots 1 and 2. In 1951, Dr. F. T. Bird, Laboratory of Insect Pathology, Sault Ste. Marie, Ont., had sprayed each of these plots with a low concentration of a virus disease that attacked *N. sertifer* larvae, (Bird 1953). As a result, populations declined from 248,000 and 1,080,000 cocoons per acre, respectively, in 1952, to 39,000 and 256,000 in 1954. Thus predation values at six different cocoon densities were obtained. An additional sample in a neighbouring plantation in 1953 provided another value.

Predation values for *Sorex* and *Blarina* were obtained from one plantation, Plot 3, in one year, 1952. In the spring of that year, virus, sprayed from an aircraft flying along parallel lines 300 feet apart, was applied in three concentrations, with the lowest at one end of the plantation and the highest at the other. An area at one end, not sprayed, served as a control. When cocoon populations were sampled in the autumn, a line of 302 trees was selected at right angles to the lines of spray and the duff under each was sampled with one one-square-foot quadrat. The line, approximately 27 chains long, ran the complete length of the plantation. When the number of new cocoons per square foot was plotted against distance, discrete areas could be selected which had fairly constant populations that ranged from 44,000 to 571,000 cocoons per acre. The areas of low population corresponded to the areas sprayed with the highest concentration of virus. In effect, the plantation could be divided into rectangular strips, each with a particular density of cocoons. The width of these strips varied from 126 to 300 feet with an average of 193 feet. In addition to the 302 quadrats examined, the cocoons from another 100 quadrats were collected from the areas of lowest cocoon densities. Thus, in this one plantation in 1952, there was a sufficient number of different cocoon densities to show the response of consumption by *Sorex* and *Blarina* to changes of prey density.

The methods used to estimate predator densities in each study plot require some further comment. In Plots 1 and 2 this was done with grids of Sherman traps run throughout the summer. In Plot 3 both a grid of Sherman traps and a line of snap traps were used. This grid, measuring 18 chains by 4 chains, was placed so that approximately the same area sampled for cocoons was sampled for small mammals. The populations determined from these trapping procedures were plotted against time, and the number of "mammal-days" per acre, from the start of larval drop (June 14) to the time cocoon samples were made (Aug. 20-30), was determined for each plot each year. This could be done with *Peromyscus* and *Blarina* since the trapping technique was shown to provide an accurate estimate of their populations. But this was not true for *Sorex*. Instead, the number of *Sorex*-days per acre was approximated by dividing the number of cocoons opened at the highest density by the known number consumed by caged *Sorex* per day, i.e. 101. Since the number of cocoons opened at the highest cocoon density was

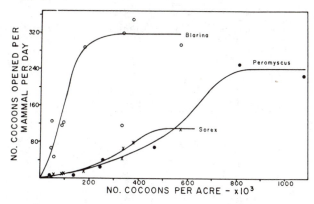

Fig. 1. Functional responses of *Blarina*, *Sorex* and *Peromyscus* in plots 1, 2, and 3.

151,000 per acre, then the number of *Sorex*-days per acre should be 151,000/101 = 1,490. This is approximately 10 times the estimate that was obtained from trapping with Sherman traps. When the various trapping methods were compared, estimates from Sherman trapping were shown to underestimate the numbers of *Sorex* by about the same amount, i.e. one-tenth.

With estimates of the numbers of predators, prey and destroyed prey available, the daily number of prey consumed per predator at different cocoon densities can be calculated. As seen in Fig. 1, the number of cocoons opened by each species increased with increasing cocoon density until a maximum daily consumption was reached that corresponded approximately to the maximum number that could be consumed in any one day by caged animals. For *Sorex* this of course follows from the method of calculation. The rates at which these curves rise differ for the different species, being greatest for *Blarina* and least for *Peromyscus*. Even if the plateaus are equated by multiplying points on each curve by a constant, the rates still decrease in the same order, reflecting a real difference in species behaviour.

The existence of such a response to cocoon density may also be demonstrated by data from the analysis of stomach contents. The per cent occurrence and per cent volume of the various food items in stomachs of *Peromyscus* captured immediately after larval drop and two months later is shown in Table I. When cocoon densities were high, immediately after larval drop, the per cent occurrence and per cent volume of *N. sertifer* material was high. Two months later when various cocoon mortality factors had taken their toll, cocoon densities were lower and

TABLE I

Stomach contents of *Peromyscus* trapped immediately before larval drop and two months later

Time trapped	Approx. no. cocoons per acre	No. of stomachs	Analysis	Plant	*N. sertifer*	Other insects	All insects
June 16–21	600,000	19	% occurrence	37%	95%	53%	100%
Aug. 17–19	300,000	14		79%	50%	64%	86%
June 16–21	600,000	19	% volume	5%	71%	24%	95%
Aug. 17–19	300,000	14		47%	19%	34%	53%

TABLE II

Occurrence of food items in stomachs of *Microtus* trapped before and after larval drop

Time trapped	Plant		*N. sertifer*		All insects	
	No. of stomachs	% occurrence	No. of stomachs	% occurrence	No. of stomachs	% occurrence
before larval drop	25	100%	2	8%	2	8%
after larval drop	29	100%	8	28%	11	38%

N. sertifer was a less important food item. The decrease in consumption of *N. sertifer* was accompanied by a considerable increase in the consumption of plant material and a slight increase in the consumption of other insect material. Plants and other insects acted as buffer or alternate foods. *Microtus*, even though they ate few non-plant foods in nature, also showed an increase in the per cent occurrence of *N. sertifer* material in stomachs as cocoon density increased (Table II). Before larval drop, when cocoon densities were low, the incidence of *N. sertifer* in *Microtus* stomachs was low. After larval drop, when cocoon densities were higher, the incidence increased by 3.5 times. Even at the higher cocoon densities, however, *N. sertifer* comprised less than one per cent of the volume of stomach contents so that this response to changes in prey density by *Microtus* is extremely low.

The graphs presented in Fig. I and the results of the analyses of stomach contents leave little doubt that the consumption of cocooned sawflies by animals in the field increases with increase in cocoon density. Similar responses have been demonstrated in laboratory experiments with three *Peromyscus*. As shown in Fig. 2, the number of cocoons consumed daily by each animal increased with increase in cocoon density, again reaching a plateau as did the previous curves. Whenever the number of prepupae consumed did not meet the caloric requirements, these were met by consumption of the dog biscuits, the alternate food provided. Only one of the animals (A) at the highest density fulfilled its caloric requirements by consuming prepupae; the remaining animals (B and C) consumed

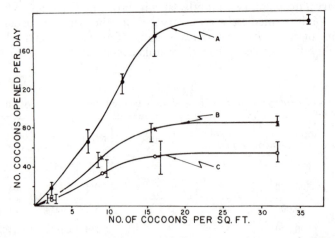

Fig. 2. Functional responses of three caged *Peromyscus* (means and ranges shown).

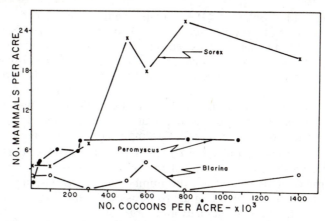

Fig. 3. Numerical responses of *Blarina, Sorex* and *Peromyscus.*

less than one-half the number of sawflies they would consume if no alternate foods were present. The cocoons used in experiments involving animals B and C, however, had been spun 12 months earlier than those involving animal A. When the characteristics of the functional response are examined in another paper, it will be shown that the strength of stimulus from older cocoons is less than that from younger cocoons, and that these differences are sufficient to explain the low consumption by animals B and C. The shape of the curves and the density at which they level is very similar for all animals, so similar that multiplying points along any one curve by the proper constant will equate all three. These curves are very similar to the ones based upon field data. All show the same form, the essential feature of which is an S-shaped rise to a plateau.

The effect of changes of prey density need not be restricted exclusively to consumption of prey by individual predators. The density of predators may also be affected and this can be shown by relating the number of predators per acre to the number of cocoons per acre. Conclusions can be derived from these relations but they are tentative. The data were collected over a relatively short period of time (four summers) and thus any relationship between predator numbers and prey density may have been fortuitous. Only those data obtained in plantations over 12 years old are included since small mammal populations were most stable in these areas. The data for the three most important species of predators are shown in the curves of Fig. 3, where each point represents the highest summer population observed either in different plantations or in the same plantation in different years.

The densities of *Blarina* were lowest while those of *Sorex* were highest. In this situation, *Blarina* populations apparently did not respond to prey density, for its numbers did not noticeably increase with increase in cocoon density. Some agent or agents other than food must limit their numbers. Populations of *Peromyscus* and *Sorex*, on the other hand, apparently did initially increase with increase in cocoon density, ultimately ceasing to increase as some agents other than food became limiting. The response of *Sorex* was most marked.

Thus two responses to changes of prey density have been demonstrated. The first is a change in the number of prey consumed per predator and the second is a change in the density of predators. Although few authors appear to recognize the existence and importance of *both* these responses to changes of prey density, they have been postulated and, in the case of the change of predator density,

197

demonstrated. Thus Solomon (1949) acknowledged the two-fold nature of the response to changes of prey density, and applied the term *functional response* to the change in the number of prey consumed by individual predators, and the term *numerical response* to the change in the density of predators. These are apt terms and, although they have been largely ignored in the literature, they will be adopted in this paper. The data available to Solomon for review did not permit him to anticipate the form the functional response of predators might take, so that he could not assess its importance in population regulation. It will be shown, however, that the functional response is as important as the numerical.

It remains now to consider the effect of predator density, the variable that, together with prey density, is essential for an adequate description of predation. Predator density might well affect the number of prey consumed per predator. Laboratory experiments were designed to measure the number of cocoons opened by one, two, four, and eight animals in a large cage provided with cocoons at a density of 15 per square foot and a surplus of dog biscuits and water. The average number of cocoons opened per mouse in eight replicates was 159, 137, 141 and 159 respectively. In this experiment, therefore, predator density apparently did not greatly affect the consumption of prey by individual animals. This conclusion is again suggested when field and laboratory data are compared, for the functional response of *Peromyscus* obtained in the field, where its density varied, was very similar to the response of single animals obtained in the laboratory.

In such a simple situation, where predator density does not greatly affect the consumption by individuals, the total predation can be expressed by a simple, additive combination of the two responses. For example, if at a particular prey density the functional response is such that 100 cocoons are opened by a single predator in one day, and the numerical response is such that the predator density is 10, then the total daily consumption will be simply 100 x 10. In other situations, however, an increase in the density of predators might result in so much competition that the consumption of prey by individual predators might drop significantly. This effect can still be incorporated in the present scheme by adopting a more complex method of combining the functional and numerical responses.

This section was introduced with a list of the possible variables that could affect predation. Of these, only the two operating in the present study — prey and predator density — are essential variables, so that the basic features of predation can be ascribed to the effects of these two. It has been shown that there are two responses to prey density. The increase in the number of prey consumed per predator, as prey density rises, is termed the functional response, while the change in the density of predators is termed the numerical response. The total amount of predation occurring at any one density results from a combination of the two responses, and the method of combination will be determined by the way predator density affects consumption. This scheme, therefore, describes the effects of the basic variables, uncomplicated by the effects of subsidiary ones. Hence the two responses, the functional and numerical, can be considered the basic components of predation.

The total amount of predation caused by small mammals is shown in Fig. 4, where the functional and numerical responses are combined by multiplying the number of cocoons opened per predator at each density by the number of effective mammal-days observed. These figures were then expressed as percentages opened. This demonstrates the relation between per cent predation and prey density during the 100-day period between cocoon formation and adult emergence. Since the data obtained for the numerical responses are tentative, some reservations must be applied to the more particular conclusions derived

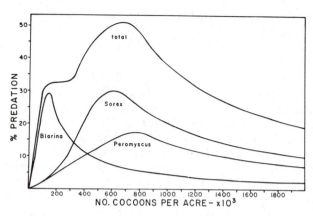

Fig. 4. Functional and numerical responses combined to show the relation between per cent predation and cocoon density.

from this figure. The general conclusion, that per cent predation by each species shows an initial rise and subsequent decline as cocoon density increases holds, however. For this conclusion to be invalid, the numerical responses would have to decrease in order to mask the initial rise in per cent predation caused by the S-shaped form of the functional responses. Thus from zero to some finite cocoon density, predation by small mammals shows a direct density-dependent action and thereafter shows an inverse density-dependent action. The initial rise in the proportion of prey destroyed can be attributed to both the functional and numerical responses. The functional response has a roughly sigmoid shape and hence the proportion of prey destroyed by an individual predator will increase with increase in cocoon density up to and beyond the point of inflection. Unfortunately the data for any one functional response curve are not complete enough to establish a sigmoid relation, but the six curves presented thus far and the several curves to be presented in the following section all suggest a point of inflection. The positive numerical responses shown by *Sorex* and *Peromyscus* also promote a direct density-dependent action up to the point at which predator densities remain constant. Thereafter, with individual consumption also constant, the per cent predation will decline as cocoon density increases. The late Dr. L. Tinbergen apparently postulated the same type of dome-shaped curves for the proportion of insects destroyed by birds. His data were only partly published (1949, 1955) before his death, but Klomp (1956) and Voûte (1958) have commented upon the existence of these "optimal curves". This term, however, is unsatisfactory and anthropocentric. From the viewpoint of the forest entomologist, the highest proportion of noxious insects destroyed may certainly be the optimum, but the term is meaningless for an animal that consumes individuals and not percentages. Progress can best be made by considering predation first as a behaviour before translating this behaviour in terms of the proportion of prey destroyed. The term "peaked curve" is perhaps more accurate.

Returning to Fig. 4, we see that the form of the peaked curve for *Blarina* is determined solely by the functional response since this species exhibited no numerical response. The abrupt peak occurs because the maximum consumption of prepupae was reached at a very low prey density before the predation was "diluted" by large numbers of cocoons. With *Sorex* both the numerical and functional responses are important. Predation by *Sorex* is greatest principally because of the marked numerical response. The two responses again determine the form of the peaked curve for *Peromyscus*, but the numerical response, unlike that of *Sorex*, was not marked, and the maximum consumption of cocoons was reached only at a relatively high density; the result is a low per cent predation with a peak occurring at a high cocoon density.

Predation by all species destroyed a considerable number of cocooned saw-flies over a wide range of cocoon densities. The presence of more than one species of predator not only increased predation but also extended the range of prey densities over which predation was high. This latter effect is particularly important, for if the predation by several species of predators peaked at the same prey density the range of densities over which predation was high would be slight and if the prey had a sufficiently high reproductive capacity its density might jump this vulnerable range and hence escape a large measure of the potential control that could be exerted by predators. Before we can proceed further in the discussion of the effect of predation upon prey numbers, the additional components that make up the behaviour of predation must be considered.

The Subsidiary Components

Additional factors such as prey characteristics, the density and quality of alternate foods, and predator characteristics have a considerable effect upon predation. It is necessary now to demonstrate the effect of these factors and how they operate.

There are four classes of prey characteristics: those that influence the caloric value of the prey; those that change the length of time prey are exposed; those that affect the "attractiveness" of the prey to the predator (e.g. palatability, defence mechanisms); and those that affect the strength of stimulus used by predators in locating prey (e.g. size, habits, and colours). Only those characteristics that affect the strength of stimulus were studied experimentally. Since small mammals detect cocoons by the odour emanating from them (Holling, 1958b), the strength of this odour perceived by a mammal can be easily changed in laboratory experiments by varying the depth of sand covering the cocoons.

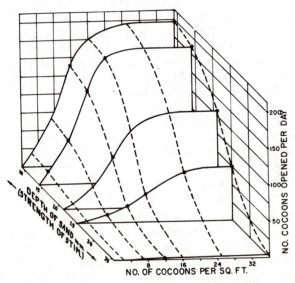

Fig. 5. Effect of strength of stimulus from cocoons upon the functional response of one caged *Peromyscus*. Each point represents the average of three to six replicates.

One *Peromyscus* was used in these experiments and its daily consumption of cocoons was measured at different cocoon densities and different depths of sand. These data are plotted in Fig. 5. Since the relation between depth of sand and strength of stimulus must be an inverse one, the depths of sand are reversed on the axis so that values of the strength of stimulus increase away from the origin. Each point represents the mean of three to six separate measurements. Decreasing the strength of the perceived stimulus by increasing the depth of sand causes a marked decrease in the functional response. A 27 mm. increase in depth (from nine to 36 mm.), for example, causes the peak consumption to drop from 196 to four cocoons per day. The daily number of calories consumed in all these experiments remained relatively constant since dog biscuits were always present as alternate food. The density at which each functional-response curve levels appear to increase somewhat as the strength of stimulus perceived by the animal decreases. We might expect that the increase in consumption is directly related to the increase in the proportion of cocoons in the amount of food available, at least up to the point where the caloric requirements are met solely by sawflies. The ascending portions of the curves, however, are S-shaped and the level portions are below the maximum consumption, approximately 220 cocoons for this animal. Therefore, the functional response cannot be explained by random searching for cocoons. For the moment, however, the important conclusion is that changes in prey characteristics can have a marked effect on predation but this effect is exerted through the functional response.

In the plantations studied, cocoons were not covered by sand but by a loose litter and duff formed from pine needles. Variations in the depth of this material apparently did not affect the strength of the perceived odour, for as many cocoons were opened in quadrats with shallow litter as with deep. This material must be so loose as to scarcely impede the passage of odour from cocoons.

The remaining subsidiary factors, the density and quality of alternate foods and predator characteristics, can also affect predation. The effect of alternate foods could not be studied in the undisturbed plantations because the amount of these "buffers" was constant and very low. The effect of quality of alternate foods on the functional response, however, was demonstrated experimentally using one *Peromyscus*. The experiments were identical to those already described except that at one series of densities an alternate food of low palatability (dog biscuits) was provided, and at the second series one of high palatability (sunflower seeds) was provided. When both foods are available, deer mice select sunflower seeds over dog biscuits. In every experiment a constant amount of alternate food was available: 13 to 17 gms. dry weight of dog biscuits, or 200 sunflower seeds.

Fig. 6 shows the changes in the number of cocoons opened per day and in the amount of alternate foods consumed. The functional response decreased with an increase in the palatability of the alternate food (Fig. 6A). Again the functional response curves showed an initial, roughly sigmoid rise to a constant level.

As cocoon consumption rose, the consumption of alternate foods decreased (Fig. 6B) at a rate related to the palatability of the alternate food. Each line indicating the change in the consumption of alternate food was drawn as a mirror image of the respective functional response and these lines closely follow the mean of the observed points. The variability in the consumption of sunflower seeds at any one cocoon density was considerable, probably as a result of the extreme variability in the size of seeds.

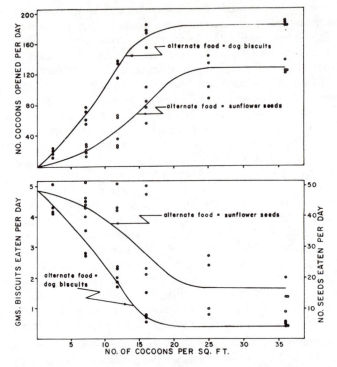

Fig. 6. Effect of different alternate foods upon the functional response of one *Peromyscus*. *A* (upper) shows the functional responses when either a low (dog biscuits) or a high (sunflower seeds) palatability alternate food was present in excess. *B* (lower) shows the amount of these alternate foods consumed.

Again we see that there is not a simple relation between the number of cocoons consumed and the proportion of cocoons in the total amount of food available. This is most obvious when the functional response curves level, for further increase in density is not followed by an increase in the consumption of sawflies. The plateaus persist because the animal continued consuming a certain fixed quantity of alternate foods. L. Tinbergen (1949) observed a similar phenomenon in a study of predation of pine-eating larvae by tits in Holland. He presented data for the consumption of larvae of the pine beauty moth, *Panolis griseovariegata*, and of the web-spinning sawfly *Acantholyda pinivora*, each at two different densities. In each case more larvae were eaten per nestling tit per day at the higher prey density. This, then, was part of a functional response, but it was that part above the point of inflection, since the proportion of prey eaten dropped at the higher density. It is not sufficient to explain these results as well as the ones presented in this paper by claiming, with Tinbergen, that the predators "have the tendency to make their menu as varied as possible and therefore guard against one particular species being strongly dominant in it". This is less an explanation than an anthropocentric description. The occurrence of this phenomenon depends upon the strength of stimulus from the prey, and the amount and quality of the alternate foods. Its proper explanation must await the collection of further data.

We now know that the palatability of alternate foods affects the functional response. Since the number of different kinds of alternate food could also have

TABLE III
The effect of alternate foods upon the number of cocoons consumed per day by one *Peromyscus*

Alternate food	No. of exp'ts	No. of cocoons opened	
		$\bar{X}$	S.E.$_{\bar{x}}$
none................................	7	165.9	11.4
dog biscuits..........................	5	143.0	8.3
sunflower seeds.......................	8	60.0	6.2
sunflower seeds and dog biscuits........	8	21.5	4.2

an important effect, the consumption of cocoons by a caged *Peromyscus* was measured when no alternate foods, or one or two alternate foods, were present. Only female cocoons were used and these were provided at a density of 75 per sq. ft. to ensure that the level portion of the functional response would be measured. As in the previous experiments, the animal was familiarized with the experimental conditions and with cocoons for a preliminary two-week period. The average numbers of cocoons consumed each day with different numbers and kinds of alternate foods present are shown in Table III. This table again shows that fewer cocoons were consumed when sunflower seeds (high palatability) were present than when dog biscuits (low palatability) were present. In both cases, however, the consumption was lower than when no alternate foods were available. When two alternate foods were available, i.e., both sunflower seeds and dog biscuits, the consumption dropped even further. Thus, increase in both the palatability and in the number of different kinds of alternate foods decreases the functional response.

DISCUSSION

General

It has been argued that three of the variables affecting predation—characteristics of the prey, density and quality of alternate foods and characteristics of the predators — are subsidiary components of predation. The laboratory experiments showed that the functional response was lowered when the strength of stimulus, one prey characteristic, detected from cocoons was decreased or when the number of kinds and palatability of alternate foods was increased. Hence the effect of these subsidiary components is exerted through the functional response. Now the numerical response is closely related to the functional, since such an increase in predator density depends upon the amount of food consumed. It follows, therefore, that the subsidiary components will also affect the numerical response. Thus when the functional response is lowered by a decrease in the strength of stimulus detected from prey, the numerical response similarly must be decreased and predation will be less as a result of decrease of the two basic responses.

The density and quality of alternate foods could also affect the numerical response. Returning to the numerical responses shown in Fig. 3, if increase in the density or quality of alternate foods involved solely increase in food "per se", then the number of mammals would reach a maximum at a lower cocoon density, but the maximum itself would not change. If increase in alternate foods also involved changes in the agents limiting the numerical responses (e.g. increased cover and depth of humus), then the maximum density the small mammals could attain would increase. Thus increase in the amount of alternate foods could increase the density of predators.

Increase in alternate foods *decreases* predation by dilution of the functional response, but *increases* predation by promoting a favourable numerical response. The relative importance of each of these effects will depend upon the particular problem. Voûte (1946) has remarked that insect populations in cultivated woods show violent fluctuations, whereas in virgin forests or mixed woods, where the number of alternate foods is great, the populations are more stable. This stability might result from alternate foods promoting such a favourable numerical response that the decrease in the functional response is not great enough to lower predation.

The importance of alternate foods will be affected by that part of the third subsidiary component — characteristics of the predators — that concerns food preferences. Thus an increase in plants or animals other than the prey will most likely affect the responses of those predators, like the omnivore *Peromyscus*, that are not extreme food specialists. Predation by the more stenophagous shrews, would only be affected by some alternate, animal food.

Food preferences, however, are only one of the characteristics of predators. Others involve their ability to detect, capture, and kill prey. But again the effect of these predator characteristics will be exerted through the two basic responses, the functional and numerical. The differences observed between the functional responses of the three species shown earlier in Fig. 1 undoubtedly reflect differences in their abilities to detect, capture, and kill. The amount of predation will similarly be affected by the kind of sensory receptor, whether visual, olfactory, auditory, or tactile, that the predator uses in locating prey. An efficient nose, for example, is probably a less precise organ than an efficient eye. The source of an undisturbed olfactory stimulus can only be located by investigating a gradient in space, whereas a visual stimulus can be localized by an efficient eye from a single point in space — the telotaxis of Fraenkel and Gunn (1940). As N. Tinbergen (1951) remarked, localization of direction is developed to the highest degree in the eye. Thus the functional response of a predator which locates prey by sight will probably reach a maximum at a much lower prey density than the response of one that locates its prey by odour. In the data presented by Tothill (1922) and L. Tinbergen (1949), the per cent predation of insects by birds was highest at very low prey densities, suggesting that the functional responses of these "visual predators" did indeed reach a maximum at a low density.

The Effect of Predation on Prey Populations

One of the most important characteristics of mortality factors is their ability to regulate the numbers of an animal — to promote a "steady density" (Nicholson, 1933; Nicholson and Bailey, 1935) such that a continued increase or decrease of numbers from this steady state becames progressively unlikely the greater the departure from it. Regulation in this sense therefore requires that the mortality factor change with change in the density of the animal attacked, i.e. it requires a direct density-dependent mortality (Smith, 1935, 1939). Density-independent factors can affect the numbers of an animal but alone they cannot *regulate* the numbers. There is abundant evidence that changes in climate, some aspects of which are presumed to have a density-independent action, can lower or raise the numbers of an animal. But this need not be regulation. Regulation will only result from an interaction with a density-dependent factor, an interaction

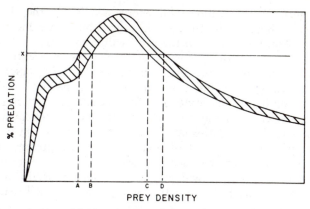

Fig. 7. Theoretical model showing regulation of prey by predators. (see text for explanation).

that might be the simplest, i.e. merely additive. Recently, the density-dependent concept has been severely criticized by Andrewartha and Birch (1954). They call it a dogma, but such a comment is only a criticism of an author's use of the concept. Its misuse as a dogma does not militate against its value as a hypothesis.

We have seen from this study that predation by small mammals does change with changes in prey density. As a result of the functional and numerical responses the proportion of prey destroyed increases from zero to some finite prey density and thereafter decreases. Thus predation over some ranges of prey density shows a direct density-dependent action. This is all that is required for a factor to regulate.

The way in which predation of the type shown in this study can regulate the numbers of a prey species can best be shown by a hypothetical example. To simplify this example we will assume that the prey has a constant rate of reproduction over all ranges of its density, and that only predators are affecting its numbers. Such a situation is, of course, unrealistic. The rate of reproduction of real animals probably is low at low densities when there is slight possibility for contact between individuals (e.g. between male and female). It would rise as contacts became more frequent and would decline again at higher densities when the environment became contaminated, when intraspecific stress symptoms appeared, or when cannibalism became common. Such changes in the rate of reproduction have been shown for experimental populations of *Tribolium confusum* (MacLagan, 1932) and *Drosophila* (Robertson and Sang, 1944). Introducing more complex assumptions, however, confuses interpretations without greatly changing the conclusions.

This hypothetical model is shown in Fig. 7. The curve that describes the changes in predation with changes in prey density is taken from the actual data shown earlier in Fig. 4. It is assumed that the birth-rate of the prey at any density can be balanced by a fixed per cent predation, and that the variation in the environment causes a variation in the predation at any one density. The per cent predation necessary to balance the birth-rate is represented by the horizontal line, x%, in the diagram and variation in predation is represented by the thickness of the mortality curve. The death-rate will equal the birth-rate at two density ranges, between A and B and between C and D. When the densities of the prey are below A, the mortality will be lower than that necessary to balance reproduction and the population will increase. When the densities of the animal are between B and C, death-rate will exceed birth-rate and the populations will decrease. Thus, the density of the prey will tend to fluctuate between densities A and B. If the density happens to exceed D, death-rate will be lower than birth-rate and the prey will increase in numbers, having "escaped" the control exerted by predators. This would occur when the prey had such a high rate of reproduction that its density could jump, in one generation, from a density lower than A to a density higher than D. If densities A and D were far apart, there would be less chance of this occurring. This spread is in part determined by the number of different species of predators that are present. Predation by each species peaks at a different density (see Fig. 4), so that increase in the number of species of predator will increase the spread of the total predation. This will produce a more stable situation where the prey will have less chance to escape control by predators.

Predation of the type shown will regulate the numbers of an animal whenever the predation rises high enough to equal the effective birth-rate. When the prey is an insect and predators are small mammals, as in this case, the reproductive rate of the prey will be too high for predation *alone* to regulate. But if other mortality occurs, density-independent or density-dependent, the total mortality could rise to the point where small mammals were contributing, completely or partially, to the regulation of the insect.

Predation of the type shown will produce stability if there are large numbers of different species of predators operating. Large numbers of such species would most likely occur in a varied environment, such as mixed woods. Perhaps this explains, in part, Voûte's (1946) observation that insect populations in mixed woods are less liable to show violent fluctuations.

I cannot agree with Voûte (1956 and 1958) that factors causing a peaked mortality curve are not sufficient for regulation. He states (1956) that "this is due to the fact that mortality only at low densities increases with the increase of the population. At higher densities, mortality decreases again. The growth of the population is at the utmost slowed down, never stopped". All that is necessary for regulation, however, is a rise in per cent predation over some range of prey densities and an *effective* birth-rate that can be matched at some density by mortality from predators.

Neither can I agree with Thompson (1930) when he ascribes a minor role to vertebrate predators of insects and states that "the number of individuals of any given species (i.e. of vertebrate predators) is . . . relatively small in comparison with those of insects and there is no reason to suppose that it varies primarily in function of the supply of insect food, which fluctuates so rapidly that it is impossible for vertebrates to profit by a temporary abundance of it excepting to a very limited extent". We know that they do respond by an increase in numbers and even if this is not great in comparison with the numerical response of parasitic flies, the number of prey killed per predator is so great and the increase in number killed with increase in prey density is so marked as to result in a heavy proportion of prey destroyed; a proportion that, furthermore, increases initially with increase of prey density. Thompson depreciates the importance of the numerical response of predators and ignores the functional response.

In entomological literature there are two contrasting mathematical theories of regulation. Each theory is based on different assumptions and the predicted results are quite different. Both theories were developed to predict the interaction between parasitic flies and their insect hosts but they can be applied equally well to predator-prey relations. Thompson (1939) assumes that a predator has a limited appetite and that it has no difficulty in finding its prey. Nicholson (1933) assumes that predators have insatiable appetites and that they have a specific capacity to find their prey. This searching capacity is assumed to remain constant at all prey densities and it is also assumed that the searching is random.

The validity of these mathematical models depends upon how closely their assumptions fit natural conditions. We have seen that the appetites of small mammal predators in this study are not insatiable. This fits one of Thompson's assumptions but not Nicholson's. When the functional response was described, it was obvious that predators did have difficulty in finding their prey and that their searching ability did not remain constant at all prey densities. Searching by small mammals was not random. Hence in the present study of predator-prey relations, the remaining assumptions of both Thompson and Nicholson do not hold.

Klomp (1956) considers the damping of oscillations of animal numbers to be as important as regulation. If the oscillations of the numbers of an animal affected by a delayed density-dependent factor (Varley, 1947) like a parasite, do increase in amplitude, as Nicholson's theory predicts (Nicholson and Bailey, 1935), then damping is certainly important. It is not at all certain, however, that this prediction is true. We have already seen that the assumptions underlying Nicholson's theory do not hold in at least some cases. In particular he ignores the important possibility of an S-shaped functional response of the type shown by small mammal predators. If the parasites did show an S-shaped functional response, there would be an *immediate* increase in per cent predation when host density increased, an increase that would modify the effects of the delayed numerical response of parasites emphasized by Nicholson and Varley. Under these conditions the amplitude of the oscillations would not increase as rapidly, and might well not increase at all. An S-shaped functional response therefore acts as an intrinsic damping mechanism in population fluctuations.

Oscillations undoubtedly do occur, however, and whether they increase in amplitude or not, any extrinsic damping is important. The factor that damps oscillations most effectively will be a concurrent density-dependent factor that reacts immediately to changes in the numbers of an animal. Predation by small mammals fulfils these requirements when the density of prey is low. The consumption of prey by individual predators responds immediately to increase in prey density (functional response). Similarly, the numerical response is not greatly delayed, probably because of the high reproductive capacity of small mammals. Thus if the density of a prey is low, chance increases in its numbers will immediately increase the per cent mortality caused by small mammal predation. When the numbers of the prey decrease, the effect of predation will be immediately relaxed. Thus, incipient oscillations can be damped by small-mammal predation.

We have seen that small mammals theoretically can regulate the numbers of prey and can damp their oscillations under certain conditions. Insufficient information was obtained to assess precisely the role of small mammals as predators of *N. sertifer* in the pine plantations of southwestern Ontario, however. Before the general introduction of a virus disease in 1952 (Bird, 1952, 1953), the sawfly was exhausting its food supplies and 70 to 100% defoliation of Scots, jack and red pines was observed in this area. Predators were obviously not regulating the numbers of the sawfly. After the virus was introduced, however, sawfly populations declined rapidly. In Plot 1, for example, their numbers declined from 248,000 cocoons per acre in 1952 to 39,000 per acre in 1954. The area was revisited in 1955 and larval and cocoon population had obviously increased in this plot, before the virus disease could cause much mortality. It happened, however, that *Peromyscus* was the only species of small mammal residing in Plot 1 and it is interesting that similar increases were not observed in other plantations where sawfly numbers had either not decreased so greatly, or where shrews, the most efficient predators, were present. These observations suggest that predation by shrews was effectively damping the oscillations resulting from the interaction of the virus disease with its host.

Types of Predation

Many types of predation have been reported in the literature. Ricker (1954) believed that there were three major types of predator-prey relations, Leopold (1933) four, and Errington (1946, 1956) two. Many of these types are merely minor deviations, but the two types of predation Errington discusses are quite different from each other. He distinguishes between "compensatory" and "noncompensatory" predation. In the former type, predators take a heavy toll of individuals of the prey species when the density of prey exceeds a certain threshold. This "threshold of security" is determined largely by the number of secure habitable niches in the environment. When prey densities become too high some individuals are forced into exposed areas where they are readily captured by predators. In this type of predation, predators merely remove surplus animals, ones that would succumb even in the absence of enemies. Errington feels, however, that some predator-prey relations depart from this scheme, so that predation occurs not only *above* a specific threshold density of prey. These departures are ascribed largely to behaviour characteristics of the predators. For example, he does not believe that predation of ungulates by canids is compensatory and feels that this results from intelligent, selective searching by the predators.

If the scheme of predation presented here is to fulfill its purpose it must be able to explain these different types of predation. Non-compensatory predation is easily described by the normal functional and numerical responses, for predation of *N. sertifer* by small mammals is of this type. Compensatory predation can also be described using the basic responses and subsidiary factors previously demonstrated. The main characteristic of this predation is the "threshold of security". Prey are more vulnerable above and less vulnerable below this threshold. That is, the strength of stimulus perceived from prey increases markedly when the prey density exceeds the threshold. We have seen from the present study that an increase in the strength of stimulus from prey increases both the functional and numerical responses. Therefore, below the "threshold of security" the functional responses of predators will be very low and as a result there will probably be no numerical response. Above the threshold, the functional response will become marked and a positive numerical response could easily occur. The net effect will result from a combination of these functional and numerical responses so that per cent predation will remain low so long as there is sufficient cover and food available for the prey. As soon as these supply factors are approaching exhaustion the per cent predation will suddenly increase.

Compensatory predation will occur (1) when the prey has a specific density level near which it normally operates, and (2) when the strength of stimulus perceived by predators is so low below this level and so high above it that there is a marked change in the functional response. Most insect populations tolerate considerable crowding and the only threshold would be set by food limitations. In addition, their strength of stimulus is often high at all densities. For *N. sertifer* at least, the strength of stimulus from cocoons is great and the threshold occurs at such high densities that the functional responses of small mammals are at their maximum. Compensatory predation upon insects is probably uncommon.

Entomologists studying the biological control of insects have largely concentrated their attention on a special type of predator — parasitic insects. Although certain features of a true predator do differ from those of a parasite, both predation and parasitism are similar in that one animal is seeking out another. If insect parasitism can in fact be treated as a type of predation, the two basic responses to prey (or host) density and the subsidiary factors affecting these responses should describe parasitism. The functional response of a true predator is measured by the number of prey it destroys; of a parasite by the number of hosts in which eggs are laid. The differences observed between the functional responses of predators and parasites will depend upon the differences between the behaviour of eating and the behaviour of egg laying. The securing of food by an individual predator serves to maintain that individual's existence. The laying of eggs by a parasite serves to maintain its progenies' existence. It seems likely that the more a behaviour concerns the maintenance of an individual, the more demanding it is. Thus the restraints on egg laying could exert a greater and more prolonged effect than the restraints on eating. This must produce differences between the functional responses of predators and parasites. But the functional responses of both are similar in that there is an upper limit marked by the point at which the predator becomes satiated and the parasite has laid all its eggs. This maximum is reached at some finite prey or host density above zero. The form of the rising phase of the functional response would depend upon the characteristics of the individual parasite and we might expect some of the same forms that will be postulated for predators at the end of this section. To summarize, I do not wish to imply that the characteristics of the functional response of a parasite are identical with those of a predator. I merely wish to indicate that a parasite has a response to prey density — the laying of eggs — that can be identified as a functional response, the precise characteristics of which are unspecified.

The effects of host density upon the number of hosts parasitized have been studied experimentally by a number of workers (e.g., Ullyett, 1949a and b; Burnett, 1951 and 1954; De Bach and Smith, 1941). In each case the number of hosts attacked per parasite increased rapidly with initial increase in host density but tended to level with further increase. Hence these functional response curves showed a continually decreasing slope as host density increased and gave no indication of the S-shaped response shown by small mammals. Further information is necessary, however, before these differences can be ascribed solely to the difference between parasitism and predation. It might well reflect, for example, a difference between an instinctive response of an insect and a learned response of a mammal or between the absence of an alternate host and the presence of an alternate food.

The numerical response of both predators and parasites is measured by the way in which the number of adults increases with increase in prey or host density. At first thought, the numerical response of a parasite would seem to be so intimately connected with its functional response that they could not be separated. But the two responses of a predator are just as intimately connected.

209

The predator must consume food in order to produce progeny just as the parasite must lay eggs in order to produce progeny.

The agents limiting the numerical response of parasites will be similar to those limiting the response of predators. There is, however, some difference. During at least one stage of the parasites' life, the requirements for both food and niche are met by the same object. Thus increase in the amount of food means increase in the number of niches as well, so that niches are never limited unless food is. This should increase the chances for parasites to show pronounced numerical responses. The characteristics of the numerical responses of both predators and parasites, however, will be similar and will range from those in which there is no increase with increase in the density of hosts, to those in which there is a marked and prolonged increase.

A similar scheme has been mentioned by Ullyett (1949b) to describe parasitism. He believed that "the problem of parasite efficiency would appear to be divided into two main phases, viz.: (a) the efficiency of the parasite as a mortality factor in the host population, (b) its efficiency as related to the maintenance of its own population level within the given area". His first phase resembles the functional response and the second the numerical response. Both phases or responses will be affected, of course, by subsidiary components similar to those proposed for predation—characteristics of the hosts, density and quality of alternate hosts, and characteristics of the parasite. The combination of the two responses will determine the changes in per cent parasitism as the result of changes in host density. Since both the functional and numerical responses presumably level at some point, per cent parasitism curves might easily be peaked, as were the predation curves. If these responses levelled at a host density that would never occur in nature, however, the decline of per cent parasitism might never be observed.

The scheme of predation revealed in this study may well explain all types of predation as well as insect parasitism. The knowledge of the basic components and subsidiary factors underlying the behaviour permits us to imagine innumerable possible variations. In a hypothetical situation, for example, we could introduce and remove alternate food at a specific time in relation to the appearance of a prey, and predict the type of predation. But such variations are only minor deviations of a basic pattern. The major types of predation will result from major differences in the form of the functional and numerical responses.

If the functional responses of some predators are partly determined by their behaviour, we could expect a variety of responses differing in form, rate of rise, and final level reached. All functional responses, however, will ultimately level, for it is difficult to imagine an individual predator whose consumption rises indefinitely. Subsistence requirements will fix the ultimate level for most predators, but even those whose consumption is less rigidly determined by subsistence requirements (e.g., fish, Ricker 1941) must have an upper limit, even if it is only determined by the time required to kill.

The functional responses could conceivably have three basic forms. The mathematically simplest would be shown by a predator whose pattern of searching was random and whose rate of searching remained constant at all prey densities. The number of prey killed per predator would be directly proportional to prey density, so that the rising phase would be a straight line. Ricker (1941) postulated this type of response for certain fish preying on sockeye salmon, and De Bach and Smith (1941) observed that the parasitic fly, *Muscidifurax raptor*, parasitized puparia of *Musca domestica*, provided at different densities, in a similar fashion. So few prey were provided in the latter experiment, however, that the initial linear rise in the number of prey attacked with increase in prey density may have been an artifact of the method.

A more complex form of functional response has been demonstrated in laboratory experiments by De Bach and Smith (1941), Ullyett (1949a) and Burnett (1951, 1956) for a number of insect parasites. In each case the number of prey attacked per predator increased very rapidly with initial increase in prey density, and thereafter increased more slowly approaching a certain fixed level. The rates of searching therefore became progressively less as prey density increased.

The third and final form of functional response has been demonstrated for small mammals in this study. These functional responses are S-shaped so that the rates of searching at first increase with increase of prey density, and then decrease.

Numerical responses will also differ, depending upon the species of predator and the area in which it lives. Two types have been demonstrated in this study. *Peromyscus* and *Sorex* populations, for example, increased with increase of prey density to the point where some agent or agents other than food limited their numbers. These can be termed direct numerical responses. There are some cases, however, where predator numbers are not affected by changes of prey density and in the plantations studied *Blarina* presents such an example of no numerical response. A final response, in addition to ones shown here, might also occur. Morris *et al.* (1958) have pointed out that certain predators might decrease in numbers as prey density increases through competition with other predators. As an example of such inverse numerical responses, he shows that during a recent outbreak of spruce budworm in New Brunswick the magnolia, myrtle, and black-throated green warblers decreased in numbers. Thus we have three possible numerical responses — a direct response, no response, and an inverse response.

The different characteristics of these types of functional and numerical responses produce different types of predation. There are four major types conceivable; these are shown diagramatically in Fig. 8. Each type includes the three possible numerical responses — a direct response (a), no response (b), and an inverse response (c), and the types differ because of basic differences in the functional response. In type 1 the number of prey consumed per predator is assumed to be directly proportional to prey density, so that the rising phase of the functional response is a straight line. In type 2, the functional response is presumed to rise at a continually decreasing rate. In type 3, the form of the functional response is the same as that observed in this study. These three types of predation may be considered as the basic ones, for changes in the subsidiary components are not involved. Subsidiary components can, however, vary in response to changes of prey density and in such cases the basic types of predation are modified. The commonest modification seems to be Errington's compensatory predation which is presented as Type 4 in Fig. 8. In this figure the vertical dotted line represents the "threshold of security" below which the strength of stimulus from prey is low and above which it is high. The functional response curves at these two strengths of stimulus are given the form of the functional responses observed in this study. The forms of the responses shown in Types 1 and 2 could also be used, of course.

The combination of the two responses gives the total response shown in the mammals is such a type, for prey characteristics, the number and variety of alternate foods, and predilections of the predators do not vary in the plantations where *N. sertifer* occurs. In this simple example of predation, the basic components of predation are responses to changes in prey density. The increase in the number of prey consumed per predator, as prey density rises, is termed the functional response. The change in the density of predators, as a result of increase in prey density, is termed the numerical response.

The three important species of small mammal predators (*Blarina, Sorex,* and *Peromyscus*) each showed a functional response, and each curve, whether it was derived from field or laboratory data, showed an initial S-shaped rise up to a constant, maximum consumption. The rate of increase of consumption decreased from *Blarina* to *Sorex* to *Peromyscus*, while the upper, constant level of consumption decreased from *Blarina* to *Peromyscus* to *Sorex*. The characteristics of these functional responses could not be explained by a simple relation between consumption and the proportion of prey in the total food available. The form of the functional response curves is such that the proportion of prey consumed per predator increases to a peak and then decreases.

This peaked curve was further emphasized by the direct numerical response of *Sorex* and *Peromyscus*, since their populations rose initially with increase in prey density up to a maximum that was maintained with further increase in cocoon density. *Blarina* did not show a numerical response. The increase in density of predators resulted from increased breeding, and because the reproductive rate of small mammals is so high, there was an almost immediate increase in density with increase in food.

The two basic components of predation — the functional and numerical responses — can be affected by a number of subsidiary components: prey characteristics, the density and quality of alternate foods, and characteristics of the predators. It was shown experimentally that these components affected the amount of predation by lowering or raising the functional and numerical responses. Decrease of the strength of stimulus from prey, one prey characteristic, lowered both the functional and numerical responses. On the other hand, the quality of alternate foods affected the two responses differently. Increase in the palatability or in the number of kinds of alternate foods lowered the functional response but promoted a more pronounced numerical response.

The peaked type of predation shown by small mammals can theoretically regulate the numbers of its prey if predation is high enough to match the effective reproduction by prey at some prey density. Even if this condition does not hold, however, oscillations of prey numbers are damped. Since the functional and numerical responses undoubtedly differ for different species of predator, predation by each is likely to peak at a different prey density. Hence, when a large number of different species of predators are present the declining phase of predation is displaced to a higher prey density, so that the prey have less chance to "escape" the regulation exerted by predators.

The scheme of predation presented here is sufficient to explain all types of predation as well as insect parasitism. It permits us to postulate four major types of predation differing in the characteristics of their basic and subsidiary components.

REFERENCES

Andrewartha, H. G. and L. C. Birch. 1954. The distribution and abundance of animals. *The Univ. of Chicago Press*, Chicago.

Stickel, L. F. 1954. A comparison of certain methods of measuring ranges of small mammals. *J. Mamm.* 35: 1-15.

Thompson, W. R. 1929. On natural control. *Parasitology* 21: 269-281.

Thompson, W. R. 1930. The principles of biological control. *Ann. Appl. Biol.* 17: 306-338.

Thompson, W. R. 1939. Biological control and the theories of the interactions of populations. *Parasitology* 31: 299-388.

Tinbergen, L. 1949. Bosvogels en insecten. *Nederl. Boschbouue. Tijdschr.* 21: 91-105.

Tinbergen, L. 1955. The effect of predators on the numbers of their hosts. *Vakblad voor Biologen* 28: 217-228.

Tinbergen, N. 1951. The study of instinct. Oxford.

Tothill, J. D. 1922. The natural control of the fall webworm (*Hyphantria cunea* Drury) in Canada. *Can. Dept. Agr. Bull.* 3, new series (Ent. Bull. 19): 1-107.

Ullyett, G. C. 1949a. Distribution of progeny by *Cryptus inornatus* Pratt. (Hym. Ichneumonidae). *Can. Ent.* 81: 285-299, 82: 1-11.

Ullyett, G. C. 1949b. Distribution of progeny by *Chelonus texanus* Cress. (Hym. Braconidae). *Can. Ent.* 81: 25-44.

Varley, G. C. 1947. The natural control of population balance in the knapweed gall-fly (*Urophora jaceana*). *J. Anim. Ecol.* 16: 139-187.

Varley, G. C. 1953. Ecological aspects of population regulation. *Trans. IXth Int. Congr. Ent.* 2: 210-214.

Voûte, A. D. 1946. Regulation of the density of the insect populations in virgin forests and cultivated woods. *Archives Neerlandaises de Zoologie* 7: 435-470.

Voûte, A. D. 1956. Forest entomology and population dynamics. *Int. Union For. Res. Organizations*, Twelfth Congress, Oxford.

Voûte, A. D. 1958. On the regulation of insect populations. *Proc. Tenth Int. Congr. of Ent.* Montreal, 1956.

CARNIVORE–MOUSE PREDATION: AN EXAMPLE OF ITS INTENSITY AND BIOENERGETICS

By Oliver P. Pearson

ABSTRACT: Populations of *Microtus, Reithrodontomys* and *Mus* reached a peak in Tilden Park, California, in June 1961, and reproduction almost ceased until the following spring. The impact of carnivores (feral cats, gray foxes, raccoons and skunks) on this standing crop of mice was measured by analysis of carnivore droppings systematically recovered from a 35-acre study area. Eighty-eight per cent of the 4,400 *Microtus*, 33% of the 1,200 *Reithrodontomys* and 7% of the 7,000 *Mus* were eaten by the carnivores before the next spring. As *Microtus* became scarce, the carnivore diet included more *Reithrodontomys, Mus*, gophers and finally wood rats. Numerous carnivores continued to hunt mice on the area even after the mice had been practically exterminated.

At the beginning of the study the standing crop per acre, in kilocalories, of various components of the food chain was: roots, 7.3 million; hay (excluding seeds), 8.1 million; seeds, 1.9 million; *Microtus*, 6,402; *Mus*, 4,543; *Reithrodontomys*, 434; and carnivores, 650. The annual caloric requirements of the peak populations (per acre) would have been: *Microtus*, 1.4 million; *Mus*, 876,000; *Reithrodontomys*, 82,000; and carnivores, 11,700. The peak population of mice could not have survived for one year on the available seed crop. The carnivores ate 55% of the calories available as mice and could have survived a full year if all mice had remained available to them, but by the end of December so many mice had been lost to other agents of mortality and by emigration that only a 12-day supply remained. In spite of the initial high density of mice, 7% of the seed crop escaped destruction and grew to form a rich vegetation in the following season.

In 1961 in Tilden Park, Contra Costa County, California, an outbreak of mice occurred under circumstances especially favorable for analyzing how effectively mammalian predators can destroy populations of mice. In this region, studied and described by Brant (1962), Hoffman (1958), Cook (1959) and Pearson (1963), a known peak population of essentially non-breeding mice served as a "standing crop" for carnivores whose droppings could be recovered systematically for analysis.

The study area is in Tilden Park east of Berkeley, and lies on the west-facing slope of a long ridge. Brant (*in* Calhoun, 1951) designated the location "California 3." The nearest residences are at the edge of Berkeley ½ mile away; in other directions there are no habitations for more than 2 miles. The study area was arbitrarily restricted to 35 acres of grassland and weeds (Plate I) bounded on three sides by roads, chaparral or strips of eucalyptus forest but continuous with similar grassy and weedy habitat on the fourth side. The most important plants are wild oats (*Avena fatua*), ripgut brome (*Bromus rigidus*), thistles, mustard and poison hemlock (*Conium maculatum*). The vegetation has been essentially undisturbed for at least 15 years except for annual bulldozing of firebreak roads and except for a grass fire on a small part of the area in 1953. Winters are rainy with occasional frost; summers are rainless but with numerous overcast days. The dominant annual grasses and weeds germinate following the first autumn rains, grow slowly during the winter and mature late in the spring. The vegetation is parched throughout the summer and early part of the autumn. The dry hay at this time provides cover (Plate I) but is nutritionally inadequate to sustain meadow mice.

Meadow mice (*Microtus californicus*) and harvest mice (*Reithrodontomys megalotis*) are usually the most abundant mammals in the grassy, weedy habitat of the study area. The *Microtus* show a spectacular cycle of abundance with a peak every 3 or 4 years; the *Reithrodontomys* fluctuate between less than 1 per acre to more than 50 per acre. The outbreak of house mice (*Mus musculus*) on the area in 1961 (Fig. 1) was unusual, as before this population began to build up in 1960 only occasional house mice had been caught since trapping records began in 1948 (Pearson, 1963).

The number of mice of each species on the study area in 1961 is shown in

PLATE I

Vegetation on part of the study area, 21 October 1961.

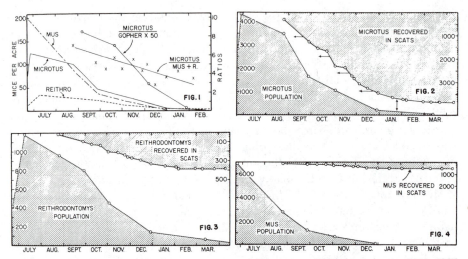

Fig. 1.—Number of mice per acre on the study area at different times in 1961–1962, and the change of ratio of *Microtus* to other prey species in scats collected at different times. Because of the small number of gophers eaten, several scat collections were combined when plotting the *Microtus*/gopher ratio.

Fig. 2.—Comparison of the size of the crop of meadow mice living on the 35-acre study area with the cumulative number of meadow mice recovered from carnivore droppings found on the same area. The narrower the unshaded band, the more effective the predation. If the carnivores caught every mouse and if the remains were found immediately, there would be *no* unshaded band. Actually the shaded area representing the carnivore catch should be shifted to the left, as indicated by the horizontal arrows, to compensate for the time elapsing between capture of a mouse by a carnivore and collection of the dropping containing that mouse. The vertical separation of the two shaded areas, as indicated in January, is a measure of the number of mice contained in scats not found and the number of mice lost through other causes.

Fig. 3.—Comparison of the size of the harvest mouse crop with the cumulative number recovered from carnivore droppings.

Fig. 4.—Comparison of the size of the house mouse crop with the cumulative number recovered from carnivore droppings.

Figs. 1 to 4. The method of censusing has been described (Pearson, 1963). An additional estimate of the density of *Microtus* is available for an area one mile farther north where Marsh (1962) recorded a maximum of 190 *Microtus* per acre in 1961 on a plot chosen because it was especially suitable for *Microtus*. By the end of June all 3 species had reached a peak. *Microtus* stopped breeding at that time (not unusual), and harvest mice also stopped breeding (unusual). House mice continued to breed through the summer, but at a low rate. As a result of the absence of reproduction of both *Microtus* and *Reithrodontomys*, the peak June population can be considered a standing crop "available" to predators. Population increase through immigration is unlikely because the area is cut off on 3 sides by unsuitable mouse habitat. On the fourth side it is continuous with several hundred acres of essentially similar habitat, so that any immigration into the study area would presumably be matched by equal emigration.

The impact of predators on the mice was measured by repeated collection and analysis of carnivore droppings. The droppings were "dissolved," with stirring, in a solution of lye, and the pairs of mandibles of each species contained in them were counted. The circumstances, in addition to the cessation of breeding mentioned above, that made collection and analysis of these scats especially satisfactory were these: Most droppings are deposited on the fire-break roads that surround and dissect the area, and these roads were scraped bare by a bulldozer on 12 June 1961. Consequently, all scats found on the roads were known to have been deposited after that date. Droppings deposited on small unscraped paths and away from the roads and paths during the spring months become hidden by the growing vegetation or disintegrated by rain, but scats deposited in such places at the end of the growing season in May or June remain intact and visible through the long rainless season until the next winter. For these reasons I am confident that almost all of the scats found in the fields and along the smaller unscraped paths were deposited after 1 May.

When scats were collected, all trails and firebreak roads enclosing and crossing the 35-acre area were searched and contributed the majority of each collection. Additional scats were collected in the fields when encountered in the course of trapping. The first collection was made on 24 August 1961, and the second on 25 September. These totaled 15 gallons and are considered to be scats that had accumulated since May or June. Subsequent collections were made at more frequent intervals through 11 April 1962, when a total of 40 gallons had been gathered. Each collection was kept separate and dated, so that most of the droppings are known to have been deposited between specific dates, but since no collection is complete, each sample is "contaminated" by an unknown number of scats that were overlooked during the previous search. Probably all scats on the fire roads were found eventually, but no systematic search of the fields was made; in fact, several large areas were never entered, so it is certain that many scats were not found. I estimate very roughly that about three-fourths of all scats deposited on the area between May 1961, and April 1962, were recovered.

The carnivores responsible for the predation were feral and vagrant cats, gray foxes, raccoons, striped skunks and spotted skunks. No weasels have been seen in the region for many years. I did not distinguish between the scats of the different species and do not know how many of each species hunted on the area. Judging by sight records and by footprints on the muddy trails, feral and vagrant cats were by far the most important. As many as 6 cats were seen on the 35 acres at one time, and 2 easily recognized individuals were seen with great regularity. Between August and January at least one cat was seen on almost every visit to the area.

In the absence of any pertinent observations on the hunting range of the predators that left droppings on the study area, or of their defecatory habits, I have assumed that the probability of a mouse's being caught elsewhere and deposited on the study area was the same as the probability that a mouse would be caught on the area and deposited in a dropping elsewhere. This assumption is supported by the fact that droppings seemed to be equally abundant on other areas close to the study area. A complicating corollary of this assumption must be kept in mind, however. If prey species A is not evenly distributed throughout the hunting and defecating range of the carnivores, then scats deposited on a part of the carnivores' range where species A is scarce will contain a disproportionately large number of individuals of species A (because these species A in process of digestion will be imported more frequently than exported). Conversely, species A living at high density in a small area will be relatively poorly represented in droppings at that place. Widely spaced traplines indicated that the mice were distributed in a satisfactorily uniform manner on the 35-acre study area, but little can be said of their distribution outside of the study area. House mice were known to have been irregularly distributed (Pearson, 1963), and trapping indicated that they were living more densely on the 35-acre study area than in parts of the similar habitat nearby. Consequently, more house mice would be caught by carnivores on the study area and carried away than would be caught elsewhere and carried onto the area, and the number of house mice in the collected scats would be lower than the number actually eaten. I have no reason to believe that meadow mice and harvest mice were not uniformly distributed on the open hillsides. In any event, in the following account no adjustment has been made for possible non-uniform distribution of the prey.

RESULTS

On the basis of the censuses made on the live-trapped grid in the center of the study area, and confirmed by Calhoun traplines closer to the edges of the area, the populations on the entire 35-acre area in June 1961, were 4,400 *Microtus*, 7,000 *Mus* and 1,200 *Reithrodontomys*. The following numbers were recovered in carnivore scats through 11 April 1962: 3,870 *Microtus*, 462 *Mus*, 382 *Reithrodontomys*, 39 gophers (*Thomomys*), 21 brush rabbits (*Sylvilagus*), 13 shrews (*Sorex*), 13 wood rats (*Neotoma*), 5 *Peromyscus*, 44 reptiles (mostly *Sceloporus* and *Gerrhonotus*), 8 birds and a large number of Jerusalem crickets (*Stenopelmatus*). Numerous moles lived on the study area, but none was eaten. Since a few young *Microtus* began to appear in traps and in scats at the end of February, a more conservative measure of the impact of the carnivores on the standing crop of *Microtus* is the number recovered from scats before 6 February, which was 3,782.

Obviously the carnivores had eaten a significant portion of the population of each of the 3 common species of mice and apparently had consumed 86% of the *Microtus* present on the area at the end of breeding in June (88% of the "available" *Microtus* when the 93 *Microtus* trapped and removed from the area are subtracted). Possible errors in deriving this percentage may arise from misestimation of the June population, inclusion of scats deposited before the population peak, failure to find all of the scats on the area or error derived from possible unequal density of *Microtus*, as described above. The size and, in 2 instances, the direction of these possible inaccuracies is not known; it is hoped that they cancel. When it is recalled that no accounting has been made of the predation by numerous hawks, owls and reptiles, one can conclude only that the meadow mouse population was nearly annihilated by predation, primarily by carnivores.

Only 32% of the estimated 1,200 harvest mice living on the area appeared in the droppings (33% after subtracting trapped mice), and 6.6% of the estimated 7,000 house mice (6.7% after subtracting trapped mice). These lower percentages suggest that the carnivores were selecting *Microtus* in preference to harvest mice and house mice. This is confirmed when one compares the *Microtus* : *Reithrodontomys* + *Mus* ratio in different scat collections with the ratio of these species existing in the population at the same time (Fig. 1). In the August collection, which contained large numbers of scats that had been accumulating on the ground since May or June, there were 7 times as many *Microtus* as *Mus* and *Reithrodontomys* combined. Gradually the ratio dropped until the carnivores were catching only 3 times as many *Microtus* as *Reithro-dontomys* and *Mus* combined (Fig. 1). At no time, however, were living *Microtus* even twice as abundant as *Reithrodontomys* and *Mus* combined, so it seems likely that the carnivores preferred *Microtus* and that as *Microtus* became scarce the carnivores turned more often to harvest mice and house mice, causing the ratio to drop in the manner shown in Fig. 1.

In a similar manner gopher remains occurred more frequently, relative to *Microtus* remains, as *Microtus* became scarcer (Fig. 1). This does not reflect an increase in the number of gophers living on the area, for they do not reproduce during the summer and autumn. It reflects instead a change in the hunting habits of the predators caused by the scarcity of mice or by the increased vulnerability of gophers as the season progresses, or by both. Gophers make comparatively few surface mounds during the hot, dry summer months and so presumably are not caught as easily at that time.

The distribution of wood rat (*Neotoma fuscipes*) remains in the scat collections also illustrates a distinct change of food habits of the carnivores. The first *Neotoma* did not appear in the droppings until the 30 October collection, before which time 1,667 *Microtus* had been recovered. Before 15 January, 3 *Neotoma* had been eaten, compared with a cumulative total of 3,476 *Microtus*. But between 15 January and 26 March, 10 *Neotoma* appeared in the same scats with 378 *Microtus*. Since wood rats do not roam into the grassland and weeds inhabited by *Microtus*, it is clear that the carnivores, after they had killed off the *Microtus*, hunted more frequently in the brush and woods inhabited by *Neotoma*.

The carnivores caught a disproportionately large number of *Microtus* either because *Microtus* is more easily caught than other species of mice or because it may be hunted more avidly. It is tempting to believe that the presence of other species of prey such as *Mus* and *Reithrodontomys* relieves the predation pressure on *Microtus*, but actually the reverse is probably true. If *Microtus* were the only palatable species present, the carnivores would catch most of them and then would be forced by hunger to move elsewhere. If other less desirable prey species were present, however, the carnivores would satisfy their hunger with other species when the density of *Microtus* became low. In this way the carnivores could remain on the area longer, hunting for meadow mice and reducing their numbers to a lower level than would occur if other kinds of prey were not present. Jerusalem crickets, gophers and harvest mice probably served as reserve food species in this manner.

At least one cat was seen on almost every visit I made to the area until February 1962. On 26 September 1961, in spite of the sharp decline in the number of mice (Fig. 1), 5 cats were seen on the area, and on 29 December, when the *Microtus* population was down to 7 per acre, *Reithrodontomys* to 4 per acre and *Mus* to only 1 per acre, 6 cats were seen on the area. These cats were still feeding almost entirely on mice. It would have required the standing crop of mice on several acres each day to nourish 6 cats. Since none of the species of mice was reproducing, they could not afford this tax. Consequently, the mouse population dropped to such low levels in February that the Calhoun traplines on 27–29 February (360 trap nights) caught only 1 *Microtus*, 1 *Reithrodontomys* and 2 shrews, and extensive trapping on the 1-acre central grid on 8–10 March revealed no *Microtus*, no *Mus* and only 2

Reithrodontomys and 2 shrews. In spite of the scarcity of mice, at least two cats were hunting on the area. Even in April predators and their tracks were still seen on the area, and small numbers of scats continued to appear on the trails.

Everyone knows that cats catch mice. Laymen are amused to observe the surprise shown by naturalists who discover that cats catch large numbers of mice. Nevertheless, I think it is important to document the extent of predation on mouse populations because many ecologists have convinced themselves that predators subsist on "surplus" prey animals, or on sick or weakened individuals. Undoubtedly this is often true. It may have been occurring during the present study, for the one or 2 California quail represented in the scat collection may well have been surplus individuals from the large covey that lived (and persisted) on the study area, and the gophers caught by the carnivores may well have been surplus members of a population that persisted at normal densities at the close of the study. But the carnivores had not merely skimmed the cream off of the *Microtus* population, they had taken almost every one.

I have watched cats hunting *Microtus*. The consistent success of their vigils beside runways makes *Microtus*-catching seem absurdly easy. Bradt (1949) and Toner (1956) have documented this aptitude. Even humans without an effective sense of smell have little difficulty recognizing burrows and runways that are being used by *Microtus*. Cats, foxes, raccoons and skunks undoubtedly can do as well, if not better, so even the last *Microtus* in an area is in serious danger if any carnivores remain. The evidence given above shows that the carnivores do remain until the mice have been almost exterminated.

There is no reason to believe that catastrophic reduction of mouse populations by carnivores as described in this report is abnormal or even unusual. Another high population of *Microtus* (250 per acre) was destroyed by carnivores and horned owls at the same time 3½ miles southeast of the study area, and Brant (1962) found that the 1951 peak population of *Microtus* and *Reithrodontomys* on his study area 0.8 mile northwest of the present area was destroyed by carnivores, especially raccoons.

Mice livetrapped on the 1-acre grid situated near the center of my 35-acre study area were marked with numbered metal clips in the ears. If these mice never wandered off of the 35-acre area, if carnivores ate all of them (including the tags), never carried them off of the area and never defecated off of the area, and if all carnivore droppings were found, then all of the ear tags should have been recovered. Thirty-two per cent of the harvest mouse tags were recovered in carnivore scats, 22% of the meadow mouse tags and 4% of the house mouse tags. The extent of departure from 100% is in each instance an indication of how closely the suppositions were fulfilled. It is unrealistic to expect that all scats on the area were found, or that the carnivores never defecated off of the area; undoubtedly these two reasons account for why many if not most of the ear tags were never recovered. However, they do not account for the great difference in recovery of *Mus* and *Reithrodontomys*. It seems possible that the carnivores were less able or less willing to catch *Mus*, or that *Mus* emigrated, died of disease or were killed by other kinds of predators.

Consideration of the bioenergetics of this carnivore–mouse relationship provides an independent appraisal of whether it is reasonable to expect carnivores to eat so many mice on such a small area. From June, when the mice had almost stopped reproducing and had stopped gaining weight, until the end of December, when the mice were almost gone, 3,481 *Microtus*, 427 *Mus* and 329 *Reithrodontomys* appeared in the scats. These totaled about 119,000 g or 180,000 kcal (based on Golley, 1960, 1961). Assuming that the period of scat deposition represented in the collections until the end of December is 6 months, then the carnivores were digesting about 24 mice (1,000 kcal) per day. The basal rate of metabolism of a 3-kg carnivore is about 150 kcal per day. Assuming that this is raised 50% by exercise, digestion and suboptimal environmental temperatures, and assuming complete utilization of each mouse carcass by the carnivores, then 4½, 3-kg carnivores would have been needed to eat the number of mice recovered in the scats during this 6-month period. Allowing ½ more carnivore to account for about 14 kg (20,000 kcal) of other prey eaten, such as Jerusalem crickets, rabbits and gophers, gives an estimate of 5, 3-kg carnivores on the 35-acre area. An average of one feral cat per 20 acres has been estimated for parts of central California by Hubbs (1951). Making allowance for the presence of other carnivores such as raccoons, foxes and skunks, and making allowance also for a probable high density of carnivores fostered by the unusually high density of mice, then 5, 3-kg carnivores, the number necessary to metabolize 200,000 kcal of mice and other prey in 6 months, does not seem unrealistic for 35 acres.

The transfer of energy through the various links of a terrestrial food chain is of great theoretical interest to ecologists but has rarely been measured. My estimates are admittedly crude and are based on so many assumptions that the results may be said to fall halfway between speculation and observation, but they offer some insight into the energy balance between vegetation, carnivores and mice at one stage in a microtine cycle. The most comparable previous study is an analysis of a vegetation–*Microtus*–weasel food chain in Michigan (Golley, 1960). Circumstances in Tilden Park in 1961 make possible a simpler analysis with fewer assumptions because an essentially non-reproducing mouse population was feeding on a non-growing food source, and because the carnivore catch was known through recovery of droppings.

The vegetation samples were taken at the end of the growing season between 17 May and 25 May 1962. Mice and insects were so scarce during this spring that very little of the plant production had been eaten. More of the crop undoubtedly was consumed before maturity during the mouse outbreak in 1961, but vegetation samples were not taken in that season. In 1960, the vegetation on sample plots about 1½ miles from the study area reached a maximum late in May, and measurements of the standing crop in that year were within 10% of my measurements for 1962 (Ratliff and Heady, 1962).

Estimates of the standing crop of various components of the food chain and of the rate of energy flow through the components are listed and annotated in Table 1 and illustrated in Fig. 5. The total plant crop weighed 2,100 times as much as the peak mouse population (dry weight) and contained 1,500 times as many calories. Perhaps a more meaningful measure of potentially available food for the mice is the seed crop which, at the beginning of the accounting, weighed 200 times as much as the mice (dry weight) and contained 170 times as many calories. The peak population of mice weighed 17 times more than the carnivores, contained 17 times as many calories and was metabolizing 200 times as fast as the carnivores. At this rate the peak mouse population would have exhausted the annual seed crop in less than 10 months. *Microtus* and

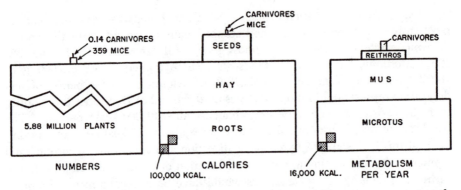

FIG. 5.—Pyramids of numbers, caloric content and energy utilization on one acre at the time of peak plant and animal standing crops. The pyramid of calories is approximately to scale for biomass also.

Mus would surely have starved if they had remained at such high densities and would, of course, have carried *Reithrodontomys* with them into starvation. Furthermore, more than 5,881,000 seeds per acre escaped being consumed, perhaps by falling into deep crevices in the parched adobe soil, and sprouted to become the 1962 crop of vegetation. These surviving seeds amount to more than 7% of the total seed crop and might contain 7% of the calories in the total seed crop. Seven per cent, therefore, might reasonably be deducted from the calories "available" to seed-eating mice.

TABLE 1.—*Size of standing crop of plants, prey and predators on one acre, and the metabolic impact of prey and predators at peak population levels*

	STANDING CROP		RATE OF USE PER YEAR	
	kg (dry wt)	kcal	kcal	% of crop
Roots[1]	2,131	7,269,000[2]		
Hay[1]	2,097	8,141,000[2]		
Seeds[1]	442	1,920,000[2]		
Microtus	1.24[3]	6,402[6]	1,368,750[7]	71[12]
Mus	0.88[3]	4,543[6]	876,000[8]	46[13]
Reithrodontomys	0.084[3]	434[6]	81,650[9]	4[13]
Other prey	0.13[4]	671[6]	27,000[10]	
Carnivores	0.126[3, 5]	650[6]	11,700[11]	97[14]

[1] Based on five sample plots, each containing 1.7 square feet, evenly spaced on the 1-acre census grid, and each harvested as the seeds matured in May 1962. Stems (5,881,000 per acre) were cut one by one at ground level with scissors; roots were dug to a depth of 5 inches; seeds (80 million per acre) were weighed after being husked by hand. Weights are of air-dry material. The item "Hay" includes all aboveground parts of the plants except the husked seeds. Not included are 1,762 kg of dead vegetation remaining on the ground from previous years.
[2] I am most grateful to Dr. G. P. Lofgreen of the University of California at Davis for the following calorimetric determinations of this plant material: roots, 3,411 kcal/kg air dry; hay, 3,882 kcal/kg air dry; husked seeds, 4,345 kcal/kg air dry. Almost all of the seed crop by weight consisted of oats and brome.
[3] Live weight × 0.294 = dry weight (from Golley, 1960).
[4] Crude estimate including rabbits, gophers, lizards and Jerusalem crickets.
[5] Assuming five 3-kg carnivores on the 35 acres.
[6] 5,163 kcal/kg dry weight (Golley, 1961).
[7] 30 kcal/*Microtus*/day, based on data in Wiegert (1961) and Jameson (1958).
[8] 12 kcal/*Mus*/day, based on data in Pearson (1947).
[9] 6.58 kcal/harvest mouse/day (Pearson, 1960).
[10] Crude estimate based on 100 g of homeotherms and 330 g of heterotherms per acre.
[11] From the mouse–elephant basal metabolism curve plus 50%.
[12] Per cent of seed crop. *Microtus* cannot survive on the dry vegetation standing aboveground during the summer and autumn. Undoubtedly some stems and roots are eaten also; the per cent of total vegetation including roots, hay and seeds is 8.
[13] Per cent of seed crop.
[14] Per cent of all prey. Per cent of *Microtus* is 183; per cent of all mice is 103.

224

The carnivores could have survived almost exactly one year on the standing crop of mice and other prey—if all of the prey had remained on the area, available to them. But other mortality factors were operating and these, combined with possible emigration of many of the *Mus*, reduced the prey population before January to much too low a level to support 5 carnivores. Judging by sight records and by the number of scats being deposited, this number of carnivores still remained at the end of December, but their existence on the area was hopeless. The caloric content of all of the mice on the area on 31 December would have sustained 5 carnivores only 12 days and would not have kept them alive until the resumption of reproduction by the mice.

In Golley's (1960) vegetation–*Microtus*–weasel food chain, the weasels are estimated to have consumed 31% of the energy available to them in the form of *Microtus*. In Tilden Park the predatory mammals consumed 88% of the energy available to them in the form of *Microtus* and 55% of the energy available in the form of mice of all 3 species.

It is obvious that I was not observing an equilibrium between vegetation, herbivores and carnivores. The plants, as usual, produced a surplus of food in the spring, with little production during the rest of the year. The mice, as usual, reproduced during the spring while plant production was far above their ability to consume it, but in this particular season many more mice were produced than could have subsisted until the next spring on the vegetation produced. At the same time carnivores appeared in such numbers that to survive they would have had to eat every mouse, leaving none for other agents of mortality. The carnivores' position was made more precarious by failure of the mice to reproduce during the summer, autumn and early winter. Before the next growing season could bring the resources for a new population of mice, the old population had been killed. Enough seeds had survived, however, to produce a rich new crop of vegetation in 1962.

The exorbitant number of carnivores compared to prey reminds one of the avian predator–lemming relation in the arctic where "the summer predator load deals a stupendous blow to the lemming population" (Pitelka, Tomich and Treichel, 1955). In Tilden Park, however, the carnivores continued their depredation into the winter until almost all of the mice had been killed.

LITERATURE CITED

BRADT, G. W. 1949. Farm cat as predator. Michigan Conservation, 18: 23–25.
BRANT, D. H. 1962. Measures of the movements and population densities of small rodents. Univ. Calif. Publ. Zoöl., 62: 105–183.
CALHOUN, J. B. 1951. North American census of small mammals. Release No. 4. Jackson Memorial Lab., Bar Harbor. 136 pp.
COOK, S. F., JR. 1959. The effects of fire on a population of small rodents. Ecology, 40: 102–108.
GOLLEY, F. B. 1960. Energy dynamics of a food chain of an old-field community. Ecol. Monogr., 30: 187–206.
———. 1961. Energy values of ecological materials. Ecology, 42: 581–584.
HOFFMAN, R. S. 1958. The role of reproduction and mortality in population fluctuations of voles (*Microtus*). Ecol. Monogr., 28: 79–109.
HUBBS, E. L. 1951. Food habits of feral house cats in the Sacramento Valley. Calif. Fish and Game, 37: 177–189.
JAMESON, E. W., JR. 1958. Consumption of alfalfa and wild oats by *Microtus californicus*. J. Wildl. Mgmt., 22: 433–435.

Marsh, M. P. 1962. Food as a factor regulating the numbers of the California vole, *Microtus californicus*. Ph.D. Thesis, Univ. Calif. Berkeley. 201 pp.

Pearson, O. P. 1947. The rate of metabolism of some small mammals. Ecology, 28: 127–145.

————. 1960. The oxygen consumption and bioenergetics of harvest mice. Physiol. Zoöl., 33: 152–160.

————. 1963. History of two local outbreaks of feral house mice. Ecology, 44: 540–549.

Pitelka, F. A., P. Q. Tomich and G. W. Treichel. 1955. Ecological relations of jaegers and owls as lemming predators near Barrow, Alaska. Ecol. Monogr. 25: 85–117.

Ratliff, R. D. and H. F. Heady. 1962. Seasonal changes in herbage weight in an annual grass community. J. Wildl. Mgmt., 15: 146–149.

Toner, G. C. 1956. House cat predation on small animals. J. Mamm., 37: 119.

Wiegert, R. G. 1961. Respiratory energy loss and activity patterns in the meadow vole, *Microtus pennsylvanicus pennsylvanicus*. Ecology, 42: 245–253.

Museum of Vertebrate Zoology, University of California, Berkeley. Received 2 January 1963.

Plant-Herbivore Coevolution: Lupines and Lycaenids

Abstract. *Predation on lupine flowers by larvae of a lycaenid butterfly was studied by comparison of inflorescences exposed to and protected from infestation, and by comparison of lupine populations exposed to different degrees of attack. The lycaenids caused striking reduction in seed set, indicating that this small herbivore could act as a potent selective agent in lupine populations.*

Coevolutionary interactions between plants and herbivores have been studied (*1*) and may be a major source of organic diversity (*2*). The selective effect of herbivore attack on plants, except the most extreme attacks which lead to extensive defoliation, are usually discounted as having little influence on plant populations. Also discounted is the primary role of plant biochemicals as herbivore poisons (*3*). Kemp (*4*) described an example of extreme selection for procumbency in pasture plants under heavy grazing. A seemingly insignificant herbivore, the small (wing length ± 14 mm) lycaenid butterfly *Glaucopsyche lygdamus* Doubleday, may have a profound effect on the reproductive capacity of the herbaceous perennial lupine *Lupinus amplus* Greene. This supports the contention that plants are under powerful evolutionary attack by herbivores, an attack not apparent to the casual observer.

Lupine populations in the vicinity of Gothic and Crested Butte, Gunnison County, Colorado, were investigated in June and July of 1968. Female butterflies oviposited only on pubescent portions of immature inflorescences of *L. amplus*. No oviposition was observed on an inflorescence in which some flowers were opened. A comparison of two inflorescence types, both of which occur on the same plants, was made on 7 July. Eggs and egg shells were counted on 125 inflorescences without open flowers (Fig. 1) and 130 inflorescences which had open flowers at the base only (Fig. 1). The unopened portion of the inflorescence presented an oviposition environment to a female butterfly which we are unable to distinguish from an immature inflorescence, except for the presence of opened flowers below, and increased distance from, the crown of the lupine

Fig. 1. (Left) Inflorescence of *Lupinus amplus* without open flowers; (right) inflorescence with open flowers at base and unopened flowers at apex.

plant. Table 1 shows the very significant difference ($P \ll .01$) in egg distribution on the two types of inflorescences. Note that since the eggs and egg shells remain attached after the flowers open, all of the eggs found at this time on open flowers may have been laid on the inflorescence when it was immature.

Larvae feed primarily on the wing and keel of the corolla and the stamens which are contained within the keel (54 of 78 larvae observed were feeding in these areas). Other parts of the flower, including the ovary, are less frequently attacked. Flowers attacked by lycaenids often do not reach anthesis and subsequently absciss.

One hundred immature inflorescences (of the type shown in Fig. 1) on 36 plants of the Gothic population were tagged on 5 July. Egg counts were made on all inflorescences and roughly half were designated controls. Controls either had no eggs on them, or had unhatched eggs removed. The tagged inflorescences were censused subsequently on 6, 9, 11, 14, and 17 July. Great care was taken not to damage the flowers. Periods between censuses were not long enough to permit egg hatch, so that we could, by removing all new eggs at each census, keep the controls free of attack by *G. lygdamus* larvae. On 17 July all inflorescences were collected and examined microscopically for damage. Floral scars were counted to give the total number of flowers which could have been produced on the inflorescence (potential

production). At this date all inflorescences were fully mature and each flower had ovarian development. The lycaenid larvae found ranged in size from small (newly hatched) to large (presumably last instar). Most larvae, however, were intermediate in size. Clearly, further damage would have been done if the inflorescences had been permitted to progress to seed set. We feel, however, that such damage would have been relatively minor since the ovaries were all well developed and were subject to little attack.

Eight inflorescences were destroyed in the course of the study, leaving 41 controls and 51 exposed to attack. A total of 111 eggs were laid on the exposed inflorescences, 2.18 per inflorescence. The 41 control inflorescences had a potential production of 967 mature flowers. This group actually produced 693, or 71.66 percent of potential. The experimental group had a potential production of 1433 mature flowers and actually produced 533, or 37.19 percent of potential. Of these mature flowers 138 were so badly damaged that they would have abscissed without setting seed, so that a more realistic estimate of realized potential in the experimental group is 395/1433, or 27.56 percent. Both experimental groups (with and without damage) are, of course, highly significantly different from the controls ($P \ll .01$).

A sample of 100 large inflorescences was taken on 15 July from the Crested Butte population of *L. amplus* on which *G. lygdamus* is rarely seen. This population of lupines is essentially continuous with that at Gothic, some 5 miles (8 km) away. Of a potential of 4169 flowers, 3149 (75.53 percent) were realized, and 3091 (74.14 percent) were judged sufficiently undamaged to set seed. Only 11 egg shells or larvae were found on these plants. In contrast, an additional sample of 100 large inflorescences from the Gothic population, where *G. lygdamus* was abundant, was censused on 16 July. Of a potential of 4277 flowers, 2434 (57.31 percent) matured. Of these 2152 (50.67 percent) matured and were judged sufficiently undamaged to set seed. On

Table 1. Distribution of *Glaucopsyche* eggs on the two types of inflorescences shown in Fig. 1.

Number of eggs	Number of inflorescences	
	No open flowers	Open flowers
0	43	120
1	53	8
2	14	2
3	9	0
4	3	0
5	1	0
6	1	0
7	0	0
8	1	0

these inflorescences 126 *G. lygdamus* egg shells or larvae were found. The differences between the two areas are highly significant ($P \ll .01$).

The damage done to the Gothic population of *L. amplus* by this small butterfly is stunning. In 1968 nearly 50 percent of the potential seed production was destroyed by *G. lygdamus*, which has been abundant at Gothic in every season since 1960 except 1964–65 (when no observations were made). There is no reason to believe that the 1968 density was unusual. Presumably the lupines have been subject to a long-term attrition of their seed production. This has a drastic selective effect on the plant population. Lupines are dependent on having an abundance of seeds widely distributed in the soil since they germinate only upon disturbance and scarification.

We can guess at one selective response of the plant to *Glaucopsyche* attack—advancement of flowering time. The Gothic population of *L. amplus* seems to have been pushed to its earliest limit, as many examples of frost-killed and damaged inflorescences were observed this year. The butterflies oviposit strictly on the immature inflorescences (Table 1), indicating that plants on which flowers mature before the adult butterflies emerge, or early in the flight season, would be least subject to damage. There is no other obvious reason for the early flowering, as seed production is completed with more than a month of growing season remaining. At this time, other explanations cannot be excluded.

DENNIS E. BREEDLOVE
Department of Botany, Botanical Gardens, University of California, Berkeley 94720

PAUL R. EHRLICH
Department of Biological Sciences, Stanford University, Stanford, California 94305

References and Notes

1. For example D. Janzen, *Evolution* **20**, 249 (1966).
2. P. R. Ehrlich and P. H. Raven, *ibid.* **18**, 586 (1965); P. R. Ehrlich, *Oreg. State Univ. Biol. Colloq.*, in press.
3. For example, C. H. Muller, *Bull. Torrey Bot. Club* **93**, 332, 351 (1966); *Z. Pflanzenkr. Pflanzenpathol., Pflanzenschutz* **74**, 333 (1967); and personal communication: Professor Muller considers the toxic compounds of plants to be "primarily metabolic wastes."
4. W. B. Kemp, *J. Heredity* **28**, 328 (1937).
5. We thank J. A. Hendrickson, R. W. Holm, and P. H. Raven, for criticizing our manuscript. Supported by NSF grant GB-5645 and by a Ford Foundation grant.

5 August 1968 ■

Part III

METABOLISM: ENERGETICS AND PRODUCTIVITY

The general introduction suggested that a way of examining complex interactions in a community, whether of people or of plants and animals, is to identify the materials of exchange, and the routes and modes of movement of these materials. A similar scheme can be made using energy as the currency.

The major results of the radiant energy of the sun falling on the earth are the oceanic currents and atmospheric winds. Together, these produce the major features of climate. Oceanic circulation is of further interest to ecologists because it permits nutrient substances settled in the ocean depths to be returned to the surface, and helps control the climate of an area. The sun's energy also keeps the water cycle in motion through warming, evaporation, and precipitation. Warming and evaporation are two modes of dissipating radiant energy from the sun. Together, they account for weather, and for many differences in habitats from place to place. A third function of sunlight is to bring about photosynthesis. Eventually, all of the incoming solar energy is reradiated to space, except for a minute fraction which may be stored in fossil fuels such as coal and oil.

A good way to evaluate the flow of photosynthetic energy in an ecosystem is to study a food chain. Energy enters a food chain initially as radiant energy, by means of photosynthesis. Chemical substances enter the chain initially as they are absorbed by plants. Green plants constitute the lowest, or producer, level of the chain. Herbivorous animals—for example, the snowshoe hare or pine sawfly—occur at the next level, that of primary consumers. Carnivores, such as lynx, occur at the levels of secondary and tertiary consumers. Thus, radiant energy entering the ecosystem is converted by photosynthesis to chemical energy and passes in this form step by step through the system. De-

231

composing organisms are a necessary part of a food chain if it is to remain in steady state, not only because they are part of the scheme of energy flow but also because they return substances to the environment in a form usable by plants. A comparable examination of the movement of substances could be examined in a similar way; this is discussed in the last section. Energy, however, does not cycle; it enters an ecosystem and is thereafter dissipated from it.

A schematic accounting of solar radiation impinging on the earth has been given by Gates (1963). On an average, the energy budget for the northern hemisphere is shown in Figure 1.

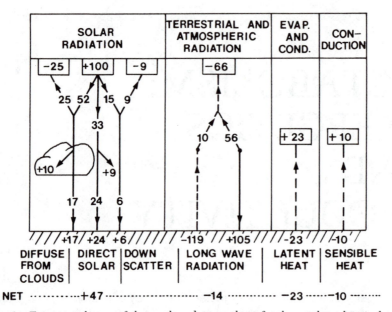

Figure 1. Energy exchange of the earth and atmosphere for the northern hemisphere (100 units = 0.485 cal per cm² per min). Based on the solar constant value of 1.94 cal per cm² per min.

Considering 100 units of solar radiation passing across a horizontal surface at the top of the atmosphere, clouds reflect 25 to space, absorb 10, and permit 17 to pass to the ground. Of the 33 units passing directly through the atmosphere, 9 are absorbed and 24 are transmitted to the ground. Scattering of the incoming radiation sends 6 of the total to the surface, whereas back-scatter reradiates 9 units to space.

Similar to the immediate energy input from the sun, a budget can be constructed for long-wave radiation, and is brought about by radiation from the warm surface of the earth and the atmosphere. The net change here is − 14. The energy of evaporation transmits 23 units to the atmosphere, and the combination of conduction and convection carry away 10 units from the earth, depositing them in the atmosphere. Photosynthesis uses a very small fraction of the total.

For any organism, an energy budget can be given schematically as

$$S + IR + M = IR_0 \pm C + LE_1$$

where the energy absorbed or produced by the organism is on the left and consists of the components S, direct radiation, IR, infrared radiation from the sky

232

and surroundings, and M, metabolic energy produced through respiration. The right-hand side gives the losses of energy through IR_0, infrared radiation to the environment, C, convection and less importantly conduction, and LE, evaporative heat loss. For many organisms conduction from the surroundings is unimportant, but it may be a significant part of the total for a lizard pressed against a rock.

So far we have characterized the total energy environment of organisms. The ecologist is primarily concerned with the quantity of incident radiation and the efficiency with which it is converted by organisms into other forms of energy. The first conversion, photosynthesis, changes one to five per cent of the incident radiation into the chemical energy of plant tissue. Phillipson (1966) gives the formal relation

$$\begin{matrix} \text{Solar energy} \\ \text{assimilated by} \\ \text{plant(s)} \end{matrix} = \begin{matrix} \text{Chemical energy of} \\ \text{growth and reproduction} \end{matrix} + \begin{matrix} \text{Heat energy} \\ \text{of respiration} \end{matrix}$$

At the next level, herbivores, we have the relations

$$\begin{matrix} \text{Chemical energy} \\ \text{eaten by} \\ \text{herbivores} \end{matrix} = \begin{matrix} \text{Chemical energy} \\ \text{assimilated by} \\ \text{herbivores} \end{matrix} + \begin{matrix} \text{Chemical energy} \\ \text{of faeces produced} \\ \text{by herbivores} \end{matrix}$$

and

$$\begin{matrix} \text{Chemical energy} \\ \text{assimilated by} \\ \text{herbivores} \end{matrix} = \begin{matrix} \text{Chemical energy of} \\ \text{growth of herbivores} \\ \text{(including production} \\ \text{of young and excretory} \\ \text{products)} \end{matrix} + \begin{matrix} \text{Heat energy} \\ \text{of} \\ \text{respiration} \end{matrix}$$

The heat energy is dissipated to the environment and is eventually reradiated. The effective functioning of ecosystems depends upon the transfer of energy from plant to herbivore, from herbivore to carnivore, and from all of these to decomposers.

More complete discussions of aspects of energy relations among organisms are found in Gates (1963), Phillipson (1966), and in the series of lectures published by the American Society of Zoology, and in the symposium on animal nutrition in the same volume.

LITERATURE CITED

American Society of Zoologists. 1968. Energy Flow in Ecological Systems. A refresher course arranged by Frederick B. Turner. American Zoologist 8(1):10–69.
American Society of Zoologists. 1960. Animal Nutrition. A symposium arranged by R. M. Darnell. American Zoologist 81:70–174.
Gates, D. M. 1963. Energy Exchange in the Biosphere. Harper & Row: New York. 151 pp.
Phillipson, J. 1966. Ecological Energetics. St. Martin's Press: New York. 57 pp.

THE TROPHIC-DYNAMIC ASPECT OF ECOLOGY

RAYMOND L. LINDEMAN

Osborn Zoological Laboratory, Yale University

Recent progress in the study of aquatic food-cycle relationships invites a re-appraisal of certain ecological tenets. Quantitative productivity data provide a basis for enunciating certain trophic principles, which, when applied to a series of successional stages, shed new light on the dynamics of ecological succession.

"COMMUNITY" CONCEPTS

A chronological review of the major viewpoints guiding synecological thought indicates the following stages: (1) the static species-distributional viewpoint; (2) the dynamic species-distributional viewpoint, with emphasis on successional phenomena; and (3) the trophic-dynamic viewpoint. From either species-distributional viewpoint, a lake, for example, might be considered by a botanist as containing several distinct plant aggregations, such as marginal emergent, floating-leafed, submerged, benthic, or phytoplankton communities, some of which might even be considered as "climax" (cf. Tutin, '41). The associated animals would be "biotic factors"

of the plant environment, tending to limit or modify the development of the aquatic plant communities. To a strict zoologist, on the other hand, a lake would seem to contain animal communities roughly coincident with the plant communities, although the "associated vegetation" would be considered merely as a part of the environment[1] of the animal community. A more "bio-ecological" species-distributional approach would recognize both the plants and animals as co-constituents of restricted "biotic" communities, such as "plankton communities," "benthic communities," etc., in which members of the living community "co-act" with each other and "re-act" with the non-living environment (Clements and Shelford, '39; Carpenter, '39, '40; T. Park, '41). Coactions and reactions are considered by bio-ecologists to be the dynamic effectors of succession.

The trophic-dynamic viewpoint, as adopted in this paper, emphasizes the relationship of trophic or "energy-availing" relationships within the community-unit to the process of succession. From this viewpoint, which is closely allied to Vernadsky's "biogeochemical" approach (cf. Hutchinson and Wollack, '40) and to the "oekologische Sicht" of Friederichs ('30), a lake is considered as a primary ecological unit in its own right, since all the lesser "communities" mentioned above are dependent upon other components of the lacustrine food cycle (cf. figure 1) for their very existence. Upon further consideration of the trophic cycle, the discrimination between living organisms as parts of the "biotic community"

---

[1] The term *habitat* is used by certain ecologists (Clements and Shelford, '39; Haskell, '40; T. Park, '41) as a synonym for *environment* in the usual sense and as here used, although Park points out that most biologists understand "habitat" to mean "simply the place or niche that an animal or plant occupies in nature" in a species-distributional sense. On the other hand, Haskell, and apparently also Park, use "environment" as synonymous with the *cosmos*. It is to be hoped that ecologists will shortly be able to reach some sort of agreement on the meanings of these basic terms.

Reproduced with permission from Ecology, 23: 399-418, 1942. Published in cooperation with The Ecological Society of America by The Brooklyn Botanic Garden, Brooklyn, New York.

234

and dead organisms and inorganic nutritives as parts of the "environment" seems arbitrary and unnatural. The difficulty of drawing clear-cut lines between the living *community* and the non-living *environment* is illustrated by the difficulty of determining the status of a slowly dying pondweed covered with periphytes, some of which are also continually dying. As indicated in figure 1, much of the non-living nascent ooze is rapidly reincorporated through "dissolved nutrients" back into the living "biotic community." This constant organic-inorganic cycle of nutritive substance is so completely integrated that to consider even such a unit as a lake primarily as a biotic community appears to force a "biological" emphasis upon a more basic functional organization.

This concept was perhaps first expressed by Thienemann ('18), as a result of his extensive limnological studies on the lakes of North Germany. Allee ('34) expressed a similar view, stating: "The picture than finally emerges . . . is of a sort of superorganismic unity not alone between the plants and animals to form biotic communities, but also between the biota and the environment." Such a concept is inherent in the term *ecosystem*, proposed by Tansley ('35) for the fundamental ecological unit.[2] Rejecting the terms "complex organism" and "biotic community," Tansley writes, "But the more fundamental conception is, as it seems to me, the whole *system* (in the sense of physics), including not only the organism-complex, but also the whole complex of physical factors forming what we call the environment of the biome. . . . It is the systems so formed which, from the point of view of the ecologist, are the basic units of nature on the face of the earth. . . . These *ecosystems*, as we may call them, are of the most various kinds and sizes. They form one category of the multitudinous physical systems of the universe, which range from the universe as a whole down to the atom." Tansley goes on to discuss the ecosystem as a category of rank equal to the "biome" (Clements, '16),

___

[2] The ecological system composed of the "biocoenosis + biotop" has been termed the *holocoen* by Friederichs ('30) and the *biosystem* by Thienemann ('39).

but points out that the term can also be used in a general sense, as is the word "community." The *ecosystem* may be formally defined as the system composed of physical-chemical-biological processes active within a space-time unit of any magnitude, i.e., the biotic community *plus* its abiotic environment. The concept of the ecosystem is believed by the writer to be of fundamental importance in interpreting the data of dynamic ecology.

TROPHIC DYNAMICS

Qualitative food-cycle relationships

Although certain aspects of food relations have been known for centuries, many processes within ecosystems are still very incompletely understood. The basic process in trophic dynamics is the transfer of energy from one part of the ecosystem to another. All function, and indeed all life, within an ecosystem depends upon the utilization of an external source of energy, solar radiation. A portion of this incident energy is transformed by the process of photosynthesis into the structure of living organisms. In the language of community economics introduced by Thienemann ('26), autotrophic plants are *producer* organisms, employing the energy obtained by photosynthesis to synthesize complex organic substances from simple inorganic substances. Although plants again release a portion of this potential energy in catabolic processes, a great surplus of organic substance is accumulated. Animals and heterotrophic plants, as *consumer* organisms, feed upon this surplus of potential energy, oxidizing a considerable portion of the consumed substance to release kinetic energy for metabolism, but transforming the remainder into the complex chemical substances of their own bodies. Following death, every organism is a potential source of energy for saprophagous organisms (feeding directly on dead tissues), which again may act as energy sources for successive categories of consumers. Heterotrophic bacteria and fungi, representing the most important saprophagous consumption of energy, may be conveniently differentiated from animal consumers as special-

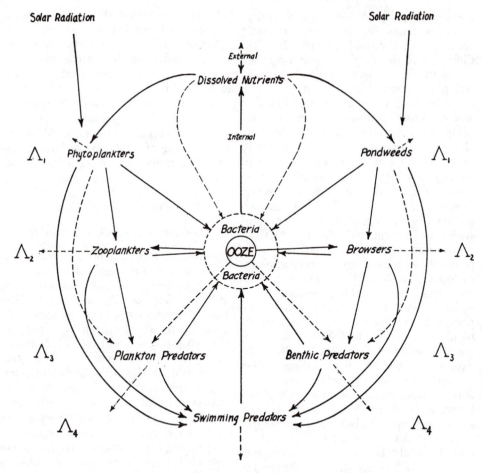

Solar Radiation   Solar Radiation

FIG. 1. Generalized lacustrine food-cycle relationships (after Lindeman, '41b).

ized *decomposers*[3] of organic substance. Waksman ('41) has suggested that certain of these bacteria be further differentiated as *transformers* of organic and inorganic compounds. The combined action of animal consumers and bacterial decomposers tends to dissipate the potential energy of organic substances, again transforming them to the inorganic state. From this inorganic state the autotrophic plants may utilize the dis-

[3] Thienemann ('26) proposed the term *reducers* for the heterotrophic bacteria and fungi, but this term suggests that decomposition is produced solely by chemical reduction rather than oxidation, which is certainly not the case. The term *decomposers* is suggested as being more appropriate.

solved nutrients once more in resynthesizing complex organic substance, thus completing the food cycle.

The careful study of food cycles reveals an intricate pattern of trophic predilections and substitutions underlain by certain basic dependencies; food-cycle diagrams, such as figure 1, attempt to portray these underlying relationships. In general, predators are less specialized in food habits than are their prey. The ecological importance of this statement seems to have been first recognized by Elton ('27), who discussed its effect on the survival of prey species when predators are numerous and its effect in enabling predators to survive when their

236

usual prey are only periodically abundant. This ability on the part of predators, which tends to make the higher trophic levels of a food cycle less discrete than the lower, increases the difficulties of analyzing the energy relationships in this portion of the food cycle, and may also tend to "shorten the food-chain."

Fundamental food-cycle variations in different ecosystems may be observed by comparing lacustrine and terrestrial cycles. Although dissolved nutrients in the lake water and in the ooze correspond directly with those in the soil, the autotrophic producers differ considerably in form. Lacustrine producers include macrophytic pondweeds, in which massive supporting tissues are at a minimum, and microphytic phytoplankters, which in larger lakes definitely dominate the production of organic substance. Terrestrial producers are predominantly multicellular plants containing much cellulose and lignin in various types of supporting tissues. Terrestrial herbivores, belonging to a great number of specialized food groups, act as *primary consumers* (sensu Jacot, '40) of organic substance; these groups correspond to the "browsers" of aquatic ecosystems. Terrestrial predators may be classified as more remote (secondary, tertiary, quaternary, etc.) consumers, according to whether they prey upon herbivores or upon other predators; these correspond roughly to the benthic predators and swimming predators, respectively, of a lake. Bacterial and fungal decomposers in terrestrial systems are concentrated in the humus layer of the soil; in lakes, where the "soil" is overlain by water, decomposition takes place both in the water, as organic particles slowly settle, and in the benthic "soil." Nutrient salts are thus freed to be reutilized by the autotrophic plants of both ecosystems.

The striking absence of terrestrial "life-forms" analogous to plankters[4] (cf.

figure 1) indicates that the terrestrial food cycle is essentially "mono-cyclic" with macrophytic producers, while the lacustrine cycle, with two "life-forms" of producers, may be considered as "bi-cyclic." The marine cycle, in which plankters are the only producers of any consequence, may be considered as "mono-cyclic" with microphytic producers. The relative absence of massive supporting tissues in plankters and the very rapid completion of their life cycle exert a great influence on the differential productivities of terrestrial and aquatic systems. The general convexity of terrestrial systems as contrasted with the concavity of aquatic substrata results in striking trophic and successional differences, which will be discussed in a later section.

Productivity

Definitions.—The quantitative aspects of trophic ecology have been commonly expressed in terms of the productivity of the food groups concerned. Productivity has been rather broadly defined as the general rate of production (Riley, '40, and others), a term which may be applied to any or every food group in a given ecosystem. The problem of productivity as related to biotic dynamics has been critically analyzed by G. E. Hutchinson ('42) in his recent book on limnological principles. The two following paragraphs are quoted from Hutchinson's chapter on "The Dynamics of Lake Biota":

The dynamics of lake biota is here treated as primarily a problem of energy transfer . . . the biotic utilization of solar energy entering the lake surface. Some of this energy is transformed by photosynthesis into the structure of phytoplankton organisms, representing an energy content which may be expressed as Λ_1 (first level). Some of the phytoplankters will be eaten by

---

[4] Francé ('13) developed the concept of the *edaphon*, in which the soil microbiota was represented as the terrestrial equivalent of aquatic

plankton. This concept appears to have a number of adherents in this country. The author feels that this analogy is misleading, as the edaphon, which has almost no producers, represents only a dependent side-chain of the terrestrial cycle, and is much more comparable to the lacustrine microbenthos than to the plankton.

zooplankters (energy content Λ_2), which again will be eaten by plankton predators (energy content Λ_3). The various successive levels (i.e., stages[5]) of the food cycle are thus seen to have successively different energy contents (Λ_1, Λ_2, Λ_3, etc.).

Considering any food-cycle level Λ_n, energy is entering the level and is leaving it. The rate of change of the energy content Λ_n therefore may be divided into a positive and a negative part:

$$\frac{d\Lambda_n}{dt} = \lambda_n + \lambda_n',$$

where λ_n is by definition positive and represents the rate of contribution of energy from Λ_{n-1} (the previous level) to Λ_n, while λ_n' is negative and represents the sum of the rate of energy dissipated from Λ_n and the rate of energy content handed on to the following level Λ_{n+1}. The more interesting quantity is λ_n which is defined as the true *productivity* of level Λ_n. In practice, it is necessary to use mean rates over finite periods of time as approximations to the mean rates λ_0, λ_1, λ_2. . . .

In the following pages we shall consider the quantitative relationships of the following productivities: λ_0 (rate of incident solar radiation), λ_1 (rate of photosynthetic production), λ_2 (rate of primary or herbivorous consumption), λ_3 (rate of secondary consumption or primary predation), and λ_4 (rate of tertiary consumption). The total amount of organic structure formed per year for any level Λ_n, which is commonly expressed as the annual "yield," actually represents a value uncorrected for dissipation of energy by (1) respiration, (2) predation, and (3) post-mortem decomposition. Let us now consider the quantitative aspects of these losses.

Respiratory corrections.—The amount of energy lost from food levels by catabolic processes (respiration) varies considerably for the different stages in the life histories of individuals, for different levels in the food cycle and for different seasonal temperatures. In terms of annual production, however, individual deviates cancel out and respiratory differences between food groups may be observed.

[5] The term *stage*, in some respects preferable to the term *level*, cannot be used in this trophic sense because of its long-established usage as a successional term (cf. p. 23).

Numerous estimates of average respiration for photosynthetic producers may be obtained from the literature. For terrestrial plants, estimates range from 15 per cent (Pütter, re Spoehr, '26) to 43 per cent (Lundegårdh, '24) under various types of natural conditions. For aquatic producers, Hicks ('34) reported a coefficient of about 15 per cent for Lemna under certain conditions. Wimpenny ('41) has indicated that the respiratory coefficient of marine producers in polar regions (diatoms) is probably much less than that of the more "animal-like" producers (peridinians and coccolithophorids) of warmer seas, and that temperature may be an important factor in determining respiratory coefficients in general. Juday ('40), after conducting numerous experiments with Manning and others on the respiration of phytoplankters in Trout Lake, Wisconsin, concluded that under average conditions these producers respire about $\frac{1}{3}$ of the organic matter which they synthesize. This latter value, 33 per cent, is probably the best available respiratory coefficient for lacustrine producers.

Information on the respiration of aquatic primary consumers is obtained from an illuminating study by Ivlev ('39a) on the energy relationships of *Tubifex*. By means of ingenious techniques, he determined calorific values for assimilation and growth in eleven series of experiments. Using the averages of his calorific values, we can make the following simple calculations: *assimilation* (16.77 cal.) — *growth* (10.33 cal.) = *respiration* (6.44 cal.), so that respiration in terms of growth = $\frac{6.44}{10.33}$ = 62.30 per cent. As a check on the growth stage of these worms, we find that $\frac{growth}{assimilation}$ = 61.7 per cent, a value in good agreement with the classical conclusions of Needham ('31, III, p. 1655) with respect to embryos: the efficiency of all developing embryos is numerically similar, between 60 and 70 per cent, and independent of temperature within the range of biological tolerance. We may therefore conclude that the worms were growing at nearly maximal efficiency, so that the above respiratory coefficient is nearly minimal. In the absence of further data, we shall tentatively accept 62 per cent as the best available respiratory coefficient for aquatic herbivores.

The respiratory coefficient for aquatic predators can be approximated from data of another important study by Ivlev ('39b), on the energy transformations in predatory yearling carp. Treating his calorific values as in the preceding paragraph, we find that *ingestion* (1829 cal.) − *defecation* (454 cal.) = *assimilation* (1375 cal.), and *assimilation* − *growth* (573 cal.) = *respiration* (802 cal.), so that respiration in terms of growth $= \frac{802}{573} = 140$ per cent, a much higher coefficient than that found for the primary consumer, *Tubifex*. A rough check on this coefficient was obtained by calorific analysis of data on the growth of yearling green sunfishes (*Lepomis cyanellus*) published by W. G. Moore ('41), which indicate a respiratory coefficient of 120 per cent with respect to growth, suggesting that these fishes were growing more efficiently than those studied by Ivlev. Since Moore's fishes were fed on a highly concentrated food (liver), this greater growth efficiency is not surprising. If the maximum growth efficiency would occur when $\frac{growth}{assimilation}$ = 60–70 per cent (AEE of Needham, '31), the AEE of Moore's data (about 50 per cent) indicates that the minimum respiratory coefficient with respect to growth might be as low as 100 per cent for certain fishes. Food-conversion data from Thompson ('41) indicate a minimum respiratory coefficient of less than 150 per cent for young black bass (*Huro salmoides*) at 70° F., the exact percentage depending upon how much of the ingested food (minnows) was assimilated. Krogh ('41) showed that predatory fishes have a higher rate of respiration than the more sluggish herbivorous species; the respiratory rate of *Esox* under resting conditions at 20° C. was $3\frac{1}{2}$ times that of *Cyprinus*. The form of piscian growth curves (cf. Hile, '41) suggests that the respiratory coefficient is much higher for fishes towards the end of their normal life-span. Since the value obtained from Ivlev (above) is based on more extensive data than those of Moore, we shall tentatively accept 140 per cent as an average respiratory coefficient for aquatic predators.

Considering that predators are usually more active than their herbivorous prey, which are in turn more active than the plants upon which they feed, it is not surprising to find that respiration with respect to growth in producers (33 per cent), in primary consumers (62 per cent) and in secondary consumers (>100 per cent) increases progressively. These differences probably reflect a trophic principle of wide application: the percentage loss of energy due to respiration is progressively greater for higher levels in the food cycle.

Predation corrections.—In considering the predation losses from each level, it is most convenient to begin with the highest level, Λ_n. In a mechanically perfect food cycle composed of organically discrete levels, this loss by predation obviously would be zero. Since no natural food cycle is so mechanically constituted, some "cannibalism" within such an arbitrary level can be expected, so that the actual value for predation loss from Λ_n probably will be somewhat above zero. The predation loss from level Λ_{n-1} will represent the total amount of assimilable energy passed on into the higher level (i.e., the true productivity, λ_n), plus a quantity representing the average content of substance killed but not assimilated by the predator, as will be discussed in the following section. The predation loss from level Λ_{n-2} will likewise represent the total amount of assimilable energy passed on to the next level (i.e., λ_{n-1}), plus a similar factor for unassimilated material, as illustrated by the data of tables II and III. The various categories of parasites are somewhat comparable to those of predators, but the details of their energy relationships have not yet been clarified, and cannot be included in this preliminary account.

Decomposition corrections. — In conformity with the principle of Le Chatelier, the energy of no food level can be completely extracted by the organisms which feed upon it. In addition to the energy represented by organisms which survive to be included in the "annual yield," much energy is contained in "killed" tissues which the predators are unable to digest and assimilate. Average coefficients of indigestible tissues, based largely of the calorific equivalents of the "crude fiber" fractions in the chemical analyses of Birge and Juday ('22), are as follows:

Nannoplankters	ca. 5%
Algal mesoplankters	5–35%
Mature pondweeds	ca. 20%
Primary consumers	ca. 10%
Secondary consumers	ca. 8%
Predatory fishes	ca. 5%

Corrections for terrestrial producers would certainly be much higher. Although the data are insufficient to warrant a generalization, these values suggest increasing digestibility of the higher food levels, particularly for the benthic components of aquatic cycles.

The loss of energy due to premature death from non-predatory causes usually must be neglected, since such losses are exceedingly difficult to evaluate and under normal conditions probably represent relatively small components of the annual production. However, considering that these losses may assume considerable proportions at any time, the above "decomposition coefficients" must be regarded as correspondingly minimal.

Following non-predated death, every organism is a potential source of energy for myriads of bacterial and fungal saprophages, whose metabolic products provide simple inorganic and organic solutes reavailable to photosynthetic producers. These saprophages may also serve as energy sources for successive levels of consumers, often considerably supplementing the normal diet of herbivores (ZoBell and Feltham, '38). Jacot ('40) considered saprophage-feeding or coprophagous animals as "low" primary consumers, but the writer believes that in the present state of our knowledge a quantitative subdivision of primary consumers is unwarranted.

Application.—The value of these theoretical energy relationships can be illustrated by analyzing data of the three ecosystems for which relatively comprehensive productivity values have been published (table I). The summary account of Brujewicz ('39) on "the dynamics of living matter in the Caspian Sea" leaves much to be desired, as bottom animals are not differentiated into their relative food levels, and the basis for determining the annual production of phytoplankters (which on theoretical grounds appears to be much too low) is not clearly explained. Furthermore, his values are stated in terms of thousands of tons of dry weight for the Caspian Sea as a whole, and must be roughly transformed to calories per square centimeter of surface area. The data for Lake Mendota, Wisconsin, are

TABLE I. *Productivities of food-groups in three aquatic ecosystems, as g-cal/cm²/year, uncorrected for losses due to respiration, predation and decomposition. Data from Brujewicz ('39), Juday ('40) and Lindeman ('41b).*

	Caspian Sea	Lake Mendota	Cedar Bog Lake
Phytoplankters: Λ_1	59.5	299	25.8
Phytobenthos: Λ_1	0.3	22	44.6
Zooplankters: Λ_2	20.0	22	6.1
Benthic browsers: Λ_2		1.8*	0.8
Benthic predators: Λ_3	20.6	0.9*	0.2
Plankton predators: Λ_3			0.8
"Forage" fishes: $\Lambda_3(+\Lambda_2?)$	0.6	?	0.3
Carp: $\Lambda_3(+\Lambda_2?)$	0.0	0.2	0.0
"Game" fishes: $\Lambda_4(+\Lambda_3?)$	0.6	0.1	0.0
Seals: Λ_5	0.01	0.0	0.0

* Roughly assuming that ⅔ of the bottom fauna is herbivorous (cf. Juday, '22).

taken directly from a general summary (Juday, '40) of the many productivity studies made on that eutrophic lake. The data for Cedar Bog Lake, Minnesota, are taken from the author's four-year analysis (Lindeman, '41b) of its food-cycle dynamics. The calorific values in table I, representing annual production of organic matter, are uncorrected for energy losses.

TABLE II. *Productivity values for the Cedar Bog Lake food cycle, in g-cal/cm²/year, as corrected by using the coefficients derived in the preceding sections.*

Trophic level	Uncorrected productivity	Respiration	Predation	Decomposition	Corrected productivity
Producers: Λ_1	70.4±10.14	23.4	14.8	2.8	111.3
Primary consumers: Λ_2	7.0±1.07	4.4	3.1	0.3	14.8
Secondary consumers: Λ_3	1.3±0.43*	1.8	0.0	0.0	3.1

* This value includes the productivity of the small cyprinoid fishes found in the lake.

Correcting for the energy losses due to respiration, predation and decomposition, as discussed in the preceding sections, casts a very different light on the relative productivities of food levels. The calculation of corrections for the Cedar Bog Lake values for producers, primary consumers and secondary consumers are given in table II. The application of similar corrections to the energy values for the food levels of the Lake Mendota food cycle given by Juday ('40), as shown in table III, indicates that Lake Mendota is much more productive of producers and primary consumers than is Cedar Bog Lake, while the production of secondary consumers is of the same order of magnitude in the two lakes.

In calculating total productivity for Lake Mendota, Juday ('40) used a blanket correction of 500 per cent of the annual production of all consumer levels for "metabolism," which presumably includes both respiration and predation. Thompson ('41) found that the "carry-

TABLE III. *Productivity values for the Lake Mendota food cycle, in g-cal/cm²/year, as corrected by using coefficients derived in the preceding sections, and as given by Juday ('40).*

Trophic Level	Uncorrected productivity	Respiration	Predation	Decomposition	Corrected productivity	Juday's corrected productivity
Producers: Λ_1	321*	107	42	10	480	428
Primary consumers: Λ_2	24	15	2.3	0.3	41.6	144
Secondary consumers: Λ_3	1†	1	0.3	0.0	2.3	6
Tertiary consumers: Λ_4	0.12	0.2	0.0	0.0	0.3	0.7

* Hutchinson ('42) gives evidence that this value is probably too high and may actually be as low as 250.
† Apparently such organisms as small "forage" fishes are not included in any part of Juday's balance sheet. The inclusion of these forms might be expected to increase considerably the productivity of secondary consumption.

ing-capacity" of lakes containing mostly carp and other "coarse" fishes (primarily Λ_3), was about 500 per cent that of lakes containing mostly "game" fishes (primarily Λ_4), and concluded that "this difference must be about one complete link in the food chain, since it usually requires about five pounds of food to produce one pound of fish." While such high "metabolic losses" may hold for tertiary and quaternary predators under certain field conditions, the physiological experiments previously cited indicate much lower respiratory coefficients. Even when predation and decomposition corrections are included, the resultant productivity values are less than half those obtained by using Juday's coefficient. Since we have shown that the necessary corrections vary progressively with the different food levels, it seems probable that Juday's "coefficient of metabolism" is much too high for primary and secondary consumers.

Biological efficiency

The quantitative relationships of any food-cycle level may be expressed in terms of its efficiency with respect to lower levels. Quoting Hutchinson's ('42) definition, "the efficiency of the productivity of any level (Λ_n) relative to the productivity of any previous level (Λ_m) is defined as $\dfrac{\lambda_n}{\lambda_m}\,100$. If the rate of solar energy entering the ecosystem is denoted as λ_0, the efficiencies of all levels may be referred back to this quantity λ_0." In general, however, the most interesting efficiencies are those referred to the previous level's productivity (λ_{n-1}), or those expressed as $\dfrac{\lambda_n}{\lambda_{n-1}}\,100$. These latter may be termed the *progressive efficiencies* of the various food-cycle levels, indicating for each level the degree of utilization of its potential food supply or energy source. All efficiencies discussed in the following pages are progressive efficiencies, expressed in terms of relative productivities $\left(\dfrac{\lambda_n}{\lambda_{n-1}}\,100\right)$. It is important to remember that efficiency and productivity are not synonymous. Productivity is a rate (i.e., in the units here used, cal/cm²/year), while efficiency, being a ratio, is a dimensionless number. The points of reference for any efficiency value should always be clearly stated.

The progressive efficiencies $\left(\dfrac{\lambda_n}{\lambda_{n-1}}\,100\right)$ for the trophic levels of Cedar Bog Lake and Lake Mendota, as obtained from the productivities derived in tables II and III, are presented in table IV. In view of the uncertainties concerning some of the Lake Mendota productivities, no definite conclusions can be drawn from their relative efficiencies. The Cedar Bog Lake ratios, however, indicate that the progressive efficiencies increase from about 0.10 per cent for production, to 13.3 per cent for primary consumption, and to 22.3 per cent for secondary consumption. An uncorrected efficiency of tertiary consumption of 37.5 per cent ± 3.0 per cent (for the weight ratios of "carnivorous" to "forage" fishes in Alabama ponds) is indicated in data published by Swingle and Smith ('40). These progressively increasing efficiencies may well represent a fundamental trophic principle, namely, that the consumers at progressively higher levels in the food cycle are progressively more efficient in the use of their food supply.

At first sight, this generalization of increasing efficiency in higher consumer groups would appear to contradict the previous generalization that the loss of energy due to respiration is progressively greater for higher levels in the food cycle. These can be reconciled by remembering that increased activity of predators considerably increases the chances of encountering suitable prey. The ultimate effect of such antagonistic principles would present a picture of a predator completely wearing itself out in the process of completely exterminating its prey, a very improbable situation. However, Elton ('27) pointed out that food-cycles rarely have more than five trophic levels. Among the several factors involved, increasing respiration of successive levels of predators contrasted with their successively increasing efficiency of predation appears to be important in restricting the number of trophic levels in a food cycle.

The effect of increasing temperature is alleged by Wimpenny ('41) to cause a decreasing consumer/producer ratio, presumably because he believes that the "acceleration of vital velocities" of consumers at increasing temperatures is more rapid than that of producers. He

TABLE IV. *Productivities and progressive efficiencies in the Cedar Bog Lake and Lake Mendota food cycles, as g-cal/cm²/year*

	Cedar Bog Lake		Lake Mendota	
	Productivity	Efficiency	Productivity	Efficiency
Radiation........	≦118,872		118,872	
Producers: Λ_1......	111.3	0.10%	480*	0.40%
Primary consumers: Λ_2............	14.8	13.3%	41.6	8.7%
Secondary consumers: Λ_3....	3.1	22.3%	2.3†	5.5%
Tertiary consumers: Λ_4....	—	—	0.3	13.0%

* Probably too high; see footnote of table III.
† Probably too low; see footnote of table III.

cites as evidence Lohmann's ('12) data for relative *numbers* (not biomass) of Protophyta, Protozoa and Metazoa in the centrifuge plankton of "cool" seas (741:73:1) as contrasted with tropical areas (458:24:1). Since Wimpenny himself emphasizes that many metazoan plankters are larger in size toward the poles, these data do not furnish convincing proof of the allegation. The data given in table IV, since Cedar Bog Lake has a much higher mean annual water temperature than Lake Mendota, appear to contradict Wimpenny's generalization that consumer/producer ratios fall as the temperature increases.

The Eltonian pyramid

The general relationships of higher food-cycle levels to one another and to community structure were greatly clarified following recognition (Elton, '27) of the importance of size and of numbers in the animals of an ecosystem. Beginning with primary consumers of various sizes, there are as a rule a number of food-chains radiating outwards in which the probability is that predators will become successively larger, while parasites and hyper-parasites will be progressively smaller than their hosts. Since small primary consumers can increase faster than larger secondary consumers and are so able to support the latter, the animals at the base of a food-chain are relatively abundant while those toward the end are progressively fewer in number. The resulting arrangement of sizes and numbers of animals, termed the pyramid of Numbers by Elton, is now commonly known as the Eltonian Pyramid. Williams ('41), reporting on the "floor fauna" of the Panama rain forest, has recently published an interesting example of such a pyramid, which is reproduced in figure 2.

The Eltonian Pyramid may also be expressed in terms of biomass. The weight of all predators must always be much lower than that of all food animals, and the total weight of the latter much lower than the plant production (Bodenheimer, '38). To the human ecologist, it is noteworthy that the population density of the essentially vegetarian Chinese, for example, is much greater than that of the more carnivorous English.

The principle of the Eltonian Pyramid has been redefined in terms of productivity by Hutchinson (unpublished) in the following formalized terms: the rate of production cannot be less and will almost certainly be greater than the rate of primary consumption, which in turn cannot be less and will almost certainly be greater than the rate of secondary consumption, which in turn . . . , etc. The energy-relationships of this principle may be epitomized by means

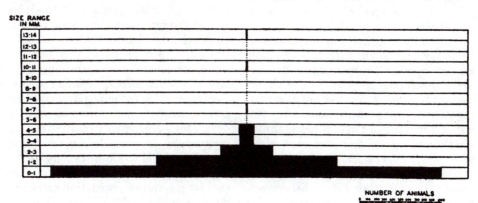

Fig. 2. Eltonian pyramid of numbers, for floor-fauna invertebrates of the Panama rain forest (from Williams, '41).

243

of the productivity symbol λ, as follows:

$$\lambda_0 > \lambda_1 > \lambda_2 \ldots > \lambda_n.$$

This rather obvious generalization is confirmed by the data of all ecosystems analyzed to date.

TROPHIC-DYNAMICS IN SUCCESSION

Dynamic processes within an ecosystem, over a period of time, tend to produce certain obvious changes in its species-composition, soil characteristics and productivity. Change, according to Cooper ('26), is the essential criterion of succession. From the trophic-dynamic viewpoint, succession is the process of development in an ecosystem, brought about primarily by the effects of the organisms on the environment and upon each other, towards a relatively stable condition of equilibrium.

It is well known that in the initial phases of hydrarch succession (oligotrophy → eutrophy) productivity increases rapidly; it is equally apparent that the colonization of a bare terrestrial area represents a similar acceleration in productivity. In the later phases of succession, productivity increases much more slowly. As Hutchinson and Wollack ('40) pointed out, these generalized changes in the rate of production may be expressed as a sigmoid curve showing a rough resemblance to the growth curve of an organism or of a homogeneous population.

Such smooth logistic growth, of course, is seldom found in natural succession, except possibly in such cases as bare areas developing directly to the climax vegetation type in the wake of a retreating glacier. Most successional seres consist of a number of *stages* ("recognizable, clearly-marked subdivisions of a given sere"—W. S. Cooper), so that their productivity growth-curves will contain undulations corresponding in distinctness to the distinctness of the stages. The presence of stages in a successional sere apparently represents the persistent influence of some combination of limiting factors, which, until they are overcome by species-substitution, etc., tend to decrease the acceleration of productivity and maintain it at a more constant rate. This tendency towards *stage-equilibrium* of productivity will be discussed in the following pages.

Productivity in hydrarch succession

The descriptive dynamics of hydrarch succession is well known. Due to the essentially concave nature of the substratum, lake succession is internally complicated by a rather considerable influx of nutritive substances from the drainage basin surrounding the lake. The basins of lakes are gradually filled with sediments, largely organogenic, upon which a series of vascular plant stages successively replace one another until a more or less stable (climax) stage is attained. We are concerned here, however, primarily with the productivity aspects of the successional process.

Eutrophication. — Thienemann ('26) presented a comprehensive theoretical discussion of the relation between lake succession and productivity, as follows: In oligotrophy, the pioneer phase, productivity is rather low, limited by the amount of dissolved nutrients in the lake water. Oxygen is abundant at all times, almost all of the synthesized organic matter is available for animal food; bacteria release dissolved nutrients from the remainder. Oligotrophy thus has a very "thrifty" food cycle, with a relatively high "efficiency" of the consumer populations. With increasing influx of nutritives from the surrounding drainage basin and increasing primary productivity (λ_1), oligotrophy is gradually changed through mesotrophy to eutrophy, in which condition the production of organic matter (λ_1) exceeds that which can be oxidized (λ_1') by respiration, predation and bacterial decomposition. The oxygen supply of the hypolimnion becomes depleted, with disastrous effects on the oligotrophconditioned bottom fauna. Organisms especially adapted to endure temporary anaerobiosis replace the oligotrophic species, accompanied by anaerobic bacteria which during the stagnation period cause reduction rather than oxidation of the organic detritus. As a result of this process, semi-reduced organic ooze, or *gyttja*, accumulates on the bottom. As oxygen supply thus becomes a limiting factor of productivity, relative efficiency of the consumer groups in utilizing the synthesized organic substance becomes correspondingly lower.

The validity of Thienemann's interpretation, particularly regarding the trophic mechanisms, has recently been challenged by Hutchinson ('41, '42), who states that three distinct factors are involved: (1) the edaphic factor, representing the potential nutrient supply (primarily phosphorus) in the surrounding drainage basin; (2) the age of the lake at any stage, indicating the degree of utilization of the nutrient supply; and (3) the morphometric character at any stage, dependent on both the original morphometry of the lake basin and the age of the lake, and presumably influencing the oxygen concentration in the hypolimnion. He holds that true eutrophication takes place only in regions well supplied with nutrients, lakes in other regions developing into "ideotrophic types." The influx of phosphorus is probably very great in the earliest phases, much greater than the supply of nitrogen, as indicated by very low N/P ratios in the earliest sediments (Hutchinson and Wollack, '40). A large portion of this phosphorus is believed to be insoluble, as a component of such mineral particles as apatite, etc., although certainly some of it is soluble. The supply of available nitrogen increases somewhat more slowly, being largely dependent upon the fixation of nitrogen by microorganisms either in the lake or in the surrounding soils. The photosynthetic productivity (λ_1) of lakes thus increases rather rapidly in the early phases, its

quantitative value for lakes with comparable edaphic nutrient supplies being dependent on the morphometry (mean depth). Since deep lakes have a greater depth range for plankton photosynthesis, abundant oxygen and more chance for decomposition of the plankton detritus before reaching the bottom, such deep lakes may be potentially as productive as shallower lakes, in terms of unit surface area. Factors tending to lessen the comparative productivity of deep lakes are (1) lower temperature for the lake as a whole, and (2) greater dilution of nutrients in terms of volume of the illuminated "trophogenic zone" of the lake. During eutrophication in a deep lake, the phosphorus content of the sediment falls and nitrogen rises, until a N/P ratio of about 40/1 is established. "The decomposition of organic matter presumably is always liberating some of this phosphorus and nitrogen. Within limits, the more organic matter present the easier will be such regeneration. It is probable that benthic animals and anion exchange play a part in such processes" (Hutchinson, '42). The progressive filling of the lake basin with sediments makes the lake shallower, so that the oxygen supply of the hypolimnion is increasingly, and finally completely, exhausted during summer stagnation. Oxidation of the sediments is less complete, but sufficient phosphorus is believed to be regenerated from the ooze surface so that productivity in terms of surface area remains relatively constant. The nascent ooze acts as a trophic buffer, in the chemical sense, tending to maintain the productivity of a lake in stage-equilibrium (*typological equilibrium* of Hutchinson) during the eutrophic stage of its succession.

The concept of eutrophic stage-equilibrium seems to be partially confused (cf. Thienemann, '26; Hutchinson and Wollack, '40) with the theoretically ideal condition of complete *trophic equilibrium*, which may be roughly defined as the dynamic state of continuous, complete utilization and regeneration of chemical nutrients in an ecosystem, without loss or gain from the outside, under a periodically constant energy source—such as might be found in a perfectly balanced aquarium or terrarium. Natural ecosystems may tend to approach a state of trophic equilibrium under certain conditions, but it is doubtful if any are sufficiently autochthonous to attain, or maintain, true trophic equilibrium for any length of time. The biosphere as a whole, however, as Vernadsky ('29, '39) so vigorously asserts, may exhibit a high degree of true trophic equilibrium.

The existence of prolonged eutrophic stage-equilibrium was first suggested as a result of a study on the sediments of Grosser Plöner See in Germany (Groschopf, '36). Its significance was recognized by Hutchinson and Wollack ('40), who based their critical discussion on chemical analyses (ibid.) and pollen analyses (Deevey, '39) of the sediments of Linsley Pond, Connecticut. They reported a gradual transition from oligotrophy to eutrophy (first attained in the oak-hemlock pollen period), in which stage the lake has remained for a very long time, perhaps more than 4000 years. They report indications of a comparable eutrophic stage-equilibrium in the sediments of nearby Upper Linsley Pond (Hutchinson and Wollack, unpublished). Similar attainment of stage-equilibrium is indicated in a preliminary report on the sediments of Lake Windermere in England (Jenkin, Mortimer and Pennington, '41). Every stage of a sere is believed to possess a similar stage-equilibrium of variable duration, although terrestrial stages have not yet been defined in terms of productivity.

The trophic aspects of eutrophication cannot be determined easily from the sediments. In general, however, the ratio of organic matter to the silt washed into the lake from the margins affords an approximation of the photosynthetic productivity. This undecomposed organic matter, representing the amount of energy which is lost from the food cycle, is derived largely from level Λ_1, as plant structures in general are decomposed less easily than animal structures. The quantity of energy passed on into consumer levels can only be surmised from undecomposed fragments of organisms which are believed to occupy those levels. Several types of animal "microfossils" occur rather consistently in lake sediments, such as the carapaces and post-abdomens of certain cladocerans, chironomid head-capsules, fragments of the phantom-midge larva *Chaoborus*, snail shells, polyzoan statoblasts, sponge spicules and rhizopod shells. Deevey ('42), after making comprehensive microfossil and chemical analyses of the sediments of Linsley Pond, suggested that the abundant half-carapaces of the planktonic browser *Bosmina* afford "a reasonable estimate of the quantity of zooplankton produced" and that "the total organic matter of the sediment is a reasonable estimate of the organic matter produced by phytoplankton and littoral vegetation." He found a striking similarity in the shape of the curves representing *Bosmina* content and total organic matter plotted against depth, which, when plotted logarithmically against each other, showed a linear relationship expressed by an empirical power equation. Citing Hutchinson and Wollack ('40) to the effect that the developmental curve for organic matter was analogous to that for the development of an organism, he pressed the analogy further by suggesting that the increase of zooplankton (*Bosmina*) with reference to the increase of organic matter (λ_1) fitted the formula $y = bx^k$ for allometric growth (Huxley, '32), "where $y = Bosmina$, $x =$ total organic matter, $b =$ a constant giving the value of y when $x = 1$, and $k =$ the 'allometry constant,' or the slope of the line when a double log plot is made." If we represent the organic matter produced as λ_1 and further assume that *Bosmina* represents the primary consumers (λ_2), neglecting benthic browsers, the formula becomes $\lambda_2 = b\lambda_1^k$. Whether this formula would express the relationship found in other levels of the food cycle, the development of other stages, or other ecosystems, remains to be demonstrated.[6] Stratigraphic analyses in Cedar Bog Lake (Lindeman and Lindeman, unpublished) suggest a roughly similar increase of both organic matter and *Bosmina* carapaces in the earliest sediments. In the modern senescent lake, however, double logarithmic plottings of the calorific values for λ_1 against λ_2, and λ_2 against λ_3, for the four years studied, show no semblance of linear relationship, i.e., do not fit any power equation. If Deevey is correct in his interpretation of the Linsley Pond microfossils, allometric growth would appear to characterize the phases of pre-equilibrium succession as the term "growth" indeed implies.

The relative duration of eutrophic stage-equilibrium is not yet completely understood. As exemplified by Linsley Pond, the relation of stage-equilibrium to succession is intimately concerned with the trophic processes of (1) external influx and efflux (partly controlled by climate), (2) photosynthetic productivity, (3) sedimentation (partly by physiographic silting) and (4) regeneration of nutritives from the sediments. These processes apparently maintain a relatively constant ratio to each other during the extended equilibrium period. Yet the food cycle is not in true trophic equilibrium, and continues to fill the lake with organic sediments. *Succession* is

<hr/>

[6] It should be mentioned in this connection that Meschkat ('37) found that the relationship of population density of tubificids to organic matter in the bottom of a polluted "Buhnenfeld" could be expressed by the formula $y = a^x$, where y represents the population density, x is the "determining environmental factor," and a is a constant. He pointed out that for such an expression to hold the population density must be maximal. Hentschel ('36), on less secure grounds, suggested applying a similar expression to the relationship between populations of marine plankton and the "controlling factor" of their environment.

continuing, at a rate corresponding to the rate of sediment accumulation. In the words of Hutchinson and Wollack ('40), "this means that during the equilibrium period the lake, through the internal activities of its biocoenosis, is continually approaching a condition when it ceases to be a lake."

Senescence.—As a result of long-continued sedimentation, eutrophic lakes attain senescence, first manifested in bays and wind-protected areas. Senescence is usually characterized by such pond-like conditions as (1) tremendous increase in shallow littoral area populated with pondweeds and (2) increased marginal invasion of terrestrial stages. Cedar Bog Lake, which the author has studied for several years, is in late senescence, rapidly changing to the terrestrial stages of its succession. On casual inspection, the massed verdure of pondweeds and epiphytes, together with sporadic algal blooms, appears to indicate great photosynthetic productivity. As pointed out by Wesenberg-Lund ('12), littoral areas of lakes are virtual hothouses, absorbing more radiant energy per unit volume than deeper areas. At the present time the entire aquatic area of Cedar Bog Lake is essentially littoral in nature, and its productivity per cubic meter of water is probably greater than at any time in its history. However, since radiant energy (λ_0) enters a lake only from the surface, productivity must be defined in terms of surface area. In these terms, the present photosynthetic productivity pales into insignificance when compared with less advanced lakes in similar edaphic regions; for instance, λ_1 is less than $\frac{1}{3}$ that of Lake Mendota, Wisconsin (cf. table IV). These facts attest the essential accuracy of Welch's ('35) generalization that productivity declines greatly during senescence. An interesting principle demonstrated in Cedar Bog Lake (Lindeman, '41b) is that during late lake senescence general productivity (λ_n) is increasingly influenced by climatic factors, acting through water level changes, drainage, duration of winter ice, snow cover, etc., to affect the presence and abundance of practically all food groups in the lake.

Terrestrial stages.—As an aquatic ecosystem passes into terrestrial phases, fluctuations in atmospheric factors increasingly affect its productivity. ⋅ As succession proceeds, both the species-composition and the productivity of an ecosystem increasingly reflect the effects of the regional climate. Qualitatively, these climatic effects are known for soil morphology (Joffe, '36), autotrophic vegetation (Clements, '16), fauna (Clements and Shelford, '39) and soil microbiota (Braun-Blanquet, '32), in fact for every important component of the food cycle. Quantitatively, these effects have been so little studied that generalizations are most hazardous. It seems probable, however, that productivity tends to increase until the system approaches maturity. Clements and Shelford ('39, p. 116) assert that both plant and animal productivity is generally greatest in the subclimax, except possibly in the case of grasslands. Terrestrial ecosystems are primarily convex topographically and thus subject to a certain nutrient loss by erosion, which may or may not be made up by increased availability of such nutrients as can be extracted from the "C" soil horizon.

Successional productivity curves.—In recapitulating the probable photosynthetic productivity relationships in hydrarch succession, we shall venture to diagram (figure 3) a hypothetical hydrosere, developing from a moderately deep lake in a fertile cold temperate region under relatively constant climatic conditions. The initial period of oligotrophy is believed to be relatively short (Hutchinson and Wollack, '40; Lindeman '41a), with productivity rapidly increasing until eutrophic stage-equilibrium is attained. The duration of high eutrophic productivity depends upon the mean depth of the basin and upon the rate of sedimentation, and productivity fluctuates about a high eutrophic mean until the lake becomes too shallow for maximum growth of phytoplankton or regeneration of nutrients from the ooze. As the lake becomes shallower and more senescent, productivity is increasingly influenced by climatic fluctuations and

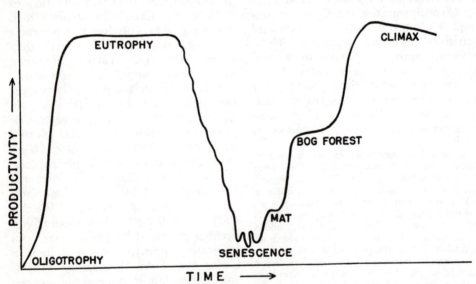

FIG. 3. Hypothetical productivity growth-curve of a hydrosere, developing from a deep lake to climax in a fertile, cold-temperate region.

gradually declines to a minimum as the lake is completely filled with sediments.

The terrestrial aspects of hydrarch succession in cold temperate regions usually follow sharply defined, distinctive stages. In lake basins which are poorly drained, the first stage consists of a mat, often partly floating, made up primarily of sedges and grasses or (in more coastal regions) such heaths as *Chamaedaphne* and *Kalmia* with certain species of sphagnum moss (cf. Rigg, '40). The mat stage is usually followed by a bog forest stage, in which the dominant species is *Larix laricina*, *Picea mariana* or *Thuja occidentalis*. The bog forest stage may be relatively permanent ("edaphic" climax) or succeeded to a greater or lesser degree by the regional climax vegetation. The stage-productivities indicated in figure 3 represent only crude relative estimates, as practically no quantitative data are available.

Efficiency relationships in succession

The successional changes of photosynthetic efficiency in natural areas (with respect to solar radiation, i.e., $\frac{\lambda_1}{\lambda_0} 100$) have not been intensively studied. In lake succession, photosynthetic efficiency would be expected to follow the same course deduced for productivity, rising to a more or less constant value during eutrophic stage-equilibrium, and declining during senescence, as suggested by a photosynthetic efficiency of at least 0.27 per cent for eutrophic Lake Mendota (Juday, '40) and of 0.10 per cent for senescent Cedar Bog Lake. For the terrestrial hydrosere, efficiency would likewise follow a curve similar to that postulated for productivity.

Rough estimates of photosynthetic efficiency for various climatic regions of the earth have been summarized from the literature by Hutchinson (unpublished). These estimates, corrected for respiration, do not appear to be very reliable because of imperfections in the original observations, but are probably of the correct order of magnitude. The mean photosynthetic efficiency for the sea is given as 0.31 per cent (after Riley, '41). The mean photosynthetic efficiency for terrestrial areas of the earth is given as 0.09 per cent $\pm$ 0.02 per cent (after Noddack, '37), for forests as 0.16 per cent, for cultivated lands as 0.13 per cent, for steppes as 0.05 per cent, and for deserts as 0.004 per cent. The mean photosynthetic efficiency for the earth as a whole is given as 0.25 per cent. Hutchinson has suggested (cf. Hutchinson and Lindeman, '41) that numerical efficiency values may provide "the most fundamental possible classification of biological formations and of their developmental stages."

Almost nothing is known concerning the efficiencies of consumer groups in succession. The general chronological increase in numbers of *Bosmina* carapaces with respect to organic matter and of *Chaoborus* fragments with respect to *Bosmina* carapaces in the sediments of Linsley Pond (Deevey, '42) suggests progressively increasing efficiencies of zooplankters and plankton predators. On the other hand, Hutchinson ('42) concludes from a comparison of the P : Z (phytoplankton : zooplankton) biomass ratios of several oligotrophic alpine lakes, ca 1 : 2 (Ruttner, '37), as compared with the ratios for Linsley Pond, 1 : 0.22 (Riley, '40) and three eutrophic Bavarian lakes, 1 : 0.25 (Heinrich, '34), that "as the phytoplankton crop is increased the zooplankton by no means keeps pace with the increase." Data compiled by Deevey ('41) for lakes in both mesotrophic (Connecticut) and eutrophic regions (southern Wisconsin), indicate that the deeper or morphometrically "younger" lakes have a lower ratio of bottom fauna to the standing crop of plankton (10–15 per cent) than the shallower lakes which have attained eutrophic equilibrium (22–27 per cent). The ratios for senescent Cedar Bog Lake, while not directly comparable because of its essentially littoral nature, are even higher. These meager data suggest that the efficiencies of consumer groups may increase throughout the aquatic phases of succession.

For terrestrial stages, no consumer efficiency data are available. A suggestive series of species-frequencies in mesarch succession was published by Vera Smith-Davidson ('32), which indicated greatly increasing numbers of arthropods in successive stages approaching the regional climax. Since the photosynthetic productivity of the stages probably also increased, it is impossible to determine progressive efficiency relationships. The problems of biological efficiencies present a practically virgin field, which appears to offer abundant rewards for studies guided by a trophic-dynamic viewpoint.

In conclusion, it should be emphasized that the trophic-dynamic principles indicated in the following summary cannot be expected to hold for every single case, in accord with the known facts of biological variability. *à priori*, however, these principles appear to be valid for the vast majority of cases, and may be expected to possess a statistically significant probability of validity for any case selected at random. Since the available data summarized in this paper are far too meager to establish such generalizations on a statistical basis, it is highly important that further studies be initiated to test the validity of these and other trophic-dynamic principles.

SUMMARY

1. Analyses of food-cycle relationships indicate that a biotic community cannot be clearly differentiated from its abiotic environment; the *ecosystem* is hence regarded as the more fundamental ecological unit.

2. The organisms within an ecosystem may be grouped into a series of more or less discrete trophic levels (Λ_1, Λ_2, Λ_3, . . . Λ_n) as producers, primary consumers, secondary consumers, etc., each successively dependent upon the preceding level as a source of energy, with the producers (Λ_1) directly dependent upon the rate of incident solar radiation (productivity λ_0) as a source of energy.

3. The more remote an organism is from the initial source of energy (solar radiation), the less probable that it will be dependent solely upon the preceding trophic level as a source of energy.

4. The progressive energy relationships of the food levels of an "Eltonian Pyramid" may be epitomized in terms of the productivity symbol λ, as follows:

$$\lambda_0 > \lambda_1 > \lambda_2 . . . > \lambda_n.$$

5. The percentage loss of energy due to respiration is progressively greater for higher levels in the food cycle. Respiration with respect to growth is about 33 per cent for producers, 62 per cent for primary consumers, and more than 100 per cent for secondary consumers.

6. The consumers at progressively higher levels in the food cycle appear to be progressively more efficient in the use of their food supply. This generalization can be reconciled with the preceding one by remembering that increased activity of predators considerably increases the chances of encountering suitable prey.

7. Productivity and efficiency increase during the early phases of successional development. In lake succession, productivity and photosynthetic efficiency increase from oligotrophy to a prolonged eutrophic stage-equilibrium and decline with lake senescence, rising again in the terrestrial stages of hydrarch succession.

8. The progressive efficiencies of consumer levels, on the basis of very meager data, apparently tend to increase throughout the aquatic phases of succession.

ACKNOWLEDGMENTS

The author is deeply indebted to Professor G. E. Hutchinson of Yale University, who has stimulated many of the trophic concepts developed here, generously placed at the author's disposal several unpublished manuscripts, given valuable counsel, and aided the final development of this paper in every way possible. Many· of the concepts embodied in the successional sections of this paper were developed independently by Professor Hutchinson at Yale and by the author as a graduate student at the University of Minnesota. Subsequent to an exchange of notes, a joint preliminary abstract was published (Hutchinson and Lindeman, '41). The author wishes to express gratitude to the mentors and friends at the University of Minnesota who encouraged and helpfully criticized the initial development of these concepts, particularly Drs. W. S. Cooper, Samuel Eddy, A. C. Hodson, D. B. Lawrence and J. B. Moyle, as well as other members of the local Ecological Discussion Group. The author is also indebted to Drs. J. R. Carpenter, E. S. Deevey, H. J. Lutz, A. E. Parr, G. A. Riley and V. E. Shelford, as well as the persons mentioned above, for critical reading of preliminary manuscripts. Grateful acknowledgment is made to the Graduate School, Yale University, for the award of a Sterling Fellowship in Biology during 1941–1942.

Literature Cited

Allee, W. C. 1934. Concerning the organization of marine coastal communities. Ecol. Monogr., 4: 541–554.

Birge, E. A., and C. Juday. 1922. The inland lakes of Wisconsin. The plankton. Part I. Its quantity and chemical composition. Bull. Wisconsin Geol. Nat. Hist. Surv., 64: 1–222.

Bodenheimer, F. S. 1938. Problems of Animal Ecology. London. Oxford University Press.

Braun-Blanquet, J. 1932. Plant Sociology. N. Y. McGraw-Hill Co.

Brujewicz, S. W. 1939. Distribution and dynamics of living matter in the Caspian Sea. Compt. Rend. Acad. Sci. URSS, 25: 138–141.

Carpenter, J. R. 1939. The biome. Amer. Midl. Nat., 21: 75–91.

——. 1940. The grassland biome. Ecol. Monogr., 10: 617–687.

Clements, F. E. 1916. Plant Succession. Carnegie Inst. Washington Publ., No. 242.

—— and **V. E. Shelford.** 1939. Bio-Ecology. N. Y. John Wiley & Co.

Cooper, W. S. 1926. The fundamentals of vegetational change. Ecology, 7: 391–413.

Cowles, H. C. 1899. The ecological relations of the vegetation of the sand dunes of Lake Michigan. Bot. Gaz., 27: 95–391.

Davidson, V. S. 1932. The effect of seasonal variability upon animal species in a deciduous forest succession. Ecol. Monogr., 2: 305–334.

Deevey, E. S. 1939. Studies on Connecticut lake sediments: I. A postglacial climatic chronology for southern New England. Amer. Jour. Sci., 237: 691–724.

——. 1941. Limnological studies in Connecticut: VI. The quantity and composition of the bottom fauna. Ecol. Monogr., 11: 413–455.

——. 1942. Studies on Connecticut lake sediments: III. The biostratonomy of Linsley Pond. Amer. Jour. Sci., 240: 233–264, 313–338.

Elton, C. 1927. Animal Ecology. N. Y. Macmillan Co.

France, R. H. 1913. Das Edaphon, Untersuchungen zur Oekologie der bodenbewohnenden Mikroorganismen. Deutsch. Mikrolog. Gesellsch., Arbeit. aus d. Biol. Inst., No. 2. Munich.

Friederichs, K. 1930. Die Grundfragen und Gesetzmässigkeiten der land- und forstwirtschaftlichen Zoologie. 2 vols. Berlin. Verschlag. Paul Parey.

Groschopf, P. 1936. Die postglaziale Entwicklung des Grosser Plöner Sees in Ostholstein auf Grund pollenanalytischer Sedimentuntersuchungen. Arch. Hydrobiol., 30: 1–84.

Heinrich, K. 1934. Atmung und Assimilation im freien Wasser. Internat. Rev. ges. Hydrobiol. u. Hydrogr., 30: 387–410.

Hentschel, E. 1933–1936. Allgemeine Biologie des Südatlantischen Ozeans. Wiss. Ergebn. Deutsch. Atlant. Exped. a. d. Forschungs- u. Vermessungsschiff "Meteor" 1925–1927. Bd. XI.

Hicks, P. A. 1934. Interaction of factors in the growth of *Lemna*: V. Some preliminary observations upon the interaction of temperature and light on the growth of *Lemna*. Ann. Bot., 48: 515–523.

Hile, R. 1941. Age and growth of the rock bass *Ambloplites rupestris* (Rafinesque) in Nebish Lake, Wisconsin. Trans. Wisconsin Acad. Sci., Arts, Lett., 33: 189–337.

Hutchinson, G. E. 1941. Limnological studies in Connecticut: IV. Mechanism of intermediary metabolism in stratified lakes. Ecol. Monogr., 11: 21–60.

——. 1942. Recent Advances in Limnology (*in manuscript*).

—— and **R. L. Lindeman.** 1941. Biological efficiency in succession (Abstract). Bull. Ecol. Soc. Amer., 22: 44.

—— and **Anne Wollack.** 1940. Studies on Connecticut lake sediments: II. Chemical analyses of a core from Linsley Pond, North Branford. Amer. Jour. Sci., 238: 493–517.

Huxley, J. S. 1932. Problems of Relative Growth. N. Y. Dial Press.

Ivlev, V. S. 1939a. Transformation of energy by aquatic animals. Internat. Rev. ges. Hydrobiol. u. Hydrogr., 38: 449–458.

——. 1939b. Balance of energy in carps. Zool. Zhurn. Moscow, 18: 303–316.

Jacot, A. P. 1940. The fauna of the soil. Quart. Rev. Biol., 15: 28–58.

Jenkin, B. M., C. H. Mortimer, and W. Pennington. 1941. The study of lake deposits.
Nature, 147: 496–500.

Joffe, J. S. 1936. Pedology. New Brunswick,
New Jersey. Rutgers Univ. Press.

Juday, C. 1922. Quantitative studies of the
bottom fauna in the deeper waters of Lake
Mendota. Trans. Wisconsin Acad. Sci.,
Arts, Lett., 20: 461–493.

——. 1940. The annual energy budget of an
inland lake. Ecology, 21: 438–450.

Krogh, A. 1941. The Comparative Physiology
of Respiratory Mechanisms. Philadelphia.
Univ. Pennsylvania Press.

Lindeman, R. L. 1941a. The developmental
history of Cedar Creek Bog, Minnesota.
Amer. Midl. Nat., 25: 101–112.

——. 1941b. Seasonal food-cycle dynamics in
a senescent lake. Amer. Midl. Nat., 26:
636–673.

Lohmann, H. 1912. Untersuchungen über das
Pflanzen- und Tierleben der Hochsee, zu-
gleich ein Bericht über die biologischen Ar-
beiten auf der Fahrt der "Deutschland" von
Bremerhaven nach Buenos Aires. Veröffentl.
d. Inst. f. Meereskunde, N.F., A. Geogr.-
naturwissen. Reihe, Heft 1, 92 pp.

Lundegårdh, H. 1924. Kreislauf der Kohlen-
säure in der Natur. Jena. G. Fischer.

Meschkat, A. 1937. Abwasserbiologische Untersuchungen in einem Buhnenfeld unterhalb
Hamburgs. Arch. Hydrobiol., 31: 399–432.

Moore, W. G. 1941. Studies on the feeding
habits of fishes. Ecology, 22: 91–95.

Needham, J. 1931. Chemical Embryology.
3 vols. N. Y. Cambridge University Press.

Noddack, W. 1937. Der Kohlenstoff im Haushalt der Natur. Zeitschr. angew. Chemie,
50: 505–510.

Park, Thomas. 1941. The laboratory population as a test of a comprehensive ecological
system. Quart. Rev. Biol., 16: 274–293,
440–461.

Rigg, G. B. 1940. Comparisons of the development of some Sphagnum bogs of the Atlantic coast, the interior, and the Pacific
coast. Amer. Jour. Bot., 27: 1–14.

Riley, G. A. 1940. Limnological studies in
Connecticut. III. The plankton of Linsley
Pond. Ecol. Monogr., 10: 279–306.

——. 1941. Plankton studies. III. Long Island Sound. Bull. Bingham Oceanogr. Coll.
7 (3): 1–93.

Ruttner, F. 1937. Limnologische Studien an
einigen Seen der Ostalpen. Arch. Hydrobiol., 32: 167–319.

Smith-Davidson, Vera. 1932. The effect of
seasonal variability upon animal species in a
deciduous forest succession. Ecol. Monogr.,
2: 305–334.

Spoehr, H. A. 1926. Photosynthesis. N. Y.
Chemical Catalogue Co.

Swingle, H. S., and E. V. Smith. 1940. Experiments on the stocking of fish ponds.
Trans. North Amer. Wildlife Conf., 5: 267–
276.

Tansley, A. G. 1935. The use and abuse of
vegetational concepts and terms. Ecology,
16: 284–307.

Thienemann, A. 1918. Lebensgemeinschaft
und Lebensraum. Naturw. Wochenschrift,
N.F., 17: 282–290, 297–303.

——. 1926. Der Nahrungskreislauf im Wasser. Verh. deutsch. Zool. Ges., 31: 29–79.
(or) Zool. Anz. Suppl., 2: 29–79.

——. 1939. Grundzüge einen allgemeinen
Oekologie. Arch. Hydrobiol., 35: 267–285.

Thompson, D. H. 1941. The fish production
of inland lakes and streams. Symposium
on Hydrobiology, pp. 206–217. Madison.
Univ. Wisconsin Press.

Tutin, T. G. 1941. The hydrosere and current
concepts of the climax. Jour. Ecol. 29: 268–
279.

Vernadsky, V. I. 1929. La biosphere. Paris.
Librairie Felix Alcan.

——. 1939. On some fundamental problems
of biogeochemistry. Trav. Lab. Biogeochem.
Acad. Sci. URSS, 5: 5–17.

Waksman, S. A. 1941. Aquatic bacteria in
relation to the cycle of organic matter in
lakes. Symposium on Hydrobiology, pp.
86–105. Madison. Univ. Wisconsin Press.

Welch, P. S. 1935. Limnology. N. Y. Mc-
Graw-Hill Co.

Wesenberg-Lund, C. 1912. Über einige eigen-
tümliche Temperaturverhaltnisse in der Lito-
ralregion. . . . Internat. Rev. ges. Hydrobiol. u. Hydrogr., 5: 287–316.

Williams, E. C. 1941. An ecological study of
the floor fauna of the Panama rain forest.
Bull. Chicago Acad. Sci., 6: 63–124.

Wimpenny, R. S. 1941. Organic polarity:
some ecological and physiological aspects.
Quart. Rev. Biol., 16: 389–425.

ZoBell, C. E., and C. B. Feltham. 1938. Bacteria as food for certain marine invertebrates.
Jour. Marine Research, 1: 312–327.

ADDENDUM

While this, his sixth completed paper, was in
the press, Raymond Lindeman died after a long
illness on 29 June, 1942, in his twenty-seventh
year. While his loss is grievous to all who knew
him, it is more fitting here to dwell on the
achievements of his brief working life. The
present paper represents a synthesis of Lindeman's work on the modern ecology and past
history of a small senescent lake in Minnesota.
In studying this locality he came to realize, as
others before him had done, that the most profit-
able method of analysis lay in reduction of all
the interrelated biological events to energetic
terms. The attempt to do this led him far

beyond the immediate problem in hand, and in stating his conclusions he felt that he was providing a program for further studies. Knowing that one man's life at best is too short for intensive studies of more than a few localities, and before the manuscript was completed, that he might never return again to the field, he wanted others to think in the same terms as he had found so stimulating, and for them to collect material that would confirm, extend, or correct his theoretical conclusions. The present contribution does far more than this, as here for the first time, we have the interrelated dynamics of a biocoenosis presented in a form that is amenable to a productive abstract analysis. The question, for instance, arises, "What determines the length of a food chain?"; the answer given is admittedly imperfect, but it is far more important to have seen that there is a real problem of this kind to be solved. That the final statement of the structure of a biocoenosis consists of pairs of numbers, one an integer determining the level, one a fraction determining the efficiency, may even give some hint of an undiscovered type of mathematical treatment of biological communities. Though Lindeman's work on the ecology and history of Cedar Bog Lake is of more than local interest, and will, it is hoped, appear of even greater significance when the notes made in the last few months of his life can be coordinated and published, it is to the present paper that we must turn as the major contribution of one of the most creative and generous minds yet to devote itself to ecological science.

G. Evelyn Hutchinson.
Yale University.

ECOLOGICAL ENERGY RELATIONSHIPS AT THE POPULATION LEVEL*

L. B. SLOBODKIN

Department of Zoology, University of Michigan, Ann Arbor, Michigan

I will be concerned with the ecologically significant energy relationships of single species populations. The theoretical analysis and data deal primarily with laboratory populations of *Daphnia pulex*, but I believe that the conclusions have significance for nature as will be indicated in the discussion.

The number and kind of organisms found in nature is variable from year to year and even from day to day. Despite this variability, it can be said that a sufficiently detailed and temporally extensive examination of any one species, or even of an isolated population of a species, will show that the number of organisms and volume of protoplasm represented by that species or population remain approximately constant. Some populations may vary in size in a cyclic way, either annually or possibly with some other period; others may vary in a random way, but in any case there is some definite mean population size, if data over a period of the order of ten times the mean generation time is considered.

Mean population size does not represent an equilibrium value in the sense that the position of a pendulum bob at rest represents an equilibrium, but rather represents a steady state. The steady state can be characterized by the fact that it requires energy for its maintenance. Just as the steady state temperature gradients in a metal bar heated at one end would disappear in the absence of an energy source, so the steady state properties of the ecological world would vanish in the absence of the radiant energy of sunlight.

It is possible to conceive of a series of metal bars in contact at their ends, with the terminal bar converting radiant energy into heat and this heat then being transmitted by conduction through the whole series of bars. Again a steady state temperature gradient would characterize each bar. Similarly in nature radiant energy is converted into potential energy by the green plants and this potential energy is transmitted through a chain of organisms. There will be various steady state values characterizing this chain of organisms. We will be concerned with some of the values that are more or less immediately recognizable as functions of energy, in particular the potential energy, contained in the various single species populations, that is, the standing crops, and with the ratios between the various steady state rates of energy transfer in the system, that is, the efficiencies (Lindeman, 1942).

*Presented at "Interactions in Nature: A Symposium on Modern Ecology" at the meeting of the American Society of Naturalists, cosponsored by the Ecological Society of America and the American Society of Limnology and Oceanography, Chicago, Illinois, December 27–28, 1959.

I have confined myself to steady state values since a short period of very high ecological efficiency or standing crop maintenance has very little applicability to long term values that are likely to occur in nature. Non-steady state efficiencies or standing crops must eventually receive intensive study, but I feel that more immediate progress will be made by considering them as minor perturbations of the steady state values for the moment.

Examining the analogy between metal bars, electric wires, flowing water and other inanimate models on one hand and an ecological community on the other, it is seen that the analogy breaks down almost immediately. In a heat transmission system or in an electric wiring diagram the continued physical existence of the energy transmitting elements is not contingent on the maintenance of energy flow. In a biological system, if energy flow ceases there is almost immediate dissolution of the system's components.

The process of energy flow in ecological systems does not lend itself to discussion in terms of gradients or flow diagrams, except on the most rudimentary level. Flow diagrams are primarily suitable to discussion of heat or radiant energy transport in which physical contact or simply suitable geometric distribution of the physical elements will permit energy flow to occur. In ecological interactions the energy involved is in the form of potential energy, which in general can not be transmitted between parts of a system without displacement or distortion of the physical elements. That is, energy flows from a plant population to an animal population only when a concrete plant or piece of plant is physically removed into the body of some particular animal. It only remains for the ecologist, if he is to concern himself with energy at all, to develop his theories and concepts on a biological basis rather than by assuming the direct applicability of the laws developed for the simple systems of physics and electronics.

Even such elementary concepts as efficiency and energy, and such universal generalizations as the second law of thermodynamics have very peculiar properties on the level of the ecological community.

I will therefore discuss the concepts of efficiency, energy and entropy as they apply to ecology. Ecological efficiency will then be shown to have at least three distinct, operationally defined meanings. These three different concepts of efficiency will be evaluated from the data on *Daphnia pulex*. I will then suggest that certain kinds of efficiency are actually constant for most populations in nature. I will finish with some speculations on the relation between energetics and the future development of a complete theory of community ecology.

AN ELEMENTARY CLARIFICATION OF EFFICIENCY, ENTROPY AND ENERGY IN ECOLOGICAL SYSTEMS

The superficial simplicity of the concept of ecological efficiency requires careful analysis.

The efficiency of an energy machine is easy to define. A machine, in general, is designed and constructed to do a particular kind of work or to produce a particular form of energy. The ratio of the output to the input (both in energy units) is the efficiency of the machine. The output of a moving locomotive is in energy used to overcome the forces that tend to stop the train; the input is in the potential energy of coal or oil burned in the process. The output of a light bulb is in visible radiation; the input in electrical energy and the ratio of the two is the efficiency. But notice that it is possible to read by the light of a coal locomotive's fire box or to warm oneself at a cloth-draped light bulb. These do not seem particularly clever ways to read or to keep warm, but they are conceivable. From the standpoint of a moronic bookworm the efficiency of a locomotive might be measured as the ratio of visible radiant energy from the fire box to potential energy consumption. For most locomotives this efficiency is lower than our initial calculations of the efficiency of the locomotive. Our chilled illiterate in front of the draped light bulb might measure efficiency as total radiant energy output over total electrical energy input and this ratio would be higher than our original estimate of the efficiency of the bulb. I conclude from this that the magnitude of an efficiency need have nothing to do with the importance of the process to which the efficiency ratio refers, even in the case of a machine.

An organism must do many things that require energy. Movement of its internal parts, movement of itself in its environment, producing new protoplasm to compensate for attrition of its own body, adding new protoplasm to its own body and producing offspring are all energy utilizing processes involving single organisms. On the level of the individual we will be concerned with the efficiency of the last two of these only.

This limitation of our concern is due to a peculiar property of ecological interactions. In order to maintain an ecological community of several kinds of animals and plants at a steady state, the new protoplasm made by any population of organisms of any one species, above and beyond replacement requirements, must be consumed during the process of maintaining the steady state of one or more of the other species present. The new protoplasm produced by any population is in one sense a sum of the new growth occurring in all the individuals of that population. I will therefore consider only new protoplasm to be an ecologically useful kind of potential energy and will largely ignore other possible uses of energy on the individual level.

It is impossible to refer to *the efficiency* of a population. The term must, at all times, be qualified. We can speak only of the efficiency of producing energy in some form which we arbitrarily consider useful (the output) from some other form which we arbitrarily define as useless (the input).

The concept of energy is used rather loosely in ecological literature, and recently the concepts of entropy, negative entropy and information have been used equally loosely. We have statements in print that organisms live on order or that communities consume negative entropy, eat information, etc. It therefore seems appropriate to present a statement of the role of energy in ecology.

Radiant energy is absorbed by green plants and part of this is converted to potential energy by the process of photosynthesis. The slow conversion of this potential energy to kinetic energy permits ecological communities to survive.

Particular compounds in the plant will be converted into other compounds in the herbivore. To the extent that individual reversible chemical reactions are being considered the various terms in the equation

(1) $$\Delta H = \Delta F + T \Delta S$$

may be evaluated and the change in entropy per mole computed. An appropriate summation of the entropy contributions of all the reactions that occur in the process of incorporating plant material into the herbivore might be considered the entropy production of the herbivore, were it not that:

1. All of the reactions tend to interact with each other.
2. Phase differences and structural restrictions of complicated kinds occur in both plants and animals and the reactions producing these phase differences are, in general, not reversible in any practical sense, at least in the aggregate.

In other words, it is very difficult by simply supplying energy to get an organism to undigest a meal and thereby measure the ΔF associated with the digestion process. The entropy associated with the process of food assimilation is therefore not conveniently measurable.

It is possible to consider the state of all materials entering an organism and the state of the material leaving the organism, duplicate the degradation process in a reversible way and make the appropriate entropy calculation. To my knowledge this has never been explicitly done for all of the ingested and waste products of any particular organism. It is clear, in principle, that it could be done and if it were done we would find an increase in entropy associated with this passage through the organism as illustrated:

$$\Delta H \longrightarrow \boxed{\text{organism}} \longrightarrow \Delta F + T \Delta S + Q'$$

(2) $$\Delta H = \Delta F + Q' + T \Delta S$$

This requires explication. ΔH can be defined as calories ingested per unit time and ΔF in this context is the calories egested which are still of use to organisms as a supply of energy. $T \Delta S + Q'$ are the caloric equivalent of the heat produced in the utilization of the energy ΔH.

$T \Delta S$ is the heat that would be produced in the various transformations occurring in the organism on the assumption that all reactions were reversible, independent, and of infinitely slow occurrence. None of these conditions is met.

Q' is the heat produced from friction within the organism and from work done by the organism on its environment. In principle, Q' can be evaluated experimentally, but the problem is technically difficult; and except for very simple systems is not likely to be done. It is possible, in an ecological steady state, to write the equation:

Caloric equivalent of the potential energy ingested = caloric equivalent of the potential energy removed from the population by egestion, predation, mortality, etc., plus the heat produced by the population.

It may be legitimate to equate this heat to entropy, but it is not clear what proportion of the potential energy ingested actually shows up as entropy. Estimates of anywhere from two to 50 per cent might be offered.

The notion of entropy content of a living organism is extremely complex. Normal thermodynamic theories apply to an equilibrium state, which is equivalent in one sense to death. The theory of thermodynamics of steady states (Denbigh, 1951) is not yet capable of handling elaborate multiphasic systems. The Onsager equations which permit some development of steady state thermodynamics depend on the rigorous definition of fluxes and on their associated forces.

Any energy gradient of an appropriate sort can be considered a generalized force. This·is particularly evident in the relation between a temperature gradient and heat flow. The interesting ecological energy flow is in the form of potential energy. Potential energy can have a gradient, as in the glucose gradient in a single cell. Ecologically, however, the gradient is a rather coarse histogram, of standing crop vs. trophic level. The precise procedure for the interpretation of this histogram as a generalized force seems unclear.

The fluxes can, therefore, be stated but the forces can only be dealt with on an almost metaphorical level in ecology. While metaphor leads to certain sorts of insight it does not have predictive power.

A further complication in the application of thermodynamics to steady state systems has been considered by Foster, Rappoport and Trucco (1957) who find that Prigogine's theorem, which states that steady state systems tend to a condition of minimum entropy production, is not applicable to certain types of feedback systems. It is now generally conceded that individual organisms, populations of organisms, and natural communities must be treated as complex feedback systems and it is quite likely that Prigogine's theorem does not apply to ecological systems, or at least its validity can not simply be assumed.

Potential energy (ΔH) can be approximately measured by direct combustion of dried tissue. A certain amount of entropy ought to be subtracted from the combustion calories but this is not practical for reasons indicated above. Some free energy is lost prior to combustion in the drying process but this has not yet been evaluated.

When I speak of the energy content of an organism I will be referring to the calories released by burning that organism under normal atmospheric conditions and measured as heat. This is equal to the difference in potential energy per gram between dried protoplasm and the various oxidation products of that protoplasm and includes both the free energy and the entropy.

When I refer to a flow of energy through a population I will be considering only the steady state in which the rate of energy accumulation is zero.

THEORY OF ECOLOGICAL EFFICIENCIES AND THEIR INTERACTIONS

A population of organisms is characterized by new animals being born, by animals dying or being consumed (by other animals or by man). I will be concerned with the potential energy content of the animals removed from the population by predators or man as a useful energy output and will consider the food consumed by the population as the energy input. That is, when I speak of ecological efficiency, I am assuming the viewpoint of a predator.

In one sense, the removal of an animal by a predator can be considered a divergence of energy from the other possible roles it might play in the population. In particular, the greater the rate at which yield is removed from the population the smaller the standing crop that the population is capable of maintaining. The yield to the predator divided by the difference between the energy used in maintaining a population in the absence of predation and that used in maintaining the same population under predation will be called the population efficiency.

The ratio of the potential energy in an individual organism to the potential energy utilized in its birth and growth will be called growth efficiency, or individual growth efficiency.

The interrelation between these three concepts of efficiency is discussed below.

The gross inflow will be in units of calories per time per volume and will be designated I_F. This will be the amount of food made available to the population from some outside source. In nature food is available to an animal population as a result of the activities of some other population or populations of plants, animals or both. In the laboratory I_F is the potential energy in the food made available to the population by the experimenter. The population does not necessarily consume all of this food. In nature part of it may pass through the ecological space of a particular population without being altered at all. In the laboratory the experimenter may periodically remove excess food.

We must therefore distinguish between I_F, the food available, and I, the energy input or ingested food. $I_F \geq I$ is always trivially valid.

I is the potential energy ingested per day per population and therefore is slightly different in concept from I_F, unless the volume considered only contains one population. In experimental situations discussed here this difference is not significant.

Population size is effectively constant at a steady state in the absence of cropping, fishing and predation. In a typical experimental study of efficiency the population is cropped and censused at regular intervals so that a plot of population size as a function of time would be saw-toothed. For our present discussion we will consider the population size as the size at the base of the saw teeth. This is equivalent to assuming that no energy must be expended in maintaining those animals which are destined to be cropped at the next census. This assumption is not dangerous so long as the ratio $\left(\dfrac{\text{yield/census interval}}{\text{population size}} \right)$ is small. (See Armstrong, 1960.)

Let P' be the caloric content of the standing crop of a population subjected to some arbitrary predation process and let P be the caloric content of the appropriate control population in the absence of predation. P and P'

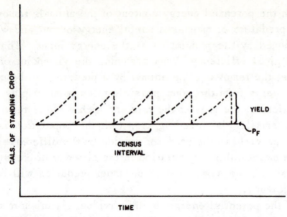

FIGURE 1. The term standing crop (P_F) is used as indicated in this diagram, ignoring the maintenance cost of the animals destined to constitute yield. A more precise but less convenient measure of standing crop would be the dotted line.

have the dimensions of calories and represent the potential energy maintained in the living protoplasm of the population. Occasionally we will use the letters P and P′ as names for populations.

In order to maintain living protoplasm, energy must be expended. The greater this energy expenditure per calorie of standing crop per time the smaller will be the value of P that can be maintained by a given energy income per day (I).

In general, increase of I will imply increase of P. The precise relation between P and I is not obvious *a priori* since the maintenance cost per calorie of standing crop may be a complicated function of the interactions between individual organisms in the population.

In the most general case, since there is a unique age distribution and total number of organisms corresponding to any steady state caloric content we can write

(3) $$I = Pc + P^2c′ + P^3c″ \ldots$$

where c is the proportion of the total cost in (calories/calorie day) of maintaining one calorie of standing crop which is assignable to first order interactions in the population, c′ the proportion assignable to second order interactions, etc.

It has been experimentally demonstrated in Daphnia that only first order interactions are significant over a wide range of population densities (Slobodkin, 1954) so that for the present discussion (3) reduces to

(3′) $$I = Pc.$$

When a population is subjected to predation it either becomes extinct or it comes to a new steady state caloric content P′. If the population can survive steady predation potential energy now leaves the population at some steady state rate as yield to the predator. The ratio of yield (Y) in calories per day to I is the ecological efficiency.

260

The age and size of the individuals that make up the yield is determined by the interaction between the predator's method and intensity of capturing the yield animals and the population dynamics of the prey and predator.

Assuming that I is not altered by predation, we can take account of the change in maintenance cost associated with predation writing

$$(4) \qquad I = P'(c + \Delta c) + (P')^2(c' + \Delta c')$$

and in the case of Daphnia populations

$$(4') \qquad I = P'c + P'\Delta c .$$

Assume the prey to consist only of animals of age i, taken by the predator at the rate Y_i calories/day. Then

$$(5) \qquad P'\Delta c = \frac{Y_i}{E_{pi}}$$

where E_{pi} is the efficiency, in one sense, of this predation process. An efficiency of this type will be referred to as a population efficiency. Since

$$(5') \qquad E_{pi} = \frac{Y_i}{P'\Delta c}$$

population efficiency can be interpreted as the ratio of yield of a particular kind to the increase of maintenance cost associated with the production of that yield. It will vary with the kind of organism taken as yield. It is independent of the intensity of predation so long as the linearity implicit in equation (4') holds.

The precise value of E_{pi} depends on growth and survival and their interaction with age in an intimate way which will be indicated below.

In order to clarify the meaning of E_{pi} we must examine an individual organism more closely. At the time an individual organism begins to take nourishment, say age j, it already represents the end product of a series of metabolic processes, all of which have involved the degradation of potential energy. As it grows to some arbitrary age, say i, it will consume more potential energy and may have increased its caloric content. In any case the total potential energy that must be used to replace an animal of age i > j will be greater than that required to replace an animal of age j.

If we designate the total energetic cost of replacing an animal age i as $\frac{S_i}{E_i}$, in which S_i is the caloric content of the animal age i, then E_i is the growth efficiency of this animal. The caloric content (S_i) is usually proportional to the size of the animal. E_i can be evaluated as the inverse of the total calories consumed in the production of one calorie of protoplasm at age i and is the "individual growth efficiency" of an animal aged i. It varies with the age and feeding rate of the animal concerned and with the energy expended by the parents of that individual in producing it.

The concept of growth efficiency has suffered in the past from failure to specify precisely the time interval over which the growth of the animal is to be considered. Here we have taken this as the entire life span over which an energetic cost can be meaningfully associated with the individual, following the suggestion of Armstrong (1960).

The relation between E_i and E_{pi} can be clarified as follows.

Let N_0 and N'_0 be the number of newborn animals produced per day in populations P and P' respectively, and let l_x and l'_x be the per cent survival to age x in the two populations respectively. Define q_x as

$$q_x = \frac{l_x - l_{x+1}}{l_x}$$

and correspondingly define q'_x.

Also let

(6) $\qquad\qquad d_x = q_x\, l_x$ and similarly for d'_x

and

(7) $\qquad\qquad D_x = d_x N_0$ and similarly for D'_x.

The deaths per day in population P is $\sum_0^\infty D_x$ and in population P', $\sum_0^\infty D'_x$. The primary characteristic of a steady state population is that births and deaths are equal and there is no change in mean total biomass with time.

The caloric cost per day of replacing the dying individuals and maintaining biomass constancy is $\sum \frac{D_x S_x}{E_x}$ in population P and assuming that caloric content as a function of age and growth efficiency are both dependent on predation $\sum \frac{D'_x S'_x}{E'_x}$ in population P'.

In other words

(8) $\qquad\qquad I = \sum_0^\infty \frac{D_x S_x}{E_x} = Pc$

$\qquad\qquad\qquad = \sum_0^\infty \frac{D'_x S'_x}{E'_x} = P'(c + \Delta c)$

whence

(9) $\qquad\qquad c = \frac{1}{P} \sum_0^\infty \frac{D_x S_x}{E_x}$

and

(10) $\qquad\qquad \Delta c = \frac{1}{P'}\left(\sum_0^\infty \frac{D'_x S'_x}{E'_x}\right) - \frac{1}{P}\left(\sum_0^\infty \frac{D_x S_x}{E_x}\right)$

and substituting (10) in (5') we define the population efficiency of animals age i as

$$(11) \qquad E_{pi} = \frac{Y_i}{\left(\sum_0^\infty \frac{D'_x S'_x}{E'_x}\right) - \frac{P'}{P}\left(\sum_0^\infty \frac{D_x S_x}{E_x}\right)}$$

or if food ingestion is constant under predation simply:

$$(11') \qquad E_{pi} = \frac{Y_i}{I\left(1 - \frac{P'}{P}\right)}$$

From equation (11) it can be seen that population efficiency varies inversely with the depletion of standing crop population size associated with the removal of the yield. Decrease in life expectancy with predation also lowers population efficiency. A predator would be acting with maximum prudence if he removed yield from his prey in such a way as to maximize population efficiency.

We will return to this concept after we have considered ecological efficiency. The commonest usage of the term efficiency in ecological literature is the ratio of the energy per unit time taken from some population (the prey) as yield by some other population (the predator) to the energy per unit time ingested by the prey population. I am deliberately ignoring the often made distinction between ingestion and assimilation, since the meaning of ingestion seems fairly clear while it is an almost arbitrary matter to decide when, or what portion of, a particular mouthful of food is assimilated.

Food chain efficiency (a term borrowed from LaMont Cole) is similar to ecological efficiency except that the denominator is the food available (I_F) rather than the food ingested (I).

Ecological efficiency (E) is therefore defined by $\frac{Y}{I}$. Since population efficiency is defined for any constant predation method, if I is not changed by predation

$$(12) \qquad E = E_p\left(1 - \frac{P'}{P}\right),$$

from which it is clear that for any predation method

$$(13) \qquad E \leq E_p .$$

The relation $E = E_p$ will hold only for a scavenger or for a predator which replaces some other source of mortality. If there is any selective advantage in maintaining a large standing crop, a predator population will tend to maximize yield from its prey. This is equivalent to maximizing food chain efficiency $\left(\frac{Y}{I_F}\right)$. As predation becomes more intense, the food consuming capacity and standing crop of the prey population will decrease. The decrease of prey standing crop associated with a given yield can be minimized by the predator if he chooses his yield in such a way as to maximize population efficiency. This can generally be accomplished by taking yield animals which are about to die in any case, so that their replacement cost would have to be paid even in the absence of the predator.

APPLICATION OF THE THEORY

First order evaluations of the various concepts of efficiency have been made in laboratory populations of *Daphnia pulex* by Richman (1958), Armstrong (1960) and Slobodkin (1959). All three workers have depended on the caloric determinations of *D. pulex* and *Chlamydomonas reinhardi* made by Richman.

Richman (1958) analyzed the growth and feeding of *Daphnia pulex*.

Slobodkin provided an initial theoretical analysis of laboratory predation experiments (1959) and that analysis has been considerably amplified and modified in the present paper.

Armstrong has reconsidered certain of the theoretical assumptions of both Richman and Slobodkin and has amplified their calculations, in addition to providing new data on growth and predation.

All three workers dealt with a system consisting of *Daphnia pulex* and *Chlamydomonas reinhardi* in which the Daphnia were maintained in conditioned tap water and the algae were grown on sterile agar. Algae was fed to the Daphnia by washing it off the agar, measuring its optical density with a photometer and adding an aliquot of suspension to the Daphnia. Any of the three above cited papers will provide more detailed information on culture techniques.

Richman collected 50 mg. dry samples of Chlamydomonas. These were combined with 250 mg. of benzoic acid and burned in a semi-micro calorimeter bomb. Twelve determinations gave a mean of 5289 cal./gm. on a dry weight basis or 5506 on an ash-free dry weight basis. These figures are very close to those for other Chlorophyceae. The mean of 17 analysis of five species reported by Ketchum and Redfield (1949) is 5340 cal./gm. dry weight and 6154 cal./gm. ash-free dry weight. The caloric content of one Chlamydomonas cell is given by Richman as 1.308×10^{-6} cal.

He sorted *Daphnia pulex* into three size categories. Dried samples of 10–25 mg. were combined with c. 275 mg. of benzoic acid and burned. Mean caloric contents per gram were 4059 ± 203, 4124 ± 229 and 5075 ± 235 respectively for animals of mean length 0.7, 1.3 and 1.8 mm.

Trama found from 5295 to 5975 cal./gm. in the may fly *Stenonema pulchellum* (Trama, 1957). Golley (undated mimeographed sheets) reports cal./gm. determinations for a variety of animals. The extremes are 1780 for the mud crab *Panopius herbsti* and 6273 for *Mus musculus*. Presumably the cal./gm. ash-free dry weight would be somewhat higher since all his reported values for whole Malacostraca seem low, indicating possible inclusion of the mineralized exoskeletons in the samples.

There is sufficiently close agreement between Richman's analyses and the various values reported by Golley and Ketchum and Redfield, to indicate that neither *Daphnia pulex* nor Chlamydomonas are at all extraordinary

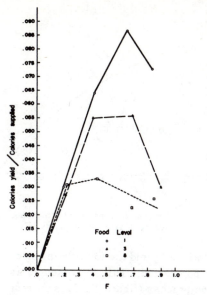

FIGURE 2a. Food chain efficiency on the ordinate vs. F on the abscissa for populations in which adult animals were preferentially removed as yield.

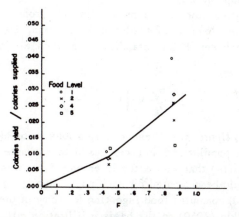

FIGURE 2b. Identical with 2a except that young animals were preferentially removed as yield.

in caloric content. This point is of some importance since I will later make the claim that ecological efficiencies are quite likely as similar as caloric contents.

Using Richman's caloric content data Slobodkin (1959) assumed three conversion constants which were used to translate numerical census and yield data, derived from 22 laboratory populations, into terms of calories. In addition, the number of Chlamydomonas cells provided for these populations was estimated and translated into calories by using Richman's value for calories per algal cell. This provides a direct estimate of I_F.

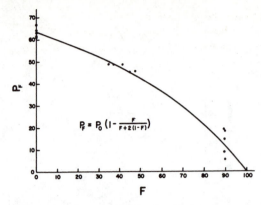

FIGURE 3. P_F, for populations in which young animals were preferentially removed, vs. F.

From I_F and the calories of yield the food chain efficiency could be evaluated directly for each population. This is presented as a function of the intensity of the predation process (figure 2). This measure of fishing intensity is defined elsewhere (Slobodkin, 1957, 1959) and for present purposes we need simply indicate that it is a fishing rate set as a per cent of the births occurring in the population.

Daphnia population standing crops are linearly proportional to their food consumption in the absence of predation (Slobodkin, 1954). There is a simple relation between F and standing crop when all food is consumed, namely

$$(14) \qquad \frac{P_F}{P_O} = \left(1 - \frac{F}{2-F}\right)$$

(Slobodkin, 1957) figure 3. These two relations were assumed generally valid for Daphnia populations and were used to estimate the proportion of the food provided (I_F) that was actually eaten. From this, values of I, the food ingested, could be computed for each population.

Armstrong (1960) computed food ingestion for some of the populations discussed by Slobodkin (1959) on the basis of filtration rate estimates. Comparative values are shown in table 1 and are seen to be of the same order of

TABLE 1

| Population | Armstrong (1960) | Slobodkin (1959) | |
		I	I'
1.25 A	8.1	8.3	8.6
1.50 A	8.1	7.1	7.9
1.75 A	8.1	8.1	7.7
1.90 A	7.7	6.2	4.9
1.50 Y	8.1	8.1	9.0
1.90 Y	8.0	7.3	9.5

magnitude, but in general somewhat lower estimates of I are derived by the method of Slobodkin than by the more direct method of Armstrong.

Having estimates of I/four days, standing crop calories and also yield/four days of small animals, large animals and eggs, for 22 experimental populations, an equation of the form

$$(15) \qquad I = P'c + \sum \frac{Y_i}{E_{pi}}$$

was set up for each population. The subscript i can take the values A for large animals, S for small animals and E for eggs.

This system of 22 equations was then reduced to a set of four equations:

$$(16) \quad
\begin{aligned}
\sum_{1}^{22} P'I &= (c) \sum (P')^2 + \frac{\sum P'Y_A}{E_{pA}} + \frac{\sum P'Y_Y}{E_{pY}} + \frac{\sum P'Y_E}{E_{pE}} \\
\sum Y_A I &= (c) \sum Y_A P' + \frac{\sum Y_A{}^2}{E_{pA}} + \frac{\sum Y_A Y_Y}{E_{pY}} + \frac{\sum Y_A Y_E}{E_{pE}} \\
\sum Y_Y I &= (c) \sum Y_Y P' + \frac{\sum Y_Y Y_A}{E_{pA}} + \frac{\sum Y_Y{}^2}{E_{pA}} + \frac{\sum Y_Y Y_E}{E_{pE}} \\
\sum Y_E I &= (c) \sum Y_E P' + \frac{\sum Y_E Y_A}{E_{pA}} + \frac{\sum Y_E Y_Y}{E_{pY}} + \frac{\sum Y_E{}^2}{E_{pE}}
\end{aligned}$$

This set of equations was then solved for c, and the three E_{pi}.

$$c = 1.68 \ cal./cal. \ day, \ E_{pA} = .48, \ E_{pY} = .036, \ E_{pE} = .062.$$

We have implicitly assumed that the increments in standing crop maintenance cost associated with the various kinds of yield are additive. This assumption probably does not hold at high rates of yield production but precise analysis of the interaction has not yet been made. The E_{pi} are dimensionless, while c has the dimensions $\dfrac{cal.}{cal. \times days}$

The values E_{pi} found from equation (16) are the population efficiencies that would presumably be associated with predation that took only one category of organism as yield. The calculated value of c successfully predicted the mean standing crop of five control populations which did not enter directly into the analysis of equation (15). (Observed 4.8, calculated 4.7). The control populations were used in computing I for each population by means of the relation shown in figure 3.

There also exists a population efficiency for any distribution of the age and size of yield organisms at a steady state in a particular population.

From our previous assumptions and equations (11) and (14) this can be determined for each population, as

$$(17) \qquad E_p = \frac{\dfrac{2Y}{F} - Y}{I}.$$

The only explicit free variables in this equation are Y and F, since I has already been adjusted in value by the use of (14). In addition, the age and

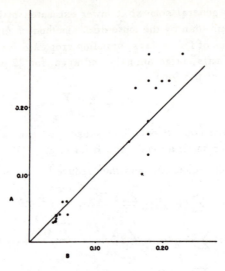

FIGURE 4. The ordinate (A) is given by $E_p = \dfrac{\dfrac{2Y}{F} - Y}{I}$. The abscissa (B)

is $E_p = \sum \dfrac{Y_i/\sum Y_i}{E_{pi}}$. The line assumes A = B.

size distribution of the yield are free to vary from population to population, thereby permitting the estimation of E_p from the composition of the yield and the E_{pi} as

(18) $$\frac{1}{E_p} = \sum \frac{Y_i/\sum Y_i}{E_{pi}}$$

The relation between population efficiency estimated from (17) and from the relative composition of the yield (18) is shown in figure 4.

The I′ values listed in table 1 are the result of substituting c and the E_{pi} from the solution of equation (16) back into equation (15) for each population and solving for the input. The fact that the individual values I′ tend to diverge from Armstrong's estimates more than do the values of I must be attributed to non-linear effects. Ecological efficiency, expressed as $\dfrac{Y}{I'}$ is presented in figure 5 as a maximum estimate of ecological efficiency. The maximum estimate obtained is 12.5 per cent and it seems clear that ecological efficiency would not exceed 14 per cent under any conceivable experimental circumstances.

Values for ecological efficiency of animals in the field, summarized by Patten (1959) include a value of 75 per cent from Teal (1957) which seems almost impossible, a rather high value of 21 per cent (Lindeman, 1942) and eight other non-zero values ranging from 5.5 per cent to 13.3 per cent. There is no significant relation between trophic level and efficiency in these eight values. Top trophic levels have zero ecological efficiency by definition.

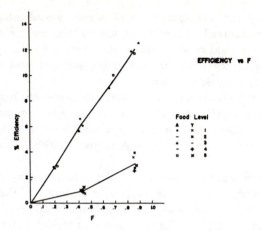

EFFICIENCY vs F

Food Level
A   Y   1
•   x   2
—   ■   3
▲   —   3
▼   ♦   4
□   x   5

FIGURE 5. A maximum estimate of ecological efficiency in the Daphnia
populations. Ordinate: Y/I'; abscissa: F.

The Daphnia experimental maximum is therefore in good accord with other
data. It seems likely on general grounds that any population in nature will
be producing yield at close to its maximum steady state efficiency.

Combining life table data with growth data Armstrong could compute a
table of E_i for the age categories "eggs," "young," "small," "large" and
"adult." The process of solution was remarkably ingenious but would involve excessive digression to present here. These efficiencies are presented diagrammatically in figure 6, with the omission of the data for eggs.

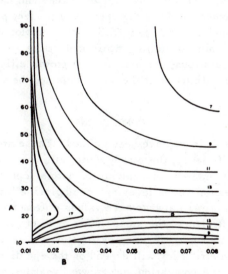

FIGURE 6. Individual growth efficiency × 100 of *Daphnia pulex* as a function of
Chlamydomonas concentration in thousands of cells per ml. (ordinate) and the caloric content of the animals (abscissa). (Using data from Armstrong, 1960).

In excessively low concentrations of algae, growth efficiency is low, since the effort involved in feeding is not compensated adequately by the food acquired. As algal concentrations increase, individual efficiencies increase and then decrease as the rate of ingestion of food exceeds the capacity of the gut to digest the food.

Individual growth efficiencies in Daphnia are somewhat higher in maximum value than ecological efficiencies. They are dependent on the food consumption and growth of individual animals as a function of time and on the energetic cost of producing an egg. (See Armstrong, 1960; Slobodkin, 1959, Appendix B.)

The rather startling difference in age dependence between population efficiency and growth efficiency is explicable in terms of the distribution of life expectancy and food consumption as a function of age. Frank, Boll and Kelly (1957) and Pratt (1943) have shown that Daphnia life expectancy decreases as a function of age, after the first week of life. Various workers (Richman, 1958; Ryther, 1954) have shown the rate of filtration to be considerably greater for an adult Daphnia than for a small Daphnia. · Removal of an adult Daphnia will therefore be expected to make relatively little difference in the mean life expectancy of the animals in the population, not only because the adult animals' probability of survival in the absence of predation is not particularly high but also because its removal results in a food increase for the survivors which tends to lengthen their life expectancy. This, in effect, decreases the denominator of equation (11). At the same time the large size of an adult tends to increase the numerator. The older and bigger an animal gets, the greater this effect. To remove animals that are growing slowly, have lived most of their time and have a low reproductive value (see Fisher, 1958) is the epitome of prudent predation and therefore has a high population efficiency. The consumption of old sows will do little to deplete a pig population, while consuming suckling pig in equal quantity will be disastrous, despite the high growth efficiency of the piglet and the low growth efficiency of the sow. This may be verified at any meat market.

CONCLUSIONS

Three types of efficiency have been defined. These are:

1. Ecological efficiency, the steady state ratio of yield to food ingested. This is of primary interest in analysis of natural community interactions. There is some reason to believe that ecological efficiency, at least in aquatic environments, will always have values of from five to 15 per cent.

2. Population efficiency, the steady state ratio of yield to the alteration in population maintenance produced by the removal process. The precise value of population efficiency will depend on the age distribution of the animals removed and the population and growth dynamics of the population in question. It may have values greater than one, under some circumstances. In Daphnia it varies from four per cent for the removal of young animals to

48 per cent for old animals. It is of primary interest in establishing criteria for the removal of yield, by relating efficiency to standing crop size.

3. Growth efficiency, the ratio of the calories in an individual organism to the calories expended in the course of its development. This is dependent on a variety of physiological responses of the organism to its immediate environment and has no direct relation to community dynamics. In Daphnia the extreme values found by Armstrong (1960) are 37 per cent for eggs at 20,000 algal cells per ml. and six per cent for adults at algal concentrations of 70,000 cells per ml.

The Daphnia values for all three types of efficiency may be considered typical, at least until more data are available for other species, since the ecological efficiencies determined from Daphnia seem of the same order as those determined from various natural situations.

SPECULATION

A single laboratory population requires approximately two to five hours of work per week for a year, not counting data reduction time or effort. A significant number of populations must be run in any one experiment.

Field studies are even more time consuming and expensive. The laboratory suffers from a lack of reality and the field from a lack of repeatability. At those points where concepts are comparable, the Daphnia laboratory studies agree with various field studies, enhancing my faith in the applicability of the laboratory and the reliability of the field.

As the phenomena that cry for explanation by the physiologist and biochemist are the simple observational facts of animal life, so the phenomena that must be predictable from any ecological theory are the facts of natural history and species abundance distributions. So far we are a long way from explaining these facts. The hope is raised by the present study that just as the metabolism of all organisms turned out to be essentially the same, so the economy of all populations may turn out to be roughly the same. The only way to tell is to repeat these rather painful studies on as many organisms as possible in the laboratory, if possible with considerable increase in precision. I expect to find that ecological efficiency will have approximately the same maximum throughout the animal kingdom, that growth efficiency will vary as a function of age to the same degree as growth rate and that population efficiency as a function of age will vary somewhat more widely, just as population growth curves are more variable than individual growth curves.

In further field studies, it is more difficult to make clear predictions of the pattern that future data will show. I can, however, make a guess. Sampling errors and errors in the conversion of animals to energy units and errors due to failure to have steady state data will all diminish.

In my own laboratory, Richman and I are getting equipment in operating order which will permit us to measure the calories released on combustion of tissue samples weighing as little as four mg. Golley, in Georgia, is now collecting data on larger animals. In a few years it should be possible to convert biomass data from field studies directly into energetic units, not only for large animal studies but for studies of terrestrial and aquatic microfauna. I expect that the use of direct conversion constants for each species will considerably increase the precision of field studies of energetics.

Concurrently, the laboratory predation studies are now being repeated on two species of Hydra and on Chlorohydra. I hope that this will test the applicability of the efficiency values determined for Daphnia to carnivorous animals.

The apparent differences between the estimates of food chain efficiency of corresponding trophic levels in different communities will also tend to vanish. I would guess that herbivores in general will have an efficiency of from ten to 13 per cent. Higher trophic levels may quite likely have slightly lower efficiencies. The presently accepted order of magnitude for food chain efficiencies of from c. six to c. 15 per cent is almost certainly correct.

In the absence of yield removal, the corpses in a laboratory Daphnia population represent five per cent of the energy input. Even on high trophic levels, in which predation in the normal sense is not occurring, an efficiency of conversion to decomposer of the same order as the other efficiencies in the system might be expected.

Assuming that we do find constancy of the food chain efficiencies in a steady state community, what type of theoretical structure can be built with this information? By itself, it tells us relatively little that would not have been predictable from elementary thermodynamics or elementary biochemistry. In combination with other ecological information it may provide a set of restrictions that will severely limit the range of possible ecological speculation.

The basic theoretical problem of community ecology is to construct a model or metamodel (Slobodkin, 1958) based on a simple set of assumptions that will generate not only the steady state conditions of the biosphere at a particular instant but the responses of these steady states to various climatic and geologic perturbations. These responses will constitute a theoretical reconstruction of evolution and almost incidentally will be a guide to exploitation of the natural world by man.

It seems possible that the following ecological generalizations are valid.

1. Food chain efficiencies can only have a narrow range of values.

2. Species abundance distribution patterns can only take the form of distributions generated from the theory of interspecific competition (Hairston, 1959; MacArthur, 1957).

3. Pairs of competing species must have a certain minimum of ecological difference if they are to coexist in a steady state (Hutchinson, 1959).

If we now demand that all models of the ecological world that make any pretense to reality must meet all of these conditions simultaneously we will be saved from unbridled speculations and misleading metaphors.

To the degree that these and other generalizations hold we may eventually be able to turn to the mathematician or even to his idiot cousin, the IBM machine, and ask him, or it, to build us all the theoretical models which will meet our restrictions and still maintain steady states and evolve properly under perturbation. At that time, community and population ecology will enter the company of the exact sciences.

In the interim we must increase the precision of those measurements which we know must be made and test the range of applicability of those generalizations which now seem valid.

SUMMARY

The energetic relation between different trophic levels and populations in a community involves primarily potential energy transfer in complex feedback systems, making the applicability of existing steady state thermodynamic theory questionable, since the requirements for direct evaluation of entropy are not met by ecological systems. The only form of energy considered here was potential energy.

The efficiency of a population does not have a unique meaning. Three different concepts of efficiency were defined and evaluated for *Daphnia pulex*. Two of these, the ecological efficiency and population efficiency, refer to the population level. The growth efficiency refers to individual organisms.

Ecological efficiency is a function of the rate of removal of yield and of the kind of yield animals removed. Population efficiency is a function of the kind of animals removed as yield and the interaction between these animals and the population. Growth efficiency does not depend on the removal of yield at all. It is a function of individual food consumption, growth rate and the energetic cost of reproduction.

These three are interrelated. In general, for a particular system of predation ecological efficiency is proportional to population efficiency. Population efficiency is related to the individual growth efficiency through the effect of the removal of animals on the maintenance cost per calorie of standing crop, which in turn is a function of growth efficiency.

The maximum ecological efficiencies found in the Daphnia experiments are of the same order as ecological efficiencies found in nature, implying that ecological efficiency is effectively constant. Presumably the observed value of c. ten per cent has selective significance.

In speculating on the future development of community ecology, I suggested that certain generalizations now available, including the approximate constancy of ecological efficiency, restrict the development of possible theories. When a sufficient number of these generalizations have been stated and tested a comprehensive predictive general theory of community ecology will appear, if only by the elimination of all conceivable theories whose predictions do not conform to the generalizations.

ACKNOWLEDGMENTS

The studies reported here were initially supported by The Rockefeller Foundation and The Phoenix Memorial Project of the University of Michigan.

For the past three years they have been supported by the National Science Foundation.

I am grateful to the staff and graduate students that have participated in the community ecology seminar at the University of Michigan for their discussion of this work. Drs. Armstrong and Richman have been particularly helpful. Dr. Peter Ovenburg has criticized the mathematical presentation. Profs. G. E. Hutchinson, Anatol Rappoport and Karl Guthe have been liberal with their knowledge and encouragement.

LITERATURE CITED

Armstrong, J. T., 1960, Ph.D. dissertation, Department of Zoology. University of Michigan, Ann Arbor, Mich.

Cole, L. C., 1959, Personal communication.

Denbigh, K. G., 1951, The thermodynamics of the steady state. 103 pp. Methuen & Co., London, England.

Fisher, R. A., 1958, The genetical theory of natural selection. pp. 27-30. Dover Publications, Inc., New York, N. Y.

Foster, C., A. Rappoport and E. Trucco, 1957, Some unsolved problems in the theory of non-isolated systems. General Systems 3: 9-29.

Frank, P. W., C. D. Boll and R. W. Kelly, 1957, Vital statistics of laboratory cultures of *Daphnia pulex* DeGeer as related to density. Physiol. Zool. 30: 287-305.

Golley, F. B., 1959, Table of caloric equivalents. Mimeographed, 7 pp. Available from the author. Department of Zoology, University of Georgia, Athens, Ga.

Hairston, N. G., 1959, Species abundance and community organization. Ecology 40: 404-416.

Hutchinson, G. E., 1959, Homage to Santa Rosalia or why there are so many kinds of animals. Amer. Nat. 93: 145-159.

Ketchum, B. H., and A. C. Redfield, 1949, Some physical and chemical characteristics of algae grown in mass culture. J. Cell. and Comp. Physiol. 33: 281-300.

Lindeman, R. L., 1942, The trophic-dynamic aspect of ecology. Ecology 23: 399-418.

MacArthur, R. H., 1957, On the relative abundance of bird species. Proc. Nat. Acad. Sci. U.S. 43: 293-295.

Patten, B. C., 1959, An introduction to the cybernetics of the ecosystem: the trophic-dynamic aspect. Ecology 40: 221-231.

Pratt, D. M., 1943, Analysis of population development in Daphnia at different temperatures. Biol. Bull. 85: 116-140.

Richman, S., 1958, The transformation of energy by *Daphnia pulex*. Ecol. Monogr. 28: 273-291.

Ryther, J. H., 1954, Inhibitory effects of phytoplankton upon the feeding of *Daphnia magna* with reference to growth, reproduction, and survival. Ecology 35: 522-533.

Slobodkin, L. B., 1954, Population dynamics in *Daphnia obtusa* Kurz. Ecol. Monogr. 24: 69-88.

1957, A laboratory study of the effect of removal of newborn animals from a population. Proc. Nat. Acad. Sci. U. S. 43: 780-782.

1958, Meta-models in theoretical ecology. Ecology 39: 550–551.

1959, Energetics in *Daphnia pulex* populations. Ecology 40: 232–243.

Teal, J. M., 1957, Community metabolism in a temperate cold spring. Ecol. Monogr. 27: 283–302.

Trama, F. B., 1957, The transformation of energy by an aquatic herbivore, *Stenonema pulchellum* (Ephemeroptera). Ph.D. dissertation, Department of Zoology, University of Michigan, Ann Arbor, Mich.

GLOSSARY OF SYMBOLS

Symbol	Units	Meaning
c	calories/(calories × days)	Maintenance cost of one calorie of standing crop for one unit of time
Δc	calories/(calories × days)	Increment in maintenance cost per calorie of standing crop attributable to the removal of yield.
d_x	animals/animals	The fraction of animals born at time 0 that die during the age interval x.
D_x	animals/days	The number of animals that die during the age interval x.
E	$\dfrac{\text{calories/time}}{\text{calories/time}}$	Yield calories divided by input calories. Ecological efficiency.
E_i	$\dfrac{\text{calories}}{\text{calories}}$	Potential energy in an individual of age i, divided by the potential energy needed to replace that individual. Growth efficiency.
E_p	$\dfrac{\text{calories/time}}{\text{calories/time}}$	Yield calories divided by the difference in maintenance cost between the population producing the yield and a corresponding control population. Population efficiency.
E_{pi}	$\dfrac{\text{calories/time}}{\text{calories/time}}$	Population efficiency for the situation in which the yield consists exclusively of animals age i.
i and j	days	Age categories.
l_x	animals/animals	The fraction of animals born at time 0 that survive to time x.
N_o	animals/days	Number of newborn animals produced in a population during one time interval.
P	calories	Steady state standing crop caloric content of a population.
q_x	animals/animals	The proportion of animals that survive up to an age interval that die during that interval.

Symbol	Units	Meaning
S_x	calories	The calories of potential energy contained in an animal of age x.
$\sum$		Summation sign.
x	days	An age category. (Occasionally used as a size category.)
Y	calories/time	Total steady state yield removed from a population per unit time.
Y_i	calories/time	Steady state yield of animals age i removed from a population per unit time.

Note: Except for c' and $\Delta c'$, in equations (3) and (4), a symbol with a prime (that is, P' or S'_x) refers to a property of a population subject to predation, but is otherwise understood to have the same meaning as the corresponding symbol without the prime (that is, P or S_x).

In the discussion of entropy the symbols all have their conventional meanings.

Symbol	Meaning
ΔF	Change in free energy
ΔH	Change in enthalpy
Q'	Non-entropic heat.
ΔS	Change in entropy.
T	Absolute temperature

The limits to the productivity of the sea

I. Morris

The primary productivity of the oceans is a measure of the rate at which phytoplankton convert inorganic nutrients into living material by the process of photosynthesis. This is the starting point for all life in the sea. The rate at which it occurs ultimately determines the amount of food available for man. The carbon-14 method is a sensitive and convenient means of measuring phytoplankton photosynthesis and, despite problems of interpretation, there are widely accepted values for the primary productivity of the sea. From these estimates it is clear that, for most of the ocean, the level of primary production is much less than many areas on land. The total amount of carbon assimilated each year in the oceans is only large because of the large area involved and not because of any increased productivity per unit area. Two environmental factors seem to be important in limiting the primary productivity of the sea. The first is light intensity; absorption of light in the water confining photosynthesis to the upper layers. The second is nutrient concentration; the extremely dilute solution of many essential nutrients severely limiting the density of phytoplankton which can be supported by a given volume of seawater. Current experimental approaches try to define the precise physiological and biochemical mechanisms by which the various environmental factors determine the activity of phytoplankton. To date, these experiments have merely highlighted the unsolved problems of phytoplankton productivity.

Introduction

The productivity of the sea depends ultimately on the rate of photosynthesis by the phytoplankton. These microscopic algae float in the surface layers of the oceans, absorb the energy of sunlight and convert the dissolved carbon dioxide and other inorganic nutrients into the organic matter of their living cells. The rate at which this process continues is a measure of the *primary productivity* of the sea.

In this review I want to consider five aspects of the ecology of marine phytoplankton: (1) the methods of measuring primary production in the oceans, (2) the errors and uncertainties in these methods, (3) some of the published values for primary productivity of the sea, (4) the measurement of standing crop and its relevance to estimates of primary productivity, and (5) the environmental factors which limit the primary productivity of the sea.

Dr Morris is a Lecturer in the Department of Botany and Microbiology, University College London, Gower Street, London WC1E 6BT.

Produced with permission from *Science Progress*, 61:39–122.

Methods of measuring primary production in the oceans

Essentially, there are two methods of measuring primary productivity. One is to measure the change in weight of plant material on a given area over a relatively long period of time (of the order of months). The second is to measure the rate of photosynthesis by a given amount of plant material over a shorter period of time (generally several hours) and, from this, calculate the production rates over the longer time periods. The first approach is of little use in studies of phytoplankton. It is not possible to measure an increase in phytoplankton numbers over a relatively prolonged period of time, since grazing by herbivores and sinking will take them out of the sampling area. (A possible exception to this is the increase in numbers of phytoplankton during the 'spring burst' in temperate waters, but this merely gives a minimum estimate of primary production at one time of the year.) Hence, all direct measurements of primary productivity in the oceans are based on measurements of phytoplankton photosynthesis over relatively short periods of time.

There are two main methods used in the measurements of photosynthesis by phytoplankton; the assimilation of radioactive carbon dioxide (the 'carbon-14 method') and the evolution of oxygen. Of these, the carbon-14 method, first introduced by Steemann-Nielsen,[1] has now almost completely superseded the earlier, less-sensitive method of measuring oxygen production.[2] The advantages of the carbon-14 method come both from its sensitivity and from its convenience. The procedure depends simply on incubating a bottle of seawater (containing phytoplankton) with a known amount of sodium bicarbonate-^{14}C. After being illuminated for a suitable period of time (generally 4 hr) the contents are filtered. The suspended phytoplankton are retained on the filter and, after drying, the amount of radioactive carbon fixed by the algae can be counted. Usually, a second bottle is incubated for the same length of time in darkness and the radioactivity on the filter from this 'dark bottle' is subtracted from the light bottle so that the rate of photosynthetic carbon dioxide fixation can be determined. Ideally, the incubation is done *in situ*; that is, the bottles containing the radioactive bicarbonate are suspended in the water at the same depths as those used for sampling. However, it is often inconvenient for the ship to remain 'on station' for 4 hr. Frequently, therefore, the bottles are incubated in a 'deck incubator' with artificial illumination.

Some errors and uncertainties in the measurement of phytoplankton photosynthesis

1. *Problems of counting and contamination*

Despite its convenience and sensitivity, the carbon-14 method is not without its problem. These arise both from the errors inherent in the technique and from the interpretation of the results. The former difficulties include self-absorption of the β-radiation by various thickness on the filter[3,4] and the possible presence of contaminating carbon-14 from unassimilated bicarbonate. Attempts to remove this have included fuming with concentrated hydrochloric acid[1] or washing them with dilute acid or filtered seawater.[4] However, the errors from such contamination do not appear to be very large and many workers do not treat the filters before counting, arguing that subtraction of the 'dark bottle' value corrects for such errors. Recently, Williams *et al.*[5] have suggested that the presence of particulate organic ^{14}C-labelled contaminants in some batches of radioactive bicarbonate can introduce a considerable error in the estimation of low rates of primary production in oligotrophic waters.

2. *Problems arising from excretion*

Another possible source of error in the carbon-14 technique arises from the excretion of some of the assimilatory products (see reviews of Fogg[6,7] and Hellebust[8]). Briefly, this concept of excretion states that a proportion of the products of carbon dioxide fixation are rapidly excreted from the cell. These 'extracellular products' appear in the seawater which passes through the filters and so get omitted from the measurement of radioactivity on the filter. Thus, if a significant proportion of the photosynthetic product is excreted, the level of primary production is seriously underestimated.

There has been some controversy of the precise level of excretion and the papers of Anderson & Zentschell,[9] Watt,[10] Horne *et al.*,[11] Ryther *et al.*[12] and Thomas[13] are recommended. Estimates have varied from less than 2 per cent to about 50 per cent of the rate of photosynthesis. It has been generally agreed that excretion is proportionally highest in those parts of the ocean (notably the surface layers of tropical and sub-tropical regions) where the phytoplankton density is lowest.[13] The main difficulty surrounding excretion centres around the paper of Williams *et al.*[5] Briefly, the problem has to do with contamination by radioactive soluble compounds in the original sodium bicarbonate. Such contaminants appear in the filtrate after filtration and give an artificially high value for excretion. This value remains constant in all samples, thus appearing as a higher *proportional* excretion in those samples showing lower rates of primary productivity (that is, those with low phytoplankton densities). Because of this complication it is doubtful whether the high values reported from waters with low phytoplankton densities are valid.

3. *The need to correct for respiration*

Other, possibly more serious, errors arise from the interpretation of the relationship between the rate of photosynthesis determined by the carbon-14 technique and primary production. One of the problems arises from the difficulty of correcting for respiration. There is no direct way of measuring respiration in natural phytoplankton populations. Steemann-Nielsen & Hansen[14] estimated phytoplankton respiration indirectly from the photosynthesis/light curve. This curve relates the rate of photosynthesis to light intensity. These authors extrapolated the line back to the point where it cuts the light intensity axis (this gives the compensation intensity—the amount of light needed to balance respiration) and then continued the extrapolation on to the photosynthesis axis and suggested that this was the amount of carbon needed to satisfy respiration. From this crude estimate has developed the idea that respiration in phytoplankton continues at about 10 per cent of the rate of photosynthesis. This estimate agrees with studies of actively growing cultures of algae which exhibit respiration rates of 5–10 per cent the photosynthetic rate.[15,16] Similar results have been obtained by McAllister *et al.*[17]

Doubt about respiration has centred mainly around the question of whether the photosynthesis/respiration ratio changes significantly with the changing growth conditions. Ryther,[15] for example, observed that, with the onset of nutrient deficiency, photosynthesis by the green flagellate *Dunaliella* declined more rapidly than did respiration. However, Steemann-Nielsen & Hansen[14] agrued that the photosynthesis/respiration ratio remained constant in the oceans because nutrient-deficient cells are not normally found in the photic zone, since they are usually removed by sinking and grazing.[4]

Another problem concerned with respiration and the carbon-14 technique is the question of whether this technique measures *net* or *gross* photosynthesis (where gross photosynthesis = net photosynthesis + respiration). Ryther[18] concluded that the carbon-14 method measured net photosynthesis. This was based on the observation that, at the compensation intensity determined by the oxygen method, there was no measurable fixation of ^{14}C-bicarbonate. Such a fixation would have been expected if the carbon-14 technique measured gross photosynthesis. However, Steemann-Nielsen & Hansen[14] concluded that the carbon-14 method only measured net photosynthesis over long periods of time, in short-term experiments it was thought to measure some value intermediate between gross and net photosynthesis.

4. *Validity of subtracting dark ^{14}C-fixation*

Another problem of interpretation arises from the validity of subtracting the dark ^{14}C-carbon dioxide fixation from that fixed in the light. In many parts of the oceans this problem is not quantitatively significant, the dark fixation generally being less than 1 per cent of the rate of light-saturated photosynthesis. However, there are areas of the oceans, notably the oligotrophic waters of sub-tropical and tropical regions, where the dark carbon dioxide fixation can be as much as 20–30 per cent of photosynthesis.[19] Although Steemann-Nielsen[20] has suggested that the high ratios of dark/light carbon dioxide fixation arise from contamination of the filters, this does not appear to be a sufficient explanation of all the published data. In particular, Morris *et al.*[19] observed that the ratio of dark to light fixation depended on the phytoplankton density, being highest at the lowest cell densities.. These authors have questioned the validity of subtracting the dark value in oligotrophic waters with low phytoplankton densities.

5. *Problems of calculating long-term productivity values from short-term measurements of photosynthesis*

In addition to the problems of techniques and interpretation, there are difficulties in converting rates of light-saturated photosynthesis (expressed as units of carbon fixed/unit *volume* of water/*hour*) to productivity values (expressed as units of carbon fixed/unit *area* of ocean/*day* or *year*). There are two basic problems. One is the integration of photosynthesis in the entire water column beneath a unit area of ocean surface. This can be done most reliably when photosynthesis measurements are made *in situ*; that is, when bottles are suspended throughout the photic zone. This is too rarely done. A more frequent type of experiment is one in which the rate of light-saturated photosynthesis by the phytoplankton from the surface is measured under artificial illumination on deck. This single direct determination of photosynthesis is then converted to a figure integrated over the entire water column by knowing three more parameters; the penetration of light in that particular part of the ocean, the distribution of chlorophyll with depth, and the relationship between photosynthesis and light intensity (determined from studies with algal cultures in the laboratory). Thus, in practice, integrating the photosynthetic rate throughout the water column depends on a large number of assumptions, primarily concerned with the relationship between photosynthesis and light intensity (this will be discussed later when I examine the concept of light intensity as a limiting factor). Yet further problems arise during the conversion of an hourly rate to longer periods of time such as days, or even years. This involves assumptions about respiration rates during the night, about changing rates of photosynthesis with changing light intensity throughout the day, changing temperatures and light intensities throughout the year, etc.

Some accepted values for the primary productivity of the oceans

Despite the difficulties of methodology and the large number of assumptions which have to be made there is surprising agreement between many workers on the approximated values of primary production by marine phytoplankton. For example, from measurements at 194 stations during the cruise of the R.V. 'Galathea', Steemann-Nielsen & Jansen estimated the total primary production of the oceans to be $1.2–1.5 \times 10^{10}$ tons of carbon fixed per year.[21] Later, after studying data from 7000 stations, Koblentz-Mishke et al. (cited by Ryther[22]) revised the estimate to $1.5–1.8 \times 10^{10}$ tons of carbon fixed per year.

There is also general agreement on the main zones of productivity in the oceans. Table 1 is taken from the review of Ryther[22] and compares the productivity of open ocean, coastal regions and the somewhat specialized areas of upwelling (these last named are regions of the oceans where nutrient-rich water is brought from the deeper layers up to the surface where photosynthesis by the phytoplankton can occur at an enhanced rate). Although, when integrated over the entire ocean, the open sea makes the greatest contribution to primary production, this arises from the much greater area of ocean involved and not from any greater productivity *per unit area*. Indeed, on an area basis, the productivity of the open ocean areas is significantly lower than that of coastal regions or of upwelling areas (Table 1).

Table 1. Divisions of the oceans into provinces according to their level of primary organic production (from Ryther [22])

Province	Percentage of ocean	Area (km²)	Mean productivity (g carbon/m²/year)	Total productivity (10^9 tons carbon/year)
Open ocean	90	326×10^6	50	16.3
Coastal zone	9.9	36×10^6	100	3.6
Upwelling areas	0.1	3.6×10^5	300	0.1
Total				20.0

It is of some interest to compare the productivity figures summarized in Table 1 with the maximum theoretical productivity which might be expected. The paper of Ryther[16] and the more recent one by Vishniac[23] are recommended for details of this analysis. Essentially, the calculation depends on knowing: (1) the total energy received by this planet, (2) the amount of this which reaches the earth's surface, (3) the proportion of this which reaches the surface of the oceans, (4) the proportion absorbed by the oceans, (5) the efficiency of photosynthesis so as to calculate the amount of energy absorbed by the phytoplankton, (6) the energy needed to convert carbon dioxide to organic matter during photosynthesis. From this we can calculate the upper limit to the amount of living matter than can be produced by photosynthesis of phytoplankton in the oceans. The calculation made by Vishniac[23] is summarized in Table 2. Vishniac estimated the potential productivity of the oceans to be about 1.9×10^{11} metric tons of carbon fixed per year. Since a metric ton is little over a ton, we can say that the maximum potential productivity is about ten times the published estimates of primary production in the oceans. (It is worth nothing that Vishniac accepts Russell-Hunter's[24] opinion that the average productivity of the oceans is greater than is suggested by most workers and concludes that the observed primary productivity is about 25–30 per cent of the theoretical maximum.)

It is also of interest to compare the estimated primary productivity values for

Table 2. An estimation of the theoretical maximum organic production in the oceans (taken from the text of Vishniac's review)

1. Energy from the sun reaching the upper atmosphere of earth	$1 \cdot 25 \times 10^{24}$ cal
2. Energy reaching earth's surface after 60 per cent loss by scattering and absorption	5×10^{23} cal
3. Energy reaching surface of ocean after subtracting 50 per cent for infrared radiation and 28 per cent reaching land	$1 \cdot 6 \times 10^{23}$ cal
4. Energy available for absorption by phytoplankton after 10 per cent reflection	$1 \cdot 2 \times 10^{23}$ cal
5. Estimated efficiency of photosynthesis of 2 per cent giving maximum energy available for primary production	$2 \cdot 5 \times 10^{21}$ cal
6. Energy required to assimilate 1 g of carbon into living material	$1 \cdot 3 \times 10^{4}$ cal
7. Upper limit of living matter which can be produced in the ocean $\dfrac{(2 \cdot 5 \times 10^{21})}{(1 \cdot 3 \times 10^{4})}$	$1 \cdot 9 \times 10^{17}$ g carbon/year or $1 \cdot 9 \times 10^{11}$ metric tons carbon/year

the oceans with those for terrestrial environmentals. Westlake[25] has made such a comparison and a selection of some of his data is presented in Table 3. I have also added to the same table the data of Ryther[22] selected from Table 1 and some generalized data of Odum[26] quoted by Phillipson.[27]

These kind of comparisons are extremely difficult to make. They are filled with many assumptions and many possible errors. However, despite these difficulties, certain general conclusions remain valid. When calculated on an

Table 3. Comparison of marine primary productivity with selected terrestrial communities

Community	Annual mean productivity (g carbon/m²/year)	Growing season mean productivity (g carbon/m²/day)	Reference
Open ocean	50	—	Ryther (1969)[16]
Coastal zone	100	—	
Upwelling areas	300	—	
Maximum site, freshwater phytoplankton	860	1·2	Westlake (1963)[25]
Marine phytoplankton (good site)	240	0·32	
Littoral seaweed (maximum site)	1600–2100	2·1–2·8	
Uncultivated herb temperate (maximum site)	2400	9·0	
Tropical rain forest (maximum site)	5900	7·6	
Temperate grain (maximum site)	2400	8·1	
Open ocean	—	1·0	Odum (1959) (referred by Phillipson, 1966)[27]
Coastal zone	—	0·5–3·0	
Most forest, hollow lakes, most agriculture	—	3–10	
Intensive agriculture	—	10–25	
Grasslands	—	0·5–3·0	
Deserts	—	0·5	

area basis the productivity of phytoplankton in the oceans is considerably less than that of terrestrial plants. The only conditions under which the primary productivity of aquatic environments approaches that of most terrestrial situations are those when the former is influenced by the macroscopic plants growing at the edges of the water; for example, the seaweeds on the shore or the reeds and other macrophytes at the edge of shallow lakes and ponds. In larger bodies of water where the major contribution to primary production comes from the activity of phytoplankton, the productivity is comparable to the poorest kinds of terrestrial environments. In comparison with most terrestrial environments, therefore, oceans (particularly of the open ocean areas) are truly 'deserts'.

Measurements of standing crop and its relevance to estimates of primary productivity

Another parameter used in analyses of primary productivity is that of 'standing crop' (or 'standing stock'). This is the amount of plant material on a given area of land or in a given volume of water. Many of the earlier estimates of primary productivity were based simply on measurements of standing stock, and to a large extent, present-day work also relates primary production in the sea directly to the amount of phytoplankton. That is, it is still often assumed that areas with high standing stocks are equivalent to areas of high primary productivity. In many parts of the ocean this assumption remains valid. However, the relationship between the amount of phytoplankton and the rate of photosynthesis can vary considerably, particularly with changing light intensity. It is for this reason that the standing stock is best related to primary production when the light intensity is measured and when the relationship between planktonic photosynthesis and light intensity is known (see below).

One of the reasons for seeking to use the standing stock as an index of primary productivity on the oceans is the convenience of measuring chlorophyll. In most marine work chlorophyll measurements have almost entirely superseded the earlier attempts to measure cell size, cell number, surface area or dry weight of phytoplankton. Basically two methods exist, one a spectrophotometric method depends on the absorption of light of selected wavelengths by the chlorophyll; the other a fluorometric method depends on the fact that chlorophyll fluoresces with light of certain wavelengths.[28-32] The spectrophotometric method is much less sensitive than the fluorometric method and is only convenient for use in coastal waters containing high phytoplankton densities.

One of the problems in using a measurement of chlorophyll concentration as an indication of the standing stock of phytoplankton is the suspicion that some of the measured chlorophyll is not photosynthetically active. In both the spectrophotometric and fluorometric methods it is possible to correct for this by measuring the so-called 'acid ratio'. This depends on measuring the absorption (or the fluorescence) before and after acidification of the extract. The value after acidification measures the amount of phaeophytin; that is, the amount of degraded chlorophyll. This acid ratio is least useful when the fluorescence technique is used on samples of phytoplankton containing significant amounts of chlorophyll c.[33]

One interesting question is to ask whether the large differences between the productivities of marine and terrestrial environments are paralleled by similar differences in the standing crop. These comparisons are difficult to make, since standing crop measurements from terrestrial environments are generally ex-

Table 4. A comparison of the standing crop (expressed as chlorophyll concentration) of marine phytoplankton with that of plants from selected terrestrial environments. Data from the phytoplankton are taken from the review of Yentsch[4] and for land plants from Bray[34]

Location	Chlorophyll concentration (mg/m^2)
Waters off New York	
September 1956	45
December 1956	175
February 1957	190
March 1957	250
April 1957	200
July 1957	75
Red Sea	38
Sargasso Sea	42
Central Minnesota	
Zea mays	2700
Soja max.	900
Native prairie	700
Coniferous–hardwood forest	3100

pressed in units quite different from these used in the measurements of phytoplankton densities. For example, Westlake[25] expresses the biomass of terrestrial communities as kg/m^2 and that of phytoplankton populations as $mm^3/litre$. In Table 4 I have compared some of the values or chlorophyll concentrations in various parts of the oceans (taken from the review of Yentsch[4]) with the selected values of the chlorophyll content of some plant communities reported by Bray.[34] At the time of maximum phytoplankton density in temperate coastal waters the chlorophyll beneath 1 m^2 of ocean surface is one-third to one-tenth of that supported above a square metre of reasonably fertile land. When the more oligotrophic waters are considered the difference is twenty- to eighty-fold. From the data in Tables 3 and 4 it appears that the chlorophyll concentration (standing crop) and the productivities (calculated from photosynthesis measurements) of phytoplankton in the oceans are lower than those of terrestrial environments by similar orders of magnitude. The data do not permit more critical comparisons.

Factors limiting the primary productivity of the sea

It is clear from the above remarks that the rate of photosynthesis by the phytoplankton in the sea is relatively low; even the richest parts of the oceans giving rates of primary production comparable to some of the poorer terrestrial environments. It is clear too that much of this difference reflects the striking disparity in the density of plant material; the amount of phytoplankton beneath a unit area of ocean surface being much less than the amount of plant material supported by unit area of all but the poorest of terrestrial environments. Our question therefore is this: what are the factors which determine this low plant biomass and the accompanying low primary productivity of phytoplankton in the oceans?

Over the past thirty to forty years measurements of biological activity in the oceans have been routinely accompanied by relevant physical and chemical measurements. Because of this, we understand much about the basic factors which determine the primary productivity of the sea, although there is considerable doubt about their quantitative effects and of the precise mechanism by which they operate. The two most important factors are thought to be *light intensity* and *nutrient concentration*. *Temperature* is generally thought to have little direct effect, although this idea is being challenged recently (see below).

1. *Light intensity*

(a) *Absorption of light and the depth of the photic zone*. Primary productivity depends on light and so will be confined to the surface layers of the ocean; the so-called photic zone (or 'euphotic zone'). This is the zone which receives enough light to permit the rate of photosynthesis by phytoplankton to be greater than the rate of respiration. (The light intensity at which the rates of photosynthesis and respiration balance each other is known as the compensation intensity.) The depth of the photic zone varies considerably throughout the day and throughout the year, and varies geographically throughout the world's oceans. Factors which affect it include (1) the incident light intensity, (2) the proportion of this which is reflected, and (3) the attenuation of light in the water column. The proportion of light reflected from the surface of the ocean depends on the angle of the sun (at a low angle reflection may be as much as 40 per cent and when the sun is high be as little as 3 per cent) and on wave action (reflection is greatly increased by waves). The factors which attenuate light in the sea are: (1) absorption by water, (2) scattering by water molecules, (3) absorption by dissolved organic substances, (4) absorption by coloured particles, and (5) scattering by coloured particles.

As an approximate working guide the photic zone is generally assumed to extend down to the depth where the light intensity is about 1 per cent of the surface light intensity. However, there is considerable variation in this figure. For example, Steemann-Nielsen & Hansen[35] observed that in Danish coastal waters the compensation depth varied throughout the year to be between 1 and 5 per cent of the surface light on so-called bright days and between 3 and 30 per cent on so-called dark days. Jerlov[36] showed that 1 per cent of the surface light intensity occurred at a depth of 87 m in the clearest open ocean waters, at 25 m in the most turbid open ocean regions and varied from 24 to as low as 5 m in coastal waters. In the open ocean the transparency of the water is determined largely by the phytoplankton themselves but in coastal waters other dissolved and suspended materials can reduce the transparency.[4,21,37,38]

Not all the wavelengths of light are absorbed to the same extent in seawater. Thus, not only does the light *intensity* change with depth, the *spectral composition* also alters. The maximum transmission of light in pure water is between 470 and 490 nm and the transmission decreases sharply towards the longer wavelengths and gradually towards the shorter.[38,39] The spectral composition of the clearest ocean waters does not differ significantly from that of pure water, but in coastal waters the transmission maximum is shifted to higher wavelength because of absorption of shorter wavelength light by dissolved yellow organic materials[40,41] and by phytoplankton.[38]

(b) *Relationship between light intensity and photosynthesis*. Certain basic features of the relationship between light intensity and photosynthesis are common to all algae. At low light intensities there is a linear relationship between the amount of light and the rate of photosynthesis; at higher light intensites the rate of photosynthesis 'saturates' and is then limited by some process which does not depend on the amount of light received by the cells; at higher intensities still the rate of photosynthesis declines from this maximum saturated value. There are considerable differences between the various algae in the intensities required to saturate photosynthesis. Working with cultures Ryther[42] observed that photosynthesis by green algae saturated at 5000–7500 lux, that by diatoms required between 10,000 and 20,000 lux and dinoflagellates required 25,000–30,000 lux.

This known relationship between photosynthesis and light intensity allows one to predict the photosynthesis rates down through the water column merely from measuring the incident light intensity and the transparency of the water. For example, Fig. 1 shows the calculated relative rates of photosynthesis at different depths in water of varying transparencies.[4] In the clearest water photosynthesis occurs to a depth of 83 m with a maximum at 10–20 m; in waters of minimum clarity photosynthesis occurs to a depth of only 25 m with a maximum at 3 m. Intermediate conditions can be found between these extremes. In all waters the light intensities at or near the surface are inhibitory.

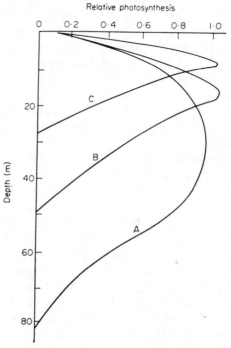

Fig. 1. The vertical distribution of photosynthesis by marine phytoplankton in waters of varying transparencies. A: maximum transparency; B: average transparency; C: minimum transparency. The photosynthesis values are relative and caculated from the photosynthesis–light relations of Ryther[18] and the transparency data of Jerlov.[37] The figure is taken from Yentsch.[4]

The values in Fig. 1 are relative. They can be converted into absolute values by measuring photosynthesis at saturating light intensity, measuring the chlorophyll concentrations throughout the water column, the incident light intensity and the transparency of the water. There is good agreement between the observed and the calculated values.

(c) *The concept of adaptation to light intensity.* Prediction of photosynthetic rates throughout the photic zone from the observed relationship between light intensity and photosynthesis is not so simple and straightforward if the phytoplankton *adapt* to high or low light intensities in the sea. That is, if the layers in the photic zone do not become adequately mixed by wind action then the various plankton can be exposed to periods of constant high or low intensities. There has been some controversy as to whether, under these conditions, they become adapted to the intensities sufficiently to modify the photosynthesis/light intensity relationship derived from culture studies. The basic question has been whether phytoplankton resemble some plants in showing 'sun' and 'shade'

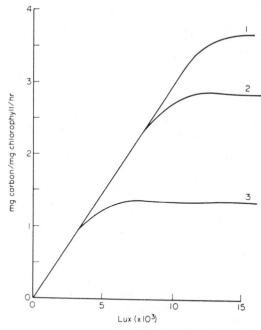

Fig. 2. The rate of photosynthesis as a function of light intensity. The experiment was done with natural populations of phytoplankton from (1) surface, (2) depth of 27 m, and (3) depth of 50 m. The rate of photosynthesis is expressed per weight of chlorophyll. (From Steemann-Nielsen & Hansen.[43])

forms (those adapted to high and low light intensities respectively). Steemann-Nielsen & Hansen[43] observed that natural populations from 27 and 50 m differed from those at the surface in two ways. They exhibited lower rates of light-saturated photosynthesis and also required lower light intensities in order to saturate photosynthesis.

These results of Steemann-Nielsen & Hansen are summarized in Figs. 2 and 3. In Fig. 2 the rate of photosynthesis is related directly to light intensity. The most obvious difference between the populations from the various depths is in the rate of light-saturated photosynthesis, the populations from lower down having lower rates at saturating light intensities. There is no difference in the photosynthetic rates at low light intensities. However, there is a difference in the light intensity at which photosynthesis saturates. This value is known as I_k. The differences in I_k values shows up most strikingly when the data from the 'direct' graph in Fig. 2 are normalized to correct for difference in the rates of photosynthesis at saturating light intensities. This is done by plotting P/P_{max} (where P is the photosynthetic rate at each light intensity and P_{max} is the rate at light-saturation) against light intensity (Fig. 3).

This shift in I_k values towards lower light intensities is generally interpreted as a characteristic of 'shade' organisms. However, Yentsch & Lee,[44] working with algae cultures, could produce the same effect merely by measuring photosynthesis at lower temperatures and concluded that the characteristics observed by Steemann-Nielsen & Hansen reflected an 'inferior environment' and were not indicative of any specialized adaptation to lower light intensities.

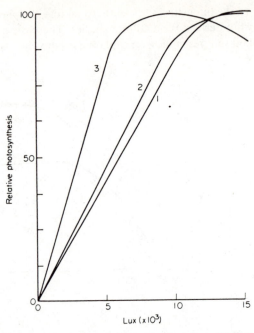

Fig. 3. The *relative* rate of photosynthesis as a function of light intensity. This figure contains the same data as in Fig. 2 except that the rate of photosynthesis at each light intensity (P) is related to the maximum rate (P_{max}) at saturating light intensities. That is, P/P_{max} is plotted against light intensity. (From Steemann-Nielsen & Hansen.[43])

In essence, the issue of light adaptation is concerned with the question of whether growth at low light intensities increases the ability of algae to assimilate carbon dioxide at those low light intensities. In the data of both Steemann-Nielsen & Hansen[43] and Yentsch & Lee[44] there is no evidence for adaptation of this kind. That is, although photosynthesis by algae grown at low light intensities saturates at lower intensities, the rate of photosynthesis at the saturating light intensities is also lower, so that the absolute rate of photosynthesis at low light intensities is not enhanced by previous growth in reduced light (see Fig. 2).

Later, Steemann-Nielsen & Jørgensen[45] clarified the question of light adaptation further. From work with cultures of *Chorella pyrenoidosa* these authors emphasized the difference between expressing rates of photosynthesis *per unit amount of chlorophyll* and expressing them *per unit cell number*. When the latter is done there is good evidence of real adaptation to low light intensities; that is, that photosynthesis at these low light intensities is enhanced by previous growth at reduced light intensities (Fig. 4). (The previous work had expressed photosynthesis per unit amount of chlorophyll.) The difference arises because growth at low light intensities increases the chlorophyll content of algae. Although not all algae adapt to light intensity in the same way[45–47] this change in the chlorophyll concentration is the main reproducible physiological response of algae to growth at reduced light intensities.

The implication of the above discussion of adaptation is that, when the productivity figures are expressed per unit amount of chlorophyll, it is unlikely that the rate of photosynthesis at the bottom of the photic zone can be higher than the calculated value. That is, by measuring chlorophyll, we have already taken account of the main adaptive change, namely the increased chlorophyll content per cell at reduced light intensities.

2. *Temperature*

It seems to be generally agreed that temperature is not an important limiting factor in the sea. For example, Steemann-Nielsen[20] writes: 'Recent investigations have shown, however, that the direct influence of temperature on organic production in the sea is fairly insignificant.' And Eppley[48] has recently written: 'Temperature does not seem to be very important in the production of phytoplankton in the sea.'

This view comes essentially from the fact that over wide ranges of temperature in the oceans the primary productivity (expressed per unit amount of chlorophyll) is remarkably constant. That is, between about 5 and 30°C there appears to be little difference in the rate of photosynthesis by the phytoplankton in the sea. (At lower temperatures in the polar regions temperature can begin to limit the photosynthetic rate.) This constancy over a wide temperature range is assumed to result from temperature adaptation of the marine algae and several attempts have been made to investigate the mechanism of adaptation of algae to sub-optimal temperatures.[45,49-51] The most widely accepted hypothesis suggests that algae grown at reduced temperatures have increased levels of the enzymes required for carbon dioxide fixation. However, recently we have suggested that this apparent higher levels of enzymes in algae grown at lower temperatures are artifacts resulting from variable physiology of algae at different stages during growth in batch culture (Morris *et al.*, unpublished).

Recently, Eppley[48] has re-examined the role of temperature in the primary productivity of the sea. His general conclusion is that temperature in the oceans sets the upper limit for phytoplankton growth rate and for the rate of photosynthesis per unit amount of chlorophyll but that, due to other factors becoming important (for example, light intensity and nutrient concentration), phytoplankton growth seldom approaches the upper limit which would be limited by

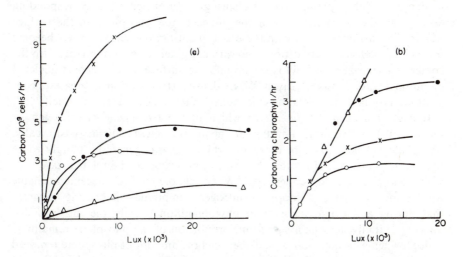

Fig. 4. The effect of light intensity on the rate of photosynthesis by *Chlorella pyrenoidosa*. The alga was grown at four different light intensities; 0·32 klux (○), 1 klux (×), 3 klux (●) and 21 klux (△). In (a) photosynthesis is expressed on a per cell basis; in (b) on a per chlorophyll basis. (From Steemann-Nielsen & Jørgensen.[45])

temperature. To a large extent the experimental approaches of Morris *et al.*[52] support these conclusions of Eppley. These workers observed that growth of a natural population of phytoplankton in the laboratory required temperatures significantly higher than the temperature of the water from which the sample was taken. Although these experiments are open to the objection that natural populations have been brought into the laboratory (with all the attendant problems) they nevertheless show that, under appropriate conditions, temperature can limit phytoplankton growth, but that other factors presumably mask this in the oceans. It is also clear from these laboratory experiments with natural phytoplankton populations that adaptation to temperatures occurs by selection of different species and not through changes to single species as suggested by work with algal cultures.

3. *Nutrients*

(a) *Nitrogen and phosphorus as limiting nutrients.* Many of the dissolved nutrients required for phytoplankton growth are probably present in the oceans in concentrations in excess of those required. These include such elements as inorganic carbon, sodium, calcium, potassium, bromine, boron, magnesium and sulphur. However, others may be present in limiting concentrations. The most notable examples of these seem to be inorganic nitrogen and inorganic phosphorus; both essential nutrients required for the growth of phytoplankton and both present in seawater at concentrations which are orders of magnitude less than those found in soils.

There are several obvious reasons for believing nitrogen and phosphorus are the important limiting factors determining the primary productivity of the sea. For example, the geographical variation in primary productivity parallels the variation in phosphate and nitrogen concentrations. That is, the regions of high productivities such as coastal and upwelling areas also show the highest concentrations of those two elements in their surface layers; whereas the oligotrophic waters of the open ocean (particularly in tropical and sub-tropical regions) show lowest levels of these nutrients. Similarly, in those waters showing seasonal periodicity of phytoplankton growth (such as the temperate waters) the increase in density of phytoplankton in the spring is paralleled by a corresponding decrease in the concentrations of the nitrogen and phosphate in the surface waters. This arises because, with the onset of spring, the surface layers become warmer and density stratification (the warmer lighter waters not mixing with the cooler heavier waters below) is set up and the surface layers become depleted of nutrients. As Yentsch[4] says: 'When density stratification is greatest, concentrations of both nutrients and chlorophyll in the surface layers are small.[53,54]

It has often been debated as to which of the two elements (nitrogen or phosphorus) is the more limiting in the marine environment. Historically, phosphate was held to be the more important and was generally thought to be the 'master nutrient'. However, this was, in part, due to the relative ease with which phosphate could be measured. When reliable methods became available for the measurements of inorganic nitrogen compounds, it became apparent that during a seasonal increase in phytoplankton density the nitrogen disappeared rapidly, leaving a significant proportion of the phosphate remaining. Indeed, when a comparison is made between the amount of phosphate removed and the amount which might have been expected to be removed by the observed growth of phytoplankton, there is discrepancy which is generally resolved by assuming a fairly rapid recycling of phosphate.[39,55] An alternative source of phosphate comes from the organic phosphorus compounds dissolved in the surface layers of the sea. The concentration of these appears to be as much as five to ten times the concentration of inorganic phosphate[56] and recently alkaline phosphatase activity (an enzyme allowing the utilization of organic phosphorus compounds) has been detected in marine phytoplankton.[57,58]

It seems unlikely that phosphate is a limiting factor in the marine environments; emphasis is placed, instead, on nitrogen. Inorganic nitrogen is found in the oceans as nitrate, nitrite and ammonium. Dissolved elemental nitrogen is also present, but, despite the existence of blue-green algae in surface layers generally devoid of combined nitrogen, the significance of nitrogen fixation in the sea is not established. Similarly, the role of the organic nitrogen compounds in the ocean is poorly understood. Thus most of the emphasis has been placed on the combined forms of inorganic nitrogen—nitrate, nitrite and ammonium. Evidence from work with algal cultures suggests that algae are able to utilize all three forms, ammonium being preferentially assimilated when all three are present.[59-61]

(b) *Nitrogen deficiency of natural phytoplankton populations*. Recent experimental work has tried to establish whether phytoplankton from waters apparently devoid of inorganic compounds are physiologically nitrogen-deficient. The general approach has been to define various characteristics of nitrogen-deficient alagae from work with cultures, measure these parameters in natural populations of marine phytoplankton and so conclude whether the population has the characteristics of nitrogen-deficient algae. A number of different biochemical features have been emphasized. Yentsch & Vaccaro[62] and Manney[63] emphasized the ratio of carotenoid to chlorophyll concentration. During the onset of nitrogen deficiency in cultures the chlorophyll content decreases more rapidly than does the carotenoid level. Steele & Baird[64,65] have used a similar approach in measuring the carbon/chlorophyll ratio. These latter workers observed that for both Loch Nevis and the Fladen Ground in the North Sea the carbon/chlorophyll ratios were at a maximum in the summer and a minimum in the spring and the autumn (this was most marked in the North Sea). Such a change is consistent with the idea of developing nitrogen deficiency after the spring bloom of phytoplankton.

The attention of other workers has been focused on the nutrient-deficient surface layers of tropical and sub-tropical waters. Thomas[66] compared the assimilation numbers (the rate of photosynthesis per weight of chlorophyll) from nutrient-rich and nutrient-poor waters in an attempt to discover whether the phytoplankton from the former were nitrogen deficient. He concluded that there was little significant difference between the two regions. More recently, Morris *et al.*[67] have adopted a slightly different approach. The basis for their experiments was the fact that nitrogen-deficient cultures of algae display an ammonium enhancement of dark carbon dioxide fixation.[59] That is, the rate of dark fixation of carbon dioxide by nitrogen-deficient cells is markedly increased by the addition of ammonium; this phenomenon is not observed with 'normal' cells. Morris *et al.*[67] could not obtain any evidence of ammonium enhancement of dark carbon fixation in any phytoplankton populations off the coast of South Florida, even in water apparently devoid of inorganic nitrogen sources. These workers concluded that level of nutrients might limit the size of a phytoplankton population but will not yield a population which is physiologically nutrient-deficient (a concept which agrees with the results of Eppley *et al.*[68] and Thomas[66]).

Recently Thomas & Dodson[69] have adopted an interesting approach to the problem of nitrogen deficiency in sub-tropical waters. These workers grew a marine diatom *Chaetoceros gracilis* in a nitrogen-limited chemostat and measured various biochemical parameters at various degrees of limitation. These parameters included the rate of photosynthesis per unit chlorophyll, the chlorophyll content per cell, the carbon/chlorophyll ratio, and the carbon/nitrogen ratio. They then measured some of those biochemical parameters in the Pacific ocean and concluded that the natural population was growing at less than its maximum possible growth rate. It is doubtful whether such an extrapolation can be made from this kind of culture work to the natural situation, but the approach could be pursued further in an attempt to understand the problem of nutrient deficiency in the ocean.

(c) *Nutrient concentration and the species composition of the phytoplankton population*. One further aspect of nutrient limitation in the oceans has also been studied extensively over the past ten years; the question of the species composition of phytoplankton from nutrient-poor and nutrient-rich waters. Yentsch[70] has recently emphasized the work of Hulburt[71-73] on the diversity of phytoplankton from waters of various nutrient status. The general point to emerge from this work is that phytoplankton populations of high cell densities are less diverse; that is, that diversity generally increases from eutrophic coastal waters to oligotrophic conditions of the open ocean.

Complementing this work on the species composition has been extensive attempts to measure the biochemical characteristics of nutrient uptake by different species of phytoplankton and so discover what determines the species distribution relative to nutrient concentration. The basis of this approach has been the idea that the uptake of nutrient and the growth of the organisms show a Michaelis-Menton relationship with increasing nutrient concentration. This assumes that the uptake of the nutrient (substrate) (or the growth of the organism) interacts with the nutrient (substrate) concentration in a way which can be described by a hyperbolic curve. That is, at certain concentrations of substrate the uptake and growth is satisfied (saturated). The affinity of the organism for the nutrient (substrate) can be shown by the 'half-saturation' constant, K_s. This is comparable to the Michaelis constant (K_m) for enzymes. The interesting idea behind this approach was the question of whether species of phytoplankton from oligotrophic waters relatively low in nutrients had K_s values different from algae isolated from water rich in nutrients.[68,74,78]

Most of this work has been concerned with determining the half-saturation constants for ammonium and nitrate uptake of phytoplankton isolated from oligotrophic and eutrophic waters. MacIssac & Dugdale[74] observed lower K_s values for uptake by natural populations from oligotrophic water than by those from eutrophic regions. Eppley & Thomas[75] measured the growth rates (not nutrient uptake) of several species of phytoplankton isolated from oligotropic and eutrophic waters, but could not detect any reproducible differences in the half-saturation constants with respect to both nitrate and ammonium.

Thomas[77] has measured the growth of a natural population of phytoplankton in the presence of increasing concentrations of ammonium or nitrate and, from this, determined the K_s and μ_{max} (maximum growth rate at saturating nutrient concentrations). With this information he then measured the concentration of nitrate and ammonium in the water and from this estimated the growth rate of the phytoplankton population in the sea. He obtained growth rates which agreed well with those estimated from the carbon-14 method. Despite the problem attending laboratory experiment on natural populations of phytoplankton, this is nevertheless an interesting approach to the problem of determining the growth rates of phytoplankton in the oceans. The kinetic approach outlined

292

above has yielded interesting results but has not explained satisfactorily the distribution of certain species in nutrient-poor and nutrient-rich waters.

(d) *Metals and vitamins as possible limiting nutrients.* So far we have emphasized nitrogen and phosphorus as the important limiting nutrients in the sea and placed particular emphasis on nitrogen. However, other nutrients have been suggested as likely candidates for limiting the growth of marine phytoplankton. The most important of these are certain metals and vitamins. The most important metals are iron and manganese.[4,39] These metals are easily adsorbed on to particulate matter of all kinds and it is conceivable that the photic zone could be stripped of both elements in this way.[79] Indirect evidence to support the limiting role of these two metals comes from Harvey's observations[79] that phytoplankton growth could be stimulated by the addition of iron and manganese to water already enriched with nitrogen and phosphorus. Similarly, the rate of ^{14}C-carbon dioxide fixation by populations from the Sargasso Sea was not stimulated by the addition of nitrate, phosphate or vitamins, but increased several fold by the addition of a trace metal solution.[80,81] The effective metal was found to be iron. This work has not been pursued and it seems uncertain as to its general implications.

Many phytoplankton require vitamin B_{12}, biotin or thiamin for growth. The amounts needed are extremely small, of the order of $\sim 10^{-9}$ g/litre. The debate has surrounded the question of whether the levels of vitamins in the sea can limit the growth of the phytoplankton. Originally, Droop[82] doubted whether phytoplankton growth in the sea was ever limited by vitamin B_{12}. But later, Menzel & Spaeth[83] observed that its concentration in the surface waters of the Sargasso Sea reached extremely low levels and that the spring increase in diatoms coincided with an increase in vitamin B_{12} content of the surface water. However, it has been difficult to extend these essentially qualitative observations to more critical quantitative descriptions of vitamins as limiting factors.

One approach towards the latter has been to determine the yield of algae in culture as a function of concentration of the vitamin and then to calculate the maximum yield of phytoplankton which could be expected from the observed vitamin level.[82,84] In coastal waters at least, there appears to be a sufficiently high concentration of vitamins to permit the observed highest phytoplankton crops. More detailed investigations of the kinetics of phytoplankton growth in the presence of increasing vitamin concentration is difficult. The problem seems to be associated with the fact that most of the vitamin enters the cell very rapidly and that specific growth rates in chemostats do not depend on the vitamin concentration in the medium but on its concentration in the cells.[84,85] To date these attempts at more quantitative measurements of the effects of vitamins have not clarified their ecological role. It seems unlikely that they are limiting in the same sense that nitrogen might be, but the selection of certain species could depend on their requirements for vitamins.[70]

In discussing the role of nutrients, I have omitted one important factor. It is becoming increasingly apparent that nutrients alone cannot determine the size of the phytoplankton stock. It seems necessary to take account also of grazing by the herbivorous zooplankton and for this to be superimposed on nutrient availability in both nutrient-rich and nutrient-poor waters. As Yentsch[70] says: 'It is indeed apparent that the emphasis once placed between nutrient availability and phytoplankton population dynamics must now be shared between nutrient availability and zooplankton grazing.'

Conclusions

The main object of this review has been threefold; to outline some of the more generally accepted views on the primary productivity of the oceans and of the factors which limit this, to point out the more important doubts surrounding these views, and to illustrate some of the more recent attempts which have been made to resolve these doubts.

It is clear that, despite a sensitive and convenient method of measuring the rate of photosynthesis by a natural phytoplankton population (the carbon-14 method) there is considerable doubt surrounding the calculation of primary productivity. Despite these doubts, certain general conclusions about marine productivity may be drawn. The primary productivity of phytoplankton in the sea (when expressed per unit area) is about the same as the less productive and desert areas on land. This lower productivity of the marine environment is accompanied by striking differences in the standing crop of plants supported by the environment; terrestrial environments being able to support five to ten times the maximum chlorophyll levels which can be present in the sea.

The important limiting factors affecting the standing crop and the subsequent primary production appear to be light and nutrient concentration. The absorption of light by sea water limits photosynthesis to the top 100 m (in the clearest water), and the phytoplankton density cannot be increased without reducing the depth of the photic zone. The most important nutrient limiting the size of the population in the sea appears to be nitrogen. The recent experimental approaches have tried to define in precise terms the physiological and biochemical mechanisms by which these various environmental factors determine the activity of phytoplankton. These attempts have merely emphasized the unsolved problems which remain in the study of primary productivity in the oceans.

References

1. STEEMANN-NIELSEN E. (1952) *J. Cons. perm. int. Explor. Mer.* **18,** 117.
2. GAARDER T.C. & GRAN H.H. (1927) *Rapp. Cons. Explor. Mer.* **42,** 48.
3. JITTS H.R. & SCOTT B.D. (1961) *Limnol. Oceanogr.* **6,** 116.
4. YENTSCH C.S. (1963) *Oceanogr. mar. Biol. A. Rev.* **1,** 157.
5. WILLIAMS P.J.LeB., BERMAN T. & HOLM-HANSEN O. (1972) *Nature, Lond.* **236,** 91.
6. FOGG G.E. (1964) *Chem. Weekbl.* **60,** 515.
7. FOGG G.E. (1966) *Oceanogr. mar. Biol. A. Rev.* **4,** 195.
8. MELLEBUST J.A. (1967) In *Estuaries* (Ed. by G. L. Lauff). A.A.A.S. No. 83, p. 361.
9. ANDERSON G.C. & ZENTSCHELL R.P. (1970) *Limnol. Oceanogr.* **15,** 402.
10. WATT W.D. (1966) *Proc. R. Soc. B* **165,** 521.
11. HORNE A.J., FOGG G.E. & EAGLE D.J. (1969) *J. mar. biol. Ass. U.K.* **49,** 393.
12. RYTHER J.H., MENZEL D.W., HULBURT E.M., LORENZEN C.J. & CORWIN N. (1971) *Investigación pesq.* **35,** 43.
13. THOMAS J.P. (9171) *Mar. Biol.* **11,** 311.
14. STEEMANN-NIELSEN E. & HANSEN V.K. (1959) *Deep Sea Res.* **5,** 222.
15. RYTHER J.H. (1954) *Deep Sea Res.* **2,** 134.
16. RYTHER J.H. (1959) *Science, N.Y.* **130,** 602.
17. McALLISTER C.D., PARSONS T.R., STEPHENS K. & STRICKLAND J.D.H. (1961) *Limnol. Oceanogr.* **6,** 237.
18. RYTHER J.H. (1956) *Nature, Lond.* **178,** 861.
19. MORRIS I., YENTSCH C.M. & YENTSCH C.S. (1971) *Limnol. Oceanogr.* **16,** 854.
20. STEEMANN-NIELSEN E. (1960) *Physiologia Pl.* **13,** 348.
21. STEEMANN-NIELSEN E. & JENSEN E.A. (1957) *Galathea Rep.* **1,** 49.
22. RYTHER J.H. (1969) *Science, N.Y.* **166,** 72.
23. VISHNIAC W. (1971) In *Microbes and Biological Producivity* (Ed. by D. E. Hughes and A. H. Rose), Vol. 21, p. 355. Soc. Gen. Microbiol. Symp.
24. RUSSELL-HUNTER W.N. (1970) *Aquatic Productivity.* MacMillan, London.
25. WESTLAKE D.F. (1963) *Biol. Rev.* **38,** 385.
26. ODUM E.P. (1959) *Fundamentals of Ecology,* 2nd edn. Saunders, New York.

27. PHILLIPSON J. (1966) *Ecological Energetics*. Inst. Biol. Studies in Biol. No. 1, Arnold, London.
28. YENTSCH C.S. & MENZEL D.W. (1963) *Deep Sea Res.* **10,** 221.
29. LORENZEN C.J. (1966) *Deep Sea Res.* **13,** 223.
30. STRICKLAND J.D.H. & PARSONS T.R. (1968) *A Practical Handbook of Seawater Analysis*, Bulletin 167, Fisheries Research Board, Canada.
31. GOLTERMAN H.L. (Ed.) (1969) *Methods for Chemical Analaysis of Freshwaters*. IBP Handbook No. 8. Blackwell Scientific Publications, Oxford.
32. LOFTUS M.E. & CARPENTER J.H. (1971) *J. mar. Res.* **29,** 319.
33. HOLM-HANSEN O., LORENZEN C.J., HOLMES R.W. & STRICKLAND J.D.H. (1965) *J. Cons. perm. int. Explor. Mer.* **30,** 3.
34. BRAY J.R. (1960) *Can. J. Bot.* **38,** 313.
35. STEEMANN-NIELSEN E. & HANSEN V.K. (1961) *Physiol. Pl.* **14,** 593.
36. JERLOV N.G. (1951) *Rep. Swed. deep Sea Exped.* **3,** 3.
37. YENTSCH C.S. (1960) *Deep Sea Res.* **7,** 1.
38. YENTSCH C.S. (1962) In *Physiology and Biochemistry of Algae* (Ed. by R. A. Lewin), p. 771. Academic Press, London.
39. HOLMES R.W. (1957) In *Treatise on Marine Ecology and Paleoecology* (Ed. by J. W. Hedgpeth), Vol. 1, p. 109. Mem. geol. Soc. Ass. No 67.
40. FOGG G.E. & BOALCH G.T. (1958) *Nature, Lond.* **181,** 789.
41. YENTSCH C.S. & REICHART C.A. (1962) *Bot. Mar.* **3,** 65.
42. RYTHER J.H. (1956) *Limnol. Oceanogr.* **1,** 61.
43. STEEMANN-NIELSEN E. & HANSEN V.K. (1959) *Physiologia Pl.* **12,** 353.
44. YENTSCH C.S. & LEE R.W. (1966) *J. mar. Res.* **24,** 319.
45. STEEMANN-NIELSEN E. & JØRGENSEN E.G. (1968) *Physiologia Pl.* **21,** 401.
46. JØRGENSEN E.G. (1964) *Physiologia Pl.* **17,** 136.
47. JØRGENSEN E.G. (1964) *Physiologia Pl.* **17,** 407.
48. EPPLEY R.W. (1972) *Fishery Bulletin* (in press).
49. STEEMANN-NIELSEN E. & JØRGENSEN E.G. (1968) *Physiologia Pl.* **21,** 647.
50. JØRGENSEN E.G. (1968) *Physiologia Pl.* **21,** 425.
51. MORRIS I. & FARRELL K. (1971) *Physiologia Pl.* **25,** 372.
52. MORRIS I., STRUBE L.S., YENTSCH C.M. & YENTSCH C.S. (1973) (In preparation).
53. KETCHUM B.H., VACCARO R.F. & CORWIN N. (1958) *J. mar. Res.* **17,** 282.
54. RYTHER J.H. & YENTSCH C.S. (1958) *Limnol. Oceanogr.* **3,** 327.
55. REDFIELD A.C., SMITH H.P. & KETCHUM B.H. (1937) *Biol. Bull. mar. biol. Lab., Woods Hole* **73,** 421.
56. KETCHUM B.H., CORWIN N. & KEEN D.J. (1955) *Deep Sea Res.* **2,** 172.
57. KUENZLER E.J. & PERRAS J. P. (1965) *Biol. Bull. mar. biol. Lab., Woods Hole* **128,** 271.
58. YENTSCH C.M., YENTSCH C.S. & PERRAS J.P. (1972) *Limnol. Oceanogr.* (in press).
59. SYRETT P.J. (1962) In *Physiology and Biochemistry of Algae* (Ed. by R. A. Lewin), p. 171. Academic Press, London.
60. KESSLER E. (1964) *Ann. Rev. Pl. Physiol.* **15,** 57.
61. MORRIS I. (1972) In *Physiology and Biochemistry of Algae* (Ed. by W. D. P. Stewart), Chap. 14. Academic Press, London.
62. YENTSCH C.S. & VACCARO R.F. (1958) *Limnol. Oceanogr.* **3,** 443.
63. MANNEY B.A. (1969) *Limnol. Oceanogr.* **14,** 69.
64. STEELE J.H. & BAIRD I.E. (1962) *Limnol. Oceanogr.* **1,** 42.
65. STEELE J.H. & BAIRD I.E. (1962) *Limnol. Oceanogr.* **1,** 101.
66. THOMAS W.H. (1970) *Limnol. Oceanogr.* **15,** 380.
67. MORRIS I., YENTSCH C.M. & YENTSCH C.S. (1971) *Limnol. Oceanogr.* **16,** 859.
68. EPPLEY R.W., RODGERS J.N. & MCCARTHY J.J. (1969) *Limnol. Oceanogr.* **14,** 912.
69. THOMAS W.D. & DODSON A. (1972) *Limnol. Oceanogr.* (in press).
70. YENTSCH C.S. (1973) *Oceanogr. mar. Biol. A. Rev.* (in press).
71. HULBERT E.M. (1956) *Biol. Bull. mar. biol. Lab., Woods Hole* **110,** 156.
72. HULBERT E.M. (1963) *J. mar. Res.* **21,** 81.
73. HULBERT E.M. (1970) *Ecology* **51,** 475.
74. MACISAAC J.J. & DUGDALE R.C. (1969) *Deep Sea Res.* **16,** 415.
75. EPPLEY R.W. & THOMAS W.H. (1969) *J. Phycol.* **5,** 375.
76. CARPENTER E.J. & GUILLARD R.R.L. (1970) *Ecology* **52,** 183.
77. THOMAS W.H. (1970) *Limnol. Oceanogr.* **15,** 386.
78. THOMAS W.H. & OWEN R.W., JR (1971) *Fishery Bulletin* **69,** 87.
79. HARVEY H.W. (1955) *The Chemistry and Fertility of Sea Waters*. Cambridge University Press.
80. MENZEL D.W. & RYTHER J.H. (1961) *Deep Sea Res.* **7,** 276.
81. MENZEL D.W. & RYTHER J.H. (1961) *Limnol. Oceanogr.* **7,** 282.
82. DROOP M.R. (1957) *Nature, Lond.* **180,** 1041.
83. MENZEL D.W. & SPAETH J.P. (1962) *Limnol. Oceanogr.* **7,** 151.
84. CARLUCCI A.F. & SILBERNAGEL S.B. (1969) *J. Phycol.* **5,** 64.
85. DROOP M.R. (1968) *J. mar. biol. Ass. U.K.* **48,** 689.

ENERGY DYNAMICS OF A FOOD CHAIN OF AN OLD-FIELD COMMUNITY

FRANK B. GOLLEY

*Department of Zoology, Michigan State University, East Lansing, Michigan**

INTRODUCTION

In recent years there has been a growing interest in the study of the transfer of energy through natural systems (ecosystems, Tansley 1935). Park (1946) stated that "probably the most important ultimate objective of ecology is an understanding of community structure and function from the viewpoint of its metabolism and energy relationships." Aquatic biologists have taken the initiative in the study of community energetics, and most of the information available today concerns fresh water or marine communities. A great need exists for similar studies on terrestrial communities.

In this study a food chain of the old field community, from perennial grasses and herbs to the meadow mouse, *Microtus pennsylvanicus pennsylvanicus* Ord, and to the least weasel, *Mustela rixosa allegheniensis* Rhoads, was chosen for investigation. This food chain included the dominant vertebrate of the community (*Microtus*) and one of its main predators (*Mustela*) but excluded the otherwise important insects, other invertebrates, bacteria, and fungi. The primary objectives of the study were to determine (1) the rate of synthesis of organic matter by the primary producers—the vegetation, (2) the path of this energy from the vegetation through the mouse to the weasel, and (3) the losses of energy at each step in the food chain.

The writer wishes to acknowledge with gratitude the suggestions and guidance of Dr. Don W. Hayne, Institute of Fisheries Research, Michigan Department of Conservation, especially concerning that portion of the study dealing with the population dynamics and productivity of the *Microtus* population. The writer also thanks Dr. John E. Cantlon, Department of

* Present Address: Department of Zoology, University of Georgia, Athens, Georgia.

Botany, and Dr. Robert C. Ball, Department of Fisheries and Wildlife, Michigan State University, for aid given throughout the project. The investigation was supported by the Michigan Agricultural Experiment Station through a project administered by Dr. Hayne.

DESCRIPTION OF THE AREA

The study area was located in a large field on the Michigan State University State Farm approximately one mile south-east of Okemos, Ingham County, Michigan (sec. 27, T. 4N, R. 1W). As far as is known, this farm was last tilled in 1918 when it was given to the State of Michigan by Mr. John Fink. It was acquired by Michigan State University in 1940 and was pastured from 1940 to 1942. The study area has been undisturbed since 1942, with the exception of some tree planting by the Department of Forestry, Michigan State University, and probably occasional burning. The tree plantings appeared to be only slightly successful. The vegetation on the area was unburned from January 1952 to March 1957.

The field in which the study area was located was situated on the north terrace of the Red Cedar River, approximately 20 ft above the level of the river. The topography was gently undulating, with a relief of 15 ft or less. A shallow depression ran through the center of one of the trapping areas and served as a drain during the heavy rains in the winter and spring. On February 9, 1957, the snow melt-water was approximately 7 in. deep in this drainage area. As the snow melted in February and March much of the study area was inundated, with grass hummocks and hillocks on the border of the trap area providing the only dry sites.

The soils on the study area were predominantly Conover and Miami loam (determined from the soil map by Veatch *et al.* 1941).

On the east the field was separated from similar habitat by a paved county road. The north boundary was predominantly pasture land and orchard. The west boundary was an experimental alfalfa field left uncut in 1957. To the south the field was bounded by an unused gravel road, which ran along the ridge top above the river terrace and separated the field from other old field vegetation containing more woody cover and indicating a later stage of old field development. The field itself contained approximately 10 ha of relatively homogeneous habitat.

The climate in this area of Michigan is characterized by cold winters and mild summers (Baten & Eichmeier 1951). Yearly precipitation at East Lansing (1911-1949) averages 31 in.; growing season (last day in spring to the first day in fall when the temperature reaches 32°F) precipitation averages 17 in. The mean annual temperature is approximately 47°F, with extremes ranging from −20° to +102°F. The growing season averages 147 days. Solar radiation at East Lansing (3 mi west of the study area) is peculiar in that a plateau in the insolation curve may be expected about April 25 to May 20. When solar energy received at East Lansing is compared with that at most of the 92 weather stations in North America measuring solar insolation, it is evident that East Lansing receives annually less solar heat than any other station, with the exception of Fairbanks, Alaska (Crabb 1950b).

No attempt was made to make a complete survey of the flora and fauna of the community. The vegetation of the study area was transitional between the perennial grass stage (perennial grasses predominant) and the perennial herb stage (perennial herbs co-dominant with the grasses) of old field succession (Beckwith 1954). The vegetation is considered similar to the bluegrass-upland association of Blair (1948) and the upland community of Evans & Cain (1952).

Canada blue grass, *Poa compressa*[1], was dominant over the entire area, with three herb species, *Daucus carota*, *Cirsium arvense*, and *Linaria vulgaris*, sharing dominance in portions of the area. The study area was divided into four facies on the basis of co-dominance of the above herbs with *Poa compressa*. Mosses, undeveloped small herbs, and grass shoots formed a subordinate layer beneath the grass and perennial herb layer. A woody overstory occurred sporadically over the area, consisting primarily of *Crataegus* spp., *Pyrus communis, Prunus pennsylvanica*. The woody plants were a relatively unimportant component of the vegetation, the percentage cover for all woody plants averaging approximately 0.5.

The vertebrate dominants of the community, excluding birds, were *Microtus pennsylvanicus* and *Blarina brevicauda*, when total number observed was used as the criterion of dominance.

[1] Authorities for vascular plant binomials are those given in Fernald (1950).

METHODS

As energy flows through a terrestrial food chain there is a successive transfer and loss of energy at each step in the chain (Fig. 1). As a result of the continual loss of energy through respiration and through nonutilization of food, each successive population is faced with a smaller energy source. In this report the writer's approach has been to study the energy flow through each separate population, rather than to emphasize the energy exchange through the food chain as a whole. In the traditional style of presenting research methods and results separately, this concern for each species population becomes especially evident and necessarily obscures the picture of energy flow through the entire food chain. The writer believes that this method of presentation is most satisfactory for an exploratory study of this nature. However, by referring to Fig. 1, the reader will be able to follow the flow of energy through the food chain without difficulty.

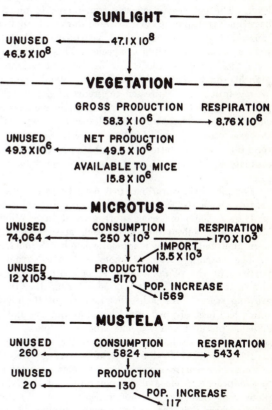

Fig. 1. The energy flow through the food chain from May, 1956 to May, 1957, on one hectare. All figures are Calories per hectare. Solar input represents that for the 1956 growing season.

Measurement of Solar Insolation

Records of solar insolation (the rate at which solar energy is received on a horizontal surface at the surface of the earth) were obtained from the Michigan Hydrologic Research Station (the Agricultural Research Service, USDA, and the Michigan Agricultural

Experiment Station cooperating). The station operates an Eppley ten-junction thermopile, thermoelectric pyrheliometer, mounted on a small instrument house on an isolated section of the Michigan State University Farm, East Lansing. There is little smoke contamination at this location (Crabb 1950a) and it is assumed that the records obtained at the pyrheliometer were applicable to the study area approximately 3 mi to the east.

Studies of Vegetation

The vegetation was studied from August 1956 to September 1957. Midway through the investigation (March 1957) a fire destroyed the vegetation on one-half of the study area, and it was necessary to move the entire operation to another portion of the same field. Fortunately there was no discernible difference in vegetation or topography at these two locations.

Square clip-plots (0.5 × 0.5 m) were used to estimate the standing crop of vegetation. All plant stems within the quadrats were clipped at the ground level. The cut vegetation was transferred to plastic bags and transported to the laboratory, where live grasses, live herbs, and dead vegetative materials were separated according to species. These materials were then dried at 100°C for 24 hrs and weighed. Monthly data were averaged and the standing crop of vegetation was expressed in grams of dry weight per 0.25 m². Ten to twenty random clip-plots were chosen for investigation each collection period, with the exception of late March. The adverse weather conditions in the latter part of March allowed an estimate to be made of green vegetation on only two plots.

Samples of several months' collections of dried grasses and herbs were randomly chosen for calorific analyses. These materials were ground in a Wiley Mill. Three subsamples from each species sample were analyzed in a Parr adiabatic bomb calorimeter.

The standing crop of roots and above-ground portions of the plants which escaped clipping were also determined at three periods during the 1957 growing season. At each collection, five of the plots which had been clipped were chosen at random and a 225-cm² piece of sod was cut from each plot. The sod was later washed in running water, oven dried at 100°C and weighed to determine average weight of roots per square meter. The samples were taken to a depth of 15 cm and did not represent the complete root biomass. Although Shively & Weaver (1939) show that the roots of many prairie plants extend at least several feet into the soil, for this study it was assumed that the main mass of roots in the old field community were concentrated within 15 cm of the surface.

The standing crop of vegetation measured here was less than the total amount of organic matter synthesized over the growing season. This is because the standing crop includes neither the amount of vegetation which grew and died between the periods of measurement, nor the amount of vegetation consumed by animals. In this study, some dead vegetation of the current growing season was unavoidably included with the green vegetation since no effort was made to separate the dead and living portions of one leaf or small plant. The material that grew and died back to the ground during the current growing season could not be separated from the dead vegetation and is therefore a source of error in determination of net production. The magnitude of this error was not estimated.

The amount of vegetation consumed by *Microtus* was estimated from feeding experiments and stomach sample analyses. The food consumption of herbivorous insects and other invertebrates, which in the pasture community may be of considerable magnitude (Wolcott 1937), was undetermined.

Another source of error in estimating the net production of the vegetation is pointed out by Pearsall & Gorham (1956). They suggest that in perennial vegetation the peak standing crop is formed from (1) the accumulation of the organic matter during the present season and from (2) the organic matter stored in the roots the previous season. The techniques used in this study allowed no estimate of the contribution of the previous season's production to the current peak standing crop.

To obtain a complete estimate of the energy utilization of vegetation (gross production, Odum 1956), the energy used in respiration of the vegetation must be added to the net production. A field respirometer was devised to make a rough measure of the respiration of the vegetation and the soil organisms. Two 5-qt oil cans were forced 5 cm into the ground at randomly chosen sites on the study area. Gases were withdrawn from the cans into Bailey gas analysis bottles. Carbon dioxide and oxygen content of the air in the cans was determined in an Orsat-Henderson gas analysis apparatus. The cans were placed in the ground and the first samples were withdrawn approximately 1 hr after dark. The second sample was taken in the early morning when the air temperature at the ground surface was approximately equal to the air temperature observed when the first samples were withdrawn the previous night. The consumption of oxygen and production of carbon dioxide over the night (12 hrs) was determined as the differences in the percentage composition of oxygen and carbon dioxide in the air in the cans at the first and second sampling. No measurement was made of the diffusion of gases between the soil and the air under the cans. The RQ (CO_2/O_2) was calculated and the thermal equivalent (in Calories) of the oxygen used and the carbon dioxide produced was extrapolated from the tables in Brody (1945). Respiration was then expressed as Calories used per gram of plant tissue per hour respiration during the night.

Studies of the *Microtus* Population

The energy dynamics of the *Microtus* population were studied both in the field and by laboratory experiments. In the field a live-trapping program was

TABLE 1. Dynamics of the *Microtus* population on one hectare

Date	Average Number Captured Per Line	Fraction[1] Per cent	Population Density Per Hectare Numbers	Size of Trap Area Hectares	Average Individual Weight Grams	Standing Crop per Hectare Calories[2]	MORTALITY BETWEEN SUCCESSIVE TRAPPING PERIODS	
							Rate[3]	Calories
May 22-28.........	4	29.4	5.2	2.6	29	205	75	393
July 24-30.........	12	41.7	9.6	3.0	29	382	37	232
Sept. 4-10.........	20	41.0	16.5	3.0	29	654	52	539
Oct. 9-15..........	19	32.4	21.2	2.7	31	898	42	710
Nov. 17-23.........	28	22.2	42.4	2.4	29	1685	39	1162
Jan. 6-23.........	22	(13.3)[4]	77.3	2.1	27	2847	27	1245
Feb. 21-27.........	39	13.0	139.1	2.1	29	5525	(55)[4]	3284
March 19-26.......	22	13.6	75.3	2.2	25	2578	35	937
April 25-1.........	43	30.4	53.2	2.6	32	2330	57	1931

[1] The percentage of total captures taken in common to both lines.
[2] Caloric value of *Microtus* was 1.37 Calories per gram.
[3] Percentage disappearing from one trap period to the next.
[4] Estimated values.

initiated in May 1956 and continued to September 1957. This paper includes only the data for one annual cycle, May 1956 to May 1957. The program was designed to yield information on population density, mortality, growth rate, and production of young. The trapping design was developed by D. W. Hayne and consisted of two crossed trap lines, 100 m long, with the live traps spaced 2 m apart. One trap line was operated for 24 hrs, it was then unset and the line crossing it was set for 24 hrs. The total trapping period extended for 6 days, with 3 days for each line. Since by the sixth day of trapping unmarked animals were generally caught only in the end traps in a line, it was assumed that six days of trapping was adequate to capture most of the animals living in the trap area. It was desirable to use as short a trapping period as possible because trap mortality tended to increase progressively during the trapping period.

Captured animals were toe clipped, sexed, aged, weighed, and examined for breeding condition before being released. Traps were baited with oatmeal, and during the colder months corn was also placed in the traps to serve as a high energy supplement. It was thought that the use of corn materially reduced trap mortality during the winter. Covers, made of asphalt shingles covered with aluminum foil, shielded the traps from sunlight, rain, and snow and were thought to reduce trap mortality especially in the summer.

A ratio method was used to estimate population density. The following formula was suggested by D. W. Hayne:

$$P = \frac{bc}{ad} \qquad (1)$$

where a is the number of animals captured in common to both lines, b the average number of animals captured in each of the two lines (both a and b exclude those animals dying in the traps during the trapping period), c average for the two lines of all captures including deaths due to trapping, d the effective area trapped, and P the population density per unit area.

The trap area, bisected by each trap line, was a square of 10,000 m². Since the home ranges of the mice extended an unknown distance beyond these lines the square was increased on both sides and ends. On each side the area added was set arbitrarily as the fraction $\frac{a}{b}$ (in Formula 1) times one-half the trap line length, 50 m, times the length of one side, 100 m. At each end of the trapping square, the area was increased by a semicircle with a radius of one-half the length of the trap line plus the fractional increase computed above. Information on numbers captured and population estimates are shown in Table 1.

In calculating the production of (or total weight grown by) the *Microtus* population, it was necessary to use one method for the animals which were susceptible to capture (the adults and an unknown proportion of the juveniles) but to use an entirely different method for the nestling young which do not enter traps. For the trapped animals, production was calculated from the rates of growth and mortality observed among the trapped individuals, while for the nestling young, production was inferred from the observed rate of pregnancy, the known rate of growth of young, and the calculated rate at which the young entered the trap-susceptible population.

In calculations of production, the use of instantaneous rates has been advantageous (Clarke 1946, Clarke Edmondson & Ricker 1946, Ricker 1946). Assuming constant rates, the products of the instantaneous rates and the mean population for a period will yield, respectively, the production of animal tissue by the population and the quantity of tissue lost from the population. This approach is especially useful here since it allows estimation of the biomass or number of animals which were produced, grew, and were lost between measurements of the standing crop.

The recapture of resident animals in two consecutive trapping periods allowed an estimate to be made of the rate of weight gain or loss of the individuals.

This rate was estimated separately for the animals in a number of 10-gm weight classes, since the rate of growth changes with body weight (Table 2). For each weight class, the daily instantaneous rate of growth was multiplied by the mean biomass for the period to calculate the daily production by growth or the daily weight loss in that particular weight class. A proportionate weight change of less than one indicated that the animals in that class lost weight (Table 2).

To determine the production of the nestling young, it was necessary to establish (1) the potential production of young by the population (potential natality), (2) the number of young which entered the trap-susceptible population, and (3) the growth rate of the young. The estimate of the potential production of young was based on the rate of pregnancy determined in the field and on the gestation period and litter size as reported in the literature. Pregnancy rates were established by abdominal palpation of all females. Davis (1956) suggests that pregnancy is "visible" for 18 days in small rodents—this would mean that 86% of the pregnancies could be determined by abdominal palpation. Although Davis's findings could probably be extended to *Microtus,* the percentage of adult females found to be pregnant in this study (Table 3) was so large during most of the breeding season that Davis's correction could not be made. The average number of days required for a female in the population to produce one litter can be found by dividing the gestation period (21 days, Hamilton 1941) by the proportion of females pregnant, here termed f. With the additional assumptions that there is an even sex ratio and an average of five young per litter (Hamilton 1941, Hatt 1930, Blair 1940), we can infer that in each time interval of $21/f$ days, one female increases to 3.5 females—2.5 young females plus the mother. With the use of the following formula it is then possible to calculate the production of young:

$$\frac{\text{nat log } 3.5}{\dfrac{21}{f}} \times t \times p' \qquad (2)$$

where f is the percentage pregnancy among females, t is the time between trapping periods, and p' is the mean population.

The number of young entering the trap-susceptible population was assumed to equal the number of adults and juveniles lost to mortality plus the number needed to fulfill the population increase.

The growth rate of the nestling young was based on the weight increase from an assumed birth weight to the weight of the lightest juvenile captured in the live traps between trapping periods. Whitmoyer (1956) showed that the mean birth weight of laboratory *Microtus pennsylvanicus* was approximately 3 gm. The lightest weights of live-trapped juveniles ranged from 10 to 16 gm. The products of the instantaneous rate of growth of the nestling young and the mean biomass of young yielded the increase

TABLE 2. Tissue production of juveniles and adults per hectare.

Interval	PROPORTIONATE WEIGHT CHANGE WEIGHT CLASSES IN GRAMS				DAILY INSTANTANEOUS RATE OF GROWTH[1]		Growth Calories	Weight Loss Calories
	11-20	21-50	31-40	41-50	+	−		
May......	data not available							
July......	data not available							
Sept.....	2.06	1.00	1.10	—	3.08	—	74	—
Oct......	1.86[2]	1.20	1.00	.96	3.03	.19	81	5
Nov.....	1.70	1.04	.82	.69	1.32	2.28	56	95
Jan......	—	.99	.86	—	—	5.15	—	123
Feb......	—	—	.94	—	—	8.20	—	152
March....	1.71	1.27	.99	.91	20.92	.68	516	17
April.....	1.87	1.21	1.03	.91	9.92	1.72	190	33

[1] Positive and negative daily instantaneous rates of growth derived from proportionate weight gains and losses of all weight classes within the month.
[2] Boldface growth rates were calculated by the increment method.

TABLE 3. Potential production of new *Microtus* per hectare.

Date	Time Interval Between Trapping Days	Pregnancy Rate Per Cent	Mean Adult Population Numbers	POTENTIAL PRODUCTION	
				Numbers	Calories
May..........	64	90	7.2	24.8	102
July..........	42	90	12.6	28.5	117
Sept..........	35	90	18.5	34.8	143
Oct..........	39	90	30.7	64.5	265
Nov..........	61	65	58.2	137.9	567
Jan..........	35	00	104.7	—	—
Feb..........	27	00	103.7	—	—
March........	36	11	63.5	15.2	63
April.........	28	92	51.5	79.3	326
Totals.....				385.0	1583

in mouse tissue due to the nestlings between the two trapping periods. The contribution of nestling young is shown in Table 4.

TABLE 4. Growth of nestling young per hectare.

Date	Mean Biomass Grams	Growth Rate	TOTAL GROWTH	
			Grams	Calories
May........	144	5.33	242	331
July........	135	5.33	226	309
September...	180	5.33	302	414
October.....	333	4.67	516	706
November...	893	7.67	1231	1686
March......	100	4.67	154	211
April........	361	3.30	435	596
Totals....			3106	4253

When the amount of energy leaving the *Microtus* population through respiratory processes is added to the production of tissue, the result is a measure of the assimilation of the population. Assimilation is defined here as the energy which enters the population and is actually used in productive or maintenance processes. An estimate of the respiratory energy loss was made by studying the metabolic rate of *Microtus* by the McLagan-Sheahan (1950) closed circuit method. This technique utilized a series of desiccator jars connected to a pure O_2 source, a vacuum pump, and mercury manometers. Soda lime, in the bottom of jars, absorbed CO_2. The system was of known volume (approximately 2600 ml) and was kept at a constant temperature of 26°C. Wild *Microtus* were trapped the day before the experiment and fasted over night (12 hrs). Three or four mice of the same sex and weight were placed in each jar and, after air was evacuated from the jars to a negative pressure of 200 mm Hg, pure O_2 was introduced until pressure returned to equilibrium. As the O_2 was consumed in the jars, the pressure changes were measured on mercury manometers. The mice were allowed about 30 min to become accustomed to the apparatus before readings were made on the manometers. After this initial period, the mice were maintained in the jars for 1 hr. A respiratory quotient (RQ) of .85 was assumed in the computations of metabolic rate.

Metabolic rate determined by this method can not be considered a basal rate (BMR) because the animals were slightly active in the jars during the experiments. Rather than basal rate, this study determined the fasting metabolic rate (FMR) of *Microtus*. The FMR (Table 5) was calculated in terms of cc of O_2 consumed per gm mouse tissue per hour and in Cal per 24 hrs per individual mouse. The respiration of the adult biomass was estimated by multiplying the metabolic rate in Cal per 24 hrs per mouse by the population density at a trap period and by the number of days between succeeding trap periods. The product of the metabolic rate of the young (assumed to be 1.7 Cal per 24 hrs), the mean population of young, and the time interval between trapping periods yielded the respiration of the nestling young.

TABLE 5. Respiration of experimental animals.

Date	Ave. Weight Individuals Grams	Oxygen Consumption cc/gm/hr	Calories Per 24 Hours Per Mouse
Oct.	25.5	2.86	8.2
Feb.	34.9	2.55	10.6
April	31.0	2.83	10.2
Average	29.9	2.75	9.7

The FMR when applied to animals in the field should be considered a minimal figure of metabolism. Brody (1945: 477) considers that the maintenance energy expense is twice the basal metabolic rate. The energy cost of maintenance is the net dietary energy needed to carry on life processes, excluding the production of flesh, milk, or young.

To determine the caloric value of *Microtus* carcasses, four wild mice were sacrificed, minced, and dehydrated in a lyophilizing apparatus. This dried material was then burned in the bomb calorimeter to determine average caloric value per gm of dry mouse tissue. The wild mice were of average weight, rang-

ing from 10 to 39 gm, and did not exhibit large fat deposits around the internal organs.

Food consumption by mice was studied both in the field and in the laboratory. For the field studies, wild *Microtus* were snap-trapped every three months in other areas which were characterized by a bluegrass-perennial herb vegetation similar to that found on the study area. At least 24 mice were captured during each trapping period (Table 6). These mice were brought into the laboratory and their stomachs were removed and weighed. A portion of the stomach contents was placed on a glass slide with several drops of Turtox CMC-10 mounting media. A smear was made of this mixture and, after a cover glass was placed on the slide, the slide was examined under the low power objective of a microscope.

TABLE 6. Percentage importance of food materials from stomach samples.

Food Material	Fall	Winter	Spring	Summer
Number of stomachs	35	27	31	24
Grass	54	75	74	54
Herbs	28	18	23	44
Insects	T	T	1.8	T
Fruits	17	3	.1	1
Wood	1	4	.3	—
Seeds	T	—	.6	T
Moss	T	—	.1	T
Fungi	T	—	T	1
Grasses and herbs alone				
Grass	66	81	76	55
Herbs	34	19	24	45

A stomach content key was devised by feeding in the laboratory 5 *Microtus* on diets of natural foods, each mouse receiving only one food substance. These animals were sacrificed and slides of their stomach contents served as a reference key when examining the stomachs of wild mice. Under the microscope it was possible to distinguish the following food types: grasses, herbs, woody materials, roots, seeds, fruits, mosses, fungi, and insect remains. These identifications were made on the basis of cell shape, cell wall structure, arrangement of stomata, presence of parenchyma cells, sclereids, tracheids, and other elements. An estimate was made of the percentage that each food type contributed to the bulk of the plant material on each slide. The percentage importance of the food types was determined for the collection period by averaging the data for each individual stomach.

The quantity of food consumed was measured for caged mice in two laboratory experiments. In the first experiment, 15 mice in 5 cages were fed a "standard" laboratory diet of lettuce, carrots, and oatmeal (Whitmoyer 1956) for 30 days. In the second experiment, 5 mice were maintained on fresh-cut alfalfa for 30 days. Water was available in both experiments. Animals gained weight, bred, and gave birth to normal litters on both diets. Food materials were weighed in and out of the cages daily; the weight loss of fresh food between weighings was determined by using a control cage. The information on food consumption is summarized in Table 7. The caloric value of the standard diet was determined from Wooster & Blanck (1950) and that of the alfalfa by combustion in the bomb calorimeter.

TABLE 7. Daily food consumption of individual mice on experimental diets.

| | Standard Diet | | | | Alfalfa Diet Alfalfa |
	Lettuce	Carrot	Oatmeal	Total	
Consumption gms wet wgt...	24.8	10.2	4.4	39.4	28.1
Consumption gms dry wgt...	1.3	1.2	4.0	6.5	12.0
Caloric value of food per gm wet wgt................	.18	.45	3.96	—	—
Caloric value of food per gm dry wgt................	—	—	—	—	4.1
Calories consumed..........	4.5	4.6	17.4	26.5	49.3
Ave wgt mice (gms).........				46.0	46.0
Gms food consumed per gm mouse tissue..............				.14	.26
Food Calories consumed per gm mouse tissue.........				.58	1.07

The digestibility of the experimental diets was studied by collecting mouse feces in the cages for a 5-day period during each experiment. The feces were oven-dried and the caloric value determined in the bomb calorimeter. By this method it was possible to estimate the amount of gross energy in the feed which was undigested.

STUDIES OF THE LEAST WEASEL

The energetics of the least weasel were given a more superficial treatment than those of the vegetation, or of the *Microtus* population. Population estimates were inferred from the capture of weasels in live traps during the mouse trapping program and from counts of weasel tracks in the snow during December, January, and February. During any one trapping period, captured individuals were identified by weight under the assumption that only one individual of a particular weight would be present on the trap area. On the basis of trap records and tracking observations it appeared that there were two adult weasels on the area of 2.5 ha in the late fall of 1956. It was assumed that these weasels had been present and had produced young during the summer. The number of litters produced per year (two) and the number of young per litter (five) were accepted as reported by Burt (1948) and by Hall (1951). June and August were arbitrarily chosen as the birth dates of the litters.

Since no data on the growth of the least weasel were available, growth rates of adult and young weasels were estimated from the weights of captured animals. The initial weight for the adults in the early summer of 1956 was assumed to be 46 gm (average of 4 captures of young adults). These adults were assumed to have grown to an average adult weight of 60 gm by August (based on one cap-

ture) and to have maintained this weight through the spring of 1957. It was further assumed that the birth weight of the young was 3 gm and that each individual in the litter grew approximately 6 gm per month for the first 5 months and then 3 gm per month for the next 5 months. As with *Microtus*, production measurements were based on the instantaneous rate of growth of adults and young. Production was calculated separately for three 4-month periods (Table 8). Biomass measurements were converted to their caloric equivalent by using the factor obtained for mice carcasses.

Mortality was arbitrarily estimated as a loss of approximately 5 young, weighing 15 gm each, from September to December, 1956, and of one young, weighing 35 gm, from January to May, 1957.

Food consumption and digestibility of food were studied in the laboratory with one captured weasel (Table 9). In the course of two feeding experiments, one live mouse was placed in the weasel cage daily. The remains of the dead carcass of the mouse fed the previous day were transferred to a hardware-cloth envelope within the cage to indicate evaporation loss from the carcass. White mice (*Mus musculus*) were fed in the first study and laboratory-raised *Microtus* in the second study. Each experiment was run for a total of 30 days.

During the feeding experiment using *Microtus*, feces were collected for a 6-day period to measure food digestibility. The caloric value of these feces was determined in the bomb calorimeter.

The metabolic rate used for the least weasel was that obtained by Morrison (1957).

RESULTS

SOLAR ENERGY

The annual insolation per ha for 1956 and 1957 is shown in Table 10. Baten & Eichmeier (1951) indicate that the average agricultural growing season at East Lansing is from May 8 to October 4, with extremes ranging from April 8 to November 16. Field observations suggested that the growing season for natural vegetation of the old field was slightly longer than that for cultivated crops and extended from approximately April 1 (when spring plant growth became obvious) to approximately November 1 (when the accumulated production peak was reached in 1956). The total insolation during the 1956 growing season was 94.2×10^8 Cal per ha. Since approximately 50% of the incident energy (that in the ultraviolet and infrared portions of the spectrum) is not used by plants in photosynthesis (Terrien, Truffaut & Carles 1957, Daubenmire 1947), the total growing-season insolation was divided by two to give the usable insolation available to the plants. The data presented in Table 10 represent total solar insolation at the ground surface, and at the bottom of the table is shown the 50% correction of growing-season insolation. The corrected insolation value for 1956 is used in Fig. 1 and in all calculations of the ratio of insolation and production of the vegetation. The 50%

302

TABLE 8. Dynamics of least weasel population on one hectare.

Season	AVERAGE POPULATION NUMBER		TOTAL BIOMASS GRAMS		PROPORTIONATE WEIGHT CHANGE		PRODUCTION GRAMS		MORTALITY GRAMS		Respiration Loss Calories
	Adults	Young	Adults	Young	Adults	Young	Adults	Young	Adults	Young	
May-Aug......	.80	2.0	42.4	10.3	1.30	2.58	11.1	10.0	0.0	0.0	1091
Aug.-Dec......	.80	2.8	48.0	34.9	0.00	3.04	0.0	38.8	0.0	31.5	1884
Jan.-May.....	.80	1.6	48.0	61.9	0.00	1.76	0.0	35.5	0.0	10.5	2459

TABLE 9. Food consumption of the least weasel fed on live mice.

Species	FOOD CONSUMPTION		Caloric Value of Feces	Per Cent of Food Digested
	Grams	Calories		
Microtus....	14.7	19.99	2.02	89.9
White mice..	15.1	29.50	—	—

reduction may be excessive during April, May and June when the total insolation at ground surface is reduced due to increased cloudiness. Clouds reduce the amount of ultraviolet and infrared radiation because of diffusion and absorption by water molecules (Terrien, Truffaut & Carles 1957) and it might be anticipated that under clouds more than 50% of the insolation at the ground would be usable by the plants.

TABLE 10. Solar insolation on the study area in calories per hectare per month for 1956 and 1957.

Month	1956	1957
January......................	4.2 x 10⁸	5.0 x 10⁸
February.....................	7.3	6.1
March.......................	9.5	11.0
April........................	10.8	9.9
May.........................	14.7	13.9
June........................	17.8	16.8
July........................	15.3	18.2
August......................	13.6	15.2
September...................	12.2	11.7
October.....................	9.8	7.9
November...................	4.5	3.9
December...................	2.7	3.8
Total.......................	122.4	123.4
Total growing season (April 1 to Oct. 31)..................	94.2	93.6
Growing season correction[1].....	47.1	46.8

Data from the Michigan Hydrologic Research Station of the USDA and the Michigan Agricultural Experiment Station.
[1] 50 per cent of the total insolation during the growing season to allow for ultraviolet and infrared radiation which are not utilized in photosynthesis.

DYNAMICS OF THE VEGETATION

The production of the vegetation can be separated into two different components: (1) the production of the plant tops and the root biomass over the growing season, and (2) the photosynthate which is lost to consumption by animals and to respiration of the plant biomass. The production of tops and roots plus the material eaten by animals comprise the net production; the inclusion of the respiration yields the gross production of the vegetation. In measure-

ments of net production by the harvest method, consumption of green plant material by animals often is not included in the estimate of total net production. Here, food consumption by the mouse population is added to the production of the roots and tops, while food consumption by insects and other herbivores is not estimated or included.

The dry weight standing crop of vegetation (Fig. 2) shows a typical cycle of growth, death, and decay of vegetation. The grass-herb ratio shows cyclical fluctuations; grasses predominate in fall and winter, with a tendency toward equality in midsummer. A slight change in caloric content of the vegetation also occurred seasonally (Tables 11, 12). The peak aboveground standing crop was 385 gm per m² (3.85 × 10⁶ gm per ha) in 1956 and 251 gm per m² (2.51 × 10⁶ gm per ha) in 1957, these values being accepted as minimum estimates of production. The average caloric value of green vegetation was 4.08 Cal per gm dry weight (average of the values in Table 2).

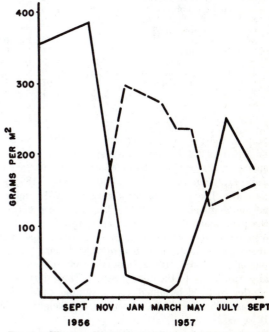

FIG. 2. The standing crops of living (solid line) and dead (broken line) vegetation by months in 1956 and 1957.

Standing crop of roots was measured three times during the 1957 growing season. The initial standing

303

TABLE 11. Above-ground standing crop of living and dead vegetation, and average caloric value of green grasses and herbs per square meter plot, and living grass-herb ratio.

Date Collected	Number of Plots	Standing Crop Live		(Grams Dry Weight) Dead		Caloric Values Cal/gram Dry Weight	Grass:Herbs (Weight)
		Mean	SD	Mean	SD		
7/21/56	2	—	—	—	—	4.12	—
8/ 8/56	10	358.0	±49.2	55.6	±30.4	4.12	3.5:1
9/24/56	16	372.4	±81.2	8.0	—	4.30	9.1:1
11/ 2/56	20	385.2	±91.2	28.0	—	4.17	49.2:1
2/ 9/57	10	31.2	±12.8	300.0	±60.0	—	—
3/22/57	15	8.0	± 2.4	274.0	±75.2	—	—
4/24/57	14	18.4	± 6.8	234.8	±97.2	3.99	16.0:1
5/22/57	14	67.6	±12.8	236.0	±66.4	3.99	6.9:1
7/ 1/57	15	147.2	±49.6	126.8	±47.6	3.90	2.6:1
8/ 5/57	15	250.8	±71.2	140.4	±42.8	—	1.4:1
9/29/57	14	184.0	±71.2	164.0	±42.4	—	—

TABLE 12. The caloric value per gram of oven-dried plant tissue for various plant species collected during the study.

Date Collected	Species	Number of Samples	Cal/gm (Aver.)	S.D.
7/22/56	Poa compressa	5	4.12	±.08
8/ 8/56	Poa compressa	9	4.18	±.20
9/24/56	Poa compressa	14	4.31	±.45
11/ 2/56	Poa compressa	15	4.18	±.08
5/22/57	Poa compressa	3	4.02	±.05
7/ 1/57	Poa compressa	3	3.99	±.11
8/ 8/56	Linaria vulgaris	5	4.28	±.07
9/24/56	Linaria vulgaris	5	4.34	±.10
8/ 8/56	Daucus Carota	5	3.92	±.45
8/ 8/56	Cirsium arvense	6	3.93	±.22
8/ 8/56	Trifolium repens	2	4.09	±.20
8/ 8/56	Verbascum Thapsus	3	3.98	±.14
8/ 8/56	Plantago spp.	2	3.79	±.09
8/ 8/56	Dead grass	6	3.91	±.05
2/ 9/57	Dead grass	15	4.25	±.06
4/24/57	Grass and herbs	3	3.99	±.10
5/22/57	Herbs combined	3	3.97	±.12
7/ 1/57	Herbs combined	3	3.81	±.12
8/ 8/56	Roots	6	3.30	±.20

TABLE 13. Food consumption of *Microtus* populations during the 1956 and 1957 growing seasons.

Date	Interval Days	Density Mice Per Hectare	Individual Mean Weight Grams	Population Biomass Grams	Consumption Grams Per Hectare
1956					
April 1	52	5.0	29	145	1,056
May 22	63	5.2	29	151	1,329
July 24	42	9.6	29	278	1,634
Sept. 4	35	16.5	29	479	2,349
Oct. 9	22	21.2	31	657	2,024
Total					8,392
1957					
April 1	53	64.2[1]	32	2054	15,243
May 22	26	49.8	26	1295	4,714
June 18	36	65.4	28	1831	9,227
July 24	61	61.4	30	1842	15,732
Sept. 23	38	111.2	26	2891	15,379
Total					60,295

[1] Average of March and April population estimates.

gm of plant per night are shown in Table 14. The product of the rate of respiration in Cal, the mean standing crop of vegetation and the number of days between measurements of respiration yielded the Cal used in night respiration by the vegetation over the growing season, 146.2 Cal per m² plot or 1.46×10^6 Cal per ha (Table 15).

TABLE 14. Night respiration of old field vegetation.

Date	CO_2 Produced cc./night	O_2 Consumed cc./night	RQ	Calories per cc. Oxygen	Grams Vegetation[1]	Calories per Gram per Night
5/17/57	1.96	3.50	.56	.0045	.398	.041
5/25/57	1.36	1.91	.72	.0047	.589	.016
6/13/57	1.17	1.20	.97	.0050	.866	.007
7/20/57	.90	.68	1.31	.0053	1.905	.002

[1] Grams of vegetation on area covered by cans (86.6 cm²) derived from the graph of standing crop of vegetation (Fig. 1).

crop (1493 gm per m², 15 cm deep) was measured on April 13, 1957 when the vegetation was beginning spring growth. The second measurement was made on July 11, when the root standing crop was 1805 gm per m². The peak standing crop was 2516 gm per m² on September 29, 1957. The difference between the peak and initial standing crop approximated the organic matter synthesized and stored in the roots above 15 cm depth over the growing season (1023 gm per m²) in 1957. It was assumed that this rate was also applicable to the 1956 season. The caloric value of the roots, determined for a sample collected in August 1956 was 3.30 Cal per gm dry weight (Table 12).

The amount of live vegetation calculated to have been consumed by mice during the growing seasons in 1956 and 1957 is shown in Table 13.

Data on respiration of the vegetation were collected during four nights in the summer of 1957. The CO_2 released, O_2 consumed, RQ, and Cal used per

Thomas & Hill (1949) in their field studies on the respiration of alfalfa showed that night respiration of the tops was approximately one-half the day respiration and that the root respiration was about equal to the combined day and night top respiration.

TABLE 15. Night respiration of the vegetation biomass during growing season.

Date	Interval Days	Mean Standing Crop Vegetation Grams	Respiration Rate Cal/gm/night	Respiration Loss/m² Cal.
April 1 to May 21.......	51	6.1	.041	50.4
May 22 to June 2........	12	16.7	.016	12.4
June 3 to July 2........	30	27.6	.007	23.2
July 3 to Nov. 1........	121	62.2	.002	60.2
Total..............				146.2

If we assume that these findings can be applied to the old-field vegetation, the day respiration of the tops would equal 2.92×10^6 Cal per ha, and respiration of the roots, 4.38×10^6 Cal per ha. Total respiration of the entire plant biomass would be approximately 8.76×10^6 Cal per ha or 15% of the total assimilation. This estimate is slightly less than those of Transeau (1926) and Thomas & Hill (1949). These workers suggest that respiration of the plant biomass amounts to 25-35% of the total production. It is not known if the discrepancy between estimates made in this study and those by Transeau and Thomas & Hill is due to a diffusion of gases between the soil and air under the cans, or if it represents a real difference between the respiration of natural vegetation and cultivated crop plants.

In 1956 and 1957 the production was made up of the following components:

	1956	1957
Production of tops	3.85×10^6gm/ha	2.51×10^6gm/ha
Root production	$10.23 \times$ "	$10.23 \times$ "
Consumed by *Microtus*	$.01 \times$ "	$.06 \times$ "
Weight net production	$14.09 \times$ "	$12.80 \times$ "
Caloric net production	49.51×10^6Cal/ha	44.25×10^6Cal/ha
Respiration	$8.76 \times$ "	$8.76 \times$ "
Caloric gross production	$58.27 \times$ "	$53.01 \times$ "

THE DYNAMICS OF THE *Microtus* POPULATION

The energy dynamics of the Microtus population were separated into several components: (1) the tissue production, (2) energy expense of respiration, and (3) the intake of energy through foods. The estimate of tissue production was, in turn, based on determinations of the standing crop of mice, production of young, and rate of growth of mice in all age categories. To relate *Microtus* to the vegetation base of the food chain, determinations of consumption and digestibility of foods were used to estimate the percentage of the available food consumed by the mice, and the percentage of the consumed food used in metabolic processes and stored as tissue production. Finally, each separate component was brought together in Fig. 1 to show the entire exchange through the *Microtus* population.

Standing Crop of *Microtus*

The standing crop of *Microtus* showed some unexpected variations during the investigation (Table 1). The population at the beginning of the study was at a very low level (5.2 mice per hectare). In fact, following the first trapping program in May 1956, an attempt was made to relocate the study on another area with a higher population of *Microtus*. It was not known whether this "low" was the result of adverse weather, heavy predation, or "cyclical behavior."

The estimated peak population (139 mice per hectare) determined in this study could not be considered unusual for the species. Other workers have arrived at greater estimates of population density for *Microtus pennsylvanicus*, 291 per hectare (Bole, 1939), 395-567 per hectare (Hamilton, 1937), and 165 per hectare (Townsend, 1935). The months in which the peak density occurred was unusual. Hamilton (1937), Martin (1956) and others showed that *Microtus* generally reach a peak population in the fall (September to November) after which the population decreases until breeding begins again in the spring. Linduska (1950), on the contrary, found that the annual peak population at Rose Lake, Michigan, approximately seven miles north of this study, occurred in January and February, as in the present study. Linduska was unable to explain the difference between his results and those of Hamilton, but suggested that the winter peak may be a local adaptation to "xerophytic" conditions.

A more detailed knowledge of the population density and topography of the study area enabled the writer to suggest another explanation for the winter population high. A region of dense cover, composed primarily of bluegrass sod, occurred in the center of the trap area. This dense cover may have served as a place of refuge for the mice during alternately wet and freezing weather occurring in January, February, and March. The number of new captures per day of trapping was correlated with snowfall (Table 16) suggesting that snow storms stimulated increased movement of the mice. Since in November and January the increased captures of new animals occurred late in the trapping period, it was thought that these captures represented new animals moving into the trap area rather than movement of the resident population. The movements immediately before and during snowfall were considered to be due to a migration of mice from upland areas into the areas with heavier cover, resulting in an increased population on the study area during the storm periods and possibly throughout the winter.

The fraction of animals captured in common to both lines decreased in January, February, and March (Table 1). This seasonal variation may have been

TABLE 16. Snowfall and new captures of *Microtus* in three winter months compared with a typical summer month.

Day of Trapping	NOVEMBER		JANUARY		FEBRUARY		JULY	
	Snow[1]	Captures	Snow	Captures	Snow	Captures	Snow	Captures
1	.00	2	.00	1	.00	3	.00	4
2	.00	3	.05	1	.00	4	.00	11
3	.00	4	.01	2	.10	10	.00	4
4	.00	3	.28	8	.00	9	.00	6
5	.10	8	.17	2	.00	3	.00	9
6	.50	2	.01	1	.00	7	.00	3
7	T	0	T	2	T	1	.00	2
8			.85	11				
9			.05	0				

[1] Snowfall or sleet in inches, taken from U. S. Department of Commerce, Local Climatological Date for East Lansing, Michigan.

the result of decreased size of the home range of the mice and consequent shorter daily movements. These in turn, may have resulted from increased density of mice or from some characteristic of winter weather acting on mouse behavior. Further information is needed before the cause for the decrease in number of captures in common in the winter can be established.

The observed fraction of animals captured in common to both lines for January (4.5%) was lower than that fraction used in Table 1. The January trapping period was interrupted by heavy snowfall and it was possible to run the trap lines only 3 days in one period and 4 days in another. If the unusually low fraction .045 is used to determine population density a very high population estimate (256 per ha) results. It was thought that this high a density was unlikely, since it would require a six-fold increase in the population in two months. Therefore, the fractions of common captures for the other winter months (February and March) were averaged and this average was used to estimate the January population.

Caloric Value of Microtus Tissue

Since the objective of this study was to determine the energy transfer and losses between the levels of the food chain, it was necessary to convert the production data, calculated initially in terms of weight, into Calories (Table 17). In the process of preparing mice for calorific analysis, the mice lost approximately 71% of their body weight. Since mouse production figures were computed in terms of live weight, the average caloric value per gm of mouse tissue had to be converted from dry weight (4.65 Cal per gm) to live weight (1.37 Cal per gm).

Mortality or Emigration of the Mice

Mortality and emigration both result in the disappearance of mice and are considered collectively in this report. When an animal was not caught again, it was impossible to determine whether it had died or had moved out of the trapping area. In a few instances animals were trapped in one month and not retrapped until several months later. Where these

TABLE 17. The wet weight, dry weight, and the average caloric value per gram dry *Microtus* tissue determined for four male mice (standard deviation in parenthesis).

Individual	Age	Live Weight	Dry Weight	Caloric Value of Tissue
1	adult	39.1	11.9	4.49 (± .21)
2	adult	24.5	7.0	4.67 (± .25)
3	adult	28.0	8.1	4.63 (± .26)
4	juvenile	10.0	2.9	4.82 (± .07)
average (pooled data)				4.65 (± .21)

animals resided in the intervening period is unknown, but it is here assumed that they were on the trap area.

The mortality of juveniles and adults was greatest immediately after the peak population was reached in February (Table 1). This peak was possibly correlated with periodic inundation of the low portions of the study area in February and March. As was mentioned previously this population decrease was expected to occur in December but may have been postponed by an immigration of mice into the trap area in January and February. Because of the fire on the study area in March, a measure of the mortality rate was unavailable for February. Mortality was assumed to be 55% in this month (based on the difference between the population estimates for February and March on the two adjacent areas).

Production of Young by Adults

The potential number of young produced by the population showed a consistent increase from 24.8 mice per ha in May to 137.9 mice per ha in November 1956, and from 15.2 mice per ha in March to 79.3 mice per ha in April 1957 (Table 3). During January and February no females were judged to be in breeding condition and it was assumed that no breeding occurred. This assumption is consistent with the findings of Hamilton (1937). During the first four months of the study data on the breeding condition of the females were not collected. The pregnancy rate for these periods was later assumed to be approximately 90%.

TABLE 18. Population dynamics of nestling young on one hectare.

Date	Potential Production Numbers	Replacements[1] Numbers	Survival Rate Per Cent	Mean Biomass of Young Grams	MORTALITY		Immigration Numbers
					Grams	Calories	
May.................	24.8	14.5	58	144	78	107	—
July................	28.5	12.7	45	135	108	148	—
Sept................	34.8	18.3	53	180	114	156	—
Oct.................	64.5	38.0	59	333	176	241	—
Nov.................	137.9	63.8	46	893	693	949	—
Jan.................	0.0	0.0	—	—	—	—	96.0
Feb.................	0.0	0.0	—	—	—	—	—
March..............	15.2	27.4	100	100	0	0	13.4
April...............	79.3	44.1	56	361	209	286	—

[1] Number of young replacing adults disappearing through death or migration.

The potential natality suggests the maximum possible number of young which could be produced by the population, and may be the source of most of the population increase and of replacements for adults disappearing from the population. The number of young entering the trap-susceptible population was assumed to be equal to the number of adults and juveniles disappearing between trapping periods. These replacement young also showed a consistent increase from spring to fall (Table 18) and in all but March were fewer in number than the potential production of young.

Production of Tissue

Production of tissue in the mouse population was calculated for each trapping period from a knowledge of the average population biomass and the observed rates of growth. This calculation was carried out separately for the various weight classes, the production of tissue being estimated by methods described earlier. For each class the average biomass between times of trapping was estimated as the mean value of the corresponding population biomass determinations made at each trapping. The rates of growth were determined from weights of individual mice recaptured in two consecutive trapping periods.

On occasion certain weight classes, while obviously contributing to the population biomass, were not represented by recaptured animals, and hence, no growth rates were available for these classes. In Table 2 these instances are distinguished. Since it was known that some of the classes not represented by recaptured mice contributed to the production of tissue, it was necessary to estimate appropriate rates of growth for weight classes known to be producing tissue.

To estimate missing growth rates, use was made of the fact that growth rates decreased progressively with increasing weight, in each time period. This fact is obvious in Table 2 where the proportional weight changes, unadjusted for length of interval, show that over the year the average weight change for mice in the 11-20 gm class exceeded the average change for the 21-30 gm class by a factor of 0.66. Similarly, the 21-30 gm mice exceeded the 31-40 gm animals by 0.30. For those classes for which information was lacking on growth rates, as detailed above,

substitute values were approximated by adding the above average increment in proportionate growth to the observed proportionate change for the next heaviest weight class. For example, in October 1956, 0.66 was added to the value of 1.20 observed for the 21-30 gm mice to estimate the missing value for the 11-20 gm animals.

In every instance survivors in the 41-50 gm class lost weight (Table 2). Hamilton (1941) suggests that the heavier adult mice lose weight only in the winter, but these data indicate that weight loss is characteristic of the 41-50 gm weight class throughout the year. This weight loss does not appear to be correlated with senility because in no instance did a heavy animal showing a weight loss disappear in the trapping period immediately following the loss in weight. Over the winter months of January and February mice in most other weight classes also lost weight. These losses probably represent the exhaustion of body fat stored over the fall months.

The weight distribution graph (Fig. 3) reflected the internal dynamics of the mouse population. Since weight may be considered a rough criterion of age, it would be expected that the greatest number of mice would fall in the lightest weight classes. However, no mice were caught in the 1-10 gm weight class, except in May. Whitmoyer (1956) found in his study of the growth rate of laboratory-raised *Microtus pennsylvanicus* that the eyes of all young were open at 11 days of age, at an average weight of 9 gm. Hamilton (1941) also showed that young *M. pennsylvanicus* did not leave the nest until they were 10 gm in weight, at 9-13 days of age. Therefore, it was assumed that nestling young did not leave the nest before they attained a weight of 10 gm, and that the probability of capturing an animal weighing less than 10 gm was very small.

Blair (1948) states that small meadow mice old enough to leave the nest may be caught by live traps. If the probability of capture were the same for all weight classes, in those months in which reproduction occurred we would expect the highest number of captures to be in the 11-20 gm class. However the 11-20 gm class in each month except one (May) had fewer mice than did the 21-30 gm class (Fig. 3). The home range of very young mice may be smaller than

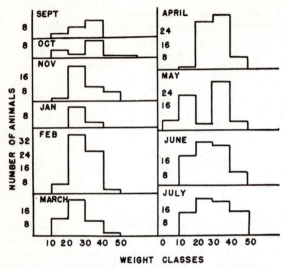

FIG. 3. The number of animals per weight class captured during each trapping period.

that of adults, resulting in a lower probability of capture of juvenile mice and a proportionately lower representation of this class of mice in the data. A second explanation for fewer animals in the 11-20 gm class than expected may be that the rapid growth of these mice shortens the period of exposure to trapping for individuals in this weight class. Hamilton (1941), observing the lower proportion of light-weight mice in his trapping data, suggested that exceptionally heavy mortality in this weight class may be further cause for the phenomenon. Whatever the cause, if the probability of capture for the 11-20 gm mice is less than for the 21 gm and heavier animals, the determination of the biomass of the population based on live-trapping data might underestimate the contribution of the 11-20 gm weight class.

The growth rates of nestling young (Table 4) were generally quite similar over the year since the growth rates were calculated from a constant birth weight of 3 gm and the relatively constant weight of the lightest juvenile captured in the traps. Since the nestling young had the highest growth rates, they contributed a larger share of the tissue growth or production over the period of study (Table 4) than did the adults and juveniles (Table 2).

Immigration into the Study Area

In January and March the potential production was insufficient to account for the increase in the population and/or the mortality of adults and juveniles. To account for the discrepancy between the potential production and the number of young entering the trap-susceptible population, it was assumed that mice migrated into the study area. In March this type of immigration was of a relatively minor nature, amounting to only 21% of the mean adult population. In January, however, the immigration was of greater importance since the population almost doubled between January and February (Table

1). There were no young produced in January; therefore, all of this increase must have been due to immigration. This assumption is supported by the previous information of the winter movements of mice immediately before or during snow storms (Table 16), which were interpreted to mean a migration of mice into the study area.

Theoretically, since the population increased in size over the period of study, the energy lost to mortality should not exceed that appearing in tissue production. However, Table 19 shows that mortality exceeded production in every period studied. Since the standing crop increased over the year by 1569 Cal (Table 1), production plus immigration must have exceeded mortality plus emigration by this amount. These last two processes exceeded production alone by approximately 12,000 Cal (Table 19).

TABLE 19. Tissue production, mortality, and respiration of mouse population in calories per hectare.

Period	Production		Mortality		Respiration	
	Entire Period	Per Day	Entire Period	Per Day	Entire Period	Per Day
May to July........	331	5	500	8	4,871	76
July to Sept.........	309	8	380	9	5,007	119
Sept. to Oct.........	488	14	695	20	6,808	195
Oct. to Nov.........	787	20	951	24	10,578	271
Nov. to Jan.........	1742	29	2,111	35	33,245	575
Jan. to Feb........	—	—	1,245	36	27,055	773
Feb. to March......	—	—	3,284	122	37,544	1391
March to April......	727	20	987	26	27,710	770
April to May........	786	28	2,217	79	17,059	609
Total............	5170		17,200		169,877	

The conclusion follows that immigration (termed import in Fig. 1) must have contributed approximately 13,500 Cal. The estimates of immigration in Table 18 account only for the difference in calculated production of young and the young needed to replace trap-susceptible adults and juveniles. These estimates are included in the above calculations.

Energy leaving one population of mice by emigration joins another by immigration. Over all populations, these gains and losses must balance, just as production of all populations must equal the sum of mortality and population change. In this particular instance, immigration appears to have involved over twice as much energy transfer as production within the population itself. It is not known whether this population, sustaining a heavy population pressure as calculated from the weasels alone, represents a "sink" with energy flowing only inward, or whether it may approach an energy equilibrium, with the weasel and other predators being in equilibrium with the local production and there being a sizable exportation of energy from the population.

Immigration adds energy to a population, increasing the biomass, but not by any process defined here as production. Production of these animals took place elsewhere, and hence, cannot be credited to the local population. On the other hand, energy losses from the respiration of immigrants may have considerable influence on the energy balance in the community. Inspection of Table 1 and 19 will show that immigration increased the biomass greatly during January and February, accounting for a large part of the high population metabolism or respiration.

Respiration of the Mouse Population

An estimate of the minimum number of Calories used by the mouse population in respiration was obtained from the fasting metabolic rate of *Microtus*. These rates showed very little variation seasonally (Table 5). Although an analysis of variance in the metabolic rates of individual groups in each calorimeter jar showed that no significant differences in the rates between seasons or within experiments, seasonal variations are to be expected. These were probably obscured by confining the mice in the laboratory at a constant temperature while measurements were being made. The average metabolic rate of 10 Cal per 24 hrs per mouse was used as the minimum metabolic constant to determine the minimum respiration of the mouse biomass (Table 20).

TABLE 20. Respiration of the mouse population.

Date	Respiration of Young	Respiration of Adults
	Calories per Hectare	
May	1,575	3,296
July	975	4,032
Sept.	1,050	5,758
Oct.	2,329	8,249
Nov.	7,381	25,864
Jan.	—	27,055
Feb.	—	37,544
March	620	27,090
April	2,177	14,882
Total	16,107	153,770

The average metabolic rate determined in the present study, 2.75 cc O_2 per gm per hr, compares favorably with the determinations on *Microtus pennsylvanicus* made by Pearson (1947), 1.9—2.8 cc/gm/hr, and Morrison (1948), 1.8—2.8 cc/gm/hr. Hatfield (1939) studied metabolism in *Microtus californicus* but arrived at a much higher figure of metabolism, 5.2 cc/gm/hr. Pearson suggested that the higher metabolic rates obtained by Hatfield were due to greater activity during the periods of measurements. The metabolic rate determined by this study was a minimal rate and when used in calculations of energy loss by respiration underestimated the actual loss. The average metabolic rate of *Microtus* in the wild is unknown. Morrison (1948) gives some indication of what this average rate would be; in his studies, the average metabolic rate of Microtus held in the calorimeter for 24 hrs, with food and water provided, was 18-42% above the minimum rate of metabolism.

Summary of *Microtus* Energy Assimilation

The summary of the energy assimilation of the *Microtus* population (Table 19) shows the assimilation of a population changing from a low density to a higher density. With the exception of January and February, when growth of young and adult mice did not occur, tissue production rose continuously during the spring, summer, and fall of 1956, and the spring of 1957. Mortality, including the disappearance of mice from the population by death, predation, or emigration, also showed a smooth rise, with a disproportionate increase in February. Respiration was proportional to the population biomass and increased until the population drop in March. Following this, the energy loss due to respiration began a second increase. Laboratory metabolic measurements allowed no estimate to be made of expected seasonal changes in the respiration energy cost.

The respiration loss, though a minimal estimate, accounted for by far the greatest amount of energy used by the *Microtus* population. Respiration accounted for 68% of the energy passing through the mouse population yearly. In comparison, the mean biomass of mice (1900 Cal per ha) represented a storage at any one time of only 1.0% of the annual energy consumption; the maximum biomass (Table 1) was only 3% and the minimum biomass 0.1% of the annual energy consumption.

Digestibility of Food

The amount of food ingested and its energy value may be understood in relation to the metabolism of the mouse population only through some knowledge of the digestive processes and their efficiency. The gross energy in the food minus the energy in the feces equals the digestible energy (Brody 1945). The feces include secretions and cells sloughing into the digestive tract. Thus the digestible energy indicates only the excess of food energy taken into the blood stream over excretion into the gut.

The digestibility of the food was investigated briefly in the laboratory, with results from three animals as indicated in Table 21. Although requiring confirmation, they indicate an exceptionally high digestibility for alfalfa in *Microtus* (90% of the gross energy as against the figure of 50% given by Morrison 1949 for cattle and sheep.) Further, with the diet of lettuce, carrots, and oatmeal, 82% of the gross energy was digested, equalling the presumed digestive efficiency of humans with the same diet, as calculated from the tables of Merrill & Watt (1955).

Further work in this direction is needed to understand the trophic ecology of *Microtus*, as well as other small mammals. Attempts should be made to determine the digestibility for various single dietary components and for complete diets. The qualitative composition of the diet also requires investigation, as suggested in the following section.

Consumption of Food

The amount of food consumed, considered with digestibility, constitutes the trophic levy upon the

TABLE 21. Digestibility of laboratory diets.

Day	Caloric Intake in Food	Caloric Loss in Feces	Undigested (per cent)
Alfalfa diet—2 female *Microtus*			
1..........	128.7	20.2	15.7
2..........	183.1	15.2	8.3
3..........	83.3	12.9	15.5
4..........	143.5	12.0	9.0
5..........	176.1	12.4	7.0
average (pooled data).........			10.2 (±4.2)[1]
Standard diet— 1 male *Microtus*			
1..........	26.1	4.3	16.5
2..........	21.3	4.3	20.2
3..........	28.9	4.4	15.2
4..........	21.5	4.3	20.0
5..........	23.3	4.2	18.0
average (pooled data).........			17.8 (±2.2)

[1] Standard deviation in parenthesis.

environment by the population. Food consumption may be estimated in several ways; here it has been done by laboratory means (Table 7) and by examination of the stomach contents of wild mice (Table 22).

TABLE 22. Weight of stomach contents of snap-trapped mice.

Season	Number Weighed	Mean Wgt Mice Grams	Mean Weight of Contents Grams	Standard Deviation Grams	Calculated[1] Daily Food Consumption Grams
Fall..........	28	28	1.15	±.83	23.0
Winter........	27	28	1.35	±.68	27.0
Spring........	21	35	1.17	±.59	23.4
Summer.......	24	27	1.31	±.68	26.2
average.......					24.9

[1] Under the assumption that the mean weight of stomach contents represents one-half the stomach capacity and that the mice have 10 feeding periods per day.

Food consumption of *Microtus* has long been of interest to investigators, partly for economic reasons. Bailey (1924) fed *Microtus* a diet of clover, cantaloupe, grain, and seeds and found that they consumed 55% of their body weight daily. Regnier & Pussard (1926) obtained similar results with *Microtus arvalis* on a mixed diet of oat seeds, oat stems, and mangolds. In an experiment on which *Microtus* were fed a diet of dry feed (rolled oats, dry skim milk, dry meat, and seeds), Hatfield (1935) found an average consumption of 3.48 gm of food per mouse per day.

In the present study the mice on the standard diet consumed more fresh food than did the mice on the alfalfa diet. When dry weight of the food and caloric value was considered the reverse was true. It appears from these results and with comparison with Hatfield's findings that inclusion of dry foods in the diet re-

duced food consumption on a weight basis. The dry food materials (oatmeal, seed, etc.) have a much higher caloric value than fresh leafy foods such as lettuce and alfalfa, and animals on a fresh diet of succulent foods might have to consume a greater quantity of food to satisfy their energy requirements. In the present study, the mice on the alfalfa diet consumed 61% of their body weight daily and those on the "standard" diet consumed 86%. In both instances, the food consumption as a percentage of body weight was greater than that found by Bailey (1924) and Regnier & Pussard (1926).

Since blue grass appeared to be the dominant food plant of the environment in the study, attempts were made to maintain *Microtus* on a diet of fresh-cut, mature blue grass, with water available. In two attempts most of the animals lost considerable weight, or died, as indicated below:

Trial	Number Mice	Number Dying	Number Losing Weight	Number Gaining Weight
1	6	2	2	2
2	4	2	2	0

Dice (1922) was able to maintain *Microtus ochrogaster* on blue grass; possibly he fed immature grass or grass sod which might have a higher nutritive value. The energy content of the blue grass was 4.13 Cal per gm dry weight, which was closely similar to the caloric value of alfalfa (4.12 Cal per gm); however, the protein content of mature blue grass (6.6%, Morrison 1949) is much lower than that of alfalfa (14.8%, Morrison 1949). Lack of protein may be a cause of my failure to maintain *Microtus* on a blue grass diet. Regnier & Pussard (1926) found *Microtus arvalis* ate meat readily, consuming other voles and insects (Carabidae). They suggest that this consumption of protein might influence the numbers of mice during plague years. During one experiment in the present study, one *Microtus* ate 15 large grasshoppers within 24 hours. *Microtus* may thus supplement a low protein diet with insects or other high protein foods.

The stomach contents of animals taken by snap-traps reveal the proportional composition of the diet, assuming all components to be digested at the same rate (Table 6). To infer food consumption from the information on the volume of food in stomachs further, information on the rate of stomach clearance through digestion is required. Such information is not available, but one may infer from the observations of Hatfield (1940), Davis (1933), and Pearson (1947) that wild mice characteristically have 8-12 activity periods during a 24-hr day, and that these periods are concerned with feeding activity, to fill a nearly empty stomach.

The quantitative information on stomach contents (Table 22) may be examined, under the assumption of 10 activity periods a day, and a filling of the stomach to twice the mean observed contents at each activity period. The assumption that the mean stomach content equalled half a full stomach is supported not only by theoretical sampling considerations, but also by the observation that the observed stomachs ranged from full to almost empty, with most being "half-full."

The overall estimate of about 25 gm of food eaten per day (.86 gm wet food per gm mouse), for all sizes of capture-susceptible mice, agrees fairly well with the laboratory-determined values of 39 and 28 gm (.86 and .61 gm wet food per gm mouse) for two different diets. It is not known whether the indicated seasonal fluctuations are real or reflect bias from either shifting activity patterns, changing age structure, or sampling variation. However, this method of observation seems to offer a practical, if approximate, method of measuring food consumption.

The differential seasonal consumption of available food materials in Table 6 showed that grass (grass and sedges) was the dominant food at all seasons. Dead vegetation (with the exception of wood) was not found in the stomach slides, therefore, it was assumed that dead vegetation was not used by *Microtus*. Since the clip quadrat used to determine food availability and production of vegetation only sampled grasses and herbs and not mosses, fruit, and other foods, the separate percentages of grass and herbs in the stomachs were also calculated (Table 6).

The food consumption of the population was estimated by multiplying the biomass of the trap-susceptible population by the food consumption (.14 gm dry food per gm of mouse tissue per day or .58 Cal per gm of mouse tissue per day) of captive mice on the standard diet. Food consumption determined with the standard diet was used because it was thought that the standard diet more closely represented the diet of wild mice. Total consumption of vegetation per trap period by the mouse population was 250 × 103 Cal.

THE LEAST WEASEL POPULATION

During the study least weasels were captured in 15 live-traps and were tracked on three different days during the winter. The largest number of individuals captured in one trap period was 4 (May 1957). Examination of the entire area on three days in winter (in each instance the morning following a snowfall of the previous day) yielded the tracks of one weasel in December, two in January, and three in February. According to Polderboer (1942) the maximum home range of the least weasel is 2 acres. Since the study area averaged 6.2 acres in size, it was assumed that at least three or four adult weasels could live on the area. Although the first evidence of weasels was not noted until July, 1956, it was assumed that two weasels were present at the beginning of the study in May, 1956.

Burt (1948) states that two litters of young are born per year. Litter size ranges from 4 to 10 (Burt 1948) and averages 5 (Hall 1951). If 2 litters of 5 young were produced by the weasels over the year, it is estimated that approximately 12 weasels were present on the area in September, 1956. This population of 12 animals decreased to 6 animals in May 1957.

The mean weight of the young dying in the period August to December was estimated at 15 gm, and in January to May at 35 gm. Although the population values may appear unusually high since the least weasel has been considered a rarity in Michigan (Hatt 1940), the evidence available supports these estimates.

Under the assumption that the population of least weasels followed the model developed in the section on methods and further elaborated in the above introductory paragraphs, the production of tissue by the weasels remained rather steady throughout the year (Table 8). In the summer, production of tissue was due to growth of both adults and young. In the fall and winter, the population of young, decreasing from 10 to approximately 5 animals, contributed all of the growth in this period. In the late winter and spring, the population of young, decreasing from 5 to 4 animals, again furnished all of the growth of tissue.

The respiration energy loss of the weasel population, based on an average minimum rate of O_2 consumption of 1.61 cc per gm per hr (Morrison 1957), increased over the year of study (Table 8). As observed with *Microtus*, the energy used in respiration of the weasel biomass was considerably greater than that involved in tissue production.

The laboratory feeding experiments were used to evaluate the role of the least weasel as a predator on *Microtus*. *Microtus* were assumed to be the sole food used by the weasel (Hatt 1940). In the laboratory experiments, the captive weasel consumed either 15.1 gm of white mice or 14.7 gm of *Microtus* per day (Table 9). Llewellyn (1942) found a similar rate of consumption in studies with a 32-gm weasel, i.e. 19.7 gm of mice per day. An average food consumption of 15 gm of mouse tissue per day was assumed to represent the true food consumption of adult weasels over the year. The young weasels, like other mammals (Morrison 1949), would probably use less food per day than the adults, and the daily food consumption of young was estimated to be 5 gm per day from May to August and 8 gm per day from August to December. Using these constants as a basis for calculating true food consumption, the effect of the weasel on the *Microtus* population was estimated. The weasel population consumed 5,824 Cal annually; this consumption was 3.07 times the mean biomass of *Microtus* (1900 Cal) over the year. Since net production of the *Microtus* population totaled only 5,170 Cal per ha annually, the weasel population appears to have required energy in excess of that produced by its principal prey. As previously noted, the production of the *Microtus* population did not allow for the energy imported by the mice which moved into the area. Further, it is possible that the weasel had other sources of food, such as *Blarina* which existed in moderately large numbers on the area, and insects, which were abundant during the summer, or perhaps the calculations of weasel population density here are in error.

The percentage of the energy in the mouse carcasses which was digested by the least weasel was determined in the digestibility experiments. When the weasel was on the *Microtus* diet, he was able to digest 89.9% of the energy in the mouse bodies (Table 9). This rather high efficiency of digestion is comparable with the somewhat lower efficiency of digestion (70-80% of a dry-feed diet, McCay 1949) for the dog.

DISCUSSION

In the transition of energy between two steps of the food chain there are two main pathways by which energy can be lost or diverted from the food chain itself. First, in tracing the energy from one population to the next not all the food organisms will be consumed by the consumer species; some of this energy could be dispersed to another food chain by migration of the food species out of the study area, by consumption of the food species by organisms outside of the food chain, or by death. These are considered to be energy losses of the first order. Second, not all the energy consumed is used in growth or in production of young; some of it is diverted to the maintenance of the organism and some passes through the body unused. These are energy losses of the second order. In energy losses of the first order the energy lost from the food chain is still in a form available for use by other animals. In energy losses of the second order, the loss is primarily heat derived from metabolic processes which is unavailable for further use by the food chain; that passing through the body is, of course, available to various other organisms in the food web.

Energy Losses of the First Order

Of the solar energy available to the vegetation over the growing season (one-half of the total incident insolation during the growing season), 1.2% was utilized in the gross production, and 1.1% in the net production of the vegetation (Fig. 1). These figures can be compared with the giant ragweed ecosystem in Oklahoma, 1.2%, and alfalfa growing in experimental plots for 6 months, 3.1% (data converted from tabular material in Odum, 1959—net production was divided by incident energy data for Michigan). Data on the percentage of solar energy utilized by the vegetation of different communities are still too limited to allow any comparison of the efficiencies of a successional community with a stable one. At this time we may say only that terrestrial vegetation of the old field community on this soil, at this site, and for these years appeared to utilize approximately 1% of the available solar energy during the growing season.

The net production of the vegetation can be considered as the energy available to the herbivorous animals in the community. *Microtus* is primarily a herbivore, with animal food appearing only in trace amounts over the year (see Table 6). It was assumed in this study that only the production attributed to the above-ground vegetation could be utilized by *Microtus*. Some of the root biomass was undoubtedly also used by the mice, but no estimate of the extent of root utilization was available. Lantz (1907) and Bailey (1924) state that consumption of roots is relatively unimportant, except during the winter, and roots were not recorded among the stomach contents in the present study. It is assumed here that use of roots was negligible.

Of the energy in the vegetation presumably available to the mice (15.8×10^6 Cal), 1.6% was consumed, with 1.1% utilized by the mice in production and respiration. These percentages assume no loss of vegetation due to cutting of stems and leaves by *Microtus*. The utilization of the energy in the vegetation not consumed by mice was not traced further in this study. Some of this energy was probably diverted through invertebrate food chains. Wolcott (1937) indicated that insects ate $.94 \times 10^6$ gm (3.76×10^6 Cal) of above-ground vegetation per ha in a pasture in New York over the summer. This level of consumption would amount to 23.9% of the available energy in the old field vegetation of the present study. If these data are correct, insects may be considered as more important herbivores in this old field community than are the meadow mice.

As mentioned previously, the energy in the *Microtus* population (production) available to predators was augmented by an import of energy through immigration of mice into the study area. This immigration was particularly noticeable in the winter and spring of 1957. Of the total energy available in the *Microtus* population (production plus immigration, Fig. 1) the least weasel consumed 31% as food and used 30% in production and respiration; considering only the production of the mice, the weasel consumed over 100%. When the energy consumed by the weasel and the energy retained in the mouse population through an increase in population size from May 1956 to May 1957 was subtracted from the production plus energy imported through immigration, 43% of the energy of the mouse population was unaccounted for. This loss may be attributed to emigration, to death from disease or accident, and degradation through microorganism food chains, or to capture in other predator chains. Some possible predators are *Blarina brevicauda* (Eadie 1952), *Felis domesticus* (Toner 1956, Korschgen 1957), or Owls, Red-tailed hawks, Red-shouldered hawks, and Cooper's hawks (Linduska 1950). All of these predators were seen on the study area during the investigation.

Most of the calculated production of the weasel population could be accounted for by the increase in the size of the population from May 1956 to May 1957. The expansion of the weasel population presumably was directly related to the expansion of the *Microtus* population. Only 10% of the production was not accounted for (Fig. 1). The least weasel may itself serve as food for certain predators, such as the great-horned owl, the barn owl, long-tailed weasel, and domestic cat (Hall 1951), but no information was gathered on mortality of weasels during this investigation.

ENERGY LOSSES OF THE SECOND ORDER

The energy losses of the second order, due to respiration (fasting metabolism), nonassimilation of energy in the food, and the energy cost of maintaining the body under normal activity, can be further separated into energy losses available and unavailable to the biosphere. Energy losses available to the biosphere include the energy in fecal matter which is composed primarily of unassimilated food but also contains intestinal secretions and cellular debris. Energy in the feces would serve as the base for food chains of coprophagous organisms. The energy lost to the biosphere as heat derived from animal metabolism can be considered an increase in the positive entropy of the ecosystem.

Respiration loss (respiration energy/energy consumed) determined for each step of the food chain is as follows: Vegetation—15.0%, Mice—68.2%, Least Weasels—93.3%. The respiration coefficient for the vegetation may be underestimated as stated earlier; Transeau (1926) and Thomas & Hill (1949) suggest that it may run as high as 25-30%. The data confirm the statement of Lindeman (1942) that as energy passes through the trophic levels an increasing percentage is lost in respiration. It must be remembered that the percentages cited above for the mice and weasel were both determined as minimum metabolic rates and, therefore, indicate basic differences in the loss due to metabolism and not mere differences in activity. Taking activity into account would presumably act to increase the difference.

The energy consumed but not assimilated by *Microtus* and *Mustela* was measured in the digestion trials. Of the energy consumed, 10-18% was recovered in the feces of *Microtus* and 10% in the feces of *Mustela*.

When these losses were subtracted from the energy loss of the second order for each species, 14-22% of the energy consumed was unaccounted for in *Microtus* and all the energy loss was accounted for in the least weasel. It is highly unlikely that the energy loss in respiration and in the feces comprises the total energy losses in the organism. For instance, energy is also lost in the urine, in fermentation gases, and in specific dynamic action of feeding (energy used in the processes of food utilization). Estimates of the energy loss in the urine are 15% for cattle and 7% for rabbits after fecal losses are subtracted from the gross food energy (Brody 1945: 28), and the loss in specific dynamic action varies from 40% of the intake energy for lean meat, 15% for fat, and 6% for sucrose (Brody 1945: 61).

An additional energy loss not included above is the expense of normal body activity above rest. Very few investigators have been concerned with this maintenance cost according to Brody (1945), although he estimates that this loss is twice the basal metabolic rate. The minimum energy expended when the animal is confined and fasting (fasting metabolism) is known for *Microtus* and *Mustela* and was used to determine the loss of energy in respiration; but the energy used by these animals as they live in their natural environment is completely unknown. This latter energy expense reduces the efficiency of conversion by widening the gap between energy intake and production. The maintenance losses are reflected in the coefficients of production. Plants are the most sedentary and have the highest coefficient, 94.3% (net production/gross production). The weasel is the most active, since it must hunt for its food, and probably has the highest maintenance cost, with a low coefficient, 2.2% (production/energy intake). Possibly the energy expense of hunting by the predator will vary with different densities of the prey population. *Microtus* which is primarily dependent on vegetative material could be expected to have a low cost of maintenance and to display a higher coefficient than that shown in the study (2.1% production/energy intake). If the total energy losses in respiration and in the feces plus hypothetical maintenance cost are added to the production, the energy used totals more than the energy consumed by both the *Microtus* and *Mustela* populations. The reasons for this discrepancy were not determined, but food consumption rates estimated in the laboratory possibly underestimate the true food consumption of the more active animals in the field.

Since the maintenance cost is irreducible, the percentage of energy converted to production will be highest when the birth of new animals and the growth rate of living animals are the highest. This surge of production can most easily occur when sources of high energy food are available. *Microtus* conforms to this model, since the young are born and the rate of growth is highest during periods of greatest growth of the vegetation. It would further increase the year-round efficiency of the population to have the lowest population density during the period of little or no production by plants since at that time the dangers of over-exploitation of the food supply would be greatest. A low density at times of low plant production is the usual observation in field studies of the population dynamics of *Microtus* (Blair 1940, Martin 1956, Greenwald 1957, and others).

Finally, *Microtus* appears, on the basis of energy relationships, to be a relatively unimportant component of the community. Even when the energy consumption of insects (estimated as approximately 24% of the net production) is added to that of the mice, only 25% of the net production of the plants is accounted for. Odum (1959) emphasizes the distinction between the herbivores which eat green plants directly and the delayed feeders which eat dead plant material. Apparently, in this stage of old field succession the major portion of the plant net production is directed through these decomposer food chains.

SUMMARY

The energy dynamics of the perennial grass-herb vegetation—*Microtus pennsylvanicus*—*Mustela rixosa* food chain of the old field community was studied from May 1956 to September 1957.

Solar insolation for the growing season, measured

at East Lansing, Michigan, totaled 94.2×10^8 Cal per ha in 1956.

Primary net production by plants was broken down into the following components: (1) production of tops, (2) production of roots, and (3) consumption by *Microtus*. The net production of vegetation for 1956 was 49.5×10^6 Cal per ha and for 1957 was 44.3×10^6 Cal per ha. Respiration of the vegetation during the growing season amounted to approximately 15% of the net production, determined by crude field calorimetry. Gross primary production ranged from 58.27×10^6 Cal per ha in 1956 to 53.01×10^6 Cal per ha in 1957.

Population dynamics and weight changes of the *Microtus* population were studied by live-trapping. Tissue production of young and adult mice was 5,170 Cal per ha per yr. The fasting metabolic rate of mice determined in the laboratory was approximately 10 Cal per mouse per day. Energy lost to respiration equalled 169,877 Cal per ha per yr. The total energy used in growth of the weasel population were 130 Cal per ha per yr and in respiration, 5,434 Cal per ha per yr.

Stomach sample analysis indicated that *Microtus* ate primarily green grass and herbs. Weasels were assumed to feed predominantly on *Microtus*. Total yearly food consumption of the study area as determined from laboratory experiments, was 250,156 Cal per ha for Microtus and 5,284 Cal per ha for *Mustela*.

Of the solar energy available during the growing season, the vegetation used 1.2% in gross production and 1.1% in net production. These results compared favorably with the coefficients for primary production of terrestrial and aquatic communities determined by other workers. Of the energy available to the mice, 1.6% was consumed and 1.1% was utilized in growth and respiration. The weasel population consumed 31% of the energy available to it in the form of *Microtus*, and used 30% of the energy consumed in growth and respiration.

Twenty-one % of the production of the *Microtus* population and only 10% of the weasel production was lost from the food chain. These losses were diverted to other food chains through other predators or through micro-organisms.

Of the energy consumed only a portion was used in production; most of the energy went to respiration or passed through the digestive tract unused. Respiration cost increased from the vegetation level to the carnivore level of the food chain. The gross energy in the experimental diets which was recovered in the feces amounted to 10-18% for *Microtus* and 10% for *Mustela*.

LITERATURE CITED

Bailey, V. 1924. Breeding, feeding and other life habits of meadow mice (Microtus). Jour. Agr. Res. 27: 523-536.

Baker, J. R. & R. M. Ranson. 1932. Factors affecting the breeding of the field mouse (*Microtus agrestis*)
Part 1. Light. Proc. Royal Soc. London (B) 110: 313-322.

Baten, W. D. & A. H. Eichmeier. 1951. A summary of weather conditions at East Lansing, Michigan prior to 1950. Mich. State College Ag. Exp. Stat. 63 pp.

Beckwith, S. L. 1954. Ecological succession on abandoned farm lands and its relationship to wildlife management. Ecol. Monog. 24: 349-376.

Blair, W. F. 1940. Home range and population of the meadow vole in southern Michigan. Jour. Wildlife Mangt. 4: 149-161.

———. 1948. Population density, life span, and mortality rates of small mammals in the bluegrass meadow and bluegrass field associations of southern Michigan. Amer. Midland Nat. 40: 395-419.

Bole, B. P., Jr. 1939. The quadrat method of studying small mammal populations. Cleveland Mus. Nat. Hist. Sci. Publ. 5(4): 15-77.

Brody, S. 1945. Bioenergetics and growth. New York: Reinhold Publ. Corp. 1023 pp.

Burt, W. H. 1948. The mammals of Michigan. Ann Arbor: Univ. Mich. Press. 288 pp.

Clarke, G. L. 1946. Dynamics of production in a marine area. Ecol. Monog. 16: 321-335.

Clarke, G. L., W. T. Edmondson & W. E. Ricker. 1946. Mathematical formulation of biological productivity. Ecol. Monog. 16: 336-337.

Crabb, G. A., Jr. 1950a. Solar radiation investigations in Michigan. Mich. Agr. Expt. Sta. Tech. Bull. 222. 153 pp.

———. 1950b. The normal pattern of solar radiation at East Lansing, Michigan. Mich. Acad. Sci., Arts, and Letters 36: 173-176.

Daubenmire, R. F. 1947. Plants and Environment. New York: J. C. Wiley Co.

Davis, D. E. 1956. Manual for analysis of rodent populations. Ann Arbor, Mich.: Edwards Bros. 82 pp.

Davis, D. H. S. 1933. Rhythmic activity in the short-tailed vole, *Microtus*. Jour. Anim. Ecol. 2: 232-238.

Dice, L. R. 1922. Some factors affecting the distribution of the prairie vole, forest deer mouse, and prairie deer mouse. Ecology 3: 29-47.

Eadie, W. R. 1952. Shrew predation and vole populations on a localized area. Jour. Mammal. 33: 185-189.

Evans, F. C. & S. A. Cain. 1952. Preliminary studies on the vegetation of an old-field community in southeastern Michigan. Contrib. Lab. Vert. Biol. Univ. Mich. 51: 1-17.

Fernald, M. L. 1950. Gray's Manual of Botany. 8th Ed. New York: Amer. Book Co.

Greenwald, G. S. 1957. Reproduction in a coastal California population of the field mouse *Microtus californicus*. Calif. Univ. Pubs. Zool. 54: 421-446.

Hall, E. R. 1951. American weasels. Kans. Univ. Pubs. Mus. Nat. Hist. 4: 1-466.

Hamilton, W. J., Jr. 1937. The biology of microtine cycles. Jour. Agr. Res. 54: 779-790.

———. 1941. Reproduction of the field mouse, *Microtus pennsylvanicus* (Ord). Cornell Univ. Agr. Expt. Sta. Mem. 237.

Hatfield, D. M. 1935. A natural history study of *Microtus californicus*. Jour. Mammal. 16: 261-271.

————. 1939. Rate of metabolism in *Microtus* and *Peromyscus*. Murrelet 20: 54-56.

————. 1940. Activity and food consumption in *Microtus* and *Peromyscus*. Jour. Mammal. 21: 29-36.

Hatt, R. T. 1930. The biology of the voles of New York. Roosevelt Wildlife Bull. 5(4): 509-623.

————. 1940. The least weasel in Michigan. Jour. Mammal. 21: 412-416.

Korschgen, L. J. 1957. Food habits of coyotes, foxes, house cats, and bobcats in Missouri. Missouri Fish and Game Div. P-R Series No. 15. 63 pp.

Lantz, D. E. 1907. An economic study of field mice. USDA Biol. Surv. Bull. 31: 1-64.

Lindeman, R. L. 1942. The trophic-dynamic aspect of ecology. Ecology 23: 399-418.

Linduska, J. P. 1950. Ecological landuse relationships of small mammals on a Michigan farm. Mich. Dept. Cons. Game Div., Lansing. 144 pp.

Llewellen, L. M. 1942. Notes on the Alleghenian least weasel in Virginia. Jour. Mammal. 23: 439-441.

Martin, E. P. 1956. A population study of the prairie vole (*Microtus ochrogaster*) in northeastern Kansas. Kans. Univ. Pubs. Mus. Nat. Hist. 8(6): 361-416.

McCay, C. M. 1949. Nutrition of the dog. Ithaca, N.Y.: Comstock. 337 pp.

McLagen, N. F. & M. M. Sheahan. 1950. The measurement of oxygen consumption in small mammals by a closed circuit method. Jour. Endocrin. 6: 456-462.

Merrill, A. L. & B. K. Watt. 1955. Energy value of foods—basis and derivation. USDA Agr. Handbook No. 74. 105 pp.

Morrison, F. B. 1949. Feeds and Feeding. Ithaca, N.Y.: Morrison Publ. Co. 21st Ed. 1207 pp.

Morrison, P. R. 1948. Oxygen consumption in several small wild mammals. Jour. Cell. and Compar. Physiol. 31: 69-96.

Noddack, W. 1937. Der Kohlenstoff im Haushalt der Natur. Ztschr. f. Angew. Chem. 50: 505-510.

Odum, E. P. 1959. Fundamentals of Ecology. 2nd. Ed. Philadelphia: Saunders. 546 pp.

Odum, H. T. 1956. Efficiencies, size of organisms, and community structure. Ecology 37: 592-597.

Park, T. 1946. Some observations on the history and scope of population ecology. Ecol. Monog. 16: 313-320.

Pearsall, W. H. & E. Gorham. 1956. Production ecology. 1. Standing crops of natural vegetation. Oikos 7(2): 193-201.

Pearson, O. P. 1947. The rate of metabolism of some small mammals. Ecology 28: 127-145.

Polderboer, E. B. 1942. Habits of the least weasel (*Mustela rixosa*) in northeastern Iowa. Jour. Mammal. 23: 145-147.

Regnier, R. & R. Pussard. 1926. Le campagnol des champs (*Microtus arvalis* Pallas) et sa destruction. Ann. des Épiphyt. 12(6): 385-535.

Ricker, W. E. 1946. Production and utilization of fish populations. Ecol. Monog. 16: 373-391.

Shively, S. B. & J. E. Weaver. 1939. Amount of underground plant materials in different grassland climates. Nebr. Univ. Conserv. Bull. No. 21. 67 pp.

Tansley, A. G. 1935. The use and abuse of vegetational concepts and terms. Ecology 16: 284-307.

Terrien, J., G. Truffaut, & J. Carles. 1957. Light, vegetation and chlorophyll. New York: Philosoph. Libr. 228 pp.

Thomas, M. D. & G. R. Hill. 1949. Photosynthesis under field conditions. In, Photosynthesis in Plants, edited by J. Franck and W. E. Loomis. Ames: Iowa State Col. Press. 500 pp.

Toner, G. C. 1956. House cat predation on small animals. Jour. Mammal. 37: 119.

Townsend, M. T. 1935. Studies on some of the small mammals of central New York. Roosevelt Wildlife Ann. 4: 6-120.

Transeau, E. N. 1926. The accumulation of energy by plants. Ohio Jour. Sci. 26: 1-10.

Veatch, J. O., et al. 1941. Soil Survey of Ingham County, Michigan. USDA Soil Survey Series 1933, No. 36. 43 pp.

Whitmoyer, T. F. 1956. A laboratory study of growth rate in young *Microtus pennsylvanicus*. Unpubl. Master's thesis, Mich. State Univ. 62 pp.

Wolcott, G. N. 1937. An animal census of two pastures and a meadow in northern New York. Ecol. Monog. 7: 1-90

Wooster, H. A., Jr. & F. C. Blanck. 1950. Nutritional Data. Pittsburgh: H. J. Heinz Co. 114 pp.

THE ENERGETICS OF A POPULATION OF
LEPTOPTERNA DOLABRATA (HETEROPTERA: MIRIDAE)

BY S. McNEILL

Imperial College Field Station, Silwood Park, Ascot, Berkshire

INTRODUCTION

There is little published information on annual production and energy flow in low density insect populations. Most natural populations are of low density and the present study deals with the production and energetics of *Leptopterna dolabrata* (L.), a mirid bug, with this characteristic.

The lifecycle has been studied and the various stages described by Osborne (1918), Tullgren (1919), Garman (1926), Kullenberg (1946) and Jewett & Townsend (1947). Briefly *L. dolabrata* is univoltine, the eggs, laid in late June and early July, enter diapause at a very early stage of embryogenesis (Cobben 1968) and do not hatch until the following May. The nymphal stages are of short duration and adults first appear in mid-June. These mature in about 10 days and the females usually lay all their eggs into the bases of the grass stems within 24 h.

The detailed numerical population data will be published in a separate paper.

THE STUDY AREA

The study was carried out on an area of unmown grassland at Silwood Park, Ascot, Berkshire over the period September 1964–July 1969. The dominant grasses on the area were *Holcus mollis* Linn., *H. lanatus* Linn. and *Agrostis tenuis* Sibth. being present in 79, 38 and 54% respectively of a sample of sixty-eight random $\frac{1}{4}$ m^2 quadrats but showing clear dominance in only 56, 17 and 12% of the quadrats respectively.

METHODS

Numbers and net production

The numbers of each instar present in the field were determined as far as possible each day, by counting the numbers present in permanent $\frac{1}{4}$ m^2 quadrats without removing the insects. The position of each quadrat was fixed by dividing the area into a $\frac{1}{4}$ m^2 grid using random number tables to determine the co-ordinates of each quadrat. In 1965, fifty quadrats were laid out and this was increased to 100 in 1966.

The experimental site included a large area of mixed *Holcus mollis*–*Agrostis* grassland but very few *Leptopterna dolabrata* were found on this mixed vegetation and the results from this area were not considered. Thus the twenty-eight quadrats placed on the remaining 1850 m^2 in 1965 of the experimental area gave a standard error of the estimated total number of insects of between 70 and 30% (using the formula of Cochran 1963); when this was increased to sixty-eight quadrats in subsequent years the standard errors were reduced to between 50% and 24–15% depending on the numbers found. The insects were never very abundant, the peak numbers/m² being 6·4, 2·4, 3·0, 5·5 and 7·1 in 1965–69 respectively.

Of the individuals collected during 1965, some were weighed immediately and others were freeze-dried for 24 h before being weighed, all weighings were made on a Cahn Gram Electrobalance reading to 0·0005 mg. Since samples were taken regularly over the whole of a season a mean dry weight and a mean wet weight could be obtained for each instar. Further collections in 1966, 1967 and 1968 showed no significant differences in the means for the instars.

Calorific values were obtained by use of a Gallenkamp Ballistic Bomb Calorimeter in which the resistance bridge had been modified to enable samples with a heat output of 0·2–1·2 kcal to be used instead of 2·0–6·0 kcal. The material for instars 1–3, and 4–5 were bulked in order that more than one determination could be carried out for each type of material.

The values for exuviae were determined by weighing dried exuviae for each stage; these were converted to calories using the value of 5·187 kcal/g obtained by Wiegert (1964) for the cuticle of *Philaenus spumarius*.

Feeding rates

Leptopterna dolabrata feeds by emptying the cells of the leaves and ovules on which it feeds and, unlike many other sucking insects, does not normally feed on phloem or xylem sap. This makes the estimation of feeding rates much easier than, for example, in aphids.

The feeding of *L. dolabrata* on a grass blade is marked by a small white patch where the mesophyll cells have been emptied. The mean number and size of feeds taken/h/insect were found by counting and measuring the maximum width and breadth of the white marks produced, at a range of temperatures simulating those measured in the field, by individual insects confined to unmarked grass blades for 48 h. Experiments were continued for more than 24 h in order to obtain both a realistic 24 h mean and to minimize the variation due to the state of hunger of the experimental animals at the beginning of the experiment.

In order that these relationships could be used to give the food intake of an insect at any given temperature it was necessary to find the weight or calorific value of the cell contents/unit area of leaf surface. This was achieved by establishing a relationship between the surface area, dry weight and calorific value of unpunctured leaves.

A known weight of dry leaves was then taken, thoroughly crushed and extracted with ethanol in a Soxhlet extractor for 48 h. The dry weight of the cell walls remaining in the thimble after extraction was found and hence the proportion by weight of the cell contents could be found. This was converted to calorific terms by determining the calorific value/g of the cell walls; as a check, the extract was freeze-dried and its calorific value/g determined.

Respiration

The respiration of this insect was measured in the laboratory using a constant pressure respirometer (Klekowski 1968). Respirometer runs were made on insects collected from the field during the whole of the season in 1967 and check runs were made at intervals in the following seasons to ensure that the response to temperature did not vary from year to year.

The range of temperatures used was 14–25° C (lower temperatures were not available) and more than one run was made consecutively with each insect so that compensation effects could be measured; however, no significant effects were noted in this species.

Table 1. *Weight and calorific value for all stages of Leptopterna*

Stage	No. examined	Mean wet weight (mg)	SE (%)	No. examined	Mean dry weight (mg)	SE (%)	kcal/g dry weight	No. of firings	SE (%)	Mean cal/insect	Approximate SE (%)	Mean dry weight of exuvium	No. examined	SE (%)
Egg	22	0·100	2	29	0·096	2	6·30	2	3·0	0·605	5·0	· —	—	—
1	23	0·373	5	20	0·083	12	} 5·81	} 2	} 0·2	0·482	12·2	0·003	10	9·6
2	24	0·598	4	27	0·157	8				0·912	8·2	0·01	3	0
3	31	1·385	4	36	0·363	5				2·109	5·2	0·03	10	6·6
4	18	3·582	10	48	0·820	6	} 5·86	} 6	} 1·5	4·805	7·5	0·06	20	6·6
5	30	9·380	6	111	2·826	3				16·560	4·5	0·20	6	56·6
Male	22	10·645	2	81	3·551	2	6·05	6	0·7	21·480	2·7			
Female	43	25·974	4	116	10·359	3	6·06	8	1·1	62·810	4·1			

Nymphal stages: 1–5

At the end of the last run with each insect it was freeze-dried and its calorific value was calculated from the calorific value/gram dry weight as determined above.

RESULTS

Numbers and net production

An estimate of the standing crop for each day was obtained by multiplying the estimated number/m² for each instar by the corresponding calorific value/individual for that instar

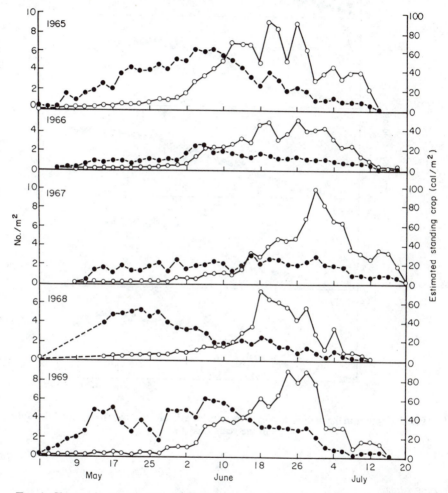

FIG. 1. Changes in the standing crop of *Leptopterna dolabrata*, expressed as cal/m², over the period May–July in the years 1965–69. Only every second estimate is shown. ●, Number/m²; ○, cal/m².

(Table 1) and summing over all instars for each day. The results are shown in Fig. 1. Estimated standing crop for each day was then divided by the total number/m² on each day in order that a mean value/individual in the population could be obtained (see Fig. 2) for substitution in the predictive equations for respiration and feeding.

Fig. 3 shows the inverse of developmental time (see Table 2) plotted against temperature and it can be seen that the developmental zero is approximately 10° C and since, during the period of active growth, the temperature seldom drops below 10° C (daily mean), the mean individual growth will always be positive and can be estimated, for each day, by reading the increase in mean individual size during that day from the graph of mean individual size against time (Fig. 2).

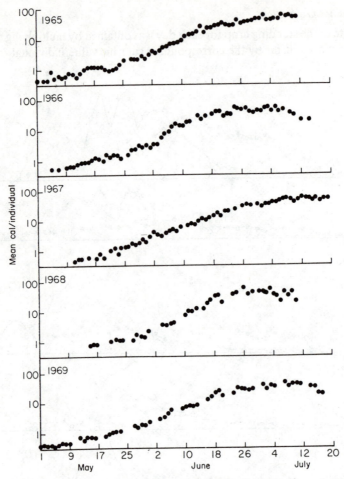

Fig. 2. Changes in the daily estimates of mean calories/individual over the period May–July in the years 1965–69.

Feeding rates

Leptopterna dolabrata has many different food plants in parts of its wide range; on the present experimental plot, however, it was mainly confined to the two species of *Holcus*, feeding mostly on the leaves of *H. mollis* during the early instars and moving on to the flower heads of *H. lanatus* at the time of maturation (see Table 3).

The mean number of feeds/insect/h in relation to environmental temperature is shown in Table 4, where it can be seen that the mean number of feeds/individual increased with temperature, size of insect having no effect.

Although temperature increase could be correlated with an increase in the number of feeds it in no way influenced the size (surface area) of individual feeds. Fig. 4 shows a close correlation between the size of a feed and the size (dry weight) of an individual insect. This relationship may be explained by the increasing length of the stylets, as the insect increases in size, allowing more cells to be reached from one puncture.

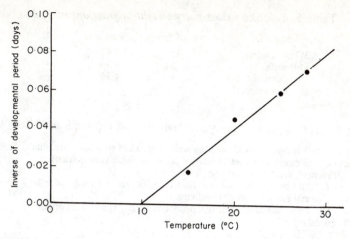

Fig. 3. Relationship between, inverse of developmental time (days) to the final moult and temperature, showing that the developmental zero is approximately 10° C. $1/D = 0.0041T - 0.0410$, where D = developmental period and T = degrees Centigrade.

Table 2. *The development of* Leptopterna *at constant temperature*

Temperature (° C)	1	2	Instar 3	4	5	Total duration (days)
15	9	9	10	16	16	60
20	3	4	4	5	6	22
25	2	4	2	5	4	17
28	2	3	2	3	4	14

All durations from moult to moult in days to the nearest day. All means of 16.

Table 3. *Relationship between* Leptopterna dolabrata *and* Holcus lanatus

Stage of L. dolabrata	Coefficient of interspecific association (Cole 1949)			
	1966	1967	1968	1969
Nymphal stages 1	0.22	0.60*	0.21	0.02
2	0.45*	0.55*	0.06	0.04
3	0.08	0.25	0.02	0.01
4	0.16	0.56*	0.19	0.02
5	0.22	0.66*	0.41*	0.14
Male	0.63*	0.64*	0.55*	0.29*
Female	0.58*	0.65*	0.58*	0.22*

* Significant at 5% using t test.
Total samples sixty-eight in all cases.

The estimation of food intake, for energy budget purposes, of different individuals depended on a knowledge of the relative proportions of cell contents and cell walls in *Holcus* leaves; plus a knowledge of the total leaf area and its calorific values. The appropriate information is provided in Tables 5 and 6.

Table 4. *The relationship between temperature and feeding rate in* Leptopterna dolabrata

Temperature (°C)	Mean feeds/insect/h
15	2.07
20	2.24
25	3.61
28	3.60

Table 5. *Calorific values/g dry weight of fractions of* Holcus

Material	No. of firings	kcal/g	SE
Whole *Holcus*	15	4·43	2
Cell walls	5	4·06	4
Cell contents (Soxhlet extract)	1	4·34	—

Table 6. *Relative proportions of cell contents and cell walls in* Holcus *leaves*

Ratio of cell contents to cell walls by weight, mean of six determinations 52·1%

Ratio of cell contents to cell walls by calorific value (cell contents by difference), six determinations 56·1%

Ratio of cell contents to cell walls by calorific value (using calorific value of cell extract), six determinations 51·1%

Total leaf 0·667 cal/mm² (ten determinations), therefore cell contents 0·380 cal/mm²

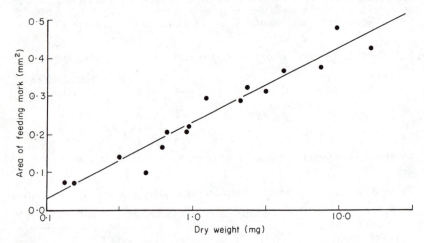

FIG. 4. The relationship between area of feeding mark and dry weight of individual in *Leptopterna dolabrata*.

It is thus possible to calculate food intake by estimating the number of feeds by an individual/unit time by reference to the prevailing environmental temperature and multiplying this by the size of feed according to insect size which gives the area of leaf emptied/unit time which can in turn be converted to calories by using the calorific values for cell contents shown in Table 6.

Respiration

In all 257 runs using 129 insects were made and the results were analysed by multiple regression techniques against temperature, calorific value of the individual and age (instar). The resultant predictive equation was:

$$\log R = -0.6537 + 0.0557I + 0.6270 \log K + 0.0310T$$

Where I is instar number, K is calorific value of the individual, T is temperature (°C) and R is respiration (μl/individual/h). Multiple R^2 was 0·9664 and F with three and 125 df was 1199·18 which is very highly significant. The extremely good fit of this equation may be spurious.

Energy budgets

Using the counts of numbers/m², age distribution and mean daily temperature deter-

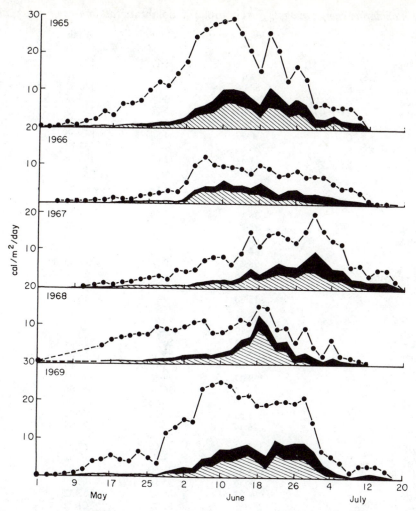

Fig. 5. Daily estimates of the energy flow parameters production (*P*, hatched areas), respiration (*R*, solid areas) and ingestion (*C*, ●) plotted against time. Only every second estimate is shown.

mined in the field, together with the relationships derived in the previous sections, estimates of each of the following parameters were made for each 24 h period for the population in calories/m²: growth, respiration, ingestion and standing crop. Assimilation was found by adding growth and respiration, and egestion from the difference between ingestion and assimilation. It was found impossible to measure faeces production accurately.

The daily pattern of energy flow is shown graphically for each year in Fig. 5.

The annual population energy budgets (Table 7) were obtained by summing the appropriate terms in the daily budgets. The total budget was then split to show the separate contributions of adults and nymphs by using the same methods on each section separately. The basic lay-out of the budgets is that used by Wiegert (1964).

DISCUSSION

The total energy flow through the population obviously varies from year to year; however, the actual pattern of energy flow rates from day to day/m² is similar in all years.

The respiration of the egg stage was not measured, but since this stage is spent largely

Table 7. *Population energy budgets for* Leptopterna dolabrata (*all figures given as cal/m^2*)

Category		Nymphs	Adults	Totals	
Eggs 1964		20·63	—	20·63	
Growth 1965	$G=P-ML$	84·96	51·17	136·13	
Moult loss (exuviae)	ML	4·10	—	4·10	Symbols after
Production	P	89·06	51·17	140·23	Petrusewicz (1967)
Respiration	R	59·58	40·98	100·56	
Assimilation	$A=P+R$	148·64	92·15	240·79	
Egestion	$FU=C-P-R$	502·35	92·43	594·78	
Ingestion	C	650·99	184·58	835·56	
Nymphs surviving	N	33·12	—	33·12	
Mortality	$E=G-N$	51·84	72·63	124·46	
Eggs 1965		11·67	—	11·67	
Growth 1966		36·42	25·59	62·00	
Moult loss		1·76	—	1·76	
Production		38·17	25·59	63·76	
Respiration		25·39	36·25	61·64	
Assimilation		63·56	61·83	125·40	
Egestion		134·71	88·56	223·27	
Ingestion		198·27	150·39	348·66	
Nymphs surviving		16·56	—	16·56	
Mortality		19·86	25·84	45·70	
Eggs 1966		16·30	—	16·30	
Growth 1967		40·61	50·84	91·46	
Moult loss		4·19	—	4·19	
Production		44·80	50·84	95·64	
Respiration		32·19	55·32	87·51	
Assimilation		76·99	106·16	183·15	
Egestion		198·07	129·86	327·93	
Ingestion		275·06	236·02	511·08	
Nymphs surviving		37·01	—	37·01	
Mortality		3·60	61·32	64·92	
Eggs 1967		26·54	—	26·54	
Growth 1968		55·71	31·60	87·31	
Moult loss		2·52	—	2·52	
Production		58·23	31·60	89·83	
Respiration		28·56	35·13	63·69	
Assimilation		86·79	66·73	153·52	
Egestion		244·63	57·09	301·72	
Ingestion		331·42	123·82	455·24	
Nymphs surviving		20·45	—	20·45	
Mortality		35·25	24·17	59·42	
Eggs 1968		27·89	—	27·89	
Growth 1969		58·67	63·30	121·97	
Moult loss		4·93	—	4·93	
Production		63·60	63·30	126·90	
Respiration		54·19	49·34	103·53	
Assimilation		117·79	112·64	230·43	
Egestion		492·64	91·18	583·82	
Ingestion		610·43	203·82	814·25	
Nymphs surviving		40·97	—	40·97	
Mortality		17·70	86·75	104·45	
Eggs 1969		22·45	—	22·45	

in diapause, the total consumption is probably low compared to the total for all the other stages.

Mean population assimilation efficiency ($A/C\%$) varies between 28·3% and 36·0% (Table 8) which is similar to the values reported for grasshoppers by Smalley (1960)—27% and Wiegert (1965)—37% but lower than the values for *Philaenus*—66% obtained by Wiegert (1964). This is, however, not constant during the whole of the life cycle as is shown by the plot of the daily estimates of this efficiency (Fig. 6). Initially it is very low,

Table 8. *Population efficiencies*

Year	Production P (cal/m^2)	Assimilation A (cal/m^2)	Ingestion C (cal/m^2)	A/C(%)	P/A(%)	P/C(%)
1965	140·23	240·79	835·56	28·8	58·2	16·8
1966	63·76	125·40	348·66	36·0	50·8	18·3
1967	95·64	183·15	511·08	35·8	52·2	18·7
1968	89·83	153·52	455·24	33·7	58·5	19·7
1969	126·90	23·43	814·25	28·3	55·1	15·6

about 10%, but rises to a peak, at about the time the first adults appear, of around 50%, thereafter it declines slowly as the population ages to about 30% at the end of the season. The peak efficiency corresponds to the time when the change over from leaf to seed feeding occurs.

The high assimilation efficiencies found in this insect (and in *Philaenus*) are presumably due to the fact that the food is already in a liquid form and hence does not contain large amounts of indigestible cell-wall material. The much lower efficiencies shown for the younger insects could be due to two main causes: (a) these do not empty most of the cells under the feeding mark, or, (b) they are unable to ingest the chloroplasts and other cell organelles due to the narrowness of the stylets.

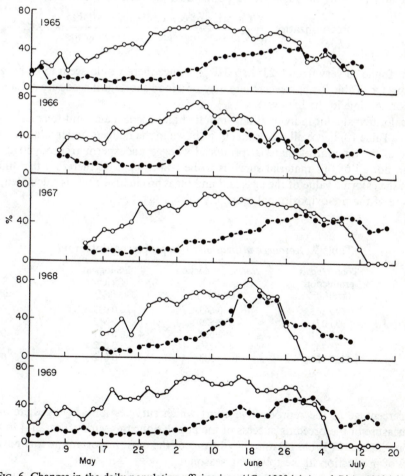

FIG. 6. Changes in the daily population efficiencies, $A/C \times 100\%$ (●) and $P/A \times 100\%$ (○) over the period May–July in the years 1965–69.

The mean net production efficiency ($P/A\%$) is very high varying from 50·8% to 58·5% (Table 8), presumably because this insect is a relatively sedentary animal living in an environment in which food is always near at hand.

The plot of the daily estimates of net population production efficiency gives a much flatter curve than population assimilation efficiency; beginning at about 20% it rises quite quickly to a plateau between 50 and 70%; finally it falls away steeply after maturation of the adults as the proportion of spent adults in the population rises (Fig. 6).

One other population efficiency that is worth consideration is the ratio of annual production to annual ingestion, since this ratio is a measure of the maximum amount of the production of the first trophic level which is made available as yield to the carnivores; Slobodkin (1960, 1962) and Wiegert (1965) have surmised that for populations which are in a steady state this efficiency cannot exceed 15–20% for any length of time. In the present study this efficiency was found to range between 15·6% and 19·7% (Table 8) which is within the limits required by the theory; because the total predation pressure on the population was not measured, the actual yield/ingestion ratio cannot be given.

The primary production of the *Holcus* during the period from 1 May to 20 July was estimated in each year by harvesting $6 \times \frac{1}{10}\,\text{m}^2$ samples at intervals and using the increase in the standing crop to give an estimate of the young grass blades and seedheads in calories per m^2 available to the population of *Leptopterna dolabrata*; this was then reduced to 56% of this figure to give an estimate of the cell contents. The percentage resource utilization by the *Leptopterna* population can then be found as:

$$\% \text{ resource utilization} = \frac{\text{Calories of cell contents available}}{\text{Calories ingested by } Leptopterna} \times 100\%$$

This was found to vary from 0·23% to 0·07%, hence there would seem to be no general food shortage (Table 9); however, there may be a food shortage if seeds are not available at the correct time in the life cycle.

The calorific value of individual new-moulted and spent males and females is almost the same (Table 10) hence all the production shown in the budgets under adults is really a measure of the amount of material produced as eggs and sperm (reproductive effort) although not all of this material survives to be laid as eggs. If therefore the difference between the calorific value of the eggs laid and the reproductive effort is calculated, this is a measure of the pre-ovipositional mortality (Table 11).

Table 9. *Resource utilization by* Leptopterna dolabrata

Year	Total *Holcus* production (kcal/m²)	*Holcus* production available (kcal/m²)	Ecological efficiency (%)	% Resource utilization
1965	649·363	360·643	0·039	0·232
1966	933·071	522·520	0·012	0·067
1967	808·271	452·632	0·021	0·113
1968	725·242	406·236	0·022	0·112
1969	1857·720	1040·323	0·012	0·078

The percentage of the reproductive effort which survives until laying therefore will give a measure of the breeding success of the population; this varies from 21·4 to 88·3% in the present study (Table 11) and may be one of the most important factors governing the level of production in the following season.

Another measure of reproductive success is the ratio of calories of eggs laid to total production; this again is highly variable ranging from 8·3 to 31·0%; this latter figure

Table 10. *Comparison of new-moulted, mature and spent adults of* Leptopterna dolabrata

Stage	No. examined	Dry weight (mg)	SE(%)
Males			
New-moulted	9	2·957	14
Mature	10	4·351	6
Spent	9	2·858	9
Females			
New-moulted	12	4·208	5
Mature	19	12·184	3
Spent	12	4·172	8

Table 11. *Reproductive efficiencies*

Year	Calories of reproductive effort	Calories of eggs laid	Calories of pre-ovipositional mortality	Reproductive efficiency (%)	Production (%)
				Eggs laid	
1965	51·17	11·67	39·50	21·4	8·3
1966	25·59	16·30	9·29	63·7	25·6
1967	50·84	26·54	24·30	52·2	27·7
1968	31·60	27·89	3·71	88·3	31·0
1969	63·30	22·45	40·85	35·5	17·7

shows how very efficient a population, in which the females lay a relatively small number of eggs (30–70), can be in its contribution to the next generation.

The percentage survival of the reproductive effort shows a relationship to the total annual production (Fig. 7) in which the higher the production the lower the reproductive success, hence this would tend to reduce the fluctuation in production from year to year.

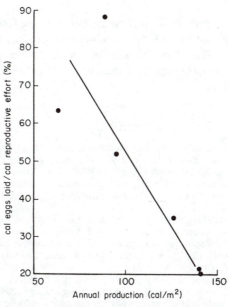

FIG. 7. Relationship between eggs/reproductive effort expressed as a percentage and annual population production/m².

Other factors affecting the level of production may also be found when more data are available on this population (e.g. the variation in total mortality may be governed by the variations in nymphal mortality, despite the fact that adult mortality, in calorific terms, is greater).

ACKNOWLEDGMENTS

I wish to thank Professor O. W. Richards, F.R.S. and Professor T. R. E. Southwood for the provision of facilities at Silwood Park, and Dr A. Duncan for the use of respirometry apparatus.

The major part of this work was carried out while the author was in receipt of an Agricultural Research Council Studentship.

SUMMARY

(1) The daily values/m² for production, respiration, and food consumption are estimated for a population of the mirid bug *Leptopterna dolabrata*.

(2) Detailed population energy budgets are presented for the years 1965–69. The total energy flow through the population varies widely from year to year but the pattern of flow in calories/m²/day is similar in all years (Fig. 5).

(3) The mean population assimilation efficiency (A/C) is similar to published figures for other insect herbivores; however, there is a large variation in the value of this ratio during the lifetime of the population, the maximum value occurring at the time the first adults appear. This corresponds to a change of feeding habits.

(4) The mean population net production efficiency (P/A) is very high and although this also shows variation this is much less than in the previous efficiency. This high value is probably due to the sedentary nature and feeding habits of this insect.

(5) The maximum possible yield/ingestion ratio (P/C) falls within the range of 15–20% predicted for steady state populations.

(6) The fraction of the available primary production utilized by the population is very low (0·23–0·07%) and hence there would appear to be no absolute food shortage in this population.

(7) Two measures of reproductive success are derived, one (calories of eggs produced/ total production) shows that up to 31% of the material produced by the population may be in the form of eggs. The other (calories of eggs produced/calories of reproductive effort) increases as the annual production decreases and hence has a stabilizing influence on the annual production.

REFERENCES

Cobben, R. H. (1968). Evolutionary trends in Heteroptera. Part 1. Eggs, architecture of the shell, gross embryology and eclosion. *Meded. Lab. Ent. Wageningen*, 151.

Cochran, W. G. (1963). *Sampling Techniques*, 2nd edn. Wiley, New York.

Cole, L. C. (1949). The measurement of interspecific association. *Ecology*, **30**, 411–24.

Garman, H. (1926). Two important enemies of Bluegrass pastures, I: the Bluegrass plant bug; II: the Green bug. *Bull. Ky agric. Expt Stn*, **265**, 29–47.

Jewett, H. H. & Townsend, L. H. (1947). *Miris dolabratus* (Linn.) and *Amblytytus nassutus* (Kirschbaum). Two destructive pests of Kentucky Bluegrass. *Bull. Ky agric. Expt Stn*, **508**, 1–16.

Klekowski, R. Z. (1968). A constant pressure microrespirometer for terrestrial invertebrates. *Methods of Ecological Bioenergetics* (Ed. by W. Grodzinski & R. Z. Klekowski), pp. 67–86. Polish Academy of Sciences, Warsaw & Cracow.

Kullenberg, B. (1946). Studien über die Biologie der Capsiden. *Zool. Bidr. Upps.* **23**, 1–522.

Osborne, H. (1918). The Meadow Plant Bug, *Miris dolabratus*. *J. agric. Res.* **15**, 175–200.

Petrusewicz, K. (1967). Suggested list of more important concepts in productivity studies (definitions and symbols). *Secondary Productivity of Terrestrial Ecosystems* (Ed. by K. Petrusewicz), pp. 51–8. Polish Academy of Sciences, Warsaw & Cracow.

Slobodkin, L. B. (1960). Ecological energy relationships at the population level. *Am. Nat.* **94**, 213–36.

Slobodkin, L. B. (1962). Energy in animal ecology. *Advances in Ecological Research* (Ed. by J. B. Cragg), vol. 1, 69–101. Academic Press, London.

Smalley, A. E. (1960). Energy flow of a salt marsh grasshopper population. *Ecology*, **41**, 672–7.

Southwood, T. R. E. (1966). *Ecological Methods with particular reference to the Study of Insect Populations.* Methuen, London.

Tullgren, A. (1919). Axsugaren *Miris dolabratus* L. (*Leptopterna dolabrata* L.) Centralanst. *Fösok. jordbr. Ent. Stockholm*, 182.

Wiergert, R. G. (1964). Population energetics of meadow spittlebugs (*Philaenus spumarius* L.) as affected by migration and habitat. *Ecol. Monogr.* **34**, 217–41.

Wiegert, R. G. (1965). Energy dynamics of the grasshopper populations in old field and alfalfa field ecosystems. *Oikos*, **16**, 161–76.

Wiegert, R. G. & Evans, F. C. (1967). Investigations of secondary productivity in grasslands. *Secondary Productivity of Terrestrial Ecosystems.* (Ed. by K. Petrusewicz), pp. 499–518. Polish Academy of Sciences, Warsaw & Cracow.

Energetics of Indian Cattle
in Their Environment

Stewart Odend'hal [1, 2]
Department of Veterinary Anatomy-Physiology,
College of Veterinary Medicine,
University of Missouri. Columbia, MO 65201

Received April 26, 1971; revised October 4, 1971

Cattle and other domestic animals in 5.77 square miles of rural West Bengal were enumerated on three separate occasions during an 18-month period. Feed consumption and productivity measurements involving 80 cattle-day observations were extrapolated to the entire cattle population and an energetic balance sheet was calculated for a 1-year period. The cattle population appears fairly stable despite a high density. The age distribution reveals a demographic imbalance in both the younger and older age groups which contributes toward a more efficient utilization of available feed supplies. One of the major roles of the cattle is to convert items of little human value into products of direct human utility. The gross energetic efficiency of the entire cattle population was approximately 17%. The current management of cattle appears to be appropriate for the ecological framework in which they exist.

INTRODUCTION

The total number of water buffalo (*Bubalus bubalis*) and cattle (*Bos indicus*) in India exceeds the total number of humans in the United States. The population of cattle alone is over 175 million (Food and Agriculture Organization, 1970: 316). This large cattle population has been called both the wealth and the burden of India. The cattle are appreciated because the "...primary function of the cattle ... is to supply the motive power for agricultural production and transport of the produce of the soil from village to marketing and consumer centres" (Fahimuddin, 1963: 39). However, at the same time, the cattle are abused because it "cannot be denied that there exists a tremendous surplus of useless and inefficient cattle which press upon the inadequate supplies of fodder" (Kuriyan, 1969: 77).

The number of "useless" cows has been estimated from 2.5% (Shah, M. M., 1967: 51) to 80% (Rao, cited in Whyte, 1968: 170) of the cattle population. However, what constitutes a "useless" cow is never defined in most cases. For religious and political reasons "there is thus a little chance that the [cattle] problem will be examined rationally and dispassionately" (Dandekar, 1967: 35).

This research was supported by NIH grant 5RO-TW00141-09 to the Johns Hopkins University Center for Medical Research and Training, Baltimore, Maryland 21205.

[1] John Hopkins University Center for Medical Research and Training, Baltimore, Maryland.

[2] Present address: Developmental Research Department, Agricultural Division, Pfizer, Inc., Terre Haute, Indiana.

In some of his latest publications, Whyte presents a very comprehensive review of the current Indian cattle situation (Whyte, 1964; Whyte and Mathur, 1968; Whyte, 1968). A. B. Shah (1967) discusses some of the social and religious implications of prevailing attitudes toward cattle. Harris (1966) has challenged the traditional western view of the unproductive nature of zebu cattle and suggests that ecological necessity, not religious sentiment, dictates cattle management in India. Heston (1971) in a rebuttal to Harris suggests that the general productivity of Indian cattle might be improved by the manipulation of the Indian cattle sex ratios.

Several years ago Wright (1937) pointed out the need to evaluate the cattle relative to village priorities rather than by urban or western concepts. Often Indian cattle are regarded as inefficient because of their low production of meat and milk when compared to western breeds (*Bos taurus*). However, would it be relevant to compare the amount of bullock power produced in India to that of useful work performed by steers in America? Thus, a comparison of meat and milk production between the two types of cattle as a measure of their productiveness is virtually meaningless.

A logical and objective method of evaluating the productivity of cattle would be to determine the gross energetic efficiency or the input-output ratio of consumption and production. This should be done on a population basis rather than just the "average" individual animal. The common denominator to which the input and output can be related with most accuracy is not economics, but energetics. The economic value of the parameters involved tends to fluctuate with supply and demand. The caloric values remain relatively constant.

Of critical importance in the input-output analysis is a clear definition of each term. For the purposes of this report, the following definitions are used. *Input* denotes the total caloric value of all food items fed to an entire cattle population over a 1-year period. *Output* denotes the total caloric value of all items produced from that cattle population over a 1-year period that contribute to direct human benefit. The products should fulfill the needs and priorities of the human society involved. What might be of immediate benefit to one culture might be useless and even harmful for another.

In India the major products of immediate human utility derived from cattle are dung, traction power, milk, and calves. Other products of lesser importance (e.g., meat, hides, and bones) have economic value, but they will be ignored for the purpose of the energetic calculations in this report.

The purpose of this paper is to present quantitative values which aid in the understanding of the basic ecology of cattle in rural West Bengal. To that end, a gross energetic balance sheet is presented taking a large cattle population as the basic unit of study. The gross energetic efficiency of this cattle population is equal to the products derived from the cattle used by humans [in Calories (kcal)] divided by the food consumed by the cattle (in Calories).

THE STUDY AREA

Singur *thana* (a geographical division of an administrative district) was taken as the basic unit of study. Geographically it is located (E 88 15 and N 22 50) about 25 miles northwest of Calcutta and lies within the Tropic of Cancer. The mean elevation above sea level is 21.5 ft. The physiography shows a slight sloping from the northwest to the southeast. Figure 1 shows the location of the *thana* in relation to the district, the state, and the nation.

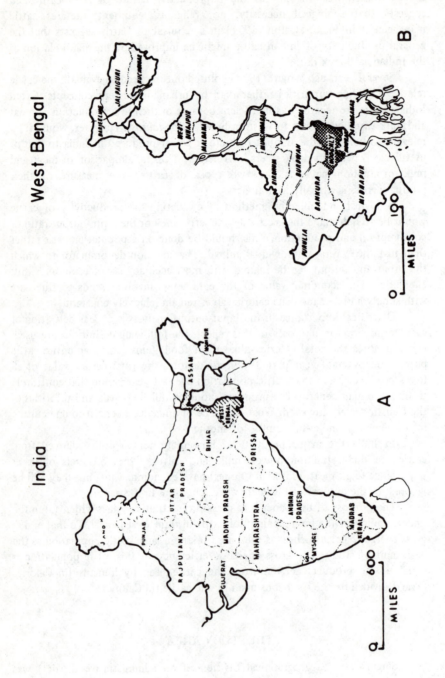

India

West Bengal

A

B

MILES
0   600

MILES
0   100

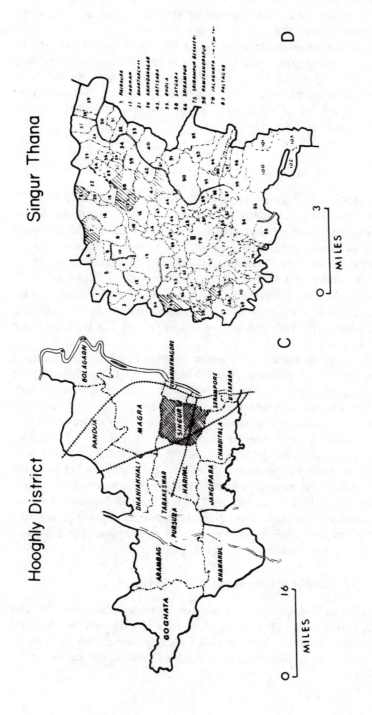

Fig. 1. Location of study areas in relation to the nation (A), the state (B), the district (C), and the *thana* (D). The cross hatched areas (study sites) are called *mauzas*.

333

The soil is recent alluvium from two sources: the Himalayas via the river Ganges and the Chotanagpur plateau via the river Damodar. The soil is fertile despite long-term continued cultivation, because of silt deposition from the occasional inundations by the rivers. The general topography consists of flat expanses of cultivated fields with meandering streams and canals. Most of the human habitation is found along or near these waterways.

The climate is monsoon-dominated with the yearly rainfall between 50 and 70 inches. Approximately 80% of the yearly rainfall occurs between May and September. Rice grain is the staple food for humans and rice straw the staple for cattle. Jute, bananas, and potatoes are among the more important cash crops. There is a large number of ponds near the houses, and fish raised in them contribute to the diet of the people.

MATERIALS AND METHODS

Singur *thana* is 56.9 square miles and is divided geographically into 103 *mauzas*. The actual study sites were selected on the basis of a random sample stratified according to land area and population density of the individual *mauzas* using figures from the 1961 census (Ray, 1965). The 11 selected *mauzas* contained 10% of the total land area as well as 10% of the total human population of Singur *thana*. Because Singur township is classified as a nonmunicipal urban area, a representative portion was included in the study. Thus, the actual study sites consisted of 11 complete *mauzas* and a portion of the town of Singur. The study sites may be seen in Fig. 1D. The total study area was 5.77 square miles.

The study was divided into four separate but interrelated projects. First, a census of humans and all domestic animals was conducted to establish the basic population parameters and to calculate the yearly milk and calf production. Second, a feed consumption and productivity study was done on randomly selected cattle to find the average daily per capita consumption and production values which could be extrapolated to the entire population. These data provided the yearly total energetic input and the work and dung production. Third, a land use study was conducted to estimate the production of rice grain and straw. Fourth, an agricultural management survey was conducted concurrent with the second and third census rounds. This was done to determine how the inputs and outputs of the cattle population were manipulated by man. Only the results of the first two projects will be reported at this time. The third and fourth projects will be covered in a subsequent paper.

Census of Humans and Domestic Animals

Each individual household[3] was contacted on three separate occasions over an 18-month period.[4] The age and sex of humans and domestic animals were recorded for each household. Also recorded for cattle were month and year of acquisition, cost or method of acquisition, kinds of food fed the day before the

---

[3] A household consists of of a group of persons who commonly live together and take their meals from a common kitchen.

[4] Muslim households (11% of total) were not contacted individually, as there was reluctance in allowing us to do so. The procedure in Muslim areas was to interrogate members of the households at one spot, i.e., near the mosque.

visit, date of last calving, date and method of last insemination, milk yield the day before the visit, etc. Three completely separate enumerations were done (July to December 1968; January to June 1969; and July to December 1969). During the second and third rounds, all changes in the population of both humans and cattle, such as births, deaths, immigrations, emigrations, and the purchase and selling of livestock, were recorded.

Interviewing of the households was conducted between 6 am and 1 pm every day, six days per week. Two Bengalis interviewed different families at the same time. The author accompanied one interviewer on one day and the other on the following day. The information was transformed to IBM punch cards for subsequent analysis.

Feed Consumption and Productivity of Cattle

Fourteen households were selected for study by a random sample of three contiguous *mauzas*. All major socioeconomic groups were represented as well as different sex and age groups of cattle. The cattle of each household were observed for one day, from the time they were taken out of the cow shed in the morning until their return that evening. During that time, all food items fed and the dung and milk produced were weighed for each animal. Also, the amount of time spent grazing and working was determined. Teams of two investigators (including the author) were assigned to each household. For seven consecutive days, two different households were observed each day. Three separate observations of the cattle at each household were completed [i.e., April (hot season), September (rainy season), and January (cold season)].

The energetic value of each food item was determined in the following manner. The total wet weight in kilograms (kg) of a particular item fed was converted to dry weight. This was divided into its fat, carbohydrate, and protein components using available proximate analysis data from the appropriate sources (Morrison, 1958; National Academy of Science–National Research Council, 1956, 1958, 1964; Sen, 1964; Schneider, 1947; Watt and Merrill, 1963). The total energetic value of the food items was determined by adding up the values of the individual components. All food items fed to one animal during one day were totaled to find the total energetic intake.

The fresh dung was weighed as it was produced from each animal. The overnight dung was weighed for each animal upon arrival at the household. Because of the spatial arrangement in the cow sheds, it was not difficult to determine from which animal the dung originated. The total dung production per animal was expressed in kilograms of wet weight. This was converted to dry weight using an estimate of 20% dry matter for adult dung and 30% for cattle 3 years old and younger (Hafez, 1968: 271). The energetic value of dried cattle manure in India has been determined to be 2.13 kcal/g (National Council of Applied Economic Research, 1965: 114).

The number of hours spent working was recorded for each bullock. In Bengal, a team of bullocks operates at 1.35 horsepower (Kurup, 1967: 567). This is an expenditure of 0.675 horsepower per bullock, which agrees with the working rate of oxen in general (Ubbelohde, 1963: 51). One horsepower is the work done at the rate of 642 Calories (kcal) per hour (Brody, 1945: 902) and thus the working rate of a bullock in Bengal is approximately 433 kcal/hr.

The percentage of fat in milk in this area has been determined to be approximately 4.7% (Panse *et al.*, 1967: 63). One kilogram of 4.7% fat milk is equal to 829 kcal (Brody, 1945).

Newborn calves in the Singur area weigh about 30 lb. Using Brody's (1945: 437) figures for dry matter content of newborn calves, the caloric value per calf was calculated to be 21,389 kcal.

RESULTS

Census of Humans and Domestic Animals

The results of the three separate enumerations may be seen in Table I. The mean population was 16,445 humans and 3770 cattle. The density was 2850 humans and 653 cattle per square mile. Considering only the cultivated (plowed) area, there were 3763 humans and 863 cattle per square mile.

The sex ratio of cattle was the same in all three surveys, i.e., 44% male and 56% female. The mean age distribution curve for cattle may be seen in Fig. 2. This graph represents 96% of the mean population. The saw-toothed configuration is typical of human age distribution curves for this area, as the exact ages of humans as well as cattle are unknown. Figures 3 and 4 show the age distribution for all three enumerations for male and female cattle, respectively. The similarity of the general profiles is evident. As a check on the reported ages, over 200 cattle were aged by their teeth. The results correlated well with that reported from the census. The aging by teeth began at the start of the second round. Subsequent to that, many villagers admitted they did not know the exact age of their older cattle. Further, they became reluctant to estimate their ages. Therefore, the number of cattle with no recorded age increased from 30 in the first round to 128 and 333 in the second and third rounds, respectively. This explains the larger number of 10-year-old bullocks reported in the first round which is evident in Fig. 3. It was not difficult to determine whether the cattle were below or above 3 years of age and the cattle population was divided into the following categories: males 4 years of age and older, 1149 (30.5%); females 4 years of age and older, 1268 (33.6%); and males and females 3 years of age and younger, 1353 (35.5%). Most of the older males were working bullocks. About 25 mature bulls were present. Approximately 80% of the bullocks were purchased, while most of the females were born and raised at the household of current residence. Over 60% of all males were purchased, but only 17% of all females were purchased.

Feed Consumption and Productivity Study

The feed consumption and production measurements involved a total of 80 cattle-days. This included data on 25 adult males (all bullocks), 29 adult females, and 26 immature cattle. All cattle were stall-fed throughout the year.

Table I. Total Number of Households Interviewed, Humans and Domesticated Animals

	Households	Humans	Cattle	Buffalos	Goats	Chickens and ducks	Pigs	Pets
1st Survey	2497	16,127	3759	28	1577	2621	5	320
2nd Survey	2603	16,566	3777	28	1964	3201	6	389
3rd Survey	2680	16,643	3776	42	1742	2952	1	398
Mean	2593	16,445	3770	32	1761	2925	4	369

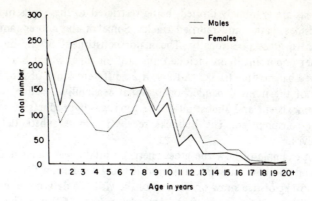

Fig. 2. Age distribution of cattle calculated from three separate surveys.

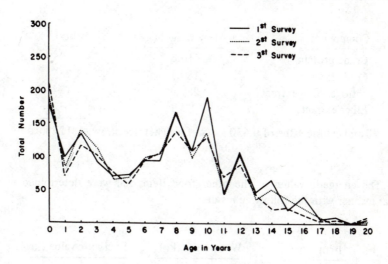

Fig. 3. Age distribution of male cattle.

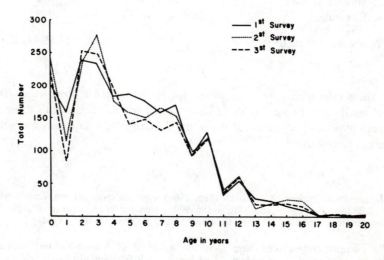

Fig. 4. Age distribution of female cattle.

Grazing areas are extremely limited, being restricted to the banks of canals and along roadsides, paths, and railroad tracks. Some of the poorer families allow their cattle to graze occasionally. The major constituent of the diet was rice straw. Other important items included mustard oil cake, wheat bran, rice hulls, and chopped banana tree trunks. A total of 24 different kinds of foods were fed, but many of the items depended on seasonal availability. Fodder crops were virtually nonexistent and almost all of the food was byproducts of crops grown for human consumption. The bullocks received a more substantial diet than cows or calves.

As an example of how the gross energetic intake was calculated, the data collected for one cow may be considered. During January, a 6-year-old female was fed 0.650 kg of rice straw on the day of the visit. To determine the energetic value, the wet weight was converted into dry weight (585 g). The proximate analysis allowed the computation of the dry weight of the individual components,[5] which can then be multiplied by their respective energetic values[6] to find the total caloric value of the rice straw:

Component	Dry weight (g)	kcal
Crude protein	16.8	95
Crude fiber	189.1	785
Nitrogen-free extract	282.9	1174
Ether extract	7.8	73

Total caloric value of 0.650 kg (wet weight) rice straw = 2127 kcal

The energetic values of the other food items fed were determined in a similar manner with the following results:

Item	Wet weight (kg)	Energetic value (kcal)
1. Rice straw	0.650	2,127
2. Tops of sugar cane	9.820	9,877
3. Mustard oil cake	0.205	872
4. Rice hulls	0.650	2,022
Total caloric value of feed		14,898 kcal

These calculations were completed for all cattle under observation. The overall results may be seen in Table II. By combining these data with those of the mean population structure of the cattle, the estimated total yearly energetic intake can be calculated.

[5] The proximate analysis of rice straw (Sen, 1964) show the crude protein component to be 2.88% of the dry weight. The comparable value for crude fiber is 32.32%; for nitrogen-free extract, 48.36%; and for ether extract, 1.33% of the dry weight.

[6] The energetic values used were (National Academy of Science-National Research Council, 1966: 15): crude protein = 5.65 kcal/g; crude fiber and nitrogen-free extract = 4.15 kcal/g; and either extracts = 9.40 kcal/g.

Age class	Mean daily consumption		Mean No. cattle		Consumption per day (kcal)
Adult males	21,688 kcal/male	X	1149 males	=	2.490×10^7
Adult females	13,585 kcal/female	X	1268 females	=	1.723×10^7
Immatures	9,016 kcal/calf	X	1353 calves	=	1.220×10^7

Total daily energy consumption by the population 5.433×10^7 kcal

Total yearly energy consumption by the population was
$(5.433 \times 10^7 \text{ kcal/day}) (365 \text{ days/year}) = 19.831 \times 10^9 \text{ kcal/year}$

Table II. Daily Per Capita Food Consumption and Dung Production of Cattle

Age class	Food energy (kcal)	Dung energy (kcal)
Adult males	21,688	4074
Adult females	13,585	2735
Immatures	9,016	1937

Output

Dung. The average daily dung production was calculated for the three different age and sex classes. These were converted to their respective energetic values and may be seen in Table II. These values were used to calculate the yearly dung production at the population level:

Age class	Mean daily dung production		Mean No. cattle		Daily production (kcal)
Adult males	4074 kcal/male	X	1149 males	=	4.681×10^6
Adult females	2735 kcal/female	X	1268 females	=	3.468×10^6
Immatures	1937 kcal/calf	X	1353 calves	=	2.621×10^6

Total energy of dung production by the population per day 10.770×10^6 kcal

Total yearly energy of dung production by the population was
$(1.077 \times 10^6 \text{ kcal/day}) (365 \text{ days/year}) = 3.931 \times 10^9 \text{ kcal/year}$

Estimates of the percentage of the total dung production used as cooking fuel vary from 40% (National Council of Applied Economic Research, 1965: 28) to 75% (Lodh, 1968: 162). For the Singur area, even 70% would appear to be a conservative estimation. In India, as a general rule, the Ministry of Food and Agriculture estimates 66% of the dung is used as fuel (National Council of Applied Economic Research, 1965: 28). Therefore, if two-thirds of the total dung produced were used as fuel, 2.62×10^9 kcal would be utilized for immediate human benefit.

Work. The average number of hours worked per bullock per day was 6 hr. Since the working rate of a bullock in Bengal is approximately 433 kcal/hr, the work accomplished in 1 day by one bullock would be 2598 kcal/day. If all the working bullocks over 5 years of age (1079) worked on a single day, the energetic value would be 2.803×10^6 kcal/day. The average number of working days in a year for bullocks in India has been estimated to range from 180 to 300 days (Joshi and Phillips, 1953). Using 200 days as a conservative figure, the total work accomplished by all the bullocks in the population in 1 year would be

$$(2.803 \times 10^6 \text{ kcal/day}) (200 \text{ days/year}) = 5.606 \times 10^8 \text{ kcal/year}$$

Milk. During the second round of the census (January to June 1969), 527 cows (about 42% of all adult cows) were reported in lactation. The average yield of milk per lactating cow was 1.37 kg/day. Therefore, a rough estimation of the total milk production by this cattle population for the first half of 1969 can be found. The daily rate of production was 722 kg of milk, which equals 131,765 kg of milk for the entire population. In the third round of the census, 433 cows (about 34% of all adult cows) were lactating an average of 1.13 kg of milk/day. This is a rate of 489 kg/day or a total estimated production of 89,243 kg of milk by the cattle population for the second half of 1969. Thus, the yearly

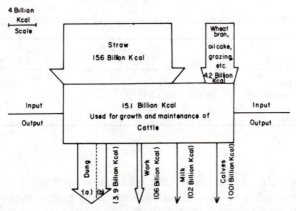

Fig. 5. Yearly energy flow through cattle population. The dung is divided into fuel (a) and fertilizer (b) components.

production would be 221,008 kg of milk. Since 1 kg of milk produced in the Singur area has an energetic value of 829 kcal, the approximate caloric value of the total milk production by this cattle population in 1 year would be

$$(221{,}008 \text{ kg/year}) (829 \text{ kcal/kg}) = 1.833 \times 10^8 \text{ kcal/year}$$

Calves. From analysis of the repeat enumeration of the population, the crude birth rate was 141.55 births per 1000 cattle. (The crude death rate was 92.76 per 1000.) The total number of births calculated for 1 year (533.64) was in close agreement with the total recorded births for 1968 (541) obtained from the census reports. If the energetic value of a newborn calf is 21,389 kcal, then the total caloric value of the calf crop in 1 year would be

$$(21{,}389 \text{ kcal/calf}) (533.64 \text{ calves/year}) = 1.141 \times 10^7 \text{ kcal/year}$$

With the above calcuations completed, an energetic balance sheet for this particular cattle population can be computed for a 1-year period. This is shown diagrammatically in Fig. 5.

The Energetic Balance Sheet

Total calculated energetic input		19.83×10^9 kcal/year
Total calculated energetic output		
Dung	=	3.93×10^9 kcal/year
Work	=	0.56×10^9 kcal/year
Milk	=	0.18×10^9 kcal/year
Calves	=	0.01×10^9 kcal/year
Total	=	4.68×10^9 kcal/year
		-4.68×10^9 kcal/year
Energy for maintenance and growth		15.15×10^9 kcal/year

In order to calculate the gross energetic efficiency, only those products derived from the cattle that have direct human utility should be considered. Direct human utility means that the products used by humans should release all or most of their contained energy soon after they are produced. Thus, dung used as fuel, work by bullocks, and milk are the significant parameters involved. Newborn calves and dung used as fertilizer represent potential energy contributions to human welfare but they are not utilized immediately. Therefore, the output column of the energetic balance sheet can be modified as follows:

Energetic output with direct human utility

Dung (at 2/3 used as fuel)	=	2.62×10^9 kcal/year
Work (at 200 working days per bullock)	=	0.56×10^9 kcal/year
Milk (at 221,008 kg/year)	=	0.18×10^9 kcal/year
Total	=	3.36×10^9 kcal/year

$$\text{Gross energetic efficiency} = \frac{\text{Calories of useful production per year} \times 100}{\text{Calories of total consumption per year}}$$

$$= \frac{(3.36 \times 10^9 \text{ kcal/year}) \times 100}{19.83 \times 10^9 \text{ kcal/year}}$$

$$= 16.9\%$$

The 16.9% gross energetic efficiency represents conservative estimations of dung used as fuel (2/3) and the number of days (200) worked by bullocks in 1 year. When the energetic efficiency is recalculated, using estimates based on 40% dung used as fuel and 100 working days per bullock, the efficiency becomes 10.3%; based on 80% dung used as fuel and 300 working days per bullock, it becomes 21.0%.

DISCUSSION

The reliability of the data used in the calculation of the energetic efficiency is substantiated by many factors. All three separate enumerations of the cattle revealed the sex ratio and the age distribution curves were similar (Fig. 3 and 4). Aging of a sample of the population by their teeth verified the age group distributions. Some of the milk yields were spot-checked immediately after they were reported and found correct. Seasonal variations in the available feed were taken into consideration and a large sample was involved in the feed consumption and production study.

One of the major assumptions was the estimation of the dry matter content of the dung. From Table II, the calculated energy in the feces varies from 18.8 to 21.5% of the gross energy intake for the different age groups. This is consistent with Mitchell's value of 20% (as cited in Brody, 1945: 83) for steers being fed at 2/3 of "full feed" (optimum plane of nutrition). It is interesting to note that, in rations above that level, the digestible energy decreases and the fecal energy increases as a percentage of the gross energetic intake. Therefore, if the cattle involved in this study received more than 2/3 of full feed, the fecal energy output calculated in Table II would probably be conservative.

The cattle population appears to be fairly stable. The rate of increase calculated from Table I is less than ½% per year. Since the birth rate exceeds the death rate, one method of maintaining a stable population is to export some of the young male calves. The resultant demographic imbalance evident in Fig. 2

contributes to a more efficient utilization of the available local feed. Food that the young male calves would have consumed can be diverted to more productive older cattle, such as pregnant and lactating females and working bullocks. There is ample evidence to indicate that the immature males are being exported to the Chotanagpur plateau region (about 200 miles to the west) where forest grazing reduces the expense of raising them. Undoubtedly, this increases the overgrazing problems in the hill areas and contributes to siltation of reservoirs which in time will reduce the amount of water available for irrigation in the intensively cultivated regions. The logistics, economics, and environmental consequences of this cattle movement would provide an interesting investigation and could lead to a better understanding of the overgrazing problem.

The total energetic input of the cattle population consisted almost exclusively of byproducts of crops grown for human consumption. There is almost no competition between cattle and humans for land or food supply. Basically, the cattle convert items of little direct human value into products of immediate human utility (see Fig. 5). For the most part, the rice straw (over 75% of the total energetic intake) necessary to feed this cattle population at the current level appears to be produced locally. The rice hulls and chopped banana tree trunks are also generally of local origin, but portions of the mustard oil cake and wheat bran may be purchased from outside the immediate area.

Most of the energetic output derived from the cattle population is utilized by humans as cooking fuel. The small portion of dung used as fertilizer does not contribute to immediate human benefit, as it is a form of capital reinvestment in next year's crop. Dung used as fuel is more efficient for cooking purposes than straw since it burns slower and with a more even heat distribution.

There is a striking difference in the use of cattle manure in the U.S. compared to India. Recent reports show cattle wastes to be a definite environmental liability in parts of the U.S. (Environmental Science and Technology, 1970; Science News, 1970), causing contamination of ground water and eutrophication of lakes. In the Singur study area, even though the monetary value of dung is low, as a substitute for coal it is extremely valuable. Over 453,000 kg of additional coal would have to be imported into the area to supply 2.62 billion kcal for cooking if the dung were not used for this purpose. This would involve a considerable cash outlay per year.

The bullock power is of obvious critical importance to agricultural production. Even if the conservative energetic output of work presented in Fig. 5 were reduced by half, it would still exceed that contained in the milk produced. With the current agricultural situation (small field size and low capital accumulation), it seems extremely unlikely that any viable alternatives to bullock power will be possible in the foreseeable future.

Much of the milk produced in the study area does not contribute directly toward local human nutrition. More than half of the households with lactating cows reported that their families did not consume all of the milk produced on a daily basis. Much of the "excess" milk is converted into casein and sent to Calcutta for the making of sweet meats. This is a source of income, but some of the nutrients are lost in transport as the whey is wasted.

The calves contribute little energetically, but are important in stimulating milk letdown in the cows. Once the dam drys up, the male calves may be sold. Unfortunately, there does not seem to be a market for female calves unless they are sold with their dams.

Other items derived from cattle, such as meat, hides, and bones, have not been considered in the energetic calculations because of the difficulty in estimating their yearly production. It is sufficient to say that the Muslims do eat beef; drums and sandals are made from hides; and the bones are collected and subsequently processed into bone meal in Calcutta. The villagers are extremely utilitarian and virtually nothing is wasted.

The range of the gross energetic efficiency (10.3 to 21.0%) of the Singur cattle is high, not because the cattle are particularly productive, but because of scrupulous product utilization by the humans. The method of calculating the gross energetic efficiency of the Singur cattle is consistent with the methods of Brody (1945) and Kleiber (1961).[7] However, some rather significant considerations were included in the calculation of the efficiency presented in this report; the work was done at the population level; the relatively less productive age groups were included; dung was regarded as a desirable product; and the length of the study was 1 year.

If the work had been done only at the individual level, some very interesting facts might have been overlooked. Through time and the pressure of numbers, the cattle population structure has been adjusted so that the available feed is maximized by reducing the number of immature males and older less productive females (the older females may be sold for slaughter either in Muslim villages or at slaughter houses). There is, thus, a greater efficiency of production from a given quantity of feed than if these less productive age groups were present.

Although similar work on cattle energetics at the population level has not been done in the United States, some comparisons are possible. The gross growth efficiency of beef cattle raised on western range land has a reported value of 4.1% (Phillipson, 1966: 49). This means that the live weight of a steer is about 4% of the total weight of food ingested from birth. However, only about one-half of the carcass is harvested as human food.

Two principles emerge from this study: the principle of increased product utilization by low-energy cultures[8] and the principle of increased energy flow in man-manipulated ecosystems.

In low-energy cultures, the people out of necessity must be very thorough in their exploitation of any available energy source. High-energy cultures tend to be wasteful because of plentiful energy supplies. The cattle in Singur supply cheap fuel, milk for household use, power to till the fields, and calves as well as milk are an income source. The main products of cattle in the U.S. are meat and milk. The work potential is not utilized and dung is becoming an environmental liability in some cases. This is because in the U.S. there are readily available alternative energy sources for cooking fuel and power to till the fields.

It is difficult for westerners to appreciate the value of dung to the typical villager in India because the westerners' frame of reference is based on easily available energy. As Myrdal (1968: 411) stated, "Reality in South Asia will be found to be a rather elusive notion when viewed through glasses shaped by western experience."

From both laboratory studies of single species (Slobodkin, 1964) and field measurements of several species at the same trophic level (Odum, 1957; Teal,

---

[7] Kleiber defines the success of animal feeding as "total efficiency," which is the energy in an animal product divided by the energy in the feed taken in during the period in which the product is formed (Kleiber, 1961: 316). This "total efficiency" is essentially the same as Brody's gross energetic efficiency.

[8] Low-energy cultures refer to the "developing countries" that have a low per capita energy consumption. High-energy cultures are those more industrialized countries with a high per capita energy consumption.

1957), the gross energetic efficiency has been found to be approximately 10%. However, in most ecological investigations, the production is usually a matter of animal tissues passed on to the next trophic level through the food chain with the excreta relegated into the decomposer aspect of the ecosytem. This is logical as the feces usually must first pass through the microbiotic community of the soil before the contained energy is utilized and this entails a considerable time lag. In Singur, the humans are speeding up the release of the fecal energy to accomplish useful work (cooking food). In essence, the humans are consuming the dung not by ingestion, but energetically. Still, this is related to the food chain indirectly since cooking allows for a more efficient extraction of the energy contained in the rice during the digestive process. The bullock power is also related to food indirectly. Odum (1971) would refer to the fecal fuel and bullock power as work gates.[9]

Perhaps this utilization of energy by humans for nonconsumptive processes is another distinguishing characteristic separating man from other animals. Man uses great quantities of energy for his convenience and comfort. Most other animals that come to mind expropriate energy from their environment mainly in the form of food per se.

Many other examples can easily be found supporting the principle of increased product utilization by low-energy cultures. The increased energy flow in man-manipulated ecosystems is also evident in eutrophication, burning of fossil fuels, timber harvests, and irrigation. Speculation as to the consequences of these two principles is beyond the scope of this paper.

The major conclusion from this study is that judging the productive value of Indian cattle based on western standards is inappropriate. The Singur cattle population appears to be efficient in supplying products of value based on the needs and priorities of the society involved. It is doubtful whether any substantial improvement in cattle productivity is possible without considerable sustained outside energetic inputs into the system.

ACKNOWLEDGMENTS

The author wishes to acknowledge Drs. F. B. Bang, C. H. Southwick, and D. W. Parrack for encouragement and advice throughout the entire project. Messrs. R. C. De, S. Singha, S. K. Dutt, and R. K. Singh provided faithful and reliable assistance during the collection of the data. Mr. J. Thomas was the statistical advisor and made many valuable suggestions. The administrative support by Mr. N. Alim was of great help. Dr. Dwain W. Parrack, above all, was of continual and consistent support. His patience and valuable assistance in the preparation of this report was particularly appreciated.

REFERENCES

Brody, S. (1945). *Bioenergetics and Growth.* Hafner Publishing Company, New York. (Reprinted in 1968.)
Dandekar, V. M. (1967). Cattle problem. In Shah, A. B. (ed.), *Cow-Slaughter, Horns of a Dilemma,* Lalvani Publishing House, Bombay, pp. 35-43.
Environmental Science and Technology. (1970). Agriculture poses waste problems. *Environmental Science and Technology* 4: 1098-1100.
Fahimuddin, M. (1963). *Animal Production in Bihar.* Asia Publishing House, Bombay.

---

[9] Work gates refer to the expenditure of energy so as to release a larger flow of energy that might not otherwise be available.

Food and Agriculture Organization. (1970). *F.A.O. Production Yearbook 1969.* F.A.O., Rome.

Hafez, E. S. E. (1968). *Adaptation of Domestic Animals.* Lea and Febiger, Philadelphia.

Harris, M. (1966). The cultural ecology of India's sacred cattle. *Current Anthropology* 7: 51-59.

Heston, A. (1971). An approach to the sacred cow of India. *Current Anthropology* 12: 191-209.

Joshi, N. R., and Phillips, R. W. (1953). *Zebu Cattle of India and Pakistan.* F.A.O., Rome.

Kleiber, M. (1961). *The Fire of Life.* John Wiley and Sons, Inc., New York.

Kuriyan, G. (1969). *India, a General Survey.* National Book Trust, New Delhi.

Kurup, C. G. R. (ed.) (1967). *Handbook of Agriculture.* Indian Council of Agricultural Research, New Delhi.

Lodh, D. C. (1968). *Will India Grow Her Food?.* Debashis Goswmi, Calcutta.

Morrison, F. B. (1958). *Feeds and Feeding.* Morrison Publishing Company, Clinton, Iowa. (Reprinted in 1967.)

Myrdal, G. (1968). *Asian Drama,* Vol. I. Pantheon, New York.

National Academy of Science−National Research Council (1956). Pub. No. 449. *Composition of Concentrate By-Product Feed Stuffs.* NAS−NRC, Washington, D.C.

National Academy of Science−National Research Council (1958). Pub. No. 585. *Composition of Cereal Grains and Forages.* NAS-NRC, Washington, D.C.

National Academy of Science−National Research Council. (1964). Pub. No. 1232. *Joint U.S. Canadian Tables of Feed Composition.* NAS−NRC, Washington, D.C.

National Academy of Science−National Research Council. (1966). Pub. No. 1411. *Biological Energy Interrelationships and Glossary of Energy Terms.* NAS-NRC, Washington, D.C.

National Council of Applied Economic Research (1965). *Domestic Fuels in Rural India.* NCAER, New Delhi.

Odum, H. T. (1957). The trophic structure and productivity of Silver Springs, Florida. *Ecological Monographs* 27: 55-112.

Odum, H. T. (1971). *Environment Power and Society.* John Wiley & Sons, New York.

Panse, V. G., Amble, V. N., and Raut, K. C. (1967). *Cost of Milk Production in West Bengal.* I.C.A.R., New Delhi.

Phillipson, J. (1966). *Ecological Energetics.* St. Martin's Press, New York.

Ray, B. (1965). *Census 1961 West Bengal, District Census Handbook; Hooghly.* Government Printing, Calcutta.

Schneider, B. H. (1947). *Feeds of the World.* Agriculture Experimental Station, West Virginia University, Morgantown.

Science News (1970). Euthrophication: feedlots contribute nitrogen. *Science News* 98: 384.

Sen, K. C. (1964). The nutritive values of indian cattle foods and the feeding of animals, Bulletin No. 25 (5th ed.), I.C.A.R., New Delhi.

Shah, A. B. (ed.) (1967). *Cow-Slaughter, Horns of a Dilemma,* Lalvani Publishing House, Bombay.

Shah, M. M. (1967). Cow slaughter: the economic aspect. In Shah, A. B. (ed.), *Cow-Slaughter, Horns of a Dilemma,* Lalvani Publishing House, Bombay, pp. 44-68.

Slobodkin, L. B. (1964). Experimental populations of Hydrida. *Journal of Animal Ecology* 33 (suppl.): 131-148.

Teal, J. M. (1957). Community metabolism in a temperate cold spring. *Ecological Monographs* 27: 283-302.

Ubbelohde, A. R. (1963). *Man and Energy.* Pelican Books, Middlesex, England.

Watt, B. K., and Merrill, A. L. (1963). *Composition of Foods.* Agricultural Handbook No. 8. ARS−USDA, Washington, D.C.

Whyte, R. O. (1964). *The Grassland and Fodder Resources of India.* I.C.A.R., New Delhi.

Whyte, R. O. (1968). *Land, Livestock and Human Nutrition in India.* F. A. Praeger Publishing, New York.

Whyte, R. O., and Mathur, M. L. (1968). *The Planning of Milk Production in India.* Orient Longmans, Bombay.

Wright, N. C. (1937). *Report on Development of Cattle and Dairy Industry in India.* Manager of Publications, Delhi.

Part IV

COMMUNITIES OF ORGANISMS

There exist two principal opposing views of the nature of biological communities. One, which seems to follow naturally from such early studies of aquatic systems as that by Möbius (1877) or Forbes (1887), suggests that communities are natural, organized systems of plants and animals having parallel structures of species presence and abundance and concomitant functional similarities. These systems have evolved and result from the consequent mutual interdependence of the organisms present. The opposing viewpoint is that what we examine are not communities in the former sense, but rather randomly collected assemblages of organisms whose physiological tolerances permit them to exist together, and that such groupings are artificial. This viewpoint appears more commonly among plant ecologists (see, for example, Gleason, 1926). Perhaps more simply, a group of organisms which do in fact occur together in time and space must coexist and function together, and therefore should be studied together.

Presumably, a community of organisms could be studied additively—that is, by investigating all the species separately and treating the community as the sum. Such a course will recommend itself to no one with practical experience, even to an ecologist who has the aid of a capacious and sophisticated computer. This simplistic view of how to study an assemblage is not only practically impossible, it is also theoretically inadequate, for such an assemblage has properties not shared by the species taken separately. There is a structure based on the kinds and proportions of species present, an organization based on the flow of energy and matter, and a succession of the populations themselves. More realistically, therefore, concepts and assumptions must be simplified to permit the community ecologist to understand his subject matter. Lindeman (1942) suggested a history of viewpoints guiding synecological theory; the principal stages he suggests are (1) the static species-distributional, (2) the dynamic species-distributional, and (3) the trophic-dynamic viewpoint.

The first should be understood to include not only the studies which give species lists—for example, lists of fish or oligotrophic and eutrophic lakes as

347

given by Forbes—but also the attempts to ascertain statistical relations among populations which will permit them to be treated as something other than mere random assemblages. An early attempt at stating this problem and suggesting a solution was Forbes' study on the local distribution of Illinois fishes for which he developed a mathematical "coefficient of association" (Forbes, 1907). Solutions to similar problems continue to be suggested, usually based either on Chi-square contingency tables or on an analysis of recurrent groups (Fager, 1957).

Once a community—which is here presumed to be, following Englemann (1961), "an assemblage of populations coexisting in time and space, mutually regulative and interdependent, and depending ultimately upon some common energy source"—is identified, a principal function of the ecologist is to try to make sense of the data. Ideally, one expects the ecologist to move now from the static to the dynamic aspect of distribution, where the causes are treated, but this expectation is seldom met. Among the attempts are the several models suggested by MacArthur (1960), the use of information theory following the suggestions of Margalef (1957), and the theories relating stability to diversity. Similarly, the studies of energetics used in the last section attempted to make functional sense out of masses of data by sorting the organism into functional goals, and investigating the flow of energy.

At present, however, the size and complexity of processes operating in ecosystems demand different kinds of investigations than those typical of ecology before about 1960, and the development of systems ecology has as its goal the construction of predictive mathematical models mimicking the essential features of ecosystems. Holling (1964), for example, has applied this approach to predator-prey systems, and a major part of the United States' effort in the International Biological Program was devoted to a functional analysis of major ecosystems. These studies attempt to develop a mathematical model of the relations between environmental variables (such as sunlight and temperature) and the quantities of substances of energy present in parts of the ecosystem, together with the rates of transfer between the parts. Once a model is developed, one can predict the effect of unusual environmental conditions, such as those induced by human use, on the ecosystem and its parts.

After a decision is reached about the use to which such a model is to be put, the first step is to define the boundaries and establish the parts of the system to be studied. Smith (1970) established an imaginary ecosystem, yet one with sufficient realism to make it helpful. The ecosystem is the water and contained plants and animals, as they might exist in an aquarium. The boundaries are the physical limits of the water; the components are the water, the plants, and the herbivores. Figure 1 is a flow diagram of the system, showing the components and the flows.

The next step is to measure the state conditions of the various components. These are, for example, the amount of each chemical element in all components if one is modeling the flow of a nutrient, or it may comprise the caloric content of each component. Next, the rates of input and output across the defined boundaries of the ecosystem are necessary, as are the rates of transfer between each pair of components in the ecosystem.

In the ecosystem we are considering, only phosphorus is measured, and the state variables, x_1, x_2, x_3, are the amount of phosphorus in the water, the plants, and the herbivores. In practice this would be measured by sampling the components and estimating the standing crop of phosphorus by quantitative chemical analysis.

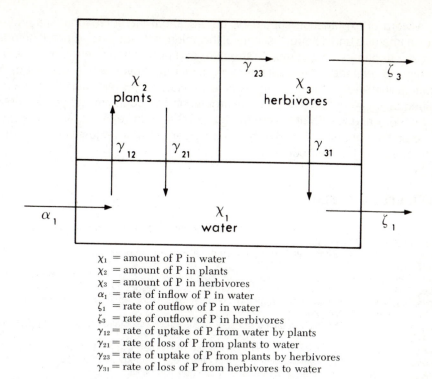

χ_1 = amount of P in water
χ_2 = amount of P in plants
χ_3 = amount of P in herbivores
α_1 = rate of inflow of P in water
ζ_1 = rate of outflow of P in water
ζ_3 = rate of outflow of P in herbivores
γ_{12} = rate of uptake of P from water by plants
γ_{21} = rate of loss of P from plants to water
γ_{23} = rate of uptake of P from plants by herbivores
γ_{31} = rate of loss of P from herbivores to water

Figure 1. Flow diagram for a very simple ecosystem composed of three components.

Next the rate of inflow, a_1, outflow, z_1, cropping, z_3, and the various rates of flow between components are measured. These describe the total set of processes leading to the state condition earlier determined. Referring to the figure we may see that

$$dx_1/dt = a_1 + y_{21} + y_{31} - y_{12} - z_1,$$
$$dx_2/dt = y_{12} - y_{21} - y_{23},$$
$$dx_3/dt = y_{23} - y_{31} - z_3.$$

A great deal of the skill and interest in this kind of study lies in not merely measuring the rates on the right side of the equation, but in establishing insight into their biological significance by relating them to more fundamental biological processes. For example, the rate y_{23} might be related to models of predation. The establishment of such relations is a first step in mathematical modeling.

By observing the system at different times, by manipulating the flow rates and the environmental conditions, more information can be gained, and the right-hand part of the differential equation given greater verisimilitude to the so-called real world. This results in a series of equations more complex and informative than the schematic ones given. It is here that our theoretical understanding of physics, chemistry, and biology is used. For these complex sets of equations purely analytical solutions are not possible, and computers must be used to obtain solutions. The model can now be used to investigate the effect of values of variables not met in nature, and so to see how manipulations of the environment may bring about an effect which interests us.

A word of explanation should be added about the selections. They reflect my own interests and, I hope, the state of the science. In the last edition I included a set of four papers on community structure and population control, only the first of which is retained. The excitement over this controversy has subsided, but I believe that the inclusion of the article by Hairston, Smith, and Slobodkin is justified as representative of a type of argument. The counter arguments by Murdoch (1966) and by Ehrlich and Birch (1967) remain relevant, as is the reply by the first set of authors (1967), but I no longer felt able to justify the use of so much space on this subject.

LITERATURE CITED

Engelmann, M. D. 1961. The role of soil arthropods in the energetics of an old field community. Ecol. Monog. *31*:221–238.

Ehrlich, P. R. and L. C. Birch. 1967. The balance of nature and population control. Amer. Nat. *101*: 97–107.

Fager, E. W. 1957. Determination and analysis of recurrent groups. Ecology *38*:586–595.

Forbes, S. A. 1887. The lake as a microcosm. Bull. Peoria Sci. Assoc., 77–87.

Forbes, S. A. 1907. On the local distribution of certain Illinois fishes: an essay in statistical ecology. Bull. Ill. Lab. Nat. Hist., 7:1–19.

Gleason, H. A. 1926. The individualistic concept of the plant association. Bull. Torrey Bot. Club *53*:7–26.

Holling, C. S. 1964. The analysis of complex population processes. Canad. Ent. *96*:335–347.

Lindeman, R. L. 1942. The trophic-dynamic aspect of ecology. Ecology 23:399–418.

MacArther, R. 1960. On the relative abundance of species. Amer. Nat. 94:25–36.

Margalef, R. 1957. La teoría de la informacíon en ecología. Mem. Real. Acad. Ciencias y Artes de Barcelona *32*:373–449.

Möbius, Karl. 1877. Die Auster und die Austernwirtschaft. Berlin. [Translated 1880, The Oyster and Oyster Culture. Rept. U.S. Fish Comm., 1880:683–751.]

Murdoch, W. S. Community structure, population control, and competition. Amer. Nat. *100*:219–226.

Slobodkin, L. C., F. E. Smith, and N. G. Hairston. 1967. Regulation in terrestrial ecosystems and the implied balance of nature. Amer. Nat. *101*:109–124.

Smith F. E. 1970. Analysis of ecosystems. *In* Ecological Studies 1. Analysis of Temperate Forest Ecosystems, ed. by David Reichle. New York: Springer-Verlag, pp. 7–18.

HOMAGE TO SANTA ROSALIA
or
WHY ARE THERE SO MANY KINDS OF ANIMALS?*

G. E. HUTCHINSON

Department of Zoology, Yale University, New Haven, Connecticut

When you did me the honor of asking me to fill your presidential chair, I accepted perhaps without duly considering the duties of the president of a society, founded largely to further the study of evolution, at the close of the year that marks the centenary of Darwin and Wallace's initial presentation of the theory of natural selection. It seemed to me that most of the significant aspects of modern evolutionary theory have come either from geneticists, or from those heroic museum workers who suffering through years of neglect, were able to establish about 20 years ago what has come to be called the "new systematics." You had, however, chosen an ecologist as your president and one of that school at times supposed to study the environment without any relation to the organism.

A few months later I happened to be in Sicily. An early interest in zoogeography and in aquatic insects led me to attempt to collect near Palermo, certain species of water-bugs, of the genus Corixa, described a century ago by Fieber and supposed to occur in the region, but never fully reinvestigated. It is hard to find suitable localities in so highly cultivated a landscape as the Concha d'Oro. Fortunately, I was driven up Monte Pellegrino, the hill that rises to the west of the city, to admire the view. A little below the summit, a church with a simple baroque facade stands in front of a cave in the limestone of the hill. Here in the 16th century a stalactite encrusted skeleton associated with a cross and twelve beads was discovered. Of this skeleton nothing is certainly known save that it is that of Santa Rosalia, a saint of whom little is reliably reported save that she seems to have lived in the 12th century, that her skeleton was found in this cave, and that she has been the chief patroness of Palermo ever since. Other limestone caverns on Monte Pellegrino had yielded bones of extinct pleistocene Equus, and on the walls of one of the rock shelters at the bottom of the hill there are beautiful Gravettian engravings. Moreover, a small relic of the saint that I saw in the treasury of the Cathedral of Monreale has a venerable and

---

*Address of the President, American Society of Naturalists, delivered at the annual meeting, Washington, D. C., December 30, 1958.

petrified appearance, as might be expected. Nothing in her history being known to the contrary, perhaps for the moment we may take Santa Rosalia as the patroness of evolutionary studies, for just below the sanctuary, fed no doubt by the water that percolates through the limestone cracks of the mountain, and which formed the sacred cave, lies a small artificial pond, and when I could get to the pond a few weeks later, I got from it a hint of what I was looking for.

Vast numbers of Corixidae were living in the water. At first I was rather disappointed because every specimen of the larger of the two species present was a female, and so lacking in most critical diagnostic features, while both sexes of the second slightly smaller species were present in about equal number. Examination of the material at leisure, and of the relevant literature, has convinced me that the two species are the common European *C. punctata* and *C. affinis*, and that the peculiar Mediterranean species are illusionary. The larger *C. punctata* was clearly at the end of its breeding season, the smaller *C. affinis* was probably just beginning to breed. This is the sort of observation that any naturalist can and does make all the time. It was not until I asked myself why the larger species should breed first, and then the more general question as to why there should be two and not 20 or 200 species of the genus in the pond, that ideas suitable to present to you began to emerge. These ideas finally prompted the very general question as to why there are such an enormous number of animal species.

There are at the present time supposed to be (Muller and Campbell, 1954; Hyman, 1955) about one million described species of animals. Of these about three-quarters are insects, of which a quite disproportionately large number are members of a single order, the Coleoptera.[1] The marine fauna although it has at its disposal a much greater area than has the terrestrial, lacks this astonishing diversity (Thorson, 1958). If the insects are excluded, it would seem to be more diverse. The proper answer to my initial question would be to develop a theory at least predicting an order of magnitude for the number of species of 10^6 rather than 10^8 or 10^4. This I certainly cannot do. At most it is merely possible to point out some of the factors which would have to be considered if such a theory was ever to be constructed.

Before developing my ideas I should like to say that I subscribe to the view that the process of natural selection, coupled with isolation and later mutual invasion of ranges leads to the evolution of sympatric species, which at equilibrium occupy distinct niches, according to the Volterra-Gause principle. The empirical reasons for adopting this view and the correlative view that the boundaries of realized niches are set by competition are mainly indirect. So far as niches may be defined in terms of food, the subject has been carefully considered by Lack (1954). In general all the indirect evi-

---

[1] There is a story, possibly apocryphal, of the distinguished British biologist, J. B. S. Haldane, who found himself in the company of a group of theologians. On being asked what one could conclude as to the nature of the Creator from a study of his creation, Haldane is said to have answered, "An inordinate fondness for beetles."

dence is in accord with the view, which has the advantage of confirming theoretical expectation. Most of the opinions that have been held to the contrary appear to be due to misunderstandings and to loose formulation of the problem (Hutchinson, 1958).

In any study of evolutionary ecology, food relations appear as one of the most important aspects of the system of animate nature. There is quite obviously much more to living communities than the raw dictum "eat or be eaten," but in order to understand the higher intricacies of any ecological system, it is most easy to start from this crudely simple point of view.

FOOD CHAINS

Animal ecologists frequently think in terms of food chains, of the form *individuals of species S_1 are eaten by those of S_2, of S_2 by S_3, of S_3 by S_4*, etc. In such a food chain S_1 will ordinarily be some holophylic organism or material derived from such organisms. The simplest case is that in which we have a true *predator chain* in Odum's (1953) convenient terminology, in which the lowest link is a green plant, the next a herbivorous animal, the next a primary carnivore, the next a secondary carnivore, etc. A specially important type of predator chain may be designated Eltonian, because in recent years C. S. Elton (1927) has emphasized its widespread significance, in which the predator at each level is larger and rarer than its prey. This phenomenon was recognized much earlier, notably by A. R. Wallace in his contribution to the 1858 communication to the Linnean Society of London.

In such a system we can make a theoretical guess of the order of magnitude of the diversity that a single food chain can introduce into a community. If we assume that in general 20 per cent of the energy passing through one link can enter the next link in the chain, which is overgenerous (cf. Lindeman, 1942; Slobodkin in an unpublished study finds 13 per cent as a reasonable upper limit) and if we suppose that each predator has twice the mass, (or 1.26 the linear dimensions) of its prey, which is a very low estimate of the size difference between links, the fifth animal link will have a population of one ten thousandth (10^{-4}) of the first, and the fiftieth animal link, if there was one, a population of 10^{-49} the size of the first. Five animal links are certainly possible, a few fairly clear cut cases having been in fact recorded. If, however, we wanted 50 links, starting with a protozoan or rotifer feeding on algae with a density of 10^6 cells per ml, we should need a volume of 10^{26} cubic kilometers to accommodate on an average one specimen of the ultimate predator, and this is vastly greater than the volume of the world ocean. Clearly the Eltonian food-chain of itself cannot give any great diversity, and the same is almost certainly true of the other types of food chain, based on detritus feeding or on parasitism.

Natural selection

Before proceeding to a further consideration of diversity, it is, however, desirable to consider the kinds of selective force that may operate on a food chain, for this may limit the possible diversity.

It is reasonably certain that natural selection will tend to maintain the efficiency of transfer from one level to another at a maximum. Any increase in the predatory efficiency of the nth link of a simple food chain will however always increase the possibility of the extermination of the $(n-1)^{th}$ link. If this occurs either the species constituting the nth link must adapt itself to eating the $(n-2)^{th}$ link or itself become extinct. This process will in fact tend to shortening of food chains. A lengthening can presumably occur most simply by the development of a new terminal carnivore link, as its niche is by definition previously empty. In most cases this is not likely to be easy. The evolution of the whale-bone whales, which at least in the case of *Balaenoptera borealis*, can feed largely on copepods and so rank on occasions as primary carnivores (Bigelow, 1926), presumably constitutes the most dramatic example of the shortening of a food chain. Mechanical considerations would have prevented the evolution of a larger rarer predator, until man developed essentially non-Eltonian methods of hunting whales.

Effect of size

A second important limitation of the length of a food chain is due to the fact that ordinarily animals change their size during free life. If the terminal member of a chain were a fish that grew from say one cm to 150 cms in the course of an ordinary life, this size change would set a limit by competition to the possible number of otherwise conceivable links in the 1-150 cm range. At least in fishes this type of process (metaphoetesis) may involve the smaller specimens belonging to links below the larger and the chain length is thus lengthened, though under strong limitations, by cannibalism.

We may next enquire into what determines the number of food chains in a community. In part the answer is clear, though if we cease to be zoologists and become biologists, the answer begs the question. Within certain limits, the number of kinds of primary producers is certainly involved, because many herbivorous animals are somewhat eclectic in their tastes and many more limited by their size or by such structural adaptations for feeding that they have been able to develop.

Effects of terrestrial plants

The extraordinary diversity of the terrestrial fauna, which is much greater than that of the marine fauna, is clearly due largely to the diversity provided by terrestrial plants. This diversity is actually two-fold. Firstly, since terrestrial plants compete for light, they have tended to evolve into structures growing into a gaseous medium of negligible buoyancy. This has led to the formation of specialized supporting, photosynthetic, and reproductive structures which inevitably differ in chemical and physical properties. The ancient Danes and Irish are supposed to have eaten elm-bark, and sometimes sawdust, in periods of stress, has been hydrolyzed to produce edible carbohydrate; but usually man, the most omnivorous of all animals, has avoided

almost all parts of trees except fruits as sources of food, though various individual species of animals can deal with practically every tissue of many
arboreal species. A major source of terrestrial diversity was thus introduced
by the evolution of almost 200,000 species of flowering plants, and the three
quarters of a million insects supposedly known today are in part a product
of that diversity. But of itself merely providing five or ten kinds of food of
different consistencies and compositions does not get us much further than
the five or ten links of an Eltonian pyramid. On the whole the problem still
remains, but in the new form: why are there so many kinds of plants? As a
zoologist I do not want to attack that question directly, I want to stick with
animals, but also to get the answer. Since, however, the plants are part of
the general system of communities, any sufficiently abstract properties of
such communities are likely to be relevant to plants as well as to herbivores and carnivores. It is, therefore, by being somewhat abstract, though
with concrete zoological details as examples, that I intend to proceed.

INTERRELATIONS OF FOOD CHAINS

Biological communities do not consist of independent food chains, but of
food webs, of such a kind that an individual at any level (corresponding to a
link in a single chain) can use some but not all of the food provided by species in the levels below it.

It has long been realized that the presence of two species at any level,
either of which can be eaten by a predator at a level above, but which may
differ in palatability, ease of capture or seasonal and local abundance, may
provide alternative foods for the predator. The predator, therefore, will
neither become extinct itself nor exterminate its usual prey, when for any
reason, not dependent on prey-predator relationships, the usual prey happens
to be abnormally scarce. This aspect of complicated food webs has been
stressed by many ecologists, of whom the Chicago school as represented by
Allee, Emerson, Park, Park and Schmidt (1949), Odum (1953) and Elton
(1958), may in particular be mentioned. Recently MacArthur (1955) using an
ingenious but simple application of information theory has generalized the
points of view of earlier workers by providing a formal proof of the increase
in stability of a community as the number of links in its food web increases.

MacArthur concludes that in the evolution of a natural community two
partly antagonistic processes are occurring. More efficient species will replace less efficient species, but more stable communities will outlast less
stable communities. In the process of community formation, the entry of a
new species may involve one of three possibilities. It may completely dis-
place an old species. This of itself does not necessarily change the stability, though it may do so if the new species inherently has a more stable
population (cf. Slobodkin, 1956) than the old. Secondly, it may occupy an
unfilled niche, which may, by providing new partially independent links, increase stability. Thirdly, it may partition a niche with a pre-existing species. Elton (1958) in a fascinating work largely devoted to the fate of species accidentally or purposefully introduced by man, concludes that in very

diverse communities such introductions are difficult. Early in the history of a community we may suppose many niches will be empty and invasion will proceed easily; as the community becomes more diversified, the process will be progressively more difficult. Sometimes an extremely successful invader may oust a species but add little or nothing to stability, at other times the invader by some specialization will be able to compete successfully for the marginal parts of a niche. In all cases it is probable that invasion is most likely when one or more species happen to be fluctuating and are under-represented at a given moment. As the communities build up, these opportunities will get progressively rarer. In this way a complex community containing some highly specialized species is constructed asymptotically.

Modern ecological theory therefore appears to answer our initial question at least partially by saying that there is a great diversity of organisms because communities of many diversified organisms are better able to persist than are communities of fewer less diversified organisms. Even though the entry of an invader which takes over part of a niche will lead to the reduction in the *average* population of the species originally present, it will also lead to an increase in stability reducing the risk of the original population being at times underrepresented to a dangerous degree. In this way loss of some niche space may be compensated by reduction in the amplitude of fluctuations in a way that can be advantageous to both species. The process however appears likely to be asymptotic and we have now to consider what sets the asymptote, or in simpler words why are there not more different kinds of animals?

LIMITATION OF DIVERSITY

It is first obvious that the processes of evolution of communities must be under various sorts of external control, and that in some cases such control limits the possible diversity. Several investigators, notably Odum (1953) and MacArthur (1955), have pointed out that the more or less cyclical oscillations observed in arctic and boreal fauna may be due in part to the communities not being sufficiently complex to damp out oscillations. It is certain that the fauna of any such region is qualitatively poorer than that of warm temperate and tropical areas of comparable effective precipitation. It is probably considered to be intuitively obvious that this should be so, but on analysis the obviousness tends to disappear. If we can have one or two species of a large family adapted to the rigors of Arctic existence, why can we not have more? It is reasonable to suppose that the total biomass may be involved. If the fundamental productivity of an area is limited by a short growing season to such a degree that the total biomass is less than under more favorable conditions, then the rarer species in a community may be so rare that they do not exist. It is also probable that certain absolute limitations on growth-forms of plants, such as those that make the development of forest impossible above a certain latitude, may in so acting, severely limit the number of niches. Dr. Robert MacArthur points out that the development of high tropical rain forest increases the bird fauna more than that of mammals, and Thorson (1957) likewise has shown that the so-called infauna show no increase of species toward the tropics while the marine epifauna becomes more diversified. The importance of this aspect of the plant or animal substratum, which depends largely on the length of the growing season and other aspects of productivity is related to that of the environmental mosaic discussed later.

We may also inquire, but at present cannot obtain any likely answer, whether the arctic fauna is not itself too young to have achieved its maximum diversity. Finally, the continual occurrence of catastrophes, as Wynne-Edwards (1952) has emphasized, may keep the arctic terrestrial community in a state of perennial though stunted youth.

Closely related to the problems of environmental rigor and stability, is the question of the absolute size of the habitat that can be colonized. Over much of western Europe there are three common species of small voles, namely *Microtus arvalis*, *M. agrestis* and *Clethrionomys glareolus*. These are sympatric but with somewhat different ecological preferences.

In the smaller islands off Britain and in the English channel, there is only one case of two species co-occurring on an island, namely *M. agrestis* and Clethrionomys on the island of Mull in the Inner Hebrides (Barrett-Hamilton and Hinton, 1911–1921). On the Orkneys the single species is *M. orcadensis*, which in morphology and cytology is a well-differentiated ally of *M. arvalis*; a comparable animal (*M. sarnius*) occurs on Guernsey. On most of the Scottish Islands only subspecies of *M. agrestis* occur, but on Mull and Raasay, on the Welsh island of Skomer, as well as on Jersey, races of Clethrionomys of somewhat uncertain status are found. No voles have reached Ireland, presumably for paleogeographic reasons, but they are also absent from a number of small islands, notably Alderney and Sark. The last named island must have been as well placed as Guernsey to receive *Microtus arvalis*. Still stranger is the fact that although it could not have got to the Orkneys without entering the mainland of Britain, no vole of the *arvalis* type now occurs in the latter country. Cases of this sort may be perhaps explained by the lack of favorable refuges in randomly distributed very unfavorable seasons or under special kinds of competition. This explanation is very reasonable as an explanation of the lack of Microtus on Sark, where it may have had difficulty in competing with *Rattus rattus* in a small area. It would be stretching one's credulity to suppose that the area of Great Britain is too small to permit the existence of two sympatric species of Microtus, but no other explanation seems to have been proposed.

It is a matter of considerable interest that Lack (1942) studying the populations of birds on some of these small British islands concluded that such populations are often unstable, and that the few species present often occupied larger niches than on the mainland in the presence of competitors. Such faunas provide examples of communities held at an early stage in development because there is not enough space for the evolution of a fuller and more stable community.

The various evolutionary tendencies, notably metaphoetesis, which operate on single food chains must operate equally on the food-web, but we also have a new, if comparable, problem as to how much difference between two species at the same level is needed to prevent them from occupying the same niche. Where metric characters are involved we can gain some insight into this extremely important problem by the study of what Brown and Wilson (1956) have called *character displacement* or the divergence shown when two partly allopatric species of comparable niche requirements become sympatric in part of their range.

I have collected together a number of cases of mammals and birds which appear to exhibit the phenomenon (table 1). These cases involve metric characters related to the trophic apparatus, the length of the culmen in birds and of the skull in mammals appearing to provide appropriate measures. Where the species co-occur, the ratio of the larger to the small form varies from 1.1 to 1.4, the mean ratio being 1.28 or roughly 1.3. This latter figure may tentatively be used as an indication of the kind of difference necessary to permit two species to co-occur in different niches but at the same level of a food-web. In the case of the aquatic insects with which I began my address, we have over most of Europe three very closely allied species of *Corixa*, the largest *punctata*, being about 116 per cent longer than the middle sized species *macrocephala*, and 146 per cent longer than the small species *affinis*. In northwestern Europe there is a fourth species, *C. dentipes*, as large as *C. punctata* and very similar in appearance. A single observation (Brown, 1948) suggests that this is what I have elsewhere (Hutchinson, 1951) termed a fugitive species, maintaining itself in the face of competition mainly on account of greater mobility. According to Macan (1954) while both *affinis* and *macrocephala* may occur with *punctata* they never are found with each other, so that all three species never occur together. In the eastern part of the range, *macrocephala* drops out, and *punctata* appears to have a discontinuous distribution, being recorded as far east as Simla, but not in southern Persia or Kashmir, where *affinis* occurs. In these eastern localities, where it occurs by itself, *affinis* is larger and darker than in the west, and superficially looks like *macrocephala* (Hutchinson, 1940).

This case is very interesting because it looks as though character displacement is occurring, but that the size differences between the three species are just not great enough to allow them all to co-occur. Other characters than size are in fact clearly involved in the separation, *macrocephala* preferring deeper water than *affinis* and the latter being more tolerant of brackish conditions. It is also interesting because it calls attention to a marked difference that must occur between hemimetabolous insects with annual life cycles involving relatively long growth periods, and birds or mammals in which the period of growth in length is short and of a very special nature compared with the total life span. In the latter, niche separation may be possible merely through genetic size differences, while in a pair of ani-

TABLE 1

Mean character displacement in measurable trophic structures in mammals (skull) and birds (culmen); data for Mustela from Miller (1912); Apodemus from Cranbrook (1957); Sitta from Brown and Wilson (1956) after Vaurie; Galapagos finches from Lack (1947)

	Locality and measurement when sympatric	Locality and measurement when allopatric	Ratio when sympatric
Mustela nivalis	Britain; skull ♂ 39.3 ♀ 33.6 mm.	(*boccamela*) S. France, Italy ♂ 42.9 ♀ 34.7 mm. (*iberica*) Spain, Portugal ♂ 40.4 ♀ 36.0	♂ 100:128 ♀ 100:134
M. erminea	Britain; " ♂ 50.4 ♀ 45.0	(*hibernica*) Ireland ♂ 46.0 ♀ 41.9	
Apodemus sylvaticus	Britain; " 24.8	unnamed races on Channel Islands 25.6–26.7	100:109
A. flavicollis	Britain; " 27.0		
Sitta tephronota	Iran; culmen 29.0	races east of overlap 25.5	100:124
S. neumayer	Iran; " 23.5	races west of overlap 26.0	
Geospiza fortis	Indefatigable Isl.; culmen 12.0	Daphne Isl. 10.5	100:143
G. fuliginosa	Indefatigable Isl.; " 8.4	Crossman Isl. 9.3	
Camarhynchus parvulus	James Isl.; " 7.0 Indefatigable Isl.; " 7.5	N. Albemarle Isl. 7.0 Chatham Isl. 8.0	James 100:140:180 100:129
C. psittacula	S. Albemarle Isl.; " 7.3 James Isl.; " 9.8 Indefatigable Isl.; " 9.6	Abington Isl. 10.1 Bindloe Isl. 10.5	Indefatigable 100:128:162 100:127
C. pallidus	S. Albemarle Isl.; " 8.5 James Isl.; " 12.6 Indefatigable Isl.; " 12.1 S. Albemarle Isl.; " 11.2	N. Albemarle Isl. 11.7 Chatham Isl. 10.8	S. Albemarle 100:116:153 100:132

Mean ratio 100:128

mals like *C. punctata* and *C. affinis* we need not only a size difference but a seasonal one in reproduction; this is likely to be a rather complicated matter. For the larger of two species always to be larger, it must never breed later than the smaller one. I do not doubt that this is what was happening in the pond on Monte Pellegrino, but have no idea how the difference is achieved.

I want to emphasize the complexity of the adaptation necessary on the part of two species inhabiting adjacent niches in a given biotope, as it probably underlies a phenomenon which to some has appeared rather puzzling. MacArthur (1957) has shown that in a sufficiently large bird fauna, in a uniform undisturbed habitat, areas occupied by the different species appear to correspond to the random non-overlapping fractionation of a plane or volume. Kohn (1959) has found the same thing for the cone-shells (Conus) on the Hawaiian reefs. This type of arrangement almost certainly implies such individual and unpredictable complexities in the determination of the niche boundaries, and so of the actual areas colonized, that in any overall view, the process would appear random. It is fairly obvious that in different types of community the divisibility of niches will differ and so the degree of diversity that can be achieved. The fine details of the process have not been adequately investigated, though many data must already exist that could be organized to throw light on the problem.

MOSAIC NATURE OF THE ENVIRONMENT

A final aspect of the limitation of possible diversity, and one that perhaps is of greatest importance, concerns what may be called the mosaic nature of the environment. Except perhaps in open water when only uniform quasi-horizontal surfaces are considered, every area colonized by organisms has some local diversity. The significance of such local diversity depends very largely on the size of the organisms under consideration. In another paper MacArthur and I (Hutchinson and MacArthur, 1959) have attempted a theoretical formulation of this property of living communities and have pointed out that even if we consider only the herbivorous level or only one of the carnivorous levels, there are likely, above a certain lower limit of size, to be more species of small or medium sized organisms than of large organisms. It is difficult to go much beyond crude qualitative impressions in testing this hypothesis, but we find that for mammal faunas, which contain such diverse organisms that they may well be regarded as models of whole faunas, there is a definite hint of the kind of theoretical distribution that we deduce. In qualitative terms the phenomenon can be exemplified by any of the larger species of ungulates which may require a number of different kinds of terrain within their home ranges, any one of which types of terrain might be the habitat of some small species. Most of the genera or even subfamilies of very large terrestrial animals contain only one or two sympatric species. In this connection I cannot refrain from pointing out the immense scientific importance of obtaining a really full insight into the ecology of the large mammals of Africa while they can still be studied under natural conditions. It is indeed quite possible that the results of studies on these wonderful animals would in long-range though purely practical terms pay for the establishment of greater reservations and National Parks than at present exist.

In the passerine birds the occurrence of five or six closely related sympatric species is a commonplace. In the mammal fauna of western Europe no genus appears to contain more than four strictly sympatric species. In Britain this number is not reached even by Mustela with three species, on the adjacent parts of the continent there may be three sympatric shrews of the genus Crocidura and in parts of Holland three of Microtus. In the same general region there are genera of insects containing hundreds of species, as in Athela in the Coleoptera and Dasyhelea in the Diptera Nematocera. The same phenomenon will be encountered whenever any well-studied fauna is considered. Irrespective of their position in a food chain, small size, by permitting animals to become specialized to the conditions offered by small diversified elements of the environmental mosaic, clearly makes possible a degree of diversity quite unknown among groups of larger organisms.

We may, therefore, conclude that the reason why there are so many species of animals is at least partly because a complex trophic organization of a community is more stable than a simple one, but that limits are set by the tendency of food chains to shorten or become blurred, by unfavorable physical factors, by space, by the fineness of possible subdivision of niches, and by those characters of the environmental mosaic which permit a greater diversity of small than of large allied species.

CONCLUDING DISCUSSION

In conclusion I should like to point out three very general aspects of the sort of process I have described. One speculative approach to evolutionary theory arises from some of these conclusions. Just as adaptive evolution by natural selection is less easy in a small population of a species than in a larger one, because the total pool of genetic variability is inevitably less, so it is probable that a group containing many diversified species will be able to seize new evolutionary opportunities more easily than an undiversified group. There will be some limits to this process. Where large size permits the development of a brain capable of much new learnt behavior, the greater plasticity acquired by the individual species will offset the disadvantage of the small number of allied species characteristic of groups of large animals. Early during evolution the main process from the standpoint of community structure was the filling of all the niche space potentially available for producer and decomposer organisms and for herbivorous animals. As the latter, and still more as carnivorous animals began to appear, the persistence of more stable communities would imply splitting of niches previously occupied by single species as the communities became more diverse. As this process continued one would expect the overall rate of evolution to have increased, as the increasing diversity increased the probability of the existence of species preadapted to new and unusual niches. It is reasonable to suppose that strong predation among macroscopic metazoa did not begin until the late Precambrian, and that the appearance of powerful predators led to the appearance of fossilizable skeletons. This seems the only reasonable hypothesis, of those so far advanced, to account for the relatively sudden appearance of several fossilizable groups in the Lower Cambrian. The process of diversification would, according to this argument, be somewhat autocatakinetic even without the increased stability that it would produce; with the increase in stability it would be still more a self inducing process, but one, as we have seen, with an upper limit. Part of this upper limit is set by the impossibility of having many sympatric allied species of large animals. These however are the animals that can pass from primarily innate to highly modifiable behavior. From an evolutionary point of view, once they have appeared, there is perhaps less need for diversity, though from other points of view, as Elton (1958) has stressed in dealing with human activities, the stability provided by diversity can be valuable even to the most adaptable of all large animals. We may perhaps therefore see in the process of evolution an increase in diversity at an increasing rate till the early Paleozoic, by which time the familiar types of community structure were established. There followed then a long period in which various large and finally large-brained species became dominant, and then a period in which man has been reducing diversity by a rapidly increasing tendency to cause extinction of supposedly unwanted species, often in an indiscriminate manner. Finally we may hope for a limited reversal of this process when man becomes aware of the value of diversity no less in an economic than in an esthetic and scientific sense.

A second and much more metaphysical general point is perhaps worth a moment's discussion. The evolution of biological communities, though each species appears to fend for itself alone, produces integrated aggregates which increase in stability. There is nothing mysterious about this; it follows from mathematical theory and appears to be confirmed to some extent empirically. It is however a phenomenon which also finds analogies in other fields in which a more complex type of behavior, that we intuitively regard as higher, emerges as the result of the interaction of less complex types of behavior, that we call lower. The emergence of love as an antidote to aggression, as Lorenz pictures the process, or the development of cooperation from various forms of more or less inevitable group behavior that Allee (1931) has stressed are examples of this from the more complex types of biological systems.

In the ordinary sense of explanation in science, such phenomena are explicable. The types of holistic philosophy which import *ad hoc* mysteries into science whenever such a situation is met are obviously unnecessary. Yet perhaps we may wonder whether the empirical fact that it is the nature of things for this type of explicable emergence to occur is not something that itself requires an explanation. Many objections can be raised to such a view; a friendly organization of biologists could not occur in a universe in which cooperative behavior was impossible and without your cooperation I could not raise the problem. The question may in fact appear to certain types of philosophers not to be a real one, though I suspect such philosophers in their desire to demonstrate how often people talk nonsense, may sometimes show less ingenuity than would be desirable in finding some sense in such questions. Even if the answer to such a question were positive, it might not get us very far; to an existentialist, life would have merely provided yet one more problem; students of Whitehead might be made happier, though on the whole the obscurities of that great writer do not seem to generate unhappiness; the religious philosophers would welcome a positive answer but note that it told them nothing that they did not know before; Marxists might merely say, "I told you so." In spite of this I suspect that the question is worth raising, and that it could be phrased so as to provide some sort of real dichotomy between alternatives; I therefore raise it knowing that I cannot, and suspecting that at present others cannot, provide an intellectually satisfying answer.

My third general point is less metaphysical, but not without interest. If I am right that it is easier to have a greater diversity of small than of large organisms, then the evolutionary process in small organisms will differ somewhat from that of large ones. Wherever we have a great array of allied sympatric species there must be an emphasis on very accurate interspecific mating barriers which is unnecessary where virtually no sympatric allies occur. We ourselves are large animals in this sense; it would seem very unlikely that the peculiar lability that seems to exist in man, in which even the direction of normal sexual behavior must be learnt, could have developed to quite the existing extent if species recognition, involving closely related sympatric congeners, had been necessary. Elsewhere (Hutchinson, 1959) I have attempted to show that the difficulties that *Homo sapiens* has to face in this regard may imply various unsuspected processes in human evolutionary selection. But perhaps Santa Rosalia would find at this point that we are speculating too freely, so for the moment, while under her patronage, I will say no more.

ACKNOWLEDGMENTS

Dr. A. Minganti of the University of Palermo enabled me to collect on Monte Pellegrino. Professor B. M. Knox of the Department of Classics of Yale University gave me a rare and elegant word from the Greek to express the blurring of a food chain. Dr. L. B. Slobodkin of the University of Michigan and Dr. R. H. MacArthur of the University of Pennsylvania provided me with their customary kinds of intellectual stimulation. To all these friends I am most grateful.

LITERATURE CITED

Allee, W. C., 1931, Animal aggregations: a study in general sociology. vii, 431 pp. University of Chicago Press, Chicago, Illinois.

Allee, W. C., A. E. Emerson, O. Park, T. Park and K. P. Schmidt, 1949, Principles of animal ecology. xii, 837 pp. W. B. Saunders Co., Philadelphia, Pennsylvania.

Barrett-Hamilton, G. E. H., and M. A. C. Hinton, 1911–1921, A history of British mammals. Vol. 2. 748 pp. Gurney and Jackson, London, England.

Bigelow, H. B., 1926, Plankton of the offshore waters of the Gulf of Maine. Bull. U. S. Bur. Fisheries 40: 1–509.

Brown, E. S., 1958, A contribution towards an ecological survey of the aquatic and semi-aquatic Hemiptera-Heteroptera (water-bugs) of the British Isles etc. Trans. Soc. British Entom. 9: 151–195.

Brown, W. L., and E. O. Wilson, 1956, Character displacement. Systematic Zoology 5: 49–64.

Cranbrook, Lord, 1957, Long-tailed field mice (Apodemus) from the Channel Islands. Proc. Zool. Soc. London 128: 597–600.

Elton, C. S., 1958, The ecology of invasions by animals and plants. 159 pp. Methuen Ltd., London, England.

Hutchinson, G. E., 1951, Copepodology for the ornithologist. Ecology 32: 571–577.

1958, Concluding remarks. Cold Spring Harbor Symp. Quant. Biol. 22: 415–427.

1959, A speculative consideration of certain possible forms of sexual selection in man. Amer. Nat. 93: 81–92.

Hutchinson, G. E., and R. MacArthur, 1959, A theoretical ecological model of size distributions among species of animals. Amer. Nat. 93: 117–126.

Hyman, L. H., 1955, How many species? Systematic Zoology 4: 142–143.

Kohn, A. J., 1959, The ecology of Conus in Hawaii. Ecol. Monogr. (in press).

Lack, D., 1942, Ecological features of the bird faunas of British small islands. J. Animal Ecol. London 11: 9–36.

1947, Darwin's Finches. x, 208 pp. Cambridge University Press, Cambridge, England.

1954, The natural regulation of animal numbers. viii, 347 pp. Clarendon Press, Oxford, England.

Lindeman, R. L., 1942, The trophic-dynamic aspect of ecology. Ecology 23: 399–408.

Macan, T. T., 1954, A contribution to the study of the ecology of Corixidae (Hemipt). J. Animal Ecol. 23: 115–141.

MacArthur, R. H., 1955, Fluctuations of animal populations and a measure of community stability. Ecology 35: 533–536.

1957, On the relative abundance of bird species. Proc. Nat. Acad. Sci. Wash. 43: 293–295.

Miller, G. S., Catalogue of the mammals of Western Europe. xv, 1019 pp. British Museum, London, England.

Muller, S. W., and A. Campbell, 1954, The relative number of living and fossil species of animals. Systematic Zoology 3: 168–170.

Odum, E. P., 1953, Fundamentals of ecology. xii, 387 pp. W. B. Saunders Co., Philadelphia, Pennsylvania, and London, England.

Slobodkin, L. B., 1955, Condition for population equilibrium. Ecology 35: 530–533.

Thorson, G., 1957, Bottom communities. Chap. 17 in Treatise on marine ecology and paleoecology. Vol. 1. Geol. Soc. Amer. Memoir 67: 461–534.

Wallace, A. R., 1858, On the tendency of varieties to depart indefinitely from the original type. In C. Darwin and A. R. Wallace, On the tendency of species to form varieties; and on the perpetuation of varieties and species by natural means of selection. J. Linn. Soc. (Zool.) 3: 45–62.

Wynne-Edwards, V. C., 1952, Zoology of the Baird Expedition (1950). I. The birds observed in central and southeast Baffin Island. Auk 69: 353–391.

COMMUNITY STRUCTURE, POPULATION CONTROL, AND COMPETITION

NELSON G. HAIRSTON, FREDERICK E. SMITH, AND LAWRENCE B. SLOBODKIN

Department of Zoology, The University of Michigan, Ann Arbor, Michigan

The methods whereby natural populations are limited in size have been debated with vigor during three decades, particularly during the last few years (see papers by Nicholson, Birch, Andrewartha, Milne, Reynoldson, and Hutchinson, and ensuing discussions in the Cold Spring Harbor Symposium, 1957). Few ecologists will deny the importance of the subject, since the method of regulation of populations must be known before we can understand nature and predict its behavior. Although discussion of the subject has usually been confined to single species populations, it is equally important in situations where two or more species are involved.

The purpose of this note is to demonstrate a pattern of population control in many communities which derives easily from a series of general, widely accepted observations. The logic used is not easily refuted. Furthermore, the pattern reconciles conflicting interpretations by showing that populations in different trophic levels are expected to differ in their methods of control.

Our first observation is that the accumulation of fossil fuels occurs at a rate that is negligible when compared with the rate of energy fixation through photosynthesis in the biosphere. Apparent exceptions to this observation, such as bogs and ponds, are successional stages, in which the failure of decomposition hastens the termination of the stage. The rate of accumulation when compared with that of photosynthesis has also been shown to be negligible over geologic time (Hutchinson, 1948).

If virtually all of the energy fixed in photosynthesis does indeed flow through the biosphere, it must follow that all organisms taken together are limited by the amount of energy fixed. In particular, the decomposers as a group must be food-limited, since by definition they comprise the trophic level which degrades organic debris. There is no a priori reason why predators, behavior, physiological changes induced by high densities, etc., could not limit decomposer populations. In fact, some decomposer populations may be limited in such ways. If so, however, others must consume the "left-over" food, so that the group as a whole remains food limited; otherwise fossil fuel would accumulate rapidly.

Any population which is not resource-limited must, of course, be limited to a level *below* that set by its resources.

Our next three observations are interrelated. They apply primarily to terrestrial communities. The first of these is that cases of obvious depletion of green plants by herbivores are exceptions to the general picture, in which

---

the plants are abundant and largely intact. Moreover, cases of obvious mass destruction by meteorological catastrophes are exceptional in most areas. Taken together, these two observations mean that producers are neither herbivore-limited nor catastrophe-limited, and must therefore be limited by their own exhaustion of a resource. In many areas, the limiting resource is obviously light, but in arid regions water may be the critical factor, and there are spectacular cases of limitation through the exhaustion of a critical mineral. The final observation in this group is that there are temporary exceptions to the general lack of depletion of green plants by herbivores. This occurs when herbivores are protected either by man or natural events, and it indicates that the herbivores are able to deplete the vegetation whenever they become numerous enough, as in the cases of the Kaibab deer herd, rodent plagues, and many insect outbreaks. It therefore follows that the usual condition is for populations of herbivores *not* to be limited by their food supply.

The vagaries of weather have been suggested as an adequate method of control for herbivore populations. The best factual clues related to this argument are to be found in the analysis of the exceptional cases where terrestrial herbivores have become numerous enough to deplete the vegetation. This often occurs with introduced rather than native species. It is most difficult to suppose that a species had been unable to adapt so as to escape control by the weather to which it was exposed, and at the same time by sheer chance to be able to escape this control from weather to which it had not been previously exposed. This assumption is especially difficult when mutual invasions by different herbivores between two countries may in both cases result in pests. Even more difficult to accept, however, is the implication regarding the native herbivores. The assumption that the hundreds or thousands of species native to a forest have failed to escape from control by the weather despite long exposure and much selection, when an invader is able to defoliate without this past history, implies that "pre-adaptation" is more likely than ordinary adaptation. This we cannot accept.

The remaining general method of herbivore control is predation (in its broadest sense, including parasitism, etc.). It is important to note that this hypothesis is not denied by the presence of introduced pests, since it is necessary only to suppose that either their natural predators have been left behind, or that while the herbivore is able to exist in the new climate, its enemies are not. There are, furthermore, numerous examples of the direct effect of predator removal. The history of the Kaibab deer is the best known example, although deer across the northern portions of the country are in repeated danger of winter starvation as a result of protection and predator removal. Several rodent plagues have been attributed to the local destruction of predators. More recently, the extensive spraying of forests to kill caterpillars has resulted in outbreaks of scale insects. The latter are protected from the spray, while their beetle predators and other insect enemies are not.

Thus, although rigorous proof that herbivores are generally controlled by predation is lacking, supporting evidence is available, and the alternate hypothesis of control by weather leads to false or untenable implications.

The foregoing conclusion has an important implication in the mechanism of control of the predator populations. The predators and parasites, in controlling the populations of herbivores, must thereby limit their own resources, and as a group they must be food-limited. Although the populations of some carnivores are obviously limited by territoriality, this kind of internal check cannot operate for all carnivores taken together. If it did, the herbivores would normally expand to the point of depletion of the vegetation, as they do in the absence of their normal predators and parasites.

There thus exists either direct proof or a great preponderance of factual evidence that in terrestrial communities decomposers, producers, and predators, as whole trophic levels, are resource-limited in the classical density-dependent fashion. Each of these three can and does expand toward the limit of the appropriate resource. We may now examine the reasons why this is a frequent situation in nature.

Whatever the resource for which a set of terrestrial plant species compete, the competition ultimately expresses itself as competition for space. A community in which this space is frequently emptied through depletion by herbivores would run the continual risk of replacement by another assemblage of species in which the herbivores are held down in numbers by predation below the level at which they damage the vegetation. That space once held by a group of terrestrial plant species is not readily given up is shown by the cases where relict stands exist under climates no longer suitable for their return following deliberate or accidental destruction. Hence, the community in which herbivores are held down in numbers, and in which the producers are resource-limited will be the most persistent. The development of this pattern is less likely where high producer mortalities are inevitable. In lakes, for example, algal populations are prone to crash whether grazed or not. In the same environment, grazing depletion is much more common than in communities where the major producers are rooted plants.

A second general conclusion follows from the resource limitation of the species of three trophic levels. This conclusion is that if more than one species exists in one of these levels, they may avoid competition only if each species is limited by factors completely unutilized by any of the other species. It is a fact, of course, that many species occupy each level in most communities. It is also a fact that they are not sufficiently segregated in their needs to escape competition. Although isolated cases of non-overlap have been described, this has never been observed for an entire assemblage. Therefore, interspecific competition for resources exists among producers, among carnivores, and among decomposers.

It is satisfying to note the number of observations that fall into line with the foregoing deductions. Interspecific competition is a powerful selective force, and we should expect to find evidence of its operation. Moreover, the evidence should be most conclusive in trophic levels where it is necessarily present. Among decomposers we find the most obvious specific mechanisms for reducing populations of competitors. The abundance of antibiotic substances attests to the frequency with which these mechanisms have been developed in the trophic level in which interspecific competition is inevitable. The producer species are the next most likely to reveal evidence of competition, and here we find such phenomena as crowding, shading, and vegetational zonation.

Among the carnivores, however, obvious adaptations for interspecific competition are less common. Active competition in the form of mutual habitat-exclusion has been noted in the cases of flatworms (Beauchamp and Ullyott, 1932) and salamanders (Hairston, 1951). The commonest situation takes the form of niche diversification as the result of interspecific competition. This has been noted in birds (Lack, 1945; MacArthur, 1958), salamanders (Hairston, 1949), and other groups of carnivores. Quite likely, host specificity in parasites and parasitoid insects is at least partly due to the influence of interspecific competition.

Of equal significance is the frequent occurrence among herbivores of apparent exceptions to the influence of density-dependent factors. The grasshoppers described by Birch (1957) and the thrips described by Davidson and Andrewartha (1948) are well known examples. Moreover, it is among herbivores that we find cited examples of coexistence without evidence of competition for resources, such as the leafhoppers reported by Ross (1957), and the psocids described by Broadhead (1958). It should be pointed out that in these latter cases coexistence applies primarily to an identity of food and place, and other aspects of the niches of these organisms are not known to be identical.

SUMMARY

In summary, then, our general conclusions are: (1) Populations of producers, carnivores, and decomposers are limited by their respective resources in the classical density-dependent fashion. (2) Interspecific competition must necessarily exist among the members of each of these three trophic levels. (3) Herbivores are seldom food-limited, appear most often to be predator-limited, and therefore are not likely to compete for common resources.

LITERATURE CITED

Andrewartha, H. G., 1957, The use of conceptual models in population ecology. Cold Spring Harbor Symp. Quant. Biol. 22: 219-232.

Beauchamp, R. S. A., and P. Ullyott, 1932, Competitive relationships between certain species of fresh-water triclads. J. Ecology 20: 200-208.

Birch, L. C., 1957, The role of weather in determining the distribution and abundance of animals. Cold Spring Harbor Symp. Quant. Biol. 22: 217-263.

Broadhead, E., 1958, The psocid fauna of larch trees in northern England. J. Anim. Ecol. 27: 217-263.

Davidson, J., and H. G. Andrewartha, 1948, The influence of rainfall, evaporation and atmospheric temperature on fluctuations in the size of a natural population of *Thrips imaginis* (Thysanoptera). J. Anim. Ecol. 17: 200–222.

Hairston, N. G., 1949, The local distribution and ecology of the Plethodontid salamanders of the southern Appalachians. Ecol. Monog. 19: 47–73.

1951, Interspecies competition and its probable influence upon the vertical distribution of Appalachian salamanders of the genus Plethodon. Ecology 32: 266–274.

Hutchinson, G. E., 1948, Circular causal systems in ecology. Ann. N. Y. Acad. Sci. 50: 221–246.

1957, Concluding remarks. Cold Spring Harbor Symp. Quant. Biol. 22: 415–427.

Lack, D., 1945, The ecology of closely related species with special reference to cormorant (*Phalacrocorax carbo*) and shag (*P. aristotelis*). J. Anim. Ecol. 14: 12–16.

MacArthur, R. H., 1958, Population ecology of some warblers of northeastern coniferous forests. Ecology 39: 599–619.

Milne, A., 1957, Theories of natural control of insect populations. Cold Spring Harbor Symp. Quant. Biol. 22: 253–271.

Nicholson, A. J., 1957, The self-adjustment of populations to change. Cold Spring Harbor Symp. Quant. Biol. 22: 153–172.

Reynoldson, T. B., 1957, Population fluctuations in *Urceolaria mitra* (Peritricha) and *Enchytraeus albidus* (Oligochaeta) and their bearing on regulation. Cold Spring Harbor Symp. Quant. Biol. 22: 313–327.

Ross, H. H., 1957, Principles of natural coexistence indicated by leafhopper populations. Evolution 11: 113–129.

Resource Partitioning in Ecological Communities

Research on how similar species divide resources helps
reveal the natural regulation of species diversity.

Thomas W. Schoener

Biologists have long been intrigued by differences in morphology and habit among closely related species, for to comprehend the manner and extent of such differences is to comprehend much of the natural control of organic diversity. Ecologists especially have concentrated on differences in the way species in the same community utilize resources. Studies of this resource partitioning are currently enjoying great popularity. In fact, in the 12 years since Hutchinson (1) posed his celebrated riddle: "Why are there so many kinds of animals?" such studies have grown exponentially at a rate four times that typical of scientific works (2).

The major purpose of resource-partitioning studies is to analyze the limits interspecific competition place on the number of species that can stably coexist. That such limits exist was suggested by the mathematical models of two early 20th-century theoreticians, Lotka and Volterra (3). The idea was supported by experiments of Gause (4) and later workers on simple organisms in laboratory containers, in which similar species tended to cause one anoth-

The author is associate professor of biology at the Biological Laboratories, 16 Divinity Avenue, Harvard University, Cambridge, Massachusetts 02138.

er's extinction. The infusion of models and data crystallized into the Gause principle, one version of which states that species cannot coexist for long if they too similarly use the same kinds of resources. The application of this idea to natural communities, however, was begun primarily in the 1940's during the time of the New Systematics. Although at first interested in differences between species that might ensure reproductive isolation, evolutionists quickly seized upon the idea of reducing competition as an alternative rationale for those differences (5). So rapidly, in fact, did this idea take hold that David Lack, eventually its principal proselytizer, was placed by a publication lag in the awkward position of having two quite different explanations for bill differences in Darwin's finches appear simultaneously (6)!

Hutchinson's (7) reformulation of the concept of ecological niche provided a precise language for the description of resource partitioning. In essence, he proposed that a species' population could be characterized by its position along each of a set of dimensions ordering environmental variables such as ambient temperature, prey size, and so on. Ideally, these dimensions would be few and independent. Hutchinson originally conceived of the niche as comprising intervals of population survival along each dimension. Now, however, many ecologists consider the frequency distribution of utilization or occurrence along dimensions as the niche.

What evidence demonstrates that the pattern of resource utilization among species results from competition? Mere presence of differences is not enough, for even if niches were arranged randomly with respect to one another, differences would exist. Hence a sufficiently precise search for differences would be bound to result in their detection, a state of affairs that led Slobodkin (8) to rephrase the Gause principle as a "rule of ecological procedure" rather than a verified or even verifiable proposition.

Ecologists now follow two approaches in their attempts to make a case for the importance of competition in nature. One approach is experimental, the other is observational.

At its most extreme, the experimental approach argues that a descriptive investigation of the equilibrium state of a process reveals little about what that process is. To prove that a particular dynamics operates, one must perturb the system away from equilibrium by adding or removing individuals. Such experiments, mostly quite recent, have demonstrated that compensatory changes sometimes occur in population numbers and in the condition of individuals (9, 10). When such changes are accomplished at several places along an environmental gradient, they show how competition maintains niche differences in nature (11–13). For example, Connell (11) has shown for barnacles, and Grant and others (12) for rodents, that habitat differences can result from competitive interactions.

Simple perturbation experiments in themselves, however, have several shortcomings. First, while demonstrating the effect of one species on another, they fail to reveal the mechanism of the competition. For example, one species may reduce the abundance of a second in a particular habitat by directly depleting its resources, by interfering with its ability to obtain those resources, or by using up in aggressive encounters energy obtained from those resources. Additional information, both observational and experimental, is required to evaluate these alternatives [for example, see (14)]. Second, they shed little light on the origin of differences. Indeed, if species differences have a strong genetic component, short-term experiments will not result in much niche expansion, even though competition may have caused those differences in the first place. Even long-term experiments, however, may fail to show the evolutionary consequences of competition if it acts rarely but with intense selective pressure (15). Third, perturbation is sometimes impractical—it is best when generation time is short, populations are insular, and only a small number of populations need to be studied.

The observational approach lacks some of these drawbacks but has others. In exchange for a direct demonstration of ongoing competition, it attempts to implicate competition indirectly. This can be done by elaboration of the predictions of competition models in such a way as to rule out other mechanisms that might cause species differences, such as selection for reproductive isolation to avoid interbreeding or for divergence in appearance to avoid habit-forming predators. In the remainder of this article I examine such predictions in detail. I attempt to show to what extent they are confirmed by patterns of resource partitioning and how they allow a better understanding of those patterns.

The evidence (see Table 1) is drawn from 81 studies that, explicitly or not, bear on resource partitioning in groups of three or more species. The studies heavily favor terrestrial vertebrates, probably reflecting my own interests as well as a real bias in the literature. Autotrophs are not included, because the way in which they partition resources is somewhat different and, in particular, seldom involves food types (16). Table 1 shows, for each group, the number of its species and genera, its location, its trophic position, and the dimensions, ranked according to importance, that separate its species

(*17–20*). Many of these dimensions order continuous variables such as food size. Some, however, such as food taxon, are easier to give as nominal categories, though these could probably be ordered along one or more axes.

Most investigators do not state how they delimit the group studied. Usually species of some taxonomic category, especially the genus, are studied in a small area. This procedure centers on theaters of most intense competition, but it introduces arbitrariness: if a species becomes too different in morphology or behavior, it is taxonomically defined out of the system, and if it becomes too different in habitat, it is geographically defined out of the system. These effects must differ for different kinds of animals and may bias the generalizations made in the following sections.

Sometimes it is convenient or necessary to estimate resource differences by using species characteristics, usually morphological, that indicate the position of its utilization on the resource dimension. The commonest *indicator* is the size of feeding structures, which is correlated usually with mean food size, hardness, or depth in some protective medium. But many other indicators (see Table 1) exist, such as body temperature for activity time and hindleg length for habitat (*21*). Indicators not only short-cut the compilation of data, but they imply strong functional relations between utilization and phenotype, relations which constrain resource partitioning.

Overdispersion of Niches

Although if species had no influence on each other's resource utilization their niches would still differ, competition should result in an overdispersion of niches in niche-space. Where niches are regularly and widely spaced over one or more dimensions, the alternative or "null" hypothesis of randomly generated differences must be rejected. Overdispersion patterns can be arranged under three headings.

Regular spacing along a single dimension. In 1959 Hutchinson (*1*) called attention to certain groups whose otherwise similar species differed in the size of their feeding apparatus by a constant factor of 1.2 to 1.4. Using this morphological indicator, one may infer that species adjacent on a size scale differ in mean food size by a constant ratio and thereby have their niches regularly spaced. Subsequent work has often, but not always, supported Hutchinson's generalization (*19, 22–28*). Certain lizards seem regularly to show higher ratios (*29*). Furthermore, insectivorous birds and lizards sometimes increase ratios with increasing body size (*27, 29*).

Why should sizes be a constant or increasing multiple of one another rather than be separated by a constant difference? If populations were close to numbers that would make extinction probable, the pattern might result from those species feeding on large items, which are often rare (*30*), having to be spaced farther apart on the size axis to maintain a viable population size (*27*). It is likely, however, that the limit of minimum population size is not as important as an increased variance in food-size utilization for large species: the larger the variance for a given distance separating the niches of two species, the greater the overlap and, for a certain set of assumptions detailed below, the more intense the competition. Hence, to hold competition just below a certain intensity, larger species must space more widely (*31*). The increased variance results from two factors: (i) large individuals usually eat a greater range of food sizes than smaller ones, probably because their optimal food is relatively rare; and (ii) species whose adults are large have a greater diversity of sizes because of their younger, smaller individuals. An increased niche variance is probably also responsible for lizards having greater ratios than birds. Lizard populations comprise individuals of many sizes, whereas birds mature quickly relative to their life spans and reach a monomorphic size.

Increase in number of important di-

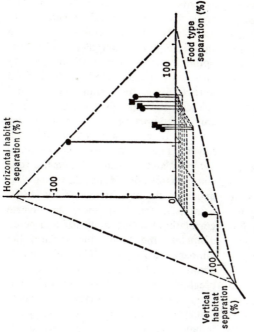

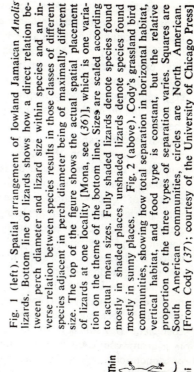

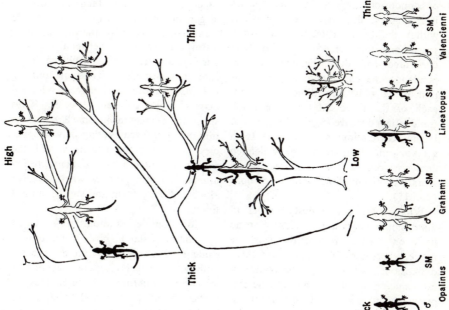

Fig. 1 (left). Spatial arrangement of lowland Jamaican *Anolis* lizards. Bottom line of lizards shows how a direct relation between perch diameter and lizard size within species and an inverse relation between species results in those classes of different species adjacent in perch diameter being of maximally different size. The top of the figure shows the actual spatial placement of lizards at one locality [Mona, see (36)], which is one variation on the theme of the bottom line. Sizes are scaled according to actual mean sizes. Fully shaded lizards denote species found mostly in shaded places, unshaded lizards denote species found mostly in sunny places. Fig. 2 (above). Cody's grassland bird communities, showing how total separation in horizontal habitat, vertical habitat, and food type is constant, but the relative proportion of the three types of separation varies. Squares are South American communities, circles are North American. [From Cody (37); courtesy of the University of Chicago Press]

mensions with increase in species number. Levins (*32*) and MacArthur (*33*) argue that in a competitive system, as the number of species accumulates, those species will eventually have to segregate on more and more dimensions to preserve minimal resource overlap. This argument assumes an eventual incompressibility of a species niche on any one dimension, an assumption which must be true because of the energy requirements and perceptual constraints of the individuals comprising the species. In contrast, if species were thrown together randomly, there should be no tendency for the number of important dimensions (defined as dimensions separating some minimal percentage of species pairs) to increase with species number. In practice, because of difficulties in ascertaining importance and determining nonindependence of dimensions, it will be hard to disentangle random effects.

Table 1 allows a crude investigation of the dimensionality of species separation. The Spearman rank correlation coefficient (r_s) of number of species in a group compared with the number of dimensions segregating the species is .277 ($P < .01$). Because dimensions within the broad categories of food, space, and time tend to be the most correlated, to reduce the effect of dependence one can recompute the relation using only one dimension from each of the three categories. But the trend is less decisive ($r_s = .146$, $P < .1$). Higher correlations should result from a taxonomically more narrowly defined analysis: our sample includes representatives from slime molds to lions (*34, 35*).

What is the commonest number of dimensions separating species? For no limit on the maximum, three is the mode, whereas for a maximum of three dimensions, two is by far the commonest value. Even if one admits the imprecise identification of important dimensions, separation appears generally to be multidimensional.

Separation of species along complementary dimensions. For groups where more than one dimension is important, similarity of species along one dimension should imply dissimilarity along another, if resources are to be sufficiently distinct. Such complementarities illustrate especially well the trouble individuals and their genes seem to take to avoid other species' niches, for they often fly in the face of expected functional relationships between phenotype and ecology. For example, small lizards optimally should eat small insects, and they can use small perches. Yet if food were limiting, this arrangement would result in the spatially most overlapping animals competing for the most similar sizes of food. How is this conflict resolved? The dilemma is not imaginary but real, and we can examine the four common lowland *Anolis* lizards of Jamaica to discover their solution (*36*). Curiously, the four show an inverse correlation between body size and perch diameter: the larger the species, the thinner the perches! The situation is complicated by the fact that the species break down into classes of different-sized individuals (a class is uniquely defined by age and sex, and adult females are usually considerably smaller than adult males). Moreover, within species, larger individuals appropriate larger perches. As Fig. 1 shows, the arrangement whereby there is a direct intraspecific relation between size and perch diameter, and an inverse interspecific relation, results in maximizing the size difference between adjacent classes from different species. Thus sizes are staggered in space so as to minimize resource overlap between species. The way the lizards solved the awkward problem of balancing heavy animals on thin perches was to evolve elongated body form and short-femured limbs.

More complex examples are provided by the grassland bird communities studied by Cody (*37*): in each community, the species separate according to various mixtures of differences in vertical habitat, horizontal habitat, and food type. The proportional importance of the three dimensions varies from community to community, but the total separation is remarkably constant (Fig. 2).

Cases of complementarity involve

nearly all possible combinations of kinds of dimensions:

1) Food type and habitat: The tendency for species that overlap in habitat to eat different foods is perhaps the commonest combination. In addition to having been reported for birds (23, 37–39) and lizards (20, 36, 40, 41), it has also been reported for fish (42, 43) and crustaceans (22, 44). The *Anolis* lizards of Bimini provide a precise example of this combination. In Fig. 3, overlap in food size is plotted against overlap in structural habitat (perch height and diameter) for all pairwise combinations of classes of Bimini lizards. For pairs from different species, where structural habitat is similar, food size is not, and vice versa. For pairs from the same species, similarity in one dimension implies similarity in another. This indicates the relative effectiveness of competition in spacing similarly sized individuals, depending upon whether those individuals are in the same gene pool and reproductively attractive to one another.

Many otherwise similar species are separated, often with extraordinarily small overlap, in geographic range. When that separation parallels changes in habitat variables, such as in Diamond's numerous examples (28) of altitudinal separation for New Guinea birds, the situation is similar to those just described. However, other cases of geographic separation do not appear to covary with any dimension and are particularly common in archipelagos, where terrain is fragmented (10, 28, 45).

2) Food type and time: Temporal separation can be on a daily or a yearly basis and both sorts can complement separation by food type. For example, two similarly sized terns feed at different times of the day (23), and similarly sized lizards (46), crustaceans (22, 44), and gastropods (47) reach peak abundance at different times of the year.

3) Habitat and time: Lizards in habitats where climatic factors vary substantially during the day can show nonsynchronous spatial overlap (36, 40, 48).

4) Habitat and habitat: In addition to Cody's birds, other species similar in horizontal habitat often differ in vertical habitat—seabirds partition depth under water (49), while woodland passerines partition foraging height (50).

5) Food type and food type: McNab constructed a matrix whose columns index food size and whose rows index food taxon; members of the Trinidad bat fauna fill this matrix fairly evenly (51, 52).

Despite there being so many cases of complementarity, there are more cases where similarity of species along one dimension implies similarity along another. This is because the dimensions that ecologists recognize are rarely independent: for example, moisture and food size can be correlated (30). The point is not to compare numbers of examples. Rather, given correlations between environmental variables and functional relations between consumer and resource characteristics, one must explain why examples of complementarity should exist at all.

Importance of Particular Dimensions in Resource Partitioning

The data just reviewed raise the questions of which dimensions are important for which groups and why some kinds of animals show greater dimensionality than others. To approach these questions, we need to answer two others: (i) What is the absolute heterogeneity of resources and, in particular, what resource kinds renew as separate populations, and (ii) to what degree is it adaptive or necessary for consumers to distinguish that heterogeneity?

Phrased another way, we need a theory of the feasibility of resource partitioning as it relates to particular dimensions. This theory is now in a formative stage, in which the qualitative sorting out of biologically important effects is critical. To obtain suggestions about the directions that such a theory might take, we can examine the data of Table 1. Five major generalizations emerge.

Habitat dimensions are important more often than food-type dimensions,

Table 1. Ecological differences between similar species. Numbers in columns "Macrohabitat" through "Time" denote importance rank of that decision. Abbreviations are as follows. Rank: A, thought to be strictly an aspect of separation on another dimension; b, breeding time; f, feeding time; i, indicator used; n, thought not to be important; X, known not to be important partitioning; Dis, foraging distance from land; For, marine formation; Geo, dimension. Macrohabitat: Alt, altitude; Aqu, aquatic-terrestrial gradient; Soi, soil; Str, stream size or part of stream; Veg, vegetation type; Wat, size geographic; Hor, aquatic horizontal zone; Lat, latitude; Microhabitat: s, used as shelter; structural habitat, food or perch substrate in vegetation. Food type: B, artificial baits; F, feeding type; H, hardness; S, size; T, taxonomic category [letters following T refer to species of food (S), higher taxonomic category (H), life stage of host (L), part of an individual prey (P)]. Indicators: 1, body size; 2 bill size; 3, head size; 4, ovipositor length; 5, bill shape; 6, body temperature; 7, mouth shape; 8, body form; 9, hindleg length; 10, hair quantity; 11, group size; 12, nutrient-utilization ability.

| Consumers | | | | Rank and description of resource dimensions | | | | |
Group, location, and reference	No. of species	No. of genera	Food	Macrohabitat	Microhabitat	Food type	Time Day	Time Year
Simple organisms								
Slime molds, forest, eastern North America (93)	4	2	Bacteria	X		1-TS		
Paramecium, near Ann Arbor, Mich. (94)	5	1	Organic minutia	1-Wat	2 (X) -Depth	1-TH; X-S		1
Triclads, shallow littoral zone of lakes, Britain (95)	4	3	Invertebrates			3-F		
Nematodes, psammolittoral, Gulf of Mexico (96)	46	?	Invertebrates, plants	1-Hor	1-Depth	3-F		
Rotifers, small lake, central Sweden (97)	5	1	Flagellates		1-Depth	1'-S[1]		
Tubificid oligochaetes, Toronto Harbor (98)	3	3	Bacteria		X			
Polychaetes, soft bottom, Beaufort, N.C. (99)	5	3	Deposit feeder		1-Sediment type; 2-Vertical zone	1'-TS[12]		
Chaetognaths, Agulhas Current, Indian Ocean (100)	18	4	Mostly copepods	2-Hor	2-Depth	1'-S		2
Mollusks								
Gastropods, shallow water, Florida (47)	8	6	Invertebrates			1-TS		
Conus, Hawaii (101)	25	1	Polychaetes, fish, gastropods	3-For	2-Substrate	1-TSH	4	
Conus, Pacific atolls (102)	17	1	Mostly polychaetes		2-Substrate	1-TSH		
Crustacea								
Crabs, intertidal bench, Tasmania (103)	11	9	Algae, invertebrates, detritus	1-Hor	1-As macrohabitat[10]; 2-Cover; 5-Vertical zone	3-TH		3[b]
Hermit crabs, intertidal, San Juan Islands, Wash. (61)	3	1	Detritus		1-Shell shape[8]; 2-Shell weight[8]; 3-Bed and tidepool type[8,n]			

Organism, location (ref)			Food						
Diaptomus copepods, Clarke Lake, Ontario (*44*)	3	1	Plant, animal particles		1'-Depth		1'-S	X	1
Diaptomus copepods, Saskatchewan ponds (*104*)	7	1	Plant, animal particles	1-Geo	4 (X)-Depth		2'-S		2
Amphipods, marine sand beaches, Georgia (*44*)	5	5	Mostly detritus, algae, protozoa	1-Hor	2-Depth in sand		2-S^1 / 5-TH		2^{b,1}
Crustaceans, cave streams, West Virginia (*105*)	4	3	Leaves, microorganisms		1^s-Riffles or type pool		X		
Insects									
Grasshoppers, prairie, northeastern Colorado (*106*)	14	11	Grasses, forbs				1-TS; 1-TS		2
Melanoplus grasshoppers, grasslands, Boulder, Colo. (*107*)	3	1	Mostly grasses	2-Veg			1-TS		2
Termites, Savannah-woodland, West Africa (*108*)	5	1	Grasses	1^n-Veg			4-TS; 4-S	3	2
Psocids, larch trees, Britain (*109*)	9	5	Bark algae, fungi	4-Alt	2-Twig condition		1-THP		
Butterflies, lowland rain forest, Costa Rica (*110*)	12	7	Decaying fruit		X-Microclimate		X-B	1^n	3
Carabid beetles, fen, England (*111*)	8	2	Mainly scavengers	1-Veg			A-TH; A-S		2^f
Whirligig beetles, Michigan (*112*)	3	1	Predators, scavengers	1-Lat	1-Lake size				3(X)^b
Euglossa bees, Panama (*113*)	19	1	Nectar	2-Veg	3^1-Microclimate		1'-S	X	
Ants, Colorado (*114*)	4	3	Animals	1-Veg	3-Type log or cover		2'-S		
Ants, Colorado (*114*)	5	2	Seeds	2-Veg	3-Type log or cover		1'-S		
Megarhyssa wasps, beech-maple, Michigan (*115*)	3	1	Parasitoids		1^1-Depth of food⁴ / X-Leaf type⁵		X	2	X
Wasps, *Neodiprion*, Quebec (*19*)	11	9	Parasitoids	4-Veg	1^1-Depth of host		1-TL; 1'-S / 4-TS		
Other arthropods									
Millipedes, maple-oak forest, central Illinois (*116*)	7	7	Leaf litter, decaying wood		1-Position in log, litter		X-F		
Mites, deciduous forest, central Maryland (*117*)	7,9	1	Invertebrates	1-Veg	1-Depth in soil		1'-S		4
Water mites, ponds, central New York (*118*)	20	1	Parasites	3-Wat			1-TS; 2-P		4
Fish									
Stream fish, dry season, Panama, moist tropics (*42*)	12	12	Animals, plants	2-Str	2-Depth		1-TH	3	
River fish, River Endrick, Scotland (*119*)	5	4	Arthropods, algae	1-Str			1-TSH		
Lake fish, eastern Ontario (*43*)	17	15	Animals, plants	1-Hor³	5-Depth⁸		1-TH / 5^a-S^{1,7}	3	3
Intertidal fish, Brittany (*120*)	13	12	Invertebrates, algae	1-Hor	1-As macrohabitat		2-TH		

Consumers				Rank and description of resource dimensions				
Group, location, and reference	No. of species	No. of genera	Food	Macrohabitat	Microhabitat	Food type	Time — Day	Time — Year
Salamanders								
Desmognathus, Appalachians (121)	5	2	Arthropods	1-Aqu, 2-Alt		2-S[1], A-TH		X
Triturus, ponds, England (122)	3	1	Invertebrates	2?-Alt	2-Temperature	1-S, 4-TH		
Frogs								
Tropical Rana, streamsides, rain forest, Borneo (123)	3	1	Small animals	1?-Wat	1-Distance from stream	3-S, 3-TH		X
Temperate Rana, northeastern North America (124)	6	1	Small animals	2-Aqu, 3-Lat		3[1]-S		1[b]
Lizards								
Ameiva teids, Osa, Costa Rica (40)	3	1	Arthropods, fruit	1-Veg	4-Plant cover[c,9]	2-S[1]	2[1]	
Ctenotus skinks, desert, Australia (21)	7	1	Arthropods			3-S[2], 1-TH	5[a]	2
Cnemidophorus whiptails, Trans-Pecos (125)	5	1	Arthropods	1-Veg		2-TH		
Cnemidophorus, south and central New Mexico (126)	4	1	Arthropods	1-Veg		2-TH; 2-S[1]	5[1]	4[b]
Anolis, Bimini (20)	4	1	Arthropods	5-Veg	1-Structural habitat	2-S[2], 2-TH	2	
Anolis, Jamaica (35)	6	1	Arthropods, fruit	3-Veg	1-Structural habitat	1[1]-S	4	
Anolis, Puerto Rico (127)	10	1	Arthropods, fruit	2-Veg	1-Structural habitat	3[1]-S	4?	
Phyllodactylus geckos, Sechura desert, Peru (128)	4	1	Mostly arthropods	2-Alt, 3-Soi	3-Plant species, 5-Foraging substrate	1-TH, 6-S	X	
Other reptiles								
Sternothaerus turtles, southeastern United States (129)	4	1	Mollusks, arthropods	1-Wat		3 (X)-TH	1	
Garter snakes, Michigan (130)	3	1	Animals	2-Veg		1-TH		3
Birds								
Alcids, Olympic Peninsula (49)	6	6	Fish, invertebrates	1-Dis	2-Feeding depth	2-TH		X[b]
Alcids, St. Lawrence Island, Alaska (131)	3	2	Invertebrates	4-Dis	X-Feeding depth	1-S[3], 1-TH[6]	3	X[b]
Terns, Christmas Islands (23)	5	4	Fish, invertebrates	2-Dis		1-S[1,3], A-TH	2	
Sandpipers, tundra, Alaska (132)	4	1	Insects	1-Veg		1-TS, 3-S		

Resource-niche dimensions for selected studies (rotated table, page 379).

Taxon, location (ref)	N1	N2	Principal foods	Classification	Niche dimensions	Code	Extra
Herons, Lake Alice, Fla. (133)	4	4	Animals	3-Veg / 2-Veg / 1-Veg	2-Feeding place / 2-Feeding method / 1-Kind of plant / 4-Feeding height / 3-Vegetation density	1-THS; 3-S / 1-THP / 2-S[1,2] / 1[1]-S[1,2] / A-TH	
Ducks, Medway Island, Britain (24)	7	3	Plants, animals				
Hummingbirds, Arima Valley, Trinidad (38)	9	8	Nectar, insects				3
Flycatchers, deciduous forest, south West Virginia (134)	5	5	Insects				
Flycatchers, deciduous forest, eastern United States (39)	5	4	Insects	1-Veg		2-S[1]	
Titmice, broadleaved woods, Britain (18)	5	1	Insects, seeds	1-Veg / 2-Alt	2-Structural habitat / 2-Foliage layer	X-TH / 2-S	
Vireos, New World (135)	17	1	Insects	1-Geo / X		4[1]-S	
Warblers, boreal forests, Vermont (136)	5	1	Insects	1-Veg	1-Part of tree / 2-Feeding style	X-TH	X
Icterids, channeled scabland, Washington (137)	4	4	Insects (for nestlings)	1-Veg	1-As macrohabitat	2-TH	
Tanagers, Trinidad (138)	10	5	Fruit, insects	2-Veg	1-Structural habitat	2-THS	
Honeycreepers, Trinidad (138)	5	4	Fruits, insects	3-Veg	1-Structural habitat	2-THS	
Finches, southeastern United States (139)	5	5	Seeds, insects	1-Veg	1-Height	3 (A)-S	
Finches, near Oxford, England (140)	10	5	Seeds, insects, buds	3-Veg	4-Ground, air, or foliage	1-TSH[6,2]	5
Geospiza finches, central Galápagos Islands (18)	5	1	Seeds, fruit, buds, insects	2-Veg		1-S[3]	
Camarhynchus finches, central Galápagos Islands (18)	4	1	Insects	3-Veg	3-Structural habitat	1-S, H	
Grassland birds, ten sites, New World (37)	2-4	2-4	Seeds, insects	2-Veg	1-Structural habitat / 1-Foraging method / 3-Vertical / 3-Substrate	3-S	X
Foliage gleaners, oak woods, California (25)	5	3	Insects		4-Foraging layer	1[1]-S / 1-S	X
Upland birds, broadleaved woods, Britain (50)	22	17?	Insects	2-Veg	1-Structural habitat / A-holes[a]	1-TH / 2-TH	A
Mammals							
Pocket gophers, Colorado (71)	4	3	Plants	1-Soi		X-FT	
Chipmunks, Sierra Nevada, Calif. (141)	4	1	Seeds, fruits	1-Alt	1-Foliage height	X[?]-S	X
Rodents, deserts, North America (142)	10	3	Seeds	1-Veg / 3-Soi			
Peromyscus, Ozarks, Mo. (143)	3	1	Insects, seeds	1-Veg / 1-Alt / 3-Veg	2-Height in trees	X-THP / 3-THP	
Giant rats, western Malaysia (144)	4	3	Plants, insects				
Carnivores, Serengeti, Africa (145)	7	5	Large animals	2-Veg		1-S[1,11]	3
Bats, central Iowa (146)	8	6	Insects	2-Veg		3	1
Bats, Central American lowlands (52)	31	21	Animals, plants	2-Veg		1[1]-S;2-TH	

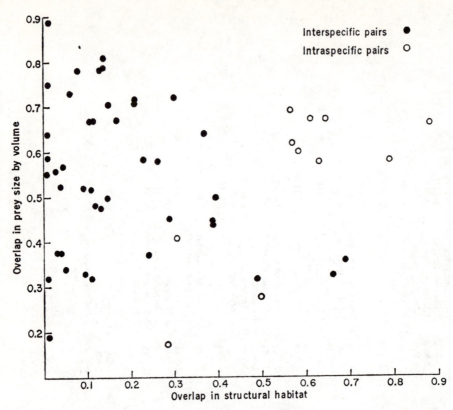

Fig. 3. Similarity in prey size (weighted by prey volume) plotted against similarity in structural habitat for all pairwise combinations of classes of Bimini *Anolis* lizards. Overlap is expressed as percentages. For interspecific pairs, similarity in habitat implies dissimilarity in prey size and vice versa, whereas the reverse is true for intraspecific pairs. More exactly, divide the plot into four sections bounded by the axes and two lines corresponding to 0.5 overlap for habitat and 0.5 for food. Then 25 interspecific pairs fall into the top left or lower right sector, whereas no pairs fall into the top right sector. In contrast, the same figures for intraspecific pairs are 0 and 8 ($P < .001$, in either separate or combined binomial tests).

which are important more often than temporal dimensions. There are two ways to show the considerable magnitude of these differences. First, we can give the percentage of groups where the most important dimension falls into one of the three categories. The result is as follows: 55 percent of the groups fall into the habitat category, 40 percent into the food category, and 5 percent into the time category. Second, we can give the percentage of groups where each kind of dimension is known to separate species. The result is: in 90 percent of the groups the species are separated by habitat; in 78 percent, the species are separated by food; and in 41 percent, the species are separated by time.

We can begin to assess the likelihood of partitioning by habitat as compared to food type with MacArthur and Pianka's (53) foraging-strategy scheme. Picture a set of habitat patches between which individuals of a given species travel and within which they forage, and suppose that individuals of a second species invade and reduce food density in certain kinds of patches. Then it may no longer be worth the while of the given species to visit patches of that habitat kind, since the time spent there might better be spent traveling to and feeding in less depleted places. However, picture now the situation within such a habitat patch, where a competing species reduces the density of certain kinds of items. The yield per unit time spent there for individuals of the original species must go down, but if those individuals still find it optimal to feed in that kind of habitat patch, they should at least eat all the types of food that they ate before competition and should probably eat other kinds of food as well. In short, competition changes the value, per unit time, of feeding in kinds of patches once they are entered, but does not affect the per-unit-time value of eating types of food once they are found (*54*).

Thus, at first, species will partition habitats. However, evolution should eventually redistribute phenotypes of the consumers, those phenotypes better at extracting energy from the more abundant food types becoming more prevalent. Unless the competing species eliminate the possibility of such evolution by their separating into nonoverlapping habitats and quickly becoming genetically fixed in them, the result can be a narrowing of diet with consequent specialization. Hence, the Mac-Arthur-Pianka argument may not be sufficient to explain the preponderance of separation by habitat.

Perhaps a more critical factor relates to the contrasting ways in which habitat and food are distributed in space and encountered by consumers. An individual must encounter many food items (and to a lesser extent microhabitats) in its foraging and if it skips too many it will lose too much energy and time in searching relative to its energy input. However, because macrohabitat patches are more continuously distributed and are large relative to the need and ability of individuals to range through them, it is feasible for an individual to spend most of its time in a single macrohabitat. Thus, when it becomes impossible to specialize further on food types, species can continue to partition macrohabitats.

Despite these arguments, there is no statistically significant overall trend for habitat rank to increase or food-type rank to decrease with increasing species number in an assemblage. Certain kinds of animals, such as lizards [for their microhabitats, see (*35*)], do seem to show an overall trend, but others, such as terrestrial mammals, do not. Indeed, in the latter group, separation by macrohabitat is more important than it is in any other group and species often seem to be separated only in this way. This is in contrast to groups such as birds, which are able to partition space vertically and which often show greater horizontal overlap (*13*).

Should the partitioning of time be more like habitat or food type? As for habitats, competitors reduce the value of foraging in certain time periods by lowering the density of available food. However, there is a fundamental difference. In deciding not to forage in a particular type of habitat, a consumer is simultaneously deciding instead to forage in or travel between other habitat types; he is weighing one positive energy gain against what is nearly always another. But in deciding to omit certain time periods, the consumer is usually trading something—a lowered but positive yield in the time period frequented by competitors—for nothing, no yield at all. Only where ability to process food is limited relative to risk of being eaten during feeding should temporal specialization be marked. A similar argument can be made for seasonal activity, where what is at stake is some reproduction as opposed to no reproduction. No wonder temporal partitioning is relatively rare (*55*).

The importance of seasonal differences between species decreases with increasing species number ($r_s = .377$, $P < .05$). So does the importance of diel differences ($r_s = .313$). Although the latter is not quite statistically significant, both of the temporal correlations are substantially greater than those for other dimensions. Hence it seems that the possibility for temporal partitioning is rapidly exhausted as species are added to an assemblage.

Predators separate more often by being active at different times of the day than do other groups. Of the 63 groups for whose species no differences in daily activity were noted, 49 percent are primarily predators, 27 percent are primarily herbivores or scavengers, and 24 percent are primarily omnivores. Of the 17 groups showing partitioning by daily activity, 82 percent are predators and 12 percent herbivores [$P < .025$ (*56*)].

The most likely hypothesis for this pattern gives a second reason for the rarity of temporal partitioning: resources cannot often be separated into independently renewing populations by their own daily activity. This is obviously true for plants and most plant products—a leaf not eaten during the day can be eaten at night. It is least likely to be true for animal foods, which themselves often show peaks of activity. Therefore, predators will be more likely to partition resources by being active at different times of the day than will other animals.

Terrestrial poikilotherms relatively often partition food by being active at different times of the day. Of the 23 such groups, 43 percent segregate by having different periods of daily activity, whereas only 12 percent of other animals do [$P < .005$ (*56*)]. Those animals most sensitive to diel climatic variation are poikilotherms, because they are less buffered against external temperature change. And such changes are greater on land than in water. Therefore, both consumer-perceived and absolute temporal heterogeneity is high for terrestrial poikilotherms.

Vertebrates segregate less by seasonal activity than do lower animals. Forty-four percent of invertebrates but only 13 percent of vertebrates differ in seasonal activity or breeding ($P < .01$). The obvious explanation for this trend is that animals whose generation times are relatively long cannot partition the year as finely as those that mature in shorter time periods. What is more, even when there is unusual opportunity for vertebrates to stagger breeding, as for birds in tropical climates, the species simply expand their breeding periods so that overlap is no less than for temperate species (*57*).

Segregation by food type is more important for animals feeding on food that is large in relation to their own size than it is for animals feeding on relatively small food items. This trend holds separately for predators and for other trophic types. For the groups whose food items are relatively large, the combined totals are as follows: 71 percent separate by food type and 33 percent separate by habitat; for groups whose food items are small, 28 percent separate by food type and 72 percent by habitat [$P < .05$; $P < .01$ (*58*)].

The reasons for this pattern may be several. First, unless some kind of small food is abundant, a necessary condition for individual specialization is that the animal eat only a few items, as do those animals feeding on relatively large foods. Many herbivorous insects, for example, spend most of their lives on a single "item." Second, animals that eat relatively large prey are often pursuers, and several models of foraging strategies argue that pursuers should specialize on food of a limited size range (*53*, *59*).

In addition to these five patterns, there are others which are not quite statistically significant but which may be real.

For example, animals that mature in size quickly relative to their life span, or whose adults are ecologically dissimilar to their young, partition food by size more often than do others (59 percent as opposed to 39 percent). A striking exception is mammals, and if these are deleted, the result is statistically significant ($P < .025$). The pattern supports the idea that specializing on food size is difficult for consumer species whose populations at any one time comprise many sizes because, for a given range of available food sizes, overlap must be greater among such species.

There is another rough tendency shown by the data in Table 1. Habitat is less often the most important dimension in aquatic animals than it is in terrestrial animals (43 percent as opposed to 65 percent). A striking exception to this pattern is terrestrial arthropods. If real, the pattern is hard to explain except on the basis of a lower absolute habitat heterogeneity in aquatic systems. As a terrestrial ecologist, I fear this hypothesis may be near-sighted. Yet there is agreement among ecologists working on benthic marine

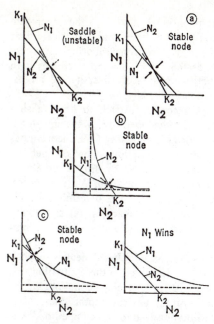

Fig. 4. (a) The two kinds of equilibria for Lotka-Volterra competition equations. (b) Equilibrium in a competition model where each species has exclusive resources (Eq. 3). (c) The two possible outcomes of competition in an "included niche" model, where one species has exclusive resources but the other does not. Either the first species wins. or there is stable coexistence.

systems (60) that spatial heterogeneity there is often low. In addition, because of the high specific heat of water compared to air, spatial climatic variation in aquatic systems should often be less severe. Finally, because of greater resource mobility, spatial dimensions may characterize resource kinds less well in aquatic than in other systems [for example. see (61)].

Limiting Similarity

Although niche overdispersion falsifies the hypothesis of randomly placed niches, it fails to rule out alternatives to competition, such as predation and reproductive isolation, that can cause species differences. Analysis of the particular dimensions used by particular kinds of animals may to some extent enable us to discriminate among the hypotheses. For example, instead of

the divergence in time of activity or in time of reproduction that would be expected from competition, predation might sometimes result in these times becoming synchronized so as to saturate the predators, as in the case of periodical cicada species (62). However, an entirely different approach is through a theory specifying quantitatively just how similar species could be and yet coexist. This number, called the limiting similarity, could then be checked against differences in hypothetically equilibrial communities. The theory, only begun during the last several years. links properties of the niche to dynamical models that specify the outcome of competition between populations.

The dynamical system that has served as the basis for models of limiting similarity is that of Lotka-Volterra for n competing species:

$$dN_i/dt =$$
$$(r_i N_i / K_i)(K_i - N_i - \sum_{\substack{j=1 \\ j \neq i}}^{n} \alpha_{ij} N_j)$$
$$i = 1, \ldots, n \quad (1)$$

where N_i is the population size of the ith competitor, r_i is its intrinsic rate of increase, K_i is its carrying capacity (the number of individuals at equilibrium with no competing species), and α_{ij} is a competition coefficient (the effect of an individual of competitor j on the growth of competitor i relative to the effect of an individual of competitor i). Depending upon the K's, the α's, and (for $n > 2$) the r's, Eq. 1 can give mathematical equilibrium with some nonpositive $\hat{N}_i$, in which case those species are excluded from the community (63). When equilibrium occurs with all positive $\hat{N}_i$, it can be stable or unstable. Figure 4a illustrates the two possible kinds of equilibria for two competitors: a stable node (64) and a saddle (the "unstable equilibrium" of some texts). Both positivity and stability are necessary for coexistence.

Conditions for coexistence were investigated with deterministic models first by MacArthur and Levins (65) and then by Roughgarden (66) and

May (67). These investigators assumed that competitors separate along one dimension and obey Eq. 1. To incorporate niches into the differential equations, they calculated competition coefficients as

$$\alpha_{ij} = \sum_k p_{ik}p_{jk} / \sum_k p_{ik}^2 \qquad (2)$$

or the continuous analog. Here, p_{ik} is the percentage of utilization of resource k by competitor i. Thus the p's specify the niche of competitor i along the dimension indexed by k. They also assumed that species have niches with the same shape and variance (w^2) and with means differing from those of adjacent niches by a constant amount, d. Not only does this last assumption collapse the algebra, but it also sets the stage for predictions about how variation in d, w, and niche shape affects α and thereby affects coexistence.

MacArthur and Levins dealt with the survival of a species trying to wedge its niche between the niches of two species that were already established. For bell-shaped niches and equal K's, limiting d/w for invasion is 1.56, and this decreases as the invader's K increases. Roughgarden dealt with the survival of the peripheral as well as the "sandwiched" species and determined how variation in niche kurtosis (a shape parameter) affects limiting similarity. As utilization curves with constant w vary from normal to back-to-back exponentials, limiting similarity decreases. He speculated that concave niches may characterize species whose resources show little long-term dependability. He also predicted a bimodality in the distribution of d/w in nature. Species with d/w larger than the upper bound of a certain interval can always coexist. Below the lower bound, successful invasion can often result in one of the peripheral species becoming extinct, giving a small d/w between the two survivors. May examined limiting similarity for arbitrary numbers of species and showed that the more species along the resource dimension, the less tightly they can be packed. It is interesting that Pianka (41) has evidence from desert lizards for this "diffuse competition," that is, the aggregate competition from many species rather than just from neighboring ones. He finds that niche overlap decreases with increasing species diversity of an assemblage.

A second approach to limiting similarity, developed by May and MacArthur (31) and May (67), incorporates stochastic variation. For competition coefficients given by Eq. 2, equilibria involving all positive $\hat{N}_i$ are necessarily stable for the deterministic version of Eq. 1. Hence, as far as stability is concerned, there is no limiting similarity, so that the deterministic approaches just discussed deal with positivity. However, the situation is different for a stochastic analog. By incorporating environmental fluctuations (white noise) into the competitors' K's, May showed that over a wide range of the fluctuations' amplitude, limiting d/w is close to one (Fig. 5). Again, the more species along a resource dimension, the less tightly they can be packed, although this effect diminishes rapidly for $n > 4$.

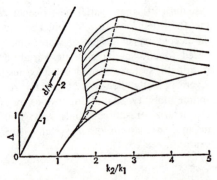

Fig. 5. Conditions of coexistence for three species arrayed along a resource dimension. The K's of peripheral species (1 and 3) are equal; species with d/w and K_2/K_1 within the limiting curves will coexist; Λ, the eigenvalue that determines stability in May's stochastic model and sets the rate of return to equilibrium in the deterministic model, is plotted as a third dimension (contours spaced 0.2 d/w-units apart). Note the rapid rise of Λ past $d/w = 1$. Dashed line shows Λ's for which all equilibrium populations are equal. [From May (147); courtesy of the American Mathematical Society]

There are many cases in nature of species separating on one dimension having $d/w \cong 1$. Examples are birds separating by prey size and feeding height, and parasitic wasps separating by depth of prey in wood. There are also cases in which limiting similarity appears to be much less than 1, for example, tropical frugivorous birds (66, 68). According to the theory just presented, such exceptions may occur in extremely stable environments or among species whose niches are concave rather than bell shaped. Most of these new and exciting ideas have yet to be tested in detail.

Other Mathematical Approaches to Resource Partitioning

While providing the gateway to the current theory of limiting similarity, the Lotka-Volterra equations (Eq. 1) are less than ideal for modeling resource utilization. This is because they fail to incorporate explicitly the mechanism of that utilization. Indeed, interpreted literally they seem better to model competition by direct interference (69, 70), though if considered a Taylor series, they can approximate a variety of more complex equations. Alternatives to Eq. 1 now exist for both one and several trophic levels, and I shall review three examples.

Without much explicit justification, Eq. 1 is sometimes said to model the situation where each competing species has an exclusive set of resources, this resulting in the stable node of Fig. 4a. However, if competition were effected purely through exploitation of resources, it would be difficult to imagine how, as Eq. 1. implies, one species could reduce the other's abundance to zero, much less how this reduction could be linear. A model (70) for one trophic level that incorporates resource partitioning explicitly is

$$\frac{dN_1}{dt} = R_1 N_1 \left(\frac{I_{E1}}{N_1} + \frac{I_{01}}{N_1 + \beta N_2} - C_1 \right)$$

$$(3)$$

where R_1 is the number of individuals of consumer 1 produced from a unit

of processed energy, C_1 is the cost in energy of the death and maintenance of an individual of competitor 1, I_{E1} is the energy extractable from competitor 1's exclusive resources per unit time, I_{01} is the energy that individuals of competitor 1 can extract from resources used by both species per unit time, and β is the relative likelihood of an individual of competitor 2 getting a unit of the overlapping resource relative to an individual of competitor 1.

The equation for competitor 2 is similar to Eq. 3 but has a β multiplying the second term; the format easily generalizes to n species. Equation 3 is not appropriate where the $\hat{N}$'s are small relative to the I's but is better close to equilibrium. Figure 4b shows the equilibrial solutions for two competing species, neither of which can be reduced below the level of that population size supportable on its exclusive resources.

When two competitors are mimicked by equations such as Eq. 3, there is always a single stable equilibrium. By including more resources, the equations can be made more complicated and less tractable. However, they can also be simplified so as to model coexistence or extinction for Miller's (71) "included niche" phenomenon. Here one species has its resource kinds contained entirely within those of the other, whereas the other has resource kinds not used by the first. The appropriate model for the broad-niched species is Eq. 3, and for the included species, $dN_2/dt = R_2 N_2\{[I_2\beta/(N_1 + \beta N_2)] - C_2\}$ is the appropriate model (70). The broad-niched species always persists, but the narrow-niched species survives if and only if $K_1 C_2 < I_2 \beta$ (Fig. 4c). Among other things, this condition requires that individuals of the narrow-niched species be sufficiently better than those of the broad-niched species at appropriating the overlapping resources, and that those resources be sufficiently abundant and calorically worthwhile. This model thus conditions coexistence on parameters more directly related to resource utilization than K and α.

Instead of fluxes through the food

processing machinery of competitors, resources can be modeled as reproducing populations. MacArthur's (72) two-level system is the best-known example:

$$dN_i/dt = R_iN_i(\sum_i a_{ik}b_{ik}F_k - C_i)$$
$$i = 1, \ldots, n$$
$$dF_k/dt = r_kF_k - (r_kF_k^2/K_k) - F_k\sum_i a_{ik}N_i \quad k = 1, \ldots, m$$
$$(4)$$

where F_k is the number of resource k, a_{ik} is the consumption rate of resource k by competitor i, b_{ik} is the net energy per item of resource k extractable by an individual of competitor i, r_k is the intrinsic rate of increase of resource k, K_k is the carrying capacity of resource k, and other symbols are as before. At equilibrium, Eqs. 1 and 4 are structurally equivalent, whence

$$\alpha_{ij} = \left[\sum_{k=1}^m \frac{a_{ik}a_{jk}b_{ik}K_k}{r_k}\right] \Bigg/ \left[\sum_{k=1}^m \frac{a_{ik}^2 b_{ik}K_k}{r_k}\right] \quad (5)$$

A second two-level system (73) has consumers the same as in Eq. 4 but resources growing according to

$$dF_k/dt = S_k - F_k\sum_i a_{ik}N_i$$
$$k = 1, \ldots, m \quad (6)$$

where S_k is the number of resource k entering the system per unit time (15, 69, 70). At equilibrium, Eq. 6 is structurally the same as models of the type of Eq. 3.

Two-level models show explicitly how many key variables affect competition. For example, Eq. 5 says that the larger a resource kind's net caloric value to consumers and the smaller its intrinsic rate of increase (a measure of recovery), the greater that resource's contribution to the magnitude of the competition coefficient, α. When resources have a one-to-one correspondence with habitats, Eq. 5 shows that the more similar the habitat preferences (reflected in the a's), the greater α. This interpretation of resources provides an approximate justification for the form of Eq. 2, since the a's are proportional to the p's. When dietary utilizations are known, a_{ik} in Eq. 5 must be replaced by n_{ik}/f_k, where n_{ik} is the number of items of resource k an individual of competitor i eats per unit time, and f_k is the standing relative abundance of resource k (74). Then the more similar the diets, the greater α; the smaller the standing frequency of a resource kind relative to its utilization, the greater its contribution to α.

While yielding intriguing results, to achieve tractability the mathematical theory of resource partitioning has had so far to ignore major kinds of biological variability. Most of its restrictive assumptions are too technical to give here. Rather, we can condense the major ones by stating that the theory is one of species with static niches or abilities. That is, the utilizations (p's), consumption rates (a's), and efficiencies (b's) vary neither with abundance of the resources nor with time. Yet often in reality individuals saturate with too much food (75), restrict the kinds of resources eaten when food is abundant (59), and apparently change their ability to perceive (76) and digest (77) resource kinds, depending on abundances. Aside from these adjustments of individuals, natural selection, with some lag, should change a species' utilization and efficiency parameters by redistributing its phenotypes (78). Niches that change in tandem with abundance of consumers and resources could lead to highly complicated systems behavior, including multiple equilibria and periodic rather than point equilibria. Nonetheless, in situations of tightest species-packing the niches themselves may approach some limiting form.

The most critical problem in applying the models is identification of resources in nature. Theorems have appeared for various model-systems stating that a necessary condition for coexistence of n consumers is that there be at least n resources (79). In what may well become a classic paper, Haigh and Maynard-Smith (80) examine the question of when population units can act as resources in the theorems. They conclude that, to act as resources, populations need only not be functionally dependent (81); for example, different parts of the same plant and different life stages of an insect species could be separate resources even if their abundances were highly correlated. One way to determine such units is to examine demographic properties of the prospective resources themselves. Another is to demonstrate or assume resource competition, then employ statistical techniques such as discriminant or multiway-contingency-table analysis (36, 82) to determine what axes and categories best separate consumer niches. Incidentally, the hoopla over resource identification has obscured what, from a resource's viewpoint, is an equivalent problem, and that is consumer identification. Indeed, in certain pollination systems, plants and insects seasonally reverse the roles of competitors and resources (83)!

Finally, an entirely different approach to interspecific habitat separation is to consider the habitat kinds as units within which species come to competitive equilibrium separately. This assumption would certainly be true were the habitat patches completely isolated from one another. But if individuals distributed their utilizations among habitats so as to balance their habitat-specific caloric benefits and costs, the assumption could be approximately met. Then spatial niches would not be static in population-dynamics time. The α's could be estimated by regression, with habitat-specific K's and $\hat{N}$'s being used as variables. Complementary occurrences of species among the habitats then could indicate the outcome of strong competition rather than the weak competition that Eq. 2 implies (70).

Cross-Community Comparisons

Another way to assess the importance of competition is to examine changes in properties of single species across communities. When such changes correlate with presence or absence of especially similar species, one may infer a causal relationship. When the properties are morphological, the changes are labeled character displacement (84); when they are ecological, the changes are labeled ecological shift (85).

Unfortunately, such simple comparisons fail to discriminate between changes resulting from competition and changes resulting from other mechanisms, such as reproductive isolation. Again, elaboration of predictions are required. For example, one can examine the modality of character change: characteristics especially effective for reproductive isolation, such as voice and plumage for birds, should differ from those most facilitating resource partitioning, such as bill and body size. Or one can ask whether the various mechanisms should always produce displacement. Interestingly, the answer for competition is no. Several models using population-dynamics equations like Eqs. 1 and 4 predict convergence for generalized feeders or homogeneous resources (33, 65). Another model, based on an optimal-feeding argument, predicts that a generalist species should shrink in size when contacting another, whether that other is larger or smaller. Thus, convergence should be associated with and only with shrinking, a prediction verified for *Anolis* lizards (see 59).

Interaction of Predation and Competition

The theory of how predation affects species differences and diversity is much less well-developed than is the theory for competition. Several major elements for the former have already appeared, however. (i) Predation in which the consumption rates per unit prey (the a's in Eqs. 4 and 6) are constant can reverse the outcome of competition among prey, whether that outcome be extinction or coexistence. For a wide range of parameters, however, such predation has no effect (86). (ii) Predation in which prey-specific consumption rate (a) monotonically decreases as that prey's relative abundance decreases and goes to zero as that prey vanishes allows prey species to coexist with greater α's and correspondingly lesser ecological differences (87). (iii) Prey when rare may evolve differences in appearance so as to escape predators whose prey-specific consumption rates vary with that prey's abundance (88). (iv) The premium placed on the consumer gaining energy quickly while feeding is set in part by the likelihood of the consumer being eaten while feeding (59). Hence predators may reinforce selection for feeding efficiency, including resource specialization, rather than obviate it.

To disentangle the possible effects of predation and to show how these effects interact with competition is now one of the major challenges of ecology. To discriminate between the effects described in (ii) and (iii), for example, again requires an examination of the modality of differences: differences relating to resource partitioning should decrease, whereas those relating to predator avoidance should increase. And whether competition or predation is dominant will depend on size and trophic position: herbivores (89) and small animals (90) are more likely to be regulated by predation than are secondary consumers and large animals. Most of the classical examples of slight ecological differences, such as Ross' leafhoppers (91), do seem to fit one or both of the two former categories. And large predatory animals, such as *Accipiter* hawks, kingfishers, and mustelids, provide classical cases of resource partitioning (15, 27, 92). But the tendency has yet to be investigated in detail.

Conclusion

To understand resource partitioning, essentially a community phenomenon, we require a holistic theory that draws upon models at the individual and population level. Yet some investigators are still content mainly to document differences between species, a procedure of only limited interest. Therefore, it may be useful to conclude with a list of questions appropriate for studies of resource partitioning, questions this article has related to the theory in a preliminary way.

1) What is the mechanism of competition? What is the relative importance of predation? Are differences likely to be caused by pressures toward reproductive isolation?

2) Are niches (utilizations) regularly spaced along a single dimension?

3) How many dimensions are important, and is there a tendency for more dimensions to be added as species number increases?

4) Is dimensional separation complementary?

5) Which dimensions are utilized, how do they rank in importance, and why? How do particular dimensions change in rank as species number increases?

6) What is the relation of dimensional separation to difference in phenotypic indicators? To what extent does the functional relation of phenotype to resource characteristics constrain partitioning?

7) What is the distance between mean position of niches, what is the niche standard deviation, and what is the ratio of the two? What is the niche shape?

References and Notes

1. G. E. Hutchinson, *Am. Nat.* 93, 145 (1959).
2. Based on data of Table 1, using studies from 1959 through 1972. Growth of papers during that period is exponential ($N_t = N_o e^{rt}$), with $r \simeq 0.25$ year^{-1}. In contrast, D. J. de Solla Price [*Little Science, Big Science* (Columbia Univ. Press, New York, 1963)] finds that exponentially growing scientific publications have $r \simeq 0.05$ to 0.07, a doubling time of about four times as long. Although the small interval of time (14 years) and the tendency to select newer studies for a review place the magnitude of the difference in question, the relation is quite regular and the true difference probably still substantial.
3. A. J. Lotka, *J. Wash. Acad. Sci.* 22, 461 (1932); V. Volterra, *Mem. R. Accad. Lincei Ser.* 6, II (1926).
4. G. F. Gause, *Struggle for Existence* (Hafner, New York, 1934).
5. J. Huxley, *Evolution, the Modern Synthesis* (Allen & Unwin, London, 1942); E. Mayr, *Systematics and the Origin of Species* (Dover, New York, 1942).
6. E. Mayr, *Ibis* 115, 432 (1973).
7. G. E. Hutchinson, *Cold Spring Harbor Symp. Quant. Biol.* 22, 415 (1957).
8. L. B. Slobodkin, *Growth and Regulation of Animal Populations* (Holt, Rinehart & Winston, New York, 1962).
9. R. G. Jaeger, *Ecology* 52, 632 (1971); B. A. Menge, *ibid.* 53, 635 (1972).
10. E. Nevo, G. Gorman, M. Soulé, S. Y. Yang, R. Clover, K. Javonović, *Oecologia (Berl.)* 10, 183 (1972).
11. J. H. Connell, *Ecology* 42, 710 (1961).
12. P. R. Grant, *Annu. Rev. Ecol. Syst.* 3, 79 (1972); R. F. Inger and B. Greenberg, *Ecol-*

ogy **47**, 746 (1966); D. H. Sheppard, *ibid*. **52**, 320 (1971); W. Sheppe, *Can. Field Nat*. **81**, 81 (1967).

13. J. R. Koplin and R. S. Hoffmann, *Am. Midl. Nat*. **80**, 494 (1968).
14. J. L. Menge and B. A. Menge, *Ecol. Monogr*. in press.
15. R. H. MacArthur, *Geographical Ecology* (Harper & Row, New York, 1972).
16. J. L. Harper [*Brookhaven Symp. Biol*. **22**, 48 (1969)] writes "the essentially similar requirements of all green plants—solar radiation, water, carbon dioxide, and a basic set of mineral nutrients—provide little opportunity for diversification in relation to food supply." Discussions of resource partitioning in plants are given by R. H. Whittaker [*Science* **147**, 250 (1965) and F. D. Putwain and J. L. Harper [*J. Ecol*. **58**, 251 (1970)].
17. Because it is of central interest to this article to rank dimensions in order of importance for separating species-pairs within groups, Table 1 excludes groups of two species, in which evaluation can be made for only one pair. I rank dimensions as follows. Usually, I prepare a matrix comparing all possible pairs of the species of interest, then ask for each pair whether they differ "significantly" (that usually being a matter of the author's opinion or particular comparative technique) in each of the dimensions investigated. Then for each dimension I total the number of pairs that differ significantly in that dimension, and rank the dimensions on the basis of that number. The method is similar to that of Lack (*18*), except he only counts that dimension most important in separating each pair, whereas I count all important dimensions for each pair. If only morphological indicators, such as size, are available, I total the number of pairs differing by at least a ratio of 1.33 [this procedure is a conservative one for estimating significant food differences (*19*, *20*)]. If numerical overlap values are available or can be calculated, I rank dimensions according to their average overlap values, the average being taken over all possible pairs. All dimensions are treated as if they were independent, not because they all are independent, but because dependence is hard to ascertain and to correct for in most studies. Grouping of dimensions under major headings was usually not difficult except for distinguishing macro- from microhabitat. This was especially hard in aquatic groups and is somewhat arbitrary.
18. D. Lack, *Ecological Isolation in Birds* (Harvard Univ. Press, Cambridge, Mass., 1972).
19. P. W. Price, *Ecology* **51**, 445 (1970); *ibid*. **53**, 190 (1972).
20. T. W. Schoener, *ibid*. **49**, 704 (1968).
21. E. R. Pianka, *ibid*. **50**, 1012 (1969).
22. R. A. Croker, *Ecol. Monogr*. **37**, 173 (1957).
23. N. P. Ashmole, *Syst. Zool*. **17**, 292 (1968).
24. R. T. Holmes and F. A. Pitelka, *ibid*., p. 305.
25. R. B. Root, *Ecol. Monogr*. **37**, 317 (1967).
26. E. J. Maly and M. P. Maly, in preparation.
27. T. W. Schoener, *Evolution* **19**, 189 (1965).
28. J. M. Diamond, *Science* **179**, 759 (1973).
29. T. W. Schoener, *Am. Nat*. **104**, 155 (1970).
30. ——— and D. H. Janzen, *ibid*. **101**, 207 (1968).
31. R. M. May and R. H. MacArthur, *Proc. Natl. Acad. Sci. U.S.A*. **69**, 1109 (1972).
32. R. Levins, *Evolution in Changing Environments* (Princeton Univ. Press, Princeton, N.J., 1968).
33. R. H. MacArthur, *Biol. Rev. (Camb.)* **40**, 510 (1965).
34. In fact, correlation coefficients for lizards are .400 and .536 (*35*), but these are less likely to be different from zero because of the smaller sample size.
35. T. W. Schoener, in *Biology of the Reptilia*. C. Gans, Ed. (Academic Press, New York, 1974).

36. ——— and A. Schoener, *Breviora* **368**, 1 (1970); T. W. Schoener, *Ecology* **51**, 408 (1970).
37. M. L. Cody, *Am. Nat*. **102**, 107 (1966).
38. B. K. Snow and D. W. Snow, *J. Anim. Ecol*. **41**, 471 (1972).
39. H. A. Hespenheide, *Ibis* **113**, 59 (1971).
40. P. E. Hillman, *Ecology* **50**, 476 (1969).
41. E. R. Pianka, paper presented at symposium for R. H. MacArthur, Princeton, N.J. (1973).
42. T. M. Zaret and A. S. Rand, *Ecology* **52**, 336 (1971).
43. A. Keast, in *Marine Food Chains*, J. H. Steele, Ed. (Oliver & Boyd, Edinburgh, 1970), p. 377.
44. G. A. Sandercock, *Limnol. Oceanogr*. **12**, 97 (1967).
45. T. W. Schoener, in preparation.
46. D. G. Broadley, *Zool. Afr*. **3**, 1 (1967).
47. R. T. Paine, *Ecology* **44**, 63 (1963).
48. R. F. Inger, *ibid*. **40**, 127 (1959).
49. M. L. Cody, *ibid*. **54**, 31 (1973).
50. J. M. Edington and M. A. Edington, *J. Anim. Ecol*. **41**, 331 (1972).
51. B. K. McNab, *Ecology* **52**, 352 (1971). However, Fleming *et al*. (*52*) found for Central America that this procedure crowds cells corresponding to small species, perhaps because of greater importance of habitat or food-species partitioning on the mainland.
52. T. H. Fleming, E. T. Hooper, D. E. Wilson, *Ecology* **53**, 555 (1972).
53. R. H. MacArthur and E. Pianka, *Am. Nat*. **100**, 603 (1966).
54. This argument is put into precise form as follows. Contingency models of optimal feeding specify that resource kind x should be added to a diet not including x, if and only if

$$(e_x/t_x) > (\sum_{\text{diet}} e_i p_i - C_s T_s)/(\sum_{\text{diet}} t_i p_i + T_s)$$

where p_i is the environmental frequency of food type i, e_i is the net energy gained from an item of type i once found, t_i is the time it takes to eat an item of food type i, T_s is the search time between two items of encountered food, C_s is the caloric cost per unit search time, and summations are over those item kinds actually eaten. Since the inequality does not contain p_x (nor in rearranged form does it contain the absolute abundance of type x), competitors that reduce item x's abundance do not affect choice. But if i indexes types of habitat patches, the situation is different. Then competitors by eating in particular patches can change the value of the e's and t's and thereby change the inequality's direction.
55. This subject is discussed in greater detail in T. W. Schoener, *Proc. Natl. Acad. Sci. U.S.A*., in press.
56. Significance determined by χ^2 or exact tests.
57. R. E. Ricklefs, *Evolution* **20**, 235 (1966); R. H. MacArthur, *Am. Nat*. **98**, 387 (1964).
58. Exact data on mean sizes of resources and consumers are generally not given in the references. Therefore, my classification is somewhat imprecise, and others would probably differ in the way they classified the data, but the trend is so strong that it would probably not be qualitatively affected.
59. T. W. Schoener, *Am. Nat*. **103**, 277 (1969); *Annu. Rev. Ecol. Syst*. **2**, 369 (1971).
60. H. L. Sanders and R. R. Hessler, *Science* **163**, 1419 (1969); P. K. Dayton and R. R. Hessler, *Deep-Sea Res*. **19**, 199 (1972).
61. R. R. Vance, *Ecology* **53**, 1062 (1972).
62. M. Lloyd and H. S. Dybas, *Evolution* **20**, 466 (1966).
63. C. Strobeck, *Ecology* **54** 650 (1973).
64. The terminology is that of nonlinear differential equations; an introduction very suitable for biologists is given in N. Keyfitz,

389

Introduction to the Mathematics of Population (Addison-Wesley, Reading, Mass., 1968).

65. R. H. MacArthur and R. Levins, *Am. Nat.* **101**, 377 (1967).
66. J. Roughgarden, *Theor. Pop. Biol.*, in press.
67. R. M. May, *Stability and Complexity in Model Ecosystems* (Princeton Univ. Press, Princeton, N.J., 1973).
68. J. Terborgh and J. M. Diamond, *Wilson Bull.* **82**, 29 (1970).
69. T. W. Schoener, *Theor. Pop. Biol.* **4**, 56 (1973).
70. ——, *ibid.*, in press.
71. R. S. Miller, *Ecology* **45**, 256 (1964); *Adv. Ecol. Res.* **4**, 1 (1967).
72. R. H. MacArthur, in *Population Biology and Evolution*, R. C. Lewontin, Ed. (Syracuse Univ. Press, Syracuse, N.Y., 1968).
73. Independently devised by MacArthur (*15*) and Schoener (*69, 70*).
74. A detailed discussion of this modified competition coefficient is given in T. W. Schoener, *Am. Nat.*, in press.
75. C. S. Holling, *Can. Entomol.* **91**, 385 (1959); *Mem. Entomol. Soc. Can.* **48**, 1 (1966).
76. L. Tinbergen, *Arch. Neerl. Zool.* **13**, 265 (1960).
77. R. T. Paine, personal communication.
78. J. Roughgarden, *Am. Nat.* **106**, 683 (1972). Roughgarden (unpublished manuscript) has recently modeled faunal buildup in which niche distance (*d*) undergoes evolutionary change between invasions. Then, the greater the number of species, the smaller *d*—the opposite of what is expected for species packed at limiting *d/w*.
79. S. A. Levin, *Am. Nat.* **104**, 413 (1970); A. Rescigno and I. W. Richardson, *Bull. Math. Biophys.* **27**, 85 (1965); A. Rescigno, *ibid.* **30**, 291 (1968).
80. J. Haigh and J. Maynard-Smith, *Theor. Pop. Biol.* **3**, 290 (1973).
81. In the sense that there exists a function *g* such that $g(x_1, x_2) = 0$, where x_1 and x_2 are the abundances of the two resources.
82. R. H. Green, *Ecology* **52**, 543 (1971); S. E. Fienberg, *ibid.* **51**, 419 (1970).
83. T. Mosquin, *Oikos* **22**, 398 (1971).
84. W. L. Brown and E. O. Wilson, *Syst. Zool.* **5**, 49 (1956); P. R. Grant, *Biol. J. Linn. Soc.* **4**, 39 (1972).
85. R. H. MacArthur and E. O. Wilson, *Theory of Island Biogeography* (Princeton Univ. Press, Princeton, N.J., 1967); J. Diamond, *Proc. Natl. Acad. Sci. U.S.A.* **67**, 529 (1970); A. Keast, *Biotropica* **2**, 61 (1970).
86. N. F. Cramer and R. M. May [*J. Theor. Biol.* **34**, 289 (1971)], trying to model R. T. Paine's results on predator removal in the intertidal zone [*Am. Nat.* **100**, 65 (1966)].
87. J. Roughgarden and M. Feldman, in preparation.
88. B. Clarke, *Syst. Assoc. Publ.* **4** (Taxonomy and Geography), 393 (1962); G. B. Moment, *Science* **136**, 262 (1962); A. S. Rand, *Atas do Simpósio sobre a Biota Amazônica* **5**, (Zoology), 73 (1967).
89. N. G. Hairston, F. E. Smith, L. B. Slobodkin, *Am. Nat.* **94**, 421 (1960).
90. D. S. Wilson, in preparation.
91. H. H. Ross, *Evolution* **11**, 113 (1957). But see D. E. Breedlove and P. R. Ehrlich, *Oecologia (Berl.)* **10**, 99 (1972); D. G. Dodds, *J. Wildl. Manage.* **24**, 52 (1960); P. J. Jarman, *Oecologia (Berl.)* **8**, 157 (1971).
92. B. K. McNab, *Ecology* **52**, 845 (1971); R. W. Storer, *Auk* **83**, 423 (1966).
93. E. G. Horn, *Ecology* **52**, 475 (1971).
94. N. G. Hairston, *Evolution* **12**, 440 (1958).
95. T. B. Reynoldson and R. W. Davies, *J. Anim. Ecol.* **39**, 599 (1970).
96. C. E. King, *Ecology* **43**, 515 (1962).
97. G. E. Hutchinson [*The Ecological Theater and the Evolutionary Play* (Yale Univ. Press, New Haven, Conn., 1965)] discussing B. Berzins' analysis.

98. R. O. Brinkhurst and K. E. Chia, *J. Fish. Res. Board. Can.* **26**, 2659 (1969).
99. C. P. Magnum, *Limnol. Oceanogr.* **9**, 12 (1964).
100. J. H. Stone, *Ecol Monogr.* **39**, 433 (1969).
101. A. J. Kohn, *ibid.* **29**, 47 (1959); *Limnol. Oceanogr.* **16**, 332 (1971).
102. ——, *Ecology* **49**, 1046 (1968).
103. D. J. G. Griffin, *J. Anim. Ecol.* **40**, 597 (1971).
104. V. T. Hammer and W. W. Sawchyn, *Limnol. Oceanogr.* **13**, 476 (1968).
105. D. C. Culver, *Ecology* **51**, 949 (1970).
106. D. N. Ueckert and R. M. Hansen, *Oecologia (Berl.)* **8**, 276 (1971).
107. E. B. Caplan, *Ecology* **47**, 1074 (1966).
108. W. A. Sands, *J. Anim. Ecol.* **34**, 557 (1965); *Entomol. Exp. Appl.* **4**, 277 (1961).
109. E. Broadhead, *J. Anim. Ecol.* **27**, 217 (1958).
110. A. M. Young, *Am. Midl. Nat.* **87**, 146 (1972).
111. N. Dawson, *J. Anim. Ecol.* **34**, 299 (1965).
112. C. A. Istock, *Evolution* **20**, 211 (1966).
113. R. E. Ricklefs, R. M. Adams, R. L. Dressler, *Ecology* **50**, 713 (1969).
114. D. C. Culver, *ibid.* **53**, 126 (1972).
115. H. Heatwole and D. M. Davis, *ibid.* **46**, 140 (1965).
116. R. V. O'Neill, *ibid.* **48**, 983 (1967).
117. H. W. Hurlbutt, *Syst. Zool.* **17**, 261 (1968).
118. C. A. Lanciani, *Ecology* **51**, 338 (1970).
119. P. S. Maitland, *J. Anim. Ecol.* **34**, 109 (1965).
120. R. N Gibson, *ibid.* **41**, 189 (1972).
121. N. G. Hairston, *Ecol. Monogr.* **19**, 47 (1949).
122. R. A. Avery, *Oikos* **19**, 408 (1968).
123. R. F. Inger and B. Greenberg, *Ecology* **47**, 746 (1966).
124. J. A. Moore, in *Genetics, Paleontology, and Evolution*, G. L. Jepsen, E. Mayr, G. G. Simpson, Eds. (Princeton Univ. Press, Princeton, N.J., 1949), p. 315.
125. W. W. Milstead, *Tex. J. Sci.* **9**, 410 (1957).
126. P. A. Medica, *Bull. South Calif. Acad. Sci.* **66**, 251 (1967).
127. A. S. Rand, *Ecology* **45**, 745 (1964); T. W. Schoener and A. Schoener, *Breviora M.C.Z.* **375**, 1 (1971).
128. R. B. Huey, thesis, University of Texas (1969).
129. D. W. Tinkle, *Tulane Stud. Zool.* **6**, 3 (1958).
130. C. C. Carpenter, *Ecol. Monogr.* **22**, 235 (1952).
131. J. Bédard, *Can. J. Zool.* **47**, 1025 (1969).
132. D. A. Jenni, *Ecol. Monogr.* **39**, 245 (1969).
133. P. J. S. Olney, *Trans. Congr. Int. Union Game Biol.* **6**, 309 (1963).
134. D. W. Johnston, *Auk* **88**, 796 (1971).
135. T. H. Hamilton, *Condor* **64**, 40 (1962).
136. R. H. MacArthur, *Ecology* **39**, 599 (1958).
137. G. H. Orians and H. S. Horn, *ibid.* **50**, 930 (1969).
138. B. K. Snow and D. W. Snow, *Auk* **88**, 291 (1971).
139. H. R. Pulliam and F. Enders, *Ecology* **52**, 557 (1971).
140. I. Newton, *Ibis* **109**, 33 (1967).
141. H. C. Heller and D. M. Gates, *Ecology* **52**, 424 (1971).
142. M. L. Rosenzweig and J. Winakur, *ibid.* **50**, 558 (1969).
143. L. N. Brown, *J. Mammal.* **45**, 189 (1964).
144. B. Lim, *ibid.* **51**, 730 (1970).
145. G. B. Schaller, *The Serengeti Lion* (Univ. of Chicago Press, Chicago, 1972).
146. T. H. Kunz, *J. Mammal.* **54**, 14 (1973).
147. R. M. May, in *Some Mathematical Problems in Biology* (American Mathematical Society, Providence, R.I., 1974), vol. 5.
148. I thank P. E. Hertz, R. B. Huey, J. Roughgarden, A. Schoener, R. L. Trivers, and E. E. Williams for criticism of an earlier draft of this article and R. B. Huey, A. Keast, E. J. Maly, R. M. May, B. A. Menge, J. L. Menge, E. R. Pianka, J. Roughgarden, and D. S. Wilson for access to unpublished material. Supported by NSF grant GB-37731X.

Lake Erie's Fish Community: 150 Years of Cultural Stresses

H. A. Regier and W. L. Hartman

Lake Erie's biotic community is not dead, although its condition is far from the healthy state that humans find most appealing. Fortunately, the reduction of various stresses, such as nutrient loading from metropolitan waste-treatment effluents, and the prevention of major new stresses, will permit the habitat and biota to recover many of their more desirable characteristics. In no event, however, will the recovery be complete; some taxa are extinct, new taxa have colonized the lake, and parts of the habitat have been irreversibly damaged. Millions of humans will continue to use Lake Erie directly and indirectly in many ways inimical to full recovery, despite our highest resolve and best collective efforts. But perhaps full recovery is not the ultimate goal; if, for example, it meant the return of mosquitoes in their original numbers, with the attendant epidemics of malaria, few of us would choose it.

We distinguish here between natural and cultural stresses. Natural stresses result from extreme or unusual manifestations of physical, chemical, and biological variables that are largely independent of man's activities; some examples are climatic warming or cooling and unseasonably heavy precipitation.

Dr. Regier is professor of zoology at the University of Toronto, Toronto 5, Ontario, Canada, and Dr. Hartman is investigations chief of the Lower Great Lakes Fisheries, U.S. Bureau of Sport Fisheries and Wildlife, Sandusky, Ohio 44870.

Cultural stresses, on the other hand, are the direct or indirect consequences of man's activities; two examples are commercial fishing and cultural eutrophication—the steady increase in nutrient supply that results from agricultural, industrial, and population growth in the drainage basin.

In this review we contrast primeval Lake Erie with Lake Erie today (Fig. 1), identify the major ecological stresses, consider the effects of the fishery and other cultural stresses on the lake's resources, explore the difficulties in managing common property resources, and outline current initiatives of fishery research and management.

Conflict between Nature and Culture

Lake Erie has changed greatly since 1669, when it was "discovered" by Louis Joliet; today more than 13 million people live in its watershed. Even in the late 1700's, when the human population was less than one-thousandth its present size, the land in the drainage basin still supported large stands of timber—primarily beech-birch, maple-hemlock, and oak-hickory associations. Interspersed were vast savannahs of grass and wild oats 2 to 3 meters high. Large marshes bordered the lake. The Great Black Swamp at the southwest corner of the lake was a wet forest of roughly a million hectares. Because of the thick vegetative cover, soil erosion

Reproduced with permission from *Science*, 180:1248–1255, 1973. Published by the American Association for the Advancement of Science, Washington, D.C.

was limited, runoff waters were generally clean and soft, stream and river bottoms were free of clayey silts, and marshes and protected shallow bays supported luxuriant aquatic vegetation. By 1870, most of the woodlands had been cleared, the savannahs burned, and some swamplands drained; these areas had been turned into rich farmlands (*1, 2*). Exposed soil was washed into rivers and inshore lake areas, and the increased deposits of clay and fine silt covered valuable spawning grounds of many species of fish such as the walleye and the lake whitefish. Aquatic vegetation in nursery marshes and bays declined. Nearly all the swamps were eventually drained in the early 1900's, which destroyed more spawning and nursery areas. Meanwhile, hundreds of mill dams impeded or blocked walleye, sturgeon, and other fishes from their traditional river spawning areas (*1*).

The quality of Lake Erie's water when its shores were first settled was solely the result of natural processes: organic and inorganic materials were leached from the watershed; water containing low concentrations of nutrient ions and organic substances flowed into Lake Erie from the upper Great Lakes; and precipitation contributed some ions and particles. Inflow rates of nutrients were relatively low. Most lake water was clear throughout the year, and free from blooms of algae. Today, nutrients that flow into the lake at high rates feed dense blooms of planktonic algae —especially the blue-green algae that are now so prevalent and obnoxious in late summer in the shallow western end of the lake. Death of the algae periodically reduces oxygen throughout the bottom waters of the lake, especially in the large Central Basin.

At the time of settlement, the great quantity and variety of fish inhabiting the lake and its tributaries included many of the larger, preferred food and game fishes—smallmouth and largemouth bass, muskellunge, northern pike, and channel catfish inshore; and lake herring, blue pike, lake whitefish, lake sturgeon, walleye, sauger, freshwater drum, and white bass in the open lake (*3*). Even lake trout maintained a moderate population in the eastern end of the lake. Some of these species moved into tributaries to spawn and were readily captured by Indians and the early settlers. Today, the blue pike, sauger, and native lake trout are gone; very few sturgeon, lake herring, lake whitefish, and muskellunge remain; and the numbers of walleye and northern pike are greatly reduced (*4*). The present fish community is dominated by yellow perch, white bass, channel catfish, freshwater drum, carp, goldfish, and rainbow smelt.

Ecological Stresses: Cultural and Natural

Obviously, Lake Erie, as well as many other great lakes of the world—Washington, Huron, Michigan, Ontario, Geneva, Maggiore, Vatter, and Constance (the Bodensee), has been adversely affected by man's activities (*5*). Consequently, the development of a general classification of cultural stresses on aquatic ecosystems is a matter of practical urgency. We distinguish here the following major cultural stresses in Lake Erie: the commercial fishery as a predatory process, in which the predator has been to some extent external to the system; cultural eutrophication; the introduction of, or invasion by, nonindigenous aquatic species; tributary and shoreline restructuring (for example, mill-dam construction and marsh drainage); turbidity and siltation caused by the continuing inflow of fine, inert materials; the release of toxic materials from industrial sources, vessels, and vehicles; and the unintended introduction of biocides.

No natural stress that has waxed and waned during the past 200 years has had a more profound, long-term, direct effect than any one of the above cultural stresses. Certainly a violent storm that causes a pronounced seiche may have marked effects on a system, some of which may persist for a considerable period. Short-term climatic effects are also widely recognized as being ecologically important. It has often been argued that a gradual increase of from 1° to 2°C in the average annual air temperature, recorded since about 1920 in the Lake Erie region (6), may have seriously stressed certain species of fish that approach their southernmost zoogeographic limits in this lake (7). For various reasons, we doubt that such natural stresses have been *primarily* responsible for most of the imbalance in the lake's ecosystem or in any major component of it. In the presence of pronounced cultural stresses, however, the severity of natural stresses may be compounded. Thus, if the spawning grounds of a species have been progressively reduced to a few vulnerable locations by intensive fishing or by environmental degradation, small climatic deviations may then lead to periodic failures of the reproductive process. Of course, climatic fluctuations alone may inhibit the reproductive process as well as reproductive success.

The Commercial Fishery

The commercial catch of fish from Lake Erie over the past 150 years has exceeded that of the other four Great Lakes combined. The fisheries for lake herring, lake whitefish, blue pike, and now yellow perch and rainbow smelt have been outstanding: total fish harvests have averaged about 9 kilograms per hectare per year.

The commercial fishery began after the War of 1812, while the south shore of Lake Erie was being rapidly settled and development of the north shore was advancing at a more deliberate pace. Subsistence fishing was practiced in the streams and coves of the lake. At the outset, populations of towns were small, the preferred species were readily caught, and transportation systems were inadequate; consequently, no market or commercial fishing of appreciable scope developed until about 1820. During the ensuing 70 years, however, social, economic, and technological developments were so rapid that the catches increased at an average rate of about 20 percent per year (Fig. 2). (The intensity of fishing—although not the size of the catches—continued to increase, with some minor dips, long beyond 1890, and probably did not peak until the late 1950's.)

Transportation was improved, and new markets were made available by the opening or improvement of canals: the Erie Canal linking the Niagara River at Buffalo and the Hudson River was completed in 1825, the Welland

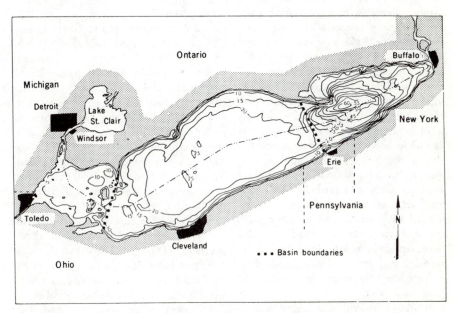

Fig. 1. Lake Erie, with depth contours shown in meters. Dashed lines separate the Central Basin from the Western and Eastern basins.

Canal which directly linked lakes Erie and Ontario was opened in 1829, and the Erie-Ohio Canal to the Maumee River upstream from Toledo was opened in 1832.

The efficiency of fishing gear improved rapidly during this early period. Before 1850, fishermen used hooks, seines, and small stationary gear, such as traps and weirs. Gill nets and pound nets first came into use in the 1850's. The American Civil War then spurred development of the Lake Erie fishery; gill nets and pound nets began to be used progressively further offshore, and by 1880 fishing gear was being operated throughout the lake.

The lake sturgeon was the species most seriously affected in the 1860's, as it became a serious problem to the early gill-net fishery, which was directed chiefly at lake trout, lake herring, and lake whitefish (8). Because the sturgeon was large (sometimes over 80 kg) and had external bony armor, it readily tore the nets set for smaller species. Fishermen then devised heavier nets with large mesh to capture sturgeon and destroyed the fish caught with them—often by piling them like cordwood on the beaches, dousing them with oil, and burning them. As this species grows slowly, does not mature until it is 15 to 25 years old, and is highly vulnerable to most fishing gear, it was rapidly reduced to commercial insignificance. Lake Erie fishermen saw no value in this fish until the 1860's, when an immigrant from Europe arrived with a knowledge of how to smoke it, render its oil, manufacture caviar from its eggs, and make isinglass from its air bladder. By 1870 the sturgeon had become a valued species, but also a much less abundant one. Although stream and marsh populations were probably damaged by other cultural stresses, some sturgeon spawned toward the eastern end of Lake Erie, where environmental conditions must have remained nearly ideal long after sturgeon had dwindled to insignificance. A few are still taken in commercial gear each year.

In the mid-19th century, construction of railroads released the fishery from its dependence on canal transport and greatly expanded the market for fish. The development of reliable methods of refrigeration soon reduced the need for smoking and salt curing. New fishing gear suited to nearshore and offshore waters were introduced from Europe and New England and modified for local conditions. Steamboats large enough to weather almost all Lake Erie storms began to operate, and steam power was also soon applied to the laborious task of setting and hauling gear (9). Capital investments were apparently large, and the industry gradually moved from a labor-intensive to a capital-intensive state; much of the capital was under the control of a relatively small number of American firms.

After the near destruction of the sturgeon population, the fishing for lake trout became excessively intense in the 1880's (10) and for lake whitefish about 1890 (11). Lake trout catches diminished rapidly. Lake whitefish and lake herring catches fluctuated for some decades, being supported in each case by a number of exceptionally large year classes, and ultimately became insignificant (Fig. 2).

The United States dominated the Lake Erie fishery until rather recently. In the early years, U.S. catches were much greater than those in Canadian waters (12) because of the earlier development of the fishery in the United States, some fishing by Ohio and New York fishermen in Canadian waters (originally with Canadian concurrence), and some direct offshore commerce between Canadian fishermen and dealers from the United States. Fishing in Canadian waters and the offshore commerce were officially discouraged beginning in the 1880's and largely discontinued by 1920, not without some objections from both sides of the border. Thereafter, U.S. dealers generally purchased Canadian catches at Canadian ports and transported them overland. (During the past two decades fishing in Lake Erie has been dominated by Canadians, in part because of lower labor costs, a more innovative industry, government price supports, and the greater stocks of marketable species in

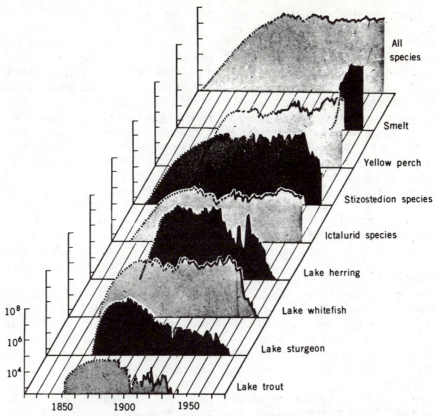

Fig. 2. Annual catches of selected species, and of all species combined, by the Lake Erie commercial fishery since 1820. The vertical scale is logarithmic. Continuous lines represent data reported annually by commercial fishermen, dashed lines represent less firm data that involve considerable interpolation, and dotted lines are based on a number of semiquantitative accounts. *Stizostedion* species include walleye, blue pike, and saugers; *Ictalurid* species include channel catfish and bullhead.

Canadian waters; in addition, the increasing popularity of water recreation has led to a substantial shift in user demands in U.S. waters.)

It was inevitable that undesirable economic and ecological effects would result from the combination of large markets, a technologically advanced fishery which had a free choice of fishing practices, unrestrictive regulations, and the lack of effective breeding programs to compensate for high rates of fish removal. As early as the 1890's, some U.S. fishing enterprises on Lake Erie collapsed because of low catch rates of preferred species. The intensity of fishing by other companies remained high, and the abundance of various species soon began to oscillate irregularly. During the 1890's a number of fishery experts worked strenuously for

regulations that would have effectively reduced fishing intensity. Some regulations were in effect by 1905, but full acceptance of stringent restrictions was impossible to achieve. The fish culturists' faith in their approach was pitted against the conservationists' faith in regulations.

The intense debate about stringent fishing regulations versus hatcheries in the period 1890 to 1910 apparently assisted anglers in their attempts to reserve certain species in U.S. waters as sport fish. In Lake Erie these species included smallmouth bass, largemouth bass, nothern pike, and muskellunge. Canadians lagged in this respect, partly because Ontario is well blessed with small inland lakes that satisfy local sportsmen and also because it has no large population centers on Lake Erie.

During the last half of the 19th century, with the new problems, new approaches to fishery management began to develop. Because of concern over the depletion of valued stocks in other areas and of lake trout and lake whitefish stocks in Lake Erie, a number of government fishery agencies were created in Canada and the United States in the 1860's and 1870's. Each state and province soon had its own agency, whose interests turned to the collection of catch statistics, fish culture, the introduction of new species of fish, catch regulations, and other methods of fishery management. A need for catch statistics was felt, not only because certain Lake Erie fishes were dwindling, but also because international disputes were developing on the Atlantic Coast and elsewhere in the 1870's. Governments concerned with potential disputes over Lake Erie apparently wished to have adequate data from which to bargain, and therefore created the agencies to collect them.

A voluminous literature on all aspects of fish and fisheries in Lake Erie documented these activities in the period 1870 to 1900. (By comparison the literature on activities during the 1900 to 1930 period is scant; modern fishery science in North America dates from about 1930.)

France in 1850 developed a new technology—the use of fish hatcheries—with the aim of improving the natural reproduction of fish (13). The glowing hopes of European fish culturists infected North Americans, including the Lake Erie fishermen, who knew even in 1870 that the most preferred fish were becoming increasingly difficult to take. Consequently, one of the first, and ultimately the most extended, responses of government agencies to falling catch rates in Lake Erie was the development of hatchery and fish stocking programs. Between 1867 and 1920, some 18 hatcheries were constructed on or near Lake Erie. They continued to operate for varying lengths of time, from a couple of years to half a century. All but one have been quietly phased out, because studies in various waters, including Lake Erie, failed to find evidence of significant returns from the stocking of fish fry.

A great enthusiasm for exporting and importing organisms was closely associated with the hatchery program. Many fish species were put into or taken out of Lake Erie. These early introductions were not preceded by careful study, nor were they subsequently monitored (14). The great majority failed completely, a few had catastrophic effects on the native fish population, others proved harmless, and some have been generally acclaimed as great successes.

During World War I, laissez faire and partial regulation were superseded by incentives to increase fish production. Fish prices rose, and the industry began to thrive.

Development of new gear and materials greatly increased fishing efficiency, partly by reducing the degree to which each gear was selective for a particular species. A very efficient, large, gill net—the so-called bull net—was introduced in 1905 and soon became widely used. Because of its efficiency, particularly in taking immature whitefish, the net was considered excessively wasteful. Between 1929 and 1934, its use was outlawed in one jurisdiction after another. The U.S. fisheries then became dominated by Ohio trap netters, who were more conservative in their fishing practices. The Canadians concentrated on the use of gill nets and pound nets.

The efficiency of gill nets, originally made of cotton or linen, improved markedly—by a factor of at least 2 or 3—when nylon materials were introduced in the early 1950's. Nylon had a further important advantage: because few microorganisms attack nylon, it is not necessary for fishermen to rack and dry the nets every few days. Consequently, effective fishing time per unit of gear also increased significantly.

When Canadian fishermen experienced high catch rates with nylon gill nets, Ohio fishermen increased their fishing effort with this new gear, without reducing the number of trap nets. The result was the most intensive fishing in Lake Erie's history for walleye, blue pike, and yellow perch in the mid- and late 1950's. By 1960, the stocks of blue pike and walleye had been depleted, and commercial catches in gill nets and trap nets consisted primarily of medium-value fish such as yellow perch, smelt, and white bass. Bottom trawling for smelt was successful in Canadian waters, and sizable landings of low-value fish such as carp, goldfish, and freshwater drum were made with haul seines in the shallow bays. Unfortunately, during the 1960's, large numbers of immature walleye continued to be caught in gill nets with the yellow perch and white bass. This added further stress to the depleted stocks of walleye (*15*).

Other Cultural Stresses

Another powerful cultural stress exerted on Lake Erie has been the nutrient loading of the aquatic environment from agricultural, industrial, and metropolitan sources. Its effects have differed considerably in different parts of the lake, because of differences in the morphometry of the three main basins and in their proximity to the sources of nutrients.

The Western Basin is the smallest and shallowest. It has an average depth of 7.4 m and encompasses only 13 percent of the total area of the lake and 5 percent of its volume. The many shoals and rocky reefs in this basin continue to be swept clean by storms, but deeper areas are filling with recent sediments. This basin has long been considered to have the most valuable fish spawning and nursery grounds in the lake and is the site of extensive boating, fishing, and other recreational activities. Because of its small size and proximity to the large urban areas of Detroit and Toledo, however, it has been especially vulnerable to pollution and nutrient loading. The Detroit River, for example, contributes 6×10^9 liters of industrial and domestic waste per day. This basin seldom stratifies thermally during the summer because of its small size and shallow depth and the large inflows from the Detroit, Raisin, and Maumee rivers.

The Central Basin is the largest. It averages 18.5 m in depth and has a large, flat, muddy plain at a depth of between 18 and 24 m. It makes up 63 percent of both the area and the volume of the lake. In contrast to the Western Basin, the Central Basin is deep enough so that it stratifies in summer, but not so deep that its bottom waters have a large reserve of dissolved oxygen at the onset of summer stratification, which is the period of isolation from atmospheric recharging.

The Eastern Basin has an average depth of 24.4 m and a maximum depth of 64 m. It encompasses 24 percent of the lake's surface area and 32 percent of its volume. Only here do the glacial relict, benthic populations of the opossum shrimp, *Mysis relicta,* and the burrowing amphipod, *Pontoporeia affinis,* persist in significant numbers. The Eastern Basin has received less sediment and nutrients than the other basins because most of the material that flows into the lake is deposited in the Western and Central basins.

Cultural eutrophication has caused several marked changes in Lake Erie. Among these is the great increase in total concentrations of most major ions over the past 50 years (*16*). Total dissolved solids have risen from 133 to 183 milligrams per liter, and concentrations of calcium, chloride, sodium plus potassium, and sulfate have risen by 8, 16, 5, and 11 mg/liter, respectively. The nutrient ions, nitrogen, and phosphorus, appear to have increased threefold since 1930.

The algae of Lake Erie have also undergone enormous changes (*17*). Average summer densities have increased only threefold, but the broad extension of spring and fall maximum densities are reflected in the nearly 20-fold increase since 1919 in the algal biomass produced annually. Qualitative changes have also occurred. Oligotrophic forms of *Asterionella* and *Synedra* once dominated the phytoplankton pulses in spring and fall; then the eutrophic *Melosira* and *Fragilaria* began to dominate the spring pulses, and by 1970 the fall pulses were dominated by three eutrophic blue-green algae—*Anabaena, Microcystis,* and *Aphanizomenon.*

The fallout of dead organic material

from greatly increased phytoplankton pulses has had profound effects on the bottom fauna. By 1953 the chemical oxygen demand in the sediments of the Western Basin was so high that after a 28-day period of calm weather in mid-summer, during which the water was thermally stratified, dissolved oxygen in the bottom waters dropped from the usual concentration of about 9 mg/liter to about 1 mg/liter (*18*). As a consequence, the dominant benthic form, the large burrowing mayfly, *Hexagenia*, which requires adequately oxygenated water for survival, was nearly eradicated (*19*). Nutrient loading continued, phytoplankton pulses enlarged, and oxygen demands in the sediments increased, until by 1963 only 5 days of hot, calm weather in summer were required for dissolved oxygen concentrations in bottom waters to drop to extremely low levels. *Hexagenia* has now been replaced primarily by oligochaetes and chironomids, which have a low oxygen tolerance.

The impact of nutrient loading and oxygen depletion on the fish community of Lake Erie has been most clear-cut in the Central Basin. Some reductions in hypolimnetic oxygen concentrations were first noted in 1929 in the heavily enriched southwest end, and by the late 1950's large areas of the basin's hypolimnion were becoming anoxic for weeks during mid- and late summer. The area and duration of hypolimnial anoxia has increased progressively since then (*20*). In the small, deep Eastern Basin, the oxygen in the cold bottom waters is only now reaching low concentrations in late summer.

The metalimnion and hypolimnion of the Central and Eastern basins were summer sanctuaries for many valued cold-water fishes—lake trout, lake herring, lake whitefish, and blue pike. During this century, catches of all these species have fluctuated greatly and all populations have declined to commercial extinction (the first three species) or possible biological extinction (the blue pike).

We suspect that the increasing fluctuations in the catches of these cold-water species have been due partly to year-to-year differences in oxygen regimes and algal food as the environment worsened because of accelerated eutrophication. The variability may also have been generated or reinforced by periodic intense predation (including cannibalism) by an occasional large year class (cohort) in succeeding year classes. The flexible, opportunistic, and intense fishing, which was already heavily stressing the fishery resources, probably acted in concert with the developing environmental stresses to increase the fluctuations in catches and extend them to a series of species.

Eutrophication of the Central Basin prior to 1900 should have caused a marked increase in the production of fish, accompanied by a gradual trend toward an increase in numbers of the more pelagic species. As the areas of low oxygen content increased, mobility of the fish should have increased, and this greater mobility should have brought about higher catch rates in stationary gear. Published catch statistics show that the largest catches usually immediately preceded the great declines. Abundance estimates based on these higher catch rates were probably excessive, however, when compared with those based on catch rates in earlier times of less environmental stress and normal fish mobility.

The major effect of eutrophication may have been a gradual restriction of suitable spawning, resting, and feeding habitats—a process that tended to make the affected species more vulnerable to other stresses. Thus the abundance of blue pike, whitefish, and lake herring, like that of lake trout and lake sturgeon, might eventually have become greatly reduced, even in the absence of fishing. If rainbow smelt (discussed below) had not invaded the lake, however, and if the fishing had been suitably regulated, it seems likely that all these preferred species would still be present in at least moderate numbers.

Although eutrophication of the Central Basin, together with intense fishing, has been implicated in the fluctuations and collapse of the dominant species in the hypolimnion, the analysis cannot end there. All these species also inhabited the Eastern Basin, which only now is approaching the degree of hypolimnetic anoxia that directly stresses mature fish. However, fishing and eutrophication were not responsible for the *final* collapse of the dominant fish populations. We suggest that the final collapse was caused by predation by smelt, cannibalistic interactions between year classes of blue pike, predation of blue pike on other species, and species desegregation (*21*)—all intensified by the effects of the fishery.

The rainbow smelt invaded Lake Erie around 1931. Its numbers increased rapidly in the late 1940's, and it became extremely abundant by 1951. Smelt generally occupy pelagic areas of Lake Erie down to the metalimnion during the summer thermal stratification in the Central and Eastern basins (*22*). Young smelt feed on plankton and crustaceans, and yearling and older smelt feed to some extent on small fish. By 1950, the stocks of lake whitefish and lake trout were greatly reduced, and during the late 1950's the blue pike and sauger had almost disappeared and the stocks of walleye were decimated. When predatory pressure on the smelt from trout, blue pike, and sauger was relieved, it became the most abundant fish in the pelagic area of central and eastern Lake Erie. Consequently, the predatory stress exerted on the young of other species by ever-increasing numbers of smelt during the 1950's and 1960's was a significant factor in the severe reduction or extirpation of the young of the remnant stocks of lake herring, sauger, blue pike, lake whitefish, and walleye (*15*).

The sea lamprey invaded Lake Erie via the Welland Canal (*23*) sometime before its first capture in 1921, but it has never become a serious parasite there. It appeared after the major losses of lake trout, lake sturgeon, and lake whitefish, although it probably killed some of each species. Of greater significance is the fact that spawning grounds for the sea lamprey in tributary streams are sharply limited; consequently, lampreys may never become a serious problem—even if the fish communities of Lake Erie are restructured to include

large numbers of salmonids, which are the favored prey of sea lampreys in other lakes (*24*).

An additional cultural stress on Lake Erie biota, of unknown effect, is that of toxic pollutants. Persistent biocides, toxic metallic materials, and various organic compounds are found in the flesh of fish in the lake. The discovery in walleye and white bass of concentrations of mercury higher than those deemed acceptable by the U.S. Food and Drug Administration and its Canadian counterpart has led to sharp restrictions in the commercial fishery in the Western Basin. Although the effects of the current levels of DDT, mercury, or selenium in Lake Erie fish on their growth, fecundity, and mortality are suspected to be small, research on this matter is far from complete.

Having mentioned a variety of cultural stresses, we now tentatively list them in order of their net effects on the fish community of Lake Erie, from greatest to least: an opportunistic, uncontrolled fishery; erosion and nutrient loading; invading species; stream destruction and shoreline restructuring; and toxic pollutants and biocides. The adverse effects of exploitation have been relatively sharp, whereas those of nutrient loading, for example, have developed slowly and subtly (although their damage to the fish community may recently have become fully as great).

Common Property Resources: Lake Erie and the Bodensee

When citizens share a resource, its management has generally been very difficult, especially when the responsibility has been divided between two or more jurisdictions. This situation has characterized the management of such resources as water, land, forests, and village commons (*25*)—and certainly the fishery resources of the Great Lakes. In Lake Erie, four U.S. states sovereign in these matters (Michigan, Ohio, Pennsylvania, and New York) and one Canadian province (Ontario), acting generally for Canada, share in the management of fishery resources. Although certain sedentary inshore populations, such as those of smallmouth bass and channel catfish, may rarely move across political boundaries, most of the valued fishes, like lake whitefish and walleye (and perhaps yellow perch), wander or migrate long distances, at least within each of the lake's basins.

Competition between jurisdictions for the same stock has complicated the usual problems of common property that occur within sovereign jurisdictions. The difficulty is further compounded when other users of the lake, like campers, swimmers, boaters, and water skiers, also demand high-quality aquatic resources. Additional complexities arise from the uses of Lake Erie for disposal of wastes, water level regulation, ship channel dredging, ship transport, and other activities that can produce harmful effects across boundaries.

Many attempts have been made, at state and at international levels, to develop institutional mechanisms to deal with the problem of managing Lake Erie as a resource; most have failed (26). No attempt has been effective enough to halt the progressive degradation of water quality. The Great Lakes Fishery Commission was established in 1955 to implement a program of sea lamprey control, to formulate and coordinate research programs, and to advise governments on measures to improve fisheries. Yet, regulatory powers remain vested with the various states and Canada, and these powers continue to be jealously guarded; consequently the few multilateral, international measures adopted have failed to adequately protect the common fishery resources in Lake Erie from overexploitation.

Some headway is being made towards regulating a number of transboundary processes inimical to water quality and fish habitat. The International Joint Commission was set up in 1911 to prevent disputes regarding the use of boundary waters and to settle other transboundary questions as they arose. The commission has frequently coordinated investigations by various agencies, and its recent activities have culminated in the "Agreement between Canada and the United States of America on Great Lakes Water Quality" of 15 April 1972. The announced objectives of this agreement were the protection and rehabilitation of the water quality of the Great Lakes, and programs were planned to operate within a specified time period. Although the agreement was signed by President Nixon and Prime Minister Trudeau, ratification and funding by the legislatures of the respective governments have yet to take place.

Lake Erie's degraded state is typical of that of many waters near population centers in North America. By way of contrast, we point to the rehabilitation of the Bodensee in central Europe, where international management of shared fishery resources and water quality has been more successful.

The Bodensee, the largest lake in Europe, is about 50 kilometers long, 10 km wide, and more than 252 m deep. On the southern edge of Germany, it is bordered by two German states, two Swiss cantons, and one Austrian state. The lake's most valuable commercial fish has been the Blaufelchen, a whitefish not unlike the lake herring of the Great Lakes.

Since World War II, industry, tourism, and the resident populace have all grown rapidly in the watershed of the Bodensee. The effluent wastes that were generated added greatly increased quantities of the chief algal growth agents, phosphorus and nitrogen, to the lake. Water quality of the Bodensee became degraded, and the valuable commercial fishery declined and was nearly lost (27).

In 1935, the Bodensee had not yet been seriously affected by cultural stresses: phosphorus was almost undetectable, and the nitrate level was about 600 micrograms per cubic meter; open-lake Blaufelchen were the most abundant commercial species, while yellow perch were confined to the shallow-water zones; and most of the Blaufelchen, which were more than 310 millimeters long and being caught in 38-mm mesh gill nets, were sexually mature and had already spawned once.

By 1963, cultural stresses had brought

about drastic changes: phosphate concentrations had reached 26 μg/m^3 and nitrate levels more than 800 μg/m^3; phytoplankton had increased 20-fold, and a late winter oxygen deficit at the bottom was beginning to occur; intensified fishing pressure, cultural eutrophication, and proliferation of yellow perch and roach in pelagic zones contributed to the decline of the Blaufelchen; both the growth rate of Blaufelchen and their length at maturity had increased, so that by 1960 few 310-mm Blaufelchen were sexually mature, and by 1963 almost none of them were; finally, the age of Blaufelchen in the catch had considerably decreased—whereas most Blaufelchen caught in 1935 were 5 years old, most taken in the 1950's were 2 to 3 years old, and nearly 80 percent of those caught in the early 1960's were less than 2 years old.

The crisis for Blaufelchen and the commercial fishery had obviously arrived by 1963. As recently as 1956, the catch of Blaufelchen was 839,000 kg, but by 1963 it had dwindled to 100,000 kg—the lowest recorded catch since the recording of catch statistics began in 1922. Of even greater gravity was the virtual absence of sexually mature fish among those taken during the 1963 fall fishing season. Nearly all of the more rapidly growing Blaufelchen were being caught before they reached sexual maturity. The Blaufelchen was headed toward complete collapse.

The International Commission for the Bodensee Fishery, at its annual meeting in 1963, heard the International Biological Subcommission recommend the closing of the Blaufelchen fishery in 1964 and an increase in the gill net mesh size to 43 mm, a size in which Blaufelchen of a minimum length of about 350 mm can be caught. After the 1-year moratorium, 400,000 kg of Blaufelchen were caught in 1965, and the catch has slowly increased since then. The age of fish in the catch has increased and the proportion of sexually mature Blaufelchen in the catch has climbed sharply.

The International Water Protection Commission for the Bodensee recom-
mended in the 1960's that the discharge of pollutants into the lake be limited uniformly. All bordering states and cantons have enlarged their mechanical and biological sewage treatment works. In addition, chemical plants are being constructed that will soon eliminate 90 percent of the phosphorus entering the lake in domestic wastes.

This example of successful multilateral international coordination of fishery and water management, with biological evidence and recommendations contributed by scientific advisors, complements a very few successful multilateral programs for marine fish and mammals. The jurisdictional mechanisms needed to duplicate this program in the Great Lakes of North America are available. Only the requisite resolve and action by the responsible parties is lacking.

Fishery Research Initiatives

There is, of course, general agreement that species interact in Lake Erie, that environmental changes may favor a new species over an established one, and that great reductions in one species because of overexploitation or other stresses can favor proliferation of less intensely stressed species. Yet, most fishery research on Lake Erie to date has dealt with single-species problems, or with a particular variety of stress. This type of research will always be necessary. But we infer from the story of Lake Erie and similar lakes (5) that broader and more comparative studies of the structure and dynamics of ecosystems are necessary if we are to achieve the insight into the roles of cultural and natural stresses required for predicting the consequences of fishery and environmental management. We need to understand the *mechanisms* that control the flow of energy and material within ecosystems under growing or diminishing stresses.

The environmental degradation of Lake Erie and its effect on the fishery resources has resulted in other new research. Concentrations of such contaminants as mercury, DDT, and polyvinyl chlorides in the flesh of fish will continue to be monitored. Other contaminants may be added to the list. The trophic paths taken by these contaminants must be understood so that it will not be necessary to treat each one as unique.

The historical sequence of eutrophication in western Lake Erie is generally agreed upon, but more analyses of the Central Basin are needed. The rate of healing—the reversal of the stress sequence which should follow intensive international programs for the abatement of nutrient loading and water pollution—can then be more accurately predicted.

The fish community will respond to pollution abatement. Oligotrophication—the recovery process that will accompany substantial reductions in nutrient loading from metropolitan waste effluents—is now under way in a series of lakes in Europe and North America (28). Continued and expanded monitoring of the abundance, distribution, and biological characteristics of fish species is critically necessary for making short-term predictions. During oligotrophication, the recovery sequences in Lake Erie can be compared with those in similar lakes to provide broad inferences about the characteristics and rates of response of the ecosystem (29).

Finally, much research remains to be done to provide a firmer basis for an interpretation of present surveys and analyses. Historical studies can be done in archives and libraries; biological samples from earlier years now stored in museums and laboratories have not been fully examined; and more historical samples are still in the sediment layers of the lake.

Fishery Management Initiatives

Fishery management initiatives in Lake Erie are being shaped by the forces of cultural stress on the environment and fishery resources of the lake; by the growing demands for use of the resources by sport fishermen, especially in U.S. waters; and by the proposed massive lake cleanup.

The current management objective in Lake Erie is not full restoration of historical fish communities. Such restoration is impossible for several reasons: (i) Viable spawning populations of certain valued fish cannot be easily reestablished because lake tributaries are blocked by dams or silted in, marshes have been destroyed by drainage, and many inshore lake spawning grounds have been covered with silt. (ii) Predation by rainbow smelt (now the most abundant pelagic species of fish) would probably inhibit restoration of lake whitefish and lake herring, or a percid like the blue pike if it were to be introduced. (iii) The existing large populations of freshwater drum (the most abundant nonpelagic species in western Lake Erie), carp, and goldfish might effectively resist the reintroduction of such species as northern pike, lake whitefish, and lake herring.

The current management objective, on the other hand, is the conservation of existing valued species, such as the walleye, yellow perch, and white bass, and an effective restructuring or engineering of new fish communities.

Recreational angling is expanding rapidly in U.S. waters. Competition for certain species—particularly walleye—between American anglers and commercial fishermen from both the United States and Canada is reaching serious proportions. Canadian anglers are also beginning to develop an interest in Lake Erie. Nevertheless, a viable commercial fishery worth millions of dollars still persists in the lake. Perhaps fishery management agencies will further modify their laissez-faire policies. For several decades, they maintained that no regulation was justified unless the need in a particular system was convincingly shown. Their stance was buttressed by an unwillingness to consider fully the data and inferences from Lake Erie and similar lakes, and changes in policy came slowly. But some regulatory measures are being reinstated. Obviously, all fishery managers must be cognizant of, and respond to, the shift in user demands toward angling in both American and Canadian waters.

To respond to the increased demands of anglers, the American states have released hundreds of thousands of fingerling Pacific salmon in Lake Erie—coho since 1968 and chinook since 1971. The results have been mildly encouraging. Growth has been satisfactory, and some mature adults have returned to the streams where they were released, along the south shore of the lake. Yet an open-lake sport fishery has not developed in U.S. waters. Evidently the salmon move north in the summer into Canadian waters, where they remain at depths of about 15 to 20 m, in the coldest waters that still have adequate oxygen. A problem is that some of these salmon are caught by commercial fishermen, particularly in Canadian waters. One proposed solution is regulation of the fisheries so that these salmon are unlikely to be caught. This proposal has not been popular with Ontario fishermen, however, because it might severely restrict Canadian landings of other species.

Species other than the Pacific salmon are being considered as replacements for fish that have been severely reduced or lost during the past century due to cultural stress. Lake trout, steelhead trout, and striped bass lead the list. The abundance of these fish, with the possible exception of striped bass, can be closely regulated by adjustments in stocking because natural spawning areas for such fish are now virtually absent in the lake and its tributaries.

Massive U.S. and Canadian programs to reduce nutrient loading from municipal sewage and detergents have already begun. Reduction of air pollution has already diminished outfall into the lake. If programs proposed in the water quality agreement signed in April 1972 by the United States and Canada are supported by the respective legislatures and adequately funded, the water quality of Lake Erie will improve markedly within the next decade or so. The initial goal of a reduction in nutrient loading is to reduce plankton production sufficiently to ensure that the oxygen in the Central Basin's bottom waters is not reduced to nil in the late summer. Higher standards may be necessary if a satisfactory response by the fish community is to be assured. Once the cold bottom water again becomes available to cold-water fish during the summer, a more desirable fish community may be possible.

Epilogue

With the advent of oligotrophication in Lake Erie, our partial understanding of the effects of 150 years of eutrophication should prove useful in defining variables to be monitored and in making short-term and long-term predictions. Fish are in many ways integrators of our insults to their environment. A clearer understanding of the separate and joint effects of cultural and natural stresses is now developing.

Fisheries, whether recreational or commercial, must be regulated in a way that is meaningful in an ecological, as well as a social, context. The operative principal of recent decades—that very simple regulations with an absolute minimum of constraints are best—is now thoroughly discredited. International and interstate regulatory mechanisms must be strengthened and supported; the tragedies that have resulted from laissez-faire management must be averted in the future.

The separate and joint ecological implications of the demands of various users on Lake Erie must be more clearly identified. Some demands are inconsistent with others, and thus some must be ruled inappropriate. Large amounts of toxic industrial wastes and plant nutrients from domestic sources cannot be accommodated in the future. Many other uses can be fitted together, sometimes in mutually beneficial ways. Recreational and commercial fisheries should be complementary; enlightened and energetic fishery managers can develop regulations to make them so.

In general, the opportunities to use Lake Erie will increase when the opportunism of those who have abused the lake in the past is effectively constrained, and when all agencies involved in protection, wise use, and enhancement of the fishery and associated aquatic resources move forward together in the task with far greater resolve and cooperation than ever before.

References and Notes

1. M. B. Trautman, *The Fishes of Ohio* (Ohio State Univ. Press, Columbus, 1957), p. 683.
2. T. H. Langlois, *Portage River Watershed and Fishery* (Publication IV-130, Ohio Division of Wildlife, Toledo, 1965), p. 22.
3. W. L. Hartman, *J. Fish. Res. Bd. Can.* **29**, 899 (1972).
4. ———, *The Explorer* **12**, 6 (1970).
5. *J. Fish. Res. Bd. Can.* **29** (No. 6) (1972), pp. 611–986.
6. A. M. Beeton, *Trans. Amer. Fish. Soc.* **90**, 153 (1961).
7. G. H. Lawler, *J. Fish. Res. Bd. Can.* **22**, 1197 (1965).
8. W. J. K. Harkness and J. R. Dymond, *The Lake Sturgeon* (Ontario Department of Lands and Forests, Toronto, 1961), p. 121.
9. V. C. Applegate and H. D. Van Meter, *U.S. Fish. Wildl. Serv. Fish. Leafl. 630* (1970), p. 1.
10. J. Moenig, "The lake trout of Lake Erie," manuscript, Univ. of Toronto Library, Toronto, Ontario, 1972.
11. G. B. Goode, *The Fisheries and Fishery Industries of the United States* (Government Printing Office, Washington, D.C., 1884), p. 895; C. M. Keyes, *U.S. Fish. Comm. Bull.* **13**, 349 (1893); W. B. Scott, *Contrib. Royal Ont. Mus. Zool.* **32**, 1 (1951).
12. N. S. Baldwin and R. W. Saalfeld, *Great Lakes Fish. Comm. Tech. Rep. 3* (1962), p. 1; *ibid.* (1970), supplement.
13. H. A. Regier and V. C. Applegate, *J. Fish. Res. Bd. Can.* **29**, 683 (1972).
14. K. H. Loftus, Ed., *A Symposium on Introductions of Exotic Species* (Research Report 82, Ontario Department of Lands and Forests, Toronto, 1968), p. 111; W. J. Christie, J. M. Fraser, S. J. Nepszy, *J. Fish. Res. Bd. Can.* **29**, 969 (1972).
15. H. A. Regier, V. C. Applegate, R. A. Ryder, *Great Lakes Fish. Comm. Tech. Rep. 15* (1969), p. 101.
16. A. M. Beeton, *Limnol. Oceanogr.* **10**, 240 (1965).
17. C. C. Davis, *ibid.* **9**, 275 (1964).
18. J. F. Carr, *Great Lakes Res. Div. Publ. 9* (1962), p. 1.
19. ——— and J. K. Hiltunen, *Limnol. Oceanogr.* **10**, 551 (1965).
20. H. H. Dobson and M. Gilbertson, in *Proceedings of the 14th Conference on Great Lakes Research* (International Association for Great Lakes Research, Ann Arbor, Mich., 1971).
21. H. A. Regier, in *Proceedings of the 11th Conference on Great Lakes Research* (International Association for Great Lakes Research, Ann Arbor, Mich., 1968).
22. W. R. MacCallum and H. A. Regier, *J. Fish. Res. Bd. Can.* **27**, 1823 (1970).
23. H. D. Van Meter and M. B. Trautman, *Ohio J. Sci.* **70**, 65 (1970).
24. S. H. Smith, *J. Fish. Res. Bd. Can.* **29**, 717 (1972).
25. G. Hardin, *Science* **162**, 1243 (1968).
26. H. R. Gallagher and J. Van Oosten, in *Proceedings of the International Board of Inquiry for the Great Lakes Fisheries* (Government Printing Office, Washington, D.C., 1943), p. 213.
27. W. Nümann, *J. Fish. Res. Bd. Can.* **29**, 833 (1972).
28. E. Grimaldi and W. Nümann, *ibid.*, p. 931.
29. A. M. Beeton and W. T. Edmondson, *ibid.*, p. 673; P. J. Colby, G. R. Spangler, D. A. Hurley, A. M. McCombie, *ibid.*, p. 975; H. A. Regier and H. F. Henderson, *Trans. Amer. Fish. Soc.* **102**, 56 (1973).
30. We thank P. H. Eschmeyer, N. E. Fogle, R. Hile, R. B. Kenyon, K. H. Loftus, S. J. Nepszy, R. L. School, W. F. Shepherd, S. H. Smith, and H. D. Van Meter for reviewing the manuscript and making suggestions.

RELATIVE STABILITY OF MINERAL CYCLES IN
FOREST ECOSYSTEMS[*]

Carl F. Jordan,[†] Jerry R. Kline,[†] and Donald S. Sasscer[‡]

Mineral cycling is the term used to describe the movement of certain materials into, through, and out of an ecosystem. These materials are the elements of the periodic table, and although the cycles are described in terms of the element studied, the material does not cycle in elemental form. Nevertheless, it has been convenient to analyze ecosystem compartments and flows between compartments for an element of interest, and describe a cycle of just that particular element.

There are many descriptive studies of mineral cycles, and one notable work (Rodin and Bazilevich 1967) synthesizes terrestrial studies into a world picture. There also has been some experimental work on mineral cycling, such as that of Likens et al. (1970), who looked at changes in element cycles following deforestation. However, very little is known about the properties of the mineral-cycling systems themselves. Patten and Witkamp (1967) analyzed a microcosm's cesium system, but studies of the properties of natural mineral cycling systems are virtually nonexistent.

Here we measure and compare the stability of various forest mineral-cycling systems, analyze some hypothetical systems to determine what factors control stability, and then relate these factors to our empirical results.

STABILITY

Steady-state systems can be either stable, unstable but bounded, or unstable. Each of these three types of systems reacts differently to a perturbation of the steady state. A stable system returns monotonically (fig. 1, line A) or with decreasing oscillations (fig. 2, line A) toward the steady state. An unstable system continues to depart from steady state, either monotonically (fig. 1, line C) or with increasing oscillations (fig. 2, line C). An unstable but bounded system either assumes a new steady-state level (fig. 1, line B) or oscillates, but the amplitude of the oscillations remains constant (fig. 2, line B).

Mineral cycles in ecosystems which remain intact are all monotonically

* Work performed under the auspices of the U.S. Atomic Energy Commission.

† Radiological Physics Division, Argonne National Laboratory, Argonne, Illinois 60439.

‡ Department of Nuclear Engineering, University of Puerto Rico, Mayaguez, Puerto Rico, and Division of Nuclear Engineering, Puerto Rico Nuclear Center, Mayaguez, Puerto Rico.

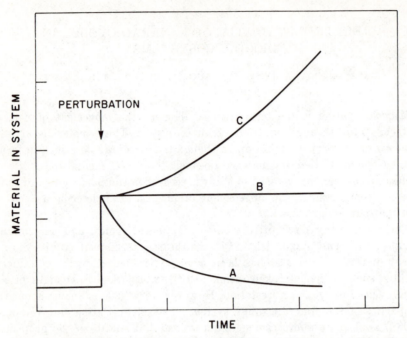

Fig. 1.—Response of a stable system (line *A*), unstable system (line *C*), and an unstable but bounded system (line *B*) to a perturbation. Systems respond monotonically.

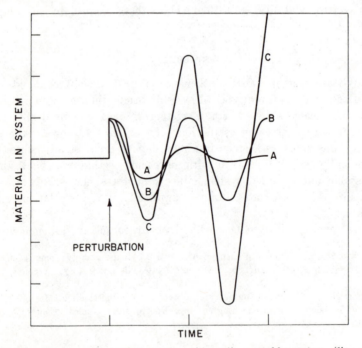

Fig. 2.—Response of a stable system (line *A*), unstable system (line *C*), and an unstable but bounded system (line *B*) to a perturbation. Systems respond by oscillating.

stable (fig. 1, line A). For example, if ^{90}Sr is deposited via fallout on a climax forest at levels which do not interfere with growth and metabolism, the amount of isotope in each ecosystem compartment returns toward zero asymptotically. If the ecosystem does not remain intact, as was the case when a portion of the Hubbard Brook Forest was deforested (Likens et al. 1970), then mineral cycling systems may become unstable. Here we are concerned only with the stability of intact ecosystems.

When all systems under investigation are basically stable, the problem of measuring relative stability arises. Our measure of relative stability is based on the equation of Patten and Witkamp (1967), which is

$$S = \left(\frac{x_j(\text{eq})}{\Delta x_j} \right) \left(\frac{\delta_j t}{\Delta_j t} \right) \tag{1}$$

where S = relative stability, $x_j(\text{eq})$ = the equilibrium amount of material in a compartment, Δx_j = the perturbation in the same units as the equilibrium amount, $\delta_j t$ = the duration of the perturbation, and $\Delta_j t$ = the time for a compartment to return to original equilibrium.

We modify this equation in two ways. (1) Instead of letting x_j equal the amount of material in a given compartment, we let it equal the total amount of material in the entire system. Thus we measure the stability of entire systems, whereas Patten and Witkamp measured the stability of individual compartments. (2) In order to compare systems, Δx should be the same proportion of x in all systems. Stability then depends on the ratio of length of time of perturbation (δt) to length of time to recover after perturbation (Δt). However, for a fixed ratio $x/\Delta x$, δt depends on the rate at which the perturbation is introduced into the system. To eliminate the effect of varying perturbation rates, we introduced a third term, the ratio of the perturbation rate to the steady-state input.

Our equation for relative stability then is

$$S = \left[\frac{r(\text{pert})}{r} \right] \left[\frac{x}{\Delta x} \right] \left[\frac{\delta t}{\Delta t} \right], \tag{2}$$

where S = relative stability, $r(\text{pert})$ = perturbation rate, r = steady-state input, x = total amount of material in the steady-state system, Δx = total perturbation, δt = duration of the perturbation, and Δt = time for the system to return to steady state.

For convenience, Δx always equals $0.05x$, and $[r(\text{pert})/r]$ always equals 10.0. With $x/\Delta x$ and $[r(\text{pert})/r]$ thus fixed, stability depends only on the ratio $\delta t/\Delta t$. If this ratio is relatively high, that is, if recovery time is short compared with perturbation time, the system has a high stability. A high-stability system returns quickly to its initial state. Conversely, if the ratio $\delta t/\Delta t$ is relatively low (i.e., if recovery time is long compared with perturbation time), the system has a low stability. Low-stability systems require a long time to return to their initial state.

Because any steady-state system which is perturbed returns to its initial state asymptotically following cessation of the perturbation, we arbitrarily assume that steady state is reached when the amount in the system is within 1% of the steady-state value.

The cycling system of elements which do not occur in gaseous form is abstracted into a steady-state four-compartment model (fig. 3); we determined stabilities of these systems following a perturbation of the steady state.

Aside from our own mineral-cycling studies, we found no report which quantified input, output, and a complete internal cycle, as in figure 3, in a steady-state forest ecosystem. However, two studies give data that fit our model provided a few assumptions are made. (1) Cole, Gessel, and Dice (1967) reported input, output, and internal cycling over a short period of time for a nonlinear system in which the wood compartment was increasing. We use their data by modifying it to represent a steady-state system. (2) Bormann and Likens (1970) reported a cycle very close to steady state. Output was only 2.5% greater than input. We modify their data to achieve steady state. These authors reported only total vegetation data, rather than leaf and wood compartments as required in our model. Therefore we divide total vegetation into leaves and wood, using a proportion calculated from deciduous temperate-zone trees (Rodin and Bazilevich 1967). We also assume that, in Bormann and Likens's data, the flux from trees to litter was

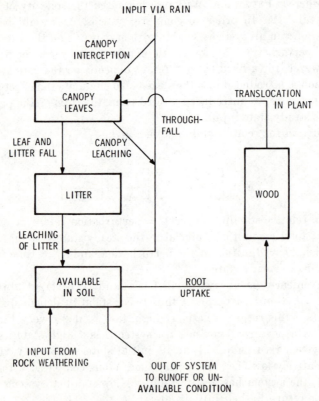

Fig. 3.—Block diagram of cycling system of elements which do not occur in gaseous form. Of the input flux via rain, 16% is intercepted by the canopy, and 84% moves directly to the soil. Material moves out of the soil compartment via runoff for most of the elements studied, but for iron, manganese, and cesium, movement is to an unavailable condition. Jordan, Kline, and Sasscer (1971) give details of systems measurements and model construction.

equal to flux from litter to soil, and that flux from wood to leaves was equal to flux from soil to wood.

Compartmental content, flow rates between compartments, and input and output fluxes for the systems analyzed are shown in table 1. These data were used to derive the transfer coefficients described below.

One other system was analyzed, for which compartmental contents and flow rates were not available, but for which transfer coefficients were available (table 2).

MATHEMATICAL FORMULATION

The rate of change of amount of material in a compartment is equal to the difference between the rates at which the element enters and leaves the compartment. The net flux for n compartments of an ecosystem may be represented by n simultaneous linear differential equations:

$$DX_j(t) = \sum_{\substack{i=0 \\ i \neq j}}^{n} \lambda_{ij} X_i(t) - \sum_{\substack{i=0 \\ i \neq j}}^{n} \lambda_{ji} X_j(t) \qquad j = 1, 2, 3, \ldots n, \qquad (3)$$

where subscripts $1, 2, 3, \ldots n$ and 0 designate compartments of the ecosystem and a compartment outside the ecosystem, respectively; X = amount of material per unit area in a compartment at any time t; and λ_{ij} = transfer coefficient for element from compartment i to compartment j.

Each transfer coefficient was calculated from the equation

$$\lambda = \frac{f}{X}, \qquad (4)$$

where f = flux of material out of a compartment, and X = amount of material in the compartment from which the flux originates. Values of f and X are from steady-state cycles (table 1).

A program for the analytical solution to equation (1) was written for the Argonne IBM 360-50/75 computer. Input to the program is in three parts: (1) an (n,n) transfer matrix $||\lambda_{ij}||$, which gives routes and permits computation of the flux of material between compartments; (2) transfer coefficients from inside to outside the system λ_{i0}, $i = 1, 2, 3, \ldots n$; and (3) the flux from a compartment outside the ecosystem (X_0) into compartment i, f_{0i}.

For every input, the program solves the series of equations and evaluates compartmental content at any desired time interval. The amount in the entire system at any time is simply the sum of the compartmental contents at that time.

RESULTS

Relative stabilities of various systems vary from a low of 0.59 for calcium in the Puerto Rican rain forest to a high of 1.34 for cesium in the rain forest (table 3), when the perturbation is positive and 5% of the total amount in the system, and when the perturbation rate is 10 times the steady-state input rate. The response of the calcium system, which has a relative stability similar to most of the other element systems in table 3, and of the cesium system are compared in figure 4. The durations of the perturbations (δt) are similar in both cases. It is primarily the recovery time

TABLE 1
MINERAL-CYCLING DATA USED IN STABILITY ANALYSIS

TYPE OF ECOSYSTEM AND ELEMENT STUDIED	COMPARTMENTAL CONTENT (kg/ha)				FLUX (kg/ha/yr)								
	Leaves	Litter	Soil	Wood	In Via Rain	In Via Rock Weathering	Leaf and Litter Fall	Stem Flow and Through Fall	Litter to Soil	Litter to Wood	Soil to Wood	Runoff from Soil	Wood to Leaves
Northern hardwoods, New Hampshire:*													
Calcium	40	1740	690	530	2.6	9.4	40	9.7	40	0.0	49.3	12.0	49.3
Douglas fir, Washington State:†													
Calcium	73	137	741	260	2.8	1.7	11.1	2.2	11.1	0.0	12.9	4.5	12.9
Potassium	62	32	234	158	0.8	0.2	2.7	11.7	2.7	0.0	14.2	1.0	14.2
Tropical rain forest, Puerto Rico:‡													
Calcium	55	11	176	380	21.8	21.3	49.9	13.00	49.9	0.0	59.3	43.1	59.3
Potassium	24	1	31	143	18.2	2.6	2.1	136.8	2.1	0.0	135.7	20.8	135.7
Magnesium	26	6	155	95	4.9	10.1	12.0	4.3	12.0	0.0	15.6	15.0	15.6
Sodium	21	1	156	218	57.2	7.3	4.2	26.0	4.2	0.0	20.8	64.5	20.8
Iron	1.3	23.6	28.5	9.6	0.0	0.10	1.10	1.09	1.14	0.0	2.24	0.10	2.24
Manganese	3.4	0.6	3.4	15.2	0.04	0.00	2.26	0.16	0.17	2.09	0.33	0.04	2.41
Copper	0.08	0.10	0.19	0.59	0.68	0.00	0.05	0.47	0.05	0.0	0.42	0.68	0.42
Strontium	0.39	0.12	8.86	4.17	0.14	0.02	0.33	0.10	0.33	0.0	0.41	0.16	0.41

* Information for New Hampshire from Bormann and Likens (1970).
† Information for Washington State from Cole et al. (1967). Data modified to obtain steady-state conditions (see text).
‡ This is the first finished presentation of the complete Puerto Rican mineral-cycling data. Compartment concentrations, flow rates, and litter and soil masses are from Jordan (1969). Biomass of leaves and wood are from Ovington and Olson (1970). Concentration times compartment mass yields total compartmental content.

TABLE 2
TRANSFER COEFFICIENTS FOR CESIUM THROUGH THE TROPICAL RAIN FOREST*

Flux	Transfer Coefficient
Canopy to litter†	0.59
Litter to soil†	0.53
Soil to wood‡	0.01
Available in soil to unavailable in soil§	0.99
Wood to canopy	0.0057‖

* To obtain a steady-state cycle with these transfer coefficients, input and output rates per year must have a value of 3.5 times greater than the total steady-state amount in the canopy.
† From Kline (1970).
‡ From Kline and Mercado (1970).
§ From Jordan (1970).
‖ When the ratio of cesium in wood to cesium in leaves is the same as the ratio for potassium (from table 1), the wood-to-canopy transfer coefficient must have this value for the wood compartment to remain in steady state.

(Δt) after the perturbation ceases which determines the relative stability in these two cases. Rate of return to steady state is slower for the calcium system than for the cesium system; consequently, the calcium system has a lower relative stability.

Changing sizes, rates, and signs of perturbations change the absolute values of stabilities but not their relative sizes. For example, in table 3, stability of the cesium is approximately twice that of the copper system. If the perturbation is changed so that it is negative, 90% of the steady-state rate, and equal in amount to 5% of the entire system, then the stability of the copper system is 5.4 and that of the cesium is 10.8.

No generally accepted method of determining the error term around predictions generated by a systems analysis such as ours exists. We are working on an approach involving stochastic models which generate a series of predictions for which an error term can be calculated. Discussion of these models is beyond the scope of this paper. The quality of the data going into the models can be assessed from Bormann and Likens (1970), Cole et al. (1967), and Jordan, Kline, and Sasscer (in preparation).

TABLE 3
RELATIVE STABILITY OF VARIOUS MINERAL-CYCLING SYSTEMS

Ecosystem and Element	Relative Stability
Northern hardwoods, New Hampshire:	
Calcium	0.61
Douglas fir, Washington State:	
Calcium	0.64
Potassium	0.62
Tropical rain forest, Puerto Rico:	
Calcium	0.59
Potassium	0.60
Magnesium	0.60
Sodium	0.76
Manganese	0.62
Strontium	0.62
Iron	0.62
Copper	0.64
Cesium	1.34

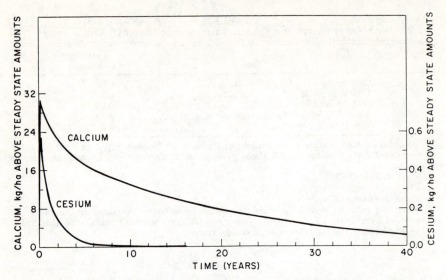

FIG. 4.—Response of the calcium and cesium systems in the Puerto Rican tropical rain forest, when the perturbation is positive and 5% of the total amount in the system, and the perturbation rate is 10 times the steady-state input rate.

ANALYSIS OF HYPOTHETICAL SYSTEMS

In order to discover the important factors in mineral-cycling stability, we analyzed a series of hypothetical four-compartment models as in figure 3. In every system the leaf compartment contained 100 g/hectare of an element, litter contained 100 g/hectare, and soil contained 1,000 g/hectare. In one system, wood contained 100 g/hectare, in a second system it contained 1,000

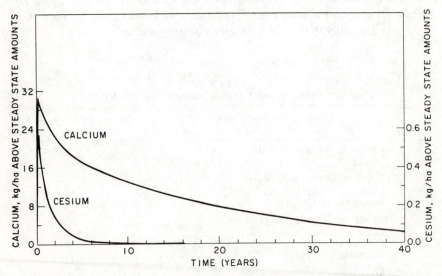

FIG. 4.—Response of the calcium and cesium systems in the Puerto Rican tropical rain forest, when the perturbation is positive and 5% of the total amount in the system, and the perturbation rate is 10 times the steady-state input rate.

(Δt) after the perturbation ceases which determines the relative stability in these two cases. Rate of return to steady state is slower for the calcium system than for the cesium system; consequently, the calcium system has a lower relative stability.

Changing sizes, rates, and signs of perturbations change the absolute values of stabilities but not their relative sizes. For example, in table 3, stability of the cesium is approximately twice that of the copper system. If the perturbation is changed so that it is negative, 90% of the steady-state rate, and equal in amount to 5% of the entire system, then the stability of the copper system is 5.4 and that of the cesium is 10.8.

No generally accepted method of determining the error term around predictions generated by a systems analysis such as ours exists. We are working on an approach involving stochastic models which generate a series of predictions for which an error term can be calculated. Discussion of these models is beyond the scope of this paper. The quality of the data going into the models can be assessed from Bormann and Likens (1970), Cole et al. (1967), and Jordan, Kline, and Sasscer (in preparation).

ANALYSIS OF HYPOTHETICAL SYSTEMS

In order to discover the important factors in mineral-cycling stability, we analyzed a series of hypothetical four-compartment models as in figure 3. In every system the leaf compartment contained 100 g/hectare of an element, litter contained 100 g/hectare, and soil contained 1,000 g/hectare. In one system, wood contained 100 g/hectare, in a second system it contained 1,000 g/hectare, and in a third, 10,000 g/hectare. For each type of structure, we varied rates of input and recycling from 10^{-2} g/hectare per year to 10^6 g/hectare per year and calculated the stability for each combination.

Size of wood compartment and ratio between input (I) and recycling (F) are important factors in the relative stability of the systems (fig. 5). Figure 5 also shows that for any system in which the wood compartment is approximately the same size or larger than the sum of the rest of the compartments ($M = 1,000$, $M = 10,000$ in the illustration), the system has two major regions of stability, one relatively high and one relatively low, with a sharp transition between regions.

Under high recycling conditions, that is, when recycling is as large or larger than system input and output, all systems have equal stabilities (stability $= 0.62$; fig. 5). This stability value is approximately equal to the minimum stability values of the naturally occurring systems (table 3). Minimum stabilities are all equal because of the following. With high recycling, the perturbation is quickly distributed throughout the system, and all compartments have the same proportion of the total material after the perturbation as before the perturbation. Because Δx, the total perturbation for each system, is the same proportion of all the systems (5%), soil compartments all have proportionately the same increase in material. From equation (4), because λ from soil to outside the system remains constant, an increase in X which is always proportionate to X results in an f which is always the same proportion of X. Because flow out of all systems (f) is always the same proportion of X, the recovery time after the perturbation, Δt, is always a constant proportion of X. From equation (2), if Δt is always the same proportion of X, stability (s) will be the same in all systems.

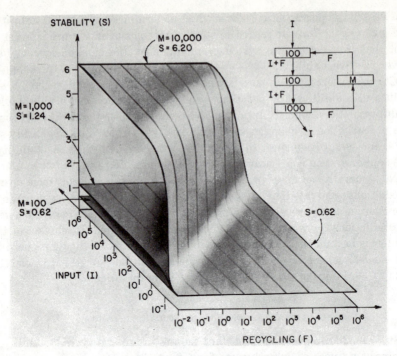

FIG. 5.—Stability of three hypothetical systems as a function of input into the system and recycling through the system. The three systems have wood compartments, designated M in the figure, of 100, 1,000, and 10,000. In the text, compartmental contents are given as grams per hectare, and flow rates, as grams per hectare per year. In the figure, units are omitted because relationships are independent of units.

When recycling rates in the hypothetical systems are low—that is, when recycling is less than one-tenth as large as input—stability depends upon the size of the wood compartment. The reason is as follows. The larger the wood compartment, the larger is the perturbation because the perturbation is always 5% of the total amount in the system. Also, in contrast with the high recycling condition where material from the perturbation is quickly distributed proportionately throughout the system, under low recycling conditions most of the perturbation remains in the soil. Because most of the material remains in the soil, the increase in soil following perturbation is nearly proportional to the size of the wood compartment. With a constant transfer coefficient from the soil to runoff, a large increase in the soil compartment results in a large increase in the flow of the excess material out of the system. In terms of equation (4), if λ stays constant, an increase in X results in an increase in f. The higher the flow rate out (f), the shorter is the recovery time of the system (Δt) and the higher is the system's stability.

In the system $M = 100$ (fig. 5), Δx is so small that even under low recycling conditions the perturbation did not seriously alter the proportionate distribution of the material. As a result, stability did not increase detectably.

Here size of wood compartment affects stability only because it determines the size of the perturbation (the perturbation was always equal to 5% of the material in the system). In natural systems, of course, there is no relationship between environmental perturbations and size of compartments such as wood. Thus, this aspect of the modeling has no significance for natural systems.

In contrast, stability changes due to changes in the ratio between input and recycling are not dependent upon size of the perturbation. Regardless of the value of the perturbation, the sharp transition between high relative stability and low stability occurs when recycling is one-tenth of the input and output (fig. 5). If recycling is less than one-tenth of input, the system has a high relative stability; that is, with constant ratios of $[r(\text{pert})/r]$ and $(x/\Delta x)$, Δt, the time to recover after a perturbation, is short relative to δt, the duration of the perturbation. If the recycling is greater than one-tenth of the input, stability is relatively low, and the system takes a long time to recover from the perturbation. Explanation of causes of this systems behavior, and of its relevance to natural systems, constitutes the remainder of this paper.

STABILITY MECHANISMS DEPENDENT UPON RECYCLING RATE

Mechanisms by which recycling influences stability can be shown by comparing the calcium and cesium systems mentioned earlier. If the steady-state input rate of calcium into the system is doubled for a period of 10 years and then the steady-state input rate is resumed, response of the entire system and the wood and soil compartments is as shown in figure 6. Because the calcium system is a high recycling system, after calcium begins to accumulate in the soil, the wood compartment increases rapidly. With a high recycling rate, the probability that a particle will move from the soil into the wood is greater than the probability that it will move from the soil out of the system. Rate of increase of calcium in the entire system is fairly uniform. When the perturbation ceases, total amount in the system dies away relatively slowly, because the majority of particles that enter the soil are recycled rather than lost to the system.

When the steady-state input of cesium is doubled, total amount in the system increases very rapidly at first, then very slowly (fig. 7), a consequence of low recycling. Almost all of the cesium that stays in the system is in its initial compartment, the soil. The probability that a particle will recycle into the wood compartment is very low. As soon as the amount of cesium in the soil approaches equilibrium with the new input (about 6 years after the beginning of the perturbation; fig. 7) the rate of increase of cesium in the system decreases greatly. As soon as the perturbation ceases, cesium in the soil drops off quickly because the probability of any particle in the soil becoming unavailable is very great. Total cesium in the system also drops quickly, resulting in a low value of Δt, a high ratio of $\delta t/\Delta t$, and a high stability.

The initial fast decrease of cesium in the system does not drop all the way to a steady-state value (fig. 7), but rather it drops to a level approximately equal to the amount in the wood compartment. During perturbation, a small amount of cesium recycles and enters the wood compartment. Because of the low recycling rate, cesium which entered the wood leaves the system extremely slowly after perturbation ceases. After the initial fast decrease ends at about 20 years (fig. 7), die-away of the cesium is very slow.

If a cutoff value, such as the value of 1% of steady state used in the above

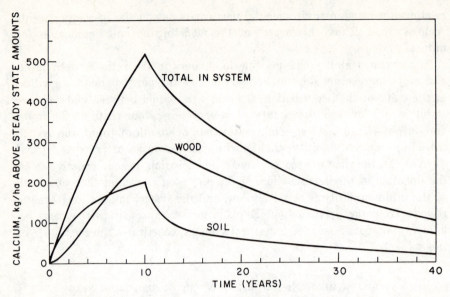

FIG. 6.—Response of the Puerto Rican tropical rain forest calcium system when the perturbation is a doubling of the steady-state input rate for a period of 10 years.

examples, is not used to define when the system effectively returns to steady state, the asymptotic return of the system toward steady state renders stability calculations meaningless. Thus, if we set our criteria for a system as having effectively returned to steady state when absolutely none of the

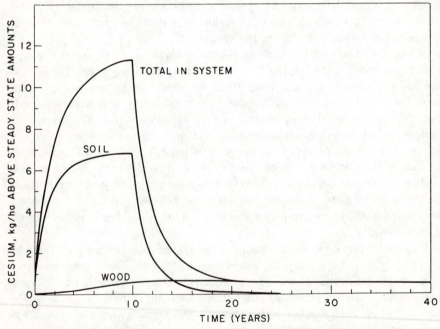

FIG. 7.—Response of the Puerto Rican tropical rain forest cesium system when the perturbation is a doubling of the steady-state input rate for a period of 10 years.

perturbation remained in the system instead of a value of 1% (see Stability section), then all systems would have stabilities with equal values, and these values would be exactly zero.

To illustrate the response of the calcium and cesium systems to negative perturbations, and to show that stability is independent of the sign of the perturbation, input into both systems was stopped for 10 years, and then steady-state input resumed (figs. 8, 9). Results are almost mirror images of positive perturbations (figs. 6, 7). Total amount in the calcium system drops off proportionately to the rate at which calcium is recycled from the wood, through the canopy and litter, into the soil. Total amount in the cesium system drops quickly until the soil empties, then drops slowly, the rate of decrease being governed by the rate of movement out of the wood.

After resumption of input, the calcium system fills more slowly than the cesium system, because a major portion of calcium coming in goes into wood, whereas most of the cesium goes into soil. A compartment which is relatively far away from the source, as is the wood compartment in the calcium system, fills up more slowly than a compartment nearer the source, as is the soil in the cesium system (fig. 9).

INTERPRETATION OF EXPERIMENTAL RESULTS

Now that an understanding of the mechanisms of stability has been achieved, we can interpret stability values presented in table 3.

A certain minimum flow of nutrient elements through a system is required to maintain the system's structure. For example, consider calcium flow through the wood and leaves of the Puerto Rican tropical rain forest. Due to certain evolutionary adaptations, leaf fall occurs, and the rate at which it occurs is such that the probability that an atom of calcium moves from the

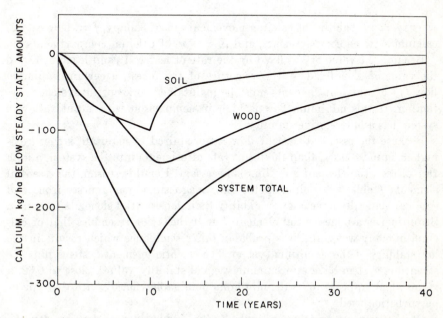

FIG. 8.—Response of the rain forest calcium system when the perturbation is an elimination of the input rate for a period of 10 years.

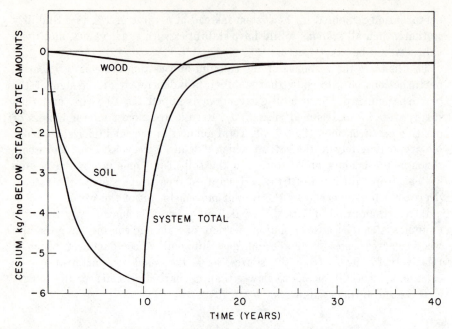

Fig. 9.—Response of the rain forest cesium system when the perturbation is an elimination of the input rate for a period of 10 years.

leaves to the litter in one year is 91%. With this probability of calcium loss from the canopy, the transfer of calcium into leaves from wood, and into wood from soil must be 59 kg/hectare per year, in order to maintain the wood and leaf structure. In mathematical terms,

$$\lambda = \frac{f}{X}, \qquad (5)$$

where λ = probability of calcium movement out of canopy, f = flow rate of calcium between compartments, and X = size of calcium compartments.

Because the value of λ is fixed by the rate of leaf fall (and leaching), and the value of X is fixed by the structure of the forest, a certain minimum flow (f) of nutrient elements must be maintained to keep the system functioning. If this minimum flow is high in comparison with input rate, the system has a low relative stability.

Because the essential-element flow rate required to maintain structure is higher, in most cases, than the input rate of elements into the system, a high rate of essential-element recycling is necessary. For this reason, the essential elements (table 3: calcium, potassium, magnesium, manganese, iron, and copper) generally have a lower stability than nonessential elements (cesium). Strontium is a nonessential element, but its behavior resembles that of calcium in many ways, and it is probably this resemblance which results in the low stability of the strontium system. The essential-element systems plus the strontium system have approximately equal stability values, close to 0.62, a value which appears to be the minimum obtainable (fig. 5) with the type of perturbation used.

Of the element systems in table 3, the cesium system has by far the greatest stability. Cesium is a nonessential element, and its uptake rate by plants is very low. We have shown that low recycling results in high stability. High stability means that an input of cesium over and above the steady-state rate should quickly move out of the system. Kline (1970) has validated this prediction with his observation that the half time in a tropical rain forest ecosystem of [137]cesium from fallout, intercepted and adsorbed by canopy leaves, was equal to the half time of the leaves on the trees. As soon as the leaves fell, the [137]cesium was essentially lost from the cycling system. Data of Peters, Olson, and Anderson (1970) from the [137]cesium-labeled forest at Oak Ridge, Tennessee, further show the high stability of the cesium cycle. They found an exponential decay of this isotope in the forest leaves with no indication of leveling toward steady state and no indication of uptake of cesium by the trees from the soil.

The high stability of the cesium systems in the tropics and temperate zone does not mean that cesium will move rapidly out of all systems. Miettinen (1967) described the adsorption of [137]cesium by lichens in the tundra, and the consequent retention of this isotope in the tundra food chains.

Depending upon the confidence limits chosen, the stability of the sodium system (table 3) may or may not be significantly greater than the average of the rest of the elements' systems, excluding cesium. We think it is significantly greater because the recycling rate of sodium is lower than the input and output rates of that system. Sodium recycling may be low in relation to input for one of two reasons. (1) Sodium may be a nonessential element. In most cases when there is no shortage of potassium, sodium is nonessential for plants (Hewitt 1963). (2) Recycling of sodium may be low only in relation to input of sodium. Input may be exceptionally high because of the proximity of the Puerto Rican tropical rain forest to the ocean.

Wherever there happens to be a superabundant supply of an element that is recycled by plants, as in the case of sodium in the rain forest, the stability of that element system is high. From the stability numbers in table 3, none of the essential elements appears to have a supply rate approaching superabundance.

The idea that essential elements generally have greater recycling rates relative to input than nonessential elements (with a few exceptions like strontium) is partially confirmed by data of M. Stewart (unpublished), who applied radioactive isotopes of mercury and silver (nonessential elements) and zinc (essential) to the soil of an old field ecosystem. He found that the ratio of uptake by plants per square meter to amount applied to the soil was 1/35 for mercury, 1/28 for silver, and 1/7 for zinc. Above we showed that the critical ratio above which recycling is important is about 1/10.

ECOLOGICAL IMPLICATIONS

Because of the interest in strontium and cesium cycling in ecosystems, due to the danger of radioactive isotopes of these elements, we computed the half time (time required for half the material to disappear from the system) of these stable elements in the Puerto Rican tropical rain forest following an instantaneous input pulse. The half time of strontium, an element with a high recycling rate, was 50.2 years. The half time of cesium, an element with a low recycling rate, was 0.9 years.

It is interesting to speculate on whether low stability (but not instability) confers any advantages or disadvantages upon a system. A comparison of figures 6 and 7 shows that in response to a positive perturbation, the less stable system (fig. 6) retains a greater proportion of the perturbation for a longer time than the highly stable system (fig. 7) and therefore, perhaps, is better able to utilize fortuitous inputs into the system. In contrast, figures 8 and 9 show that, in response to a negative perturbation, the less stable system (fig. 8) takes longer to recover, a characteristic which could be disadvantageous.

CONCLUSION

There is a certain finite rate of element loss from plants, caused in part by leaf fall. Leaf fall is an evolutionary adaptation, the significance of which may be unrelated to nutrient cycling. Because of the more or less continuous element loss from plants via leaf fall, there must be a continuous uptake of elements in order to maintain the plants' structure. This uptake and loss of elements constitutes the recycling discussed here.

We show in forest ecosystems that when mineral recycling rates are high relative to input and output rates, the systems have a low relative stability. This means that recovery of the systems, following perturbation, takes a relatively long time. Because, in general, essential elements are recycled by trees more than nonessential elements, essential-element systems in forests often have a lower relative stability than systems of nonessential elements. If the rate of element input into a forest system is higher than the recycling rate, the stability of that system will be high. This appears to be a generally uncommon situation for essential elements. In contrast with essential-element systems, recycling of nonessential elements in forest ecosystems may be low relative to input and output, with the result that these systems are highly stable. Elements such as strontium, which are nonessential but behave similarly to essential elements, are exceptions to this generalization.

A final point is in regard to the linearity of the models presented here, which contrasts with the nonlinearity of the real world. Were the models nonlinear, the return of the systems toward a steady state following perturbation would have been discontinuous instead of the smooth curve generated by the linear model. In the models of the Puerto Rican forest, the discontinuities would be so small as to be almost indistinguishable from a smooth curve, because of the very minor seasonal changes which occur in Puerto Rico. In the model of the northern hardwoods ecosystem, the discontinuities would be much larger because of the distinct seasonality in the North Temperate Zone. While including nonlinear functions in these models would make them more realistic, it would not change the conclusions drawn from them regarding the basic relative stability of mineral element cycles in forest ecosystems.

SUMMARY

Relative stability of a mineral cycle within a forest ecosystem is a function of the length of time it takes for the mineral-cycling system to recover from a perturbation. Recovery time is a function of the ratio of recycling of material through the system to steady-state input of material. Mineral-cycling systems with low ratios of recycling to steady-state input are more stable than systems with high ratios. Although there are exceptions, essential-element systems in forests generally have a lower stability than nonessential systems, because recycling of essential elements is greater than recycling of nonessential elements.

LITERATURE CITED

Bormann, F. H., and G. E. Likens. 1970. The nutrient cycles of an ecosystem. Sci. Amer. 223:92–101.

Cole, D. W., S. P. Gessel, and S. F. Dice. 1967. Distribution and cycling of nitrogen, phosphorous, potassium, and calcium in a second-growth Douglas-Fir ecosystem, p. 197–233. *In* Symposium on primary productivity and mineral cycling in natural ecosystems. Univ. Maine Press, Orono.

Hewitt, E. J. 1963. The essential nutrient elements: requirements and interactions in plants, p. 137–360. *In* F. C. Steward [ed.], Plant physiology. Vol. 3. Academic, New York.

Jordan, C. F. 1969. The Rain Forest Project annual report. Puerto Rico Nucl. Center Pub. 129.

———. 1970. Movement of ^{85}Sr and ^{134}Cs by the soil water of a tropical rain forest, p. H-201–H-204. *In* H. T. Odum [ed.], A tropical rain forest. Div. Tech. Information, U.S. At. Energy Comm., Washington, D.C.

Kline, J. R. 1970. Retention of fallout radionuclides by tropical forest vegetation, p. H-191–H-198. *In* H. T. Odum [ed.], A tropical rain forest. Div. Tech. Information, U.S. At. Energy Comm., Washington, D.C.

Kline, J. R., and Mercado, N. 1970. Preliminary studies of radionuclide cycling in understory plants in the rain forest, p. H-205–H-210. *In* H. T. Odum [ed.], A tropical rain forest. Div. Tech. Information, U.S. At. Energy Comm., Washington, D.C.

Likens, G. F., F. H. Bormann, N. M. Johnson, D. W. Fischer, and R. S. Pierce. 1970. Effects of forest cutting and herbicide treatment on nutrient budgets in the Hubbard Brook watershed-ecosystem. Ecol. Monogr. 40:23–47.

Miettinen, J. K. 1967. Enrichment of radioactivity by arctic ecosystems in Finnish Lapland, p. 23–31. *In* Proceedings of the Second National Symposium on Radioecology. CONF-670503. Biology and medicine (TID-4500). Dep. of Commerce, Springfield, Va.

Ovington, J. D., and J. S. Olson. 1970. Biomass and chemical content of El Verde lower mountain rain forest plants, p. H-53–H-77. *In* H. T. Odum [ed.], A tropical rain forest. Div. Tech. Information, U.S. At. Energy Comm., Washington, D.C.

Patten, B. C., and M. Witkamp. 1967. Systems analysis of ^{134}cesium kinetics in terrestrial miscrocosms. Ecology 48:813–824.

Peters, L. N., J. S. Olson, and R. M. Anderson. 1970. Trends of foliage and soil data on ^{137}Cs in a tagged Appalachian forest dominated by *Liriodendron tulipfera*, p. 25–26. *In* Ecological Sciences Division annual progress report for 1970. ORNL-4634 (Oak Ridge National Laboratory. Tenn.).

Rodin, L. E., and N. I. Bazilevich. 1967. Production and mineral cycling in terrestrial vegetation. Oliver & Boyd, Edinburgh. 288 p.

SYSTEMS ANALYSIS OF THE ALEUT ECOSYSTEM

J. M. HETT* AND R. V. O'NEILL

Environmental Sciences Division
Oak Ridge National Laboratory†
Oak Ridge, TN 37830

ABSTRACT

The benefits of applying systems analytic techniques at an early stage of research are examined by developing and analyzing a preliminary model for the Aleutian ecosystem. The model is developed to address certain specific questions about the Aleut ecosystem. The Aleut population is considered in its role as consumer in the total cycling of carbon. The model and data are crude as is appropriate at this preliminary stage of knowledge. Analyses of the model indicate the need for extensive research on the marine food supply and offer hypotheses for the dependence of Aleuts on the sea. The analyses also explore the possible role of the human population in maintaining or affecting the stability of the system. The study indicates the feasibility of applying environmental systems analysis to anthropological questions and suggests the benefits to be derived from application of modeling techniques in continuing studies of the Aleut ecosystem.

INTRODUCTION

The Aleuts have occupied the chain of islands off the Alaskan Peninsula for more than 8,500 years. Prior to first contact with civilization, they were intimately dependent on their physical and biological environment for shelter, clothing and food (Laughlin 1970a, b). As a marine hunting and gathering people, the Aleuts depended on the ocean to provide a major portion of their food, clothing and materials for fabrication, while the terrestrial system provided food supplements, in the form of plant tubers and birds' eggs, in addition to grasses for basketry. Coastal configuration determined the location of village and camp sites and population deployment (Laughlin, *et al.* 1969, Laughlin 1970a, b). Thus, the Aleuts form an integral part of the natural ecological system and cannot properly be understood outside this context.

The Aleutian ecosystem is a complex of physical and biological components with continuous transformation, accumulation and systematic movement of materials and energy through the system (Van Dyne 1969). This environmental system should be considered as a dynamic whole to understand the role of the Aleut population. Systems analysis techniques were applied in this study so all components and interactions of the Aleut ecosystem could be considered simultaneously.

Systems analysis is becoming increasingly important as a methodology in many sciences. Since it was first developed during World War II (White and Tauber 1969), systems analysis techniques have been applied in many fields such as medicine, hydrology, aerospace and control engineering and physiological kinetics. More recently, the methods have been applied in natural resource management and ecology (Patten 1959, Olson 1963, Van Dyne 1965, Christiansen 1968, Watt 1969). The U.S. International Biological Program is relying heavily on a systems analysis approach in the Analysis of Ecosystems Program (Smith 1970).

The potential benefits of systems analysis can be optimized by introducing the methods as early as possible in the development of a research project. The model and analyses presented in this paper should be regarded as the first of several iterations

*Present address: Coniferous Forest Biome Program, College of Forest Resources, University of Washington AR-10, Seattle, WA 98195.

†Operated by the Union Carbide Corporation for the U.S. Atomic Energy Commission.

Contribution No. 153 from the Eastern Deciduous Forest Biome, and contribution No. 70 from Coniferous Forest Biome, US/IBP.

in which systems analysis is applied to the Aleutian system. At this early stage of development, it is inappropriate to develop a model which exceeds the limits of our current knowledge of the system. In a like manner, it is impossible to include completely satisfactory data on the system since research projects on this system are still in progress. Rather, a simple model is developed which attempts to describe our preliminary insights on the Aleut population as a component of the natural ecosystem. An attempt is made to establish approximate values for the parameters of the model and a few analyses, sophisticated but preliminary, are attempted. The objectives to which the model is directed must, therefore, be realistically limited to pointing new directions for research and perhaps developing some modest additional insight into the nature of the Aleut ecosystem.

Systems analysis proceeds in an orderly sequence of steps to solve complex problems by: (1) defining the hypotheses to be tested or question to be answered, (2) placing bounds on the system of interest, (3) choosing a set of state variables that define the major components of the real system at a given point in time, (4) defining functions that express changes in state variables over time (in complex ecosystems most changes will involve interactions with other parts of the system), (5) quantifying the model specified by these functions [parameter identification techniques (O'Neill 1971) can be applied when adequate data are available], and (6) utilizing the model as an analogue of the real system to test the established hypotheses.

For the purposes of this study, the Aleuts are considered one component of a biogeochemical carbon cycle. Some ecologists have analyzed ecosystems using energy (Odum 1970) while others have considered radioisotopes, e.g., radiocesium (Olson 1965). Carbon has several advantages: (1) it is an essential component of living organisms in the system, (2) carbon can be found in all important components of the Aleutian system, and (3) carbon tends to flow steadily through this system, in contrast to some elements which remain immobile for long periods and then undergo rapid transformation—making it difficult to treat the system as continuous with respect to time. It should be noted that the use of carbon does not imply that it is a limiting factor in the system. Carbon is simply used as a tracer to elucidate the basic trophic relationships within the ecosystem.

MODEL DEVELOPMENT

Three questions, more precisely defined in the following section, are addressed in this paper. (1) How dependent were the Aleuts on various components of the system? This question also can be phrased in terms of the sensitivity of the Aleut population to minor changes in other environmental components. (2) Are there properties inherent in the system which made it advantageous for the Aleuts to utilize the marine environment more extensively than the terrestrial environment? (3) How important were the Aleuts in affecting the stability of the total system? It must be stressed that these questions cannot be fully answered at this time. Rather, an initial model of the system is used to refine our insight and to point out new directions for research. The model will be designed in simplest manner adequate to address these questions. The boundaries of our systems were defined following Laughlin, *et al.* (1969). The Aleut domain includes the linear island chain from Port Moller on the Alaskan Peninsula in the east to Attu Island in the west, a distance of approximately 2016 km. A north-south distance of 65.5 km was used to estimate the total area of the region.

The carbon cycle model emphasizes man as a consumer—the top of a natural foodchain (Figure 1). State variables for the model are specified as follows: atmosphere, land plants, dead organic matter (terrestrial), man, phytoplankton, zooplankton and marine animals, dead organic matter (marine), surface water and deep sea. These were chosen to include components most utilized by man (marine animals and land plants) and major variables involved in cycling carbon through these components. Although the deep sea is not explicitly contained within the Aleutian coastal system, it was included in order to encompass the total marine carbon cycle.

The amount of carbon in each state variable (excluding man) was obtained by multiplying average world figures (Bolin 1970) by 2.5×10^{-4}, the approximate percentage of the world's surface occupied

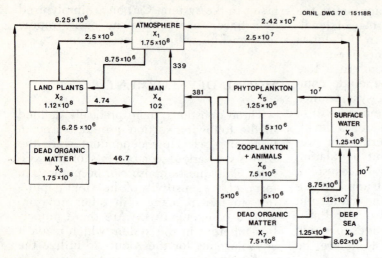

ORNL DWG 70 15118R

Figure 1. Carbon model for the Aleutian ecosystem. The values in each compartment represent metric tons (10^3) of carbon at steady state. Numbers on the arrows represent the flux of carbon (metric tons year^{-1}) between compartments.

by the Aleut domain. For zooplankton and sea animals, Bolin estimates "<5 billion metric tons" of carbon. We assumed 3 billion metric tons as a more specific estimate. To calculate the amount of carbon in the Aleut component, an estimate of 16,000 persons (Kroeber 1939, Laughlin, *et al.*, 1969) was used. The population was subdivided by age class with mean weight for each age class (Aigner 1970 personal communication), and an approximate biomass for the total population was calculated. This biomass was multiplied by 17.5%, given by Sienko and Plane (1961) as the percentage carbon in the human body. This value also was assumed to apply to marine animals utilized as food by the Aleuts.

The amount of carbon moving from the jth component to ith component per unit time is called the flux and is denoted as f_{ij}. For example, in our model (Figure 1), f_{12} is the amount of carbon (metric tons year^{-1}) as respired CO_2 in metric tons moving to x_1 (atmosphere) from x_2 (land plants). Except for those discussed below, Bolin's (1970) fluxes were multiplied by 2.5×10^{-4}.

To calculate inputs to x_4 (man), it was estimated that 95% of the Aleut diet was obtained from sea animals and 5% from land plants (Laughlin 1971 personal communication). Average daily intake of food was assumed to be 10.8 g per kg body weight per day (Spector 1956). The main vegetable diet of the Aleuts was bulbs and tubers; 4.21% carbon was used to convert fresh weight to carbon equivalent (Spector 1956).

Outputs from x_4 include respiration and excretion. Mortality data were not available but mortality was considered insignificant in relation to the other fluxes. The amount of carbon excreted per year in urine and feces was estimated (Spector 1956) and then added to give flux f_{34}. By assuming a mass balance of the population (i.e., inputs = outputs), respiration (f_{14}) can be calculated as the difference between input and excretion fluxes.

In our model, all fluxes were considered proportional to the value of the donor state variable. A transfer coefficient (a_{ij}) can be calculated as

$$a_{ij} = f_{ij}/x_j.$$

This transfer is defined as the instantaneous fractional transfer to component i from component j. Table 1 shows the matrix of transfer coefficients. Diagonal figures, a_{ii}, are, by definition (e.g., Funderlic and Heath 1971) the negative sum of the other column elements or negative sum of outputs from component i.

When transfer coefficients and amounts of carbon present in each component were calculated, it was possible to write equations that describe the rate of change of each component with respect to time. The rate of change, dx_i/dt, is the sum of the inputs minus the sum of the outputs.

$$dx_i/dt = x_i = \Sigma \text{ inputs} - \Sigma \text{ outputs}$$

where   inputs $= \sum\limits_{\substack{j=1 \\ j \neq i}}^{n} f_{ij}$

and   outputs $= \sum\limits_{\substack{j=1 \\ j \neq i}}^{n} f_{ji} = -f_{ii}.$

Therefore, $x_i = \sum\limits_{j=1}^{n} a_{ij} x_j$

in terms of fractional rates, or in matrix notation

$$\dot{x} = Ax$$

where A is a matrix of transfer coefficients and x is the vector of donor components.

The model contains two important assumptions which require some explanation and justification. The assumptions involve the linearity of transfers and the dependence of flow on the magnitude of the donor compartment but not on the magnitude of the recipient compartment. These assumptions have been found quite useful in modeling ecological systems (Olson 1965, Patten and Witkamp 1967, McGinnis, *et al.*, 1969, Kelly, *et al.*, 1969, Kaye and Ball 1969). The alternate assumption of recipient-dependent flow was rejected since it can be shown (Funderlic and Heath 1971) to result in behavior quite unlike that of an ecosystem. The assumption of linearity constrains the model to simulation of long-term changes in the system, for example, year to year. Short-term changes, for example, month to month changes, cannot be adequately represented. Since the purposes of the present study do not require resolution of less than a year, the linear model would seem to be adequate. Indeed, recent studies (O'Neill 1972, Rykiel and Kuenzel 1971) indicate that the linear model is probably more accurate for modeling ecological systems at this larger scale. Therefore, the assumptions do not appear to impose unreasonable constraints and the model appears adequate for the analyses performed below.

It should be pointed out again that systems analysis begins by establishing specific objectives or questions, such as those presented at the beginning of this section.

A model is then developed to address these questions. There is little justification for making the model more complex than required. Our intention is not to develop a general model of the Aleut ecosystem and the criteria for judging the model must be limited to the present objectives. Indeed, no single model should be expected to consider all aspects of the system. At the present state of knowledge about the Aleut system, it seems prudent to limit oneself to simple questions and develop simple models to answer them.

ANALYSIS OF THE MODEL

After parameter values of the model were developed and estimated, analytic techniques were used to address the questions posed concerning the role of the Aleut in the ecosystem. Although insight can be gained into the kinetics of the system, many questions cannot be fully answered without further elaboration and quantification of the model. Thus, we will find the inferential power of the native model is quite limited. Nonetheless, the analyses will serve to confirm and extend our insight into the system.

Using the equations in Table 2, a sensitivity analysis was performed on components and interactions directly affecting the Aleuts. If indirect flows through intermediate compartments are ignored, then the flux into compartment i due to a change, Δx, in the amount of material in compartment j is given by $a_{ij}\Delta x$. Similarly, the same amount of material, Δx, in compartment k produces the flux $a_{ik}\Delta x$ into compartment i. Thus an approximate measure of the relative effect on x_i of a change Δx in x_j compared with the same change in x_k is given by

$$\frac{a_{ij}\Delta x}{a_{ik}\Delta x} = \frac{a_{ij}}{a_{ik}}$$

The relative effect on man (x_4) to a change, Δx, in marine animals (x_6) compared with the same change in land plants (x_2) is then

$$\frac{a_{46}}{a_{42}} = \frac{5.08 \times 10^{-4}}{4.21 \times 10^{-8}} = 1.21 \times 10^4$$

The analysis indicates that the Aleuts are much more sensitive to changes in the marine system than we would have ex-

425

TABLE 1

	x_1	x_2	x_3	x_4	x_5	x_6	x_7	x_8	x_9
x_1	−0.193	0.0223	0.0357	3.32				0.194	
x_2	0.05	−0.0781							
x_3		0.0558	−0.0357	0.458					
x_4		4.21×10^{-8}		−3.78		5.08×10^{-4}			
x_5					−8.00			0.08	
x_6					4.00	−6.67			
x_7					4.00	6.67	−0.013		
x_8	0.143						0.0113	−0.354	1.3×10^{-3}
x_9							1.67×10^{-3}	0.08	$−1.3 \times 10^{-3}$

Transfer coefficient matrix (A), containing the instantaneous fractional transfer rates, a_{ij}, for each transfer in the carbon model. The coefficient $a_{ij} = f_{ij}/x_j$ where f_{ij} is the flux from component j to component i and x_j is the amount of carbon in the donor component. Each diagonal element is equal to the negative sum of the column elements, which indicates a system in equilibrium within the limits of rounding error.

Differential equations describing transient behavior of compartments for the Aleutian ecosystem model. These equations represent the rate of change of each state variable with respect to time where

$$\dot{x}_i = \sum_{j=1}^{n} x_j\, a_{ij} - x_i \sum_{\substack{j=1 \\ j \neq i}}^{n} a_{ji}.$$

They are the mathematical representation of the model in Figure 1.

TABLE 2

$$\dot{x}_1 = -0.193x_1 + 2.23 \times 10^{-2}x_2 + 3.57 \times 10^{-2}x_3 + 3.32x_4 + 0.194x_8$$

$$\dot{x}_2 = 5.0 \times 10^{-2}x_1 - 7.81 \times 10^{-2}x_2$$

$$\dot{x}_3 = 5.58 \times 10^{-2}x_2 - 3.57 \times 10^{-2}x_3 + 0.458x_4$$

$$\dot{x}_4 = 4.21 \times 10^{-8}x_2 - 3.78_4 + 5.08 \times 10^{-4}x_6$$

$$\dot{x}_5 = -8.0x_5 + 0.08x_8$$

$$\dot{x}_6 = 4.0x_5 - 6.67x_6$$

$$\dot{x}_7 = 4.0x_5 + 6.67x_6 - 1.3 \times 10^{-2}x_7$$

$$\dot{x}_8 = 0.143x_1 + 1.13 \times 10^{-2}x_7 - 0.354x_8 + 1.3 \times 10^{-3}x_9$$

$$\dot{x}_9 = 1.67 \times 10^{-3}x_7 + 0.08x_8 - 1.3 \times 10^{-3}x_9$$

pected. Intuitively, the expected sensitivity should be in the order 20:1 as the model was constructed, with the Aleuts receiving 95% of their carbon from the marine system. The model indicates that the sensitivity is more than 10,000:1, thereby confirming our qualitative impressions but leading us to additional insight into the extent of the dependence on the marine system. The analysis indicates that an error in estimating the marine food supply will be 10,000 times more important than an equal error in estimating the terrestrial food supply. The obvious conclusion to be drawn is that extensive research is required on the marine system, while very crude estimates may suffice for the land system.

Application of sensitivity analysis is also helpful in gaining insight into why the Aleut population has evolved such an intimate dependence on the marine subsystem. Although a partial answer is that the marine subsystem is a rich and readily available source of food, further understanding of the problem can be acquired by asking whether the marine or terrestrial subsystem is more likely to experience a serious disturbance if a change occurs in the environment. This can be done by examining the effects on each subsystem of a disturbance in the rate of uptake from the major carbon source (i.e., atmosphere for terrestrial and surface water for marine). In this case, examining the ratio of two partial derivatives:

$$\frac{\partial x_2(\infty)\partial a_{21}}{\partial x_6(\infty)\partial a_{58}}$$

For the existence of this ratio it is sufficient that the matrix in Table 1 has only a single zero eigenvalue and that $x_i(\infty)$ is differentiable with respect to a_{jk}. Both assumptions are valid for matrices like those in Table 1 (Funderlic and Heath 1971). It is then possible to calculate the partial derivatives by solution of the following system of equations,

$$A \ (\partial x(\infty)/\partial a_{jk}) = x_k(\infty) \ (e_k - e_j),$$

$$\sum_{i=1}^{n} \ \partial x_i/\partial a_{jk} = 0,$$

(Funderlic and Heath 1971), where A is the matrix in Table 1 and e is a vector of zeros except for a 1 in the ith component. Solving these equations, we find the magnitude of the ratio given above to be approximately 273.

This analysis shows that the terrestrial food supply is about 300 times more sensitive to a change in uptake of atmospheric carbon than the marine food supply is to changes in uptake of surface water carbon. A perturbation in the rate of carbon uptake

from the atmosphere [$(\partial x_2/\partial a_{21})$ / $(\partial x_6/\partial a_{81})$ = 9015] on the marine animals shows similar results. The large difference in sensitivity lends credence to the hypothesis that Aleuts have evolved a greater dependence on the sea because the marine subsystem is less likely to undergo serious alteration due to small changes in the environment. The sea appears to offer a more "dependable" source of food.

The final question posed above deals with the importance of the Aleut population in maintaining system stability. For the purposes of this analysis, we will assume that stability is related to the rate at which a system approaches steady state following some perturbation. This is only one of many possible definitions but is useful because it corresponds to our intuitive feeling that a more stable system will recover more rapidly from a disturbance.

The rate of recovery of a system is related to the magnitude of the eigenvalues of the matrix A in Equation 1. [Funderlic and Heath (1971) should be consulted for a more complete discussion.] For our present purposes, it is sufficient to note that the system of differential equations (Table 2) has a solution in the form of a sum of exponentials. The coefficients of these exponentials are the eigenvalues of the transfer matrix. The eigenvalues, therefore, determine the rates of change of compartment values in the model and, in a stable system, the eigenvalues will never be positive.

The rate of recovery of a system is determined by the crucial root (λ) of the matrix A. The crucial root is that nonzero eigenvalue whose real part is not less than the real part of any other eigenvalue. In other words, it is that eigenvalue, other than zero, whose absolute value is smallest. By calculating the eigenvalues for the transfer matrix in Table 1, the crucial root for the Aleutian ecosystem was found to be -6.729×10^{-3}.

The sensitivity of the crucial root to changes in the system then express how those changes affect stability. The sensitivity of the crucial root to changes in transfer rates can be calculated as

$$\frac{\partial \lambda}{\partial a_{ij}} = \frac{c_{ij} - c_{jj}}{\sum\limits_{k}^{n} c_{kk}} \qquad i,j = 1,2, \ldots ,n$$

427

where c_{ij} is the cofactor of $A - \lambda I$ (Kerlin 1967, Funderlic and Heath 1971). Cofactor c_{ij} is equal to -1^{i+j} times the determinant of the matrix remaining after the ith row and the jth column are deleted from the A matrix (Noble 1969).

Performing this analysis on the transfer matrix of the Aleutian ecosystem model shows that the smallest sensitivity coefficients were associated with transfers from the Aleut compartment. For example, $\partial \lambda / \partial a_{14}$ (transfer from man to atmosphere in respiration), was -8.34×10^{-10}. The deep sea and marine dead organic matter have the largest sensitivities (i.e., $\partial \lambda / \partial a_{97} = 0.739$). It appears, therefore, that stability of the ecosystem expressed as the rate of recovery from a disturbance is almost independent of the human population. Although the Aleuts are dependent on their environment, the system's stability shows little dependence on their activities. One should not assume this result follows from the relatively small size of the Aleut compartment. It is possible to devise matrices in which the crucial root is sensitive to small compartments.

DISCUSSION AND CONCLUSIONS

The stated purpose of this paper is to apply system analytic techniques to gain a better understanding of the role of the Aleut population in their natural environment. The analyses performed in the last section were addressed to this purpose and depended upon the carbon model developed earlier. It is appropriate, therefore, to discuss briefly how the accuracy or realism of the total model affects the analyses.

The carbon model developed here is simple and was quantified from reliable sources but with questionable applicability to the Aleutian ecosystem. Although some additional estimates of relevant parameters may be available in the literature (e.g., on Eskimos and mainland tundra), their applicability to the present problem would still remain dubious. In addition, as pointed out in the introduction, it seemed inappropriate to give the impression that our current information about the system is better than it really is. In spite of the crude estimates for transfer rates, the sensitivities calculated in the last section show differences of several orders of magnitude and the authors have specifically avoided discussions of possible effects where the differences as calculated were not so clearly obvious. For example, the estimated value of the marine animals could be in error by a factor approximating 10,000 without affecting the conclusion reached on the sensitivity of the population to the marine system. The authors have experimented with other estimates for transfer rates in the system but ceased when it became obvious that the conclusions were not being changed. In other words, although the model may be crude, the conclusions reached in the last section can still be regarded as substantially valid. Extremely large changes in variables would have to be made before the results would be altered.

The reader should not be scandalized that the model analyses confirmed his intuitive impressions about the system. The correspondence simply lends evidence that both model and intuition were correct. The model has quantified the impressions and yielded information about the magnitude of sensitivities which could not be intuited. The reader who is unfamiliar with the details of linear systems analysis must also be cautioned against concluding that the analytical results could be guessed from a superficial examination of the model. It is patent to any experienced analyst that the partial derivative of a crucial root cannot be anticipated from a glance at the matrix.

It must be emphasized that our model, or any model, cannot answer all questions directed toward the interrelationships between man and his ecosystem. However, inferences from our analyses can, in some cases, be projected to give supporting evidence to hypotheses that have been posed about the Aleutian ecosystem. Ecosystem analysis also provides an important research management tool. Our analyses clearly indicate more intensive research on the marine subsystem and its interactions with the human population is necessary if one wishes a more precise picture of the Aleut and his environment.

Ultimately, the model must be evaluated on its adequacy to address the specific questions posed. An overly complex model obfuscates subsequent analyses and may confuse rather than illuminate. Similarly, delaying model development until extensive research has been completed can result in tremendous waste of time, money and effort. The present study attempts to demonstrate that preliminary data can be utilized to structure an initial model. Analysis of this model can then be used to clarify our insights and structure future research. The preliminary carbon model appears adequate to these purposes and can serve as a first step toward a more complete understanding of the Aleut ecosystem.

Many questions which cannot be answered by this model are related to the need for more research on the marine-man interface. For example, Kenyon (1970) suggested that because sea urchins are a preferred food of the sea otter and the Aleut, both cannot coexist. To investigate this interaction, quantitative information on all three populations, including size, distribution, etc., as well as data on types of interactions between the populations, is required.

Our model appears to be the type Vayda (1969) feels show ". . . environmental phenomena are responsible in some manner for the origin or development of cultural behaviour . . .". One of the questions under investigation in the Aleut project is the origin and affinities of the Aleuts (Aigner 1970). Although this question cannot be answered precisely, our analyses support the hypothesis of a marine oriented culture during the latter stages of the Pleistocene. The hypothesis that the Aleuts migrated to the Aleutians during the Wisconsinan Stage implies arrival in their new habitat during cool climatic conditions (Laughlin, et al., 1969). There is some evidence that during glaciation, the marine productivity was not greatly affected (Black 1966). With the growth of local ice caps and glaciers, the terrestrial system could have been less productive than indicated in our data. Thus, man would have had to rely more heavily on the marine system during periods of cool climatic conditions than we have indicated in the model which is designed to approximate contemporary biological conditions.

The estimate, 16,000 persons (Sternbach 1970), of precontact Aleut population size has been questioned as being too high. Our analyses indicate the system is relatively insensitive to changes in the Aleut population. Thus the ecosystem was intrinsically capable of supporting more than 16,000 people. But to predict precise demographic characteristics much more information on village distribution, food sources, quantity and quality of food available, etc., is required.

The conclusions of this study might be summarized as follows: (1) the study demonstrates that problems of interest to the anthropologist can be feasibly approached by applying environmental systems analysis; (2) despite the simplicity of the model, analyses revealed that the model faithfully reflected the general nature of the system and confirmed prior intuitions about dependence on a marine food supply and relative stability of the marine system; (3) at the same time, the analyses indicated sensitivities to the marine system far in excess of our intuition and yielded its first benefit by pointing to the need for increased research on the marine ecosystem; (4) by predicting a more dependable food supply from the sea, the model confirmed our intuition but also indicated that freedom from large-scale fluctuations is a property of the intrinsic dynamics of the system rather than the lack of external disturbances such as fire, drought, etc.; (5) the analyses indicate that the Aleut population played a relatively minor role in maintaining or affecting the stability of the ecosystem as defined by the rate of recovery from disturbance. It should be noted that the Aleut is considered in the context of his natural state where his major effect was as a consumer. These conclusions are quite invalid when applied to civilization's present influence in the subarctic.

Perhaps the most interesting conclusion to be reached from this study is the benefit which can be derived from the early application of systems analysis in research projects on complex ecosystems. The model and data are crude, as is appropriate to our current state of knowledge, yet insights are refined and extended. Directions for future research are clearly indicated, some intuitive impressions are quantified, an hypothesis is generated to explain the Aleut's dependence on the marine system and new information has been gained about the role of the natural human population in affecting the overall stability of the system. Though modest, these contributions to our knowledge seem commensurate with the present effort and hopefully indicate the potential benefits to be derived from involvement of systems analytic approaches in the continued study of the Aleutian ecosystem.

ACKNOWLEDGMENTS

The authors would like to express their grateful appreciation to R. E. Funderlic and M. Heath for their patience and invaluable assistance in revising the manuscript. The senior author was supported in part by an NSF research grant (GB-18741) to William S. Laughlin, *et al.*, University of Connecticut. Systems analysis and manuscript preparation were supported in part by the Eastern Deciduous Forest Biome Project, International Biological Program, funded by the National Science Foundation under Interagency Agreement AG-199, 40-193-69 with the Atomic Energy Commission—Oak Ridge National Laboratory.

REFERENCES

Aigner, J. S. (1970). Configuration and continuity of Aleut culture. The Aleutian ecosystem. Invited paper, AAAS. Section 4, Chicago, December.

Black, R. F. (1966). Late pleistocene to recent history of Bering Sea—Alaska coast and man. *Arctic Anthropol.* 3(2): 7–19.

Bolin, B. (1970). The carbon cycle. *Sci. Amer.* 233(3): 125–132.

Christiansen, N. B. (1968). Forest resource management as a system. *J. Forest.* 66(10): 778–781.

Funderlic, R. E., and M. T. Heath. (1971). Linear compartmental analysis of ecosystems. Oak Ridge National Laboratory, ORNL-IBP-71-4.

Kaye, S. V., and S. J. Ball. (1969). Systems analysis of a couples compartment model for radionuclide transfer in a tropical environment. *In*: Nelson, D. J., and F. C. Evans (eds.) Symposium on Radioecology, Conference 670503, U.S. Atomic Energy Commission, Ann Arbor, Michigan, pp. 731–739.

Kelly, J. M., P. A. Opstrup, J. S. Olson, S. I. Auerbach, and G. M. Van Dyne. (1969). Models of seasonal primary productivity in Eastern Tennessee *Festuca* and *Andropogon* ecosystems. Oak Ridge National Laboratory, ORNL-4310, 305 pp.

Kenyon, K. W. (1970). Population size and behavior of sea otters. The Aleutian ecosystem. Invited paper, AAAS. Section 4, Chicago, December.

Kerlin, T. W. (1967). Sensitivities by the state variable approach. *Simulation* June: 337–343.

Kroeber, A. (1939). *Cultural and Natural Areas of Native North America.* Univ. California Press, Berkeley, California. 1963 printing.

Laughlin, W. S. (1970a). Aleutian ecosystem. *Science* 169: 1107.

Laughlin, W. S. (1970b). Delimitation and components of the Aleutian ecosystem. The Aleutian ecosystem. Invited paper, AAAS. Section 4, Chicago, December.

Laughlin, W. S., R. F. Black, and J. S. Aigner. (1969). Aleut adaptation to the Bering land bridge coastal configuration. Proposal to NSF.

McGinnis, J. T., F. B. Golley, R. G. Clements, G. I. Child, and M. J. Duever. (1969). Elemental and hydrologic budgets of the Panamanian Tropical Moist Forest. *Bioscience* 19: 697–700.

Noble, B. (1969). *Applied Linear Algebra.* Prentice-Hall, Inc., New Jersey. 553 pp.

Odum, H. T. (1971). *Environment, Power and Society.* Wiley—Interscience, John Wiley and Sons, Inc., New York, New York. 331 pp.

Olson, J. S. (1963). Energy and the balance of producers and decomposers in ecological systems. *Ecology* 44: 322–332.

Olson, J. S. (1965). Equations for cesium transfer in a *Liriodendron* forest. *Health Physics* 11: 1385–1392.

O'Neill, R. V. (1971). Tracer kinetics in total ecosystem: A systems analysis approach. Proc. Sym. Nuclear Techniques in Environmental Pollution. Int. Atomic Energy Agency, Salzburg, October 1970. pp. 693–703.

O'Neill, R. V. (1972). Error analysis of ecological models. *In*: Nelson, D. J. (ed.). Third National Symposium on Radioecology, U.S. Atomic Energy Commission, Oak Ridge, Tennessee. (In press).

Patten, B. C. (1959). An introduction to the cybernetics of the ecosystem—the trophic-dynamic aspect. *Ecology* 40: 221–231.

Patten, B. C., and M. Witkamp. (1967). Systems analysis of Cesium-134 kinetics in terrestrial microcosms. *Ecology* 48: 813–825.

Rykiel, E. J., and N. T. Kuenzel. (1971). Analog computer models of "The Wolves of Isle Royale." *In*: Patten, B. C. (ed.). Systems Analysis and Simulation in Ecology. Academic Press, New York, pp. 514–541.

Sienko, M. J., and R. A. Plane. (1961). *Chemistry.* Second edition. McGraw-Hill Book Co. Inc., New York, New York. 623 pp.

Smith, F. E. (1970). Analysis of ecosystems: *In*: *Analysis of Temperate Forest Ecosystems*, D. E. Reichle (ed.). Springer-Verlag, Berlin. pp. 7–18.

Spector, W. S. (ed.). (1956). *Handbook of Biological Data.* Nat. Acad. Sci., W. B. Saunders Co., Philadelphia, Pennsylvania. 584 pp.

Sternbach, R. (1970). Demography of Aleut communities. The Aleutian ecosystem. Invited paper, AAAS. Section 4, Chicago, December.

Van Dyne, G. M. (1965). Ecosystems, systems ecology and systems ecologists. Oak Ridge National Laboratory, ORNL-TM-3957, Oak Ridge, Tennessee. 31 pp.

Van Dyne, G. M. (1969). Some mathematical models of grassland ecosystems. *In*: *The Grassland Ecosystem*, R. L. Dix and R. G. Beidleman (eds.). Range Sci. Dept. Sci. Series No. 2, Colorado State University, Fort Collins, Colorado.

Vayda, A. P. (1969). Introduction. *In*: *Environment and Cultural Behavior*, A. P. Vayda (ed.). Natural History Press, Garden City, New Jersey.

Watt, K. E. F. (1969). *Ecology and Resource Management.* McGraw-Hill Book Co., New York, New York. 450 pp.

White, H. J., and S. Tauber. (1969). *Systems Analysis.* W. B. Saunders Co., Philadelphia, Pennsylvania. 499 pp.